They Thought They Were Free

They Thought

They Were Free

THE GERMANS 1933–45

MILTON MAYER

THE UNIVERSITY OF CHICAGO PRESS
CHICAGO & LONDON

THE UNIVERSITY OF CHICAGO PRESS, CHICAGO 60637
The University of Chicago Press, Ltd., London

ISBN: 0–226–51190–1 (clothbound); 0–226–51192–8 (paperbound)
Library of Congress Catalog Card Number: 55–5137

THIS BOOK IS DEDICATED
TO MY TEN NAZI FRIENDS:

Karl-Heinz Schwenke, *tailor*

Gustav Schwenke, *unemployed tailor's apprentice*

Carl Klingelhöfer, *cabinetmaker*

Heinrich Damm, *unemployed salesman*

Horstmar Rupprecht, *high-school student*

Heinrich Wedekind, *baker*

Hans Simon, *bill-collector*

Johann Kessler, *unemployed bank clerk*

Heinrich Hildebrandt, *teacher*

Willy Hofmeister, *policeman*

The Pharisee stood and prayed thus with himself,
"God, I thank Thee, that I am not as other men are."

Foreword to the 1966 Printing

Let a tract for the times be republished after a hundred years or a thousand and there can be no question of its having been timeless from the first. But let it be republished after ten years and the author is lucky if he gets off with no notice at all and an unbloodied head. "Things" have changed in ten years, and they have not changed as he promised (or appeared to promise) that they would. What he would give now if only he hadn't written this line or that one! Let him change them, then, and bring the work up to date —the publisher is generous in these small matters.

In the always admirable hope of playing it safe, I have taken advantage of the publisher's generosity and made all the changes in this edition that I was sure I was safe in making. They were two in number. I inserted the word "late" before a reference to Jawaharlal Nehru and I substituted "Stalin" for "Malenkov" in an abstract reference to modern dictatorship. Otherwise the book stands as it was first published, and if I must eat my words (except for those two), I must eat them.

Every thing changes. Every thing but one. Even the medieval Schoolmen admitted a limitation on God's omnipotence: He cannot change the past. He can, in his own time, disclose it, or let man stumble on it. But he cannot change it. The pre-Nazi and Nazi lives of my ten Nazi friends—and of some millions of other Germans like them—are and ever will be what they were ten years ago and twenty. To the extent that I read them right then, and wrote them right then, the account is long since complete. Nor has anything been revealed in the events of the past ten years (including the trials in Germany compelled by Eichmann's in Israel) to alter the picture that my ten Nazi friends drew of themselves.

When this book was first published it received some attention from the critics but none at all from the public. Nazism was finished in the bunker in Berlin and its death warrant signed on the bench at Nuremberg. It had gone out with a bang. Now there was nothing but rubble between the Americans and the Russians, standing face to face and armed to the teeth. Nobody wanted to hear about what was well gone and well forgotten—least of all to hear that the blood of millions of people had bought nothing definitely durable. Hitler had attacked the civilized world, and the civilized world, including by happiest accident the uncivilized Russians, had destroyed him. *Basta.*

But the civilized world was not, even then, so well satisfied with what it had done and with what, even then, it was doing, as to be able to stop doing what it was doing and take a long thoughtful look at what it had done. Nazism was a drug on the market. This book—and not this one alone— became a collector's item without collectors. But occasionally the publisher got an inquiry from a person (or a school or a college) who wanted it and couldn't get it. The inquiries increased to an interesting trickle. As "things" changed, on the whole for the worse, and the postwar world became the prewar world, and disarmament became rearmament, there arose a modestly circumscribed sentiment that it might be profitable to find out what it was that had made "the Germans" act as badly as they did.

Dreadful deeds like Auschwitz had been done before in human history, though never on so hideously handsome a scale. But they had not been done before in an advanced Christian society like—well, like ours. If we would keep such deeds from ever being done again, at least in advanced Christian societies, it might be worth digging a little deeper than the shallow grave so hurriedly dug at Nuremberg. After the heat of the long moment had gone down, it was equally difficult to cling to the pleasurable doctrine that the Germans were by nature the enemies of mankind and to cling to the still more pleasurable doctrine that it was possible for one (or two or three) madmen to make and unmake the history of the world. These were the things that had met the bloodshot eye. But man has many saving graces, and not the least of them is his impulse to sober up between brawls.

Four wonderful facts of life contributed to the sobriety. First, the Jews of Germany (and of Poland, and of where all else) were dead, and some humanistic men in America and elsewhere had supposed at one time that it was necessary to go to war with Germany to "save the Jews." That, as it turned out, had not been the way (however gratifying its taking may have been to the humanistic impulses). Second, the destruction of Hitler had involved the prior destruction of a whole nation to a degree that was possible to the technology of total war in which battlefields are only incidental areas of operation; and the nation which had been destroyed and revived (by those who had just destroyed it) was now the industrial and military titan of Europe. Third, the Germans were now civilized Christians again and, more than that, good democrats and the front-line defenders of Christian democracy against atheist tyranny. Fourth, after so much blood and wealth invested, and then balm and wealth invested, the suspicion persisted that the "German problem," whatever it was, had not been solved and would not be solved by repeated application of the same dosage.

The "German problem" moves in and out of focus as the twentieth century continues to produce—at an always accelerating tempo—more history than it can consume. Korea is forgotten, and Hungary, Cyprus, and Suez are the new sensations; Hungary, Cyprus, and Suez slide into sudden oblivion, and we are all agog at Tibet and the Congo; Tibet and the Congo vanish before we have time to find them on the map (or to find a map that has them) and Cuba explodes; Cuba subsides to something combining a simmer and a snarl, and Vietnam and Rhodesia (or is it Southern Rhodesia?) seize us. Ghana, Guiana, Guinea. Crisis is our diet, served up as exotic dishes, and dishes ever more exotic, before we are able to swallow (let alone digest) those that were just before us. Remember the "Lebanon crisis" of 1958, in which the United States was deeply involved? Of course not. Who would, these days? Who could? And why?

The "German problem" is different. It is off center stage sometimes, but it is never offstage altogether. Most Americans are inattentive to it—they can't be attentive to *everything*—unless something as pictorial as the Berlin Wall becomes a one-season wonder. (Whatever else it was, the Wall was the worst political *gaffe* since Paris snatched Helen). But to the Europeans—including the Germans—Germany and the Germans are the first order of business every season. The Englishman who remembers the summer of 1940 is dismayed to see the new German *Wehrmacht* conducting exercises on British soil, but he is undismayed to discover that the new *Bürger in Uniform* with the new *innere Führung*—the "civilians in uniform" with "self-leadership"

—were a myth successfully designed to lull the uneasiness of Germany's conquerors.

Dummer Michel, the "little man" like my ten Nazis, never accepted the myth. He drags his goose-stepping feet. He may be as provincial as he ever was, as uninformed as he ever was, as sheltered as he ever was by the shabbiest press in the western world. He may not know that the clamor for the "lost lands" beyond the Oder-Neisse has no other purpose than to keep him in line, and that that clamor, like the clamor for reunification, can be satisfied only by a Third World War. But he is not *dumm* clear out to the rind. He knows that, for the first time in his history, he can earn as as worker five times what he can as a soldier. And he knows that the United States is willing to pay him well for the privilege of maintaining its own military establishment in his country—to protect him, of course, from the godless Communist conquest that Goebbels promised.

For five, six, seven years after the Second World War, the German in his ruins wanted only to live. Today he wants to live it up—and why not?—while it lasts. Always while it lasts. The sovietized East German gets out if he can, over or under or through the Wall, to the golden West of West Berlin and then to the still more golden West of the Ruhr; and if he can't, he spends what he has as soon as he has it. *While it lasts.* In the Löwenbräu Keller in Munich the free-enterprising West German sops up the last of the butter-gravy with the last of the bread, pushes his plate away, takes a pull at his stein, lights his cigar, and says, "When I have it here," patting his stomach, "*nobody* can take it away from me."

Full, and more than full, employment is still the fact in the Federal Republic (and in the Democratic Republic, which the "lost land" irridentism of the cynical Western map-makers calls "Middle Germany"). But the bloom is off the *Wirtschaftswunder*—the economic miracle—as, soon or late, it always is. The West German inflation is so spectacular that the budget has to be cut—and the cut is achieved by eliminating the increases promised the civil servants and old-age pensioners to offset the cost of inflation. *Dummer Michel*, whose profit-sharing stocks didn't go up (or actually went down). *Dummer Michel*, who has no expense account and therefore no share in the miracle—unless he compares his condition with that of the ruins twenty years ago. *Dummer Michel*, who was honest, industrious, dependable, and who, in the general moral decline, has become so much less of some of these things that the very face of Germany, so efficiently spick and span before (and in) Hitler's time, is changed by the roadside litter. *Dummer Michel*, the legendary German Worker, whose legend (perhaps for the best) has lost its hold on him.

While it lasts. My ten Nazi friends, when I knew them ten years ago, had never believed that "it," the thousand-year Reich, would outlive them—as it didn't. Hitler got them to a pitch and held them there, screaming at them day in and day out for twelve years. They were uneasy through it all. If they believed in Nazism—as all of them did, in substantial part or in all of it—they still got what they could out of it while the getting was good. None of them was astounded when the getting turned bad.

While it lasts. The satellite East Germans have the Russians on their backs; my East German friends persuade me that not 30 per cent of them would support the regime there. The satellite West Germans ply their tools and their trades on the backs of the generous Americans whose mercenary "shield" they know themselves to be; my West German friends persuade me that not fewer than 90 per cent of them would support, and, indeed, do support, this thoroughly cynical pretense of policy. In eastern—Communist—Europe my friends persuade me that Germany, West and East, is the unchanging centerpiece of all policy and all politics in the Soviet Union, Poland and Czechoslovakia.

"The" West Germans want their place in the nuclear sun—the new Lebensraum of mass-murderous power—to erase the last insult they suffered in being demilitarized by the idealistic Americans whose ideals were so sternly pronounced and then so sternly reversed. The Russians forbid the Americans to let the Germans have that place. But as I am writing I read a sensational and authoritative headline: *GERMAN MISSILES A-TIPPED BY U.S. SIX YEARS AGO*, followed by the American government's now commonplace refusal to confirm or deny, followed, a few days later by a dispatch from Washington beginning, "A Defense Department spokesman acknowledged last night that fighter-bombers of nine North Atlantic Treaty Allies, including West Germany, were armed with American nuclear warheads." *Control* of their use was still in American hands —only the evil-minded Bolsheviks could imagine that the Germans could not be relied upon never to get out of control.

When this book was first published ten years ago, it ended, as it still does, with these words: "It is risky to let people alone. But it is riskier still to press my ten Nazi friends— and their seventy million countrymen—to re-embrace militarist anti-Communism as a way of national life." If these words had any validity ten years ago, they have some validity today—and even some small prospective relevance to my own non-Nazi country and my own non-Nazi countrymen. My ten Nazi friends and their seventy million countrymen have been ever more successfully pressed to the national way of life that they so bravely enjoyed and then, at the end, so bravely suffered in Hitler's time. The fact that two-thirds of them embrace militarist anti-Communism and the other third militarist Communism is only a detail—if a historically fatal detail. What is dreadfully, and demonstrably, bad for the Germans, and thus for the rest of the world, is their exposure to a fiery fanaticism that, in a less capable people, would burn itself out with more modest consequences.

The Germans seem to be less frightening now than they were twenty years ago. If they are, it may be because other people are more frightening now than they were then. Of the trillion dollars the world has spent for war since the Second World War ended, only an inconsequential fraction has been spent by the Germans (whose civilian enterprises, including armaments manufacture, have prospered accordingly). Things have happened elsewhere in the past twenty years that have made it impossible to claim that Auschwitz is beyond the moral comprehension of civilized men. A while back the *New York Times*' leading correspondent reported from Saigon that "there comes a time in every war when men tend to become indifferent to human suffering, even to unnecessary brutality, and we may be reaching that point in Vietnam."

The Germans are still the Germans—as aren't we all what we were, or at least no better? Who could have supposed ten years ago that they might have been otherwise? But there were some who so fondly supposed that for the world's good, and therefore for Germany's, a new way would have to be found. To say that instead their conquerors have found an old way—the educators re-educated—would be to say much too much at this date. But to say that the Germans, if a new way can be taught men, would have a harder time finding teachers today than ten years ago is not to say too little.

Where would they have found teachers ten years ago? Where but America? But it was ten years ago, and twenty, that the United States Air Force (in its own words) "produced more casualties than any other military action in the history of the world" in its great fire raid on Tokyo, and Secretary of War Henry L. Stimson, appalled by the absence of public protest in America, thought "there was something wrong with a country where no one questioned" such acts committed in its name (L. Giovannitti and F. Freed, *The Decision to Drop the Bomb* [New York: Coward-McCann, 1965]).

Still and all, I thought (and wrote) ten years ago that it might not be arrogant to assume that the Germans still looked to the Americans for light. I should change those words today if I could. I can't, for I love my country and abide in its hope and the hopes men have had of it. "We had"—always "had"—"such high hopes that the American might do *something*. Nobody else could or would, not our enemies, not our allies, or ourselves." It was not to be. "Something for the Germans," if it could have been devised, had to be abandoned to larger necessities. It is clear that it is not to be now; the time, if there was one, has passed. It passed some time before German missiles were A-tipped by the U.S. and some time after the following notice was nailed to the gate of the American prisoner-of-war camp in Babenhausen/Darmstadt in 1946:

When you, SS-man Willi Schulze, or you, Corporal Rudi Müller, stride out through this gate, your steps will lead you to freedom. Behind you lie months and years of slavish obedience, years of bloodshed, years in which human individuality suffered incredible humiliations, all of which was caused by a criminal regime whose adherents, if they have not already paid the penalty, will not escape due punishment.

You yourself are not to blame. Deluded, you blindly followed the call of a false doctrine. From now on your life in your family circle can unfold free and undisturbed. You have been freed from accursed military service, from guilt-laden German militarism. Never again will a shrill command chase you across the barracks courts or drive you to the battlefield. The ashes of your army ID card have mingled with those of Buchenwald and Dachau.

The victorious United Nations which, through their great sacrifice, have freed you and your descendants forever from military service, have assumed the responsibility of protecting your freedom. But in exchange for that great sacrifice you are duty-bound to make sure that never again in your homeland will a desire for military service arise, that never again will young Germans sacrifice the best years of their lives to the hankerings of the Prussian nobility and their war-thirsty general staff, but that they will, from now on, dedicate their strength and their gifts to peaceful ends.

The notice was signed "U.S. War Department."

Foreword

As an American, I was repelled by the rise of National Socialism in Germany. As an American of German descent, I was ashamed. As a Jew, I was stricken. As a newspaperman, I was fascinated.

It was the newspaperman's fascination that prevailed—or at least predominated—and left me dissatisfied with every analysis of Nazism. I wanted to see this monstrous man, the Nazi. I wanted to talk to him and to listen to him. I wanted to try to understand him. We were both men, he and I. In rejecting the Nazi doctrine of racial superiority, I had to concede that what he had been I might be; what led him along the course he took might lead me.

Man (says Erasmus) learns at the school of example and will attend no other. If I could find out what the Nazi had been and how he got that way, if I could spread his example before some of my fellow-men and command their attention to it, I might be an instrument of their learning (and my own) in the age of the mass revolutionary dictatorship.

In 1935 I spent a month in Berlin trying to obtain a series of meetings with Adolf Hitler. My friend and teacher, William E. Dodd, then American Ambassador to Germany, did what he could to help me, but without success. Then I traveled in Nazi Germany for an American magazine. I saw the German people, people I had known when I visited Germany as a boy, and for the first time realized that

Nazism was a mass movement and not the tyranny of a diabolical few over helpless millions. Then I wondered if Adolf Hitler was, after all, the Nazi I wanted to see. By the time the war was over I had identified my man: the average German.

I wanted to go to Germany again and get to know this literate, bourgeois, "Western" man like myself to whom something had happened that had not (or at least not yet) happened to me and my fellow-countrymen. It was seven years after the war before I went. Enough time had passed so that an American non-Nazi might talk with a German Nazi, and not so much time that the events of 1933–45, and especially the inner feeling that attended those events, would have been forgotten by the man I sought.

I never found the average German, because there is no average German. But I found ten Germans sufficiently different from one another in background, character, intellect, and temperament to represent, among them, some millions or tens of millions of Germans and sufficiently like unto one another to have been Nazis. It wasn't easy to find them, still less to know them. I brought with me one asset: I really wanted to know them. And another, acquired in my long association with the American Friends Service Committee: I really believed that there was "that of God" in every one of them.

My faith found that of God in my ten Nazi friends. My newspaper training found that of something else in them, too. They were each of them a most marvelous mixture of good and bad impulses, their lives a marvelous mixture of good and bad acts. I *liked* them. I couldn't help it. Again and again, as I sat or walked with one or another of my ten friends, I was overcome by the same sensation that had got in the way of my newspaper reporting in Chicago years before. I *liked* Al Capone. I liked the way he treated his mother. He treated her better than I treated mine.

I found—and find—it hard to judge my Nazi friends. But I confess that I would rather judge them than myself. In my own case I am always aware of the provocations and handicaps that excuse, or at least explain, my own bad acts. I am always aware of my good intentions, my good reasons for doing bad things. I should not like to die tonight, because some of the things that I had to do today, things that look very bad for me, I had to do in order to do something very good tomorrow that would more than compensate for today's bad behavior. But my Nazi friends *did* die tonight; the book of their Nazi lives is closed, without their having been able to do the good they may or may not have meant to do, the good that might have wiped out the bad they did.

By easy extension, I would rather judge Germans than Americans. Now I see a little better how Nazism overcame Germany—not by attack from without or by subversion from within, but with a whoop and a holler. It was what most Germans wanted—or, under pressure of combined reality and illusion, came to want. They wanted it; they got it; and they liked it.

I came back home a little afraid for my country, afraid of what it might want, and get, and like, under pressure of combined reality and illusion. I felt—and feel—that it was not German Man that I had met, but Man. He happened to be in Germany under certain conditions. He might be here, under certain conditions. He might, under certain conditions, be I.

If I—and my countrymen—ever succumbed to that concatenation of conditions, no Constitution, no laws, no police, and certainly no army would be able to protect us from harm. For there is no harm that anyone else can do to a man that he cannot do to himself, no good that he cannot do if he will. And what was said long ago is true: Nations are made not of oak and rock but of men, and, as the men are, so will the nations be.

My compulsion to go to Germany and to live there, in a small town, with my wife and children was spurred by Carl Friedrich von Weizsäcker, of Göttingen University, who, with his wife Gundi, lived in my home while he served as Visiting Professor of Physics at the University of Chicago in 1948–49. I corresponded with an old friend, James M. Read, who was serving as Chief of Educational and Cultural Relations in the United States High Commission for the Occupation of Germany. Messrs. Read and Weizsäcker converged on Max Horkheimer, Dean of the Institute for Social Research, in Frankfurt University, and he arranged my appointment. What I did after I got there (and after I got back) was my own responsibility, but where I went was the responsibility of my three friends. It was they who packed me off to live for a year, as close as possible to the Germans, as far as possible from the conquering "Ami," in the town I call Kronenberg.

MILTON MAYER

CARMEL, CALIFORNIA
December 25, 1954

Contents

Contents

PART I
Ten Men

Kronenberg

November 9, 1638:

"HEAR, YE TOWNSFOLK, HONEST MEN"

It is ten o'clock at night—give or take ten minutes. The great E-bell of the Katherine Church has begun to strike the hour. *Between its seventh and eighth strokes, the Parish bell begins to strike. You would suppose that the sacristan of the Parish Church had been awakened by the Katherine bell, pulled himself out of bed, and got to his bell rope just in time to avoid complete humiliation (like a man running shirtless and shoeless to a wedding to get there before the ceremony is over). But you would probably be wrong, for every night, ever since there have been two bells in Kronenberg, the first stroke from the Parish Church has come just after the seventh from the Katherine; in deference, perhaps, for the Katherine Church was once (up until the Reformation a century ago) a cathedral.*

Now Kronenberg has, besides two church bells and two churches, six thousand churched souls; and a university, with a theological faculty and almost a hundred students; and a Castle, which crowns the hill on which the closely packed, semicircular town is built (a hill so steep in places that some of the houses can be entered only from the top floor); and a river at the foot of the hill, the Werne. The Werne isn't navigable this far up from the Rhine, but its course around the flowering hill conspires with the Castle at the top, the massed gables of the timbered old houses that climb to the edge of the Castle park, and the cobblestoned lanes and alleys that gird the hillside like tangled hoops, to make of Kronenberg a picture-book town on a picture-book countryside.

The town has had its troubles, as what town hasn't? In the half-dozen centuries past it has changed hands a dozen times. It has been stormed, taken, liberated, and stormed and taken again. But it has never been burned; its prettiness (for it is small enough to be pretty rather than beautiful) may have shamed off the torches which have gutted so many old towns; and now, in 1638, Kronenberg is always designated as "old Kronenberg," an ancient place.

The Great War of Europe is twenty years old, but maybe it is over; the Prince of Hesse has decided to join the Peace of Prague, to drive the Protestant Swedes out of the Catholic Empire without, it is hoped, incurring submission to the Catholic Emperor in Vienna. True, Catholic France has just attacked Catholic Spain and, in alliance with Protestant Sweden, has just declared war on the Emperor. But Kronenberg has only heard vaguely about these wonderful events, and who knows what they mean? "The King makes war, and the people die"; it's an old, old saying in Kronenberg.

Times have been very hard everywhere these last years, in Kronenberg, too; taxes and tolls always higher, men, animals, and grain taken, always more, for the armies. But the war, moving from north to south, from south to north, and from north to south again, has spared the town, except for a siege which was driven off by the Protestant armies. All in all, the Kronenbergers can't complain. And they don't.

Pestilence and famine recur in Kronenberg—as where don't they?—and, where there are Jews, what is one to expect? After the Black Death of 1348, the Judenschule, or prayer-house, was burned in Kronenberg, and the Jews were driven away. (Everyone knew they had poisoned the wells, all over Europe.) A few years afterward the finances of the Prince of Hesse were so straitened that he had to pawn Kronenberg to the Jews in Frankfurt, but in 1396 Good King Wenceslaus declared void all debts to the Christ-killers. But that wasn't the end of it, because the princes always brought the Jews back, to do the un-Christian business of banking forbidden Christians by canon law. So it was, until 1525, when the Bürgermeister of Kronenberg implored the Prince to drive the Jews out again. "They buy stolen articles," he said. "If they were gone, there would be no more stealing." So the Prince drove them out again; but he exercised the imperial privilege given by Karl V to keep a certain number of Jews in the town on the condition that they pay a protection tax, a Schutzgeld. If they failed to pay the Schutzgeld, the Prince removed his protection.

Those were good times, before the Great War of Europe. Times are hard now; but they might be worse (and nearly everywhere are) than they are in Kronenberg, and tonight the burghers and their manservants and their maidservants are sleeping contented, or as contented as burghers and their manservants and maidservants may reasonably expect to be in this life. So are their summer-fattened cattle and their sheep in the meadows (it is not yet cold in early November), and their pigs and chickens and geese and ducks in the barn at the back of the house; sleeping, all, at ten o'clock.

The two church bells are dissonant, the Parish bell's A-flat ground tone against the Katherine's E; workmanship is not what it was when the Katherine bell was cast three or four centuries ago. But it takes more than the dissonance of the bells to awaken the people of Kronenberg. It takes even more than the rooster on top of the Town Hall to do it.

The Town Hall rooster is a wonderful rooster. It flaps its wings and crows a heroic crow, once for the quarter-hour, twice for the half-hour, three times for the three-quarter-hour, and four times for the hour—and then it crows the hour. If (as it does) it begins its ten o'clock crow when the Katherine bell is finished and the Parish bell has just struck its sixth stroke, the fault cannot be the rooster's, for the bell-ringers are human and fallible, but the rooster is mechanical. To say that the rooster was wrong would be to say that the Town Clock was wrong, and this no one says.

Now the dissonance of the two bells is as nothing to the cacophony of the rooster and the last four strokes of the Parish bell; still the Kronenbergers sleep. They sleep until their own flesh-and-blood roosters respond to the crowing atop the Town Hall. The response begins, naturally, in the barns and dooryards near by and fans out in an epidemic descent down the whole Kronenberg hill. The roosters awaken the ducks and the geese, then the pigs and the sheep; then the cattle stir and low. The house dogs are the last to be heard from, but, once begun barking, they are the last to stop.

All Kronenberg turns over underneath its mountainous feather beds. Everyone half-awakens with the dissymphony, remains half-awake until it is over, and then slips back, but not all the way back, into sleep. The Kronenbergers have yet to have their ten o'clock lullaby, the lullaby they have had, and their ancestors before them, every night of their lives, the Night Watchman's Stundenrufe, or calling of the hours.

Every night the Night Watchman stands in the Market Place until the clatter of the bells and the animals is ended; an old pensioner in the raiment of his office, a long green greatcoat and a high-crowned green hat, his horn slung over his back, his lantern in one hand, his pikestaff in the other. Staff, lantern, and horn, Night Watchman himself, are increasingly ornamental nowadays. As he makes his hourly round, he watches for fires, which are rare in cautious, pinchpenny old Kronenberg, and for a still rarer pig broken out from a barn.

But he has his dignity, this man who, if only symbolically these days, has the community in his care; he will not compete with roosters and geese. When the last echo of the clatter has died—and not before—he puts his horn to his lips and blows it ten times and then begins his descent through the town, clumping heavy-booted on the cobblestones, singing the Kronenbergers back to sleep:

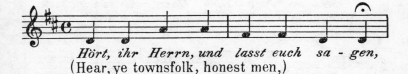

Hört, ihr Herrn, und lasst euch sa - gen,
(Hear, ye townsfolk, honest men,)

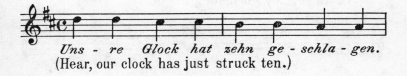

Uns - re Glock hat zehn ge - schla - gen.
(Hear, our clock has just struck ten.)

By this time, of course, the Town Hall rooster has long since crowed his one crow for 10:15.

Zehn Ge - bo - te setzt' Gott ein,
(Ten Commandments God has given,)

Gib, dass wir ge - hor - sam sein.
(Who obeys them will be shriven.)

Men - schen-wa - chen kann nichts nüt - zen;
(Watchmen's watching won't protect you;)

Gott muss wa - chen, Gott muss schüt-zen.
(God must watch you, God protect you.)

Herr, durch dei - ne Güt und Macht,
(Lord, by thy e'erlasting might,)

Gib uns ei - ne gu - te Nacht.
(Give us all a quiet night.)

Holding his lantern aloft, the Night Watchman goes through the town, as his counterpart goes through every town in Germany, singing this self-same lullaby from ten o'clock on. A few minutes before eleven (or after; who knows?) he is back at the Market Place, and when the eleven o'clock racket is over, he blows his horn and again makes his round. This time, instead of singing "Zehn Gebote setzt' Gott ein," he sings "Elf der Jünger blieben treu, Hilf dass wir im Tod ohn' Reu" ("Christ's eleven served him true, May we die without one's rue"); at twelve he sings "Zwölf, das ist das Ziel der Zeit; Mensch, bedenk die Ewigkeit" ("Twelve sets men from this day free; Think ye of Eternity"); and at one he sings "Eins ist allein der ew'ge Gott, Der uns trägt aus aller Not" ("One alone is always there, He who lifts us up from care").

From one o'clock on, until dawn, the Night Watchman sings no more. His song has no more stanzas and certainly no more listeners. Each hour, after the bells and the beasts subside, he blows his horn and makes his round, and the Kronenbergers sleep. Should one of them awaken and see a light outside, he knows whose it is and sleeps again. The town will be up at dawn; the day ends at dark. Everyone works, nobody reads, and tallow, except in the university, the hospital, and the Castle, is burned for only an hour or two to feed house stock and mend harness or stockings by.

Just outside the Town Wall, where the toll road along the Werne enters the town at the Frankfurt Gate, stand a half-dozen new houses around a burgeoning square called "Frankfurterplatz." The town is getting bigger, overflowing the new wall of two centuries ago as it has overflowed each successive ring of walls that protected it. The days when the town hugged the Castle for protection are over; this is the middle of the seventeenth century of Christianity, and men may live outside the walls without much danger.

At the corner of Frankfurterplatz, where a wide, un-cobblestoned road runs west outside the wall and along it, a nameless road known as the Mauerweg, is the new inn, the Jägerhof, the Huntsmen's Rest. It is a fine two-storied place with a commodious dormitory above, a public room and a private room (or clubroom) below, and the innkeeper's family quarters in back.

Tonight the lights are burning late in the public room of the Huntsmen's Rest. The old soldiers, the Home Reserve company, are celebrating with a stein of beer or two the fifteenth anniversary of the liberation of the homeland from the shackles of Vienna. The Home Reserve company are patriotic Hessians, of course, but first and last they are Kronenbergers, and it was fifteen years ago tonight that the siege of Kronenberg was lifted. A great event for the old soldiers, and a great anniversary.

It is after midnight when, with two steins of beer or three or four inside them, they leave the Huntsmen's Rest, some of the more patriotic old boys bent on continuing the celebration. The innkeeper does not want to get into trouble with the old soldiers or the authorities, and the instant the soldiers are gone he comes in from the back, snuffs out the lights, and goes to bed.

November 9, 1938:

The public room of the Huntsmen's Rest, at the corner of Frankfurterplatz and the Mauerweg, is alight tonight and crowded with a company of old soldiers celebrating the fifteenth anniversary of the liberation of the homeland from the chains of Versailles. It is the anniversary of the "Bloody Parade" in Munich, in which the Führer was arrested and imprisoned. The old soldiers are the Home Reserve Troop of the Nazi Sturmabteilung, or SA, and the Huntsmen's Rest is their regular meeting place.

Their regular meeting night is Friday, and this is Wednesday. But November 9, whatever the day of the week, is the greatest of all National Socialist Party celebrations. January 30 (the day the Führer came to power) and April 20 (the Führer's birthday) are national celebrations. November 9 is the Party's own.

The formal celebration was at 7:30 P.M. in the Municipal Theater. There were too many speeches, as usual, and one of the Party's poets, Siegfried Ruppel, recited too many of his Party poems. Then the four troops of the SA Kronenberg marched in uniform to their regular meeting places, the Reserve Troop to the upstairs room of the Huntsmen's Rest. Promotions were announced, as they always were on

11

November 9, and then the troop followed Sturmführer Schwenke down to the public room for a glass of beer or two. It is ten o'clock.

"HEAR, OUR CLOCK HAS JUST STRUCK TEN"

Ten o'clock, precisely, and if you want to check your watch you may get the hourly beep on the National Radio or the half-minute tone signal on Prime Meridian Time by dialing 6 on the telephone. The mechanically operated Parish Church bell begins to strike the hour after the seventh stroke of the Katherine Church bell, which is also mechanically operated. As the sixth stroke of the Parish bell dies away, the mechanical rooster crows atop the Town Hall, a fleshly rooster here and there in the town responds, a few dogs bark, an ox in a far field lows, and the town is quiet. Tradition has it that the two bells and the Town Hall rooster have been dissynchronous for centuries.

Ten o'clock. The policemen on the beat open their corner telephone boxes and report, "Schmidt speaking. All in order," and the sergeant on duty says, "Good." The lights are going out except in the cinemas, the inns and hotels, the university clinics and the students' rooms and professors' studies, in the streetcars and the railroad station and the crossings, and at the street corners dimly lighted by one high-hung bulb.

Kronenberg is a quiet little university town of twenty thousand people—two towns, really, the university and the town, although the university, like all Continental universities, is scattered through the town instead of having a campus.

Everything has always been quiet in Kronenberg. In the

years that led up to National Socialism there was an occasional street fight, and one or two meetings of Nazis or Social Democrats were broken up. (The Communists were too weak to organize meetings.) In 1930, when Party uniforms were forbidden, the Party paraded quietly in white shirts, and, when the Führer spoke in Kronenberg in 1932, forty thousand people crowded quietly into a super–circus tent on the Town Meadow to hear him. (Nazi open-air meetings were forbidden.) That was the day that a Swastika flag was run up on the Castle; in England or France it might have been taken for a college-boy prank, but in Kronenberg the culprit, who proudly admitted his guilt, was heavily fined.

Kronenberg went quietly Nazi, and so it was. In the March, 1933, elections, the NSDAP, the National Socialist German Workers Party, had a two-thirds majority, and the Social Democrats went out of office. Only the university—and not the whole university—and the hard-core Social Democrats held out until the end, and in nonindustrial Kronenberg there were no trade-unions to hold the mass base of the Social Democrats. The town was as safely Nazi now, in 1938, as any town in Germany.

Of course Kronenberg isn't Germany. To begin with, it's in Hesse, and Hesse is conservative, "backward," if you will; when city people elsewhere want to call a man stupid, they call him a blinder Hesse, a "blind Hessian." And Kronenberg, so old and changeless, off the main line and the Autobahn, is conservative even for Hesse. But its very conservatism is a better guaranty of the Party's stability than the radicalism of the cities, where yesterday's howling Communists are today's howling Nazis and nobody knows just how they will howl tomorrow. A quiet town is best.

"TEN COMMANDMENTS GOD HAS GIVEN"

The talk in the public room of the Huntsmen's Rest is (as might be expected of old soldiers) of old times, and Sturmführer Schwenke does more than his share of talking, as usual. But you have to hand it to him, he knows how to tell a story; when a character in the story roars, Schwenke doesn't say he roared—he roars himself. He tells how the SA Kronenberg got its orders fifteen years ago to assemble on November 9 and await word for the Putsch. There were 185 of them, waiting for trucks to take them to Frankfurt. They waited all day. The word never came, the trucks never came.

"I wasn't too disappointed," says Schwenke. "The time was too soon. I always said so. That's the trouble with the men at the top—they stand between the Führer and men like me who know the people and the conditions. N'ja [which in Hessian dialect means "Yep" or "So"], when the Führer got out of prison and reorganized the Party and accepted only those he knew were faithful to him, that was the right principle. With that principle, selecting the best, nothing could stop us."

The talk turns to another historic November 9, in 1918, and here again the Sturmführer does most of the talking: "I was on duty in Erfurt that night. A Bolshevik in civilian clothes came to the post and wanted to talk to the soldiers. The men chose me to represent them. The Bolshevik said we should join the townspeople and form a Workers and Soldiers Council. I said we would form our own Councils without any Reds. He said they had three cannon trained on the post, and I said we had two machine guns trained on them and we'd take our chances. They didn't have any cannon, and we didn't have any machine guns, but I hollered him down." "I'll bet you did," says one of the younger SA men, who has drifted in from another troop.

Somehow the talk drags this evening. Something is up, no one seems to know what.

Two days ago the German Councilor of Embassy in Paris, vom Rath, was shot by a Polish Jew. Immediately an intense campaign against the Jews began on the German National Radio. Are Germans to be sitting ducks all over the world for Jew murderers? Are the German people to stand helpless while the Führer's representatives are shot down by the Jew swine? Are the Schweinehunde to get off scot free? Is the wrath of the German People against the Israelite scum to be restrained any longer? "If vom Rath dies, the Jews of Germany will answer to the German People, not tomorrow, but today. The German People have suffered long enough from the parasite assassins."

This was the work of Dr. Goebbels, whom most people hated and nobody loved; even in Schwenke's loyal circle the Minister of Propaganda and Public Enlightenment was known, quietly, as Jupp der Stelzfuss, Joey the Crip. The university people didn't listen to this kind of broadcast—or, if they listened, they listened fearfully. The townspeople— the townspeople just listened. They listened as the campaign mounted hourly. Vom Rath's condition grew hourly worse. He was certain to die, and he died, on November 9, on the anniversary of the greatest day in the history of the German People, the day on which the liberators of the Homeland had shed their blood for liberty in Munich fifteen years ago.

All afternoon and evening the pitch has been mounting over the radio, and by now the Daily Kronenberger has joined in. Everywhere there are rumors. "Something will happen." What?

At the celebration in the Municipal Theater, earlier this evening, nothing was said about vom Rath or the Jews; strange. The spirit of repression is infectious; at the Huntsmen's Rest, where, ordinarily, SA men (SA men, particularly) tell stories of Jewish depravity and the SA's leadership in the Judenkampf, nothing is said this evening about the Jews, or even about the murder in Paris. No one knows why. "Something will happen." No one knows what.

"WHO OBEYS THEM WILL BE SHRIVEN"

The door of the Huntsmen's Rest opens, and the commander of the SA Kronenberg, Standartenführer Kühling, enters, in uniform.

"Attention!" says Sturmführer Schwenke.

The SA men stand.

"Heil Hitler!" says Sturmführer Schwenke, saluting.

"Heil. Be seated," says the Standartenführer, without returning the salute.

The SA men sit.

"Sturmführer, kommen Sie mal her, come here a minute," says the Standartenführer. Schwenke rises and comes to him.

The Standartenführer says, "Heute geht die Synagogue hoch, The synagogue will be burned tonight."

It is almost midnight.

CHAPTER 1

Ten Men

1. *Karl-Heinz Schwenke, Sturmführer and janitor (formerly tailor), age 54*

It was almost midnight of November 9, 1938, when Standartenführer Kühling of the SA Kronenberg entered the Huntsmen's Rest, at the corner of Frankfurterplatz and the Mauerweg, and said:

"The synagogue will be burned tonight."

As the scene was reconstructed by principals and witnesses fifteen years afterward, there were present in the public room of the inn twenty or twenty-five uniformed members of the SA Reserve Troop, composed of men over fifty, and five or ten members of other SA troops who had dropped in. There were no other customers, and the innkeeper testified in 1948 that he was "in and out" of the public room that evening and did not hear any of the conversation or remember who was present.

After Kühling spoke, Sturmführer Schwenke turned to the men in the public room and said:

"You heard what the Standartenführer said. Those who want to help, come into the private room with me."

The Standartenführer said, "I'll be back," and left the inn.

About half the men present, according to the testimony, followed Schwenke into the private room and closed the door. Schwenke reopened the door from within, said, "No more drinking," and closed it again. Those who were left in the public room sat saying nothing for a few moments and then began talking in low tones. They testified afterward that they could hear the talk, but not the words, from the other room.

Twenty minutes later the Standartenführer re-entered the Huntsmen's Rest. The dozen or so men left in the public room were eating buttered bread and drinking coffee, playing Skat, reading the paper, or just sitting there. They got to their feet and said, "Heil Hit——"

"They still in there?" said the Standartenführer.

"Yes, Herr Standartenführer."

The Standartenführer opened the door to the private room and the talk inside stopped. The dozen or so men within got to their feet and said, "Heil Hit——"

"*Jetzt mal, los! los!* Let's get going, let's get going," said the Standartenführer, standing in the doorway. "You, Sturmführer."

"Yes, Herr Standartenführer," said Schwenke. "I thought I would send two men to reconnoiter."

"You be one of them, Sturmführer."

"Yes, Herr Standartenführer. Here, Kramer, come with me. The rest of you, remain where you are until you get orders."

"I'll be back," said the Standartenführer, leaving again.

Schwenke and Kramer walked west on the Mauerweg. Half a block down, in front of the Café Schuchardt, they stopped and stood in the entrance of the darkened café. Kramer looked up and down the street. "No police," he said. "Not a sign," said Schwenke.

They crossed the street to the synagogue, pushed open the iron fence gate, and went around the building, trying the side and back doors. The furnace-room door was unlocked, and they went in. In a few minutes they left again. As they re-entered the private room of the Huntsmen's Rest, the men stood up and said, "Heil—"

"Pechmann," said Schwenke, "I want you and Heinecke and—let me see—Dowe. Upstairs. Quick. You"—to the others—"remain. This is duty. You hear me?"

The five, including Kramer, went upstairs to the SA meeting room. In a few minutes they came down.

"I don't care," Schwenke was saying, "we can use it. We have to have *something*."

"But it's floor oil," said Pechmann, "and it belongs to the Theater."

"I don't care," said Schwenke, "it's *oil*. This is duty. You heard the Standartenführer, Pechmann."

"Yes, Herr Sturmführer," said Pechmann.

Pechmann, Heinecke, and Dowe headed for the Theater, a block west of the Huntsmen's Rest, and Schwenke and Kramer returned to the furnace-room of the synagogue. In a few minutes the other three SA men entered the furnace-room, carrying, among them, four three-gallon canisters. There were footsteps above, in the synagogue.

"Can I go now?" said Pechmann to Schwenke, in a whisper. "I'm on duty at six in the morning."

"Go ahead, you s——t," said Schwenke.

"Thank you, Herr Sturmführer," said Pechmann. Heinecke and Dowe left with him, without even asking permission.

"S——ts," said Schwenke.

Pechmann testified against Schwenke after the war, but he supported Schwenke's claim that there were footsteps heard in the synagogue above when the SA men were in the furnace-room. Schwenke denied having had anything to do with the floor oil taken from the Theater; he had, he said, only reconnoitered. The four canisters were never found.

Schwenke and Kramer returned to the Huntsmen's Rest around 12:50 midnight. The Sturmführer led the way to a table in the corner of the public room. Ten minutes passed. Nobody spoke in the public room; the men in the private room, beyond the door, were still talking in a murmur. The two church bells struck 1 A.M., and the rooster atop the Town Hall crowed. Then it was quiet again. Schwenke said something to Kramer, and Kramer left the inn. None of the men in the private room raised his head. Kramer returned and said something to Schwenke. Then Schwenke left the inn and returned at once.

"SA men!" he called. "The synagogue is on fire! Outside, everybody! Close off the street! It's dangerous!"

A voice said, "Shall we call the Fire Department?"

"I'm in charge!" said Schwenke. "Close off the street! It's dangerous! *Schnell,* hurry!" And he turned and went, followed by all the SA men in the inn.

The instant the last man was out the door, the innkeeper of the Huntsmen's Rest entered the public room from the swinging door behind the bar. He closed the outer door to the street, locked it, turned out the lights, and went right to bed.

2. *Gustav Schwenke, soldier (formerly unemployed tailor's apprentice), age 26*

Neuhausen is a little summer resort on the Mariasee, an hour by the Post bus, two hours (and twenty-two cents more expensive) by the Scenic Steamer, from the old mining and textile town of Lich, in southern Austria. The Pension Goldener Engel—the Golden Angel Boarding House—

had no guests the night of November 9, 1938, except Private Gustav Schwenke of the German Military Police and his bride of a month. It was their honeymoon.

It was, as a matter of fact, their first time together since the three terrible days they'd had in Kronenberg when they were married a month before. If Gustav had decided, at the last minute, not to take the Scenic Steamer from Lich but to take the Post bus and save on the fare, it had to be admitted that he had hired a very nice room at the Goldener Engel. He got the military rate, of course, with a seasonal discount and (after hard bargaining with the host, while the bride stood by) the special three-day discount (even though the Schwenkes were going to be there only two days, the duration of Gustav's pass from his post at Lich).

Those three terrible days in Kronenberg, after the wedding in October, they had stayed at the groom's home, with the groom's father and mother and younger sister and very young brother. The groom's father, SA Sturmführer Schwenke, had been against the marriage because the bride's father was not even a Party member, and the bride (for all Sturmführer Schwenke knew; she never said anything) might even be a *Gegner*, an opponent of the regime. Frau Sturmführer Schwenke hated the bride from the first and said that the girl's family had "a history of fits." In those three days in Kronenberg, after the wedding, the bride had cried all the time (and Gustav hated crying), and Frau Sturmführer Schwenke said, "She can't help it, poor girl—it's hereditary."

Sturmführer Schwenke had wanted his oldest son to marry a strong Party woman—any strong Party woman. The boy was not a Party enthusiast, except for anti-Semitism. He was willing to join the Party in '32—glad to—when his father got him the first job he'd ever had, in the SA police.

21

But that was for the job. A job, any job, was all he cared about. A good boy, but he didn't have his father's spirit.

No wonder. And great wonder that he had any spirit at all.

Gustav Schwenke had wet his bed until he was twenty-two years old.

His mother, whose happiest topic of conversation was sickness (she herself had had plenty of it, but her husband "had never been sick a day in his life," except for his war wounds), told everybody in Kronenberg about her trouble with Gustav, the problem child. Everybody in Kronenberg knew that Gustav Schwenke was a bed-wetter, and Gustav knew that they knew, and he knew how they knew.

Long before he was twelve he hated his mother. One whistle from his father, and he came; a thousand whistles from his mother, and he hid. When he was twelve, his mother was pregnant. She said to him, "What if it's a little brother?" and he said, "If he cries at night, I'll cut his throat." Little Robert, when he came, cried at night, and when he cried Gustav wet his bed. Little Robert wet his, of course. "That's why he cries," his mother told Gustav, "because he's ashamed of wetting his bed." Gustav never cried.

Gustav had to pull his little brother around after school, in the play wagon, and the other kids, besides calling him *Bettnässer*, called him *Kindermädchen*, nurse girl. One day, in order to play, Gustav left the wagon, with little Robert in it, at the top of a long flight of stone steps leading down from the Market Place, and somehow the wagon went down the steps. A man stopped it halfway down, and Robert fell out and cried. Robert wasn't hurt, but Gustav got the worst beating of his life.

When Gustav was fifteen and his father's apprentice,

the Schwenke tailor-shop failed, and the whole family went on the dole. It was then that Gustav discovered that his father was more interested in politics than in work and would take bread out of his family's mouth in order to make himself a uniform or take a trip to the Nazi Party Day in Munich or Weimar or Nuremberg. His father a spendthrift, and the family hungry. Gustav had always been stingy, a saver of food, scraps of cloth, nails; now he became a real miser, and a miser he remained, with, unfortunately, nothing to save, even in his young manhood, but food, scraps of cloth, nails.

The room at the Goldener Engel on the Mariasee was nice but expensive. Still, a man wasn't married every day. And when Gustav was away from Kronenberg, he didn't feel so bad about spending something. He didn't feel so bad about anything. Away from Kronenberg your bride didn't cry and your mother didn't talk and your father didn't buy himself uniforms and you didn't wet your bed and the wagon didn't go down the steps and you would never go back to Kronenberg and you didn't care what they were doing there or anywhere else tonight. It was after one o'clock in the morning when Private Gustav Schwenke fell asleep by the side of his bride in the Pension Goldener Engel, three hundred miles from the burning synagogue in Kronenberg.

3. *Carl Klingelhöfer, cabinetmaker (and adjutant to the Chief of the Kronenberg Volunteer Fire Department), age 36*

The telephone rang by the side of the Klingelhöfers' bed in their house on the Altstrasse, in Kronenberg—the telephone by the bed, not the fire alarm on the wall. It was the cabinetmaker's sister calling, Frau Schuchardt, whose husband Fritz had the Café Schuchardt on the Mauerweg. Her voice was a frightened whisper: "Carl, the synagogue is burning. Inside. *Schwer*, bad." It was 1:25 A.M.

Klingelhöfer got into his clothes, his boots, and his fire coat and onto his bicycle. He could have phoned the night-alarm man or, en route to the Mauerweg, have pulled the alarm in front of the Katherine Church; but he didn't. He had to pedal slowly down the cobbled Altstrasse; but then, on the paved Hermann-Göring-Strasse and the Werneweg to Frankfurterplatz, he went at racing speed, a man who (besides flute-playing and picture-painting) had always done physical work, an old hiking-club man, who at thirty-six had the wind of a boy.

There were no policemen at the scene; the Mauerweg was closed off by SA men. But German firemen at the scene of a fire automatically have the status of uniformed policemen, and Klingelhöfer went through the SA cordon and the gate of the synagogue lawn. Smoke had begun to pour through broken windows, heavy black smoke. "Oil," said the fireman, even before he smelled it. On the side away from the smoke he shone his flashlight into the building. What caught his professional eye was the fact that the fire was burning in several separated spots: arson.

The Sturmführer Schwenke ignored him as he ran across the street to his brother-in-law's café and banged on the door; and when Fritz Schuchardt sleepily (or apparently so) opened the door, Klingelhöfer ran in and phoned the alarm man. "Got it already," said the alarm man. "Your buzzer at home rang at 1:38." Klingelhöfer, hearing the fire bells in the street, broke off.

As the first company pulled up, there was an immense *whoosh*; the rose windows in the synagogue dome had been broken by the updraft, and the sparks flew up in the sky.

The top of the wooden dome was almost as high as the wood-shingled roofs of the timbered old houses on the Adolf-Hitler-Strasse (formerly Hochstrasse), a street built up on the ruins of the old Town Wall in back of the synagogue. If the houses up there caught, the town would go. Adjutant Klingelhöfer advised the Fire Chief to send two of the three Kronenberg companies up to the Hitler-Strasse —in his excitement he called it Hochstrasse—and call the companies from the villages of Kummerfeld and Rickling, eight and eleven miles away, to replace them at the synagogue. The Chief agreed, and Klingelhöfer got a searchlight and broke in the front doors of the burning building. The benches and prayer stands had all been piled on and around the wooden stage at the center of the prayer hall, where, at the base of the updraft, the fire was fiercest. The dome was supported by four wooden pillars, issuing from the corners of the stage. The pediments of the four pillars could not be seen in the flame; up above, they were blackened.

A little groggy, the fireman went around the edge of the floor and into a smaller room, the vestry, perhaps. There was a chest. He broke it open and scooped up its contents, some sort of altar cloths and sets of embroidered hangings. He went out through the prayer hall. In front of the gate to the lawn stood a policeman now—one policeman—and Klingelhöfer turned the stuff over to him. It was three o'clock in the morning.

There was no killing the updraft; the dome itself was glowing now. A section of it fell in with a roar; a column of fire shot up in the air. It would be dangerous to enter the prayer hall now, on account of the pillars. Klingelhöfer went back in carefully. Now that the dome was partly gone, the draft was stronger above, and the lower sections of the two front pillars could be seen. One was burned, about four feet up, to a diameter of two-and-a-half inches or so; the other, though burned at the same height, looked as if it would hold. But the two back pillars could not be seen.

The smoke was being carried off faster now and, with his searchlight, Klingelhöfer saw on the east wall of the prayer hall a set of gold-embroidered hangings like those he had got from the chest. They were charred, and he saw that something was built into the wall behind them. When I asked him, many years later, if he knew what it was, he said "No," and when I told him that it was the Ark of the Covenant, he said, "The Ark of the Covenant. . . . Well, well." He himself was a vestryman of the Parish Church.

4. Heinrich Damm, Party headquarters office manager (formerly unemployed salesman), age 28

Heinrich Damm was a country boy, though he'd been in the town ten years now; he was home from the Party anniversary celebration at 9:15, and at 9:30 he was in bed and asleep in his apartment in the attic of the Kreisleitung, Party headquarters for Kronenberg. But he slept light that night; there had been talk around town, and from SA headquarters in the basement of the Kreisleitung had come rumors of out-of-town visitors and unusual activity. He heard a noise downstairs and went down. It was the Kreisleiter, the County Leader.

"What brings you here, boss?" said Damm. (Like all country people, he had a hard time with new titles like Herr Kreisleiter, but nobody cared in Damm's case; he could deal with country people like nobody else in the organization.)

"Some work to finish up," said the Kreisleiter, without looking up.

Damm went back to bed.

It was three o'clock in the morning when a crash some-where awakened him. There was a glow in the direction of the Hitler-Strasse and sparks shooting up. In ten minutes— and without awakening his hard-sleeping country-girl wife —he reached the synagogue. SA men and firemen were all over the place. One policeman stood in front of the gate to the lawn. A few spectators (remarkably few, for such a big fire) stood outside the SA cordon. Damm muttered, *"Blöd-sinn*, idiocy," and went back home. He woke up his wife and told her.

"What do you think, Heinrich?" she said. She always asked Heinrich what he thought about things.

"Blödsinn," he said. "Would they have stopped *us* by burning our headquarters?"

He was undressing when his phone rang. It was the Kreisleiter, at home. "Can you bring your car, Heinrich? We've got to go out in the country." The Kreisleiter, whose father had been a professor, always took Heinrich Damm with him when he had to go out in the country.

On the way to Spelle, the next big town, they said noth-ing. As they entered Spelle, the Kreisleiter said, "What do you think, Heinrich?"

"What do you think, boss?"

"It's as if *they* had tried to stop *us* in the old days by burning the Kreisleitung," said the Kreisleiter.

"By golly, boss, you're right," said Damm. "I hadn't thought of it that way. It's *Blödsinn.*"

"We have to cover the county," said the Kreisleiter, as they pulled up in front of the Kreisleitung in Spelle. "The Gauleiter's adjutant called. Order from Reichsmarshal Göring. It's everywhere, all over Germany. It must be stopped at once. Whoever lays a hand on *Volksgut* must be punished." Damm glanced at the Kreisleiter when he said *Volksgut*—the "German People's property"—and said nothing.

It was almost dawn when they got back to Kronenberg.

"Where to, boss?" said Damm.

"Home," said the Kreisleiter.

As he got back into bed, Damm's wife said to him, "What do you think, Heinrich?"

"*Blödsinn*," said Damm, one of the "March violets" who flocked into the Party in 1933. "It's as if *they* had tried to stop *us* in the old days by burning the Kreisleitung."

5. *Horstmar Rupprecht, high-school student, age 14*

The crash—of the synagogue dome—that awakened Heinrich Damm awakened the Rupprechts on Klinggasse, three blocks from the fire. They saw the sparks from the second-floor window of their house and went up through the hatch to the roof. There they could see the glowing half-dome. Horst's mother held his hand; he hated having his hand held.

"Papa," said his mother to his father, "It's the synagogue."

The father said nothing.

"Of course it's the synagogue," said Horst, excited. "*Juda verrecke!* May the Jews drop dead!"

"Come down," said his father.

"Golly, not yet, Pa."

His father opened the hatch.

"Can I go to the fire, Pa? They'll all be there. Can I?"

The family—Horst was an only child and the only member of either his father's or mother's family who had ever gone to high school instead of to trade school—went down the hatchway to the attic. It was pitch dark, and Horst, his mother still holding on to his hand, heard his father stop instead of opening the door to the stairs.

"They'll all be there, Pa. Can I?"

"They won't *all* be there, Horstmar. *You* won't be there."

That was a long speech for Emil Rupprecht. A long speech, and it meant that a longer speech would follow. Horst's hand stopped wriggling in his mother's.

"Where did you learn to say '*Juda verrecke*'?" said his father.

"In the *Ha-Jot*, the Hitler Youth," said Horst.

"So," said his father, "in the *Ha-Jot*."

"They don't teach it, Pa, you just hear it there. The other kids say it. They all say it."

"Like 'they'll all be there,' " said his father.

"You just hear it, Pa, don't you understand?"

"No."

Father, mother, and son stood there. At fourteen Horst couldn't stand what, when he was grown, he called his father's *Schweigsamkeit*, his taciturnity, any more than he could stand what he later called his mother's *Kadaverge-horsam*, her unresisting obedience to her husband. Horst was one of those fourteen-year-olds who *can't stand* things. And he was in the *Ha-Jot*.

"Horstmar," said his father (he never called him "Horst," and Horst couldn't stand that, either), "do you know what a synagogue is?"

"Of course," said Horst.

His father was silent.

"Tell Papa what it is, Son," said Frau Rupprecht, who was afraid of both her husband and her son.

"It's the Jews'—the Jews'—church," said Horst.

"And a church?" said his father. "What is a church, Horstmar?"

"A house of God, Pa, golly."

"A house of God, without the 'Pa, golly,' " said his father.

"Yes, Pa, a house of God."

"God's house?" said his father.

"Yes, Pa."

"And you, Horstmar, you want to go and see them burn God's house down?"

"No, Pa, golly, you don't understand. You don't—*are you for the Jews, Pa?*"

Father, mother, and son stood there.

"No, of course not, Son, of course he's not," said Frau Rupprecht, who was afraid of her husband, of her son, of God, and of Hitler.

Emil Rupprecht opened the attic door, and the family went down and back to bed. But Horst was disturbed—and excited. In a way he felt sorry for his father, in a way he had not felt before: a locomotive engineer all his life, at $144 a month, a little man with a little job and a little wife and a little house, a man who said nothing because, the fact was, he had nothing to say, a man who knew nothing of politics and the world and who *claimed* to be a Nazi. Horst had been eight when his father joined the Party in the fall of '32; now he knew that his father was just a me-tooer.

"You want to go and see them burn God's house down?" Men setting fire to houses at night. God's house. Horst's house, his father's house. Horst rolled around in his sleep and awakened, afraid. Whenever Horst was afraid at night, he looked into his parents' room to see if they were there. Now he crept to the door and opened it. The light had begun. His mother was in bed, but his father was sitting in the rocking chair at the window. It was 5:15 in the morning.

6. *Heinrich Wedekind, baker, age 51*

At 5:15 the *Brötchen*, the little breakfast rolls, had to be in the oven to be out with the boy before six. Baker Wedekind, behind his shop at the far west end of Hitler-Strasse, was at work in his slippers and trousers and apron (which needed changing), his suspenders over his quarter-sleeve heavy gray underwear. He got the *Brötchen* in and stepped to the front of the shop to open the door, have a look at the breaking light, and smoke his cigar. He had been thinking of going down to his garden plot, at the edge of town, and turning it before it got any colder, but the dawn looked like rain. He'd go tomorrow.

As he stood there, two men whom he knew came by, from the direction of Frankfurterplatz. "What's up, at this hour?" he said. They told him that the synagogue had burned down in the night. "So," he said, and went back to his *Brötchen*. The synagogue.

In 1933 Baker Wedekind had been Party manager for his block and, as he himself put it, a *flotter SA Mann*, a jaunty Storm Trooper. One day he'd been sitting in the Felsenkeller having a beer, when somebody threw a rock through the window of the Jew Mannheimer's shoestore. Wedekind rushed into the store and scooped up the money from the cash register—just to protect it—and the police came. The next day the plainclothesman, old Hofmeister, called him in and said that some of the money was missing. That was taken care of by the Party, but there was a rumor around town that Baumert, the Social Democrat Bolshevik, had taken a snapshot of the baker standing in front of the cash register with his hands full of money. It was just a rumor, of course, but Wedekind quit the SA as soon as he had a good excuse, when the Handicrafts and Trades Office

31

of the Party in Kronenberg was opened and he was offered the thankless job of mediator.

As he took his rolls from the fire, Baker Wedekind thought that he would like to see the Jew church burned down, but, on second thought, it might be better to go to the garden and work. No use looking for trouble; the shoe shop affair was enough. He would go by tomorrow, just walk past on his way to Frankfurterplatz and have a good look. That was the way to do it.

So he finished the rolls and went upstairs to eat breakfast with his wife, who was just as thick and strong as he was and did social work for the Party. He never talked to his wife, or to his son, whose wife resented her husband's low pay at the bakery, or to his daughter, who had got into trouble and could not be got rid of. The fact is that Baker Wedekind was not a jaunty man at all. He was a baker, and he baked. Each month he looked through that month's *Master-Baker*. Each day he read the headlines of the *Daily Kronenberger*. He had a copy of *Mein Kampf* (who hadn't?), but he had never opened it (who had?).

If he had been a profoundly reflective man, Baker Wedekind might have said to himself, as he ate his breakfast: This life is work. The next—if only a man knew for sure—will be different. In bad times, in this life, you work without reward. In good times, you work with reward. But in bad times and good, you work. These are good times. The regime?—the regime promised the people bread, and I bake the bread. The "Thousand-Year Reich"?—If it lasts a thousand years, fine; a hundred years, fine; ten years, still fine.

It was 6:15 A.M.

Beginning to rain. Baker Wedekind went down to the garden anyway.

7. Hans Simon, bill-collector, age 42

Hans Simon got up at 6:15, as he always did, shaved, waxed his little mustache, had his breakfast, in the course of which he reviewed the world situation, as he always did, with his wife, his son, and his daughter as audience, and set out (banging the door behind him) for the municipal electric works to pick up his morning calls. He bicycled firmly along, never swerving, preoccupied with the world situation.

He had a right to be. Cell Leader Simon—cell leader was the very lowest rank in the Party—was one of the first Nazis in Germany and the first in Kronenberg. Sturmführer Schwenke, the bankrupt tailor, always claimed to be the first. He always talked about *wir älte Kämpfer*, we Old Party Fighters, but he never gave his Party Number and no one had ever seen his Gold Party Badge. Simon wore his badge on his jacket, where everyone saw it, and whenever it was the thirteenth of the month he walked under ladders and so on and said, "Thirteen is nothing unlucky for me. My Party Number is 5813, the five thousand eight hundred and thirteenth German to join the Party, and I call that lucky. And, before that, a member of the Führer's Freiheitsbewegung, the Freedom Movement, *before* the Bloody Parade in Munich."

These reflections having taken Hans Simon across the Werne Bridge and into Frankfurterplatz, he saw a fire truck a half-block down on the Mauerweg and a small crowd held back by SA men. It was drizzling, but the bill-collector decided to pedal to the scene; it might be something of great importance.

The building was gone. The outer walls and part of the wooden dome, still smoking, were left. There was one policeman present, in front of the gate of the iron fence around the lawn. A skinny old woman was talking in a cackle to whoever would listen: "A church, a church, a church," she kept saying. SA men answered her; no one else said anything.

"A Jew church," said one SA man.

"It's not even a church," said another.

"Why don't you join, Auntie?"

"Be a Jew girl."

"A church, a church, a church," the old woman kept saying.

Bill-collector Simon, Party Number 5813, Gold Party Badge, rode on in the rain to pick up his morning calls and pondered the world situation. It was 7:30 in the morning.

8. *Johann Kessler, Labor Front inspector (formerly unemployed bank clerk), age 46*

At 7:30 Inspektor Kessler got off the local train from Kummerfeld and walked to his office in the Labor Front, in Hermann-Göring-Strasse. He got there at twenty to eight (he wasn't due until eight), and Picht came in and said, "Have you heard? They burned the synagogue last night, here, everywhere."

He and Picht picked up Euler on their way out, and the three men walked down the Werneweg to Frankfurterplatz and the Mauerweg in the drizzle. There it was, still smoking.

None of them said anything until they reached the Werneweg on their way back to the office. Then Kessler, a renegade Catholic who "preached" in the Nazi Faith Movement, said:

"This is a change. A big change."

"Burning property," said Picht, shaking his head, "burning property, whether it's a church or whatever."

"It won't make them love us abroad," said Euler.

"Do they love us now?" said Picht. Euler didn't reply.

"A big change," said Kessler again, "*eine Evolution*." Kessler liked to use flowery language.

Ahead of them Pastor Tresckow of the Katherine Church was walking slowly away from the scene of the fire, an old man who had always kept out of politics. "*Der Pfarrer guckt auch*, the pastor took a squint at it, too," said Euler. Just then there was a shout behind them:

"*Nächstesmal die Katherinenkirche!* The Katherine Church next!"

Picht and Euler raised their eyes to each other, but Kessler, the renegade Catholic, stopped sharply and looked back. People were hurrying to work on both sides of the street, some of them under umbrellas. Nobody but Kessler had stopped or raised his eyes. Pastor Tresckow was walking slowly on.

9. *Heinrich Hildebrandt, high-school teacher, age 34*

"Herr Studienrat, Herr Studienrat!" Studienrat Hildebrandt waited until Pfeffermann caught up with him. Pfeffermann was a student at the university now, but he had been one of Hildebrandt's students in the classical high school. Pfeffermann liked and admired Hildebrandt. Even though Hildebrandt was a Nazi, and an ostentatious one, he was a highly cultivated man who really knew literature and music, a true Continental. It was even said—no one knew—that before coming to Kronenberg he had once been an anti-Nazi and owed his survival to the personal influence of his father, an old Army colonel. How anxious Hildebrandt was to talk with Pfeffermann, who was a *Mischling* (his

35

father was the Jew in the marriage, which made it worse), was another question, although the teacher certainly liked the student.

"Have you heard, Herr Studienrat? They have—the synagogue has been burned."

"The synagogue?"

"Yes."

"Have you been there?"

"No. Have you time to go?"

Herr Hildebrandt had time this morning; his literature class were writing their examination, and he always made a point of arriving late on examination days to show the students that he trusted them. He hesitated a moment, began to blush, and then said, "Yes, I have time."

It was 8:45 or so when they got there. The fire had almost burned itself out, but the smoke still came through the half-fallen dome of the building. The fire trucks, one on the Mauerweg, one up above on Hitler-Strasse, were no longer pumping. It was drizzling.

"The synagogue," said Pfeffermann, shaking his head.

Hildebrandt, blushing, said nothing. The American, Henderson, a buoyant young man who was studying (not very hard) at Kronenberg University and, through Pfeffermann, had met Hildebrandt before, came over to them; he said good morning without shaking hands (American fashion), and asked, in German, "Was ist los, Herr Studienrat?" Hildebrandt shook his head, without answering. He felt himself blushing and, feeling himself blushing, blushed worse.

As he entered his classroom, the class interrupted its writing to stand until he had said good morning and sat down at his desk. He opened his briefcase and took out *Crime and Punishment*, in French, with a plain wrapping-paper cover over the binding, to read while the class continued their examination.

Always fire, always fire. The Reichstag fire. The book-burning in the Paradeplatz in Königsberg. He was an anti-Nazi then, in '33, a man who read the *Baseler Nachrichter* and *Le Temps* every day and even once in a while (with great difficulty, for his English was weak) the *Times* of London. Now he was a Nazi, reading *Crime and Punishment* in French, with a plain wrapping-paper cover over the binding. Now he was a Nazi, and the Nazis were burning synagogues.

The noon bell rang. The students brought their examination books to the desk, and each said, "*Guten Morgen, Herr Studienrat,*" but the Studienrat, reading his book in the wrapping-paper cover, did not look up.

10. *Willy Hofmeister, policeman, age 57*

It was noon, and Plainclothesman Hofmeister of the Kronenberg detective bureau was pedaling over the Werne Bridge on his way to work. Thursday was his morning to paint, but you can't paint in the rain. Hofmeister had chronic lead poisoning; he was allowed to paint once a week, out of doors. His paintings, in oil, were, like Cabinet-maker Klingelhöfer's, what a critic would call "calendar art" as far as subject, mood, and technique were concerned, but of their kind they were skilled and delicate.

Willy Hofmeister had had to give up his profession of scenery-painting when he was twenty-eight. In 1908 he had become a policeman in Kronenberg, first in the traffic police and then in the criminal division. It had not been a bad life. In thirty years there had been only three killings in Kronenberg, only one of them a murder (the other two were sex-maniac cases). In three more years he would retire on full pension. Not bad; but Willy Hofmeister had wanted to paint.

When his wife (who always made him stay in bed late and rest on Thursdays) told him that there was smoke coming up near Frankfurterplatz, Hofmeister knew right away what it was. The morning before, Oskar Rosenthal, the former Bank Director, had come to his office, stood with his hands at his side, and said, as Nazi protocol required, "*Ich bin der Jude*, Oskar Israel Rosen——"

"*Bitte, bitte,* please, please, Herr Direktor," Hofmeister said to the former Bank Director, "sit down, won't you?" When Rosenthal, the chairman of the board of the Kronenberg synagogue, told him that more windows had been broken the night before and the janitor had reported a smell of gasoline, Hofmeister said to the old man:

"A man will investigate at once, Herr Direktor, especially the gasoline smell. The windows—well, such things are difficult, you know, with, well, with the shooting in Paris yesterday."

"I understand, Herr Kriminalinspektor," said Rosenthal.

"So," said Kriminalinspektor Hofmeister, rising, "if you will excuse me a moment, I'll get the stenographer and you can dictate a report of the gasoline smell and the windows, and then we will register the complaint."

"No, no, Herr Kriminalinspektor," said Rosenthal. "I would rather not make a report, and there is certainly no complaint."

"But," said Hofmeister, "a report must be made."

"No, really," said Rosenthal, rising, "it is not at all necessary from our—from my point of view. I would much prefer not to make a report."

"But there *must* be a report, Herr Direktor," said Hofmeister.

"Only if you insist, Herr Kriminalinspektor," said Rosenthal.

The old policeman twisted his immense white mustache and said, "I shall make the report myself, Herr Direktor, after we have investigated. All possible steps will be taken." He held out his hand to the former Bank Director and said, "*Bitte*, Herr Direktor."

The old Jew took his hand and said, "*Bitte*, Herr Kriminalinspektor," and left.

Hofmeister had sent a policeman to the synagogue to investigate and, before he himself left for home at the end of the day, he wrote the report and placed it in the Kronenberg police files, which were found, incompletely burned, in the alley behind the police station when the American troops entered Kronenberg seven years later. The report, dated November 9, 1938, read:

"Synagogue, Mauerweg, report of broken windows, etc.

"Investigation at the scene established the fact that on the night of November 8, seven windowpanes in the synagogue on the Mauerweg were broken by stones thrown by unknown persons. Some of the stones lay in the prayer hall, some on the lawn. On the southeast gable side of the building, just outside the window leading to the furnace-room, which window was also found to have been broken, were the remnants of two wine bottles. These bottles had obviously been filled with a liquid, the odor of which was still present on the glass particles and in the immediate vicinity, corked with paper and rag bits, and ignited. Indications point to an explosion of small extent, i.e., of limited effect. Damage to the building, apart from a blackening on the wall, was not present.

"Criminologically valuable clues not present.

"Search for perpetrators without result, as of 5:20 P.M. instant date.

"On the side of those whose interests were injured, there was no demand for investigation."

That was the afternoon before, and now, as he pedaled over the Werne Bridge, Policeman Hofmeister was worried. The report had gone down to the chiefs of both the traffic and criminal police before 6 P.M., and Hofmeister was sure that there must have been uniformed police guarding the building during the night. The SA—of course it was the SA —did not like the police, and the police despised the SA. So there must have been trouble. Hofmeister decided to go over to the synagogue.

There were SA men everywhere, and only one uniformed policeman, Baumann, of the traffic division, in front of the synagogue gate. Hofmeister talked to him, Baumann answered, Hofmeister asked him something, and Baumann shrugged his shoulders as he replied. Then Hofmeister walked away.

"Heil Hitler, Herr Kriminalinspektor!"

It was Schwenke, the Sturmführer. "*Morgen*," said Hofmeister, getting on his bicycle. Schwenke, the Sturmführer. In 1931 Hofmeister had been sent to search Schwenke's apartment for evidence of illegal possession of arms by the SA, and Schwenke had said, "You find nothing in my mail, Herr Kriminalinspektor; do you think you will find something in my apartment?" Schwenke, the Nazi. Now it was Hofmeister, the Nazi, Schwenke and Hofmeister. The old policeman had three years to go, and then his pension, and the doctor had said that if he wasn't working he could paint.

At the office Hofmeister was told to report to the Police Chief, the Oberinspektor.

"Herr Kriminalinspektor," said the Police Chief, a young

man, "I have here an order to be executed. I will read it to you, and then I will ask you to read it yourself and sign it."

"'And sign it,' Herr Oberinspektor?" said Hofmeister.

"And sign it, Herr Kriminalinspektor."

The order said that all male Jews in Kronenberg between the ages of eighteen and sixty-five were to be taken into protective custody at once. The order was to be executed before midnight of the instant date, November 10, 1938, by the Criminal Police (who in Germany could always arrest without a warrant). Kriminalinspektor Hofmeister was to deliver the following persons, whose names began with F through M, to the storerooms of the Town Hall, which would be used for custody because of the shortage of custodial quarters.

"Clear, Herr Kriminalinspektor?"

"Yes, Herr Oberinspektor."

"You will remain on duty until all the persons on your list are in custody, and then you will get your overtime off."

"Yes, Herr Oberinspektor."

Policeman Hofmeister took his list and began his round, without his bicycle. He carried no weapon.

It was a long afternoon. It might have been longer, except that every man on the list was at home; no Jew in Kronenberg had gone out of his house since the night before. Still, it was a long afternoon, and when Policeman Hofmeister rang the apartment bell alongside Salo Marowitz's tailor-shop, it was going on nine o'clock.

Marowitz opened the door and said, "Come in, Herr Kriminalinspektor."

"Thank you, Herr Marowitz."

On the parlor table, under the green glass tulip chandelier, was a suitcase, closed. On the sofa were a man's coat and hat.

"Herr Marowitz—"

"Won't you sit down, Herr Kriminalinspektor?"

"I—. Thank you, a moment only, Herr Marowitz."

"You have come for me, Herr Kriminalinspektor."

"Yes, Herr Marowitz. Just for your own protec——"

"I understand, Herr Kriminalinspektor. Shall we go?"

"Yes, if you don't mind. . . . Herr Marowitz, may I ask if you have blankets and food, and a little money?"

"Money, yes, but not blankets. And my wife will bring me food if it's necessary."

"Why don't you take a blanket, just to have one, and maybe some bread and sausage or something, Herr Marowitz? You understand, I don't—"

"Thank you, Herr Kriminalinspektor. . . . Mama, come in and say good evening to Kriminalinspektor Hofmeister."

"No," from the other room.

"I'm sorry, Herr Kriminalinspektor. Frau Marowitz isn't so well this evening. I'll get the blanket and food."

Hofmeister sat in the room alone, and the apartment door was unlocked from the outside. Samuel, the tailor's 17-year-old *Mischling* son came in.

"Hello, Herr Kriminalinspektor. I saw Georg this afternoon, at the synagogue. They blew it up, as a safety measure."

"I know," said Hofmeister; Georg was his youngest son.

"You don't see something like that every day," said Samuel.

"No, you don't, Samuel," said Hofmeister.

"And Georg says he's sure I can get in the Air Corps;

they take half-Jews. He's going to speak to—hello, Pop, what's the blanket for, where you going?"

"Hello, Schmul. I'm going to spend the night out."

"Where?"

"At the Town Hall. Herr Hofmeister is going with me."

"Oh." The boy paused. "Can I go along?"

"Well—"

"Oh, yes," said Hofmeister, "part way, we'll all walk together."

"Well," said Marowitz, "a glass of wine, Herr Kriminalinspektor?"

"No, thank you, Herr Marowitz, not on duty, you know. Maybe just a—. No. Thank you anyway. I appreciate it."

The son carrying the father's suitcase and walking between the two older men, the three of them climbed up through the streets, around the turns, up the steps, to the Market Place which led to the Town Hall.

"We're traveling at a snail's pace," said the son.

"Herr Hofmeister and I are older than you are, Son, aren't we, Herr Kriminalinspektor?"

"Yes, Herr Marowitz," said Hofmeister, "yes, we are." Then he stopped and said, "I'm a little out of breath, if you don't mind, Herr Marowitz. I'm tired tonight. If you and Samuel care to walk on ahead, I'll catch up with you."

CHAPTER 2

The Lives Men Lead

These ten men were "little men"; only Herr Hildebrandt, the teacher, had any substantial status in the community. And when I say "little men," I mean not only the men for whom the mass media and the campaign speeches are everywhere designed but, specifically in sharply stratified societies like Germany, the men who think of themselves in that way. Every one of my ten Nazi friends—including Hildebrandt—spoke again and again during our discussions of *"wir kleine Leute,* we little people."

This self-consciousness is nonexistent—or repressed—in America. European students of our culture have all cited our egalitarianism as an affectation and an expensive one, producing a national leadership indistinguishable from its constituency. If everybody is little, nobody is little. But the rise of National Socialism involved both the elitist and the servile impulses. When "big men," Hindenburgs, Neuraths, Schachts, and even Hohenzollerns, accepted Nazism, little men had good and sufficient reason to accept it. *"Wenn die 'Ja' sagen,"* said Herr Simon, the bill-collector, *"dann sagen wir auch 'Ja.'* What was good enough for *them* was certainly good enough for us."

Foreigners speaking of the "National Socialist Party" miss the point, said the younger Schwenke; it was the

National Socialist German Workers Party, "the party of the little men like me. The only other was the Communist." Emperor and Führer both required the consciousness of littleness in the Germans, but Führer, bringing bigness down, lifted littleness up. The democratic babykisser and backslapper does the same thing, but it is more effective when an absolute ruler does it. My friends were little men—like the Führer himself.

These ten men were not men of distinction. They were not men of influence. They were not opinion-makers. Nobody ever gave them a free sample of anything on the ground that what *they* thought of it would increase the sales of the product. Their importance lay in the fact that God—as Lincoln said of the common people—had made so many of them. In a nation of seventy million, they were the sixty-nine million plus. They were the Nazis, the little men to whom, if ever they voiced their own views outside their own circles, bigger men politely pretended to listen without ever asking them to elaborate.

A year's conversations, in their own language, under informal conditions involving meals, "a glass of wine," or, more preciously, a cup of coffee, exchange of family visits (including the children), and long, easy evenings, Saturday afternoons, or Sunday walks—these were things that not one of my ten friends had supposed possible with an American. None of them had had any but official American contacts. None had been to America or England or outside Germany as civilians, excepting the teacher, who had spent much time in France. None spoke English.

My relationships with them were, in every case, established with considerable difficulty, through a third (or fourth or fifth) person who could convince them of my good faith and my good intentions. And all ten of them, with the possible exception of Baker Wedekind, seemed sooner or later to have accepted my statement of my mission: I had come to Germany, as a German-descended private person, to bring back to America the life-story of the ordinary German under National Socialism, with the end purpose of establishing better understanding of Germany among my countrymen. The statement was true, and my German academic position gave it weight with them. But my greatest asset was my total ignorance of German—the only language that any of them, except the teacher (who spoke French) could speak. They were my teachers. "Mushi," the old tailor, Schwenke, would call to his wife, "just listen to the way the Herr Professor says '*Auf wiedersehen!*' " My friends had ample opportunity to display their pedagogy and their patience with the Herr Professor, who was slow, but good-natured.

I did lie to all ten of them on two points: on the advice of my German colleagues and friends, I did not tell them that I was a Jew; nor did I tell them that I had access to other sources of information about them than my private conversations with them.

I think that I may now call all of them, with the exception of the baker, friends of mine. I think that four of the ten, Tailor Schwenke, his son Gustav, Bank Clerk Kessler, and Teacher Hildebrandt (and, possibly, Policeman Hofmeister) told me their stories as fully as the stories were in them to tell. They were none of them, except the teacher, the student, and the bank clerk, at all fluent by temperament, but none of the ten consciously lied to me (in my opinion) except, possibly, Baker Wedekind and Tailor Schwenke, and the latter only on his role in the arson of the synagogue. I found no intolerable discrepancies or contradictions in their individual accounts over months of discussion; memory lapse, normal reserve, and, above all, the confusion and repression inherent in such cataclysmic experiences as theirs seemed to me to explain the small discrepancies and contradictions I observed. At no point did I try to trap any of them.

Only one of my ten Nazi friends saw Nazism as we— you and I—saw it *in any respect*. This was Hildebrandt, the teacher. And even he then believed, and still believes, in part of its program and practice, "the democratic part." The other nine, decent, hard-working, ordinarily intelligent and honest men, did not know before 1933 that Nazism was evil. They did not know between 1933 and 1945 that it was evil. And they do not know it now. None of them ever knew, or now knows, Nazism as we knew and know it; and they lived under it, served it, and, indeed, made it.

As we know Nazism, it was a naked, total tyranny which degraded its adherents and enslaved its opponents and adherents alike; terrorism and terror in daily life, private and public; brute personal and mob injustice at every level of association; a flank attack upon God and a frontal attack upon the worth of the human person and the rights which that worth implies. These nine ordinary Germans knew it absolutely otherwise, and they still know it otherwise. If our view of National Socialism is a little simple, so is theirs. An autocracy? Yes, of course, an autocracy, as in the fabled days of "the golden time" our parents knew. But a tyranny, as you Americans use the term? Nonsense.

When I asked Herr Wedekind, the baker, why he had believed in National Socialism, he said, "Because it promised to solve the unemployment problem. And it did. But I never imagined what it would lead to. Nobody did."

I thought I had struck pay dirt, and I said, "What do you mean, 'what it would lead to,' Herr Wedekind?"

"War," he said. "Nobody ever imagined it would lead to war."

The evil of National Socialism began on September 1, 1939; and that was my friend the baker.

Remember—none of these nine Germans had ever traveled abroad (except in war); none had ever known or talked with a foreigner or read the foreign press; none ever wanted to listen to the foreign radio when it was legal to do so, and none (except, oddly enough, the policeman) listened to it when it was illegal. They were as uninterested in the outside world as their contemporaries in France— or America. None of them ever heard anything bad about the Nazi regime except, as they believed, from Germany's enemies, and Germany's enemies were theirs. "Everything the Russians and the Americans said about us," said Cabinetmaker Klingelhöfer, "they now say about each other."

Men think first of the lives they lead and the things they see; and not, among the things they see, of the extraordinary sights, but of the sights which meet them in their daily rounds. The lives of my nine friends—and even of the tenth, the teacher—were lightened and brightened by National Socialism as they knew it. And they look back at it now—nine of them, certainly—as the best time of their lives; for what are men's lives? There were jobs and job security, summer camps for the children and the Hitler Jugend to keep them off the streets. What does a mother want to know? She wants to know where her children are, and with whom, and what they are doing. In those days she knew or thought she did; what difference does it make? So things went better at home, and when things go better at home, and on the job, what more does a husband and father want to know?

The best time of their lives. There were wonderful ten-dollar holiday trips for the family in the "Strength through Joy" program, to Norway in the summer and Spain in the winter, for people who had never dreamed of a real holiday trip at home or abroad. And in Kronenberg "nobody" (nobody my friends knew) went cold, nobody went hungry, nobody went ill and uncared for. For whom do men know? They know people of their own neighborhood, of their own station and occupation, of their own political (or nonpolitical) views, of their own religion and race. All the blessings of the New Order, advertised everywhere, reached "everybody."

There were horrors, too, but these were advertised nowhere, reached "nobody." Once in a while (and only once in a while) a single crusading or sensation-mongering newspaper in America exposes the inhuman conditions of the local county jail; but none of my friends had ever read such a newspaper when there were such in Germany (far fewer there than here), and now there were none. None of the horrors impinged upon the day-to-day lives of my ten friends or was ever called to their attention. There was "some sort of trouble" on the streets of Kronenberg as one or another of my friends was passing by on a couple of occasions, but the police dispersed the crowd and there was nothing in the local paper. You and I leave "some sort of trouble on the streets" to the police; so did my friends in Kronenberg.

The real lives that real people live in a real community have nothing to do with Hitler and Roosevelt or with what Hitler and Roosevelt are doing. Man doesn't meet the State very often. On November 10, 1938, the day after the arson of the synagogues, an American news service reported a trivial incident from a suburb of Berlin. A mob of children were carrying great sacks of candy out of the smashed shop window of a Jewish-owned candy store, while a crowd of adults, including some of the children's parents (including, too, a ring of SA men in Brown Shirt uniform), stood watching. An old man walked up, an "Aryan." He watched the proceedings and then turned to the parents and said to them: "You think you are hurting the Jew. You do not know what you are doing. You are teaching your children to steal." And the old man walked off, and the parents broke out of the crowd, knocked the candy out of their children's hands and dragged them wailing away. Man, in the form of the parents, had met the State, in the form of the SA. But it is doubtful if he knew it; after all, the SA men just stood there, without interfering.

In its issue of November 11, 1938, the *Kronenberger Zeitung* carried the following report, at the bottom of page 4, under a very small headline reading *Schutzhaft*, "Protective Custody": "In the interest of their own security, a number of male Jews were taken into custody yesterday. This morning they were sent away from the city." I showed it to each of my ten friends. None of them —including the teacher—remembered ever having seen it or anything like it.

1933, 1934, 1935, 1936, 1937, 1938, 1939—until September 1, when, as the Head of the Government told them, Poland attacked their country—the little lives of my friends went on, under National Socialism as they had before, altered only for the better, and always for the better, in bread and butter, in housing, health, and hope, wherever the New Order touched them. "No one outside Germany seems to understand this," said an anti-Nazi woman, who had been imprisoned in 1943, ostensibly for listening to the foreign radio but actually for hiding Jews (which was not technically illegal). "I remember standing on a Stuttgart street corner in 1938, during a Nazi festival, and the enthusiasm, the new hope of a good life, after so many years of hopelessness, the new belief, after so many years of disillusion, almost swept me, too, off my feet. Let me try to tell you what that time was like in Germany: I was sitting in a cinema with a Jewish friend and her daughter of thirteen, while a Nazi parade went across the screen, and the girl caught her mother's arm and whispered, 'Oh, Mother, Mother, if I weren't a Jew, I think I'd be a Nazi!' No one outside seems to understand how this was."

The German language, like every other, has some glorious epithets, untranslatable, and *wildgewordene Spiessbürger* is one of them. It means, very roughly, "little men gone wild." Of themselves, such men would perhaps use the borrowed and Germanicized term *Fanatiker. Fanatiker* are not to be confused either with *Spitzbuben*, rascals, or with *Bluthunde*, hired hoodlums or goons. When I asked (of anti-Nazis and of Nazis) how many genuine *Fanatiker* there were in the Third Reich, how many little men gone wild, the hazard was never over a million. It must be remembered, especially in connection with Communism in Russia, and even with Fascism in Italy, that the National Socialist movement died young; it never had a chance to rear a whole generation of its own.

And the rest of the seventy million Germans? The rest were not even cogs, in any positive sense at all, in the totalitarian machine. A people like ourselves, who know such systems only by hearsay or by the report of their victims or opponents, tends to exaggerate the actual relationship between man and the State under tyranny. The laws are hateful to those who hate them, but who hates them? It is dangerous, in Nazi Germany, to go to Communist meetings or read the *Manchester Guardian*, but who wants to go to Communist meetings or read the *Manchester Guardian?*

In the America of the 1950's one hears, on the one hand, that the country is overcome by mistrust, suspicion, and dread, and, on the other, that nobody is afraid, nobody defamed, nobody destroyed by defamation. Where is the truth? Where was it in Nazi Germany? None of my ten Nazi friends, with the exception of the cryptodemocrat Hildebrandt, knew any mistrust, suspicion, or dread in his own life or among those with whom he lived and worked; none was defamed or destroyed. Their world was the world of National Socialism; inside it, inside the Nazi community, they knew only good-fellowship and the ordinary concerns of ordinary life. They feared the "Bolsheviks" but not one another, and their fear was the accepted fear of the whole otherwise happy Nazi community that was Germany. Outside that community they never went, or saw, or heard; they had no occasion to.

That Nazism in Germany meant mistrust, suspicion, dread, defamation, and destruction we learned from those who brought us word of it—from its victims and opponents whose world was outside the Nazi community and from journalists and intellectuals, themselves non-Nazi or anti-Nazi, whose sympathies naturally lay with the victims and opponents. These people saw life in Germany in non-Nazi terms. There were two truths, and they were not contradictory: the truth that Nazis were happy and the truth that anti-Nazis were unhappy. And in the America of the 1950's —I do not mean to suggest that the two situations are parallel or even more than very tenuously comparable— those who did not dissent or associate with dissenters saw no mistrust or suspicion beyond the great community's mistrust and suspicion of dissenters, while those who dissented or believed in the right to dissent saw nothing but mistrust and suspicion and felt its devastation. As there were two Americas, so, in a much more sharply drawn division, there were two Germanys. And so, just as there is when one man dreads the policeman on the beat and another waves "Hello" to him, there are two countries in every country.

In Russian-Communized East Germany after the second World War, a worker in a State factory is compelled to attend one meeting a week, of two hours, for purposes of what we should call "indoctrination" or "brain-washing" and what the Communists call "education." Beyond that and paying his taxes, he is compelled to do nothing more; he takes military service, secret police, and rationing for granted (as who doesn't?). Of course, he is blared at, from posters, newspapers, radio, and public address systems (as who isn't, for one purpose or another?), but he is let alone.

Most Germans—nearly all of them, after twelve years of Nazism—see nothing inordinate in this amount of compulsion. Even under Nazism (before the war), Party members were required to give only Friday evenings and Sunday mornings to Party or public work. Beyond this point, service to the tyranny was, naturally, highly advisable for the ambitious and the politically suspect, but it was not required of the man who wanted to hold a job, a home, a family, and an honored place in the *Singverein* or the *Turnverein*. I encountered a few civil servants in Kronenberg who had never joined the Party and had not been bothered; they were the kind that never joined anything, and nobody expected them to—the kind, too, that is never promoted; and I met a pastor who had not been persecuted although he had refused to let his children join the Hitler

Youth and the German Maidens until membership became automatic.

It is local conditions, even under totalitarianism, which govern the application of public authority to the individual. These conditions, which vary so much elsewhere, varied much more than I had supposed possible under National Socialism and tended almost always to relax the central controls (just as local courts everywhere tend to relax legal principles), except where the local boss was a *Fanatiker*. And these latter instances were the exceptions; local bosses, in order to function effectively, have to be locally popular.

Pastor Wilhelm Mensching, in the village of Petzen, in Lower Saxony, preached anti-Nazism to his little flock during the whole twelve years that the Nazis were in power in Germany. Every Sunday morning he stood in his pulpit and answered the speech which the Bürgermeister, an "Old Party Fighter," made every Saturday night in the Market Place. Mensching was never touched; when the Gestapo came from Hannover to arrest him, the Bürgermeister went to the Gauleiter to oppose them, and the arrest wasn't made. Wilhelm Mensching had "always" been pastor of Petzen, and to disturb him would have been an intolerable disturbance to the configuration of the village. And both he and the Bürgermeister knew it.

There were not enough thousands of Menschings in Germany, simply because such men are not born every day and the church in Germany (as elsewhere) does not nourish their multiplication. But there were dozens enough of them to make the point. To be sure, National Socialism had only a few years to achieve its great *Gleichschaltung*, its integration of man into the State; still, six of them were war years, in which the tempo could be, and was, stepped up considerably. But modern tyrants all stand above politics and, in doing so, demonstrate that they are all master politicians. They know, without having to read Florentine theorists, that politicians cannot afford to be hated. A Niemöller would have to be silenced, at whatever risk to the tyranny; the best-known of all German pastors, he had said, "God is my Führer." He was a national and an international challenge, and he had to be handled the hard way. But there were easy ways (the easiest being to ignore them) to confine the effectiveness of dozens of Menschings to their separate villages without taking steps which would have rocked any good villager on his heels and made him say, "No, not this, not this."

Ordinary people—and ordinary Germans—cannot be expected to tolerate activities which outrage the ordinary sense of ordinary decency unless the victims are, in advance, successfully stigmatized as enemies of the people, of the nation, the race, the religion. Or, if they are not enemies (that comes later), they must be an element within the community somehow extrinsic to the common bond, a decompositive ferment (be it only by the way they part their hair or tie their necktie) in the uniformity which is everywhere the condition of common quiet. The Germans' innocuous acceptance and practice of social anti-Semitism before Hitlerism had undermined the resistance of their ordinary decency to the stigmatization and persecution to come.

In the pleasant resort towns of New England Americans have seen signs reading "Selected Clientele" or "Restricted." They have grown accustomed to seeing such signs, so accustomed that, unless they are non-Caucasian or, perhaps, non-"Aryan" Americans, they take no notice of them and, in taking no notice, accept them. In the much less pleasant cottonseed-oil towns of the Deep South Americans have grown accustomed to seeing signs reading anything from "White" and "Colored" to "Nigger, Don't Let the Sun Set on You Here," and, unless they are non-Caucasian or, perhaps, northern Americans, they take no notice of them. There were enough such signs (literally and figuratively) in pre-Nazi Germany, and there was enough nonresistance to them, so that, when the countryside bloomed in 1933 with signs reading *"Juden hier unerwünscht, Jews Not Wanted Here,"* the Germans took no notice of them. So, in the body politic as in the body personal, nonresistance to the milder indulgences paves the way for nonresistance to the deadlier.

It is actual resistance which worries tyrants, not lack of the few hands required to do the dark work of tyranny. What the Nazis had to gauge was the point at which atrocity would awaken the community to the consciousness of its moral habits. This point may be moved forward as the national emergency, or cold war, is moved forward, and still further forward in hot war. But it remains the point which the tyrant must always approach and never pass. If his calculation is too far behind the people's temper, he faces a palace *Putsch;* if it is too far ahead, a popular revolution.

It is in this nonlitigable sense, at least, that the Germans as a whole were guilty: nothing was done, or attempted, that they would not stand for. The two exceptions were euthanasia, which was abandoned, and the pagan "Faith Movement" of Alfred Rosenberg, which was aborted.

Local hoodlums could beat up Communists or Social Democrats, desecrate Jewish cemeteries or smash Jews' windows by night; the local police, overseen by the Gestapo, would make a routine and invariably unsuccessful investigation of the assault; and the ordinary demands of decency would be satisfied. The Kronenbergers, being decent folk, would, perhaps, turn over in their beds—and sleep on.

The burning of a synagogue was something else; it approached, closely and almost dangerously, the point at which the community might be awakened. If not sacrilege, it was, after all, lawless destruction of valuable goods, an affront to the German property sense (much deeper than ours) and, no less, to the responsibility (much sterner than ours) of the authorities to uphold the law. When the synagogue was burned in Kronenberg, local SA men (including Tailor Schwenke, my friend) were used incidentally; but the arson was planned and directed by outsiders, from a big city forty miles away. In the pattern of American gangsterism's importation of killers from New York to Chicago or vice versa, the local officials were helpless and, by transference, the community, too.

The German community—the rest of the seventy million Germans, apart from the million or so who operated the whole machinery of Nazism—had nothing to do except *not to interfere*. Absolutely nothing was expected of them except to go on as they had, paying their taxes, reading their local paper, and listening to the radio. Everybody attended local celebrations of national occasions—hadn't the schools and the stores always been closed for the Kaiser's birthday?—so you attended, too. Everybody contributed money and time to worthy purposes, so you did, too. In America your wife collects or distributes clothing, gives an afternoon a week to the Red Cross or the orphanage or the hospital; in Germany she did the same thing in the Nazi Frauenbund, and for the same reasons. The Frauenbund, like the Red Cross, was patriotic and humanitarian;

did your wife ask the Red Cross if "Negro" plasma was segregated from "white"?

One minded one's own business in Germany, with or without a dictatorship. The random leisure which leads Americans into all sorts of afterhour byways, constructive, amusing, or ruinous, did not exist for most Germans. One didn't go out of one's way, on a day off, to "look for trouble"—there less than here. Germans were no more given to associating with nonconformist persons or organizations than we are. They engaged themselves in opposing the government much less than we do. Few Americans say "No" to the government—fewer Germans. None of my ten friends said "No" to the Nazi government, and only one of them, Teacher Hildebrandt, thought "No."

Men who are ever going to say "No" to the government are for the most part—not uniformly—men with a prior pattern of politically conscious impulse. But such men were, in Hitler's Germany, either Nazis or anti-Nazis. If they were Nazis, they said "Yes," with a will. If they were anti-Nazis, their past record, like the teacher's, hung over their heads. Far from protesting, these, the only Germans who might have protested in quantity, had the greatest incentive of all to conform. They were like men who, in McCarthy-ridden America, had been Communists in their youth, who hoped that their past was safely buried, and whose sole concern was whether or not *their* names turned up in the day's un-American activities testimony. Of all Americans, they would be the least likely to participate *now* in protest or opposition. "I never got over marveling that I survived," said Herr Hildebrandt. "I couldn't help being glad, when something happened to somebody else, that it hadn't happened to me. It was like later on, when a bomb hit another city, or another house than your own;

you were thankful." "More thankful for yourself than you were sorry for others?" "Yes. The truth is, Yes. It may be different in your case, Herr Professor, but I'm not sure that you will know until you have faced it."

You were sorry for the Jews, who had to identify themselves, every male with "Israel" inserted into his name, every female with "Sarah," on every official occasion; sorrier, later on, that they lost their jobs and their homes and had to report themselves to the police; sorrier still that they had to leave their homeland, that they had to be taken to concentration camps and enslaved and killed. But—*weren't you glad you weren't a Jew?* You were sorry, and more terrified, when it happened, as it did, to thousands, to hundreds of thousands, of non-Jews. But—weren't you glad that it hadn't happened to you, a non-Jew? It might not have been the loftiest type of gladness, but you hugged it to yourself and watched your step, more cautiously than ever.

Those who came back from Buchenwald in the early years had promised—as every inmate of every German prison had always had to promise upon his release—not to discuss his prison experience. You should have broken your promise. You should have told your countrymen about it; you might, though the chances were all against you, have saved your country had you done so. But you didn't. You told your wife, or your father, and swore them to secrecy. And so, although millions guessed, only thousands knew. Did you want to go back to Buchenwald, and to worse treatment this time? Weren't you sorry for those who were left there? And weren't you glad you were out?

"*So war die Sache.* That's the way it was." Where the community feels and thinks—or at least talks and acts— pretty much one way, to say or do differently means a kind of internal exile that most people find unattractive to undertake, even if it involves no legal penalty. Oh, it isn't so bad if you have been a lifelong dissenter or radical, or a known criminal; you're used to it. But you—you and I— you're used to saying "Hello" to everyone and having everyone say "Hello" to you. You look every man in the eye, and, though your eyes may be empty, they are clear. You are respected in the community. Why? Because your attitudes are the same as the community's. But are the community's attitudes respectable? That's not the point.

We—you and I—want the community's approval on the community's basis. We don't want the approval of criminals, but the community decides what is criminal and what isn't. This is the trap. You and I—and my ten Nazi friends —are in the trap. It has nothing to do directly with fear for one's own or his family's safety, or his job, or his property. I may have all these, never lose them, and still be in exile. Somebody somewhere in the community (it doesn't matter who or why) is telling somebody else that I'm a liar or a cheater—or a Red. Tomorrow somebody whose closer acquaintance I should never have cultivated—I have never liked him, never really respected him—will pass me without saying "Hello" to me. I am being exiled at home, isolated. My safety, unless I am accustomed to being a dissenter, or a recluse, or a snob, is in numbers; this man, who will pass me tomorrow and who, though he always said "Hello" to me, would never have lifted a finger for me, will tomorrow reduce my safety by the number of one.

In what you and I call the blessings of life—including uncritical acceptance by the whole of the undifferentiated community—every one of my ten friends, excepting Tailor Schwenke, who had once had his own shop and was now a school janitor, was better off than he had ever been before; and not just they and their families, but all their friends, the "whole" community, the widows and orphans, the aged, the sick, and the poor. Germany had been what many Americans would call a welfare state ever since Bismarck, the reactionary Junker, introduced social legislation to stave off social democracy. In the collapse after the first World War, and again in the collapse at the end of the 1920's, the Weimar Republic could not maintain its social services. Nazism not only restored but extended them; they were much more comprehensive than they had ever been before or, of course, than they have been since. Nor were they restricted to Party members; only "enemies" of the regime were excluded from them.

The war was hard, although not, until the bombing became general, anywhere near as hard as the first war, in which the German government had not anticipated the blockade and the civilian population ate acorns; this time, the conquered countries were starved and the Germans were fed. But my friends do not mean 1939–45 when they speak of "the Nazi time." They mean 1933–39. And the best time of one's life is, in retrospect, all the better when, as in Germany after 1945, one supposed that he would not see its like again.

The best time of their lives.

"Yes," said Herr Klingelhöfer, the cabinetmaker, "it was the best time. After the first war, German families began to have only two children. That was bad, bad for the family, the marriage, the home, the nation. There is where Germany was dying, and that was the kind of strength we believed that Hitler was talking about. And he was talking about it. After '33 we had more children. A man saw a future. The difference between rich and poor grew smaller, one saw it everywhere. A man had a chance. In 1935 I took over my father's shop and got a two-thousand-dollar government loan. *Ungeheuer!* Unheard of!

"The good development had nothing to do with whether we had a democracy, or a dictatorship, or what. The form of government had nothing to do with it. A man had a little money, a chance, and he didn't pay any attention to any *system*. Inside the system, you see the benefits. Outside it, when you are not benefited by it, you see the faults, I suppose. I suppose that's the way it is in Russia now. That's the way it is everywhere, always, *nicht wahr? 'Das danken wir unserm Führer.* For all this we thank our Leader,' the kids all said in school. Now they say, *'Das danken wir den Amerikanern.'* If Communism comes, they'll say, *'Das danken wir dem Stalin.'* That's the way men are. I couldn't do that myself."

But he did it.

Herr Klingelhöfer counted his blessings. Who doesn't?

This might be, I suppose, pro-Nazi propaganda. It is also a fact, in so far as men's attitudes are facts and decisive facts. No Occupation could make—or had made—anti-Nazis out of my friends. The evidence they had before their eyes for rejecting that period of their lives that was spent under National Socialism was wholly inadequate. And it was hard to see how any "recovery" under any German government in any foreseeable future (still less, under any Occupation) could make it adequate. At best, until such time as men (or at least these men) changed the root basis of their values, "things" could only some day be as "good" as they had been under Hitler. What we call freedom is not, even if they had all the freedom we have, an adequate substitute, in my friends' view, for all that they had and have lost. Men who did not know that they were slaves do not know that they have been freed.

CHAPTER 3

Hitler and I

None of these nine ordinary Germans (and even the tenth, Herr Hildebrandt, is not completely firm on the point) thought then or thinks now that the rights of man, in his own case, were violated or even more than mildly inhibited for reasons of what they then accepted (and still accept) as the national emergency proclaimed four weeks after Hitler took office as Chancellor. Only two of the ten—Hildebrandt, of course, and Simon, the bill-collector—saw the system as in any way repressive. Herr Simon thinks that it was because of what he calls his "democratic" tendency to argue that he rose only to the lowest rank in the Party, cell leader, in spite of his having been one of the oldest members of the Party in Germany. But he was never alienated from his Party faith or its leadership by what he still regards as the local perversions of its principles by "the little Hitlers."

"The little Hitlers" recurred constantly in my conversations with my friends. It did not derogate Hitler—quite the opposite. "The little Hitlers" were the local or provincial officials, fellows you knew or had heard other fellows talk about familiarly. You knew (or had reason to believe) that they were no bigger or better than you were; you detested their imitation of the Führer, above all, of his certainty and the absoluteness that springs from certainty. But, because of the old military principle of command which obtained throughout the Party, you could do nothing about it but dream at night that Schmidt, the little Hitler, had fallen on his face in public and you were chosen by acclaim to replace him.

None of my ten friends, even today, ascribes moral evil to Hitler, although most of them think (after the fact) that he made fatal strategical mistakes which even they themselves might have made at the time. His worst mistake was his selection of advisers—a backhanded tribute to the Leader's virtues of trustfulness and loyalty, to his very innocence of the knowledge of evil, fully familiar to those who have heard partisans of F. D. R. or Ike explain how things went wrong.

Having fixed our faith in a father-figure—or in a father, or in a mother or a wife—we must keep it fixed until inexcusable fault (and what fault of a father, a mother, a wife, is inexcusable?) crushes it at once and completely. This figure represents our own best selves; it is what we ourselves want to be and, through identification, are. To abandon it for anything less than crushing evidence of inexcusable fault is self-incrimination, and of one's best, unrealized self. Thus Hitler was betrayed by his subordinates, and the little Nazis with him. They may hate Bormann and Goebbels—Bormann because he rose to power at the end, and they are ashamed of the end; Goebbels because he was a runt with a "Jewish mind," that is, a facile and cunning mind unlike theirs. They may hate Himmler, the *Bluthund*, above all, because he killed in cold blood, and they wouldn't do that. But they may not hate Hitler or themselves.

"You see," said Tailor Schwenke, the littlest of my ten little men, "there was always a secret war against Hitler in the regime. They fought him with unfair means. Himmler

I detested. Goebbels, too. If Hitler had been told the truth, things would have been different." For "Hitler" read "I."

"The killing of the Jews?" said the "democratic" bill-collector, der alte Kämpfer, Simon. "Yes, that was wrong, unless they committed treason in wartime. And of course they did. If I had been a Jew, I would have myself. Still, it was wrong, but some say it happened and some say it didn't. You can show me pictures of skulls or shoes, but that doesn't prove it. But I'll tell you this—it was Himmler. Hitler had nothing to do with it."

"Do you think he knew about it?"

"I don't know. We'll never know now."

Hitler died to save my friend's best self.

Apart from the partially and secretly anti-Nazi teacher, only the bank clerk, Kessler, the natively eloquent little man who became an official Party speaker in the county, seems to have had any shadow of doubt about Hitler's personal or public goodness—and even he may be projecting his own experience: "Hitler was a spellbinder, a natural orator. I think he was carried away from truth, even from truth, by his passion. Even so, he always believed what he said." "The schemers, Himmler, Goebbels, Rosenberg, Bormann—they built him up into a man of destiny," said Salesman Damm, the Party office manager in Kronenberg. "They did it so skilfully that he finally believed it himself. From then on, he lived in a world of delusion. And this happened, mind you, to a man who was good and great." It could happen to me, Heinrich Damm, too.

These believers (for believers they certainly were) do not seem to have been worshipers any more than we believers in F. D. R. or Ike are—if anything, less so. Hitler was a man, one like ourselves, a little man, who, by doing what

65

he did, was a testament to the democracy "you Americans" talk about, the ability of us little men to become great and to rule the whole world. A *little man, like ourselves.* Such a man is the modern pattern of the demagogical tyrant, "the people's friend" of Plato's mob democracy. These Hitlers, Stalins, Mussolinis are commoner upstarts, the half-literate Hitler the commonest of the lot.

Kings and kaisers rule by God's grace, Hitlers by their own. God's grace puts a father over his children, to rule them in their interest. He is visibly and incontrovertibly endowed with wisdom appropriate to his function, and his walking stick (or his napkin ring or his rocking chair), like the Kaiser's crown, sets him wholly apart from his children. But these Hitlers wear trench coats. Are they in fact father-figures? Or are Leader and Father two separable subconscious entities?

The newest wrinkle in psychoanalytic lingo is "charismatic leader." It seems to mean (if "charismatic" is derived from the Greek *charisma*) the one to whom it is given to take care of his people. Both the Kaiser and Hitler "took care of" the German people, but the Kaiser was endowed by God. He did not have to kiss babies; he did not have to do anything. The most perfect of fathers, he lived far away, in Potsdam; you might see him once or twice in your life, in a great parade, or never at all. Unlike your own biological father, he never punished you for little things or unjustly. Unlike your biological father, he let you be "bad," in your personal life, beat your wife or get drunk or do shoddy work, without ever whipping you or withdrawing his love.

Seven of my friends (the seven oldest of them) had been brought up in a stable society, with their perfect father in Potsdam and their imperfect father at home. One of the seven, Herr Kessler, the bank clerk, had been orphaned early and was brought up by his mother. At least four of the other six feared or hated their fathers (or both), and of Hildebrandt alone am I able to say with some certainty that he neither feared nor hated his.

The old tailor, Schwenke, *still* hates his father, who is still alive, at ninety-three, in a near-by village; Schwenke has not seen him in years. He hated him always in his heart— "he drank too much," "he was cruel to my blessed mother" —and finally he hated him openly, running away from home to the army after his father ordered him to remain in the service of a master-tailor who mistreated him. Heinrich Damm, the country boy, feared his father, who, besides being an ambitious and avaricious farmer, was the village innkeeper and, after a backbreaking day in the fields, could handle any half-dozen sots who tried to keep him from closing the inn at midnight. Damm remembers that his father compelled his pregnant mother to pile rocks until she dropped; when she died, a few years later, his father said, "I guess I worked her too hard." But the son feared his father too much (and still does) to hate him.

By contrast, the five of my friends who now have children in or approaching their teens all marvel at the sassiness, the independence, of their own children. And "marvel" better describes their attitude than "disapprove" or "resent." The younger Schwenke said, "My father"—the old tailor— "would have killed me if I'd talked to him the way my boy talks to me," and he shakes his head. "It's all different now," said Cabinetmaker Klingelhöfer. "When I was a boy, I spoke when I was spoken to; otherwise, never. Now my children disagree with me about everything, and I can't do a thing. My wife is the boss," and he laughs. The clue to the change (and a radical change it seems to be) may be the emancipation of the German woman and, in particular, of the wife, which Nazism tried to overcome. The German child, today as yesterday, seems to be left almost entirely to the mother; even among my non-Nazi friends, the relationship between father and child was generally much more remote than ours. But, whereas the mother once executed the father's will upon the child, she now seems to execute her own.

My friends' youngsters are, to be sure, being brought up in a disintegrated society, in which not only the Kaiser but also the biological father have been dislodged. My friends have lost their jobs or their homes or their status or their security, and their children know it. And the Kaiser is only a character in history, gone without any supposition that he will ever return.

The true father-figure is a true *figure*, the representation of an ideal essence. Whether Wilhelm II was, as a ruler or a man, good or bad was irrelevant to his status. The failings of one's biological father could not but affect one's attitude, but the failings of the true father-figure were, like the Emperor's new clothes in the fairy tale, beyond the very presumption of his subjects to observe. There were, in Germany, daring intellectuals who attacked the Kaiser's policies before the first World War, but my friends were not daring intellectuals.

One does not presume to judge the true father-figure. One would not—but cannot help himself—judge his biological father. But one judges a man like himself by his own criteria of success and failure. Hitler was, until 1943 or 1944, a success. He displayed all the way to Stalingrad a genius which only a dozen men in the whole world's history have had, a genius for continuous success in public affairs against the odds which only public affairs present. None of my friends hesitates—every soldier is a military expert, and every German is a soldier—to say that he was wrong to invade Poland (or to invade *when* he did or *how* he did) or, perhaps, to attack Russia, which he had so brilliantly immobilized, or to ally himself with Italy or to take on the world so soon. But these wrongs were strategic mistakes. I might—my friends are talking—have made them myself. Napoleon made them.

My friends do not mourn Hitler any more than we mourn those of our own national leaders whose genius culminates in ruin; such geniuses must build their own sarcophagi with the cynical assistance of the political party hacks who find themselves with bare bones on their hands in the next campaign. My Nazi friends do not deify Hitler or (if the distinction may be made) glorify him. They never questioned his absolute right or absolute power to absolute rule. But they do not think of him—and seem never to have done so—as Führer, the Leader, and not just because the Occupation's re-educators suppressed the use of the very word. They think of him as Hitler, and, whatever they dream of reviving, they do not dream of reviving Hitlerism.

Romantic they are, but this romantic they are not. They do not repress his name; they mention it when there is occasion to mention it. But there is little occasion to do so. Old soldiers in Germany have something else to do these days besides spit on the stove and tell stories; the stove is cold. Nothing surprised my friends so much as to hear that Americans still speculate about Hitler's survival, in the flesh in Argentina or Spain or in personal spirit in Germany. He lived, succeeded, failed, died, and is dead.

Adolf Hitler was good for Germany—in my friends' view —up until 1943, 1941, or 1939, depending upon the individual's assessment of his strategy. After that—you have only to look at Germany, "at us, Herr Professor," to see that he was bad for Germany. Hitler belongs to the ages; what he left behind him belongs to my friends, who are scrabbling in the ruins. The distant future may revive him, but I think not; the distant future is not likely to leave Germany as it was or is.

CHAPTER 4

"What Would You Have Done?"

None of my ten friends ever encountered anybody connected with the operation of the deportation system or the concentration camps. None of them ever knew, on a personal basis, anybody connected with the Gestapo, the Sicherheitsdienst (Security Service), or the Einsatzgruppen (the Occupation Detachments, which followed the German armies eastward to conduct the mass killing of Jews). None of them ever knew anybody who knew anybody connected with these agencies of atrocity. Even Policeman Hofmeister, who had to arrest Jews for "protective custody" or "resettlement" and who saw nothing wrong in "giving the Jews land, where they could learn to work with their hands instead of with money," never knew anyone whose shame or shamelessness might have reproached him had they stood face to face. The fact that the Police Chief of Kronenberg made him sign the orders to arrest Jews told him only that the Chief himself was afraid of getting into trouble "higher up."

Sixty days before the end of the war, Teacher Hildebrandt, as a first lieutenant in command of a disintegrating Army subpost, was informed by the post doctor that an SS man attached to the post was going crazy because of his memories of shooting down Jews "in the East"; this was the closest any of my friends came to knowing of the systematic butchery of National Socialism.

71

I say none of these ten men knew; and, if none of them, very few of the seventy million Germans. The proportion, which was none out of ten in Kronenberg, would, certainly, have been higher among more intelligent, or among more sensitive or sophisticated people in, say, Kronenberg University or in the big cities where people circulate more widely and hear more. But I must say what I mean by "know."

By *know* I mean knowledge, binding knowledge. Men who are going to protest or take even stronger forms of action, in a dictatorship more so than in a democracy, want to be sure. When they are sure, they still may not take any form of action (in my ten friends' cases, they would not have, I think); but that is another point. What you hear of individual instances, second- or thirdhand, what you guess as to general conditions, having put half-a-dozen instances together, what someone tells you he believes is the case—these may, all together, be convincing. You may be "morally certain," satisfied in your own mind. But moral certainty and mental satisfaction are less than binding knowledge. What you and your neighbors don't expect you to *know*, your neighbors do not expect you to act on, in matters of this sort, and neither do you.

Men who participated in the operation of the atrocity system—would they or wouldn't they tell their wives? The odds are even in Germany, where husbands don't bother to tell their wives as much as we tell ours. But their wives would not tell other people, and neither would they; their jobs were, to put it mildly, of a confidential character. In such work, men, if they talk, lose their jobs. Under Nazism they lost more than their jobs. I am not saying that the men in question, the men who had firsthand knowledge, opposed the system in any degree or even resented having to play a role in it; I am saying, in the words of Cabinet-maker Klingelhöfer, that that is the way men are; and the more reprehensible the work in which they are voluntarily or involuntarily engaged, the more that way they are.

I pushed this point with Tailor Marowitz in Kronenberg, the one Jew still there who had come back from Buchenwald. On his release, in 1939, he was forbidden to talk of his experience, and, in case he might become thoughtless, he was compelled to report (simply report) to the police every day. Whom did he tell of his Buchenwald experience? His wife and "a couple of my very closest friends—Jews, of course."

"How widely was the whole thing known in Kronenberg by the end of the war?"

"You mean the rumors?"

"No—how widely was the whole thing, or anything, known?"

"Oh. Widely, very widely."

"How?"

"Oh, things seeped through somehow, always quietly, always indirectly. So people heard rumors, and the rest they could guess. Of course, most people did not believe the stories of Jews or other opponents of the regime. It was naturally thought that such persons would all exaggerate."

Rumors, guesses enough to make a man know if he wanted badly to know, or at least to believe, and always involving persons who would be suspected, "naturally," of exaggerating. Goebbels' immediate subordinate in charge of radio in the Propaganda Ministery testified at Nuremberg that he had heard of the gassing of Jews, and went to Goebbels with the report. Goebbels said it was false, "enemy propaganda," and that was the end of it. The Nuremberg tribunal accepted this man's testimony on this point and acquitted him. None of my ten friends in Kronenberg—nor anyone else in Kronenberg—was the immediate subordinate of a cabinet minister. Anti-Nazis no less than Nazis let the rumors pass—if not rejecting them, certainly not accepting them; either they were enemy propaganda or they *sounded* like enemy propaganda, and, with one's country fighting for its life and one's sons and brothers dying in war, who wants to hear, still less repeat, even what *sounds* like enemy propaganda?

Who wants to investigate the reports? Who is "looking for trouble"? Who will be the first to undertake (and how undertake it?) to track down the suspicion of governmental wrongdoing under a governmental dictatorship, to occupy himself, in times of turmoil and in wartime with evils, real or rumored, that are wholly outside his own life, outside his own circle, and, above all, outside his own power? After all, what if one found out?

Suppose that you have heard, secondhand, or even firsthand, of an instance in which a man was abused or tortured by the police in a hypothetical American community. You tell a friend whom you are trying to persuade that the police are rotten. He doesn't believe you. He wants firsthand or, if you got it secondhand, at least secondhand testimony. You go to your original source, who has told you the story only because of his absolute trust in you. You want him now to tell a man he doesn't trust, a friend of the police. He refuses. And he warns you that if you use his name as authority for the story, he will deny it. Then you will be suspect, suspected of spreading false rumors against the police. And, as it happens, the police in this hypothetical American community, are rotten, and they'll "get" you somehow.

So, after all, what if one found out in Nazi Germany

(which was no hypothetical American community)? What if one came to know? What then?

There was *nichts dagegen zu machen*, "nothing to do about it." Again and again my discussions with each of my friends reached this point, one way or another, and this very expression; again and again this question, put to me with the wide-eyed innocence that always characterizes the guilty when they ask it of the inexperienced: "What would you have done?"

What is the proportion of revolutionary heroes, of saints and martyrs, or, if you will, of troublemakers, in Stockholm, Ankara, El Paso? We in America have not had the German experience, where even private protest was dangerous, where even secret knowledge might be extorted; but what did we expect the good citizen of Minneapolis or Charlotte to do when, in the midst of war, he was told, openly and official-ly, that 112,000 of his fellow-Americans, those of Japanese ancestry on the American West Coast, had been seized without warrant and sent without due process of law to re-location centers? There was *nichts dagegen zu machen*—not even by the United States Supreme Court, which found that the action was within the Army's power—and, any-way, the good citizen of Minneapolis or Charlotte had his own troubles.

It was this, I think—they had their own troubles—that in the end explained my friends' failure to "do something" or even to know something. A man can carry only so much responsibility. If he tries to carry more, he collapses; so, to save himself from collapse, he rejects the responsibility that exceeds his capacity. There are responsibilities he must carry, in any case, and these, heavy enough under normal conditions, are intensified, even multiplied, in times of great change, be they bad times or good. My friends carried their normal responsibilities well enough; every one of them was a good householder and, with the possible exception of Tailor Schwenke, a good jobholder. But they were unaccustomed to assume public responsibility.

The public responsibilities which Nazism forced upon them—they didn't choose to assume them when they chose to be Nazis—exceeded their capacities. They didn't know, or think, at the beginning, that they were going to have to carry a guilty knowledge or a guilty conscience. Anti-Nazism of any sort, in thought or in feeling (not to say action), would have required them, as isolated individuals, already more heavily burdened than they were accustomed to being, to choose to burden themselves beyond their limit. And this, I think, is always the case with public responsibilities of a volunteer nature—in Germany, America, anywhere—which promise, at best, a deferred reward and, at worst, an imminent penalty.

The American is much better accustomed than the German to responsibilities of a volunteer character, but the principle of rejection is operative here in the United States, too, although the load limit is greater. The greater the combined load of my private and required public responsibility, the weaker my impulse to take volunteer public responsibility; if I'm building a new house and I have to enrol in Civilian Defense, my work with the Boys' Club will suffer. And anti-Nazism in a Nazi dictatorship was no Boys' Club.

Responsible men never shirk responsibility, and so, when they must reject it, they deny it. They draw the curtain. They detach themselves altogether from the consideration of the evil they ought to, but cannot, contend with. Their denial compels their detachment. A good man—even a good American—running to catch a train on an important assignment has to pass by the beating of a dog on the street and concentrate on catching the train; and, once on the train, he has to consider the assignment about which he must do something, rather than the dog-beating about which he can do nothing. If he is running fast enough and his assignment is mortally important, he will not even notice the dog-beating when he passes it by.

The Federal Bureau of Investigation, with its fantastically rapid development of a central record of an ever increasing number of Americans, law-abiding and lawless, is something new in America. But it is very old in Germany, and it had nothing to do with National Socialism except to make it easier for the Nazi government to locate and trace the whole life-history of any and every German. The German system—it has its counterpart in other European countries, including France—was, being German, extraordinarily efficient. American tourists are familiar with the police identity cards they fill out *pro forma* at Continental hotel desks. Resident nationals don't fill out a card when they come to live in a German town or leave it; they fill out a life-history for the police.

Policeman Hofmeister explained to me, with enthusiasm, how thoroughly the identity system meshed in Germany, before Nazism, during Nazism, and since Nazism. Every town has a criminal registry which contains, always up to date, the record of every person born in the town (no matter where he now lives) who has ever been in "trouble"; in addition, the registry contains the whole record of any person who has ever committed a crime (or been arrested) in the town, no matter where he was born. "Consider," said Policeman Hofmeister, an unenthusiastic Nazi, "how nearly impossible it is, and always has been, in Germany for anyone to escape or 'lose' himself. In such a country, my friend, law and order rule always."

How nearly impossible it is to escape, once a man has come into conflict with the police. Better, far, if you have ever before come into conflict with them (or if you suspect that you have ever come under their suspicion), to come into contact with them on their side; best of all, never come into contact with them at all. Don't see the dog-beating on the street or the wife-beating or the Jew-beating or anything. You have your own troubles.

Everyone everywhere has his own troubles. Two hundred miles from Kronenberg was the great chemicals plant of Tesch & Stabinow. In 1942, the manager—he is not a "little man," like my friends, but a manager—gets his first government order for Cyclon-B gas, which could be used as an insecticide but wouldn't be likely to be (especially since the order is "classified," secret). Now Tesch & Stabinow has been producing poison gases for the Army's chemical warfare service, which has a colonel of engineers attached to the plant for consultation. But this order is not for the Army, and there has been no consultation. The manager may have heard, or guessed, that the famous "final solution of the Jewish problem" was to be mass death by gas; Cyclon-B would be the most suitable preparation for this limited purpose. We learned at Nuremberg that the entire extermination program was directed without written orders, a remarkable fact in itself; still, a big man whose business is poison gas for the government may have heard, or guessed. Perhaps the manager shows the order to the colonel, who is not a "little" man, either.

What did these two big men—not little men, like the Nazis I knew—do then, at that moment, with the government order on the desk between them?

What did they say?

What *didn't* they say?

That is what we did not find out at Nuremberg. That is what we never find out at Nuremberg. That is what we have to imagine. And how are we to imagine it?—We are not colonels or plant managers or Nazis, big or little, with a government order on the desk between us, are we?

Everyone has his own troubles.

None of my ten Nazi friends ever knew—I say *knew*—of these great governmental systems of crime against humanity. None of them except possibly (quite probably, I believe) Tailor Schwenke, the SA Sturmführer, ever did anything that we should call wrong by the measure we apply to ourselves. These men were, after all, respectable men, like us. The former bank clerk, Kessler, told his Jewish friend, former Bank Director Rosenthal, the day before the synagogue arson in 1938, that "with men like me in the Party," men of moral and religious feeling, "things will be better, you'll see." And Hildebrandt, the teacher, thought that it had to be expected, under the conditions that obtained in Germany just before Nazism, that the movement would be proletarian and radical, with fools and villains in positions of leadership, "but as more and more decent citizens joined it, it would certainly change for the better and become a *bürgerlich*, bourgeois development. After all, the French Revolution had its Robespierres, *nicht wahr?*"

My friends meant what they said; they calculated wrong, but they meant what they said. And the moral and religious bank clerk was, on the basis of that mortally wrong calculation, to preach the most barbarous paganism. And the decent bourgeois teacher was to teach "Nazi literature" from Nazi textbooks provided by the Nazi school board. Teachers teach what they are told to teach or quit, and to quit a public post meant, in the early years of the Third Reich, unemployment; later on, when one had an anti-Nazi political past, it meant concentration camp. "Once you were in the Party," said Baker Wedekind, who doesn't say he ever wanted to get out, "you didn't get out easily." A man who had always been nonpolitical might get away with "dropping out"; a political man, a man who had assumed the political responsibility of citizenship, never. Policeman Hofmeister, who had done his duty in Kronenberg since 1908, did his duty in 1938 when he was ordered to arrest Jews for being Jews. One of those he arrested, the tailor Marowitz, calls him "a decent man"—*anständig* is the word he used.

All this in no degree reduces the number and awfulness of Nazi evils; it reduces the number and awfulness of Nazi evildoers. It took so few to manage it all, in a country fabled for the efficiency and faithfulness of its civil servants. Policeman Hofmeister was sworn to fidelity to the Führer in a mass-loyalty-oath ceremony at the Kronenberg Town Hall early in 1933. The whole civil service participated and heard the message from Field Marshal Göring himself: "The Führer knows that every civil servant is faithful to the oath." And so they were, to the holy oath by which Germans (more so than men of either freer or lighter consciences) bound themselves so mortally that the ultimate resistance to Hitler, which exploded July 20, 1944, lost in advance many bitterly anti-Nazi Army officers who would do anything except violate their sworn word. The decision of the resistance conspiracy to assassinate Hitler, rather than arrest and convict him, was made for this very reason; sworn fealty to the Führer bound hundreds of thousands until he was dead.

With the civil service and the military safely "faithful," it took so few at the administrative level and so few more, a million at most, of a population of seventy million, to carry out the whole program of Nazi persecution; a million ex-convicts, future ex-convicts, poolroom hoodlums, disheartened young job-seekers, of whom every large country has its million. And Germany had, especially in the north and east, a whole class of recruits better known in eastern Europe and Asia than elsewhere, the brutally bred young *Bauernknechte*, the quasi-serf farm hands, over whom the landowners up to the end of the first World War had had almost absolute feudal jurisdiction.

The "democratic," that is, argumentative, bill-collector, Herr Simon, was greatly interested in the mass deportation of Americans of Japanese ancestry from our West Coast in 1942. He had not heard of it before, and, when I told him of the West Coast Army Commander's statement that "a Jap is a Jap," he hit the table with his fist and said, "Right you are. A Jap is a Jap, a Jew is a Jew." "A German a German," I said. "Of course," said the German, proudly. "It's a matter of blood."

He asked me whether I had known anybody connected with the West Coast deportation. When I said "No," he asked me what I had done about it. When I said "Nothing," he said, triumphantly, "There. You learned about all these things openly, through your government and your press. We did not learn through ours. As in your case, nothing was required of us—in our case, not even knowledge. You *knew* about things you thought were wrong—you did think it was wrong, didn't you, Herr Professor?" "Yes." "So. You did nothing. We *heard*, or *guessed*, and we did nothing. So it is everywhere." When I protested that the Japanese-descended Americans had not been treated like the Jews, he said, "And if they had been—what then? Do you not see that the idea of doing something or doing nothing is in either case the same?"

"Very early," he went on, "still in spring, '33, one of our SA leaders protested against the dismissal of the Oberbürgermeister, a Social Democrat, a good, really nonpolitical man. The SA leader was arrested and taken away. And this, mind you, was when the SA still had great power in the regime. He never came back. His family is still here. We heard he was convicted, but we never heard for what. There was no open trial for enemies of the State. It was said it wasn't necessary; they had forfeited their right to it." "And what do you think?" "That's a legal question. If the courts say it's so, it's so, *gell?*" *Gell?* is dialect for the rhetorical "isn't it so?" "nicht wahr?" "n'est-ce pas?" and Hessian townsfolk love to use it.

A few hundred at the top, to plan and direct at every level; a few thousand to supervise and control (without a voice in policy) at every level; a few score thousand specialists (teachers, lawyers, journalists, scientists, artists, actors, athletes, and social workers) eager to serve or at least unwilling to pass up a job or to revolt; a million of the *Pöbel*, which sounds like "people" and means "riffraff," to do what we would call the dirty work, ranging from murder, torture, robbery, and arson to the effort which probably employed more Germans in inhumanity than any other in Nazi history, the standing of "sentry" in front of Jewish shops and offices in the boycott of April, 1933.

And all the other millions?

They had only to go on as they were and keep out of trouble. What could be easier? "Only Communists were in trouble," said Herr Simon.

"And in Russia," I said, "only anti-Communists."

"That's the way it is," said Herr Simon.

"But," said I, "besides the Communists, there were the

Socialists and the Jews and the religious opponents of the regime. They were 'in trouble,' too, weren't they?"

"Oh, yes," said Herr Simon, ingenuously, "but that came later. I meant at first."

Only Communists were in trouble. And all the other millions of Germans? The SA and the Hitler Youth and the German Maidens marched up the hill and down again on State occasions, which, in such a State, and especially in Germany, are frequent. The workers were dismissed by the Arbeitsfront, the State employer-employee agency, to watch the SA march, just as the government workers in Washington are given a half-day holiday to swell (or, rather, comprise) the crowd that lines the capital's streets to welcome the President of Turkey or the Emperor of Ethiopia; in Nazi Germany swelling the crowd was compulsory. Those who had uniforms strutted in them on Sundays and came home from their Friday night Storm Troop meeting to tell their wives that they had passed a Jewish acquaintance on the street and only nodded to him. And their wives said, "*Gut*," which, in German, may mean "Good" and may mean "Yes."

CHAPTER 5

The Joiners

Party membership in the NSDAP meant absolutely nothing. Like membership in many organizations, it was restricted for the purpose of whetting the appetite of the nonmembers who, by virtue of the restriction, were now excluded. It's an old come-one, known to every real estate promoter. When Hitler was released from prison in December, 1924, he announced that he would accept only 35 per cent of his previous followers, and that was all it took to bring 100 per cent of them to heel again.

In March, 1933, when membership in the triumphant NSDAP was thrown open, millions joined. These "March violets," as they were contemptuously called by both old Nazis and old anti-Nazis, were band-wagoners. Hitler never trusted them, and few of them ever rose to high rank. Hitler was right; the "March violets" joined for good reasons, bad reasons, Nazi reasons, non-Nazi reasons, and even anti-Nazi reasons; and X-number of them for no reason at all—that is, because "everybody" was doing it.

I do not mean that Party membership was the same as buying a tag on tag day in America, but neither was it without any resemblance. Nor was the Nazi block-manager system the same as the civilian defense organization in America; but neither was it entirely noncomparable. Eager beavers, who constituted a distinctly small minority of the block managers in Kronenberg, rode herd for all (and more than) they were worth, swaggering, bullying, discriminating, threatening to denounce, and occasionally denouncing. But the majority served notices of meetings or canvassed for contributions and did not keep official track of delinquency. In American-occupied Kronenberg, after the war, some of the most enthusiastic organizers of American-supported projects had been among the most enthusiastic organizers of Nazi-supported projects. Some of these people were trying to cover up for past misdeeds or mistakes; but most of them were simply enthusiastic organizers of anybody's-supported project.

Men joined the Party to get a job or to hold a job or to get a better job or to save themselves from getting a worse job, or to get a contract or to hold a contract, a customer, a client, a patient. Every third man, in time, worked for the State. In the Weimar Republic the German tradition of the nonpolitical, nonparty civil servant (always safely conservative) was broken down; the Nazis finished the politicalization of the government workers which the Social Democrats began.

It would not be reckless to estimate that half the civil servants had to join the Party or lose their jobs. The other half were well advised to do likewise, and nearly all of them did. Career men in the central and provincial governments and in the city halls, living only for their pensions, could no more resist Party membership (if they ever thought of doing so) than they can the "kickback" in our own Tammanies. In the United States the ancient, if not honorable, practice of compelling state payrollers to support the party in power with 1 per cent or even 2 per cent of their annual salaries is known colloquially as "swinging the mace." In 1954 the Governor of Pennsylvania, admitting that the sys-

85

tem was in operation there, said that there was no "macing" involved; the contributions, he said, were voluntary, and no state employee would be fired for failure to contribute.

"Governor Fine is surely not so naïve as his use of that word 'voluntary' would indicate," said the *Pittsburgh Post-Gazette* editorially. "When your political bosses, the men who got you your public job, ask you to chip in for the welfare of the party, there's very little 'voluntary' about the situation. You don't have to chip in, true enough, but if you have any brains or ambition, you'd better. To be considered uncooperative by the political bosses is not the best way to advance or even hang on in a patronage post." In Germany, where, as everywhere in Europe, party membership is formal and the party is supported by regular dues, you did not have to join the National Socialist Party if you were a government employee, but, if you had any brains or ambition, you'd better have.

The exposure of hundreds of former Nazis in the Foreign Ministry of postwar West Germany, although it revealed in a half-dozen sensational cases a real penetration by Nazism of the Adenauer regime, did not tell us, for the rest, whether they were high officials in the Ministry, stenographers, or messenger boys before, during, or after Nazism; or how many of them (if any) had joined the NSDAP for the purpose of covering their anti-Nazism, alleviating the application of inhuman policies, or even participating from within in a hoped-for (or merely dreamed-of) revolt.

Take the late Ernst von Weizsäcker, promoted by Nazi Foreign Minister Ribbentrop in 1934 from Minister to Switzerland to State Secretary for Foreign Affairs. He not only became a Nazi; he accepted the rank of brigadier general in the black-shirted Nazi SS. As Ribbentrop's State

Secretary, he signed the documents by which thousands of Jews were deported to slavery and death. At Nuremberg the American prosecutor called him "the Devil's State Secretary" and "the executive officer of Murder, Incorporated." An American tribunal convicted him of crimes against humanity.

There, certainly, was a Nazi. But at his trial, the diplomats of all the Allied countries (including the United States of America) testified to his hatred of Nazism; all the surviving leaders of the anti-Nazi resistance in Germany testified to his support and encouragement; distinguished Allied churchmen, scholars, scientists, and International Red Cross executives testified to the relentlessness of his efforts to mitigate or circumvent Nazi directives; a procession of German Jews and Jews of Nazi-occupied countries testified that his illegal assistance to them had saved their lives. Bishop Primate Berggrav, leader of the Norwegian resistance and President of the World Council of Churches, said, "Von Weizsäcker was not a Nazi; he was an anti-Nazi. I know this man in the essential character of his soul. I saw him suffer and serve. If he is condemned, we are all condemned."

Expressions like "Nazi teacher," "Nazi actor," "Nazi journalist," "Nazi lawyer," even "Nazi pastor," are as meaningless as "the Devil's State Secretary." Most teachers teach the three R's under all regimes everywhere. Most actors are looking for jobs anywhere. Most journalists are reporting fires or accidents (with most lawyers hard on their heels) and are writing what the management wants, whoever the management. And most pastors in Germany had always preached Christ crucified without seeing—who does?—that he was being crucified all around them every day.

There are many lawyers in the United States who disagree vehemently with the policies and program of the

American Bar Association; but, if they want to practice law, they had better belong to the constituent societies of the ABA. There are even more physicians in the United States who disagree even more vehemently with the policies of the American Medical Association, but, if they want to practice medicine, they had better belong to the constituent societies of the AMA. They may only pay dues, and that grudgingly; but the record shows that they belong. They are officially "guilty" of the policies of the organization which speaks in their name. In Nazi Germany the professional associations were all "blanketed" into the National Socialist organization.

"So it was," said all of my Nazi (and most, not all, of my anti-Nazi) friends and acquaintances in Germany, and always with a sigh that said, "You don't believe it, do you?"

The anti-Nazi son of a railroad worker told me his father's story. In 1931 the German state railways were letting men go because of the depression. Herr Schäfer, who had no interest in politics, learning that his local boss had joined the National Socialist Party, joined it himself in the hope of hanging on to his job. Long after the war, he learned that the local boss had been an anti-Nazi who had joined the Party in the hope of hanging on to *his* job, because *his* boss, the section superintendent, was an ardent Nazi. And the local boss, assuming that Schäfer had joined the Party from conviction, tried covertly to get him fired —unsuccessfully, because the section superintendent was protecting Nazis. "So it was," in one instance, in Kronenberg—perhaps in more than one, and not only in Kronenberg.

None of this means that there was any mass opposition —if opposition is more than unenthusiasm—to National Socialism in Germany. No attempt has ever been made to discover its genuine extent. Perhaps no attempt would be feasible. But we know how little mass opposition to National Socialism there was prior to 1939 outside Germany, where opposition would have been less dangerous than it was within. Those who, as Cabinetmaker Klingelhöfer said, lived outside the system and were not its beneficiaries could see its evils better. How many of those saw them or, seeing them, raised their voices even to demand that their own governments grant refuge to the system's victims? Some few millions of Germans, at least, listened for foreign voices to hearten their opposition: from America they heard a few; from England and France, where the Germans listened more closely, still fewer. Moral indignation outside Germany was free, but it was scarce.

Nonmembership in the Party meant no more than membership. As some men joined for good, bad, or no reasons, so some men, for good reasons, bad reasons, or no reason at all, did not join. "After the war," said Herr Hildebrandt, the teacher, "every nonmember of the Party was an 'anti-Nazi hero.' Some of these heroes weren't Nazis because of the sixty cents a month dues and for no other reason." "Opposition?" said Herr Simon, the argumentative bill-collecter. "What does 'opposition' mean? Employers opposed the Party because it raised wages, capitalists because it cut profits, loafers because it found jobs; but what do they all say now? They all say, 'The poor Jews.' All the criminals who didn't join because they were 'on the lam' —now they are 'anti-Nazi persecutees.' "

"I was a tobacco salesman," said Herr Damm, who had risen to be office manager of the Party headquarters in Kronenberg, "but I was let out when the state tobacco tax was raised 100 per cent in 1930. I reported to the Labor Office immediately and wrote applications for every job, but

I got no work. At first I drew unemployment compensation, but then, since I was still single, I was told I could go back home to the village and live on my father's farm, which, when my father died, my oldest brother would get. That's the way it was in the spring of 1932, when the National Socialists from Kronenberg held a recruiting evening in the village *Bierstube*. Only one member of each household was allowed to sign up, and my family all agreed that I was the one. I agreed, too. Why not? And, by the way, Herr Professor, it was the *only* political party that had ever held a recruiting meeting in our village as far back as anyone could remember."

Cabinetmaker Klingelhöfer was contemptuous when he spoke of those who did not want to join the Party "lest something happen, some day" but who, while the going was good, wanted it known that they were the truest of the Nazis. "My own brother-in-law was one, Schuchardt, who had the café in the Mauerweg. I used to argue with him—not to join, no, but to be *something*, either for or against. He always said it was for 'business reasons' that he was nonpolitical but, of course, that his heart was with the Party. So he made big contributions to the Winter Relief, always hung out the flag, said 'Heil Hitler' a thousand times a day, and then, when the Americans came, he wasn't a Nazi, he had never been in the Party. Such men play both sides, always. You admire them, their cunning. But you wouldn't want to be like them, would you?" "No," I said.

The notes of my conversations with Herr Klingelhöfer, made during or immediately after our meetings, quote him as saying, again and again, "*Die freiwillige Feuerwehr über alles!* The Volunteer Fire Department above everything!" and "*Mein Leben für die freiwillige Feuerwehr!* My life for the Volunteer Fire Department!" I can scarcely believe my own notes; this earnest, middle-aged German cabinetmaker is as fire-department–crazy as a boy. Kronenberg, like all German cities under one hundred thousand population, had a volunteer fire department. In 1927 the Fire Chief asked my friend Klingelhöfer to join because the department was short a trumpeter. In those days each block had a fire trumpeter. The trumpeter had an alarm in his bedroom, and when the alarm rang he blew his trumpet out the window, awakening the other firemen (and everyone else) in the block. So Klingelhöfer, who was interested in trumpeting but not, in those days, in fire-fighting, joined. "N'ja, that's me. I always joined everything."

Beginning in 1932, under the Republic, Klingelhöfer took two weeks off from his shop every summer, at his own expense, to attend the state training school for firemen. In 1933 he was a squad leader in the *freiwillige Feuerwehr* when, the Nazis having come to power, some of the "fellows" said that Party members would get promotion preference in the department. "You see," he said, "before the Hitler time, the firemen chose their own leaders, but after 1933 promotions were proposed by the company chiefs and had to be approved by the Oberbürgermeister. Of course, the Oberbürgermeister was a Nazi, and, when the old chief, who wasn't, quit in 1934, the man promoted from company chief to take his place was a Nazi, too. So I joined. Besides, I thought the Party was a good thing."

"Would you have joined if it hadn't been for the *Feuerwehr*?"

"Not then. Later, probably; oh, yes, certainly. But not then."

"Why not?"

"Because I was against a one-party State. That was one reason. And I was not a strong nationalist; a Frenchman is a man, just as I am. That was another reason. And the race politics didn't make sense; there is no pure race any more, and inbreeding is bad anyway—we know that from plants and animals and from the insanity and feeble-mindedness in the villages where everyone is related to everyone else. That was another reason. We talked about all these things in the Wandervogel, the Youth Movement, when I was young, and I had gone on hikes across the borders a little way, into both France and Switzerland."

"Well," I said, "you've given me three good reasons for not being a Nazi."

"*Und* doch *war ich in der Partei!* And *still* I was in the Party!" And he laughed exuberantly, and I with him.

Once he was in the Party, he was asked to join the SA and to be a block manager. "I said 'No.' The Volunteer Fire Department was more important, and I said so. The SA didn't like that, and *they* said so," and he laughed again. "But we were independent until (when was it?) 1934, yes, in the reorganization after the Röhm purge. Then we heard that all the fire departments would become either technical troops of the SA or a branch of the police, and at the firemen's training school that summer we were asked which we preferred. There were fifty men in training, one from each county in Hesse. All fifty of them said the same thing—they wanted neither; they wanted to remain independent.

"That's what we *said*, yes, and that fall we were put under the police, and our name was changed to *Feuerlösch-Polizei*, "fire-fighting police." How is *that* for a name, Herr Professor?" and he laughed again.

"Terrible," I said, and laughed with him.

"*So war die Sache*. That's the way it was. Well, at least it wasn't the SA. I was promoted to adjutant to the new chief. At the end of 1938 the police in the towns like Kronenberg were put under the SS, so we, the *freiwillige Feuerwehr*, were part of the Nazi SS! What do you think of *that*, Herr Professor?"

"What did you think of it?"

"*Man macht eine Faust im Sack*. One made a fist in one's pocket." He wasn't laughing now, nor was I. Then he brightened and smiled and said, "*Aber, die freiwillige Feuerwehr über alles!*"

"Opposition?" said Herr Klingelhöfer, on another occasion. "How would anybody know? How would anybody know what somebody else opposes or doesn't oppose? That a man *says* he opposes or doesn't oppose depends upon the circumstances, where, and when, and to whom, and just how he says it. And then you must still guess *why* he says what he says. So, too, even in action. The few who tried to kill Hitler and seize the Government in '44, certainly they 'opposed,' but why? Some hated the dictatorship of National Socialism, some hated its democracy, some were personally ambitious or jealous, some wanted the Army to control the country, maybe some could escape punishment for crimes only by a change of government. Some, I am sure, were pure and noble. But they all acted."

"And here in Kronenberg?"

"Here in Kronenberg? Well, we had twenty thousand people. Of these twenty thousand people, how many opposed? How would you know? How would I know? If you ask me how many *did* something in secret opposition, something that meant great danger to them, I would say, well, twenty. And how many did something like that openly, and from good motives alone? Maybe five, maybe two. That's the way men are."

"You always say, 'That's the way men are,' Herr Klingelhöfer," I said. "Are you sure that that's the way men are?"

"That's the way men are here," he said. "Are they different in America?"

Alibis, alibis, alibis; alibis for the Germans; alibis, too, for man, who, when he was once asked, in olden time, whether he would prefer to do or to suffer injustice, replied, "I would rather neither." The mortal choice which every German had to make—whether or not he knew he was making it—is a choice which we Americans have never had to confront. But personal and professional life confronts us with the same kind of choice, less mortally, to be sure, every day. And the fact that it is a platitude does not keep it from being true that we find it easier, on the whole, to admire Socrates than to envy him; to adore the Cross, especially on cloudy Sundays, than to carry it. A still young man in Berlin, an actor forbidden employment since the war, said to me: "I had my choice of acting for Hitler at home or dying for him in Russia. I preferred not to die for him in Russia, not because I was an anti-Nazi (I wasn't) but because I wasn't a hero. If I had wanted to die for Hitler or my country—and this, you understand, was the same thing in the war—I would not have waited to be conscripted. I would have enlisted, like a patriot. Tell me, Herr Professor"—he was too polite to ask me what *I* had done in *my* circumstances—"what would *you* have done in *my* circumstances?"

CHAPTER 6

The Way To Stop Communism

"It had its beginning in Munich," said my friend Herr Kessler, the one-time Catholic from Bavaria's neighboring state of Württemberg in southern Germany, "in the most artistic, cultivated, and Catholic city in Germany, the city of art and of song and of love and *Gemütlichkeit,* the only city in Germany that all the foreign tourists always insisted on visiting. There it had its beginning, a purely local affair without any *Weltanschauung,* philosophy. Nobody outside paid any attention to it. Only after it spread and took root, Bavarians asked, 'Who is Hitler? What is this Party with the fancy name? What is behind it?'

"Hitler was a simple soldier, like millions of others, only he had a *feeling* for masses of people, and he could speak with passion. The people didn't pay any attention to the Party program as such. They went to the meetings just to hear something new, anything new. They were desperate about the economic situation, 'a new Germany' sounded good to them; but from a deep or broad point of view they saw nothing at all. Hitler talked always against the government, against the lost war, against the peace treaty, against unemployment. All that, people liked. By the time the intellectuals asked, 'What is this?' it had a solid basis in the common people. It was the *Arbeiter, Sozialist* Party, the

Party of *workers controlling the social order;* it was not for intellectuals.

"The situation in Germany got worse and worse. What lay underneath people's daily lives, the real root, was gone. Look at the suicides; look at the immorality. People wanted something *radical,* a real change. This want took the form of more and more Communism, especially in middle Germany, in the industrial area, and in the cities of the north. *That* was no invention of Hitler; *that* was real. In countries like America there is no Communism because there is no desire for *radical* change.

"Hitlerism had to answer Communism with something just as radical. Communism always used force; Hitlerism answered it with force. The really absolute enemy of Communism, always clear, always strong in the popular mind, was National Socialism, the *only* enemy that answered Communism in kind. If you wanted to save Germany from Communism—to be *sure* of doing it—you went to National Socialism. The Nazi slogan in 1932 was, 'If you want your country to go Bolshevik, vote Communist; if you want to remain free Germans, vote Nazi.'

"The middle parties, between the two millstones, played no role at all between the two radicalisms. Their adherents were basically the Bürger, the bourgeois, the 'nice' people who decide things by parliamentary procedure; and the politically indifferent; and the people who wanted to keep or, at worst, only modify the status quo.

"I'd like to ask the American Bürger, the middle-class man: What would *you* have done when your country stood so? A dictatorship, or destruction by Bolshevism? Bolshevism looked like slavery and the death of the soul. It didn't matter if you were in agreement with Nazism. Nazism looked like the only defense. There was your choice."

" 'I would rather neither,' " I said.

"Of course, Herr Professor. You are a bourgeois. I was, too, once. I was a bank clerk, remember."

Of my ten friends, only two, Tailor Schwenke and Bill-collector Simon, the two *alte Kämpfer*, wanted to be Nazis and nothing else. They were both positive—still are—that National Socialism was Germany's and therefore their own, salvation from Communism, which, like the much more sensitive bank clerk, they both called "Bolshevism," "the death of the soul." "Bolshevism" came from outside, from the barbarous world that was Russia; Nazism, its enemy, was German, it was their own; they would rather Nazism.

Did they know what Communism, "Bolshevism," was? They did not; not my friends. Except for Herr Kessler, Teacher Hildebrandt, and young Horstmar Rupprecht (after he entered the university, in 1941), they knew Bolshevism as a specter which, as it took on body in their imaginings, embraced not only the Communists but the Social Democrats, the trade-unions, and, of course, the Jews, the gypsies, the neighbor next door whose dog had bit them, and his dog; the bundled root cause of all their past, present, and possible tribulations. Prior to 1930 or 1931, none of my ten friends, except Tailor Schwenke and Bill-collector Simon, hated any Communist he knew (they were few, in nonindustrial little Kronenberg) or identified him with the specter; *these* were flesh-and-blood neighbors, who would not break into your house and burn it down. After 1933 or 1934 these same neighbors were seen for "what they were"—innocently disguised lackeys of the specter. The Bolshevist specter outraged the property sense of my all but propertyless friends, the class sense of these *déclassé* Bürger, the political sense of these helpless subjects of the former Emperor, the religious sense of these *pro forma* churchgoers, the moral sense of these unexceptional characters. It was "the death of the soul."

The question was not whether Communism threatened the country, as, with the continuation of deteriorating conditions, it certainly did or soon would; the question was whether the Germans were convinced that it did. And they were. They were so well convinced, by such means as the Reichstag fire of 1933, that the Nazis were able, ultimately, to establish anti-Communism as a religion, immune from inquiry and defensible by definition alone. When in 1937 the Pope attacked the "errors" of National Socialism, the Nazi Government's defense of its policies consisted of a Note accusing the Pope of "having dealt a dangerous blow to the defense front against the world menace of Bolshevism."

Those Germans who would do anything, be anything, join anything to stop Bolshevism had, in the end, to be Nazis. And Nazism did stop Bolshevism. How it stopped Bolshevism, with what means and what consequences, did not matter—not enough, at least, to alienate them. None of its shortcomings, mild or hideous, none of its contradictions, small or calamitous, ever swayed them. To them, then and now, Nazism kept its promise.

Three of my ten friends, the bank clerk, Kessler, the salesman, Damm, and the tailor's apprentice, Herr Schwenke's son Gustav, were unemployed when they joined, and the first two were family men in middle life at the time. In all three cases they joined, I think, because they were unemployed—which is not in the least to say that they would not have joined if they hadn't been. The two Old Fighters, Tailor Schwenke and Bill-collector Simon, when they joined in 1925, were both employed (the tailor self-employed), but the inflation which had just ended had reduced them (and nearly all other *petit bourgeois* Germans) to near-starvation.

Willy Hofmeister, the old policeman, joined the Party in 1937 because the new Police Chief said that all the men must join. When I asked him if he could have refused, he said, *"Ein Millionär war ich ja gar nicht.* A millionaire I was not." (The Sicherheitspolizei, or detective force, one of whose five members he was in Kronenberg, was subsequently attached willy-nilly to the Gestapo, just as the Volunteer Fire Department was placed under the SS). Horstmar Rupprecht, the student, had been a Nazi since he was eight years old, in the Jungvolk, the "cub" organization of the Hitler Jugend; his ambition (which he realized) was to be a Hitler Youth leader; in America he would certainly have been a Scoutmaster.

The two most active churchmen of the ten, Herr Klingelhöfer, the cabinetmaker, and Herr Wedekind, the baker, both of them vestrymen of their parish church, were the two who today (and, I think, yesterday) put the most emphasis on the "everybody-was-doing-it" theme. (They were both "March violets.") The fact that they were, of the ten, the two retail tradesmen doubtless contributed to their sensitivity to this urge to go along (*mitschwimmen* was the term each of them used) with the Party as they had with the Church; the cabinetmaker freely admitted that his church activity "didn't hurt" his coffin-making, although neither he nor I would say that he was a churchman *because* it was good business to be one.

Neither Klingelhöfer nor Wedekind read the Party Program, the historic Twenty-five Points, before they joined, while they were members, or afterward. (Only the teacher, of the ten, ever read it.) But they were earnestly impressed, as were most ardent churchgoers in the early years of the

movement, by the Program's demand, of which every one
of my friends had heard, for "positive Christianity" for
Germany. The baker left the vestry board in 1937, when
the Church-Party struggle had become intense. He says he
left voluntarily, as a "good Nazi," because he felt that his
Party loyalty compromised his position on the board; his
pastor confirms his assertion. But he did not leave the
church. Herr Klingelhöfer—"I always joined everything"—
remained a vestryman to the end.

All ten of my friends, including the sophisticated Hildebrandt, were affected by this sense of what the Germans
call *Bewegung*, movement, a swelling of the human sea,
something supraparty and suprapolitical, a surge of the
sort that does not, at the time, evoke analysis or, afterward, yield to it. These men were victims of the "Bolshevik" rabies, to be sure. They were equally victims of
economic hardship and, still worse, of economic hopelessness, a hopelessness that they suffered more easily by identifying it with their country's. But they were seekers, too,
and affirmers—agents, not just patients.

Their country was torn to pieces from without, of course,
but still more cruelly from within. Germans had been
at one another's throats since 1918, and dissension grew
shriller and more bitter all the time. In the course of the decomposition, the principle of *being German*, so newly won
under Bismarck and so preciously held for fear of its slip-
ping away, was indeed being lost. The uniting of the country, of all of its people, was possible only on this one principle of *being German*, and my ten friends, even including
the old fanatic Schwenke, onlookers at the disruptive strug-
gles of the old parties and the old party politicians, at the
process of shredding the mystical fabric which supported

this principle, asked, "Where is Germany?" Nazism—Hitler, rather—knew this and knew that nothing else mattered to my friends so much as this, the identification of this Germany, the community again, in which one might know he belonged and, belonging, identify himself. This was the movement which any non-German might see at once for what it was; and this was the movement which restored my friends as the sight of home restores the lost child; or as the sight of the Lorelei Maiden, seen sitting high above the Rhine, combing her golden hair with a golden comb in the surprising late sunshine, bewitches the sailor, who overlooks the rocks beneath the river.

National Socialism was a revulsion by my friends against parliamentary politics, parliamentary debate, parliamentary government—against all the higgling and the haggling of the parties and the splinter parties, their coalitions, their confusions, and their conniving. It was the final fruit of the common man's repudiation of "the rascals." Its motif was, "Throw them all out." My friends, in the 1920's, were like spectators at a wrestling match who suspect that beneath all the grunts and groans, the struggle and the sweat, the match is "fixed," that the performers are only pretending to put on a fight. The scandals that rocked the country, as one party or cabal "exposed" another, dismayed and then disgusted my friends. (One sensed some of this reaction against the celebrated Army-McCarthy hearing in the United States in 1954—not against one side or another but against "the whole thing" as "disgusting" or "disgraceful.")

While the ship of the German State was being shivered, the officers, who alone had life-preservers, disputed their prerogatives on the bridge. My friends observed that none of the non-Communist, non-Nazi leaders objected to the

101

35,000 Reichsmark salaries of the cabinet ministers; only the Communists and the Nazis objected. And the bitterest single disappointment of Nazism—both to Simon, the insensitive bill-collector, and to Hofmeister, the sensitive policeman—was the fact that Hitler had promised that no official would get more than 1,000 Reichsmarks a month and did not keep his promise.

My friends wanted Germany purified. They wanted it purified of the politicians, of *all* the politicians. They wanted a representative leader in place of unrepresentative representatives. And Hitler, the pure man, the antipolitician, was the man, untainted by "politics," which was only a cloak for corruption. The "mink coat" scandal in the United States at the beginning of the 1950's had its counterpart in Berlin in the beginning of the 1930's, when the Nazis focused their campaign for the mayoralty on the receipt by the wife of the Social Democratic mayor of a fur coat from a man who did business with the city.

Against "the whole pack," "the whole kaboodle," "the whole business," against *all* the parliamentary politicians and *all* the parliamentary parties, my friends evoked Hitlerism, and Hitlerism overthrew them all. The power struggle within the National Socialist Party, which culminated in the Röhm purge of June 30, 1934, was in essence parliamentary and political, but my friends never knew it. They accepted it as a cleanup of moral degenerates, and if they caught a glimpse of the reality underneath the official propaganda, their nascent concern was dissipated by the fact that the Führer acted with an instant and terrible sword and the "debate" with Röhm was finished; the Führer held the country and the countrymen together.

This was the *Bewegung*, the movement, that restored

my friends and bewitched them. Those Germans who saw it all at the beginning—there were not very many; there never are, I suppose, anywhere—called Hitler the *Rattenfänger*, the "rat-catcher." Every American child has read *The Pied-Piper of Hamlin*. Every German child has read it, too. In German its title is *Der Rattenfänger von Hameln*.

CHAPTER 7

"We Think with Our Blood"

Heinrich Hildebrandt joined the Party in 1937. He may not have been the only one of my ten friends who was afraid not to join, but he was the only one of them who knew then and now, and says so, that fear was his reason—fear and advantage. ("But how," he said, "is one to separate them?") He had been an anti-Nazi, an active moderate democrat in East Prussia before he came quietly to Hesse in 1935 and, his past uneasily buried, got a job teaching literature and French in the Kronenberg *Realgymnasium*, the humanistic high school. An anti-Nazi and a cultivated man, more clearly aware than most men of the primitive considerations which directed his course of action—and yet he, too, once he was inside the system he hated, sheep that he was in wolf's clothing, found something profoundly good in it.

"Perhaps," he said, "it was because I wanted, unconsciously, to justify what I had done. If so, I succeeded. But I say it now, too, and I know it now. There were good things, great things, in the system—and the system itself was evil."

"For instance?"

"You mean about the evils?"

"No, I know about those. About 'the good things, the great things.'"

"Perhaps I should make it singular instead of plural, the good *thing*. For the first time in my life I was really the peer of men who, in the Kaiser time and in the Weimar time, had always belonged to classes lower or higher than my own, men whom one had always looked down on or up to, but never *at*. In the Labor Front—I represented the teachers' association—I came to know such people at first hand, to know their lives and to have them know mine. Even in America—perhaps; I have never been there—I suspect that the teacher who talks about 'the common people' has never known one, really known one, not even if he himself came from among them, as I, with an Army officer as a father, did not. National Socialism broke down that separation, that class distinction. Democracy—such democracy as we had had—didn't do it and is not doing it now."

"Wedekind, the baker," I said, "told me how 'we simple working-class men stood side by side with learned men, in the Labor Front.' "

"I remember Wedekind," said the teacher. "I didn't know him before I joined the Party, and I don't know him now. Why? Because he was my inferior. A baker is nothing, a teacher is something; in the Labor Front we belonged to something together, we had something in common. We could know each other in those days. Do you understand that, Herr Professor?"

"I understand it because you call me 'Herr Professor,' " I said, smiling.

"Yes. The baker calls me 'Herr Studienrat'—that was my rank—and I call you 'Herr Professor.' It is for me to accept the baker and for you to accept me."

"Neither the baker nor the teacher would call a professor 'Professor' in America," I said.

"Never?"

"Rarely. I can't remember ever having been called 'Professor,' except by friends, who in an argument might say ironically, 'Professor, you're crazy.' "

"It was never like that in Germany," he said, "or anywhere else in Europe—not even, from what I know, in England. Always in Germany, before Nazism, and again now, the title is a genuine reflection of class distinction."

I told Herr Hildebrandt of an incident a German friend, an eminent physicist, had recently reported to me. He was returning to Germany from a scientific congress in Amsterdam, and an American colleague was traveling with him. At the Netherlands-German border the American discovered he had lost his passport. My friend observed that both the Dutch and the German passport inspectors were elderly men, obviously relics of the Imperial days, and he said to the two of them, "Gentlemen, I am Professor Doktor Karl Otto, Baron von G——, and you have my word that Professor W—— possesses a valid passport properly visaed, which he has mislaid. I take personal responsibility for Professor W——'s transit." "It was a gamble," the physicist said, in reporting the incident to me, "but it succeeded. The obvious duty of the two old inspectors was overridden by the word of a Professor Doktor Baron, and W—— came in with me. He was amazed."

"Why was he amazed?" said the teacher, when I told him the story.

"Because," I said, "every side-show medicine salesman in America calls himself 'Professor,' and a man who calls himself 'Baron' or 'Count' is an obvious fraud. An American passport inspector would have turned to one of his colleagues and said, 'Here's a hot one, Joe. The "Professor" wants in and he hasn't a passport. What're you peddling, "Professor," cocaine?'"

"You exaggerate a little?" said the teacher.

"A little," I said, "but only a little."

"I understand," he said. "This is your American feeling of absolute equality. That we have never had here. But there was a democracy in Nazism, and it was real. My—how shall I say it?—my inferiors accepted me."

My inferiors accepted me.

The German schoolteacher found himself, in Nazi Germany, as, I dare say, any schoolteacher finds himself in any emerging totalitarianism, in a unique situation which constituted a compulsion upon him unknown (or less painfully known) to other kinds of workers. The National Socialist development entailed the inexorable displacement of the teaching profession from its position in the German community. The teacher everywhere in Europe is much more highly honored than his American counterpart, and more highly paid. In addition, he has had, in Europe, an education so far beyond the financial ability of nearly all his countrymen that the very fact of his being a teacher is taken as evidence of his family's having been prosperous, and the prosperous, in Europe no less than in America, are highly honored and highly paid.

In the small community, the village, and even the town, the teacher and the pastor stand alone in Germany, the two *Respektpersonen*, far above the mayor or the merchant. And, because of the Church-State identity, they stand together as the arbiters of the community's moral and cultural, as well as its religious and intellectual, life. In the village which has only a visiting pastor who comes every second Sunday, the alternative sermon is "naturally" preached by the teacher. Religious education was officially, until 1918, an element of elementary-school education. And the teacher is like as not the organist in the village church.

The pastor sits in judgment on the old, the teacher on the young and on the young's relations with the old. In the villages the parents are still literally afraid of the teacher. His knock at the door in the evening, when the child has misbehaved at school that day, means that the parents will have to promise, then and there, specific disciplinary action. The call will not be social, and the mother as well as the father will rise when he enters the house. If, on a happier occasion, he is willing to accept an invitation to call socially, the house will be cleaned and warmed, cakes will be baked, and the good wine brought out.

In Tailor Schwenke's childhood, at the end of the Nineteenth Century, the teacher had been there "all his life." He may have come to the village directly from the teachers' college, or he may have made one or two changes in his youth before he settled down to stay. The pastor, with his circuit of two or three villages, was likelier to change his residence or even go up the professional ladder. Young Karl-Heinz Schwenke's teacher had taught Karl-Heinz's father and had even taught the grandparents of some of the village children; these, grown to be parents and grandparents, saw their teacher still when he came to the door. And, where the parents might not have close contact with the pastor, they could not help having it with the teacher, who, besides learning the family secrets from the feckless offspring, had to be called in to help transact such business, especially official business, as transcended the father's grasp or self-confidence.

In the summer, in Karl-Heinz's village, the teacher went through the streets at 9 P.M., in the winter at dark; if he found a child on the street, his knock was heard at the door that same evening. At his own discretion, he himself did the disciplining with his *Rohrstock*. If the *Rohrstock* was a hazel branch, it was possible to cut it part way through when the teacher was out of the room, so that, when applied, it would fly to pieces. But Herr Pietsch, who was wise in the ways of three rising generations, had a bamboo stick, which, besides being harder to cut, had a greater flexibility than hazel, adding injury to insult.

One day when the future Sturmführer Schwenke was eleven, he ditched school in the afternoon to engage in the revolutionary act of stealing cherries. That night Herr Pietsch came by the Schwenkes'. Karl-Heinz was lucky; his father, who, like all very small farmers, was often away from home working for other farmers, was away that night, and Mother Schwenke beat the truant. The boy's luck lay in the fact that his mother's beating him meant that she would not tell his father, who would have beat him much harder. But the luck didn't last, for Herr Pietsch knew that Father Schwenke was away and that mothers' hands are sometimes unconvincingly light. The next morning, at the opening of school, Karl-Heinz received the bamboo treatment. The beating was so fierce that the boy bit the teacher's leg; then the teacher beat him harder. "Much harder?" I said. "So much harder," said the old tailor, "that the whole class howled with pain just to see it. That old man Pietsch," the arsonist of the Kronenberg synagogue went on, "he was a regular devil."

The regular devil showered down favors, too, but never on Karl-Heinz, who was poor in his studies. The favorites, who might be the best students, and who might be the worst students who belonged to the best families, were allowed a half-hour out of school to go, in turn, to the teacher's house each day to shine his shoes. Did the parents know this? Of course. Were the children paid? Of course not. What did the parents and children think about it? They didn't think about it.

The authoritative, not to say authoritarian, role that the teacher played in the German community, a role which declined very little in the "democratic" days between 1918 and 1933, is wholly foreign to the American tradition of that sad sack, the schoolteacher (as witness the life and times of Ichabod Crane in *The Legend of Sleepy Hollow*). The teacher in Germany once was, and often is now, the only person in the community who has attended a nonvocational secondary school; the fact that everyone else can read and write does not mean that the villagers do not come to him with important documents to be read or written properly. He is quite likely to be the only university graduate in the village. And he is certain to be the leading cosmopolitan, in respect not only of learning but also of mobility. Two or three merchants may be richer, the landowner certainly so, but they do not waste their money on travel. No professional in America has the status of the teacher in Germany, and to have achieved, as Herr Hildebrandt did, the rank of Studienrat (which means senior high-school teacher), with its title no less than its tenure and pension, is an eminence which no American teacher dreams of.

As the recognized repository of the community's intellect, the teacher would probably be a political conservative, a man not to be influenced by reformers. As a man who, although decently paid, still had to live on a state salary, he would still more probably want to identify himself with the wealthiest members of the community, who could afford to pay him for special lessons for their children. As a State employee, he would not be likely to disagree with Bismarck. But he would not, for all this, be a political protagonist or even a conscious political partisan. He would be above politics, not merely as the public service is above politics, but as the intellect is above politics. His business, and his alone in the community, is thinking, just as the horseshoer's, and his alone, is horseshoeing. Laymen do not presume to advise, still less to command, experts. And, while the historic sterility of German education may be laid in part to the academic's unaccountability, there was, in the pre-Hitler community, an independent, if a rigid and shallow, mind.

This mind was a bulwark, however fragile, not against National Socialism but against National Socialism's transition from practice to theory; for Nazism, unlike modern Communism, began with practice. Because the mass movement of Nazism was nonintellectual in the beginning, when it was only practice, it had to be anti-intellectual before it could be theoretical. What Mussolini's official philosopher, Giovanni Gentile, said of Fascism could have been better said of Nazi theory: "We think with our blood." Expertness in thinking, exemplified by the professor, by the high-school teacher, and even by the grammar-school teacher in the village, had to deny the Nazi views of history, economics, literature, art, philosophy, politics, biology, and education itself.

Thus Nazism, as it proceeded from practice to theory, had to deny expertness in thinking and then (this second process was never completed), in order to fill the vacuum, had to establish expert thinking of its own—that is, to find men of inferior or irresponsible caliber whose views conformed dishonestly or, worse yet, honestly to the Party line. The nonpolitical pastor satisfied Nazi requirements by

111

being nonpolitical. But the nonpolitical schoolmaster was, by the very virtue of being nonpolitical, a dangerous man from the first. He himself would not rebel, nor would he, if he could help it, teach rebellion; but he could not help being dangerous—not if he went on teaching what was true. In order to be a theory and not just a practice, National Socialism required the destruction of academic independence.

In the years of its rise the movement little by little brought the community's attitude toward the teacher around from respect and envy to resentment, from trust and fear to suspicion. The development seems to have been inherent; it needed no planning and had none. As the Nazi emphasis on nonintellectual virtues (patriotism, loyalty, duty, purity, labor, simplicity, "blood," "folkishness") seeped through Germany, elevating the self-esteem of the "little man," the academic profession was pushed from the very center to the very periphery of society. Germany was preparing to cut its own head off. By 1933 at least five of my ten friends (and I think six or seven) looked upon "intellectuals" as unreliable and, among these unreliables, upon the academics as the most insidiously situated.

Tailor Schwenke, before the first World War, had made suits for some of the prosperous professors of Kronenberg University. If, as of course he did, he resented their superior station, he was nevertheless proud and boastful of being tailor to such a distinguished trade. In 1925, when he was starving and joined the new political movement, they, although they were no longer able to order tailor-made suits, still had their sinecures, and he was no longer able to identify himself with them; they were sinking, as he was, but they had much further to sink. In 1927 he left the Party in the hope of recapturing their custom; he himself says this is why. But what he calls the "boycott" persisted (partly, of course, because the ready-made suit had taken the custom tailor's place).

In 1931, when Tailor Schwenke rejoined the Party, his Nazi indoctrination plus his personal experience had awakened his hostility toward professors in general, many of whom in Kronenberg, he told me, were Communists. (None was.) And in 1933, when the Party came to power, he was given a school janitor's job—with, of course, the title of *Hausmeister*—and the command of the local SA Reserve Troop. From that point on, he had no difficulty in placing academics (who, no doubt, had been patronizing when they were patrons) entirely outside the pale of the great community, the New Germany, which *he* now represented.

He was not, of course, sure of the New Germany or of himself; he was still, after fifty years of being Karl-Heinz Schwenke, Karl-Heinz Schwenke, and the Herr Professor was still the Herr Professor. The New Germany was, of course, Schwenke's, but the Herr Professor had something, and something German, that the New German had not. Tailor Schwenke would not, after 1933, any more than before, have failed to tip his hat to the Herr Professor; all the more joyously he received the revelation that half the academics were traitors and the other half dupes and boobies who might be tolerated—under close surveillance—by the New Germany which Tailor Schwenke, at your service, Sir, represented.

CHAPTER 8

The Anti-Semitic Swindle

Gustav Schwenke, the tailor's son, was twenty when he became a Nazi. This was in 1932. His father's business had collapsed; he himself, after his apprenticeship to his father, had never found work. There was simply no work to do for a strong, intelligent, well-trained young man of nineteen, eighteen, seventeen, sixteen. For four years he had gone on foot, like hundreds of thousands of other young men, from village to village, looking for work. Apart from an occasional odd job, he had, during this period, two months of state work relief service on the roads, for food and lodging and two dollars a week. Then his "old sickness," bed-wetting, came on him again and he had to go home and start over. But he never became a bum or a brawler; he slept only in youth hostels or in the fields. And then, in 1932, Gustav Schwenke became an SA policeman, for pocket money and a uniform—and a place in the sun.

What Gustav Schwenke wanted, and the only thing he wanted, was security. The job he wanted, and the only job he ever wanted, was a job with the State, any job with the State, with its tenure, its insurance, and its pension. Gustav was not, I imagine, the only boy born in Germany in 1912 who wanted security and thought, until 1933, that he would never have it. When he got it, when the Party Police were incorporated into the Military Police in 1935, his dream was come true. At last he *belonged*. He was a man at last.

As a boy, Gustav had clung to his father and kept away from his mother. He always did his homework in the afternoons in his father's workshop in the front of the house. There he fed on his father's manhood, which took the form of political power, and starved out his mother's womanhood, which took the form of domestic power. When he was seven he heard his father call the Weimar Constitution *Dreck*, dirt. So Gustav hated the Constitution. (He didn't know what it was.) When he was eleven, a customer came in to call for a suit, which had been ordered eight days before for 8,000 Reichsmarks; now, eight days later, 8,000 Reichsmarks would buy one pound of butter; and, when Gustav asked his father what caused the inflation, his father said, "The Jews." So Gustav hated the Jews. (He didn't know any Jews and wouldn't have bothered them if he had. His father would.)

Old Karl-Heinz Schwenke was a product of "the golden time" before the first World War. Even in the golden time he had, as he said, "only been a tailor." "But I had ten suits of my own when I married," said the iron-faced old dandy. "Twenty-five years later, when their 'democracies' got through with me in 1918, I had none, not one. I had my sweater and my pants. Even my Army uniform was worn out. My medals were sold. I was nothing. Then, suddenly, I was needed. National Socialism had a place for me. I was nothing—and then I was needed."

"And now," I said, "you are down to your sweater and pants again."

"Yes," he said, "now that their 'democracies' are through with me again."

"National Socialism," I said, gently, "didn't leave its enemies that much."

"They had it coming. You see what their 'democracies' did to us."

By "they" Herr Schwenke always meant the Jews. He was the most primitive of my ten friends. He was a very limited man. Facts, although he could apprehend them, had no use he could put them to; he could neither retain nor relate them. He could talk, but he could not listen. I let him talk.

"They say six million Jews were killed"—not that "we" or even "the Nazis" killed them—"but when you see how many there are all over the world today, there are just as many as ever. There are fifteen million in America—"

"Only six or eight, I believe," I said.

"Naturally, that's what they tell you. Do you know how many there are in Russia right now? They control the government, money, everything, everywhere."

I wanted to tell him a story, but I didn't. It's a story about a Jew riding in a streetcar, in Germany during the Third Reich, reading Goebbels' paper, the *Völkische Beobachter*. A non-Jewish acquaintance sits down next to him and says, "Why do you read the *Beobachter?*" "Look," says the Jew, "I work in a factory all day. When I get home, my wife nags me, the children are sick, and there's no money for food. What should I do on my way home, read the Jewish newspaper? 'Pogrom in Roumania.' 'Jews Murdered in Poland.' 'New Laws against Jews.' No, sir, a half-hour a day, on the streetcar, I read the *Beobachter*. 'Jews the World Capitalists.' 'Jews Control Russia.' 'Jews Rule in England.' That's me they're talking about. A half-hour a day I'm somebody. Leave me alone, friend."

National Socialism was anti-Semitism. Apart from anti-

Semitism, its character was that of a thousand tyrannies before it, with modern conveniences. Traditional anti-Semitism—what Nietzsche, beloved by the Nazis for his superman, called "the anti-Semitic swindle"—played an important role in softening the Germans as a whole to Nazi doctrine, but it was separation, not prejudice as such, that made Nazism possible, the mere separation of Jews and non-Jews. None of my ten friends except Herr Hildebrandt, the teacher, had ever known a Jew at all intimately in a town of twenty thousand, which included a nine-hundred-year-old Jewish community numbering six or eight hundred persons. The last traces of the ghetto had gone a century and more ago. Generation after generation, these people went on living together, in a small town, with a nonexistent wall between them over which the words "Good morning" and "Good evening" were tossed.

My ten friends had all had business relations with Jews, as both buyers and sellers. Springer, the Jewish jeweler, had even belonged to the town Glee Club, along with the Schwenkes, father and son. "I bought Mushi's wedding ring from Springer," said the tailor, patting his old wife's hand.

"Why from a Jew?" I asked.

"N' ja," said the arsonist of the synagogue, "we always traded with Springer. For a Jew, he was decent." I thought of Tacitus' observation on the Hessian tailor's forebears: "The Chatti [Hessians] are intelligent, for Germans."

Seven of my ten friends had known Springer over a period of years, and all seven of them, when I interrupted their animadversions on the Jews to ask them if they had ever known a decent Jew, named Springer first. They had traded with him, sung with him, marched with him (in veterans' organizations), but he had never been in any

117

of their homes nor any of them in his. None of them knew how many children he had or where his ancestors came from.

"What became of him?" I asked the tailor.

"Oh, he went away."

"Where?"

"I don't know. South America, maybe. It was early"—that meant before the synagogue burning of 1938—"and a lot of them went to South America or somewhere."

None of the seven knew what had become of Springer.

I asked Horst Rupprecht, the student and Hitler Youth leader, who had lived around the corner from the synagogue and the Hebrew school, if as a child he had had Jewish friends. "Certainly," he said at once. "I never had a fight with a Jewish boy."

"I don't mean that," I said. "I mean, did you play with any?"

"Oh, no," he said.

"Why not?"

" 'Why not?' I don't know. They played together, and we played together."

In the Dark Ages the Jews had to separate themselves to preserve their communion, just as the Christians (and the Jews) had had to do in pre-Constantine Rome; in the Middle Ages their separation had been recognized and progressively enforced by the non-Jews. But, with the elimination of the formal ghetto in Germany, under Napoleon, the causal conditions of separation had declined. Moses Mendelssohn's translation of the Pentateuch into Luther's High German, at the end of the eighteenth century, had drastically reduced (and was on its way to eliminating) the linguistic separation. In the late nineteenth and early twentieth centuries the formal economic, educational, and occupational disabilities had all been progressively lifted (the last, in the Army and the higher civil service, after the first World War).

As the disabilities against them disappeared, the Jews disappeared. They had never numbered more than 1 per cent of the German population, and their rate of apostasy was higher in modern Germany than anywhere else except Italy. After the first World War, social scientists predicted that within two generations there would be no more Jews in Germany. The progression from orthodoxy to agnosticism (via "liberalism") was the largest factor, underlying the conversion of thousands to nominal Protestantism, which had economic and, more significantly, social advantages, and even to Catholicism. Conversion tended, within limits, to remove the "cold" discrimination in the universities and the professions. Noblemen, Army officers, and professors married daughters of wealthy Jewish families, and the motivation was not always money; many Jews of consequence, having fallen away from their faith, ran as fast and as far as they could from it, and the distinguished non-Jew had his pick of not merely wealthy, but cultivated and beautiful young women. This did not, of course, affect the "little man" in Germany except, when he heard of it, to make him hate the "Jew plutocrats" a little more. Nor was he mollified when he heard that intellectuals, artists, "bohemians" intermarried without thought of religious distinction.

Jewish "suicide," by apostasy or conversion, was thus reducing the Jews without reducing anti-Semitism; on the contrary. Four years before Hitler was born in Austria, that country's great anti-Semite, Von Schönerer, said, *"Ob Jud, ob Christ ist einerlei, in der Rasse liegt die Schweinerei.* Whether he says he's a Jew or a Christian doesn't matter, he's depraved by race." Conversion and intermarriage simply shifted the emphasis from the economic and the civil to the racial basis of hatred, and, in doing so, invigorated in new and virulent form the anti-Semitism of the "little man," who, whatever else he was or wasn't, was of German "blood." Long before the first World War, lower-middle-class holiday places, such as the island of Borkum, were beginning to boast of being *judenfrei*.

After all their centuries of exclusion from all the honorable pursuits, the Jews had turned, as their liberation began in the eighteenth and nineteenth centuries, to the "free professions," those which were not organized as guilds or associations excluding them: medicine, law, journalism, teaching, research, and, of course, for the greater part, retail merchandise. (The poorer among them had turned, when they were driven out of the towns in past centuries, to the only possible occupation, the ancestor of retail trade: peddling). Thus the Jews were, on the whole, better off in the years of inflation after the first World War because a smaller proportion of them than of non-Jews were on fixed money incomes of wages, salaries, or pensions; and the "old" Jews of Kronenberg were, before Nazism, nearly all "comfortable." No one in Kronenberg was rich.

Besides the "old" Jews, there were the "new" ones, who had come principally from Poland after the first World War, who spoke Yiddish instead of German and lived as best they could—which might mean peddling and might mean pandering and might mean speculation of the pettiest or the wildest sorts. The Jewish community in Kronenberg had very few "easterners" or, as the "old" Jews called them, "kikes." There were some, of course.

The tailor, Salo Marowitz, had been a Russian soldier,

married to an "Aryan" wife after his release from a German prison camp after the first war. He was honest and respectable, a good man and a good Jew but (as the "old" Kronenberg Jews said) a "kike." There was no doubt that the Marowitzes' older son, Samuel, was born before his parents were married—the kind of scandal that died hard among the "old" German Jews, whose illegitimacy rate, even in the postwar years, was almost nil. Still, he was an honest man.

The three brothers Lipsky, from Poland, were honest, too, but their profession was less creditable. They were notion-peddlers, and they had little dignity. They couldn't afford to have, perhaps; they were none of them very bright. Even though they knew that Tailor Schwenke was a violent anti-Semite, they still came to his house trying to sell him soap. He always called them names and slammed the door on them, but they always came back. The youngest Lipsky, somehow come by the good German name of Bruno, was badly crippled from the waist down. When he walked he had to throw his legs out in front of him, which was enough to make children laugh. Back in the 1920's, when the Reichswehr was supposedly limited to 100,000 men, Kronenberg had a "nonmilitary" battalion which drilled in white shirts, and Bruno insisted on marching beside them, whistling. He would have marched later alongside the SA if they'd let him. He was not very bright.

The Kronenberg Jews were dying out fast enough before Nazism. After 1933 they began moving away from Kronenberg, and from Germany. Most of them stayed on—they didn't believe that "it" would last forever—until the synagogue burning and the pogrom laws of late 1938. But the Jewish community, as a formal organization to which almost every Jew, through choice, heredity, inertia, or social

121

compulsion belonged in a small town, was shrinking steadily *before* 1933.

There was a special reason for the decline of Kronenberg
Jewry. The Jewish community, like the town itself, was
conservative, old-fashioned, and pietistic. The younger generation, since the first World War, had been turning away
from the Tuesday and Thursday prayer service, from the
prayer shawl and the white *Kitl* to be worn at the Passover
ceremony, even from learning Hebrew. It is true that nearly
all of them attended the synagogue school rather than public school; but this was largely a hangover from the days
just gone when Christian religious services were part of the
public school program. Look at Springer, the jeweler: a
member of the community, yes, but when his father died in
the 1920's, he had the tombstone inscription carved in German instead of Hebrew!

The Kronenberg synagogue had, under this kind of pressure in the 1920's, inaugurated new, more acceptable
"German" customs and abandoned some of the old sacra-
mental and liturgical forms. It had become more liberal.
At the time the Nazis came to power, the synagogue's
Shames, or sexton, a non-Jew, lit fires in only a dozen
homes of members who still observed the rigid Saturday
Shabbath prohibition against work, and Jewish-owned shops
were open on Saturdays and closed on Sundays, just like
the Gentiles'.

The concessions to liberalism had not arrested the decline of the Kronenberg congregation. After 1933, however, it began to grow again, in spite of the fact that members were emigrating. Some of those who remained and had
fallen away from the faith came back. The Jewish Charity
was, of course, more active than it had ever been before,
with the demands imposed by the continuing boycott, and

the children (who, if they attended a public school and did not belong to the Hitler Youth, had to remain in the schoolroom alone when the rest were dismissed for celebrations) were all back in the synagogue school.

True, the Jews had been disappearing in Germany; and intermingling, at least at the higher levels of culture and society, had been increasing. But the nonexistent wall between the Jews and the "little men" of Germany was as high as ever, and it was a wall with two sides. It was not clearly and simply a matter of exclusion but, rather, of two-way separation, of the independent existence of two communities in one town, a condition which distinguished the small-town situation in Germany from anti-Semitism in, say, the United States.

In this separation the devil slumbered and in slumber built sinew before Hitler was born. "When I was a boy," said the old tailor whom the teacher had caned, "there were maybe half-a-dozen Jew boys in the village. They had their own school and learned Yiddish—"

"Hebrew," I said.

"Hebrew, if that's what it was, and they could talk to each other in it so that the German kids couldn't understand them. They could understand us, but we couldn't understand them. When there was trouble, just kid trouble, they would talk Yiddish to each other. It scared a person; do you know what I mean?" I said I did. And I did.

When my friend Kessler, the former bank clerk, was a child in a Catholic village in Württemberg, a Jewish peddler came to his village once a month. The peddler transacted all the villagers' business for them, including their banking, without charge, and in return he stayed two or three days with the families of the village, in rotation, on his monthly visits. "He was just like a member of the family to us children," said Herr Kessler, "except for one thing. After dinner, when we read from the Lives of the Saints, the peddler went into the corner and stood there facing the wall and put a shawl on and a band around his forehead and said prayers different from ours. It must have frightened us somehow, because I remember my mother's saying not to be frightened—it was because he was a Jew he did that. We did not know what 'Jew' meant.

"I remembered him only many years afterward, after the first war, when I first heard Nazi propaganda in Munich. And I remembered how I had been afraid—perhaps only mystified, but I suppose that with children the two are the same—when the Jew stood in the corner, facing the wall, with that band around his forehead, saying prayers we couldn't understand, in Yiddish."

"In Hebrew," I said.

"Yes, in Hebrew."

"Did your memory of the peddler make you anti-Semitic?"

"No—not until I heard anti-Semitic propaganda. Jews were supposed to do terrible things that the peddler had never done. And still—I had been frightened by him when he prayed, although I think I really loved him otherwise. The propaganda didn't make me think of him as I knew him but of him as a Jew. And it was as a Jew, praying alone, that he frightened us. So I suppose that, in the end, that was part of it, of my anti-Semitism. I can still make myself frightened, put myself back there. I hear my mother saying not to be frightened."

CHAPTER 9

"Everybody Knew." "Nobody Knew."

When people you don't know, people in whom you have
no interest, people whose affairs you have never discussed,
move away from your community, you don't notice that
they are going or that they are gone. When, in addition,
public opinion (and the government itself) has depreciat-
ed them, it is still likelier that you won't notice their departure or, if you do, that you will forget about it. How
many of us whites, in a white neighborhood, are interested
in the destination of a Negro neighbor whom we know only
by sight and who has moved away? Perhaps he has been
forced to move; at least the possibility occurs to us, and,
if we are particularly sensitive, and we feel that perhaps a
wrong has been done that we can't rectify, it is comforting
to hear that the Negro was also a Communist or that he
will be happier wherever he's gone, "with his own people,"
and was even paid a handsome bonus for moving.

Four of my ten Nazi friends—the tailor and his son, the
baker, and the bill-collecter—said that the only Jews taken
to *Kah-Zed*, concentration camp, were traitors; the rest
were allowed to leave with their property, and, when they
had to sell their businesses, "the courts" or "the finance
office" paid them the market value. "I've heard that the
Jews who left late could only take fifty or a hundred Marks
with them," I said to the tailor, who was talking about

125

"the courts." "I don't know about that," he said. "How should I know about that?" He had "known," a moment before, about "the courts," but I didn't remind him. "I've heard," I said to Herr Simon, the bill-collector, who was talking about "the finance office," "that they could only take part of their property with them." "Well, why not?" said Herr Simon. "If they wanted to leave, the State had a right to a share. After all, they had made their money here."

The fact is, I think, that my friends really didn't know. They didn't know because they didn't want to know; but they didn't know. They could have found out, at the time, only if they had wanted to very badly. Who wanted to? We whites—when the Negro moves away—do we want to find out why or where or with what he moved? The teacher, the student, the cabinetmaker, and the bank clerk, these four at least, suspected the truth of the "market value" myth, and the policeman, to whom you or I would intrust our goods and our chattels without hesitation after five minutes of talk, spoke with contempt of the *"weisse Juden,"* the "white Jews," the hawks who fell upon the property that the Jews had to sell in a hurry. Four of my friends suspected the truth, at the time; what should they have done?

"What would you have done, Herr Professor?" Remember: the teacher excepted, nine of my ten friends didn't know any Jews and didn't care what happened to them— all this *before* Nazism. And it was their government, now, which was carrying on this program under law. Merely to inquire meant to attack the government's justice. It meant risk, large or small, political or social, and it meant risk in behalf of people one didn't like anyway. Who but an ardent Christian, of the sort that takes Matthew 5 seriously, would undertake the risk of inquiring; who, if injustice were to be discovered by inquiry, would undertake the penalty of protesting? I am sorry to say that none of my friends was that ardent a Christian.

But Cabinetmaker Klingelhöfer, he who remained a vestryman of the church throughout Nazism, was as ardent a Christian as most vestrymen I have met, and his idea of relaxation, during our conversations, was to turn to religious questions. "I know it's not what you're interested in, Herr Professor, but I'd like your views." One day, by way of relaxation, we went through Matthew 24 together. (I didn't say that I was interested or that I wasn't, but I did say that reading aloud with a German friend improved my German.) I read, from the ninth through the thirteenth verses, to improve my German:

"Then shall they deliver you up to be afflicted, and shall kill you: and ye shall be hated of all nations for my sake.

"And then shall many be offended, and shall betray one another.

"And many false prophets shall rise, and shall deceive many.

"And because iniquity shall abound, the love of many shall wax cold.

"But he that shall endure unto the end, the same shall be saved."

I stopped, looked up, and then looked at Herr Klingelhöfer. His head—this was my ebullient friend, "My life for the Volunteer Fire Department!"—was lowered. I waited. He said, without looking up:

"Das ist schwer, Herr Professor. Das ist kolossal schwer. That's hard. That's terribly hard."

And it *is* hard. It is said to be hard to be a Christian—or even to want to be—under the most propitious of conditions. The conditions in Nazi Germany were not the most propitious. Just consider:

Jews, because they were in such high proportion in the "free professions," tended to be the people one owed money to for goods or services already delivered, for merchandise, say, or for medical care. Now I, in America, cannot well pay my doctor's bill. My doctor is a nice fellow, but his bills, however low they may be, are too high; I didn't want to be sick in the first place, and, now that I'm well, I wish I hadn't had to buy the medical care I no longer need. I wish my doctor well, believe me, and my dentist and my merchant and my lawyer and the jeweler who repaired my watch; if any of them are Jews, I still wish them well, because I am not anti-Semitic. (Remember, my Nazi friends were.)

Now let us imagine that the Jews are emigrating from America, as fast as they can. They liquidate their assets, at whatever loss, and collect such debts as are collectable in a week or a month. Small debts they don't bother with. They may send out a bill with the word "Please" written on it; but I can't pay it, not this month. What I can't avoid wondering is whether my Jewish dentist or doctor or shopkeeper is thinking of emigrating, winding up his affairs, closing his office or shop, selling out (I may still have to pay my debt some day, if he is able to sell his uncollected bills), taking his whole family with him, losing his citizenship and his power to pursue me with his bills. Of course, I'm a nice fellow, too, so I say, "I'll pay when I can."

But I won't. I won't have to. And I know I won't have to, although in my waking, honorable hours I may not know that I know I won't have to. But—oh, if that doctor and his bills, that dentist and his bills, only didn't exist. A Jewish physician in Kronenberg emigrated in 1936. I was able to talk to him after I got back to America, and, when I had asked him what decided his course in 1936 and he had given me the usual good reasons, he added: "I remember the very occasion which fixed my decision. I was in the public telephone room at the Frankfurt railroad station, and I heard the man in the next booth say, 'Don't pay him. Just don't pay him. Don't argue with him. Don't call him names. Don't waste your breath. Be polite. But don't pay him. Mark my words—in another six months or a year you won't have to pay at all. Hold him off.' It was something like that. 'Jew' wasn't mentioned; I don't know who the man was or even what he was talking about. But that decided me. It took me three, four months, to get a sponsor in America and get everything together. I sent bills out. Some were paid, some in full, some in part. I collected more than half of what was owed me; after all, these people had been my patients, and they were decent people. And 1936 was still early. Later, of course, it was different."

In 1934 I visited a family of remote relatives of mine in a country village outside Hannover. These Jews were small shopkeepers; they had been there for seven centuries, and there were too few of them to constitute a formal Jewish community. There was no anti-Semitism in Eichdorf. (There was no intermarriage, either.) In those first years of Nazism their non-Jewish friends continued to trade with them openly; later, secretly. Little children—it began with little children—who called them names on the street were taken home and spanked. The villagers, except for a few officials and a few young rowdies, simply would not let Nazism have its way, not in Eichdorf.

Nine years later, in 1943, the Jews of Eichdorf were "sent away." In such a small community they could not be "sent" unnoticed. After the war one of their neighbors was telling about it: "Everybody knew, but nobody came out on the street. Some looked from behind their curtains, not many."

"Did you?"

"No."

"Why not?"

"Why? What good is it to look?"

Kronenberg was, of course, bigger. None of my ten friends ever saw any Jews leave in a group. It wasn't required that they see. Only Policeman Hofmeister, of the ten, knew of the details of the departure of the Jews, and he only of their departure, not of their destination. And only Herr Hildebrandt, the teacher, ever corresponded with any Jews afterward or knew what had become of them. Everyone knew that Jews were moving away, from 1933 on. All of my ten friends had heard that these Jews or those were going or gone. A Jewish woman came to Herr Wedekind's bakery to pay her bill and wanted to make sure that there was nothing left owing him. "You're leaving?" he said. "Yes," she said. That was all. Three of my friends heard, during the war, that a bus load of Jews had left the Market Place at dawn one day. That was all.

Shortly after the war began, a group of Jews were seen working on the street, laying blocks in the trolley-car track (Jews were now forbidden any but common labor). Hofmeister waved a greeting to some he knew but didn't talk to them. Cabinetmaker Klingelhöfer spoke to one he knew, a lawyer, who had been a customer of his. "Did you ask him how he happened to be there?" I said.

"No. I knew."

"How?"

"Everybody knew."

"How?"

"Oh—we just knew."

"What did you say to him?"

"I asked him how he was, and he said, 'Fine.' He looked all right."

"Did you shake hands with him?"

"No. . . . One doesn't shake hands with a man who is busy with both hands, *nicht wahr?*"

"No, not in America, but you Germans always shake hands so much, I thought maybe—. By the way, Herr Klingelhöfer, do you think you were brave to talk with him on the street?"

"Brave? No, not brave. Maybe, a little. No, not really. My loyalty was known."

Herr Kessler, the unemployed bank clerk risen to Party speaker and department head in the local Labor Front, saw Stein on the Kronenberg platform waiting, as he himself was, for the northbound train. He had known Stein well, in a business way; Stein, to help him out when he was unemployed, had always hired him to audit the books of his dry-goods store. The Jew was an old man. It was—when was it? —early in 1939. "He pretended not to see me. Maybe he thought it would embarrass me, or just that I wouldn't want to talk to him. That was wrong; I wasn't a *Fanatiker*. Finally I went up to him and shook hands and asked him how he was. He said, 'Fine.' I couldn't ask him how his business was, because I knew he had sold out. Then, when the train was coming, I said, 'Are you going away, Herr Stein?' Of course he was going away, or he wouldn't have been waiting for the train, but a man may go away for a day or forever; I didn't ask that. I said, 'Are you going away, Herr Stein?' He said, 'Yes,' and then I said, 'Well, goodbye,' and held out my hand, but he had already turned away."

"Did you both get on the train?"

"Yes."

"Together?"

"No. He got on the nonsmoker end of the car, and I got on the smoker."

"Did you smoke?"

"No."

I did not initiate the discussion of the Jews with any of my ten friends. Somewhere between the beginning of the second conversation and the end of the fourth, each of them introduced the subject, and each of them, except Messrs Hildebrandt, Kessler, and Klingelhöfer, reverted to it continually. I would ask Tailor Schwenke, "Did you like the Program, in '25?" "The Party Program?" he would say. "Yes, it was very good, very. Take the Jewish question, for instance. . . ." (In a subsequent conversation he said he had never seen the Party Program.)

Of the ten men, only the teacher, Hildebrandt, was not anti-Semitic. The policeman, a fine old man, did not want to be; but he was. The student, young Rupprecht, thought he wasn't anti-Semitic, but in his case I am not at all sure; he was glib. Kessler and Klingelhöfer, the two deepest-feeling of my friends (except Hildebrandt), were the mildest; their anti-Semitism was not at all "racial" and almost entirely economic, "rational."

Klingelhöfer's father, from whom the son had taken his trade as cabinetmaker, had told him that Jews were all right: "They were people, like other people, but you couldn't trust them in money matters, that was all. If you went to a Jew to do business, that was one thing, but if a Jew came to you to do business, that was another."

"Why do you suppose that was?" I said.

"I don't know. I don't know. I remember my father telling me about Moses, whose leather-shop was in the Bahnhofstrasse. My father did lots of work for him, and they got along fine. Moses only paid his accounts on Sunday mornings and he always paid a 'round sum,' no *Pfennige*. And he always deducted 3 per cent."

"Why?"

"I don't know. That was his custom, I guess. So my father always arranged *his* accounts so that the 3 per cent was already in. You may say 'cheating the cheater,' but it wasn't like that, exactly. Moses was a nice man. My father liked him. But my father always said that you couldn't trust a Jew in money matters. And he was right."

"Were you ever cheated by a Jew?"

"No, but that was because I was warned and was careful. If you're careful, you have no trouble with them."

"Were you careful with Professor Freudenthal?" (Freudenthal, who committed suicide in 1933, had been a customer of Herr Klingelhöfer's and had sent him a wedding present, a piano shawl of which my friend was proud.)

"No. With him you didn't have to be."

The former bank clerk's thinking was much larger than the cabinetmaker's. The Jews had accumulated too much of the country's economic power; "they should have been reduced economically to their proper proportion in the population."

"How should that have been done?"

"That's what I don't know, but a way should have been found without depriving them of their citizenship or mistreating them."

"Did they exercise this power badly?"

"In a way. I suppose anybody would, especially if he was looked down on, like the Jews. But it seemed to be very bad with the Jews."

"Do you mean that they introduced a 'Jewish spirit' into

economic life? I have heard other National Socialists say that."

"Well, that was the propaganda, of course, part of the whole 'race' thing, but I wouldn't say that. There is and there isn't a 'Jewish spirit,' but certainly the aggressiveness and competitiveness of some Jews led to abuses—for instance, to pornography in the press, just to sell papers and magazines."

" 'Of some Jews,' " I said.

"Oh, yes, of some; not all."

"And of some non-Jews."

"Of course. That's why I don't like to speak of a 'Jewish spirit.' But there were so many more Jews than non-Jews in these things, proportionately. That's what I mean."

Not one of my ten friends had changed his attitude toward the Jews since the downfall of National Socialism. The five (or six, if young Rupprecht is included) who were extreme anti-Semites were, I believe, not a bit more or less so now than before. What surprised me, indeed, was that, with the war lost and their lives ruined, they were not more so. Certainly Nazism's defeat by force would not make Nazis love the Jews more; if anything, less. Nor would their country's destruction. Nor would the three-quarters of a billion dollars their conquerors compelled them to pay, as restitutive damages, to the Jews of Israel. And the five extremists had never seen the inside of the local *Amerika-Haus* or any other agency of "re-education" and never would.

They, and, to a degree, even the bank clerk, the cabinet-maker, and the policeman, took the greatest pains to convince me that the Jews were as bad as the Nazis said they were. I sat passively, every so often asking a question which betrayed my simple-mindedness, while my friends pressed their argument. If I diverted them, they came back to it. The one passion they seemed to have left was anti-Semitism, the one fire that warmed them still. I thought, as they went on, of the customary analysis: We have to justify our having injured those we have injured, or we have to persuade others to our guilty view in order to implicate them in our guilt. I thought a little, but I didn't say much. What could I have said?

CHAPTER 10

"We Christians Had the Duty"

Herr Simon, the bill-collector, was visiting me. He had brought tulips to my wife, as, when I went to his house, I took candy to his. We were drinking coffee, he and I, as, at his house, we (or, rather, I; he was a teetotaler, "like Hitler") always drank wine. He was interested in finding out about America, at least in talking about it. I was telling him about the reservation of powers to the states in our federal system—.

"Do you know any Jews over there, Herr Professor?" he said.

"Oh, yes," I said, "many, quite well. They live among us over there, you know, just like other people."

"Not like Negroes," said the "Old Fighter." "But," he went on, "I want to ask you about the Jews. Can you always tell a Jew when you see one, over there? We can, here. Always. They're not like you and me."

"How can you tell?" I said. "They sometimes *look* like you and me."

"Certainly," he said, "sometimes. It isn't by looks, though. A German can tell. Always."

"Well," I said, like a man who is saying to himself, "You learn something new every day."

"Yes," he said.

Then I said, "Could you tell, if you saw Jesus, that he was a Jew, Herr Simon?"

"I think so," he said, "if he was a Jew. *But was he a Jew?* If he was, why did the Jews kill him? Can you tell me that?"—He went right on—"I've never heard a pastor say that Jesus was a Jew. Many scientists say he wasn't. I have heard that Hitler himself said that he was the son of a Greek soldier in the Roman Army."

"I never heard that," I said. I was lying; Reinhold Hanisch, in his memoirs, says that Hitler told him that in 1910, when they were living together in a Vienna flophouse.

"Yes," said Herr Simon, "and do you know, Herr Professor, the Jews have a secret Bible, called the Talmud. Maybe you never heard that, either, but it's true. They deny it, of course. You just ask a Jew about it, and watch him when he says it doesn't exist. But every German knows about it; I've seen it myself. It has their ritual murder in it, and everything else. It tells them—mind you, it was written I don't know how many centuries ago—that they must marry German women and weaken the German race. What do you think of that?"

What did I think of that? I thought I would telephone the dean of the theological faculty at Kronenberg University and ask him, even though it was a Sunday night and a blowy one, to bring a German Talmud to my house. That, I said to myself, will do it, much better than my telling him I'm a Jew. If, I said to myself, I tell him I'm a Jew now, he will be so furious at my previous deception of him that I shall have no opportunity to point out to him that he didn't know a Jew when he saw one. I wanted a minute to think it over, first.

"You say," I said idly, "that you have seen this—this—?"

"Talmud," said the bill-collector, a small, spectacled man who needed a strong mustache (he had a weak one). "But watch out, Herr Professor, that they don't fool you.

137

I've seen the real one. The Jews would show you a fake, if you trapped them, and even in your own universities you will find professors in the pay of the Jews who will tell you that it is genuine. We had such professors here—before. And again now, of course."

What did I think of that? I thought that I would not telephone to the dean, and, later on, as I said, "We'll have to have many more talks, Herr Simon," I thought that we'll have to have many more generations of Herr Simons, emerging, somehow without being led or driven, from the wilderness in which this generation of Simons lived with their "real" Talmud.

I was visiting Tailor Schwenke, my lusty old *Fanatiker* friend. He was in his sweater and pants, and we were having soup and unbuttered bread, a meal which, German country bread being what it is, was not so light as it sounds. His wife had baked a cake, and I had brought tea. "And so," I was saying, "we come to the end of your father's life-story, and that brings us to the end of the story of all your ancestors on both sides, down to you. I marvel, Herr Schwenke, that you know so much about each one of them, for so many generations back."

"That's the way we Germans are," said my friend. "We are proud of our families. The Americans took my Bible—they sent a Jew to do it, naturally—or I could give you all the dates exactly, birth, baptism, marriage, children, death."

"Your family," I said, very carefully, "seems always to have been lucky. Never any great troubles. Never lost their homes or their land. A very unusual family, always to have had such good fortune."

"Always, always," said the tailor. "As far back as we go—up to my own bad fortune—it was always very good, with my father, my grandfathers, my great-grandfathers, all of them."

This exchange occurred in our fourteenth conversation. In the course of the second, long before we had begun the remarkably detailed examination of the lives of his ancestors, he had talked about the Jews, saying, "I had reason enough to hate them, even before, for the way they ruined my ancestors for generations back. Stole everything from them, ruined them," and his face was furious with filial wrath.

I think that my friend believed what he was saying—at the time he was saying it—both in our second conversation and in our fourteenth. I might have shot home the contradiction. It would not have made him any less anti-Semitic, and, besides, men's lives are what they think they are. So I didn't.

I was visiting Herr Damm, the country boy who, his oldest brother being destined to get the family farm under Hessian primogeniture, had come to Kronenberg to get a job. He lost it in the depression and went back home, joined the Party at the "recruiting evening" the Nazis held in the village in 1932, and rose to be office manager of the Kronenberg Party headquarters. It was the twelve hundredth anniversary of the founding of the country village, where the Damms had settled in A.D. 808, and I was attending the celebration.

"Yes," said Herr Damm, "our family were always great anti-Semites. My father and grandfather were followers of Dr. Böckel, who founded the Anti-Semitic Party in Hesse, way back in the eighties. We used to have the Party flag, with the anti-Semitic inscription on it, 'Freedom from Jewry,' out the Americans took it away."

"Did you ever have any dealings with Jews?" I said.

"Always," he said. "We had to, in the country. Before the farmers' credit union was founded by Dr. Böckel—it was anti-Semitic, to save the farmers from the Jews—we were at the mercy of the cattle dealers. They were all Jews, and they all worked together."

"How do you know that they all worked together, Herr Damm?"

"They always do. They held us in the palm of their hand. Do you know what one of them once did? He bought a calf from my father and took it to town and sold it to my father's cousin, *at a profit*."

"Yes," I said, "but that is just the profit system. You believe in the profit system, don't you? You're certainly no Communist!"

"Of course," he said, "but only think—to my father's own cousin! If my father had known his cousin wanted the calf, he could have sold it to him himself, without the Jew."

"Well—" I said.

"Look, Herr Professor, a Jew buys a cow. When he buys it, it's terrible, everything's wrong with it, he wouldn't have it for a gift. So he pays a few Marks for it. Then he goes to the next farmer with it, to sell it, and it's the most wonderful cow in the world. Do you see what I mean?"

"I think so," I said, wreathed, internally, with a smile as I thought of "the American Way," "but don't Germans," that is, non-Jews, "buy as low and sell as high as possible?"

"Yes, but that's just it. Look, Herr Professor," he went on, patiently, "Germans couldn't trade with one another. There was always a Jew between them. All Jews are *Händler*, traders, never workers or farmers. Every child knows this. All trade was in the hands of the Jews. What could

140

we poor Germans"—he was speaking of what Hitler calls, in *Mein Kampf*, the "genius-race"—"do?"

I liked Herr Damm. He was a professional clodhopper— he had been used for Party work among the farmers, whose "language," that is, whose mind, he spoke—but he was still a clodhopper. On another occasion, he was visiting me in town; or, rather, since it was to be our last talk together, I was his host at a one-dollar de luxe dinner at Kronenberg's best restaurant. I brought the talk back to one of our first conversations, in which he had told me that he was the only Kreisamtsleiter in our whole *Gau* who had refused to leave the Church. "I told them I was born in the Church," he had said, "and I would die in it, and not in the 'German Church,' but the Christian Church."

"Now," I said, as we were lighting up after dinner, "what many Christians in America cannot understand is how you Christians in Germany could accept the persecution of the Jews, no matter how bad they were. How could you accept it *as Christians?*"

It was the first time I had taken the initiative on the subject. "The Jews?"—he said—"but the Jews were the *enemies* of the Christian religion. Others might have other reasons for destroying them, but we Christians had the *Christian duty* to. Surely, Herr Professor, you know how the Jews betrayed our Lord?"

None of my friends was the least interested in Nazi race theory as such, not even the tailor or the bill-collector. Five of the ten of them laughed when they spoke of it, including the cabinetmaker. "That was nonsense," said Herr Klingelhöfer, "for the SS and the universities. Look at the shape of my head: broad as a barnside. Look at my brunette wife. Do you suppose we're not Germans? No; that they could teach to the SS and the university students. The

SS *Flott* ["cream," sacastically] would believe anything that made them great, and the university students would believe anything complicated. The professors, too. Have you seen the 'race purity' chart?" "Yes," I said. "Well, then, you know. A whole system. We Germans like systems, you know. It all fitted together, so it was science, system and science, if only you looked at the circles, black, white, and shaded, and not at real people. Such *Dummheit* they couldn't teach to us little men. They didn't even try."

What my friends believed—and believe—is an accumulation of legend, legend which comes to them no more guiltily than the cherry-tree story comes to us. Only in their case, esteeming themselves as they did as "little men," "little people," who did not amount to anything except in so far as they were Germans, the legend of a people among them who were not Germans and who, therefore, were even less than they, was especially precious.

Nobody has proved to my friends that the Nazis were wrong about the Jews. Nobody can. The truth or falsity of what the Nazis said, and of what my extremist friends believed, was immaterial, marvelously so. There simply was no way to reach it, no way, at least, that employed the procedures of logic and evidence. The bill-collector told me that Jews were filthy, that the home of a Jewish woman in his boyhood town was a pigsty; and the baker told me that the Jews' fanaticism about cleanliness was a standing affront to the "Germans," who were clean enough. What difference did the truth, if there were truth, make?

I suggested from time to time, and always in hesitant fashion, that perhaps the medieval exclusion of Jews from citizenship and landholding, their subsequent exclusion, after 1648, from guild apprenticeship, and their confinement for a thousand years to the practice of moneylending, with the attendant risk of the despicable creditor against the knightly debtor, might have required cunning of most of the Jews in most of early Europe as the condition of survival itself; that the consequent sharpening of the intellect under such circumstances would have produced a disproportionate number of unusually noble and unusually ignoble dispositions among any people, their unusualness, in the marginal occupations to which they were driven, disappearing as the great community removed the disadvantagements which produced it. I reminded the bank clerk, Kessler, that the ancestors of the Christians who now forbade Jews to be bank presidents once compelled them to be. He was a Swabian, from Württemberg, and the Swabians are humorous—"for Germans," as Tacitus would say. He appreciated the joke.

None of my ten friends argued with me when I said these things. None of them, except the bank clerk and, of course, the teacher, listened. Everything I said, all of them might have learned long ago. But there are some things that everybody knows and nobody learns. Didn't everybody know, in America, on December 8, 1941, that the Japanese, or Japs, were a treacherous people?

In the American Embassy in Berlin, in 1935, an official of the German Foreign Press Office told me the story of a North Sea town where there had never been a Jew. When Goebbels announced the boycott of the Jews for the month of April, 1933, the Bürgermeister of the town sent him a telegram: "Send us a Jew for our boycott."

CHAPTER 11

The Crimes of the Losers

Long before the second World War ended, the Allies decided that, in case they won, they would not again write a "war guilt" clause (which the Germans would again repudiate) into the peace treaty. They would this time, by a great legal proceeding, convict the Germans of their guilt under international law and convince them of it. And this time the guilt, in addition to breach of the peace, would include war crimes and crimes against humanity. The day the International Military Tribunal opened at Nuremberg, the American prosecutor, Justice Jackson of the United States Supreme Court, called the occasion "a rare moment in history," and the day after the Nazi leaders were hanged the *New York Times* said: "Mankind has entered a new world of international morality."

The Nazi leaders were hanged, but they were not impressed. They pleaded, during the legal proceeding against them, that they had all acted under orders (wasn't Nazi Germany a dictatorship?); that, if anyone were guilty, their judges were as guilty as they themselves were (especially the Russians; why, they asked, wouldn't the Tribunal press the charge it had made that it was the Germans, not the Russians, who had slaughtered the Polish officers in the Katyn Forest?); that international law was law only by analogy, that it wasn't codified, that even if it were codified it would not supersede national law (which, obviously, they had not broken), and that even if it were codified and superseded national law it would not permit one party to a suit to try another or bring only one party, rather than both, to trial.

There were Americans who wondered whether the Nuremberg gallows trap was a wide enough entrance to a new world of international morality for mankind, but such wonderers were not numerous in 1946. Most Americans were satisfied with the operation, even if they did not share the premature ecstasy of Justice Jackson. But the succeeding "international" tribunals at Nuremberg, twelve in all, had to be conducted by the United States without the co-operation of its Allies. Nuremberg, after the "big show" of the IMT trial, lost its interest, not only for the other three European Allied governments, but also for most American citizens. It was water over the dam—spilled milk, at worst.

But it was gall, if not wormwood, for the Germans, and not just for the Nazis among them. As far as my ten friends were concerned, the Nuremberg method of convincing them of their guilt was a failure. It was not that it miscarried; it simply had no fundamental effect on them at all. It was taken as an incidental penalty of losing the war, another turn of the screw.

My friends were, they all said, little men; why should they repent those acts of State (and of a dictatorship State in which they had no controlling voice) which the highest surviving ministers of the State did not repent? Repentance is not of the essence, or even of the atmosphere, of a legal proceeding anyway, still less of a military proceeding. Repentance is effectively urged when the urger stipulates in the indictment that we are all sinners, and the Nuremberg indictments made no such stipulation.

If, after all the wars of history, the losers had not been roughly treated without a formal finding of guilt, the treatment of the Germans after the last war, upon a formal finding, might have impressed my friends. As it was, they were, in their own view, simply paying the usual price of losing. "Why so much money to hang us?" said Göring to his neighbor in the dock when the American prosecutor, complaining at the trial's delays, said that the procedure was costing his government thousands of dollars a day. Five irreparable years later, the man we sent to Germany to re-educate the Germans found himself re-educated: "In looking backward," said former High Commissioner Mc-Cloy, "I wish we had been able to erect tribunals not composed exclusively of the victors." Why weren't we able to?

In 1950, in October, United States General Douglas MacArthur approved a legal procedure, modeled after Nuremberg, for trying North Korean and Chinese war criminals after the war in Korea would be won. Legal teams scoured the Korean peninsula as far north as the Yalu River, accompanied by motion-picture photographers. A year later the United Nations commander in Korea, General Matthew Ridgway, said that there were 400 "active cases and 126 suspects" of war crimes in UN custody. But a year later North Korean and Chinese war criminals went home, untried and unhung; Secretary Dulles, an international lawyer, announced the good news, as he called it, that the North Korean–Chinese command had agreed to release enemy personnel charged with war crimes on the condition that the UN command release enemy personnel so charged. The "rare moment in history" had passed; the war in

Korea had not been won; international law, like international conquest, required losers before it could operate.

Losers are hard to convince of their guilt. The suffering they have undergone in losing constitutes, as they see it, expiation and more for their own offenses, real or alleged. Boys fighting in alleys are that way. The battered and bloody vanquished is seldom magnanimous enough to admit that he got what was coming to him—about all he can be got to say is "uncle"—and more seldom still to admit that he ought to get more. Men should not be that way, but they sometimes are. My friends were.

It is a principle of animal training that, for the punishment to be effective, the offender must associate it with the crime. You must catch him in the act, on the scene, or he will have forgotten what he did and the punishment will appear abusive to him. Men, too, have a way of dating their guilt and innocence from the injuries they suffer, not from those they inflict. No matter how far back in history I went with my National Socialist friends, they would want to begin its writing with their own or their country's agonies. When I spoke of 1939, they spoke of 1945; when I spoke of 1914, they spoke of 1918; when I spoke of 1871, they spoke of 1809. As a university-educated American, I knew that there had been a Dawes Plan for the payment of German reparations after the first World War, and a Young Plan which had liberalized the payments. But seven of my ten friends—five of whom had not gone beyond six years of folk school—knew that the Young Plan payments were to have been continued until 1988, "when," said Policeman Hofmeister, "my son will be eighty years old."

My fellow-Americans in Germany were sick of the Germans' self-pity. "I'll tell you about them," said one of the Occupation officials, "in a nutshell. They're like dogs. If you don't kick them, they bite you; and, when you kick them, they whine." An American Occupation judge was trying to get transferred. "It's got so," he said, "that the minute a German starts whining, I know I'm going to find him guilty. And they all whine. They all have a hard-luck story. Well, they *have* had hard luck. But they gave other people lots harder luck first. Of course, they've forgotten that."

The judge was equating inequivalents. The hard luck the Germans have had *they* have had, while the hard luck they gave, somebody else had, somebody they don't know; and they don't even believe that it was they who gave it. Herr Damm, after losing his career and his home and possessions, was now earning $47 a month as a "black," that is, unauthorized worker; he did not see the equivalence between his boycott of Jews in the past and his own children's undernourishment now. He hadn't seen the Jews who, as the ultimate consequence of *his* legal acts were slain; and, besides, like everyone else except Hitler, who had a mandate from the German people, Herr Damm had a mandate from Hitler, the head of the government, to boycott Jews.

I am sure that the tailor, Schwenke, had a hand, and a ready one, in burning the Kronenberg synagogue. See the way *he* may see the crime (which he denies): He was a man provoked to fury by extreme misfortune, in which "the Jews" played the central role; and he was one of many; and he was a follower, not a leader; and he was being a patriot in Nazi Germany; and the victim was a building; and so on. And the loss to him (which he admits) was three years' imprisonment late in life, his job, his health, his home, his possessions, and a chance to earn a living to keep from starving. Justice has not overtaken the spirit which led to the Nazi enormities—how could it?—but it has overtaken Herr Schwenke, in his view, with a terrible vengeance.

As my ten friends, all ten of them, told me their troubles, whining, whining, whining, I sympathized with the American complaint. One of the shoemakers in Kronenberg, a man who bears the reputation, and justly so, of a philosopher, said, "I was listening to a German-Swiss soccer game at Zürich, just before you came in. The Swiss were being beaten, and it was near the end of the game. There seem to have been several fouls called on the German team in the course of the game, and here was another. The Swiss announcer said, without raising his voice, 'Foul called on the visitors,' and went on. Do you know what a German announcer would have done, if the situation were reversed and the game were in Germany?—He would have cried out, 'Another foul on the Swiss!' and he would have made the word "Swiss," *Schweitzer*, sound like "pig," *Schwein*. He would have named the Swiss player who fouled, and he would have repeated the name, saying, 'This Baltz is the same Baltz who . . .' and so on. You understand? That's our trouble."

War seems to be the German sport—if not exclusively theirs—and the Germans seem to be poor sports. Baker Wedekind, without having read the ancient Romans, who made the same point on the subject of the Germans, said, "Churchill promised the English 'blood and tears,' *and at the very beginning of the war*. That you would never hear in Germany. You might hear it at the very end, and even then you would hear that we were still winning. We won all the battles, you know; we only lost the war. We are not

149

good losers. I don't know about you. You have never lost, have you?"

Americans have not had the Germans' troubles, perhaps by happy accident, perhaps because they have not made such troubles for others as the Germans have. Americans are not injured, and they don't feel injured. And, if they do, they do not characteristically whine. There is an unbecoming childishness in all this whining, a childishness which is not mitigated by one's looking on one's self as "little." An American may be helpless, but he doesn't know it. The stiff upper lip of the Englishman may be a national affectation, but he keeps it. These Germans, hitting out because somebody tells them to (or doesn't tell them not to), are offended when somebody hits them back. Sacrifice and endurance are more arduously cultivated among the Germans than among other peoples, with strangely mixed success.

My Nazi friends were sorry for themselves because they were wrongfully injured. And they were wrongfully injured, you know; everyone is, in this life. And there seems to be a much greater accumulation of wrongful injury—injury suffered, that is, which weighs heavier than injury inflicted —in Germany than in places off the path of the last twenty centuries' wars. So Germans whine. But there was the woman who told me, "It was my own fault. I should have been more courageous"; and the man who said, "I should have been man enough to say 'No' at the very beginning"; and the priest who stood on the scaffold after the unsuccessful *Putsch* of 1944 and said to his confessor, "In a minute, Father, I shall know more than you"—these, too, were Germans.

Being a German may make whining easier, but not inevitable. In October, 1945, the Confessional church of

Germany, the "church within the Church" which had defied Hitler's "German Christians," issued the "Stuttgart Confession": "We know ourselves to be with our people in a great company of suffering, but also in a great solidarity of guilt. With great pain do we say that through us has endless suffering been brought to many peoples and countries. That to which we have often borne witness before our congregations, we declare in the name of the whole church. True, we have struggled for many years in the name of Jesus Christ against a spirit which has found its terrible expression in the National Socialist regime of violence, but we accuse ourselves for not witnessing more courageously. . . ." Those, too, were German words.

The juridical effort at Nuremberg to punish the evildoers without injuring the losers—when punishment and injury came to the same thing and the losers were identical with the evildoers—was unlikely enough to succeed. The effort to convince my ten friends that *they* were evildoers was even unlikelier. In retrospect, there was one extremely remote possibility of its having been done more successfully in Germany than it had ever been done anywhere else: It might have been possible to exploit the Germans' attachment to "the German spirit" and to have convinced them that this spirit, instead of being good, is evil. How to have gone about doing this I do not know. Certainly not by treating them hard; the Nazis used this technique on the Jews without convincing them of anything.

CHAPTER 12

"That's the Way We Are"

There was a peculiar disadvantage in trying to convince the Germans generally that they were guilty of the crimes of the Reich. The German people have never, as single individuals, had to assume the responsibility of sovereignty over their government. The self-governing American regards his government as his mere agent, an animated tool in his hand. If it doesn't suit his purposes, he discards it and tries a new one. He, the constituent, constitutes the State; his ministers minister to him. My Nazi—and most of my non-Nazi—friends in Germany simply do not understand this view of government in which the enduring fact of society, the will of the people, is represented by an instrument which is here today and gone tomorrow. The government must be *embodied*. To say that it is embodied in the law is, in their view, so much gobbledygook; laws are enacted by men. (The Nazis did not even bother to repeal the Weimar Constitution.)

The English constitutional monarchy, a monarchy they themselves never had, my friends might comprehend, with the greatest difficulty; our constitutional democracy, not at all. This seems to say that my friends want despotic rule. They do, if by despotism we mean, not the ruler's oppression, but the ruler's independent right to rule.

This does not mean totalitarianism; it does not mean that

there is no opposition. It means that the opposition is limited to matters below the level of general policy; Bismarck did not govern without the *advice* of the Reichstag; he governed without its *consent*, as the Kaiser, when he finally chose, governed without Bismarck's. The story is told of the last emperor of Austria-Hungary, the famous-visaged Franz Josef of the great white burnsides, that, having on one occasion received an Opposition delegation and heard its demands, he turned to his prime minister and said, "This is not opposition—this is *factious* opposition!" My friend Willy Hofmeister, the policeman, who, now that I think of it, looked like Franz Josef, was telling me that a German policeman never used his gun except in cases of extreme personal peril. "Well," I said, "when you order a car to stop and it doesn't, don't you fire?" "We wouldn't," he said, "but when you order a car to stop, it stops." Opposition.

The history of the Social Democratic Party of Germany is suggestive. In 1890 the Kaiser, with Bismarck gone, let the anti-Socialist laws lapse. In a single generation of legal status the Social Democratic Party transformed itself from a revolutionary underground to a governmental party, reformist, to be sure, even radically reformist, but not, as it was in England and even in Austria, an opposition with an independent program of its own for altering the very basis of government.

In 1914 the Socialists, supporting the Kaiser's demand for war credits, proclaimed that Germany was fighting a defensive war—"In the hour of danger, we will not leave our country in the lurch." A generation later, after its country had left it in the lurch, the Party was even more nationalistic than the anti-Socialist coalition of the Adenauer government; "never again," said the Socialist leader Schumacher, "will the Socialists be caught being less nationalistic than their opponents."—Thus they who of yore proclaimed "the commonwealth of man and the parliament of the world."

The formation of Germany's "black" army after 1918 had its sanction and support from the Reich Ministry of War under the Socialist leadership of Severing, and, at the end of Wiemar, only the Prussian Socialist leadership stood firm in resistance. Like all the rest of the pre-Nazi parties in Germany, left, right, and center, the Social Democratic Party as such provided no independent alternative to the Nazis and the Communists, each of which parties was ready to rule with a program of its own uninhibited by any atavistic subservience to the tradition of the suprapolitical Sovereign. "There was one thing you had to say for the Bolsheviks," said the Nazi *Fanatiker* Schwenke. "Their 'No' wasn't a three-quarters 'Yes.'"

It hadn't always been that way. Just before the first World War one-fourth of the deputies in the Reichstag were Social Democrats, at a time when parliamentary government was a rich man's game, with the deputies unsalaried; at a time, too, when to be a Social Democrat in Germany was almost as bad as being a Communist in the United States thirty years later. Regarded still in those days, as they had been under Bismarck, as traitors, the future party of loyal opposition fought to change the character of their country and the basis of its government. Their workingmen's education movement, although (unlike our own adult programs) it was education for specific social purposes, was the most advanced and widespread in Europe. Their trade-unions, and the men in them, were politically conscious and aggressive; unlike American workers, who were born with civil rights, the German and all other European workers had had to fight to win theirs.

Immediately prior to their turning respectable, at the outset of the first war, the German Social Democrats had been a force for fundamental change among perhaps one-third of all the Germans. Respectability, which the Social Democrats finally achieved by supporting the war government in 1914, killed that force and left its vestiges to the Nazis and the Communists.

Twice in our time, at Weimar and at Bonn, Germany's victorious enemies have tried to turn Germany upside down and install government (as my Nazi friends see it) without rule. Hitler turned Germany (as they see it) right side up. He was an independent Sovereign, popularly supported, in part for no other reason than that he was an independent Sovereign. *This* was government.

Were the props to be pulled out from under it, the Bonn Republic would sooner or later fall, as surely as Weimar, not because Germans find it oppressive but because they find it a *nonregnum*. The chancellor is a party politician at the mercy of party politicians who, to the extent that they are responsible to the people, derive their power, and therefore his, from those creatures furthest removed, in their own estimate, from Sovereignty. A fifty-year-old non-Nazi acquaintance of mine remembered that, when she was a teen-ager, not in the feudal east or imperial south of the country but in modern Westphalia, the farmers took off their hats when the Count's carriage went by *empty*, and Policeman Hofmeister told me, "When all is said and done, it is cheaper to pay one man, who knows how to rule, twenty million marks than to pay five thousand men ten thousand marks apiece."

Chancellor Bismarck ruled Germany; he was the Chancellor of Iron. But the King-Emperor could and did dismiss him, could and did use the independence of the

Crown (which Bismarck, in his hatred of parliamentarianism, had fortified) to launch a mad attack upon Europe in what he regarded as the interest of the German people. He may have been wrong and Bismarck right, but the German people, who regarded him as the man whose business it was to rule them, fought when he told them to. Neither Americans unlaureled nor English poets laureate believe (though the latter say) that it is not ours to reason why. But my Nazi, and some of my non-Nazi, friends believe it; "the King makes war, and the people die." They are good soldiers, these Germans; they lack only what Bismarck (of all people) said they lacked, "civilian courage," the courage which enables men neither to be governed by nor to govern others but to govern themselves.

This does not mean that my Nazi—or non-Nazi—friends are bad men. (They may be bad, but, if they are, it is for other reasons.) It means that their political history is different from ours—we should say "behind" ours. I put "behind" in quotation marks because my friends do not see it that way; they are less ready than we are to identify chronological change with progress. Without having read the Greeks, they use all the arguments against democracy that the Greeks used. "In your government," said the argumentative bill-collector, who wanted to talk about America and had read about it in Luckner, "nobody has authority. This is a fine thing, to be sure, in a big, rich, empty land, unless there is an emergency. Then you suddenly establish authority. You boast that you have elections even in wartime, but you never change governments then; *then* you say, 'Don't change horses in the middle of the stream' (we have the same saying in Germany); and you don't. We don't pretend that we can."

Nor does it mean that my Nazi—or non-Nazi—friends

are politically unconscious. Far from it; their conversation is more political than ours, and they take their politics with what Schopenhauer called *tierischer Ernst*, bovine seriousness. The German press devotes much more of its space than ours to politics and more of its political discussion to issues than to personalities. In our first conversations, when I found that my friends preferred talking about Versailles or the Polish Corridor to talking about themselves, I thought that they were running away from their guilt. I was wrong. They did not regard what they themselves did as important, and they were interested in important things like Versailles and the Polish Corridor.

To say that my German friends were nonpolitical, and to say no more, is to libel them. As in nearly all European countries, a very much larger proportion of Germans than Americans turns out for political meetings, political discussions, and local and general elections. Where the German was (in contrast with the American) nonpolitical was at a deeper level. He was habitually deficient in the *sense of political power* that the American possesses (and the Englishman, the Frenchman, the Scandinavian, and the Swiss). He saw the State in such majesty and magnificence, and himself in such insignificance, that he could not relate himself to the actual operation of the State.

One of my non-Nazi friends made a relevant point, however, in defense of his countrymen, at least against the Americans, if not against the rest of the Europeans: "Our situation differs from yours the way city life differs from the country. Ours is intensely complicated and difficult, sophisticated, so to say, while yours (at least until very recently) has been almost pastoral, primitive in its clarity and simplicity. Ours is much less readily intelligible to us than yours is to you, and our 'average citizen,' therefore, feels more inadequate than yours to deal with it." But the nonpolitical, or, more accurately, politically nonconfident, German, who minded his own business and confined his business to his *Fach* (which means both pigeonhole and specialty), was just as prevalent in business, industry, and finance, in education, in the church, and in the press as in tailoring, baking, or cabinetmaking.

The German universities were crawling with experts on the Akka pygmies of the Aruwimi Congo, but they were closed to political thinking except on the level of detached theory; in the whole state of Hesse not a single course in political science was offered. The German universities began their life with theology, and German theology began its life with the great bicker, the Luther-Melanchthon-Zwingli disputation over the Eucharist, which broke up with Luther's adherence to the literality of the words *Hoc est corpus meum*, which he carved in great letters on the table at Marburg. The German church was out of this world; the social gospel did not enter German preaching, and preaching was rigidly separated from theology (and prophecy from them both).

The press, unlike the church and the universities, was not a state institution, but it was characteristically cautious and dull in a nation where the right to suppress had never been overturned. The *Frankfurter Zeitung*, until it was picked up by the I.G. Farben trust in the 1920's, was a very conservative newspaper of great cultural interest, and the provincial press lacked even cultural interest. The fact that the trade-unions were predominantly Social Democratic said nothing of breadth of the German worker; the leadership was as independent of the membership as it was in some of the more notorious unions in the United States; strikes in Germany were called, not voted; and the

Social Democratic workers, "good citizens," were absorbed, with almost no resistance, in the Nazi Labor Front. Outside the great business, industrial, and financial combines, which influenced public policy through court camarillas, the *Kaiserreich* boss was no more politically alive than his worker. A member of the pre-Hitler Prussian cabinet, asked what caused Nazism, said: "What caused Nazism was the clubman in Berlin who, when he was asked about the Nazi menace in 1930, looked up from his after-lunch game of Skat and replied, '*Dafür ist die Regierung da.* That's what the government's there for.'"

Arguing with an American, you may ask him, with propriety, "All right—what would you have done if you had been President?" You don't ask one of my Nazi friends what *he* would have done if *he* had been Führer—or Emperor. The concept that the citizen might become the actual Head of the State has no reality for my friends. Why not?—Didn't Hitler become the Head of the State? "Not at all," said Herr Simon, the bill-collector, and then he went on to enlighten me on legitimacy. Hitler was *appointed* by the Head of the State. The true German ruler is the monarch. The first President of Germany, Ebert, was not elected by the people at all, and the second (and last), Hindenburg, was not really elected but was *chosen* by the German people as custodian for the monarchy. My friends, like all people to whom the present is unpalatable and the future unpromising, always look back. Looking back, they see themselves ruled, and well ruled, by an independent Sovereign. Their experience with even the outward forms of self-government does not, as yet, incline them to it.

The concept that the citizen actually is, as such, the Head of the State is, in their view, nothing but self-contradiction. I read to three of my friends a lecture I had prepared, in which I was going to say that I was the highest official of the United States, holding the office of citizen. I had used the word *Staatsbürger*. "But that," said all three, in identical words, "is no office at all." There we were. "But it really is the highest office in America," I said; "the citizen is the Sovereign. If I say '*souveräner Staatsbürger*,' will that be clearer?"

"Clearer, certainly," said Herr Kessler, the bank clerk, "but wronger, if I may, Herr Professor. Those two words do not go together. The idea is not a German idea. It says that the citizen is the ruler, but there are millions of citizens, so that would be anarchy. There could be no rule. A State must have a Head, not a million or fifty million or a hundred million Heads. If one of your 'sovereign citizens' does not like a law, do you allow him to break it? If not, your 'sovereign citizen' is only a myth, and you are, like us, ruled by real rulers. But your theory does not admit it."

"We hear a lot about America," said Policeman Hofmeister, "not only now, but all our lives we have heard a lot, because so many of us have relatives who have gone there. Now we always say in Germany, '*Monarchie oder Anarchie*'; there is nothing in between, and *Anarchie* is mob rule. We have heard of your American cities ruled by gangsters working with dishonest politicians who steal the people's money and give them poor service, bad roads, and such, charging them always for good roads or good sewers. That we have never known here in Germany, not under the Kaiser, not under Hitler. That is a kind of *Anarchie*, maybe not mob rule but something like it."

"You think," said Herr Simon, who did not always remember to call me Professor, "that there is one kind of dictatorship, the kind we had here. But you might have a dictatorship not by the best of your people but by all, or a majority, of your people. Isn't that possible, too?"

"I suppose so," I said, "but it is hard to believe. I should say that National Socialism had some of that in it, that dictatorship by the majority."

"Yes," said Herr Simon, "but what about the law against drinking liquor that you had in the United States. Wasn't that a majority dictatorship?"

I explained, and we went on, but my friend was trying to make a point. In Tennessee a kind of legal mob rule forbade the teaching of evolution, in California (long afterward) it forbade the teaching of internationalism as manifested in UNESCO. My Nazi friend Simon had not heard of John Stuart Mill, the philosopher of liberty, who was worried about "the tyranny of the majority," or of Alexander Hamilton's staggering dictum, "Your 'People,' Sir, is a great beast."

I think it is unfair to say that my friends are irresponsible, at least without adding that irresponsibility, which is a moral failure, may be at least in part a consequence of nonresponsibility, which is historical fact. There is a distinction between "unconscionable" and "conscienceless." The model of the conscienceless pattern of German behavior was (and is) the civil service, whose security and status are the dream of the "little man" in a world where, even in good times, to lose a job is a dreadful prospect. The magnificence of the German civil service is one side of the coin; the training and elevation of a whole conscienceless class of citizens, who hear nothing, see nothing, and say nothing undutiful, the other. The apprenticeship of a *Beamte*, a civil servant, is hard and long, and the man who is seen to do his duty reluctantly or squeamishly is never certified; he is kept on as *Angestellte*, employee. German bank employees, who are not *Beamten*, call themselves *Bankbeamten*, simply to swell their little pride.

This immense hierarchism, based upon blind servility in which the man on the third rung would never dare to imagine that the man on the second would order him to do something wrong, since, after all, the man on the second had to answer to the man on the first, nourished the buck-passing instinct to fantastic proportions. "If," said a friend of mine whose sense of humor was surprising ("for a German"), "you ask the postman whether he thinks it will rain tomorrow (and tomorrow is the day of the Communist parade, and the Communists are illegal), he will excuse himself while he gets his immediate superior's permission to answer, and his superior will take the question up through channels until it reaches an official whose sense of independent moral responsibility is so strong that he dares to lose the question rather than send it on higher. By the time the postman is able to tell you that he has no opinion on the matter, it is day after tomorrow."

Men who learn to live this way get used to it and even get to like it. It is workable, too; good discipline produces, at least in limited areas, the same performance as good self-discipline. The only objection to the scheme is that men who always do as they're told do not know what to do when they're not. Without the thoughtful habit of decision, they decide (when they must decide for themselves) thoughtlessly. If they are forbidden to beat Jews, they learn how not to want to, something a free man who wants to beat Jews never learns; then, when they are allowed to, the release of their repressed wish to beat Jews makes maniacs of them.

All Germans are not "authoritarian personalities." I imagine that most are not. But, while there have been intervals in which the German was actually allowed to concern himself with matters of State, the pattern of German life has been such, over the centuries, that free spirits either had to give up or get out. From Goethe, who said he preferred "injustice to disorder," to Thomas Mann, who gloried in being nonpolitical, German intellectuals contrived to live "above it all," in "the land of poets and thinkers," as Mme de Staël described the Germany of 1810. Those who contrived to live *in* it all fared badly.

Other nations sent their worst people away. Germany sent—drove, rather—its best. Between Prince Metternich's Mainz Commission of 1819 (the Un-German Activities Committee of its day) and the last renewal of Bismarck's anti-Socialist laws in 1888, some four and a half million Germans came to the United States alone, 770,000 of them after the suppression of the Revolution of 1848. Wave after wave, after each unsuccessful movement against autocracy, came over to constitute, wherever they went, the finest flower of immigration. Their letters back home brought new and larger waves of their friends and relatives, who were, in large measure, moved more by economic opportunity than by political hope or necessity—who, however, belonged to families or circles in which political liberalism had led to emigration. Left behind were, in the main, those who conformed, willingly or because they saw no way out. Left behind, too, for the next generation, was the dream, always madder as it was frustrated, which produced new outbreaks, new suppressions, new emigrations. National Socialism brought dream and conformism together into something satanic.

Each new generation's leadership was somewhere in Pennsylvania or the Argentine or Wisconsin or China. But millions of liberty-loving Germans remained, and all men, in whatever form they love it, love liberty. Thus throughout Germany, as everywhere where there is oppression among literate peoples, one encountered, and still encounters, more diversity, more individuality, than there is among, say, Americans, who are unoppressed; more variety in entertainment and in the arts, in political partisanship and in the political complexion of the press; all this, more individuality, more independence, stubborn or sublimated, in the land of the goose step than one finds in the land of the free. Free Americans all read the same papers, wear the same clothes, and vote for the same two transposable parties; Germans dress freely, freely read different papers, and vote a dozen different ways, but they are, in their submissiveness, the same.

Of what are these people guilty, who have never known the responsibility of the sovereign citizen? Of not assuming it, all at once, on January 30, 1933? Their offense was their national history. The crime of all but a million or so of them (and, in part, of these, too) had been committed long before National Socialism. All ten of my friends gladly confess this crime of having been Germans in Germany.

"That's the way we Germans are," said Herr Simon, the *alter Kämpfer.*

"But," I said, "is this the *Herrenrasse,* the superior race?"

"Morally and mentally, yes," he said. "We are industrious and orderly, too. But we are unfortunate in this one respect: we cannot rule ourselves; *wir brauchen eine starke Hand,* we require an iron hand."

"Why?"

"I don't know. That's the way we Germans are."

It is partly self-pity again, partly, of course, self-exculpation, the easy way out. My friends may not present an admirable spectacle. But failure to present an admirable spectacle is not a crime against humanity. Maybe it should be.

CHAPTER 13

But Then It Was Too Late

"What no one seemed to notice," said a colleague of mine, a philologist, "was the ever widening gap, after 1933, between the government and the people. Just think how very wide this gap was to begin with, here in Germany. And it became always wider. You know, it doesn't make people close to their government to be told that this is a people's government, a true democracy, or to be enrolled in civilian defense, or even to vote. All this has little, really nothing, to do with *knowing* one is governing.

"What happened here was the gradual habituation of the people, little by little, to being governed by surprise; to receiving decisions deliberated in secret; to believing that the situation was so complicated that the government had to act on information which the people could not understand, or so dangerous that, even if the people could understand it, it could not be released because of national security. And their sense of identification with Hitler, their trust in him, made it easier to widen this gap and reassured those who would otherwise have worried about it.

"This separation of government from people, this widening of the gap, took place so gradually and so insensibly, each step disguised (perhaps not even intentionally) as a temporary emergency measure or associated with true patriotic allegiance or with real social purposes. And all the crises and reforms (real reforms, too) so occupied the people that they did not see the slow motion underneath, of the whole process of government growing remoter and remoter.

"You will understand me when I say that my Middle High German was my life. It was all I cared about. I was a scholar, a specialist. Then, suddenly, I was plunged into all the new activity, as the university was drawn into the new situation; meetings, conferences, interviews, ceremonies, and, above all, papers to be filled out, reports, bibliographies, lists, questionnaires. And on top of that were the demands in the community, the things in which one had to, was 'expected to' participate that had not been there or had not been important before. It was all rigmarole, of course, but it consumed all one's energies, coming on top of the work one really wanted to do. You can see how easy it was, then, not to think about fundamental things. One had no time."

"Those," I said, "are the words of my friend the baker. "One had no time to think. There was so much going on."

"Your friend the baker was right," said my colleague. "The dictatorship, and the whole process of its coming into being, was above all *diverting*. It provided an excuse not to think for people who did not want to think anyway. I do not speak of your 'little men,' your baker and so on; I speak of my colleagues and myself, learned men, mind you. Most of us did not want to think about fundamental things and never had. There was no need to. Nazism gave us some dreadful, fundamental things to think about—we were decent people—and kept us so busy with continuous changes and 'crises' and so fascinated, yes, fascinated, by the machinations of the 'national enemies,' without and within, that we had no time to think about these dreadful

167

things that were growing, little by little, all around us. Unconsciously, I suppose, we were grateful. Who wants to think?

"To live in this process is absolutely not to be able to notice it—please try to believe me—unless one has a much greater degree of political awareness, acuity, than most of us had ever had occasion to develop. Each step was so small, so inconsequential, so well explained or, on occasion, 'regretted,' that, unless one were detached from the whole process from the beginning, unless one understood what the whole thing was in principle, what all these 'little measures' that no 'patriotic German' could resent must some day lead to, one no more saw it developing from day to day than a farmer in his field sees the corn growing. One day it is over his head.

"How is this to be avoided, among ordinary men, even highly educated ordinary men? Frankly, I do not know. I do not see, even now. Many, many times since it all happened I have pondered that pair of great maxims, *Principiis obsta* and *Finem respice*—'Resist the beginnings' and 'Consider the end.' But one must foresee the end in order to resist, or even see, the beginnings. One must foresee the end clearly and certainly and how is this to be done, by ordinary men or even by extraordinary men? Things *might* have changed here before they went as far as they did; they didn't, but they *might* have. And everyone counts on that *might*.

"Your 'little men,' your Nazi friends, were not against National Socialism in principle. Men like me, who were, are the greater offenders, not because we *knew* better (that would be too much to say) but because we *sensed* better. Pastor Niemöller spoke for the thousands and thousands of men like me when he spoke (too modestly of himself) and said that, when the Nazis attacked the Communists, he was a little uneasy, but, after all, he was not a Communist, and so he did nothing; and then they attacked the Socialists, and he was a little uneasier, but, still, he was not a Socialist, and he did nothing; and then the schools, the press, the Jews, and so on, and he was always uneasier, but still he did nothing. And then they attacked the Church, and he was a Churchman, and he did something— but then it was too late."

"Yes," I said.

"You see," my colleague went on, "one doesn't see exactly where or how to move. Believe me, this is true. Each act, each occasion, is worse than the last, but only a little worse. You wait for the next and the next. You wait for one great shocking occasion, thinking that others, when such a shock comes, will join with you in resisting somehow. You don't want to act, or even talk, alone; you don't want to 'go out of your way to make trouble.' Why not?— Well, you are not in the habit of doing it. And it is not just fear, fear of standing alone, that restrains you; it is also genuine uncertainty.

"Uncertainty is a very important factor, and, instead of decreasing as time goes on, it grows. Outside, in the streets, in the general community, 'everyone' is happy. One hears no protest, and certainly sees none. You know, in France or Italy there would be slogans against the government painted on walls and fences; in Germany, outside the great cities, perhaps, there is not even this. In the university community, in your own community, you speak privately to your colleagues, some of whom certainly feel as you do; but what do they say? They say, 'It's not so bad' or 'You're seeing things' or 'You're an alarmist.'

"And you are an alarmist. You are saying that this must

lead to *this*, and you can't prove it. These are the beginnings, yes; but how do you know for sure when you don't know the end, and how do you know, or even surmise, the end? On the one hand, your enemies, the law, the regime, the Party, intimidate you. On the other, your colleagues pooh-pooh you as pessimistic or even neurotic. You are left with your close friends, who are, naturally, people who have always thought as you have.

"But your friends are fewer now. Some have drifted off somewhere or submerged themselves in their work. You no longer see as many as you did at meetings or gatherings. Informal groups become smaller; attendance drops off in little organizations, and the organizations themselves wither. Now, in small gatherings of your oldest friends, you feel that you are talking to yourselves, that you are isolated from the reality of things. This weakens your confidence still further and serves as a further deterrent to—to what? It is clearer all the time that, if you are going to do anything, you must *make* an occasion to do it, and then you are obviously a troublemaker. So you wait, and you wait.

"But the one great shocking occasion, when tens or hundreds or thousands will join with you, never comes. *That's* the difficulty. If the last and worst act of the whole regime had come immediately after the first and smallest, thousands, yes, millions would have been sufficiently shocked —if, let us say, the gassing of the Jews in '43 had come immediately after the 'German Firm' stickers on the windows of non-Jewish shops in '33. But of course this isn't the way it happens. In between come all the hundreds of little steps, some of them imperceptible, each of them preparing you not to be shocked by the next. Step C is not so much worse than Step B, and, if you did not make a stand at Step B, why should you at Step C? And so on to Step D.

"And one day, too late, your principles, if you were ever sensible of them, all rush in upon you. The burden of self-deception has grown too heavy, and some minor incident, in my case my little boy, hardly more than a baby, saying 'Jew swine,' collapses it all at once, and you see that everything, everything, has changed and changed completely under your nose. The world you live in—your nation, your people—is not the world you were born in at all. The forms are all there, all untouched, all reassuring, the houses, the shops, the jobs, the mealtimes, the visits, the concerts, the cinema, the holidays. But the spirit, which you never noticed because you made the lifelong mistake of identifying it with the forms, is changed. Now you live in a world of hate and fear, and the people who hate and fear do not even know it themselves; when everyone is transformed, no one is transformed. Now you live in a system which rules without responsibility even to God. The system itself could not have intended this in the beginning, but in order to sustain itself it was compelled to go all the way.

"You have gone almost all the way yourself. Life is a continuing process, a flow, not a succession of acts and events at all. It has flowed to a new level, carrying you with it, without any effort on your part. On this new level you live, you have been living more comfortably every day, with new morals, new principles. You have accepted things you would not have accepted five years ago, a year ago, things that your father, even in Germany, could not have imagined.

"Suddenly it all comes down, all at once. You see what you are, what you have done, or, more accurately, what you haven't done (for that was all that was required of

171

most of us: that we do nothing). You remember those early meetings of your department in the university when, if one had stood, others would have stood, perhaps, but no one stood. A small matter, a matter of hiring this man or that, and you hired this one rather than that. You remember everything now, and your heart breaks. Too late. You are compromised beyond repair.

"What then? You must then shoot yourself. A few did. Or 'adjust' your principles. Many tried, and some, I suppose, succeeded; not I, however. Or learn to live the rest of your life with your shame. This last is the nearest there is, under the circumstances, to heroism: shame. Many Germans became this poor kind of hero, many more, I think, than the world knows or cares to know."

I said nothing. I thought of nothing to say.

"I can tell you," my colleague went on, "of a man in Leipzig, a judge. He was not a Nazi, except nominally, but he certainly wasn't an anti-Nazi. He was just—a judge. In '42 or '43, early '43, I think it was, a Jew was tried before him in a case involving, but only incidentally, relations with an 'Aryan' woman. This was 'race injury,' something the Party was especially anxious to punish. In the case at bar, however, the judge had the power to convict the man of a 'nonracial' offense and send him to an ordinary prison for a very long term, thus saving him from Party 'processing' which would have meant concentration camp or, more probably, deportation and death. But the man was innocent of the 'nonracial' charge, in the judge's opinion, and so, as an honorable judge, he acquitted him. Of course, the Party seized the Jew as soon as he left the courtroom."

"And the judge?"

"Yes, the judge. He could not get the case off his conscience—a case, mind you, in which he had acquitted an innocent man. He thought that he should have convicted him and saved him from the Party, but how could he have convicted an innocent man? The thing preyed on him more and more, and he had to talk about it, first to his family, then to his friends, and then to acquaintances. (That's how I heard about it.) After the '44 *Putsch* they arrested him. After that, I don't know."

I said nothing.

"Once the war began," my colleague continued, "resistance, protest, criticism, complaint, all carried with them a multiplied likelihood of the greatest punishment. Mere lack of enthusiasm, or failure to show it in public, was 'defeatism.' You assumed that there were lists of those who would be 'dealt with' later, after the victory. Goebbels was very clever here, too. He continually promised a 'victory orgy' to 'take care of' those who thought that their 'treasonable attitude' had escaped notice. And he meant it; *that* was not just propaganda. And that was enough to put an end to all uncertainty.

"Once the war began, the government could do anything 'necessary' to win it; so it was with the 'final solution of the Jewish problem,' which the Nazis always talked about but never dared undertake, not even the Nazis, until war and its 'necessities' gave them the knowledge that they could get away with it. The people abroad who thought that war against Hitler would help the Jews were wrong. And the people in Germany who, once the war had begun, still thought of complaining, protesting, resisting, were betting on Germany's losing the war. It was a long bet. Not many made it."

Collective Shame

My colleague came back, one day, to the subject of "this poor kind of heroism: shame." "The trouble with shame," he said, "is that it goes down deep or it doesn't. If it doesn't, one throws it off as soon as he himself is injured (as, of course, in total war, he is likely to be, in his family, his property, his position, his person). If it does, if it goes down deep enough, it is a form of suicide; it was this that led some men I knew to join the Party later on, an act of throwing themselves away. None of your 'little men,' perhaps—"

"No, not shame," I said.

"But one doesn't know this easily," said my colleague, "this deep shame. With many it took the outward form of their saying that, since National Socialist rule was here, and here for a long time to come, they would join it and reform it from within. But to be effective, they would first have to be accepted—"

"Oh, 'effectiveness,'" I said. "That I heard from my friend the teacher. For the sake of being effective he did everything required of him, and of course he wasn't effective. He knows that now. But then he had hopes of being able to oppose the excesses—"

"Yes, it was always the excesses that we wished to oppose, rather than the whole program, the whole spirit that produced the first steps, A, B, C, and D, out of which the excesses were bound to come. It is so much easier to 'oppose the excesses,' about which one can, of course, do nothing, than it is to oppose the whole spirit, about which one can do something every day."

"All of my 'little men' opposed the excesses, at least the worst excesses," I said, "and the two best of them, the teacher and the bank clerk, blamed them on the radicals who had grown up in the movement when it was irresponsible and attracted the most reckless elements—"

"Yes," said my colleague, shaking his head, "the 'excesses' and the 'radicals.' We all opposed them, very quietly. So your two 'little men' thought they must join, as good men, good Germans, even as good Christians, and when enough of them did they would be able to change the Party. They would 'bore from within.' 'Big men' told themselves that, too, in the usual sincerity that required them only to abandon one little principle after another, to throw away, little by little, all that was good. I was one of those men.

"You know," he went on, "when men who understand what is happening—the motion, that is, of history, not the reports of single events or developments—when such men do not object or protest, men who do not understand cannot be expected to. How many men would you say understand—in this sense—in America? And when, as the motion of history accelerates and those who don't understand are crazed by fear, as our people were, and made into a great 'patriotic' mob, will they understand then, when they did not before?

"We learned here—I say this freely—to give up trying to make them understand after, oh, the end of 1938, after the night of the synagogue burning and the things that followed it. Even before the war began, men who were teachers, men whose faith in teaching was their whole faith, gave up, seeing that there was no comprehension, no capacity left for comprehension, and the thing must go its course, taking first its victims, then its architects, and then the rest of us to destruction. This did not mean surrender; it meant conservation of energy, doing what little one could (now that it was too late to do anything!) and consuming one's energy doing it, to relieve the present victim (if only by brazenly saying 'Hello' to him on the street!) and to prevent, or at least postpone, the fate of the next victim (if only by writing a 'nonpolitical' letter abroad asking somebody to take an emigrant!)."

"Yes," I said.

"You say that is not much"—I tried to protest—"but I say that it is more, under the circumstances, than ordinary life, in Germany, in America, anywhere, has prepared ordinary men to do."

His wife was there. "I hope," she said, "that the Anglo-Saxons"—she obviously meant the Anglos and not the Saxons—"have characteristics that will make them less susceptible to the things we Germans could not resist."

"What would such characteristics be?" I said.

"Oh, farsightedness, I think, above all. Maybe a shorter history makes it easier for people to look ahead instead of always behind. And you are under less pressure, somehow, than we are. You are freer—I don't mean legally, of course—to take the long view." It was the first time, in my conversations in Germany, that the focus had been placed on the word *Druck*, "pressure."

Another colleague of mine brought me even closer to the heart of the matter—and closer home. A chemical engineer by profession, he was a man of whom, before I knew him, I had been told, "He is one of those rare birds among Germans—a European." One day, when we had become very friendly, I said to him, "Tell me now—how was the world lost?"

"That," he said, "is easy to tell, much easier than you may suppose. The world was lost one day in 1935, here in Germany. It was I who lost it, and I will tell you how.

"I was employed in a defense plant (a war plant, of course, but they were always called defense plants). That was the year of the National Defense Law, the law of 'total conscription.' Under the law I was required to take the oath of fidelity. I said I would not; I opposed it in conscience. I was given twenty-four hours to 'think it over.' In those twenty-four hours I lost the world."

"Yes?" I said.

"You see, refusal would have meant the loss of my job, of course, not prison or anything like that. (Later on, the penalty was worse, but this was only 1935.) But losing my job would have meant that I could not get another. Wherever I went I should be asked why I left the job I had, and, when I said why, I should certainly have been refused employment. Nobody would hire a 'Bolshevik.' Of course I was not a Bolshevik, but you understand what I mean."

"Yes," I said.

"I tried not to think of myself or my family. We might have got out of the country, in any case, and I could have got a job in industry or education somewhere else.

"What I tried to think of was the people to whom I might be of some help later on, if things got worse (as I believed they would). I had a wide friendship in scientific and academic circles, including many Jews, and 'Aryans,' too, who might be in trouble. If I took the oath and held my job, I might be of help, somehow, as things went on.

177

If I refused to take the oath, I would certainly be useless to my friends, even if I remained in the country. I myself would be in their situation.

"The next day, after 'thinking it over,' I said I would take the oath with the mental reservation that, by the words with which the oath began, '*Ich schwöre bei Gott*, I swear by God,' I understood that no human being and no government had the right to override my conscience. My mental reservations did not interest the official who administered the oath. He said, 'Do you take the oath?' and I took it. That day the world was lost, and it was I who lost it."

"Do I understand," I said, "that you think that you should not have taken the oath?"

"Yes."

"But," I said, "you did save many lives later on. You were of greater use to your friends than you ever dreamed you might be." (My friend's apartment was, until his arrest and imprisonment in 1943, a hideout for fugitives.)

"For the sake of the argument," he said, "I will agree that I saved many lives later on. Yes."

"Which you could not have done if you had refused to take the oath in 1935."

"Yes."

"And you still think that you should not have taken the oath."

"Yes."

"I don't understand," I said.

"Perhaps not," he said, "but you must not forget that you are an American. I mean that, really. Americans have never known anything like this experience—in its entirety, all the way to the end. That is the point."

"You must explain," I said.

"Of course I must explain. First of all, there is the problem of the lesser evil. Taking the oath was not so evil as being unable to help my friends later on would have been. But the evil of the oath was certain and immediate, and the helping of my friends was in the future and therefore uncertain. I had to commit a positive evil, there and then, in the hope of a possible good later on. The good outweighed the evil; but the good was only a hope, the evil a fact."

"But," I said, "the hope was realized. You were able to help your friends."

"Yes," he said, "but you must concede that the hope might *not* have been realized—either for reasons beyond my control or because I became afraid later on or even because I was afraid all the time and was simply fooling myself when I took the oath in the first place.

"But that is not the important point. The problem of the lesser evil we all know about; in Germany we took Hindenburg as less evil than Hitler, and in the end we got them both. But that is not why I say that Americans cannot understand. No, the important point is—how many innocent people were killed by the Nazis, would you say?"

"Six million Jews alone, we are told."

"Well, that may be an exaggeration. And it does not include non-Jews, of whom there must have been many hundreds of thousands, or even millions. Shall we say, just to be safe, that three million innocent people were killed all together?"

I nodded.

"And how many innocent lives would you like to say I saved?"

"You would know better than I," I said.

"Well," said he, "perhaps five, or ten, one doesn't know. But shall we say a hundred, or a thousand, just to be safe?"

I nodded.

"And it would be better to have saved all three million, instead of only a hundred, or a thousand?"

"Of course."

"There, then, is my point. If I had refused to take the oath of fidelity, I would have saved all three million."

"You are joking," I said.

"No."

"You don't mean to tell me that your refusal would have overthrown the regime in 1935?"

"No."

"Or that others would have followed your example?"

"No."

"I don't understand."

"You are an American," he said again, smiling. "I will explain. There I was, in 1935, a perfect example of the *kind* of person who, with all his advantages in birth, in education, and in position, rules (or might easily rule) in any country. If I had refused to take the oath in 1935, it would have meant that thousands and thousands like me, all over Germany, were refusing to take it. Their refusal would have heartened millions. Thus the regime would have been overthrown, or, indeed, would never have come to power in the first place. The fact that I was not prepared to resist, in 1935, meant that all the thousands, hundreds of thousands, like me in Germany were also unprepared, and each one of these hundreds of thousands was, like me, a man of great influence or of great potential influence. Thus the world was lost."

"You are serious?" I said.

"Completely," he said. "These hundred lives I saved—

or a thousand or ten as you will—what do they represent? A little something out of the whole terrible evil, when, if my faith had been strong enough in 1935, I could have prevented the whole evil."

"Your faith?"

"My faith. I did not believe that I could 'remove mountains.' The day I said 'No,' I had faith. In the process of 'thinking it over,' in the next twenty-four hours, my faith failed me. So, in the next ten years, I was able to remove only anthills, not mountains."

"How might your faith of that first day have been sustained?"

"I don't know, I don't know," he said. "Do you?"

"I am an American," I said.

My friend smiled. "Therefore you believe in education."

"Yes," I said.

"My education did not help me," he said, "and I had a broader and better education than most men have had or ever will have. All it did, in the end, was to enable me to rationalize my failure of faith more easily than I might have done if I had been ignorant. And so it was, I think, among educated men generally, in that time in Germany. Their resistance was no greater than other men's."

As I thought of my ten Nazi friends in the light of my talks with the philologist and the engineer, it occurred to me that the concept of collective guilt is at bottom a semantic failure. What is really involved is collective shame. Collective shame may be possible, but it cannot be compelled. Shame is a state of being, guilt a juridical fact. A passer-by cannot be guilty of failure to try to prevent a lynching. He can only be ashamed of not having done so.

Even a sovereign, self-governing citizen, such as an American, cannot be guilty of failure to try to prevent an act of State. It would be Nazism itself to take Americans off the street and charge them, in connection with, say, the bombing of Hiroshima, with having violated the Hague Regulations, to which their government, whose sovereign citizens they are, was signatory. Still less than a sovereign citizen can the subject of a dictatorship be guilty of an act of State. And, when the State requires him, personally and individually, to commit what he regards as a crime, and the penalty for his refusal to do so is very heavy, the common law acquits him on the ground of duress. "I was lucky," said Herr Klingelhöfer, the cabinetmaker. "I didn't have to do anything wrong."

Collective shame is something else, but it requires not merely the fact of sovereign citizenship but the most delicate sense of it. I did not discover much collective shame among my ten friends. The President of the West German Federal Republic had called upon them to feel it and had used that very expression, "collective shame." But how does one call, effectively, upon people to feel ashamed?

In the case of Horst Rupprecht, the university student and Hitler Youth leader, who blamed himself for the sins of Nazism, the sins of Germany, the sins of the whole German people, his *mea culpa* was just a little unconvincing: he was eight years old in 1933. I think his testimony is what many non-Germans wanted to hear from the lips of every German: "No, no, it wasn't Hitler and Göring and the rest, it was we Germans, every one of us, I more than any of the rest, who did it"; but I think they would have been disappointed when they heard it, as I was.

At his trial at Nuremberg, young Rupprecht's highest superior, Baldur von Schirach, the Nazi Youth Leader, said: "It is my guilt, and I must bear it before God and the German nation, that I educated German youth for a man whom I thought irreproachable, but who was a murderer millions of times over." Was this the same Baldur von Schirach who had called Hitler "Germany's greatest son," "this genius grazing the stars," who had said that the altar was not in the Church but on the steps of the Feldherrn Hall, where Hitler's *Putsch* had ended in 1923? It was. When, where, and how does one discover that an irreproachable man is a murderer millions of times over? Does it take the hangman's hood on his eyes to open them?

What I found, among my ten friends, was something like regret, regret that things, which they had not done, had been done or had had to be done. All ten of them, even the tailor, I think, *felt bad*, now, about the torture and slaughter of innocent people—not, however, about the deportation, "resettlement, relocation," or even about the expropriation. (My friends had all lost their own possessions, hadn't they, and who but they themselves felt sorry for them?) The six extremists all said of the extermination of Jews, "That was wrong" or "That was going too far," as if to say, "The gas oven was somewhat too great a punishment for people who, after all, deserved very great punishment."

My ten friends had been told, not since 1939 but since 1933, that their nation was fighting for its life. They believed that self-preservation is the first law of nature, of the nature of nations as well as of herd brutes. Were they wrong in this principle? If they were, they saw nothing in the history of nations (their own or any other) that said so. And, once there was shooting war, their situation was like that of the secret opponents of the regime whom my colleague described: there was no further need for the nation, or anyone in it, to be justified. The nation was literally fighting for its literal life—"they or we." Anything went, and what "anything" was, what enormities it embraced, depended entirely on the turn of the battle.

Even Herr Schwenke, the tailor, proud of his having refused a Jew of old acquaintance a light for his cigarette, frankly glad that the synagogue had been burned, said of the gas ovens, "If it happened, it was wrong. But I don't believe it happened." And, if he were ever able to admit that it *did* happen, he would have to admit that it was right and, to prove it, cry out, with his wound rubbed raw, in still greater anguish against the victims and ascribe to them sins even he had not yet been able to dream of.

What we don't like, what *I* don't like, is the hypocrisy of these people. I want to hear them confess. That they, or some of their countrymen and their country's government, violated the precepts of Christian, civilized, lawful life was bad enough; that they won't see it, or say it, is what really rowels. I want them to plead no extenuation. I want them to say, "I knew and I know that it was all un-Christian, uncivilized, unlawful, and in my love of evil I pretended it wasn't. I plead every German guilty of a life of hypocrisy, above all, myself. I am rotten."

I don't like the dolorous mask my friend Klingelhöfer wears when he says, "I always said no good would come of it, and no good *did* come of it." His *freiwillige Feuerwehr* ebullience is suddenly gone, and now he emerges from the wings, like a one-man troupe playing Molière, in judicious melancholy. I want to say to him, "You *Schweinehund*, what you said, and you said it to yourself, was that no good would come of it *if it lost*. And it did lose. If it had won, you'd be drinking blood with the rest of them." But what's the use?

I want my friends not just to feel bad and confess it, but to have been bad and to be bad now and confess it. I want them to constitute themselves an inferior race, self-abased, so that I, in the magnanimity becoming to the superior, having sat in calumnious judgment on them, may choose to let them live on in public shame and in private torment. I want to be God, not alone in power but in righteousness and in mercy; and Nazism crushed is my chance.

But I am not God. I myself am a national, myself guilty of many national hypocrisies whose only justification is that the Germans' were so much worse. My being less bestial, in my laws and practices, than they were does not make me more Godly than they, for difference in degree is not difference in kind. My own country's racist legislation and practices, against both foreigners and citizens, is a whole web of hypocrisies. And, if I plead that racism has been wonderfully reduced in America in the past century, that the forces of good have been growing ever more powerful, how shall I answer my friends Hildebrandt and Kessler, who believed, or affected to believe, that the infiltration of National Socialism by decent men like themselves would, in time, reduce and even eliminate the evils?

The trouble is that these national hypocrisies, which I myself am not called upon to practice in person, with my own hands, are all acts of the State or its culture. I feel bad about them, to be sure; very bad. But I do not in the least feel like a bad man, and I do not want to be punished for them. And, if I beat my breast, like my Nazi friend, young Rupprecht, and say, "It is I, I, I, who did it," I am afraid that I shall sound just as pretentious as he sounded to me. The confession that I want to hear or that I ought to make does not ring real.

What I really want, since (while I want to let my friends

off in my magnanimity) I do not want to have to reproach myself some time later with having let them escape the consequences of their unheroism, is for each of them to have cared enough at the time to have thrown himself under the iron chariot of the State, with its wheels rimmed with spikes. This none of my friends did, and this I cannot forgive them. They did not care enough.

CHAPTER 15

The Furies: Heinrich Hildebrandt

How was I to know, or to find out, how much my friends had suffered (if they had suffered at all) or whether they had suffered enough? If, as doctrine has it, man is perfected by suffering, none of my friends had suffered enough, for none of them, I could see, even in my imperfect knowledge of them, was perfect.

Seven of them ducked my question. My question, which I framed very carefully and put to them in a variety of ways in the last weeks of our conversations, was, "What did you do that was wrong, as *you* understand right and wrong, and what *didn't* you do that was right?" The instinct that throws instant ramparts around the self-love of all of us came into immediate operation; my friends, in response, spoke of what was legal or illegal, or what was popular or unpopular, or what others did or didn't do, or what was provoked or unprovoked. But I was interested, at this point, in none of these things. "Who knows the secret heart?" I was trying to know the secret heart; I knew all about Versailles and the Polish Corridor and the inflation, the unemployment, the Communists, the Jews, and the Talmud.

The eighth of my friends, young Rupprecht, the Hitler Youth leader, having taken upon himself (or having affected to take) sovereign responsibility for every first and last injustice of the whole Hitler regime, was no better able to enlighten me than Herr Schwenke, the old *Fanatiker*, who, when I was at last able to divert him, with my insistent last question, from Versailles, the Polish Corridor, etc., said, "I have never done anything wrong to any man." "Never?" said I, just to hear myself say it. "Never," said he, just to hear himself say it. But two of my friends, Herr Hildebrandt, the teacher, and Herr Kessler, the bank clerk, enlightened me, in their own time, in their own ways, without my having asked them my question.

Fear and advantage, Hildebrandt had said, were his reasons for becoming a National Socialist in 1937, a late "March violet" indeed. "Were there," I said, on another occasion, "any other reasons you joined?" He said nothing and then began to blush. "I—," he began, blushing fully, and then he said, "No, no others." It was a long time before I learned all Herr Hildebrandt's reasons for being a Nazi.

"I might have got by without joining," he said more than once. "I don't know. I might have taken my chances. Others did, I mean other teachers in the high school."

"How many?"

"Let me see. We had thirty-five teachers. Only four, well, five, were fully convinced Nazis. But, of these five, one could be argued with openly, in the teachers' conference room; and only one was a real fanatic, who might denounce a colleague to the authorities."

"Did he?"

"There was never any evidence that he did, but we had to be careful around him."

"How many of the thirty-five never joined the Party?"

"Five, but not all for the same reason. Three of the five were very religious. The teachers were all Protestants, of course, but only half a dozen, at most, were really religious; these were all anti-Nazi, these half-dozen, but only three of them held out. One of the three was the history teacher (now the director of the school), very nationalistic, very Prussian, but a strong churchman. He stood near the anti-Nazi Confessional Church, but he couldn't join it, of course, or he'd have lost his job. Then there was the theology teacher, who also taught modern languages; he was the best teacher in the school; apart from his religious opposition, his knowledge of foreign cultures made him anti-Nazi. The third was the mathematics teacher, absolutely unworldly but profoundly pietistic, a member of the Moravian sect."

"And the two who were nonreligious and didn't join?"

"One was a historian. He was not an atheist, you understand, just a historian. He was a nonjoiner, of anything. He was nonpolitical. He was strongly critical of Nazism, but always on a detached, theoretical basis. Nobody bothered him; nobody paid any attention to him. And vice versa. The other nonbeliever was really the truest believer of them all. He was a biologist and a rebel against a religious background. He had no trouble perverting Darwin's 'survival of the fittest' into Nazi racism—he was the only teacher in the whole school who believed it."

"Why didn't he join the Party?"

"He hated the local Kreisleiter, the County Leader of the Party, whose father had been a theologian and who himself never left the Church. The hatred was mutual. That's why the biologist never joined. Now he's an 'anti-Nazi.' "

"And you?"

"Yes," he said, blushing a little again. "I joined. I had my past, of course, in East Prussia. All sorts of care had been taken to bury it, but—one never knew. I had been active in the old Staatspartei, the successor of the Democratic Party in 1930. After 1930 I had lectured regularly at the local folk high school, the adult education program, which was promoted and largely attended by Social Democrats and Communists. In my book program, on the radio, I had praised the works of 'treasonable' writers after the Nazis took power.

"For eight years I held the rank of Studienassessor. It carries no tenure with it. After 1933 my name was not even included in the list of candidates for Studienrat, the rank which is usually given after five years of high-school teaching. The spring the Nazis took power, I was dismissed from my radio program and from my adult-school lectureship. Then I was transferred from the city to one small school after another. So I resigned, very quietly, and came here, to Hesse. My father, through an old Army friend of his here, got me the appointment in Kronenberg. But still I was not promoted, and I was afraid that something was suspected. I waited two years, and then I joined the Party. I was promoted to Studienrat and got married."

"And Frau Hildebrandt?" I said. I watched for the blush, but there was none; it (whatever *it* was) wasn't Frau Hildebrandt.

"Eva went just the other way from me. In 1933 she was for Hitler. Of course, she was much younger than I and her family was petty nobility, who were all in the old Nationalist Party, which threw its weight, at the end, to the Nazis. But she adored the Jewish Professor Neumann at Kiel—who didn't?—and the day of the book-burning there he instructed the secretary of his philosophy seminar to give his books to the students. Eva got three of Neumann's own books, her proudest possession—and still she believed in Nazism. She was what we call *begeistert,* bewitched.

"We first met in 1938, at the Casino, in Kassel, for officers and their families. The young men—we weren't so young any more—all went there with their parents. I was with my parents, she with hers; our fathers were both retired officers and old acquaintances. It happened to be on

January 30, the anniversary of Hitler's coming to power, but that was only an accident; the Casino society was by no means Nazi. We danced, which I was not very good at"— he blushed, just a little—"but a month later I gave a talk there and she came, and 'fell for me.'

"I was already a Party member. She was really nonpolitical, at heart. It's funny; I, with my knowledge of politics, I became more and more Nazi, and she became less and less. After the synagogue burning, at the end of '38, she was strongly anti-Nazi. She got out Neumann's books and cried. I told her she didn't understand these things. She didn't, either, but she knew them, sensed them, better than I did— or than I was willing to. From then on, until I went into the Army in '39, we quarreled all the time. But now it's all right." (It was, too. I had met the Hildebrandt family frequently.)

"She never quit the Party, of course. She had joined in '37, too, not until then; she was a teacher, and she did it to hold her job. But women are braver than men, don't you think?"

"Yes," I said (still wondering what *it* was, besides "fear and advantage," that had made a Nazi of Herr Hildebrandt).

"It's because—well, they don't face things the same way men do. They assume that the man will find a way to support the family. They could be stronger Nazis or stronger anti-Nazis than men, without thinking too much about it. Most of them." I thought I saw a faint blush, at this last, but it was late afternoon in the winter. I turned the lights on.

Hildebrandt had no guilt about his "Nazi" teaching of literature. "One could talk about other things, outside the textbooks, and there was 'un-German' literature that had been overlooked, such as Lessing's *Nathan the Wise*, which we read openly in class. *The Buddenbrooks*, too; it was not specifically forbidden, but everybody knew that the Nazis hated Thomas Mann.

"Privately, certain students read Jewish authors—it went without saying that they were not to be read—like Wassermann, Werfel, Zweig, and wrote papers on them, brought them to me, and I accepted them for credit, although they were not discussed in class. And I gave them French and English literature, more so than before, although to do so was one of those vague betrayals of the 'new spirit'; still, it had not been specifically forbidden. Of course, I always said, to protect myself (but I said it in such a way that I hoped the students would see through it), that the foreign works we read were only a reflection of German literature. So, you see, Herr Professor, a man could show some—some independence, even, so to say, secretly."

"I understand," I said.

"Many of the students—the best of them—understood what was going on in all this. It was a sort of dumb-show game that we were all playing, I with them. The worst effect, I think, was that it made them cynical, the best ones. But, then, it made the teachers cynical, too. I think the classroom in those years was one of the causes of the cynicism you see in the best young men and women in Germany today."

"In the best?"

"Yes. The others, the great majority, are disillusioned now, but that is something else. You see, the young people, and, yes, the old, too, were drawn to opposite extremes in those years. People outside Germany seem to think that 'the Germans' came to believe everything they were told, all the dreadful nonsense that passed for truth. It is a very bad mistake, a very dangerous mistake, to think this. The fact, I think, is that *most* Germans came to believe everything, absolutely everything; but the rest, those who saw through the nonsense, came to believe nothing, absolutely nothing. These last, the best, are the cynics now, young and old."

"And the others, the believers?"

"Well, the old among them are, I suppose you would say, the hopeless now. The younger, those who were teen-agers then—I don't know what to say about them except that they have lost their old illusions and see nothing new to turn to. This is dangerous, both for them and for the world ten or twenty years from now. They need, well, to be born again, somehow."

I asked Herr Hildebrandt if he could recollect specific instances of his own "dumb-show game," and the next time we met he spoke of them. "In Shakespeare, for instance, only *Macbeth* and, of course, *The Merchant of Venice*, which I never assigned, were recommended. But, again, nothing was forbidden, although *Hamlet* was denounced as embodying the 'flabbiness of soul' that the Nazis condemned in Russian writers like Dostoevski and Tolstoi, the 'soft Slavic soul' that in Tolstoi even went so far as pacifism. So in Shakespeare I could assign *A Midsummer Night's Dream*, which in normal times I should not have bothered with, just so that I could say to the students, 'The music for this was written by Mendelssohn. Your parents all know the music. Mendelssohn was a Jew. We don't play his music any more.' Perhaps that was not much to say, but it was something, don't you think?"

"Yes," I said, "certainly. . . . Tell me, Herr Hildebrandt, what about *Julius Caesar*?"

He smiled very, very wryly. "*Julius Caesar*? No . . . no."

"Was it forbidden?"

"Not that I remember. But that is not the way it was. Everything was not regulated specifically, ever. It was not like that at all. Choices were left to the teacher's discretion, within the 'German spirit.' That was all that was necessary; the teacher had only to be discreet. If he himself wondered at all whether anyone would object to a given book, he would be wise not to use it. This was a much more powerful form of intimidation, you see, than any fixed list of acceptable or unacceptable writings. The way it was done was, from the point of view of the regime, remarkably clever and effective. The teacher had to make the choices and risk the consequences; this made him all the more cautious."

"You spoke of giving certain students books by Jewish authors," I said, on another occasion. "How did you know which students you could trust not to denounce you?"

"Oh, one judges, from person to person. I may say generally that one would be safe in giving such books to *Mischlinge* [mongrels, half-Jews] and those from known liberal families. People who were so far under suspicion would never denounce one, because they would not be believed—people, that is, who were clearly beyond currying favor with the authorities. It was like complaining to Jews about the regime; it was safe."

"I can imagine," I said, "that some Jews would have resented being a sort of secret wailing wall for people who had something on their minds that they did not dare to say openly." I knew he would blush a little, and he did. "Yes. I think most Jews resented it, very deeply. That was why some people didn't do it."

"Yes," I said.

"In those times," he went on, "a student could have denounced me, but it would have been hard to make a case against me, because I was, well, clever in the way I did these things. But, even if I had been denounced, I could have got off, almost certainly, if my past were not revealed, because I was a Party member. You may say that it is a rationalization —I know it is, myself—but a Party member could get away with something, not much, but something. A non-Nazi would not dare to violate the rules. At least none in our school did."

"Were there any spies in the classes?" I said.

"No, unless students volunteered to be informers. The regime regarded informers as patriots, of course, but you know how students would feel; young people despise that kind of thing. There certainly were no spies, or even regular informers, that I heard of in our school. Not before the war, anyway. And certainly not during the war (although I was away in the Army except for my furlough in '40, after the fall of France). During the war even anti-Nazi teachers would not criticize the regime. Once the war began, all this ended. We were 'one folk.' We could not separate the regime from our country then."

"The July 20 conspirators did."

"Yes . . . yes, they did. *They* did."

I knew he was blushing, as he did so easily, but I did not look up. I was waiting—perhaps I only imagine it now, long afterward—for something that would bring his blush to a boil. I had a long time to wait.

He showed me the government manual for upper-school teaching, issued in 1938. Under *Literatur* there was this: "Of course, only such selections should be chosen as point in the direction of the New Germany, help prepare the new world outlook [*Weltanschauung*], or give instances of its innermost will. As we recognize only the vigorous as educationally valuable, everything must be avoided that weakens or discourages manliness. The thought of race will stand out strongest with a vivid knowledge of Teutonism." And then, apparently as subjects for study: "The nation as a community of fate and struggle. The struggle for living space. Soldiery (Army, Navy, Air Corps). Heroism. War poetry. The soldier of the World War as a legendary figure and a moral force. Woman in the World War. The community of National Socialist struggle. Leadership, comradeship. The fight of the German nation on our frontiers and abroad. Colonies."

"That was all," said Herr Hildebrandt, "although, of course, all these things would be explicated, but still not in detail, in the publications or meetings of the Lehrerbund, the Nazi teacher organization. But it was all very sloppy and vague. Under those headings one could teach almost anything—except, maybe, *All Quiet on the Western Front!*"

"Why was it so sloppy?" I said.

"Partly because the Nazification of the secondary schools was known to be difficult. They were stronger and better organized professionally than the primary schools. There the teachers were much more insecure, and also more susceptible, because, having to teach everything, they had been trained thoroughly in nothing. This half-educated condition made them excellent Nazi material; they could be 'taught' anything fast. We had a joke in those days: 'What is speed?'—'Speed is an instant so short that a grade-school teacher hasn't time to change his politics.'

"Then, too, the primary schools were more important to the regime. There they could reach all the children of the country, while we, in the high schools, had only one-fourth of them. So the primary schools had to be brought into line first, the secondary schools later. They never finished the job, but in another ten years, maybe even five, they would have."

"So soon?"

"So soon. One may say overnight. Resistance is low in a dictatorship. And this was, or would have become, an efficient dictatorship, even in cultural matters. There it was weakest, at the beginning, because the oldest and most trusted Nazis were uncultivated men, except for a few freaks like Rosenberg. And wherever there was a 'deserving' Party member and no other place could be found for him, he would be dumped into education. The Nazi 'educators' were illiterate, from Rust, the Minister of Education, on down. They did not know what they wanted or where to find it. Putting ignorant 'reliables,' from politics or business, over the educators was also part of the Nazi way of humiliating education and bringing it into popular contempt.

"Then, too, the Party education bosses did not know themselves when the Party line would change, and they were afraid of being caught on the wrong side when it did. Any author might suddenly prove to be 'decadent,' although, incidentally, when one hears so much of Goethe now as an anti-Nazi symbol, one recalls that all (almost all, certainly) of Goethe was recommended. His universalism was not so powerful or direct as to embarrass National Socialism. I do not mean to make light of the greatest genius of all, but if he had lived a century longer he might have wished to rewrite every word so that he could not be used by the Nazis."

"It might have ruined his poetry, Herr Studienrat."

He smiled at my form of address, and emphasized his: "Yes, *Herr Professor*, but now we sound like the classroom. I was speaking, oh, yes, of the sudden changes in the Party line. There were not so many, except the great ones, which

197

you know of, like the Russian pact of '39, and these did not immediately affect us. The difficulty was that changes could not be predicted. Living writers, unless they were Party hacks, could not be recommended at all, because they might turn anti-Nazi or be found to have been anti-Nazi or Communistic.

"It was not what a man wrote, but what his politics were (or were accused of being) that counted with the Nazis. Hans Grimm, for instance, was a great Party favorite because of his story, *Volk ohne Raum*, 'A People without Living Space'; then he became critical of the Nazis and had to be anathematized and his books forbidden—no matter what they contained. By the way, even *Wilhelm Tell* was suddenly forbidden during the war, at the time when it was thought that Switzerland might be attacked.

"In history, in biology, and in economics the teaching program was much more elaborate than it was in literature, and much stricter. These subjects were really rewritten. They had to be. But literature could not so easily be rewritten to order. The rewritten subjects were the worst nonsense, and, of course, the cynicism of the teachers and the better students was worst there. Every student had to take a biology examination to be graduated, and the biology course was a complete distortion of Mendelianism to prove that heredity was everything; such technical materials were most effective, of course, because the student had never met them before.

"But mathematics was the most interesting case. You would think that nothing could be done with such a 'pure' subject, but just this subject was handled very cleverly, and I often wondered who in the Party was so clever. I remember well, because Eva, my wife, taught mathematics. The problems to be assigned were all given, but they would almost all be taken from such subjects as ballistics or military deployment, or from architecture, with Nazi memorials or monuments as examples, or from interest rates—'A Jew lent RM 500 @ 12% interest. . . . '—or from population ratios. The students would be given the problem of projecting population curves of the 'Teutonic,' 'Roman,' and 'Slavic' peoples of Europe, with the question: 'What would be their relative sizes in 1960? What danger do you recognize for the Teutonic peoples in this?'

"Everything depended, actually, on the director of the school, everything, that is, outside the textbooks. The director of ours was a Nazi, of course, but not a real one, not a *Fanatiker*. He would tell the district superintendent, when he came for an inspection, that everything was all right, and the superintendent was too busy, and too unsure of himself academically, to look closer. And everything *was* all right, if what is meant is the absence of talk or teaching against the government. That's the same in America, I think—everywhere."

Herr Hildebrandt's hardest experience was, I felt, somewhere outside his school work. He told me, fairly freely, how hard it was to sit with fellow-members of the Party in a café and hear them vituperate Jews in ignorant passion. "I would sit there," he said, "and say nothing. This was not heroic, and yet it was something, a little something. A wild *Fanatiker* like your friend Schwenke, seeing that I never said anything in agreement, might have taken it into his head to denounce me, and my past, which would have been fatal, might have come out."

Once, in 1938 in a café in Baden-Baden, he saw a family of Jews from Kronenberg. "I was wearing my Party insignia and sitting with some Party men. Understand, I was proud to be wearing the insignia. It showed I 'be-

longed,' and the pleasure of 'belonging,' so soon after feeling excluded, isolated, is very great. Maybe in America you
don't have these feelings; in that case you are very lucky,
but also, in that case, you may have difficulty in understanding what it was like for men like me here.

"Still—I didn't want those Jews from our town to see
me wearing my insignia. I never wore it at home, except
for special events, where there were no Jews. The uniform
and insignia were a sort of anti-Semitism in themselves, and
I was not an—an anti-Semite. It hurt me to have Jews see
me wearing them. So, when I saw these Jews in the café,
I tried to sit so that they wouldn't see me. When I think
of that now, I still blush."

"Did they see you?"

"I don't think so," he said, blushing.

Prompted by the blush this time, I thought that I
might hit upon Herr Hildebrandt's secret, if he had one.
But the tack I took turned out to be empty.

"When were you *really* disillusioned with National Socialism?" I said in a later conversation.

The blush again; deeper, this time. "Only after the war
—*really*."

"That discourages me," I said, "because you are so much
more sensitive than most people, and this makes me realize
how hard it must be, under such conditions, for people,
even sensitive people, to see what is going on around them."
He continued to blush, but my blush-detector told me that
this was not *it*.

"It's all so well masqueraded," he said, "the bad always
mixed up with the good and the harmless, and you tell
yourself that you are making up for the bad by doing a
few little things like speaking of Mendelssohn in class."

"And so you were," I said.

"No. No," he said, shaking his head, "but that is very kind of you to say. No, I would not be honest with you if I told you that I was always an anti-Nazi, that I always thought and felt like an anti-Nazi. It is so easy these days to say 'anti-Nazi' and even to believe it. Before 1933 I certainly was, but then—only again after the war.

"I fooled myself. I had to. Everybody has to. If the good had been twice as good and the bad only half as bad, I still ought to have seen it, all through as I did in the beginning, because I am, as you say, sensitive. But I didn't want to see it, because I would then have had to think about the consequences of seeing it, what followed from seeing it, what I must do to be decent. I wanted my home and family, my job, my career, a place in the community. I wanted to be able to sleep nights—"

"Weren't you?" I said.

"Not in the period when I was deciding whether to join; but after the decision it was better, always better. I enjoyed doing those little things at school, 'defying' the Party, not because what I did was right (that, too, of course) but because I showed I was clever and, above all, because I 'belonged.' I belonged to the new 'nobility,' and the nobility can get away with certain things just because they are the nobility; merely getting away with them proves that they are the nobility, even to themselves. So I slept."

It was near the end of our many, many conversations that I said, "Those Jews you saw in the café, in Baden-Baden that time, when you tried not to have them see you; who were they, Herr Hildebrandt, do you remember?"

The needle on my blush-detector jumped. "Yes. Yes, of course, I remember. They were friends of the Wolff family, my—my relatives."

"Wolff?"

"Yes."

"Here in Kronenberg?"

"Yes. At the University."

"Professor Wolff? Eberhard Wolff?"

"Yes."

"But he was a Jew."

"Yes."

"How were they related to you, Herr Hildebrandt?"

"Oh, not by blood. Professor Wolff was Jewish, his wife three-quarters Jewish. Their son Erich married my cousin Sibylle."

"Sibylle," I said. "That's a very pretty—"

My two small boys broke into the room, to get their afternoon cake. Being small American boys, they did not say, "*Guten Tag, Herr Studienrat*," they said, '*Tag*'; but, being small boys in Germany, they did have the decency to shake hands all around before grabbing for the cake.

A few visits later I reverted to the Wolff family, and again the needle jumped. The Wolffs were closely related to the most illustrious Jewish name in Germany, and intermarriage between Jews and non-Jews in this great family had been common. The Wolff home in Kronenberg was a great, ancient pile on the Schlossweg, the beautiful wooded area of old mansions on the hill, beyond the Castle. I knew that the aged Frau Professor Wolff (Frau Geheimrat Wolff, her eminent husband having borne the additional eminence of "Geheimrat," or distinguished professor) still lived, alone with a servant, in the family home.

What I learned, without much difficulty (indeed, he spoke with understandable pride, although the blush remained), was that Herr Hildebrandt had saved the Wolffs' home during the Third Reich by arranging for the transfer of its ownership to another "Aryan" in-law in a pretended sale. Hildebrandt had been a frequent visitor at the Wolffs' before he joined the Party; then his visits dropped off and, finally, when the ownership of the home was transferred, although the family still lived there, stopped altogether. Why?

"I felt uncomfortable," said the teacher. "You may well believe that. I wanted to talk about the current situation and to try to explain my position, but Professor Wolff, who was quite old, would never let me talk about such things. He would not tolerate talk about National Socialism, against it or for it.

"I had always felt very much at home there. Everyone did who came. It was like the old times of books, music, poetry, art; another age. And it never changed. But after I joined the Party I felt out of place. When other people were there—it was a great house, with many friends—I knew that I was always the only Nazi. The others were not open anti-Nazis, of course, but the fact that they were there spoke for itself. And the talk always avoided politics. It did everywhere, in those days. It was—well, at the worst, it was simply that, if you had not been present when somebody said something against the regime, there was no danger of anything's being forced out of you later on. So nobody talked politics, not among non-Nazis.

"When I was there alone, after I joined the Party, it was still worse. I played chess with the Professor, or we listened to music, and he never spoke, except politely. And I knew I couldn't speak, to say (at least to try to say) how I felt. So the visits became formal, and then stopped."

"But you saved his home."

"Yes."

"Didn't that make you feel better?"

"No."

"Why not?"

"Because with him I wanted to say how I felt, and he wouldn't let me."

On one of our last visits—Herr Hildebrandt was at my house—he said, "Herr Mayer" (he had, with my help, got over calling me "Herr Professor"), "there is something else I should like to tell you about."

"Please," I said. The blush was coming up again.

"It was at the end of 1940, when I came back on leave. My wife was almost eight months pregnant, and we were living in two furnished rooms. Housing was very short. We heard an apartment was available, but only on the way there did we learn that it was the apartment of the lawyer, Dr. Stern. Have you heard of him?"

"Yes," I said. "Herr Damm, the Kreisamtsleiter, told me he once saved the Sterns' apartment for them, when an SA leader tried to get it. And Policeman Hofmeister mentioned them, too."

The blush mounted sharply. "Did Hofmeister tell you about the—the deportation of the Sterns?"

"No, except to say that they were deported and how bad he felt about it." The blush subsided a little, I thought.

"Well," said Hildebrandt, "it was a lovely apartment. We spoke in a very friendly way with the Sterns (his wife and daughter were there) and they with us. We said that we had not come as Nazis, and we explained our situation. They believed us, obviously, and Dr. Stern said he wanted to move anyway to be nearer their friends and relatives. (Most of the Jews in Kronenberg had moved into the old Bertholdstrasse; I forget what new name the Nazis gave it, but it was not a formal, compulsory ghetto.)

"We assumed that, now that Dr. Stern could have only

Jews for clients, and the Jews were becoming so poor, he could no longer afford the apartment. I felt bad, very bad, and Eva felt worse; she was already so strongly anti-Nazi, and here she felt that her condition was responsible for driving these people from their home, for our wanting an apartment so badly. It was very embarrassing. 'Still,' I said to myself, 'if we don't take it, someone else will,' and just then Dr. Stern said: 'If you don't take it, Herr Studienrat, someone else will.' So we—we took it."

The blush remained level.

It was getting on for evening again, and the room was growing dark. I was fumbling around, in my memory, and in my imagination. There was something connected with Jews, with the Wolffs, possibly with the Sterns, that Herr Hildebrandt wanted (or didn't want) to tell me.

"The Wolffs," I said, groping. "How was it you said you were related to them?"

"Erich Wolff, Eberhard's son," said the teacher. "He was a lawyer. But he'd wanted to be a musician. He played the piano, and I played the violin, and in my first two years in Kronenberg, before I joined the Party, we played duets together sometimes. He was married to—my cousin."

"Of course," I said, "Sibylle, the beautiful name."

I didn't need the light; I could feel the heat.

"What became of Erich?" I asked.

"He went to Italy, in '39, and died there. Of a heart attack. Or suicide. We don't know which."

"And his wife, Sibylle?"

This was it.

"She stayed here."

"Did you see her, after you stopped seeing the Wolffs?"

"Yes."

"How did she feel about your being in the Party?"

"She—she advised me to join. Not exactly *advised*, but accepted my reasons. She saw the necessity. She agreed with me that I might be able to help the Wolffs that way. I was to keep them advised—through her—of all developments and of any dangers and do what I could. She thought that might be helpful. And it was, up to a point."

"Up to a point?"

"Yes."

"She went on seeing her father- and mother-in-law, of course?"

"Oh, yes. We would be talking and she would say, 'You must excuse me now, I am going up to the Schlossweg, to the Wolffs', to *gaukeln*.' *Gaukeln* means 'juggle,' but it also means 'talk without saying anything,' 'beat around the bush.' It meant she was going to the Wolffs' and pretend, as one always did there now, that everything was the same as always."

"Do you know if she talked to the Wolffs about you?"

"She—tried."

"But you yourself never saw them again, after you joined the Party or after you arranged the 'sale' of their house?"

"No. Well—once. It was they that I saw in the café, in Baden-Baden that time, when I told you that it was friends of theirs that I saw. It was they I did not want to see me."

"When was that?"

"In '39, just before the war. I knew they were there, because my wife and Sibylle and I had driven down together, and, after we'd got rooms and gone out again in Sibylle's car, she stopped in front of another hotel and said to me, 'You'd better get out now.' It meant that the Wolffs were there, and she didn't want them to have to meet me."

"Or, maybe, you to have to meet them."

"Yes."

"Do you think that Sibylle would rather you hadn't joined the Party, even to help protect the family?"

"I think so, yes. . . . Yes."

"Do you think she was right, Herr Hildebrandt?"

"I—. I don't know, Herr Professor." (I noticed the lapse back to "Herr Professor.")

"I'd like to meet her," I said.

"She's dead," said Herr Hildebrandt.

It was dark in the room now, but I still tried to take notes, just a few words (the way a reporter does) to remind me, so that I could fill them out afterward. In the dark my writing ran all over the paper.

"Dead?"

"Yes. She worked in the 'underground,' Herr Mayer, to help people escape from Germany. That's why she stayed. Her husband was more than half Jewish; he couldn't help her. In '42, before the Sterns were deported, sent to the concentration camp at Theresienstadt and then to the 'East,' she was trying to arrange their escape into Italy. She must have been somewhere on the Swiss-Italian border. The Gestapo got her."

"And—?"

"Her family was told that she had been arrested and hanged herself in the jail at Constance."

"Had she?"

"No." This came like a shot. "No. She would not have hanged herself. Unless—unless things had reached the point where she knew she might talk without knowing it and endanger others."

I could not see Herr Hildebrandt now.

"Did she—did they—have any children?"

"A son."

"What happened to him?"

"I—." He stopped, and then resumed. "I—arranged it so that I was appointed his guardian. He's in the university now."

My wife rapped at the door to say it was time for dinner and to ask Herr Hildebrandt if he'd stay. He said "No," and I went to the front door with him without turning on the lights.

CHAPTER 16

The Furies: Johann Kessler

"I still say," said Herr Kessler, "that National Socialism was good for Germany."

"Was it good for you?" I said, on an off chance.

There was a pause. Then: "No."

"Why not?" I said, "if it was good for Germany?"

"Perhaps we will talk about that, one day, Herr Professor."

We did, one day, months later. It burst out. "Through National Socialism I lost my soul. I blasphemed. Every night, through all those years, I blasphemed; I said my children's prayers with them; I took the name of the Lord in vain. I wanted them to be Christians, and I myself had denied Jesus Christ."

Johann Kessler had been born and brought up a Catholic, in a Catholic village in Württemberg, in southern Germany. He was the second son in a large family; his older brother would inherit the Kesslerhof. He himself wanted to learn. At nine he had gone to the village priest and asked to be taught Latin. At ten he wanted to be a monk, and he was so insistent that his mother (his father was dead now) sent him with the priest to a Benedictine monastery nearby. The monks were kind to him, but there were no other children and he had to get up at midnight and dawn for Mass; at the end of a week he wanted to go home. The monks told him that he might come back, if he wanted to, at eighteen.

At eighteen he was a soldier. At seventeen he had been a bank clerk, leading a glorious life in town. The day the first World War began he enlisted and served as an Army regular through the war. He participated in the suppression of the Communist rebellion in Munich after the Armistice. Then he was demobilized, got a job again as a bank clerk after a year unemployed, wound up in Frankfurt, jobless again, in the depression of 1931, and moved to a village just outside Kronenberg, where he worked for a year as manager of an estate and was unemployed again.

He was very happily married to a fine, large woman, a good "free-thinking" Protestant. She had never been converted to Catholicism, but he had gone on being a Catholic, less ardently than he had been as a child, of course, and the Kesslers' two children, a boy and a girl, were being brought up in the Catholic faith. Like a good woman, Frau Kessler respected her husband and his wishes; like a good man, he was warmly devoted to his children, much more so than any of my North German friends.

Herr Kessler was an engaging personality, a semilearned man among unlearned men, and a popular public speaker, in the rolling, sententious Fourth-of-July vein, a favorite at weddings and birthdays, at veterans' meetings, and at assemblies of the nationalist Kyffhäuserbund. Politically he was a good Catholic centrist of the conservative, clerical-agricultural wing of the Center rather than its Christian Socialist–trade-union wing. But he had no compunction, in 1933, against joining the National Socialist Party in the hope of getting a job. He was placed in personnel work—where he belonged—in the Kronenberg Labor Front office and was appointed one of several "Party Orators" for the county, one of the little men with big voices who addressed small-town meetings.

He was allowed to speak on the Party's history and on German history and culture but never received (or asked for) the special permission required to speak for the Party on "the Jewish question." Every Sunday morning at ten the Party had a two-hour service at the local theater. It was not exactly a religious service, although the speakers, and especially Party Orator Kessler, often took religious or, more properly, spiritual themes.

Those who came to the Sunday-morning services, like those who spoke at them, knew that they should have been in church; at least the hours conflicted. After the Church-Party split began to develop, in 1936, the Party services became more ritualistic, more specifically a substitute for church. When, a year or two later, Church-Party relations had become bitter, it was not uncommon at the close of the Party service for the SA and the Hitler Jugend to march noisily (even singing) past the churches, whose services, beginning at eleven, were in progress. Kessler became the most popular speaker in the vicinity at the Sunday-morning meetings of the Party.

One day in 1938 Kessler was asked to perform a German Faith Movement funeral service, for a Nazi who had died in the new racist-naturalist Nordicism of Alfred Rosenberg, the official Nazi philosopher. No pastor in Kronenberg, not even Weber, who was a Nazi, would conduct such a service; Rosenberg's Faith Movement was the purest paganism, with the orb of the sun as the center of its symbolism. It was radical even for Nazism.

The man who had once been the boy who wanted to be a monk, whose dying mother had placed her missal in his hands and said, "Whatever happens to you, never stop praying," had a hard time deciding. The County Leader of the Party, who himself had not left the Protestant Church, did not order or ask him to perform the service. It was the Party red-hots who put pressure on him, men above whom, in natural gifts and feeling, Kessler stood high. But it was a chance for the man who had once wanted to be a monk to be a cleric, of some sort, and, besides, "There was no one else to conduct the service. That part of my impulse was Christian. But the service—the service was not."

That evening, when Kessler came home, he told his wife that he had left the Catholic Church and asked her to say the children's prayers with them. She looked at him and said nothing. She finished the dishes and then started to the children's room, when the two children's voices were heard in a jingle they always sang when they were ready for their father to come in for prayers: "The children will not go to sleep, 'til Daddy's asked God their souls to keep." Kessler pushed past his wife, went in himself, and said the prayers, ending with the usual words, "*In Christus Namen*, In Jesus' name."

That night, having said nothing more to his wife, he went to the parish priest and told him he was no longer a Christian. "I was going to tell him about the funeral, but he knelt and prayed—"

"Did you?"

"Kneel?"

"Yes."

"No."

"Did you pray?"

"No. No, I didn't. I waited until he stood up, and then I left."

"Were you going to tell him about the children's prayers?"

"Was I?"

"Yes."

"No."

"I went home," Herr Kessler continued. "I told my wife, and talked to her almost all that night. It wasn't so serious for her, because she was not church-connected. And she wasn't interested in politics or in history. I had read Rosenberg's *Myth of the Twentieth Century*, the 'bible' of the Faith Movement. It was on the Papal Index, and, although I could have got permission from my priest to read it, I hadn't bothered to or hadn't wanted to. Inside I had been turning against the Church ever since I'd become a Nazi, against the political Church, the Papacy as a government. Canossa, the struggle of the German kings against the popes, the right of Germany and Germans to be free from an outside government—this was the way I had been thinking. It is the way I still think, too.

"All this I told my wife. She didn't say much, almost nothing. Only at the end she said, 'And the children?' And then she added, from the Bible, 'The father's blessing builds the children's house.'

"What would happen to my children, my children?" he went on, one moment impassioned, the next didactic. "They could not go to church any more or to Sunday school. And the teaching in the public schools is not adequate for the moral development of children. Many times afterward I talked with teachers about it. I never got a satisfactory answer. *Blut und Boden*, blood and soil, the eternal life of the plants, of the animals, of nature—that's only a part of the religious story; it isn't religion.

"I told my wife: 'When they're twelve or thirteen, they

shall decide for themselves.' I knew when I said it that that was a lie, the same lie, at bottom, that dominated the Hitler Youth, the lie that children can educate themselves. Children who grow up without religion cannot decide about religion for themselves; that's a fallacy, that people can choose intelligently between what they know and what they don't know. What it was, was an excuse for me, a shimmer of hope to excuse me, hope that they would find what I had lost, that they, my little children, would absolve me!

"At the end, when I had finished talking that night, I was more tired than I have ever been before or since. I told myself—not my wife—that I could remain a Christian in soul. It wasn't true. It wasn't true. The next day I declared my intention to leave the Church before the county court. It was done. After that, I never had a quiet hour—"

"Until after the war?"

"What has the war to do with it?"

"I mean, until now, when things are changed again."

"Do you mean that because the Nazis are gone, and the outside has changed, that the inside has changed? There are things that don't change so easily, Herr Professor. When I say, 'After that I never had a quiet hour,' I mean every hour after that, this hour included."

During the next six years Herr Kessler was called upon more and more often to perform German Faith Movement funerals, baptisms, even weddings. There was no church service, of course, for the funerals, only a cemetery service, and no sermon but, rather, a speech, "no Bible, never a word about God or the soul, the whole personal afterlife denied by the clearest implication." The baptism celebrated nature as the source of life and the child's father as the "life-giver," and the wedding joined the couple as "Germans."

"But," said Herr Kessler, "man is still man, he must be comforted in the presence of death and sobered in the presence of life. Those who had left the Church—Evangelical or Catholic—had no place to go. And no—pastor."

"But the municipal marriage office performed weddings, didn't they?"

"Yes, but Germans are religious, including those who believe they are not. Especially as regards death. During the war, it was hard in the hospitals. If a wounded soldier died confessed in the Church, or even if he died unconscious and his religion was unknown, the Church would bury him. But when they died having said they had left the Church, and their identity was unknown or their relatives couldn't be found, the hospital called the Party office, and they asked me to officiate."

"Even if they were not known to be members of the Faith Movement?"

"Even then. Even if they were not known to be members of the Party. Very few, that we knew of, were members of the Faith Movement. But, if men died who had left the Church, what was there to be done? We were glad to do it. I was glad myself, although I knew it was blasphemy; so far had I fallen that I was glad to be of 'service.'

"Millions had left the Church—the Protestant much more than the Catholic—before 1933. Not just Social Democrats and, of course, Communists, but people in general. That had been going on since 1918, more and more all the time. Protestants, especially, didn't believe in the Church any more, because the Protestant Church was the official Church, the State Church, and its head was the King of Prussia, who happened to be the Kaiser, the Emperor of Germany. With the Kaiser gone, the Church didn't know where it stood; it was as if God had run away to the Netherlands. Only when the Nazi flag flew over it again did it know (or think it knew) where it stood.

"The Catholic Church was different; the head and center of the Catholic Church were outside Germany. The German Catholic—and, if you include Austria, Germany is half Catholic—had an allegiance which, while it was not temporal, had a temporal capital, Rome. This 'divided allegiance' the Nazis hated, and I hated it with them. But it was just this 'foreign loyalty' that provided a greater possibility of Catholic resistance to Nazism."

"Which, however," I said, "did not materialize."

"That's so," said Herr Kessler, "not in the masses or the priests, but for another reason. But, for one Protestant *prelate* who resisted, you found two or three or four Catholic prelates.

"Outside Catholicism only women, and especially old women, were very religious any more, except in the villages; and to some extent this was true even there. The Protestant cathedal churches stood almost empty, sometimes with more tourists than communicants. The women tried to make their husbands go to services with them for the children's sake, but they were not always successful. The sermons had always been dull, and now they had lost any great meaning, any comfort, any relevance to people's lives.

"The trouble was that the Church—Catholic as well as Protestant—was supported by taxes. Thus it did not have to consider the people's wants in order itself to survive, or minister to their needs. When their wants and needs changed, the Church, especially the Protestant Church, didn't know it. Only in the villages (those that could still support a resident pastor) were the people and the Church in real contact. Otherwise, only a few young and enthusiastic pastors ever called on their parishioners, except in great sickness. If you were ever to see your pastor, you had to call on him in his visiting hours, which were during workingmen's working hours, and then you had to sit and wait for him, as you would at the dentist's, and he would look at his watch while you talked; or perhaps you would be told to come back at the same time next week. There were exceptions, many exceptions, the whole Christian Socialist movement, for example; but, in general, the Protestant clergy acted like high civil servants, which, after all, is what they were.

"I do not mean to say that the Catholics were better, and there certainly was no more Catholic resistance to Nazism than there was Protestant. But there was a reason for this. The reason—it had both the best and the worst consequences—was that the priest was close to the people. After all, he had no more status in the German State than they had. In the Catholic villages, in the years after the first war, you would not find a Communist; everyone belonged to the Catholic Center Party; the priests had real power because they were close to the people. In the Evangelical towns it was different, especially where the industrial workers lived. In Westphalia, for instance, you would find the workers on one side, the pastor on the other. The pastor did not belong to the people; the priest did.

"But why, then, you ask, did the Catholics go Nazi? Why didn't the priests hold them, as they had held them from Communism? The answer is twofold. First, Communism was atheist and Nazism was its enemy, supposedly the defender of religion. But there was another reason, and

217

I'm told that you see this today in Italy and France, where one hears that there are actually Communist priests. And that is that the masses of the people could not be held back from Nazism, so powerful was its appeal, and this same priest, who would not leave his people, went with them to Nazism, too."

I knew something about all this. My authority was Policeman Willy Hofmeister. In 1936 or 1937 each of the Kronenberg detectives was openly assigned to a local church as observer, to report on the "loyalty" of the sermons. In addition—this the detectives were not supposed to know, but they did—there was a Gestapo agent assigned to report on the fidelity of the detective's report. One day, at the height of the Church-Party struggle, Hofmeister was ordered to inform Pastor Faber, whose sermons he reported, that he must not read the pastoral letter sent out by the Protestant bishops to be read from the pulpits on the following Sunday.

To Policeman Hofmeister's horror, Pastor Faber coldly told him that the Church, not the State, would decide what was to be read from the pulpit. Hofmeister tried to "reason" (he puts it this way, fifteen years later) with the clergyman and told him that there would be a Gestapo agent present and that they would both, Faber and Hofmeister, get into trouble if the pastoral letter were read. Faber said that Hofmeister would have to look out for himself, and rose, ending the interview.

To my amazement, Hofmeister, who had by no means been an ardent Nazi, still, fifteen years later, resented the pastor's defiance of the "law," that is, of the authorities. He no more admired Faber's heroism—the letter was read from the pulpit—now than then. He himself, Hofmeister, had violated the "law," that is, what his superiors told him to do, by revealing to the pastor that there would be a Gestapo man present, and the pastor was willing to jeopardize an innocent man along with himself. "It was like a slap in the face," said Hofmeister, and I saw that even the policeman might have a hard time of it in the police state.

I could not, at first, understand Hofmeister's persistent failure to admire the pastor's great courage. I pressed the matter and learned that the policeman had always disliked the great pastor. "He was too high and mighty for us, a great theologian, you know, above the people. I was a member of his church, you understand. He had been my pastor for years. That did not mean a thing to him. When I went to him—this was years earlier—to ask him to come to the house to christen my daughter, he said, 'There will be a charge, of course, for coming to the house.' Like a doctor; worse than a decent doctor.

"After the ceremony, my wife offered Faber and his assistant wine and *Torte*. The assistant accepted gladly, but the pastor said "No," he would not have any. As soon as the assistant finished his wine, Faber said they would have to leave, but I said that the custom was that the guests at a christening must not leave *schief*, that is, 'out of balance,' with an odd number of glasses of wine. The assistant held his glass out, but Faber would not have any. When they were leaving, I asked the pastor how much it was customary to pay for a christening. He said three Marks, so I laid a three-Mark piece in front of him and a five-Mark note in front of his assistant. That's how *I* felt, and that's what kind of Christian the great Faber is."

"Were they all like that, the pastors in Kronenberg?"

"More or less. Not all. There was Weber, the one that become a Nazi. He was a friendly man, really beloved, even by those who disagreed with him. Ask anyone. And the

Catholic priest, Father Pausch, *there* was a man you could talk to. You would visit him, and he'd show you into the parlor, and you'd sit down next to a table on which there was an open box of cigars. The housekeeper would bring wine and glasses, and the priest would hand you the cigars, and you'd sit and talk with him, about conditions, yes, even about your problems, although you were not of his faith. And he would speak of his troubles. When the government forbade the continuation of religious services in the Church schools, Father Pausch accepted it (what else could he do?) and said to me, 'This is the saddest day of my life.' There was a man you could sympathize with, a man like yourself."

So I knew something about the Protestant and the Catholic clergy, at least about one Protestant clergyman and one Catholic, the heroic Pastor Faber and the unheroic Father Pausch, as they appeared to my Protestant friend Hofmeister. What Herr Kessler, the Catholic, or former Catholic, was telling me did not sound at all incredible.

"At the beginning of National Socialism," said Herr Kessler, "there was no effort to draw people away from the Church. Just the opposite. The Weimar Republic had separated Church and State, just as it is in America, you know, and the pastors, most of them, supported the Nazis in the hope of reuniting the two and rebuilding the Church. Certainly the Party call for 'positive Christianity' was clear, so much so that, in the first days of the regime, many liberals and radicals who had left the Church hurried to join it again as a means of 'covering up,' of proving that they were not leftists.

"But by and by the Party's own spirit began by itself to fill up the emptiness of spirit in people's lives. This was where the Church had failed. And people began to turn from the Church, which in spirit they had already left, to the Party. The Church blamed the Party for this, but in the beginning it was not the Party's fault at all. The Church created this vacuum, and the Party, in the end, took advantage of it.

"On the surface there were other things, but that was what lay underneath. On the surface the Church-State fight began on the 'Jewish question,' but it is important to remember that the fight did not begin for two or three years. The Party had not expected the Church to take a stand against anti-Semitism as such, and, with some individual exceptions, it didn't. Then the Party made the claim that baptized Jews, converts to Christianity, were Jews still and had to be dismissed from the clergy and, presumably, thrown out of the Church. Of course, that was a mistake, but the Party had to make it to be consistent. And the Church had to resist if it were even to maintain the pretense of being Christian; Christianity is evangelical; its business is to win *all* souls to Christ.

"Once the fight had begun, the Church leaders blamed the Party for luring the people away. Finally that was actually the case, but that was after the trouble began. And, when a man died who had left the Church, the Church people would say it was the Party's fault that there was no one to bury him. It would look bad for the Party, you can see that, and I was a Party man."

"A Party man first, or a Christian first?"

"A Party man, then."

"And now?"

"Now?—Nothing. But," Herr Kessler went on after a pause, "it was not just a matter of how it would look for the Party. There was something else. You ask why the hospitals would call the Party office when a soldier died who had left the Church. It was because people called the Party in all difficulties arising from the reconstruction of the country, and the Party always helped. This pattern was established from the first, long before the war. It was what made the Party so strong—it would always help. In religious matters, in domestic problems, in everything. It really watched over the lives of the people, not spying on them, but caring about them.

"You know, Herr Professor, we are told that not a sparrow falls without God's care; I am not being light when I say this—that not a person 'fell,' fell ill or in need, lost his job or his house, without the Party's caring. No organization had ever done this before in Germany, maybe nowhere else. Believe me, such an organization is irresistible to men. No one in Germany was alone in his troubles—"

"Except," I said, " 'inferior races' and opponents of the regime."

"Of course," he said, "that is understood, but they were few, they were outside society, 'over the fence,' and nobody thought about them."

"But these, too, were 'sparrows.' "

"Yes," he said.

"Could these," I said, "have been 'the least of them,' of whom Jesus spoke?"

"Herr Professor, we didn't see it that way. We were wrong, sinful, but we didn't see it that way. We saw 'the least of them' among our own people, everywhere, among ordinary people who obeyed the laws and were not Jews, or gypsies, and so on. Among ordinary people, 'Aryans,' there were 'the least of them,' too. Millions; six million unemployed at the beginning. These 'least,' not all who were 'least' but most of them, had somewhere to turn, at last.

"You say, 'Totalitarianism.' Yes, totalitarianism; but perhaps you have never been alone, unemployed, sick, or penniless, or, if you have, perhaps never for long, for so long that you have given up hope; and so (you'll pardon me, Herr Professor) it is easy for you to say, 'Totalitarianism—no.' But the other side, the side I speak of, was the side that the people outside Germany never saw, or perhaps never cared to see. And today nobody in Germany will say it. But, believe me, nobody in Germany has forgotten it, either.

"In the Labor Front every person we placed in a job remained our responsibility, our care. The owner of a café tried to mistreat a girl I had placed there. She came to me. I warned him. He did it again, and his business was closed. Totalitarian?—Yes, of course. He was an *alter Kämpfer*, an Old Party Fighter, this man, and at the hearing he said to me, 'You treat me as if I were a Jew. You will lose your job for this.' He took it up with the district office of the Party, without any success. And that was not an exceptional case. Totalitarianism?—Yes. But I am proud of it."

The Party Orator was getting oratorical. "Yes," I said, "I can understand that. But—what about your children?" I had yielded to the temptation to deflate him; I was sorry, but it was too late. The Party Orator shriveled, and there was Johann Kessler.

"The children," he said, "yes, the children."

"Excuse me, Herr Kessler," I said.

"That's all right," he said, "nothing to excuse. The children."

"Did your wife say their prayers with them after their first night?"

"No. I did. I had to, Herr Professor, I had to. They were too young to understand, don't you see?"

"To understand what?"

"To understand what—what their father was. I had to say their prayers with them, and I could not talk to anyone, not anyone, about it. Not because of the danger, this was not the kind of thing that would ever mean danger, but because of the shame. It was a lonely road; it still is—lonelier, I think, than never to have believed at all."

"Did you ever pray otherwise?"

"Yes. At Faith Movement funerals. At the end of my—my talk—you know, about what a good comrade the man had been, what a good husband and father, how true to our cause and our country, at the end I would say the Lord's Prayer."

"Aloud?"

"Oh, no. But that was different, you know."

"How?"

"Well, what you do to yourself and to God, God can carry, and you yourself don't matter. But what you do to your children—."

He broke off, and I said nothing, and then he went on. "Every night, all those years, even the last night, before I left home. We were all told to go north, to fight to the end, even the old men. So I started north, on my bicycle, and surrendered like everyone else. That night, too, when I thought I might not see my children again, I said their prayers with them, after I had kissed my wife."

"What did your wife say?"

"My wife never said anything about it, ever, after that first night. We didn't talk any more about it, in all those years. But she knew."

"And you, you knew all the time that you blasphemed?"

"All the time, I knew all the time that I was damned, damned worse every day. But I wanted my children to be Christians."

"Why, Herr Kessler?"

"Why does a man want his children to be better than himself?"

A month after the night her husband left home and was captured, Frau Kessler went to the parish priest and asked for Communion for the older child, the girl Maria. She had not been able to locate her husband, and she thought that, even if he were still alive, she might not see him again; she had heard that anybody who had been a Party Orator would certainly be classified as a war criminal. Three days later she got word that he was held in the compound at Darmstadt, and she went to see him. She told him what she had done. He wept. "Why?" I asked.

"Because God had had mercy on me, a sinner. I was damned. Whatever I did, whatever they did with me, I was damned. And God had had mercy, even on the damned."

"Can't a man always be saved, Herr Kessler?"

"I didn't believe that any more. I didn't even believe that. The Faith Movement denied the Redeemer."

Every Sunday, now, Herr Kessler's grown daughter and his almost-grown son worship with the congregation in the parish church. Maria (like so many girls in Europe, and unlike most girls here) plays the violin. Hans, the boy, sings in the choir with a rich voice like his father's, the Party Orator. The Party Orator, who now works in the shipping-room of the village feed store, goes to the church alone and sits at the back, outside the congregation. He has not asked

225

to be readmitted to the faith, and the priest (who himself was a Nazi) shakes hands with him but has never spoken. "God can wait. He waited for me," the priest told Maria, who told me. In the biographical record which Johann Kessler wrote down for the United States military authorities on July 3, 1945, he gives his religion as *Gottgläubig*—non-church-connected believer in God.

CHAPTER 17

The Furies: Furor Teutonicus

Who, asks Tacitus rhetorically, would trade Asia or Africa for Germany, "a region hideous and rude, under a rigorous climate, dismal to behold or cultivate?" The German answer is obvious: the Germans. It's the wrong answer, of course; other people live in still ruder regions without getting into trouble. But for purposes of nationalist romanticism the German answer will serve.

Romanticism is the stuff of which men's dreams are made. National Socialism was a piece of this stuff, cut not from immanent villainy, "congenital criminality," but from the dream of freedom from unbearable conditions which have got to be borne. Since these conditions were more unbearable in Germany than anywhere else, who but the Germans should undertake, self-sacrificially, to free the human race from the human condition?

In their dream my friends turned, regretfully, all the way from the Christian obligation to one's fellow-men, with whom, through God, one identifies one's self, real men in a real world, feeble, fitful men, to the altogether transcendent obligation (much heavier than that which the Cross imposes) to produce Man the Imagined, Man like God, Man Who Once Was, German Man. We must remember that racial perfection was only the means—*the* means, to be sure —to moral perfection. Moral perfection was possible. And

227

moral perfection, in Germany, would alleviate the human condition everywhere, even among those who, incapable of perfection because of their lower nature, would have to have alleviation forced upon them.

Seven of my ten Nazi friends had heard the joke—it originated in Germany during Nazism—and enjoyed it: "What is an Aryan?" "An Aryan is a man who is tall like Hitler, blond like Goebbels, and lithe like Göring." They, too, had smiled at the mass Aryanization, first of the Italians and then of the Japanese. They all knew "Aryans" who were indistinguishable from Jews and Jews who were indistinguishable from Nazis. Six of my ten friends were well below middle height, seven of them brunet, and at least seven of them brachycephalic, of the category of head breadth furthest removed from "Nordic longheadedness." None of this mattered; all this was only reality, a parliamentary quibble.

The German, said the German philosopher, has a yesterday and a tomorrow, but no today. Out of my ten Nazi friends, the "German spirit," manifest in the whole unbroken history of suffering and sacrifice of the whole German people, would, tomorrow at the latest, breed yesterday's German, "blond, blue-eyed, huge," as he appeared to the Divine Julius, who happened to be dark and squat. Men too heavy-laden can—and not only can but must—dream such dreams.

Wagnerian men like gods and Faustian men like angels people these dreamy lives—raise the tailor from his steaming bench, release the farm boy from his blistering plow handles, fit the burning feet of the shop clerk with winged sandals, transport them to dark forests (darker in Germany than anywhere else), whence, stripped to sword and shield and helmet, they hew their way to the top of the mountain.

There, in a combination Walpurgis-Wartburg, they hurl Teutonic-Christian fire at the lightning, driving it and its demons away.

The incubation of Germany was terrified by *das Wütende Heer, die Wilde Jagd*, the Huntsman's Wild Horde riding the night, and in the sacred groves the protective fire has never been allowed to die. In 1951 a German mayor burns the de-Nazification records in the town square. In 1952 the Berlin police stage the greatest torchlight display since Nazism. In 1953 a German pacifist—a *pacifist*, mind you—burns the "contractual agreement" with the Allies in public in Hamburg. And all over Germany, at the fall farm festivals, at the spring school festivals, the climax of the celebration is a fire of orgiastic proportions. In 1933 the anti-Christians burned a bonfire of books in Prussia to liberate Germany from the radical Jews; in 1817 the Christians burned a bonfire of books in Saxe-Weimar to liberate Germany from the reactionary Prussians.

On the night of June 29, 1934, Adolf Hitler burned his bridges behind him. The decision was made on the terrace of a hotel at Godesberg on the Rhine. Sitting there alone in the night, the Leader stared at a thousand men on the lawn in front of him; each of the thousand men held a torch; all of the thousand torches together formed a fiery Swastika, in his honor. The Leader, staring into that fire, made the decision to decimate the Party leadership. He left the terrace, commandeered his plane, and flew to Munich at midnight. The next morning was June 30, 1934, "the day of blood," the nation-wide purge of National Socialism.

The world once purged by flood ends always again in the surer purgative of fire. Deviltry runs deep in the "Teutonic Spirit." Those two little devils, "Max und Moritz," the German counterpart of our comic-strip mischief-makers, specialize in enormities undreamed of and undreamable by Peck's Bad Boy, Kayo Mullins, and Dennis the Menace. And, while it is a long way back from "Max und Moritz" to Martin Luther, who invited the Wittenberg students to the burning of the Papal bull which split the Church, the way is not trackless. The Lutheran Reformation, libertarian in its genesis, drove out of the religious life of the German people such sunshine as there was in Roman universalism; replaced it with a gloom which still defies theological permeation; subordinated the Church Militant to the Church Military; and re-established the sect of the patriot tribe.

It was dreadfully heroic, and dreadfully dramatic, when the Augustinian monk said, *"Hier stehe ich, ich kann nicht anders,"* and defied the greatest power on earth. It was less heroic and much less dramatic but no less prophetic of the Germany to come, when he decided that to "give to him that asketh of thee" did not mean to give him what he asks but, rather, what is good for him. It had taken a century to convert the English to Christianity, seven to convert the Germans; and in some sections of the land the new faith had died out altogether as late as the end of the eleventh century.

My friend Kessler was right; the resistance of Catholics, not to dictatorship, but to nationalist dictatorship and to racism and idolatry, was stronger, if not significantly so, than Protestantism's. The strength of the Catholic Church was the strength of the Catholic Church; the strength of the Protestant Church was the strength of the German State, whose Church dominated an almost half-Catholic country. In the Protestant north one says, *"Guten Tag"*; in the Catholic south, *"Grüss' Gott*, God be with you." It is a little harder (not much, but a little) to change to "*Heil Hitler*" from "*Grüss' Gott*" than from "*Guten Tag.*"

The Catholic Church is, willy-nilly, protestant in a country whose State Church is Protestant. Bismarck's campaign against it, and later Rosenberg's and Goebbels' ("We will deal with this crew," wrote Goebbels of the Catholicism into which he was born, "when the war is over"), taught Catholics a little about living dangerously and cleaving joyously to a faith under fire. The common estimate that only 10 per cent of the nominal Protestants of Germany were (and are) free adherents to the State Church is, at least in Kronenberg, not low. Kronenberg had been 100 per cent Catholic until the Prince of Hesse, embracing Protestantism in 1521, suppressed the Catholic worship; from which instant on, Kronenberg had been 100 per cent Protestant. Under the American Occupation, after 1945, the Nazis' Sunday-morning paganism was replaced, in the same theater, by popular movies during church hours, and without any Protestant protest.

This dark Church of Luther, born not of bread and wine but of blood and iron, so remote from the universal surrender and the universal embrace in which the parent Church was born (if not bred), even in Luther's lifetime lost its libertarian impulses and has never been able to release the "little people" of Germany from the demonological terrors of the dark. They cannot resist the torchbearer who, with his torch, turns the black into day. I had several talks with a country pastor, an anti-Nazi, who, without challenging the one Scripture that "we ought to obey God rather than men," shook his head doggedly and reverted, again and again, to the other Scripture that "the powers that be are ordained of God." His three oldest sons had been killed in the German Army invasion of Russia; he will never, he said in tears, let "them" take his last son, Kurt; but I'm afraid he will.

So the Tree of Christ, freely planted in the fulfilment of perfect freedom, grows weak and dry beside the Oak of Odin. But it grows; believers and unbelievers and agnostics, big men and little, weak men and strong, good men and bad, left with me the conviction that there was one thing that would have made Nazism even worse than it was: the nonexistence of the Christian Church.

Tailor Schwenke may not have known what Christianity was; he may not have been a Christian; he may not have wanted to be; but he could not bear to look in the mirror and say, "I am not a Christian." As long as he could not, there was one way left to his heart, however hard or near-hopeless, that would have been closed had there been no Christian Church to claim him. He was, he assured me, "very religious, always," adding, as he always did when he spoke of any of the virtues, "Our whole family, always." As evidence of his religiosity, he taught me the hymns his confirmation class had sung sixty years before, *Ich will dich lieben, meine Stärke* ("I Will Love Thee, My Almighty") at the beginning of the confirmation, and *So nimm denn meine Hände* ("Take Thou My Hands") at the end. For a seventy-one-year-old man, who was almost fatally wounded in one war and served three years in prison after another, his baritone was remarkably beautiful.

"It was like this," he said. "The new National Socialist faith believed in God but not in the divinity of Christ. That's the simplest way to put it."

I thanked him for putting it simply, and he went on. "We little people didn't know whether or not to believe it. 'Is it right, or isn't it?' we asked ourselves" (after a thousand years of "very religious" Christianity). "One believed one way, one another. It wasn't ever decided. Perhaps, if the war had been won, it would have been decided finally."

"By whom?"

"By the men on top. But they didn't seem to have decided yet themselves. A man didn't know what to think."

This "very religious" old brute was the only one of my nine Protestant friends who left the Church. But he did not turn to the pagan Faith Movement, nor did he apostasize for religious reasons at all. It seems that in 1934 a fine young SA man wanted to be married ("He had to be," the tailor's wife interrupted) and told the pastor that he wanted to be married in his fine SA uniform. The pastor refused. So Tailor Schwenke, now Sturmführer Schwenke, wrote to the pastor that the young man did not have enough money to buy a suit. "Did he?" I said. "No," said Schwenke. "Maybe not," said Mother Schwenke. The pastor then agreed to the uniform.

After the regular service, on the appointed Sunday, Schwenke led his Storm Troop, all of them in uniform, into the gallery of the church. When the pastor, who had gone into the sacristy, came out and saw the Storm Troopers, he stood in front of the altar and the waiting couple and said to the congregation, "What kind of business is this?" Then he performed the ceremony, in brief and unfriendly fashion, and, when it was over and Schwenke tried to speak to him, he turned away.

The district Party office, having heard of the incident, suggested that the tailor apologize to the pastor, but he refused. Then the case reached the district Church Council, and the chief pastor summoned the tailor and suggested that he apologize. "He didn't say I had to, so I didn't. But I was disgusted by the whole thing and resigned my church membership. That's the way I am; our whole family's that way. I started a petition to get that pastor out of his church —his daughter was married to a half-Jew—and a year later he was pensioned. That's all they want anyway. They just work for a salary and a pension, like everyone else. If they weren't paid, they wouldn't work."

A few days after this conversation, a local pastor of my acquaintance, who knew I had been talking with the tailor, called on me and asked me if I thought that Herr Schwenke was a Christian, "a real Christian. I know that that is a peculiar question, but his application to re-enter the Church is before the Council."

"I should guess," I said, "that he's as real a Christian now as he ever was, but it would only be a guess."

"That isn't real enough," said the pastor.

"Why should he want to re-enter the Church if he isn't a Christian?" I said.

"Most probably," said the pastor, a bright young man, "to have the Church carry his *Überfracht,* his excess baggage, for him."

"Isn't that what the Church is for?" I said, just as brightly.

"Ah, yes," said the bright young pastor, who had recently been to America, "but there's so much *Überfracht* in Germany. We Germans seem to be born with it," and he handed me an American cigar.

PART II

The Germans

Heat Wave

Intervening events have driven from all but the hardiest memories the disaster of June 14, 1907, the day that the entire Temperate Zone was hit head on by the worst heat wave in history. Although the suffering of streetcar passengers generally was noted in the chronicles of the disaster, one of the most singular incidents (or congeries of incidents) of that singular day was, so far as I know, never reported. The press had, understandably, overlooked the fact that in those days, and on that day, June 14, the streetcars everywhere in the world carried placards which read: "Windows Are NOT To Be Opened before June 15."

In downtown Milan, where the cars round the Duomo, an Italian threw a rock through a streetcar window and ran.

In Barcelona a Spaniard fell asleep and rode to the end of the line.

In Leeds an English rider called the attention of the Yorkshire Post to the situation, in a strong letter, and, after the letter was picked up in the Times, a Parliamentary debate ensued and the Liberal Government fell—ostensibly on the issue of window regulation.

In Graz the streetcar windows were in such bad condition that, although they were closed, the breeze came through and no Austrian suffocated.

The Bucharest Surface Lines were sold to a Turkish syndicate reliably reported to represent the interests of the Government of ———.

In Lyon a tram passenger cried "Liberté!" and drove his fist through the window. At the sight of his bleeding hand, the Lyonnaise in the dreamy, picturesque Place de Ville rioted.

The Swiss Cabinet, in an emergency session, ordered fans installed at once on all the municipal railways.

In the Scandinavian capitals it was cool, even muggy.

In Omaha an American opened the streetcar window.

In Hannover a German, having read the placard and consulted his mechanical pocket calendar, sat back comfortably in his seat, kept his coat on, and read his paper; but that evening he beat his small son, who, twenty years later, joined the NSDAP, or National Socialist German Workers' Party.

CHAPTER 18

There Is No Such Thing

It is an article of the modern faith—an article all the more hotly held for its dubiety—that there is no such thing as national character. Nothing may be said about a whole people, e.g., in America about Negroes, Jews, or Catholics. This article, like others of older faiths, may, of course, be (and everywhere is) suspended for the duration of war. George Washington said that the New Englanders were "an exceedingly dirty and nasty people"; Alexander I of Russia said that the French were "the common enemy of Humanity"; and Dr. Joseph Goebbels said that the English "are a race of people with whom you can talk only after you have first knocked out their teeth." That such things are said not merely by civilized people in uncivilized times or by uncivilized people in civilized times may be seen in the observation of General Nathan DeWitt, the West Coast Area Commander of the United States Army, in 1942: "A Jap is a Jap. It makes no difference whether he is an American citizen or not. You can't change him by giving him a piece of paper. The Japanese race is an enemy race."

Between 1933 and 1945 the most curious things—some of them wrong, as things said in partisan passion sometimes are—were said of the whole German people. While the political consequences of some of the things that were said were unfortunate, I think it was right to generalize about

239

the Germans. There is such a thing as national character, even though the Nazis said there is.

This is not to say that the character is bounded by national, racial, or religious boundaries or that every member of the nation, race, or religion involved displays the character in the same degree or even in any degree. It is only to say that a sufficiently pronounced outlook—and inlook—is to be found in a sufficiently large proportion of Slobovians everywhere to manifest itself decisively in the behavior of Slobovians generally and of Slobovia as a nation; and this in spite of the radical differences among the Slobovian tribes themselves. It is only to say that we are justified in at least looking for something common, and even peculiarly common, in, say, the Germans.

What we find, in the way of national character, certainly does not entitle any whole people to do anything to any other whole people, no whole people having shown any moral superiority over any other during the whole of their collective existence. The woman who made a lampshade of the skin of innocent Jews was a German, but the man who made a blanket of the scalps of innocent Indians was an American. If every American did not so distinguish himself, neither did every German. And, if there were only one innocent German or one innocent American, the greatest wrong would inhere in associating the fact of national character with the right or, worse yet, the duty to do something to all of the nationals. Burke did not say, in behalf of the American colonists, that he could not bring himself to characterize a whole people; he said that he could not bring himself to indict them.

Nor does it follow from the fact of national character that the characteristics are either innate or indelible. The Roman character certainly changed between Romulus and

Romulus Augustus. The Spaniards were the terror of the world, a few centuries back; and so, a little later, were the Swedes. And the Americans were once sober, devout, and penurious. "Much learned trifling," says Gibbon in one of his savage little footnotes, "might be spared, if our antiquarians would condescend to reflect that similar manners will naturally be produced by similar conditions."

The distinguished Englishman who not so long since accused the German people of *congenital* criminality overlooked the view of respectable English historians that the main stream of the English character is not Celtic at all but Germanic, not to mention the London *Times* of November 11, 1870, which carried the following Letter to the Editor:

"That noble, patient, deep, pious and solid Germany should be at length welded into a Nation, and become Queen of the Continent, instead of vapouring, vainglorious, gesticulating, quarrelsome, restless, and over-sensitive France, seems to me the hopefulest public fact that has occurred in my time.—I remain, Sir, Yours truly, T. Carlyle."

It is not necessarily mischievous to speculate about the cause and the cure of the Germans, nor need such speculation involve either Germanophilia or Germanophobia. As the dust unsettles in Europe, Germany and the Germans have again emerged as the first order of unfinished, and probably unfinishable, business. If, in the present division of the world, Germany were united, for despotism or for constitutional government, there would be a substantial basis for predicting the near future of Europe and perhaps of the world. But Germany is divided, the Germans are divided, and the German is divided. Sixty million Germans are the bloodless battleground of prewar peace. The battlers have no time to inquire into the character of the prize they pursue, even though such inquiry might facilitate their pursuit. To them, in their respective hurries, Germany is so many bases, so much production or production potential, and so many units of so many men. But Germany, like Russia, America, or Slobovia, is something special. Germany is the Germans.

The national behavior of Germany between 1933 and 1945—and, it would seem, of most Germans—indicates a character that is just about as unattractive as a character can be. Among the million or so who ran, or tried to run, away from National Socialism, there were many who opposed it on principle. Maybe a million more fought it, or tried to fight it, from within. A few million more didn't like it. But so many Germans liked it (and not just some of it, but all of it) that it may justly be said to have represented the predominant national character of the time. And National Socialism, made in Germany, out of the German character, is the worst thing that modern man has made.

Worse, certainly, than Communism; for it is not the performance of political systems which justifies or condemns them, but their principles. Communism, in principle, supposes itself to represent the wretched of the earth and bars no man by nature from Communist redemption; the Nazis, in categorical contrast, took themselves to be the elite of the earth and consigned whole categories of men to perdition by their nature. The distinctions between these two totalitarianisms may not command much interest in the present temper of the Western Christian; they are still distinctions.

National Socialism could have happened elsewhere in the modern world, but it hasn't yet. Up to now it is unique to Germany. And the deception and self-deception it required were required of a people whose civilization, by common measurement, was very highly advanced. German music and art, German belles-lettres and philosophy, German science and technology, German theology and education (especially at the highest levels) were part and parcel of Western achievement. German honesty, industry, family virtue, and civil government were the pride of other Western countries where Germans settled. "I think," says Professor Carl Hermann, who never left his homeland, "that even now the outside world does not realize how surprised we non-Nazis were in 1933. When mass dictatorship occurred in Russia, and then in Italy, we said to one another, 'That is what happens in backward countries. We are fortunate, for all our troubles, that it cannot happen here.' But it did, worse even than elsewhere, and I think that all the explanations leave some mystery. When I think of it all, I still say, with unbelief, 'Germany—no, not Germany.' "

The Germans resist all ready-to-hand analysis of social behavior. Every important factor in their development has been present in the development of other peoples who have not, at least recently, behaved themselves as badly as the Germans. To say that they were Christianized late is too easy; so were the Scandinavians. To say that the notion of equality, connected or unconnected with Christianity, is new to Germany will not do, either; the Peasant Wars of the sixteenth century were certainly egalitarian. The Germans were nationalized late, it is true, but so were the Swiss, comparatively, and the Italians were just as late. Industrialism was a century late coming to Germany, but it was later still coming to Czechoslovakia and Finland, and it hasn't reached India yet.

All these tardinesses are, applied to the Germans, marginal or, at best, inconclusive. There is only one easy inference left—that there is something not just different, but uniquely different, about the Germans. The minor consequence of this easy inference is the proliferation of theories about the Germans, and of studies to bolster or undo them. This proliferation has reached the point where being studied is the most crowded single profession in Germany. The foreigner (except the Frenchman, who is immune to the Germans) cannot spend a week in the country without coming down with a pernicious case of theory.

But the major consequence of this inference is something much more dreadful—namely, its acceptance by the Germans themselves. And the Germans do not, as we know, go half-hog about anything. The theory—passion, rather; for that is what theory becomes when it falls into German hands—that there is something different about the Germans was the wellspring of National Socialism. But it pervades German culture, Nazi, non-Nazi, anti-Nazi, and pre-Nazi. It posits the existence of a "German spirit" as something apart and, above all, very interesting. Croce, a "confessed Germanophile," observing everywhere in Germany the inscriptions *deutsche Treue*, *deutsche Tapferkeit*, *deutsche Grossmut*, German fidelity, German valor, German generosity, wryly decided that the Germans had "confiscated for themselves all the common human virtues."

And, as Germans ascribed a spirit to themselves, so they infused other peoples with other, non-German and (on the basis of local pride) inferior spirits. The behavior of Jews was not to be understood in mundane terms or differentiated as between Jew and Jew; the "Jewish spirit," a notion nebulously supported by misreading the ancients from Moses to Esdras, was adequate to explain the behavior of Jews. And when the behavior of a Jew—or of an Englishman or of a crocodile—was good, as it once in a great while was, and could not be explained by the spirit peculiar to the species involved, it was dismissed as aberration. The rest of the world, falling victim to the "German spirit" fantasy, finally, in an equal and opposite reaction, accepted it as something existent, apart, very interesting, and, on the whole, objectionable.

This "German spirit," taken to the German heart as innate and indelible, created, as any such concept must, a world independent of common sense and of common experience. This "German spirit" created German philosophic idealism uninhibited by history as surely as it created German racism uninhibited by biology. But what created the "German spirit"?

CHAPTER 19

The Pressure Cooker

I have a friend, in America, with whom I once discussed the question of the indeterminate prison sentence for felonies. Himself an opponent of prison sentences of all kinds, he was by way of being a firsthand authority in the field of penology; in his time he had left a half-dozen jails and penitentiaries without, as he put it, permission. When I met him, he was on his way to the Institution for the Criminally Insane at Menard, Illinois. Nobody could break out of Menard. My friend did, a few months later, and when I last heard of him he was at Alcatraz.

"I'll tell you," said Basil Banghart, for that was his name, "what's wrong with the indeterminate sentence. If you tell me to pick up a big rock and carry it, and I say, 'Where to?' and you say, 'To that pile over there,' and the pile is a mile, or two miles, or five miles away, and I say, 'And then can I put it down? and you say, 'Yes,' I can pick it up and carry it. But if I say, 'Where to?' and you say, 'Until I tell you you can put it down,' why, I can't budge it. My condition then is that of a native I met in the United States Penitentiary on Marietta Avenue in Atlanta, Georgia; I am just too po' to tote it."

Every one of my ten National Socialist friends, and a great majority of all the Germans I met, no matter what their political history, their wealth, their status, or their cultivation, all seemed to me to be somehow overloaded with *Überfracht*, excess baggage, which, in the words of Basil Banghart's native, they were too po' to tote. There seems to be something heavy about the Germans—not, to be sure, about all of them, and not in the same degree or in the same form in those who are. How many of them are heavy? How heavy are they? I don't know. I can't imagine. All I know is (as every tourist has observed who has ever got out of the bus) that there seems to be something heavy about the Germans.

Their dumplings, their liturgy, their Blitzkrieg are heavy. So is their humor; they even have a word for the enjoyment of another's misfortune. Their bowing and scraping are heavy, and their operas (and especially their light operas). Their poetry, too, Goethe almost alone excepted (and not always he; read his *Erlkönig*). Fantasists have even said that their women's legs—Marlene Dietrich being the exception here, as Goethe is in poetry—are heavy.

We are in an uproar; our German friends pound the table (we make a note of the fact that they pound the table) and ask if we are to understand that Mozart is heavy? No, we are not; we are to understand that he came from Vienna. Are we to understand that Stefan Georg is heavy? No, we are not; we are to understand that he was exiled to Switzerland. What do we mean by talking about "the Germans"? How would we like it if somebody said that "the Americans" are money-mad? (A cry of, "They are," is heard above the uproar.) How would we like it?— Not at all, but how are we to judge our own madness?

Why is the Germans' politics so desperately heavy; their scholarship so marvelously heavy; their philosophy, with Will, Duty, and Destiny its central terms, even heavier than their public law and their public fountains? Their language—what is there left to say after Mark Twain's *The Awful German Language?*—is so deadly heavy that it cannot be got under way without being pushed from behind. *Strč prst skrz krk*, which is Czech for, "Put your finger through your throat," is a bit heavy, to be sure, but *Die, die die, die die Äpfel gestohlen haben, anzeigen*, is a no less impossible way of saying, in German, "Whoever reports the apple thieves."

You may not say of the Germans (as you do of the Swedes) that you find them dull, for the Germans are capable of the wildest excursions; or (as you do of the Swiss) that you find them smug, for the Germans are most uneasy; or (as you do of the English) that the Germans are pompously reserved, for German pomposity is always assertive (for centuries the high bust has been known to Paris dressmakers as à la prussienne); or (as you do of the Russians) that they are stolid (or, when they're on our side, stoical), for the Germans complain continuously. There is supposed to be something fascinating about the moodiness of the Hungarians; in the Germans this moodiness is manic-depressive, and depressing. What there is about the Germans, let them march or dance, let them roar or sing, is something heavy.

The German's hand is heavy, on his wife and children, on his dog, on himself, on his enemies. His heel is heavy, as we know, and his tread, even when he is mushroom-picking-bent in the woods, is heavy. His woods and his winters, his whole world, are heavy. The German—with, naturally, some several millions of exceptions, including whole provinces—seems to be a heavy, heavy man. How do a people live with the Danes on one side, the French on another, the Poles on another, and the Austrians and Italians on another, and develop a state of being at such extraordinary variance with their neighbors? Only the North Swiss and the Rhenish Dutch, both of whom love nothing less than being taken for Germans, are much like them.

This catalogue of German characteristics is, of course, a moderately mad exaggeration. The whole gamut of variations in persons and places is ignored. German *Moselwein* is as light as French *Moselle* across the river; and Goethe and Dietrich are Germans and, had they lived in the same time and town, might have been very good friends. Who has not seen a Scotsman or a Bengal with a single plane from his clavicle to his occiput—or a German likewise constructed without saying, "Look at that German's neck?" Let us say, then, that there seems to be something heavy about the Germans.

This heaviness has a character of its own. It is not solidity, for the Germans are the most volatile of human compounds; nor is it rest, for the Germans are the eagerest of beavers. It is not a dead weight which has gone just about as far as it can go and has made its peace with gravity. It has, rather, a living character, exerting a perpetual push and implying a perpetual restraint, like a buttressed wall. It betrays pressure and consequent counterpressure, which between them seem to me to account (better, at least, than any other crude notion) for German autocracy within and German aggression without.

We are speaking, of course, of living substances, persons; and the analogy of the "German spirit" with centripetal and centrifugal interaction is (besides being obvious) bound to be imperfect. Any explanation of human behavior in terms of a single condition, or set of conditions, is oversimplified anyway, and probably unsound. But no durable harm should issue from the pursuit of the analogy if, while we pursue it, we remember that analogy and will-o'-the-wisp are cousins.

To try to account for human behavior on the basis of pressure and counterpressure requires the antecedent recognition that psychological pressure is just as real as "real" pressure. The Germans have, to begin with, more than their share of "real" pressure. I am sorry to have to say that Hitler said that Germany was encircled, because I am sorry to have to say that Hitler was right. Germany has more frontiers—and they are "soft" frontiers—and more historically dissimilar neighbors than any other nation on earth. Its people first knew and became known to the world through the hostile invasion of their land.

It has, by being prepared to invade, and by invading, been defending itself against this invasion, unconsciously since the Spanish succession to the Holy Roman Empire, consciously since the destruction of the Empire by Napoleon. At the Peace of Pressburg, in 1805, the full focus of European pressure finally fell upon the future German nation, and there it remains. From Richelieu to Barthou the first principle of French policy was the encirclement of Germany; the mortality of "Schuman Plan" ministries in France since the first fine flush of post-1945 *rapprochement* suggests that the principle is still operative.

The North Sea, far from being an open coast, has been the "northern front" against Germany since the seventeenth century. A hostile Denmark and an unfriendly (and often hostile) Netherlands pressed in upon that one German outlet, with England and Sweden behind them. The French seized it in the eighteenth century, and the English sealed it in the nineteenth. The first World War ended with the "central powers," that is, Germany, more central than ever—doubly encircled, geographically by the partition of Austria-Hungary and the erection of Czechoslovakia and the Corridor, politically by the world alliance which excluded Germany and Russia. It was not anti-Semitism or socialism or the New Order that first animated the Nazis; their first slogan was, "Break the chains of Versailles." *Der alte Fritz* had broken the circle, by making peace with Russia in 1756, before it was quite completed; *der kleine Adolf* had to begin with the circle closed.

In 1888 Wilhelm II, then Crown Prince, wrote to Bismarck that Russia was "merely waiting for the favorable moment to attack us in alliance with the [French] Republic." Bismarck disagreed, but the year before, as insurance against a two-front war, he had made his secret treaty with the Tsar, agreeing to support the latter's occupation of the entrance to the Black Sea. "I wake up screaming," he wrote later, when Wilhelm accused him of being pro-Russian, "when I dream of our Russian alliance failing." He had reason to; his dismissal, and Wilhelm's abandonment of his policy, brought the French-Russian entente into being and the destruction of Imperial Germany.

What the rest of the world knows as German aggression the Germans know as their struggle for liberation. And this liberation has no more to do with individual liberty than it has in Poland or Abyssinia or South Korea—nothing whatever. "I don't want what belongs to nobody else," says the peasant in the story, "I only want what j'ines mine." Every aggression is a defense—at worst, a premature defense—including that of September 1, 1939. Were not the French and the English, in July and August, making frantic overtures to Moscow, to tighten the circle of Europe? Were they letting their ideological differences with the Communists embarrass them? Why should the Germans? Who (except, of course, the innocents who read and write the newspapers) could suppose that ideology had anything to do with it? Twelve hard years later Herr Schumacher, the Social Democratic leader, arose in the German Bundestag to say, "The German military contribution makes sense if the world democracies will defend Germany offensively to the east."

"Defend Germany offensively." Wilhelm's plea for "a place in the sun" is identical with Hitler's for "living space." In 1914 the great German economy bestrode the Continent; in 1939 Germany's population density was lower than England's. The problem had something, but only something, to do with population density and economics, still less with colonies. Germany's need was *every* place in the sun, *all* the living space. The man who dreams that he can't breathe in a telephone booth can't breathe in a circus tent. Bismarck's nightmare is the perpetual nightmare of Germany.

Proponents of the theory of aggression as a conscious, purposive pattern of German history—still more, those who propound it as German nature—have always had a hard time explaining Bismarck's indifference to both colonial expansion and Pan-Germanism. He armed Germany to the steepletops, created a naked power state faster than any man in history except Friedrich Wilhelm I and Adolf Hitler, and what was his purpose? His purpose never wavered; with power and even with war as his means, it was the perpetuation of the German Reich which he saw himself as having completed.

External pressure—real or imaginary, it doesn't matter which—produced the counterpressures of German rigidity and German outbreak, the ordered, explosive propensity of the pressure cooker. How rigid will the rigidity be, how big the outbreak? The answer is: How great is the pressure?

Ask the carrot in the cooker how far out it wants to go, or the German dictator to set a limit to his requirements. The transition from the Lincolnian sentiment of *Deutschland über Alles*, "The Union above the States," to its latter-day implication of world domination was inevitable; there is no basis for supposing that the Germany we have known recently would stop short of world domination, or stop there. How much air does the man in the nightmare need when he cries out, "I can't breathe"?

What do we find inside the pressure cooker, among the carrots? We find the perfect pattern of organization, be it in the street-cleaning department, the Church, or the concentration camp, in the Hegelian order of the morally absolute State or the Kantian order of the morally absolute universe. Who has ever reached for the stars like the Germans, breaking asunder the bindings of reality that constrict the human heart and restrain that teetering creature, the reasonable man? Reality's ambivalence makes Hamlets—cowards, say Hamlet and Hitler, who burned *Hamlet*—of us all. Hitler cut all the knots that freemen fumble with. He did not resolve the problems that immobilized his people; he smashed them. He was the grand romantic. I asked my friend Simon, the "democratic" bill-collector, what he liked best about Hitler. "Ah," he said at once, "his '*So—oder so*,' his 'Whatever I have to do to have my way, I will have my way.'"

CHAPTER 20

"Peoria über Alles"

Take Germany as a city cut off from the outside world by flood or fire advancing from every direction. The mayor proclaims martial law, suspending council debate. He mobilizes the populace, assigning each section its tasks. Half the citizens are at once engaged directly in the public business. Every private act—a telephone call, the use of an electric light, the service of a physician—becomes a public act. Every private right—to take a walk, to attend a meeting, to operate a printing press—becomes a public right. Every private institution—the hospital, the church, the club—becomes a public institution. Here, although we never think to call it by any name but pressure of necessity, we have the whole formula of totalitarianism.

The individual surrenders his individuality without a murmur, without, indeed, a second thought—and not just his individual hobbies and tastes, but his individual occupation, his individual family concerns, his individual needs. The primordial community, the tribe, re-emerges, its preservation the first function of all its members. Every normal personality of the day before becomes an "authoritarian personality." A few recalcitrants have to be disciplined (vigorously, under the circumstances) for neglect or betrayal of their duty. A few groups have to be watched or, if necessary, taken in hand—the antisocial elements, the liberty-howlers, the agitators among the poor, and the known criminal gangs. For the rest of the citizens—95 per cent or so of the population—duty is now the central fact of life. They obey, at first awkwardly but, surprisingly soon, spontaneously.

The community is suddenly an organism, a single body and a single soul, consuming its members for its own purposes. For the duration of the emergency the city does not exist for the citizen but the citizen for the city. The harder the city is pressed, the harder its citizens work for it and the more productive and efficient they become in its interest. Civic pride becomes the highest pride, for the end purpose of all one's enormous efforts is the preservation of the city. Conscientiousness is the highest virtue now, the common good the highest good. (Is it any wonder that the German people, whose nation disorders the world, have established the world's best-ordered cities, the Milwaukees of America as well as of Germany?)

What if the emergency persists, not for weeks, months, or even years, but for generations and for centuries? Unrelieved sacrifice requires compensation in the only specie available. Peoria—let Peoria be our beleaguered city—is seen, little by little, to be different from Quincy, Springfield, Decatur. It is something special to be a Peorian, something, if say so we must, heroic. Tales of the founding of Peoria, once taken lightly, reveal that our city was no ordinary city to begin with. Legends turn out to be true. No wonder Peoria sticks it out, sees it through; see the stuff Peorians are made of, always were. Peorians are superior people, superior blood and superior bone; their survival proves it.

Their ancestors, they recall, established the city against the most fearful odds; their descendants will deliver it against odds more fearful still. There will be a New Peoria, a Greater Peoria, a Thousand-Year Peoria. The world will ring with its timeless fame, kneel at its topless towers. And Peoria will be a model to mankind; Peorian courage, Peorian endurance, Peorian patriotism—these will be a model to a world that, because it has never been tried like Peoria, has grown soft, decadent, plutocratic, has fallen prey to rot and to the parasites that rot carries with it.

And whom, meanwhile, among Peorians, have we called to the helm in our hour, our aeon, of struggle, in our place of danger?—Peorians who are tried and true, men who have served their city and never disserved it, men who have represented the best of Peoria to the world, who have always known its glories and extolled them. We want the Old Guard, not the *avant-garde*; the doers, not the do-nothings; the clear thinkers, not the skeptics; the believers in Peoria, not the complainers and the cranks. We don't want the men who always wanted to make Peoria over and who see our trial as their opportunity; this, of all times, is no time for divisiveness.

The things that a country honors will be cultivated there. What shall we teach the young Peorians, who will follow us? What life shall we hold out to them as the highest life? —Why, the life they will have to live to deliver their city, in a Peoria oppressed and encircled. The flabby and effete must go, and with it the dabbling, the faddism, the free thinking that squander our people's time and their energies, divert them from the overriding need of their city, and debase their tastes and their morals. Peorianism is, as Daniel Webster would have said, foursquare, rock-ribbed, copper-sheathed; red-blooded; undoubting and undivided; staunch, stern, rugged, simple, brave, clean, and true. Every influence on our people (above all, on our young people) will be Peorian.

We Peorians cannot live as others. We would not if we could. See them—Quincy, Springfield, Decatur—hopelessly unprepared for a struggle such as ours, with their niggling parliamentarism (the Lend-Lease debate; the Army-McCarthy hearings), their democratic corruptionism (Teapot Dome; the five-per-centers), their corrosive individualism (Tommy Manville; H. D. Thoreau). See them fattening while Peoria hungers. See them exploiting Peoria's prostration. Quincy, Springfield, Decatur, have always hated Peoria. Why? The answer is suddenly obvious: because we are better than they are.

Why do the Poles, egged on by the English, or the Serbs, egged on by the Russians, begin these world wars against Germany? The chauvinist braggadocio of my ten Nazi friends—excluding the teacher and, to a lesser degree, the cabinetmaker and the bank clerk—was of an order, I thought at first, that I had never before encountered. And then I remembered: the "new boy" in the neighborhood at home, on the Calumet Avenue of my childhood, ringed round by the neighborhood gang and trying to brazen it out alive. "Betcha my father can beat your father." Betcha my fatherland can beat yours.

"The whole world has always been jealous of Germany," said my friend the bill-collector, "and why not?—We Germans are the leaders in everything."

"We Germans," said my friend the tailor, the only one of the ten who deserved to be called an ignoramus, and a lazy ignoramus to boot, "are the most intelligent people in the world, and the hardest working. Is it any wonder that they hate us? Have you ever seen a Jew or an Englishman work when he didn't have to?"

"Twice we have had to fight the whole world, all alone," said the baker. "What good are the Italians or the Japanese?"

But I could always count on the tailor to go the whole hog: "We won *both* wars, and *both* times we were betrayed."

CHAPTER 21

New Boy in the Neighborhood

Germany is the "new boy" in the neighborhood of the Western world. The one durable consequence of the first World War was the unification of a Germany some of whose states, up until then, had their own kings and courts, their own armies, ambassadors, and postal systems. And even the war did not complete the unification; Bavaria and Prussia, which hated one another, both defied the Weimar Republic with impunity, the one from the right, the other from the left.

Nationhood was nominally forced upon the dozens of "Sovereign German States" in 1871 by Prussia, of which the King of Württemberg had said, a half-century earlier, "Prussia belongs as little to Germany as does Alsace." The nonexistent Germany of 1870 was composed *entirely* of foreigners, ethnically and historically so hodgepodged that an East Prussian or a Bavarian was just as likely to be taken for a Pole or an Austrian as for a German. Only by his language could a German be distinguished, and not always then; Low and High German are as mutually unintelligible as German and Dutch.

The language itself—a *Mischmasch*, Leibniz called it—reflected the German miscegenation, the "disgrace" which the elite passed on to the populace. "I have never read a German book," the greatest of all German heroes boasted at the end of the eighteenth century; and his friend Voltaire wrote home from the Prussian court, "We all talk French. German is left for soldiers and horses." Pre-Nazi nationalism tried to drive "loan" words out of the language—even universal European terms like *Telefon*—and Nazi nationalism intensified the campaign. But in vain; German remained a *Mischmasch*.

German nationalism was, and still is, the effort to create a German nation. The independence of the old German States had its merits, in spite of the ridiculous fragmentation it perpetuated and the dozens of ossified nobilities and their clumsy Ruritania courts in imitation of a Versailles long gone. Culture flourished (to be sure, at the whim of whimsical princes), but it was under such princes, and with their self-serving patronage, that German culture was great. It would be very nice, said Goethe to Eckerman, to cross the thirty-six States without having one's trunk examined thirty-six times, "but if one imagines the unity of Germany with a single large capital for the whole nation, and that this great capital would encourage the development of genius or contribute to the welfare of the people, he is wrong."

The nationalization of Germany, although it came too late to perform the historic function it performed everywhere else, was not to be stopped. When the liberal philosopher Feuerbach wrote his friend Friedrich Kapp, "I would not give a row of pins for unity unless it rests on liberty," Kapp, a "Forty-eighter," who had left his Fatherland to find liberty, wrote back from America: "To be sure, it is disagreeable that Bismarck, and not the democrats, achieved this magnificent consolidation, that the reactionary Junkers and bureaucrats of old Prussia rule. But are not the results achieved, and does it matter *who* is responsible for such a great achievement?"

Germany was a nation, but in 1871 it was prematurely a nation; in 1914 and in 1918 still prematurely. Like all parvenus, the German nation had, and still has, a compulsion to display its wealth, its nationhood, and a desperate terror of losing it, not of being broken apart from without, but, more terribly, of falling apart within. Englishmen and Frenchmen know that they are Englishmen and Frenchmen; when I asked a Danish Communist whether, in his heart, he was a Dane or a Communist, he said, "What a silly question; every Dane is a Dane." But the German has to be reassured that he is a German. The German pressure cooker required, and still requires, the fierce, fusing fire of fanaticism under it.

Russia and the United States of America have both, until recently, at least, been spared this peculiar experience of German nationalism, partly because of their longer national history, partly because of their isolation. Like the other two "Pans," Pan-Slavism and Pan-Americanism, expansionist Pan-Germanism is the none-too-paradoxical consequence of the dread of decomposition. As long as the self-consciously fragile German nation is threatened, internally no less than externally, it will threaten the world, and foreign statesmen who divide the Germans into our friends and *their* friends would do well to be mindful that those Germans who are neither, or who are one today and the other tomorrow, are thinking of Germany, not of Democracy or Communism.

Just as German nationalism was the effort to create a nation, so German racism was the effort to create a race out of a geographical group none of whose stocks, according to all the available pre-Nazi measurements, was Nordic.

Ethnical heterogeneity is greater among the Germans (taking the Austrians as Germans) than it is among any other of the world's peoples except the Russians and the Americans.

True, my ten friends, not one of whom met or even approached the Nordic standard, rejected their own "Aryanism." But they did accept a kind of racist "Germanism," a biologized mystique which, I was surprised to discover, they were not alone in accepting. A university graduate of the pre-Nazi era, an anti-Nazi intellectual, when I asked her how many Jews there were still in Kronenberg, said, "Almost none—but, then, you would have to take biological as well as historical and religious data to find out exactly."

My friend Simon, he of the secret Talmud, when he told me that, yes, the Jew Springer was a decent man, and I asked him how there could be a decent Jew when the "Jewish spirit" was a matter of blood, replied: "Of course it's a matter of blood. It might skip a generation"—he had certainly not read Mendel—"but it would show up in the next. Only when the proportion of Jewish blood is small enough will it no longer be a danger to *Deutschtum*." "How small," I said, "would it have to be?" "The scientists have that worked out," he said.

Herr Simon was not alone in his preoccupation with "pollution." The tailor's son, Schwenke, spoke frequently of the "race injury," the relations between "Aryans" and "non-Aryans" of opposite sexes, the special province of the Nazi SS. He and Simon both told me, in some genuine terror, mixed, I felt, with some of the titillation always involved in discussing sexual relations, that Jewish householders invariably hired "German" housemaids (this much was true, since housemaids came largely from the peasant or unskilled working classes), for the express purpose of "ruining" them. Neither Schwenke nor Simon, of course, had any evidence.

Once—as far as I could learn, only once—a Jew was seen walking through the streets of Kronenberg wearing a sandwich-board sign reading, *Ich habe ein aryanisches Mädchen beschändet*, "I have ruined an Aryan maiden."

"No one looked at him," said Policeman Hofmeister.

"Why?"

"Everyone felt sorry for him."

"Why?"

"Because it was such—such nonsense."

"Nonsense?"

"Yes. Here's a Jewish boy. He has a German"—non-Jewish, the policeman meant—"girl friend. They quarrel. That can happen. They call each other names, then threaten each other. Now they hate each other, although maybe they are still in love; you know, that can happen, Herr Professor. She threatens to denounce him. He dares her to, and she does. And then this—this nonsense."

Policeman Hofmeister was less remorseful about the gypsies, whose treatment was, if anything, more horrible than that of the Jews and who had no voice anywhere in all the world to cry out for them. The gypsies, said Policeman Hofmeister, who would not have said this about the Jews, were *Menschen zweiten Grades*, second-class humans, submen. "The idea," he said, "was to preserve the pure gypsies," the biologically pure, that is, "to preserve them intact, if possible, although, of course, outside the framework of German rights. But the gypsy *Mischlinge*, the mongrels, the half-breeds, were a great danger to the race, through intermingling. Gypsy blood"—I thought of the waltz—"was bad. Still"—here was a good man speaking, who *thought* he believed in "blood" and not in social determinants—"one felt sorry for them, for the conditions in which they had to live, without homes or towns or decent provisions for their children. How could they help themselves?"

"You will have to admit, Herr Professor," said Baker Wedekind, "that Hitler got rid of the beggars and the gypsies. That was a good thing. The gypsies had lots of children, charming children, too, whom they taught to cheat and steal. In the village, in my childhood, we locked our doors when gypsies were there; otherwise, never. They were an alien race, alien blood." He, too, would not have said that I should have to admit that Hitler had done a good thing in getting rid of the Jews.

I think that what worried Policeman Hofmeister and Baker Wedekind was their own common knowledge. The achievements of Jews in every field in which the "Germans" excelled gave rise to an essentially schizoid condition in my friends. The inferior race, the Jews, was also, like the Germans themselves, superior. The gypsies would have made a better Devil for German racism, if only the Devil were not, by definition, superhuman as well as inferior. The gypsies were adequately inferior, but they were not, in German terms, superhuman. They were, quite literally, such *poor* Devils. The Jew would have to do—if he could be distinguished from the German.

CHAPTER 22

Two New Boys in the Neighborhood

In other countries governments have been willing to foment and exploit—but always deplore—anti-Semitism. In Germany, and in Germany alone, was it made the cornerstone of public policy. Why? The peculiar ferocity of civil war, the war of brother against brother, comes to mind as hypothesis. The hypothesis is not original; Rauschning says that Hitler once told him that the Germans and the Jews could not live together because they were too much alike.

The Germans and the Jews are wonderfully alike. There are, of course, great and obvious differences between them, because the Jews are few, scattered, anciently civilized, and southern in origin, while the Germans are many, concentrated, primitive, and northern. That the Jew is tasteful and epicurean, more so than the German, is the mere consequence of his geographical origin and his cultural age. That he is subtle, much more so than the German, is the mere consequence in part of his geographical origin, in part of his defenselessness. That his passion for individual independence is exalted, as the German's is not, is the mere consequence of the world's pariahism; and his interest in righteousness, which is not nearly so prominent among the Germans, the mere consequence of the unrighteousness of that pariahism.

There is (or, until very recently, was) no Jewish nation

to suffer pressure and put consequent pressure on both its members and the outside world. It is the *individual* Jew who is both object and subject of the pressures which, in Germany's case, are sustained and exerted by the nation. Germany's internal Diaspora, the first Thirty Years' War, set the stage for German romanticism and German aggressiveness. The history of the combative, incurably restless German nation begins with the reduction of Germany to the depths. The history of the individual Jew is parallel. But what the German nation could seek by weight—its restoration, its "place"—the Jewish individual had to seek by speed.

The dispersed and scattered Jews—who were once much more fiercely tribal than the Germans—were compelled by their situation to become cosmopolitans. This forced cosmopolitanism of the isolated Jew has two polar consequences. Oppressed by each nation, the Jew must be the reformer of the nation, as Germany, isolated and oppressed by the world, must be the reformer of the world. At the same time the Jew must be the most adjustable of men. Except for his religion—which, in the modern West, is weak—he has no continuing mold to contain and shape him. He has nothing to hold to, to fall back upon, to hide behind when war, revolution, famine, tyranny, and persecution sweep over him. He has nothing to turn to but God.

The German has Germany. The German individual, living his changeless generations in his own land, among his own people, and on his own soil, has had no need for adjustability and has never developed it. What for the Jew is the central problem of life does not—I must say *did* not, for times are changing—exist for the German.

From the Castle hill in Kronenberg one can still see the country German in the second half of the twentieth century—the thousand-skirted costumes (the Protestant and Catholic aprons tied differently), the oxen (and often the women and the children) pulling a perforated cheese cask on wheels through the fields for irrigation. The first World War shook the little valleys; on the walls of a village church one counts a hundred memorial wreaths from the first World War, in a village of a thousand population. The peasant youth began to move to the towns. The second World War blew the town and city people out of their houses and packed the railroad trains and the roads.

After 1918 the immobile German, incapable of adjusting to the new conditions inflicted upon him, turning romantically and meaninglessly toward the hope of restoring the old, found himself bewildered and increasingly helpless, while the Jew was in the element in which, through no fault (or virtue) of his own, he thrives best: changing conditions, requiring rapid and radical adjustment. Instead of saying that the Jews were the "decomposing element" in Imperial Rome—a favorite citation of the Nazis— Mommsen should have said that the Jew was able, because he had to be, to adjust himself to a decomposing, as to any other kind, of Rome.

Between 1918 and 1933 this marginal man, the Jew, this *Luftmensch*, this man in the air, in a situation which put a premium on speed and a penalty on weight, rose to such power in a decomposing Germany that his achievement looked dangerously like that of a superman. But wasn't the German to be the superman?—Very well, then. The order in which the Jew was usurping this role would have to be reversed, the standards of supermanliness redefined to fit the German. Superman, the German, would not adjust to this world; he would adjust it. *So—oder so.*

The pliant German, beaten into shape by centuries of

nonresistance, could not compete with the subtle Jew. Germany, the marginal nation, had always had to struggle to survive—but not the German. The German had only to do as he was told, while to do as he was told would have been fatal to the Jew. The Jew had to take chances, and so did the German nation. But the German individual, unless he was crazy drunk, could not take chances. The Jew did not drink; he had to be light to live. The German nation had to drink to lighten itself, and what do nations drink but blood?

In Germany or in England or in Russia, everywhere, indeed, except in the lost Homeland, the Jew had to be light as a feather and fast as the wind. Like Germany—but not like the German—he was hemmed in by hostile neighbors. He had to fight—honorably, if possible, dishonorably, if necessary, like the German nation. He was driven, like the German nation, to every extreme and every excess of good and evil, and his situation evoked in him whatever geniuses survival required of him. Moses Mendelssohn and the Jewish pander were both Jews, just as the Germany of Schiller and that of Streicher were both Germany. Germany is the Jew among nations.

"They are always *insisting* on something," the hostess of one of the presently decrepit but eternally fashionable resort hotels on Lago Maggiore said. She was speaking of the Germans collectively. "One can't say just what it is that they seem to be insisting on. But they are uncomfortable, and they *must* make the management and the rest of the guests uncomfortable. Just like the Jews." "*What?*" I said, collectively insulted. She laughed. "Not every Jew," she said, "and, of course, not every German; only enough of them to make one think, always, 'the Germans.' Perhaps I am prejudiced. I am half-German myself."

Being beset, in fancy and in reality, has produced in the Jews and in the German nation the compensatory assertion of superiority and messianism. Each of them must save the world; so only, saving the world, are Germany and the Jew to be saved. But neither is evangelistic. Conversion (which implies humility) and love (which implies submission) have no place in either's mission. The remaining alternative is mastery; mastery, of course, for the sake of the mastered. In the Germans the necessary means of mastery, imposed upon the benefactors by the intransigence of the prospective beneficiaries, were lately seen to be genocide. But genocide was not unknown, once, to the Jews, and, if survival requires excessive measures, the salvation of the whole world ennobles their use.

To other, less hard-pressed, peoples, the prejudice of the Jew against intermarriage is unintelligible. Among Westerners, only the Nazis share this prejudice. Doctrinal restrictions are not involved, as they are among Christians, where the prohibition against marriage is dissolved by conversion. To the Nazi the Jew is forever a Jew; to the Jew the non-Jew is always a non-Jew. In both cases the inference of taint is inescapable. And in neither the Nazi (who is nothing but the German stripped of religion) nor the Jew is there any confidence that the threatened taint might be diluted or dissipated; in both, the overriding concern is purity. That this arrogation of purity is an impudence other peoples than the Germans and the Jew will agree. But other peoples live in a different world from the Jew and the Germans. These two live in a world of their own.

The German Jew was the perfect German. The *Jewish Encyclopaedia* has, I suppose, fifty times as many citations of German specialists as of all the Jews all over the rest of the world together. Was there ever a "better" German than Bismarck's adviser, the Jew Bleichröder, or than Wilhelm II's, the Jew Ballin? And who but the Jew Stahl laid the constitutional foundations for what we call "Prussianism" in Germany? It is the *German* Jew who, in a minority, will soon or late dominate Israel; already we hear, in Israel, of what we think of as peculiarly German forms of extremist tendency, the same tendency toward "Nazi" behavior observed among the Jewish prisoners in Buchenwald by Professor Bruno Bettelheim.

And how this German Jew loved his Germany, for which he was willing to give up his Judaism! How German he seemed to be abroad, so much so that everywhere in the Allied countries in the first World War the Jew was suspected of being pro-German! What happened to him from 1933 on he could not believe; he stayed on, until 1936, until 1938, until 1942, until—. "It won't last," he told himself. What made him think it wouldn't? Why, this was Germany, his Germany. And now, in England and America, in France and Brazil and Mexico, there is a new kind of Jew, the Jew who has learned, when he speaks of those who a few years ago were his countrymen in his beloved country, to say "the Germans," to distinguish them, just as Hitler did, from the Jews.

The "Lorelei," the song of the witch of the Rhine who dazzles and wrecks the boatman, is the German people's most popular song, not today, or yesterday, but always; so popular that the Nazis did not dare eliminate it from the songbooks. Instead, they included it with the wonderful line, *Dichter unbekannt,* "Author unknown." Every German knew that the author of the most German of all German folksongs was Heinrich Heine. It took Heine, the German Jew, to write in exile:

Ich hatte einst ein schönes Vaterland.
Der Eichenbaum wuchs dort so hoch, die Veilchen
nickten sanft.
Es war ein Traum
Das küsste mich auf deutsch und sprach auf deutsch
(Man glaubt es kaum,
Wie gut es klang) das Wort, "Ich liebe dich!"
Es war ein Traum.

It is untranslatably beautiful:

Once I had a Fatherland.
The oak grew there so great, the violet so small and
sweet.
It was a dream
That kissed me in German and in German spoke
(If only you knew how good it sounded in German!)
The words, "I love you."
It was a dream.

It took Heinrich Heine, the Jewish German, to write: "Better to die than to live, best of all never to have lived." With the world—and themselves?—against them both, both Germany and the Jew appear to be indestructible. The Nazis' "final solution" of "the Jewish question" was the destruction of the Jews, as the world's "final solution" of "the German question," advanced by the Morgenthauites, was the destruction of Germany. We may assume that the Morgenthauite program to reduce Germany to a primitive peasant nation was no more final than the Nazis' program to reduce the Jews of Germany to primitive peasant persons, "working on the land." What the world was too civilized to do (or to attempt to do), the Nazis were not. But the Nazis no more succeeded in reducing the status of the Jews than the world succeeded in reducing the status of Germany. German recovery, a few years after the lost war in 1945, was the wonder of the world. And the twenty thousand Jews left in Germany were on their way to greater distinction, in both the highest and lowest endeavors, than ever before.

The survival of Germany is much more easily explained, historically and anthropologically, than the survival of the Jew, two thousand years from his Fatherland and scattered into dozens of hostile environments. He has survived. Perhaps he has survived so that the survival of Germany, and of the Germany we have lately known, might bear witness to the world that there is more in the world than meets the eye. It may be that the explanation of survival is not exhausted by historical and anthropological analysis or by social-psychological curve-making; it may be that Cain's answer to the Lord is relevant, too.

As the fate of the Jews—and of Germany—approached its climax in the last months of the second World War, the *Jüdisches Nachrichtenblatt*, published weekly by the German Jews at the order of the Nazi Government, to communicate "directives" to those of Nazism's victims who were left alive, shrank in size and content and, finally, in frequency of publication. It shrank, too, in the quality of paper allotted to it, and it is for that reason that I wish to publish, in its original form, on paper which will outlast the March 5, 1943, issue of the *Nachrichtenblatt*, a story which appeared in the lower right-hand corner, on the reverse side of the single sheet, manuscript-paper size, which constituted the publication:

Alles zum Guten

Immer gewöhne sich der Mensch zu denken: "Was Gott schickt ist gut; es dünke mir gut oder böse."

Ein frommer Weiser kam vor eine Stadt, deren Tore geschlossen waren. Niemand wollte sie ihm öffnen; hungrig und durstig musste er unterm freien Himmel übernachten. Er sprach: "Was Gott schickt, ist gut," und legte sich nieder.

Neben ihm stand ein Esel, zu seiner Seite eine brennende Laterne um der Unsicherheit willen in derselben Gegend. Aber ein Sturm entstand und löschte sein Licht aus, ein Löwe kam und zerriss seinen Esel. Er erwachte, fand sich allein und sprach: "Was Gott schickt ist gut." Er erwartete ruhig die Morgenröte.

Als er ans Tor kam, fand er die Tore offen, die Stadt verwüstet, beraupt und geplündert. Ein Schar Räuber war eingefallen und hatte eben in dieser Nacht die Einwohner gefangen weggeführt oder getötet. Er war verschont. "Sagte ich nicht," sprach er, "dass alles, was Gott schickt, gut sei? Nur sehen wir meistens am Morgen erst, warum er uns etwas des Abends versagte."

(Aus dem Talmud).

In English:

Everything Happens for the Best

We know that whatever God sends us, however good or bad it may seem to us, is good.

A pious man came to a city whose gates were closed. No one would open them to let him in. Hungry and thirsty, he had to spend the night outside the gates. Still he said, "Whatever God sends us is good," and he lay down to sleep.

Beside him stood his ass, and his lantern burned to ward off the dangers of the dark. But a storm came up and extinguished the lantern. Then a lion came up and, as the pious man slept, tore the ass to pieces. Awakening, and seeing his plight, the pious man said, "Whatever God sends us is good," and serenely awaited the sunrise.

Day broke. The pious man found the gates open, the city laid waste and plundered. A band of robbers had fallen upon the city during the night and had murdered some of the citizens and enslaved the rest. The pious man had been saved. "Didn't I say," he said to himself, "that whatever God sends us is good? We must wait until morning, and then we will understand the meaning of the night."

(From the Talmud).

CHAPTER 23

"Like God in France"

Substances move, under pressure, to extreme positions and, when they shift positions, shift from one extreme to the other. Men under pressure are drained of their shadings of spirit, of their sympathy (which they can no more give than get), of their serenity, their sweetness, their simplicity, and their subtlety. Their reactions are structuralized; like rubber balls (which we say have "life" in them because they react in such lively fashion to the living impulse outside them), the harder they are bounced, the higher they go. Such men, when they are told not to cut down a tree, won't cut down a tree, but when they are not told not to cut down a man, they may cut down a man.

The German who is dedicated to instant self-immolation for the sake of Germany is the same German whose day-to-day egotism amazes the world. This egotism, always "idealized" (that is, romanticized), is, as has often been observed, the very heart of German philosophy; but it is also the basis of the habitual callousness of ordinary life. It is as if there were, in the human heart, only so much selflessness; pressure requires so much of it of the Germans that they are left with almost none for volition.

I know that the unconcern for others displayed, say, by the American who plays a hotel-room radio late at night, is everywhere common in an individualistic civilization except, perhaps, among the English; but nowhere, not even

275

among the English, are "manners" as rigidly emphasized as they are among the Germans, and nowhere as among these people who swarm to tribal sacrifice have I seen men so invariably fail to offer old women their seats in busses, streetcars, or trains. Nowhere have I seen so many old men and women staggering through train sheds with heavy suitcases and never an offer of assistance from the empty-handed, nowhere such uniform disinclination to assist on the scene of an accident or to intervene between children fighting on the street. But the *service* in German hotels, restaurants, and stores is superb. One "minds one's own business" in the small affairs of the street, in the larger affairs of the job or the family, in the great affairs of the State.

Grimly preoccupied with themselves; deadly serious and deadly dull (only the Germans could have been unbored by Hitler); tense, hurried, unrelaxed; purpose-bedeviled, always driven somewhere to do something; taking the siesta like Communion, with determined, urgent intent; sneering, and not always genteelly, at the Frenchman sitting "doing nothing" at his café (wie *Gott in Frankreich,* "like God in France," is the German expression for "carefree"), at the Italian talking his head off over his endless dinner; incapable of quiet without melancholy or frustrated fury; insatiably hungry for the heights or the depths, stone sober or roaring drunk; forever insisting that man is born to suffer —and then begrudging the suffering; unresponsive and over-reactive; stodgy and unstable; uncalm, the inventors and prime practitioners of "stomach trouble"; tormented, exhausted, unable to remain fully awake unless they are angry or hilarious—these, with more than a little hyperbole, with millions of exceptions and contradictions and still more millions of variations, are the ways and the woes of men under pressure.

Men under pressure are first dehumanized and only then demoralized, not the other way around. Organization and specialization, system, subsystem, and supersystem are the consequence, not the cause, of the totalitarian spirit. National Socialism did not make men unfree; unfreedom made men National Socialists.

Freedom is nothing but the habit of choice. Now choice is remarkably wide in this life. Each day begins with the choice of tying one's left or right shoelace first, and ends with the choice of observing or ignoring the providence of God. Pressure narrows choice forcibly. Under light pressure men sacrifice small choices lightly. But it is only under the greatest pressure that they sacrifice the greatest choices, because choice, and choice alone, informs them that they are men and not machines.

The ultimate factor in choosing is common sense, and it is common sense that men under pressure lose fastest, cut off as they are (in besieged "Peoria") from the common condition. The harder they are pressed, the harder they reason; the harder they *must* reason. But they tend to become unreasonable men; for reasonableness is reason in the world, and "Peoria" is out of this world.

The besieged intellect operates furiously; the general intelligence atrophies. Theories are evolved of the grandest order and the greatest complexity, requiring only the acceptance of the nonworlds, the Ideas, in which they arise. The two extremist doctrines that have seized hold of our time—Marx's, denying that there is anything in man, and Freud's, denying that there is anything outside—are Made in Germany. If you will only accept Marx's "human nature has no reality" or Freud's "conscience is nothing but the dread of the community," you will find them both irresistibly scientific.

In such exquisitely fabricated towers a man may live (or even a whole society), but he must not look over the edge or he will see that there is no foundation. The fabrication is magnificent; the German is matchless in little things, reckless only in big ones, in the fundamental, fateful matters which, in his preoccupation, he has overlooked. That a Wagner should be a vulgar anti-Semite (or stand on his head, or wear a ring in his nose, or whatever) is one thing; he was "only a genius." But that one of Germany's two greatest historians, Treitschke, should be a ravening chauvinist, that the other, Mommsen, should find in Julius Caesar "the complete and perfect man"—these are something else. Max Weber could be "the father of sociology," but he could not see what was sociologically unhealthy in the institution of student dueling.

Who is this Einstein, who was "only a scientist" when he conceived the atomic bomb and now, in his old age, sees what he has done and weeps? He is the German specialist, who had always "minded his"—high—"business" and was no more proof against romanticism than his tailor, who had always minded his low business. He is the finished product of pressure, the uneducated expert, like the postal clerk in Kronenberg whose method of moistening stamps on the back of his hand is infallible. The German mind, encircled and, under pressure of encirclement, stratified, devours itself in the production of lifeless theories of man and society, deathless methods of licking postage stamps, and murderous machinery. For the rest—which is living— the German has to depend upon his ideals.

CHAPTER 24

But a Man Must Believe in Something

It is the Germans' ideals which are dangerous; their practices, when their ideals do not have hold of them, are not
a bit better or worse than other men's. Where do they get
their ideals? "The 'passions,'" says Santayana, "is the old
and fit name for what the Germans call ideals." This ideal-
ist slave of his own or another man's passions was twice
sundered from Rome, in A.D. 9 and in A.D. 1555. In the
year 9 the Germans expelled the founders of secular Europe;
in 1555 they cut themselves loose from the *Weltanschauung*
which the age of the Mediterranean fused in Italy from the
Greco-Hebraic break with Syria and Egypt. This bright
Weltanschauung rests upon the dogma of personal responsibility. This dogma is the first fact of our civilization. Its
repulse left Germany peculiarly rootless.

Thought, like feeling, took root in irresponsibility, with
subjectivism, relativism, "intelligent skepticism" its flower.
It was not only in physics or in government that the Germans excelled in producing Frankenstein's monsters but in
epistemology itself. Thought is all, but there are a thousand ways of thinking. The thinker can attach no worth
to his thinking as against another man's because there is no
reality to measure them both, only internal consistency,
"system." At the same time no other man's system is, by
definition, better than his. The superiority of the thinking
lies—somewhere—in the thinker.

"A trite, nauseatingly repulsive, ignorant charlatan without *esprit*, who with unexampled impertinence scribbled
together twaddle and nonsense, which his venal adherents
trumpeted forth . . . the hollowest farrago of words devoid
of sense that ever satisfied dunderheads . . . repulsive . . .
recalls the ravings of madmen." This is a philosophical critique by one of Germany's greatest philosophers, Schopenhauer, of another of Germany's greatest philosophers, Hegel.
The "pedantic arrogance" of which Goethe complained in
the Germans was the self-assuredness not of common,
Western dogma but of the antidogmatic who, needing, like
all men, dogma to live by, had none to fall back on but
his own. Each man was his own "school"; you did not go to
Germany to get an education but to get a man or, more
exactly, a mind. The characteristic German professor did
not know the students or meet them (and there were no
student deans or advisers). He was a thinker, and a teacher
of thinking.

Cut from its moorings in Western dogma, German thinking shot up unencumbered to the clouds. Balloons ascended
everywhere. Which basket the fortunate few boarded was
a matter of fancy and favoritism; once they were off the
ground, they were all equally impervious to puncture by
reality down below. "He stands up there," said Willy Hofmeister, the old policeman; "I stand down here. I can't
argue with him. I'm not stupid, but he's spent his whole
life studying. He knows. I don't." He was contrasting *wir
Einfachen*, we simple people, with *die Gebildeten*, the cultivated.

Down below were *wir Einfachen*, the millions who were
some day to be Nazis, the "little men" who, as Balzac put it,
seemed to have been sent into the world to swell the crowd.
When I was first in Germany I asked a German theologian

to help me find one such "little man," one whom National Socialism had confronted with *innerlicher Konflikt*, moral struggle. The theologian replied: "Moral struggle?—They had none. They are all little sausages, *Würstchen*." German thought soared away from the *Würstchen*, carrying with it the elect, for whom the educational system above the eighth grade existed, and the stage and the philharmonic and the bookstores. For the rest—let the greatest of the great German masters say it:

> He who has Science has Art,
> Religion, too, has he;
> Who has not Science, has not Art,
> Let him religious be.

For the rest, there were the churches and the songs of Heaven and Home. At the Kronenberg Singfest, held in the auditorium of Kronenberg University at Easter, I saw not one of my academic colleagues. But eight of my ten "little men" were there.

To the extent that the big men influenced the little men, it was to convince them that thought, of which they themselves were incapable, was everything. There is, besides intelligent skepticism, unintelligent skepticism, and it was a long time ago that Nietzsche asserted that Germans *as a whole* were skeptics. The ground fell away from under the churches even while, in the gradually emptying sanctuary, those who were still credulous were promised the invincibility of German arms. When German arms proved vincible, the churches lost still more of the credulous.

But people who do not have a good religion will have a bad one. They will have a religion; they will have something to believe in. Men—not just Germans—cannot bear the pressure of life, however light it may be elsewhere compared with the pressure upon the Germans. Hitlerism was a mass flight to dogma, to the barbaric dogma that had not been expelled with the Romans, the dogma of the tribe, the dogma that gave every man importance only in so far as the tribe was important and he was a member of the tribe. My ten Nazi friends—and a great majority of the rest of the seventy million Germans—swarmed to it. German thought had not bothered to take them along on its flight. It had left them on the ground. Now they are back on the ground again, rooting around the husks of old ideals for a kernel.

The Germans were, when Hitler found them, emotionally undernourished. Life in a besieged city, even relaxation, is unrelievedly rigid. Happiness is dismissed as unattainable —the German word for it is derived from *Glück*, luck—and its pursuit then disdained as decadent. But it is duty-bearers, not pleasure-seekers, who go berserk. The ordinary hours of the German person, day by day, do not feed his hunger for expression. The decline of conversation is a very modern phenomenon, and a world phenomenon wherever the most modern means of mass communication have replaced it; but the malady of repression is something else. Repression is not the same thing as reserve, any more than denial (the Germans are peerless here) is the same as self-denial.

In a stifled, lid-on atmosphere, the "German" way of thinking flourished, exoteric, meticulous, and introverted; flourished in the starved soil of German emotion. National Socialism fructified that soil, and it bloomed suddenly red with fire and blood.

CHAPTER 25

Push-Button Panic

One Saturday afternoon in Kronenberg three house-paint-ers, who were off at noon, got hold of some Weinbrand at our house, and, when we returned from a visit, we found the house torn up and the painters howling drunk. Tante Käthe, our five-foot-tall housekeeper, was with us. She handed them mops and brooms and said, "Clean up and get out." In instant, silent sobriety they cleaned up and got out. They were back Monday morning for work, without a word of apology, a blush of shame, or a man-to-man wink.

The speed of the German is the initial speed of release under pressure, soon spent. Then the pressure reasserts itself, and the German re-emerges as he is: sober, a heavy, heavy man. His personality, under pressure, is just as exces-sively submissive as it is assertive. Its essence is excess. On November 9, 1938, word went through the country that the synagogues were to be burned. A million men, released like jack-in-the-boxes, sprang to action. Pushed back in the boxes, as they were by Göring's order the following morn-ing, a million men dropped their fagots; another sixty-nine million, who had not thought much about it the night be-fore, reproached the million in silence; and the work of arson, robbery, enslavement, torture, and murder proceeded in legalized form, in *Zucht und Ordnung*.

Zucht und Ordnung, discipline and order. My two friends Hofmeister and Schwenke, the policeman and the tailor, who hated one another and who represented two incompatible moralities, agreed that "it doesn't matter whether you call it a democracy or dictatorship or what, as long as you have discipline and order." The sensitive cabinetmaker, Klingelhöfer, and the insensitive bill-collector, Simon, said the same thing. Neither morality nor religion but legality is decisive in a state of perpetual siege. And the attest of legality is order; law and order are not two things but one.

The gas ovens of Belsen were peculiarly German; the improvised slaughter pits of the Ukraine were Nazi. The distinction is a large one. Nazism, like the Lutheran Reformation and all other German upheavals, contained revolutionary elements of improvisation. But Nazism was always at war with the Army. The Army was German. The remarkable fact of the *Putsch* against Hitler of July 20, 1944, is that a handful of Army officers could be found to undertake it; that it was planned so recklessly; that it happened at all, not that it failed or might have succeeded. It was treated as treason. What it was was un-German.

What was truly German was what has come to be called the cold pogrom, the systematic persecution, legal, methodical, and precisely co-ordinated, of the "national enemies." When you have combined "cold" with "pogrom"—they appear to be uncombinable—you have Nazi Germany, the organism *as a whole* gone wild, its organs admirably co-ordinated. The universal witness of the people invaded by the Germans is the nonhumanity of the conqueror, his push-button transition from fury to formality, from fire to ice and back again, depending on whether he is under orders or out from under orders. A Nazi might be moved by a prisoner's plea that he had a wife and children; but a German would say, "So have I."

The German's incapacity for calm, consistent insubordination—for being first and last a free man—is the key to his national history. Germany has often had a counterrevolution, but never a revolution. What the Germans would call a revolution the Americans would call a *Putsch.* "The German revolutionaries," said Lenin, "could not seize the railways because they did not have a *Bahnsteigkarte*"—the ten-pfennig ticket admitting visitors to the train shed. The Reformation and the Counter Reformation were both counterreformations. (Luther's "peasant" uprising ended with Luther's tract *Against the Murderous and Rapacious Hordes of the Peasants.*) The German War of Liberation against Napoleon saddled Germany with peacetime conscription, and the revolutionary unification of the Reich in 1871 was achieved by the reactionary Junker of Prussia.

The German breakout—call it liberation, call it aggression, call it what you will—is a kind of periodic paranoid panic. In between times, the pressure from outside having supervened, and having been passed on from Germany to the Germans, the next panic cooks silently, symptomlessly, in *Zucht und Ordnung.* To blame Germany—still less the Germans—is to blame the thistle for its fruit. It is fantastic to suppose that, with the pressures of destruction, defeat, partition, foreign rule, and cold war superimposed upon those that already existed, "it" will not happen again. It not only will happen; it must, unless the life of seventy million Germans is altered at the very depth and they find a way to live *wie Gott in Frankreich,* "like God in France."

PART III

Their Cause and Cure

The Trial

November 9, 1948:

It is ten o'clock in the morning in Kronenberg, and, in the Courthouse just below the Castle, the three members of the ——th District Court of Hesse have ascended the bench to pronounce judgment. Except for the defendants and their counsel and a few close relatives of some of the defendants, the courtroom is almost empty, for the fact is that there is not much interest in the pending case in Kronenberg.

Kronenberg is a quiet town. It is one of the quiet old "picture-book towns," of which there are (or were) so very many in Germany. Most of them are partly destroyed now, some of them wholly. But old Kronenberg is (as it always has been in the wars) but lightly scarred. And, like all lightly scarred towns now, Kronenberg's prewar population is almost doubled, and around the railroad station and along the lowland of the Werne there are shacks and hovels which are not seen in picture-books.

Kronenberg must be excused for not keeping up its picture-book appearance. You see, there are no tourists now. (Who would come to Germany?) And the Kronenbergers— even those who had savings have just been wiped out by the currency stabilization—are preoccupied with staying alive. The town is shabby, very shabby, and the weeds are head-

289

high in the lot where the synagogue stood, and the iron fence, which still surrounds the lot, is rusted.

But the ruins of the war are few in Kronenberg. Two or three times sorties of planes crisscrossed the town in the night and burned a dozen houses down and fired into the streets; that was all, in quiet little old nonindustrial Kronenberg, except for the day that the bombers, apparently aiming at the railroad station, set fire to the University Eye Clinic a mile away from the station and burned up fifty-three blind-folded patients.

Still, one doesn't measure the damage entirely in ruins; one measures it, too, in years of air-raid alarms, night after night; in the price of unpasteurized milk; in the bundle of kindling that costs a day's work to buy and is gone in an hour. The Kronenbergers are tired people, too tired to climb the Castle hill to the Courthouse to hear all about it all over again.

The three judges sit silent until the Katherine bell, the Parish bell, and the Town Hall rooster have given their dissynchronous notice that it is ten o'clock; then the senior judge, having first exchanged nods with his colleagues to his right and left, begins to read the decision:

"This is the first case arising from the synagogue arson of November 9, 1938, to be decided under the full jurisdiction of the German Courts. The previous cases were adjudicated in de-Nazification proceedings under the United States High Command for the Occupation of Germany. . . .

"Every defendant in this case, as in all preceding cases, has argued that he was acting under superior orders. The doctrine was asserted by the International Military Tribunal at Nuremberg that superior orders do not constitute a de-fense of a crime against humanity. This doctrine is not clear to this court. Citizens must obey the law and the officers of the law, or anarchy will rule. And yet, no man should commit an offense against humanity. Here we have an apparent contradiction.

"But in the instant case, the truth of the charges does not require clarification of this doctrine or resolution of the apparent contradiction. We may, therefore, proceed to a finding.

"In this case we do not know who gave the original orders or whether original orders were given. We know that in one night, November 9, 1938, five hundred and eighty-six synagogues were destroyed in Germany, and the Court takes judicial notice of this fact which led to the disgrace of the German nation and a tragic misunderstanding of the German character everywhere in the world.

"In the instant case, there is testimony, which the Court does not exclude, that the synagogue was on fire many minutes, or even hours, before any of the defendants in this or in previous cases approached the scene of the crime. It seems likely that this was true and unlikely now that any more of the offenders will ever be identified. Official and unofficial records of all kinds which might have been relevant appear for the most part to have been destroyed before, during, or at the end of the war.

"But the charges here, of breach of the peace by a public mob and of criminal arson, do not require us to answer the many questions which will probably remain unanswered to the end of time. Under the statutes, participation is culpable, and, if the Court may revert to the claim of superior orders, it may be said that evidence of willingness, or even of eagerness, to carry out such orders has been considered. Such willingness and eagerness have, in some instances, been found. . . .

"In the days preceding the crime, it had to be expected,

and was in general expected, that in case of the death of the wounded Diplomatic Counselor vom Rath in Paris, there would be violent measures taken against the Jews. The widely prevailing, artificially fostered tension pressed for release. Against the threatening danger stood such institutions for the usual preservation of public order as, for example, the police, who were themselves either anti-Semitically inclined or stood aside inactive.

"It has been established that there were no police at the scene of the crime; why, we do not know judicially. Under these circumstances it was to be expected that a group of persons, even of two men, would run into no resistance worth mentioning, especially when these persons were garbed in the SA uniform. The smallest group could pose a threat to public peace. They could reckon with the fact that their measures were approved in the highest official places, and the institutions responsible for the preservation of public order would not unsheathe their weapons.

"In assigning the punishment, the Court has considered, as favorable to leniency, the fact that the defendants have never been convicted of any crime except those arising from their political activity. They did not belong to the 'criminal class.' They had been good citizens and, as far as the record is before us, honorable men. Political passion made criminals of them. As members of the Party and of the SA they were overcome by year-in-year-out propaganda. Their educational level is not high, although all of them are fully literate and all of them had religious training in school in their childhood. This is said here because they seemed to take no responsible position as individuals toward the problem of respect for human beings who believed other than they did.

"The crime was committed at a time when the leadership of the State would not punish such assaults against unpopular persons or groups or their property and in this sense favored and even urged such assault. In addition, many of the highest officials of the State competed with one another, in the interest of their own political popularity, in the most violent denunciations of such persons or groups, thus arousing the passions of ordinary citizens who look to their public officials for counsel and direction.

"Certain facts, however, argue against leniency in the instant case. . . .

"Nearly all the defendants in all the cases arising from this criminal act have denounced one another (and accused one another of denouncing them in order to exculpate themselves or gain an advantage). This has not been a spectacle of which Germans may be proud. And it has had the effect on this Court and, apparently, on others, of destroying the weight of all denunciations and counterdenunciations.

"In addition, nearly all the defendants, caught in multifarious self-contradictions, have said that they cannot remember what they said in earlier proceedings, or that the events at issue occurred too long ago for them to be sure of anything, or that too many things more important in their lives have happened since. The witness Karl-Heinz Schwenke, former SA Sturmführer, brought here from prison, where he is serving a three-year sentence for his part in the arson, has made a particularly unhappy spectacle of himself in this respect. His claim that he is an old man and cannot remember clearly would, if it were taken seriously, invalidate his repeated assertion that he should be regarded as a man of honor because he is a Christian and has applied for readmission into the Evangelical Church, which he left during National Socialism. If, at sixty-eight and, apparently, in good health, he is too old to take responsibility for his past acts, he may be equally too old to know what a Christian is. . . .

"It is true that, in the fortunes of politics and war subsequent to November 9, 1938, all the defendants in this and the other cases arising from this criminal arson have suffered loss of property, liberty, or health, or all three. But so have those of their fellow-citizens who committed no crime, including those of Jewish ancestry or faith. If this Court could turn history back, it would, and so, undoubtedly, would the defendants; but it cannot and they cannot.

"Still, the punishment of these defendants will not restore the property rights that were lost, the human rights that were lost, the lives that were afterward lost, and the abandonment by many of our people, including the defendants, of their honor and humanity, which led to the loss of these other values and shamed our German nation and our German civilization. . . .

"Since the principal perpetrator (in so far as we have evidence), the former Sturmführer Schwenke, was sentenced to three years upon conviction of this crime, the present defendants, whose roles were subsidiary to his, should receive lesser sentences. The Court therefore. . . ."

CHAPTER 26

The Broken Stones

One sunny spring afternoon our seven-year-old, Dicken, was playing in the alley outside our house in Kronenberg when a flight of four American jet planes came screaming over the town, circled it, and went away. They were the first planes of any sort we had seen or heard over Kronenberg and the first jets we had seen or heard anywhere. Everyone ran to the window. Down below we saw Dicken's playmates, six-, seven-, eight-year-olds, transfixed, like him, with wonder. But there were bigger children, too, ten or eleven and older, playing in the alley, and they, the bigger ones, ran away howling with terror, their hands clasped on top of their heads. "Didja see the jets?" said Dicken, when he came in. We said "Yes," and Dicken said, "Why did the big boys and girls run away?"

War, between 1939 and 1945, had come at last to the country of the "war men," the Germans. And from 1943 on, after Hermann Göring (who had said in 1941, "If a single bomb drops on Germany, my name is Hermann Meyer") had become Hermann Meyer, war came into the "war men's" houses to live with them, to eat with them, to sleep in their beds, and to take over the teaching of their children, the care of their sick, and the burial of their living. On May 9, 1945, Germany was a world of broken stones.

On May 9, 1945, there were no more Nazis, non-Nazis,

anti-Nazis. There were only people, all of them certainly guilty of something, all of them certainly innocent of something, coming out from under the broken stones of the real Thousand-Year Reich—the Reich that had taken a thousand years, stone by stone, to build.

Those stones were the houses—not the munitions plants or the switchyards, but the houses. In the city of Worms, the railroad roundhouse stood miraculously untouched; and a half-mile away stood a whole row of walls that were once apartment houses; and so it was in Frankfurt, where the I.G. Hochhaus, the headquarters of the world dye trust, was undamaged; and in Berlin, where the Patent Office was intact. And so it was everywhere in Germany, for the war was a war against houses. One raid knocked one-third of Freiburg over; Dresden was destroyed in twenty-four hours. And Hamburg! And Munich! And Rotterdam! Warsaw! Coventry! Stalingrad! How could Americans understand? They couldn't.

Americans, one-fifth of whom change their abode every year; Americans, building a brand-new America every fifty years; Americans visiting Antietam *battlefield*, Gettysburg *battlefield*, Bull Run *battlefield*—how could they understand the world of broken stones that once were houses? Houses mean people. The war against houses was a war against people. "Strategic bombing" was one of war's little jokes; the strategy was to hit railroads and power plants and factories—*and houses*. Right up until the total collapse of steel fabrication at the end of 1944, the Germans had four rails in the yards for every rail in use; within two to six hours after a yard was hit, it was moving again. But sleepless workers weren't moving so fast, and terrified workers were moving still slower, and workers whose homes were gone (and maybe a wife or child) weren't moving fast at all.

Americans, visiting their Civil War battlefields, wouldn't know that it isn't a man's life and his work that yields the bomb its big dividend but his *accumulated reason* for living and working. In the first case, he's only a dead enemy. In the second, he's a live ally. In the war that came—for the first time—to the "war men" of Germany, the parlor was the prime military installation and the pictures on the parlor wall the prime military objective. If the bomb hits the factory worker's parlor, it can let the factory go. The way to win wars is to hit the pictures on the worker's, the miner's, the soldier's parlor wall. And a bombardier who lets go from a mile or two up, or even five, can hardly miss over Berlin— or Kronenberg.

Words are worthless, and pictures, each of them worth a thousand words, are worthless. Seeing is not believing. Only having been there, having been hit or not hit running to or from it, and being bedeviled forever by what might have been done a half-hour before or a half-minute after is worth anything. A book might have been saved, or a pair of shoes, or a mother or a child. Or a passport. Or a child might have been saved if a pair of shoes had been let go, or a mother if a child had been let go.

And words and phrases like "hit," "got it," "kaput," "knocked over," talk about prize fights or three-balls-for-a-dime at an amusement park. All that words can say is that Stuttgart was "hit" or Bremen "hit hard" (or Coventry or Stalingrad—or Seoul). It's like saying that Christ, in the course of his carpentering, got a nail through his hand. Better not say it at all.

Those houses against which the war was waged were built —even the tenement houses—of stone or Gargantuan timbers laced together and covered with a smooth, imperme-

297

able stucco. There were, in Germany, no rural slums, no bulging, leaning, or caving barns, no tar-paper or clapboard shanties, no abandoned homesites, rotten fences, great mountains of rusting automobiles, nothing left to oxidize and blow away. Everything had been built to endure to the last generation. Maybe this was the last generation.

CHAPTER 27

The Liberators

The defeat of Germany and the Germans in 1945 was not intended to relieve the pressures which had made them what they were. And it didn't. On the contrary, to all the old pressures which produced totalitarianism and aggression, it added, necessarily, new ones—the guilt-finding and punitive processes; the dismemberment first of the country itself and then of its business and industry; reparation costs, indemnification costs, occupation costs—and the Occupation.

If any occupation ever had a chance of succeeding, it should have been the American (sometimes called the Allied) Occupation of western Germany. As occupations went, it was probably the most benign in history, in part because the fortunes of their history have nourished benignity in the American people, in part because the Occupyees turned out to have the same kinds of tastes and talents, and even cousins, as the Occupiers. That the Occupation did fail—if its object was to do any better than Versailles—is now clear, I think, to anyone who does not define peace as order or democracy as balloting. It failed because it was an occupation, and no occupation has a chance of succeeding.

The day the American troops came to Kronenberg, a sergeant rode through the town in a jeep and designated homes which were strategically located for occupancy by the troops responsible for maintaining security. One of the homes belonged to a woman with two babies; within a few hours her furniture was out on the street, along with her and her children. She addressed the corporal in charge of the eviction, explaining to him, in English, that she was not a Nazi but an anti-Nazi. His reply was not unfriendly. He said, "Too bad, lady."

It was too bad, lady, but that's the way it was. It was an occupation; worse yet, a *civilized* occupation, which, as such, violated Machiavelli's inviolable injunction either to liberate or exterminate a conquered people but under no circumstances to irritate them by halfway measures. The halfway measures of the American Occupation were halfway just, but they were halfway unjust, too. How could they, being civilized, have been otherwise?

The American determination to do something about Nazism meant that something had to be done about each of some twenty-five million Germans. It required the employment of thousands of their countrymen, selected, necessarily, in great haste by Americans who were themselves selected in great haste; and this meant the wrong men all around. Long before the de-Nazification process came of its own weight to an ignominious halt, it had become a bottomless swamp. In the absence of records—anti-Nazi and Nazi files had both been destroyed as first the Nazis and then the anti-Nazis swept through Germany—the defendants invariably accused their accusers. It was a field day for paying off old scores. Oaths piled up on every side until they reached the heavens to which they were addressed. In Kronenberg University, eight years after the war, there were still pending one hundred and sixty libel suits filed by faculty members against one another.

Of course the American Military Occupation was Draconian; men cannot be taught to hate and kill on Wednesday and to love and cherish on Thursday. But by 1948 those Americans who *wanted* to participate in the punishment of the Germans had had enough blood to drink and had all gone home. With the substitution of civilian for military control of occupied Germany, things looked up. Unfortunately (and ironically), the advent of civilian control coincided with the outbreak of war—the cold war between the United States and the Soviet Union.

The civilian High Commission for the Occupation of Germany began its work in the shadow of that new situation. United States Commissioner McCloy commuted twenty-one of the twenty-eight remaining death sentences of Nazis and vigorously pushed the program of "reorientation and re-education" that had been laid out, in dreamy detail, in the post-1945 and pre-1948 world. But the brave new program was doomed from the start. Between 1950, when the Korean War began, and 1952, when the dreamers disappeared from the American government, the program limped along, ever more lamely.

In 1952 it ended, without notice. Local "Resident Offices" of the High Commission reverted to their prior status of United States Army subposts; the re-educators and reorienters, who had been coming and going at the Germans' expense, went. German-American Youth Centers and German-American Women's Clubs closed quietly; dedications of new hospitals and schools, with German "counterpart" funds and American oratory, stopped. The members of the "United States Occupation Forces in Germany" were informed by the United States that they were now members of the "United States Defense Forces in Germany." Only the State Department propaganda establishments—the United States Information Centers, or *Amerika-Häuser*—

301

remained to mark the spot where the German character was to have been transformed.

Between mid-1950 and mid-1954 the budget of the United States High Commission and related agencies was reduced 75 per cent, and personnel was cut from 2,264 Americans and 12,131 Germans to 780 Americans and 3,650 Germans. Even more spectacular was the reduction in the number of automobiles operated (usually with German chauffeurs) to serve the urgent needs of the re-educators, from 1,545 in mid-1952 to 251 in mid-1954. The decline in civilian activity was more than matched by the rapid-as-possible redevelopment of the American military establishment in Germany. In the fall of 1954, although the remilitarization of Germany was not yet legalized, Robert S. Allen reported in his Washington column that, in addition to all American forces and facilities in Germany, there were being built by the United States a $250,000,000 weapons stockpile and a $100,000,000 food stockpile for six German Army divisions.

The failure of the American Occupation had little or nothing to do with German resistance to it. Apart from their impotence and their hunger and the Occupation's absolute control, the Germans were *ausgespielt*, played out, for a while at least. Nine of my ten Nazi friends were positive that they would never again join a political party, any party. Always credulous and submissive, the Germans had just had twelve years' intensive training in total credulity and total submissiveness; the Occupiers found them marvelously docile, even unresentful, Germans to the manner born.

They were actually indifferent to the general civil corruption—something unknown even in the Third Reich—introduced by the American black market. It was not for them, good Germans, to complain of the morals of their new rulers. They might grumble, in their poverty, at having to pay fifty cents for a package of cigarettes while the rich who had come to democratize them paid a dime, but by and by American cigarettes so saturated the black market that the grumbling was inconsequential. The rich Americans got still richer, but the poor Germans got good coffee for half the legal German price; one way or another, every third German was a direct or indirect beneficiary of the black market. In a few years they were hardened—these once pretentiously honest Bürgers—to monstrous financial scandals. The State Department's construction of "Westchester-on-the-Rhine" for American officials—including five $100,000 homes and one at $240,000—did not, in 1953, excite even the Opposition in the Bundestag. Hadn't Germany's rulers always been kings?

The failure of the Occupation could not, perhaps, have been averted in the very nature of the case. But it might have been mitigated. Its mitigation would have required the conquerors to do something they had never had to do in their history. They would have had to stop doing what they were doing and ask themselves some questions, hard questions, like, What is the German character? How did it get that way? What is wrong with its being that way? What way would be better, and what, if anything, could anybody do about it?

CHAPTER 28

The Re-educators Re-educated

From the beginning, the American Occupation was an operating model of nondemocracy and a demonstration of high-
pressure salesmanship. But where were the buyers? None of
my ten friends had ever taken advantage of the resources of
the Kronenberg *Amerika-Haus* except Herr Hildebrandt,
the only one of the ten who didn't need to be won to democracy. Besides the children who attended the ever repeated free movies of the Grand Canyon and Niagara Falls,
the *Amerika-Haus* patrons were, in the main, pro-Americans
from 'way back and students writing papers on American
subjects assigned them by their hurriedly Americanized instructors. Prior to the onslaught of McCarthyism in 1952,
the *Amerika-Häuser* still stocked American books of all
sorts, all of them, unfortunately, in English. They were no
more read by my friends—or burned—than the anti-Nazi
New York Times had been when it was available in the
fashionable hotels of Nazi Berlin.

What the Germans needed was to see what democracy
was, not to hear it touted. But in my year in Kronenberg
there was not one controversial public discussion or debate
under American sponsorship or control. In East Germany,
a few miles away, the Communists were beating the drum
for Communism; in Kronenberg the Americans were blowing the trumpet for Americanism; and in both places, not so

long since, the Nazis had been burning the torch for Nazism. But the Germans had—in their own polite phrase—had a noseful of beating, blowing, and burning.

The Germans were, after 1945, in a position to begin to judge Nazism, whose blessings and curses they had now experienced, if only they could begin to have the experience of another way. But they would first have to see another way in operation before their eyes and be attracted to its practice. They would certainly fumble it at first—or second—but who hasn't? They might misunderstand it and even misuse it. But how else would they ever discover what it was? When my little boy cuts the tail off the cat and I say, "When will you learn how to be a good boy?" he replies, "I already know—you've told me a thousand million times."

Freedom is risky business; when I let my little boy cross the street alone for the first time, I am letting him risk his life, but unless I do he will grow up unable to cross the street alone. For the American Occupation to have chosen freedom for the post-Nazi Germans would have been dangerous; even my anti-Nazi friends, so thoroughly German were they, were opposed to freedom of speech, press, and assembly for the "neo-Nazis." But it was the fear of freedom, with all its dangers, that got the Germans into trouble in the first place. When the Americans decided that they could not "afford" freedom for the Germans, they were deciding that Hitler was right.

Free inquiry on a free platform is the only practice that distinguishes a free from a slave society; and, if the post-Nazi Germans needed force, they needed it for the one purpose it had never been used for in Germany, namely, to keep the platform free. What they needed was the town meeting, the cracker barrel—to see, to hear, and at last to join the war on the totalitarianism in their own hearts.

What they needed was not the Grand Canyon or Niagara Falls but the Sunday afternoon forum in Bughouse Square and the thunderous cry of American authority: "Let 'im talk, let 'im *talk*."

My friend Willy Hofmeister, the old policeman, was amazed, and kept adverting to his amazement, that *Mein Kampf* had not been banned in America during the war. What the Germans needed, so sorely that without it no effort, no expenditure, no army would ever help them, was to learn how to talk and talk back. In the *Amerika-Häuser* and on all the other American-controlled platforms they heard lectures on Goethe's Debt to Edgar A. Guest and learned the old, old German lesson of listening to their betters tell them what was good and what was great and what was good and great for them.

What they needed, and went on needing during the whole of the American Occupation, was the peculiarly American genius for contentious and continuous talk in a framework not of law but of spirit. Everything else they needed they had genius enough, and more, to produce for themselves.

Why should America have undertaken, in 1945, to export freedom, above all to a people who had habitually squandered their own and eaten up other people's? The question may or may not have had merit, but it was too late, in 1945, to ask it. The American Occupation had added something new to the history of occupations: idealism. It had undertaken to do something more than punish, collect, and control: it had undertaken to civilize the Germans.

The two tottering old civilizations of Europe, France and England, showed small appetite for what they may have thought an impossible ambition, and they dragged their heels at every turn. But there were two new civilizations on the German scene, the United States and the Soviet Union. They, with their conflicting views of civilization, were ardent with regard to their respective areas of control, and, if either of them had not wanted to be, the other's ardor would have forced it.

It was on the East-West border of divided Germany that these two new civilizations met, each of them committed to world revolution, both of them so long isolated that they were only now, in their confrontation, compelled to consider their commitments. The Declaration of Independence did not say that all Englishmen—or their overseas colonists —were created equal. It said that *all men* were created equal, and with certain inalienable rights. The *Communist Manifesto*, too, proclaimed the equal rights of all men but, denying creation, deprived the rights of their inalienability. Down the middle of Germany the quarrel, avoidable, perhaps, if the two revolutions had not found root in the two repositories of world power at the moment, was joined in 1945.

Now, what makes civilizing so hard is that, even if the primitives recognize their own condition as primitive (which I don't know that they do), they do not always recognize that of the civilized as superior. The Germans, for example, had thought themselves, and not other people, superior. And, in addition, the impeccability of the civilizing intention is always clouded by suspicion and the suspicion fortified by events of recent memory. Being beaten is not the best immediate preliminary to being civilized or reeducated or reoriented. The post-Nazi Germans were bound to have difficulty, for a while, in believing that those who had beaten them so bloody and burned their country down had done so for their own good or were interested in their own good now. The nature of the case was against us, even in genuine peacetime conditions, which, certainly after 1948, no longer obtained.

Still, as the American Occupation learned that what was done in ten centuries cannot be undone in ten days, some small progress might have been made in time. As the sting of punishment, collection, and control was relieved, receptivity to the American world revolutionary effort might grow in Germany, and the effort itself, if only it were not abandoned in a new isolationist temper in America, might become more imaginative. By 1948 there were signs of hope. No West German would have said, outside an official statement, that his government was free, much less democratic; but words like "freedom" and "democracy" were everywhere heard, especially among the rising generation.

The public schools were full of free books, free movies, and free lectures in praise of freedom and free enterprise, in praise, above all, of peace. And the pupils were memorizing the blessings of democracy as assiduously as their older brothers had memorized the blessings of National Socialism. More significantly, the private elementary and secondary schools, from which public school reform had always emerged, were alive again in the land.

Of the universities, "it is difficult to predict . . . but a start has been made," said James M. Read, very cautiously, when he resigned as education chief of the United States High Commission in 1951. The intellectual sheep and goats were still separated at the age of ten or eleven, but, if a higher education was still beyond the children of three-fourths of the people, the West German universities, most of whose students were working their way through, no longer had to plead guilty to the Communist charge that, where the East German universities put a premium on poverty as a condition for admission, those in the West excluded the workingman's son altogether. A chair of political science or so-cial research appeared here and there, and there were, in five or six universities in the American and English (and even, at Tübingen, in the French) zones of occupation, government-supported or at least government-tolerated efforts to introduce a program of general education on the fringe of the specialized curriculum.

No American would have said in 1948, outside an offi-cial report, that a transformation had been wrought, or even wedged, in the German national character except on one point, and that was militarism. "The war-making power of Germany should be eliminated," General Eisenhower of SHEAF told Henry Morgenthau and Harry Dexter White in 1944, and everybody present and absent agreed with him. In 1945 the Americans interrogated some 13,000,000 indi-vidual Germans—and indicted some 3,500,000 of them—under a statute "for the de-Nazification and demilitariza-tion of Germany." In his 1946 speech in Stuttgart, United States Secretary of State Byrnes reaffirmed the Potsdam principle that Germany should be *permanently* demili-tarized and added: "It is not in the interest of the German people or in the interest of world peace that Germany should become a pawn or partner in a military struggle for power between the East and West"; and in 1949 the new Bonn Government pledged "its earnest determination to maintain the demilitarization of the Federal territory and to endeavor by all means in its power to prevent the re-creation of armed forces of any kind."

Everywhere the German turned, he was told that Ameri-can idealism had come to liberate him forever from the curse of militarism, from its money cost, its cost in life, and its cost in reducing his character to barracks-room servility. And, with a readiness that should, perhaps, have been disturbing, he seemed to believe what he was told.

It is hard to exaggerate the impression which this American ideal made upon the Germans—an impression supported, of course, by their own experience of the second Thirty Years' War of 1914–45. "The German people display no eagerness for military service," High Commissioner McCloy was able to report. "The distaste for military service as such [is] something new in German life." Then, suddenly, in 1948, with the cold war warming up in Berlin, the American ideal was reversed.

CHAPTER 29

The Reluctant Phoenix

The first modest proposal, heard in late 1948, was to arm the West German police, on the ground that the Russians had already armed an East German police force. But this little tit-for-tat soon gave way to the call for twelve West German divisions. "The Germans are great fighters," said Senator Thomas of Oklahoma in late 1949. "If the United States gets into a war, we shall need fighters." "It should be enough," said General Collins of the United States Joint Chiefs of Staff in 1950, "if we send arms. Our sons must not shed their blood in Europe." Shortly thereafter, the *New York Times* put it in plain American: "America has the right to demand a dollar's worth of fight for every dollar it spends."

But the phoenix showed no disposition to rise from its ashes. The "war men" were tired, dead tired, of war, and General Eisenhower of NATO felt called upon to reassure them in 1950: "If the Allies were to rearm the Germans, they would be repudiating a whole series of agreements. It has been announced officially in Washington, London, and Paris that no such action is contemplated." And so it had been. But the Germans were so tired, and so vocally tired, that the General was moved, as late as 1951, to inform Washington, London, and Paris that he wanted "no reluctant divisions in an army under my command."

He was, however, going to get them. The West German Security Commissioner—there was, of course, no War Ministry—announced that Germany would conscript 300,000–400,000 men. (It was peacetime conscription which Woodrow Wilson called "the root evil of Prussianism.") There would be, when the Germans (not to say the French) could be brought to accept the American "contractual agreement," in addition to peacetime conscription, nine new *Panzer* divisions, and "the German contingent will dispose directly of its own air force" of 75,000 men and 1,500 fighters and fighter-bombers. This "German contingent" (the Security Commissioner did not need to add) would be as strong as the forces with which Hitler attacked the West in 1939, and (the Security Commissioner did not add, but the Pleven Plan did) the national units of the European Defense Community would be, "in the beginning," under national, not international, control.

A few months after the beginning of hostilities in Korea, the American, British, and French foreign ministers took note—without expressing their own views—of "the sentiments expressed in Germany and elsewhere in favor of German participation in an integrated force." The sentiments were not confined, either in Germany or elsewhere, to governmental or militarist circles; in America, Walter Lippmann, writing in the very conservative internationalist *New York Herald Tribune*, was convinced that "Germany as a nation can be brought willingly into a Western coalition only if we can prove to them that we have the military power and that it is our strategic purpose to carry the war immediately and swiftly beyond the Vistula River." (It would not be the first time that the war had been carried immediately and swiftly beyond the Vistula River; the last time, Hitler did it.) And in Germany the very conservative nationalist *Stuttgart Zeitung* thought that "it is very probable that Great Britain's value to America as an ally will soon sharply depreciate. This would be tremendously important for us Germans. . . . If Anglo-American friction increases and Britain's position becomes weaker, we may expect that America may assign an increasing importance to Germany's role on the Continent."

After the 1953 elections in Germany, the Adenauer Government had enough power in Parliament to override the German Supreme Court's unwillingness to find that German remilitarization was permitted by the Constitution forced upon Germany by the victorious Allies of 1945. (The same thing was happening in Japan, where the new Constitution forbidding militarization forever had actually to be amended.) German industry, said General Hays, the Deputy United States High Commissioner, would be able to start turning out armaments "within six to nine months of receiving orders," and in 1953 Krupp of Essen, the company that built the Nazi war machine, displayed its new line of vehicles, complete with turret emplacements. "Once the go-ahead is given," Foreign Aid Director Stassen told the United States House of Representatives Appropriations Committee in the fall of 1954, "you will see one of the fastest jobs of building an army in modern history. The necessary equipment, most of which will be furnished by the United States, is well on the way."

Meanwhile, everything had been changed in the "Coca-Cola Zone" of West Germany. What was left of the American engine for re-education and reorientation was thrown into reverse, to serve the campaign for a new German *Wehrmacht*. The still-wet picture of the Curse of Militarism was turned to every wall, and the not-yet-dusty old masterpiece of the Defense of the Fatherland was rehung. Much could still be said, and done, against Communism. But not much could be done any more about the re-education of the Germans. Their re-education had been based too heavily on the theme that militarism had been the cornerstone of German totalitarianism, German war, and German ruin.

There were hitches here and there. At a fracas in Frankfurt in 1952 the German police picked up a flying squad of the Bund Deutscher Jugend, whose specialty was breaking up Communist, Social Democratic, and neutralist meetings. A few weeks later Minister President Zinn of the State of Hesse announced that the BDJ had been "created and financed by the United States" and that, on United States orders, it had set up a "technical service" to go into action in case of Communist invasion. This "technical service" was composed of one to two thousand former German officers up to the rank of colonel, all of them over thirty-five years of age. (*Bund Deutscher Jugend* means "German Youth League"). Many of them were former Nazi SS men. (Mere membership in the black-uniformed Schutzstaffel had been condemned at Nuremberg as criminal.) The "technical service" was being trained, with all kinds of light weapons, in a disguised lumber camp maintained by the United States in the Odenwald. (The penalty, under the Allied Control Law, for arming Germans was death and was still in force.)

What most exercised President Zinn—a Social Democrat—was the "technical service's" list of West German "unreliables" to be "removed." The list included fifteen Communists—and eighty Social Democrats, including the entire national leadership of the latter party. It included, in addition, the only Jewish member of the German Parliament. The "technical service," said President Zinn, cost the United States taxpayers $11,000 a month. HICOG—

the United States High Commission for the Occupation of Germany—knew nothing about it. Neither did General Eisenhower of NATO or President Truman of the United States or, of course, Chancellor Adenauer of Germany.

But everybody else knew something about it. The "technical service" was maintained by the United States Central Intelligence Agency, created by the United States National Security Council with a rumored budget of $500,000,000 completely concealed in the departmental appropriations of the United States Congress. "One would like to assume," said the pro-West *Frankfurter Rundschau*, "that the secret American sponsors knew nothing of the assassination plans. However, their support of a Fascist underground movement is bound to produce distrust of American officials. We refuse to fight Stalinism with the help of Fascism."

It was only a hitch, of course. And the Germans had been taught to have short memories. Still—. Two years later, in the hullabaloo that attended the disappearance of Dr. Otto John, "West Germany's J. Edgar Hoover," it developed that John, who reappeared in East Germany, did not like Nazis and had been having trouble with the Süddeutsche Industrieverwertung, or South German Industrial Development Organization. The Development Organization was, as it developed, a barbed-wire-surrounded compound of 30 acres in the dreamy Bavarian village of Pullach, in the American Zone. The Development Organization was developing a spy network of 4,000 agents in the Soviet Union. The cost of the development, according to the moderate, right-of-center *Paris-Presse* of August 27, 1954, was six million American dollars a year. And the Director of the Development was former Brigadier-General Rheinhardt Gehlen, Nazi intelligence chief in the Soviet Union during

the second World War. His new job, said the *Paris-Presse,*
was "to carry on for the United States the work he had
begun for Hitler."

It was only a hitch, of course, but such hitches are mortal to mewling idealism. The Germans had been taught to
have short memories, but there were a few whose memories carried them all the way back to the former German
captain who persuaded the Allies to let his "Freedom
Movement" have a few rusty old guns to repulse the Communists in Bavaria after the first World War. The captain's
name was Röhm, Ernst Röhm. Could it have been the
same Captain Ernst Röhm who founded the National Socialist Party?

CHAPTER 30

Born Yesterday

All the Germans were not born yesterday. But some of them were; and youth is the time of ideals. When the West German Security Commissioner announced the details of remilitarization—including peacetime conscription—the London *Observer's* correspondent reported, on the basis of public opinion polls, that "the percentage of support for a German defense contribution dropped below 15, and the percentage of outspoken opposition, about 40 to 50 for the population in general, reached nearly 75 for the age groups directly concerned"—that is, for the young people. Student polls taken in three universities in Germany—without official sanction or supervision—showed opposition so nearly unanimous that the scientific basis of the polling went unchallenged. Youth is the time of ideals, and in the German generation that had known only war's horrors and none of its glories the pre-1948 American Occupation had planted an ideal that was brand-new in Germany.

The American "exchange programs" for German students, professors, journalists, and public officials had been screened from the start, to bring only pro-American Germans to America. Now—after 1948—the candidates were asked what they thought of the remilitarization of their country. "I'm against it," one of the high-school seniors who was accepted for the program told me, "but I said I was for it. You know, 90 per cent of our graduating class at the *Realgymnasium* signed a petition against remilitarization a month before my examination for the program. My name was on the petition, but I assumed that the American officials in our town had not sent it to the American examiners in Frankfurt, and I was right."

"Why," I said, "did you guess that the petition had never been sent to Frankfurt?"

"Because everybody tells his superior what his superior wants to hear, and the superior in Frankfurt does not want to hear about opposition to remilitarization. Look, Professor, we are used to this in Germany."

The young people's resistance to remilitarization was led by German churchmen, Protestant and Catholic, especially in the anti-Nazi Confessional Church, the "church within the Church" which is the most vigorous and numerous branch of German Protestantism. In mid-1950, when Pastor Mochalski, Secretary of the Confessional Church Council, established the Darmstadt Action Groups against remilitarization, the movement spread from the Darmstadt Institute of Technology to the Universities of Frankfurt, Mainz, Heidelberg, Tübingen, and Freiburg. Americans who were "warned" by the United States Consul in Frankfurt to keep away from this "Communist-dominated outfit" and who asked to see the evidence were told, "That's impossible. The evidence is classified."

Notices of meetings of the Niemöller-Heinemann-Wessel group of Protestants and Catholics opposing militarization were torn down by culprits unknown. But in Kronenberg, late in 1952, huge posters appeared on the kiosks showing a hairy red hand, tattooed with the hammer and sickle, seizing the thin white arm of a woman, over the caption *"Deine Frau, Herr Ohne Mich!"* "Your Wife, Mr. 'I-Won't-Fight-in-the-Next-War'!" The source of the posters being unknown, they would ordinarily have been confiscated by the police. But they weren't. "We are used to this, too," said my friend, the exchange student. "It may be that this poster was left over in Dr. Goebbels' storeroom."

Cynicism, the deepest cynicism, in Germany, among a people who, rather than believe in nothing, will turn to the most fantastic of faiths; cynicism among the young people, and youth is the time for ideals. Not that their elders were any less cynical, but, then, age is the time for disenchantment. "I suppose," said my friend Klingelhöfer, the cabinetmaker, "that the Occupation law 'for the de-Nazification and demilitarization of Germany' is repealed, now that we are to be remilitarized. Are we to be re-Nazified, too?"

Were they? A transition had set in among the Germans, a transition from the view that the American Way was, perhaps, better than their own to the view that the American Way was very good, indeed, but no better than theirs. The German press, controlled as it was by the Occupation, expressed itself by the amount of space it gave news, and it gave an extraordinary amount of space to the development of "McCarthyism" in the United States and especially to the incursion of book-burning into the libraries of the *Amerika-Häuser*. The bolder newspapers expressed themselves editorially, the anti-Communist *Münchner Merkur* nominating Senator McCarthy for honorary membership in the Communist Party and the anti-Communist

Weser-Kurier saying that Goebbels would have appreciated the Wisconsin Senator. "We in Germany," said the anti-Communist *Mannheimer Morgen*, "are fed up with what we had last time, when a whole party of McCarthys tried to control our thinking."

Some Germans were born yesterday; not all of them.

CHAPTER 31

Tug of Peace

The new German joke was: "How do the Germans feel about the situation?"—"Well, how does a bone feel between two dogs?" Pressure, once more, new pressure on top of all the old pressures unrelieved by war, destruction, and defeat. The Nazi rallying cry had been, "Germany, awaken!" Now the Americans and the Russians were crying the same cry. In time the Germans would yield to the new pressures. It would certainly be easier to re-re-educate Germans to militarism than to re-educate them away from it. "I wish," said a German pastor, "that we Germans didn't believe so easily."

The consequences of the pressure, of being needed, wanted, for war again, of being wooed wherever they went, they who so recently had been the world's untouchables, can only be guessed at; but they *can* be guessed at. "The German tragedy," said Reinhold Schneider, one of Germany's great living men of letters, "is as deep as ever. It is that nothing can be regarded as having a life of its own. Everything—whether music, or art, or religion, or literature —is judged almost exclusively on its conceivable political bearing. The most tortured and far-fetched conclusions are drawn from productions that were only created out of the urge to create or, if they had a goal, to enhance the outreach of the human spirit. Of course I am aware of the social re-

321

sponsibility of the artist, but to go over to the Marxist thesis, as the West seems to be doing, that everything is only an incident to a great political, and ultimately economic, movement is to sell out something that will impoverish the world, certainly to sell out that early hope that something new in the human plastic might emerge out of Germany's pain."

That was one way of putting it, but there were not many putting it that way. There were more who saw remilitarization as the only way to sovereignty; these were the nationalists. There were more who saw it as the way to professional activity; these were the ex-officers. There were more who saw it as the way to a job; these were the unemployed. And there were some ten million "expellees" (nobody had ever bothered to count them) forced into post-Nazi Germany from the liberated countries by the victors who decided at Potsdam that Hitler was right, after all: there was such a thing as a "German race," and its members, classified at Potsdam as "German ethnics," would have to live in Germany. The "expellees" were an immense and ever growing force for war against Russia as their only hope of getting back home.

Growing, too, among the Germans, was the most intense pressure of all, the pressure to reunite their country, infinitely more intense than the pressure to regain the lost colonies in the twenties. West (and East) Germans had no relatives in German West Africa, but they all had relatives in East (and West) Germany. A new Hitlerism, if it arose in West Germany, would need only one plank in its platform: reunification. In 1953 the West Germans re-elected a Chancellor who told them, à *l'Américaine*, "We talk a lot about unification. Let us talk of liberation." But, when any speaker in Germany, West or East, used the word *Einheit*, unity, no matter how he used it, he was interrupted by wild, *Sports-Palast*-like cheering.

Unfortunately, *Einheit* was an old Nazi term, too. Still more unfortunately, *Einheit*, along with *Friede*, peace, was the slogan the hated Communists had painted on walls and billboards all over East Germany—on walls and billboards facing the West. The Germans, East and West, wanted the Americans out of Germany—five minutes after the Russians were out. But the Russians, who lost 17,000,000 people in the last war, would not get out, and neither would the Americans, who did not want to lose 17,000,000 people in the next one. The Occupation—West as well as East—was a matter of might. Might was something the Germans could understand without being re-educated or reoriented.

The Germans in the East did not appear to believe that they would get both *Einheit* and *Friede* from the Russians. The Americans did not speak of *Einheit* and *Friede* to the Germans in the West. They spoke of *Verteidigung*, defense, and offered it free. Well, the Germans wanted defense, too, above all against "Bolshevism." But defense was the offer made them by their own government in 1914 and in 1939, and in 1914 and in 1939 defense meant war. The Germans did not want war. They did not want peace at any price, but they did not want war at the price of death, and that was the price, when they were allowed to think about it, that they thought they would have to pay.

The German dilemma was, perhaps, most acute in Germany, but it wasn't really a German dilemma; it was the dilemma of Europe. If defense meant death, one had to consider defense very seriously. But the Germans could see the dilemma most acutely, because they could see that the Americans and the Russians were agreed that, if they had to fight each other, they would both prefer to do it in Germany. The Germans could see that, wherever the third World War ended, it would begin where they were, and their broken stones would be reduced to dust.

In the re-election of the conservative coalition of Adenauer in 1953, the central issue was the economy. Almost half the Bonn budget was going for social services; one-fifth of the population was directly supported by the State on pensions or doles. Still, the day after V-E Day, five-fifths were unsupported by anybody, and in 1953 the Germans were not in the mood to shoot even a thin Santa Claus. In the fall elections of 1954 the mood had changed—or, rather, the focus. Everywhere, even in Catholic Bavaria, Adenauer lost support and lost it radically. What had happened? What had happened was that the "European Defense Community," with its façade of an international army, had collapsed, and the Adenauer Government, under the most intense pressure from the United States, was trying to deliver a German Army, complete with a German General Staff, under the new "London Agreement."

The phoenix was dragging its talons. Professor Hans Morgenthau, of the University of Chicago, returned from a visit to his native land in the summer of 1954 and reported that he had raised the question of German rearmament "with scores of all kinds of people. I found only one man who came out in favor of it, and he is closely identified with the Adenauer Government." He added that "all four living ex-chancellors of Germany, representing the most diverse colors of the political spectrum from the extreme right of Papen to the extreme left of Wirth, have declared their opposition to the Western orientation of the Bonn regime." In the winter of 1954–55 the West German "Security Commissioner" was having the greatest difficulty in persuading young men to register voluntarily for the when-

and-if "defense force." At a mass meeting in Cologne, the magazine *U.S. News & World Report* said that the Security Commissioner "found more conscientious objectors than anything else. A check in key areas of West Germany indicates that the attitude of the young men at Cologne is typical of much of the country. Hardly anyone signs up. Antimilitarism suddenly has become one of the most popular political issues."

"Conscientious objectors" to volunteering are not, of course, conscientious objectors to conscription. "Actually," *U.S. News & World Report* concluded, "nobody in West Germany seriously doubts any more that the country will have an army by one means or another. But it is becoming apparent that the German soldiers of the future will be very different from the German troops who went to war in 1870, 1914, and 1939." "Fight?" said one of those anonymous officials with whom I spoke in Berlin. "Of course the Germans will fight. But they will fight a tired war, the way the French fought in 1940."

The Germans want, not at all oddly, to live. They would like to live well, but in any case they would like to live, well or badly. Their attitude may be unheroic; they ought, perhaps, to prefer dying on their feet to living on their knees. But they don't; and, unlike us, who have had neither experience, they have had both. What we, who have never been slaves, call slavery, they, who have always been what we call slaves, find less abhorrent than death. They hate Communism—under that name—but they do not love what we call liberty enough to die for it. If they did, they would have died for it against Hitler.

Americans who saw the love of liberty in the East-West refugee traffic and the East German riots needed to remind themselves that these same East Germans lived under totalitarian slavery for twelve years, 1933–45, and loved it. They did not even call it slavery. Those of them who hated it (and there were, of course, many) could have emigrated in much better style than those who are now arriving from the East, but emigration during those twelve years, except for those whom the totalitarian dictatorship drove away, was almost nil.

CHAPTER 32

"Are We the Same as the Russians?"

The nineteenth century of Europe left untouched only three great bulwarks of autocracy—Russia, Prussia, and Austria. These were, in the phrase of the time, the three eastern great powers, in which the pattern of postfeudal absolutism, serving an agrarian and military nobility, with a subservient church appended, still survived in the West. German royalty's predilection for France and England—and its intermarriage with the latter's ruling house—gave the world an easy impression of Western orientation, which was fortified by the spectacular industrialization of the new Reich under Bismarck. But the perennial preoccupation of German scholarship with Russia (and vice versa) might have been a better clue to the future of Europe than the didoes of court society.

Russia (whose history has been epitomized as the search for a warm-water port) and Germany are the two have-nots, subjectively, with a long history of like, and co-operative, behavior, beginning with their postmedieval continental colonization (including a half-dozen amiable partitions of Poland) and their failure (or inability) to colonize abroad. Bismarck's support of Russia's Black Sea ambitions; the German General Staff's support of the October Revolution; Rapallo; the Molotov-Ribbentrop Pact—all these are seen, quite rightly, as German policy in a perpetual pincers situation. But German-Russian relations have always been happier than the relations of either one with the other European great powers. Behind the events of the immediate past are five centuries of remarkably peaceful penetration of the western Slav world by German traders and agriculturists and the concomitant Slavic influence on the East Prussian and Silesian temperaments.

We are late in discovering the essential resemblance of Communism and Nazism, diverted perhaps by the "advanced" condition of the Germans, perhaps by the confusion of Soviet Communism with democratic socialism; perhaps by both. But the circulatory course of anti-Semitism—from fourteenth century Germany to Russia (via the partitioning of Poland at the end of the eighteenth century), from Russia to Austria in the nineteenth, and from Austria back to Germany in the twentieth—should itself have been a sign of the singular congeniality of the Pan-German and Pan-Russian nationalisms. But it was not until the 1930's, when National Socialism overcame Germany, that we discovered, to our amazement, that the aboriginal "folk family," the herd sense of the tribe, was as deeply set in the Germans as it was in the Russians.

Some of the Germans have not discovered it yet. In Hamburg I was meeting with a group of students, and the discussion turned to Russia. "You don't know the Russians," said one of the students, addressing, apparently, not just me but the group generally. "I say that you do not know the Russians. I do. They have no idea of freedom. They would not know how to use it if they had it. They are a primitive, animal-like people. They simply have no conception of humanity or of human rights. I had a friend who was in a

Russian concentration camp. What they do there is hideous. You wouldn't believe it." Another student spoke up: "I had a friend who was in a German concentration camp. What they did there was hideous. You wouldn't believe it." The first student was enraged. "Are you saying," he shouted, "that we are the same as the Russians?"

CHAPTER 33

Marx Talks to Michel

"When two Russians fight," so the joke goes, "they tear each other's clothes off and then shake hands. When two Germans fight, they kill each other, but there won't be a button missing." The German's bourgeois development came late—the Russian's never—and his private property sense is as overdeveloped as a child's. But the Thirty Years' War of 1914–45 has proletarianized this man of private property, especially the bourgeoisie. In the inflation of 1945–48, as in 1919–23 (when, however, the retailers with stocks survived), the farmer not only held his own but traded food for whatever he wanted, and there were "Persian rugs in pigsties." Then the currency reform, on both occasions, hit the farmer, and his downward course began to follow that of the bourgeoisie.

The higher bourgeois were the first and the hardest and the most persistently proletarianized. They may not know it yet; Herr Doctor Schmidt or Herr Lawyer Schmidt or Herr Professor Schmidt or Herr Architect Schmidt or Herr Engineer Schmidt still has his professional title, and his title is property, as it is nowhere else in the Western world. But he has no real property, no tangible stake left in the social order. He has nothing to sell but his labor. Marx is talking to him.

A university department head in Kronenberg had no hot

water and no central heat in his four-room apartment, with a household of four adults and two children. Eight years and more after the war his family still gladly accepted gifts of used clothing, the crumbs of charity. I see him now, sifting his pipe dottle, looking for unburned flakes; I see his wife using tea leaves a second time, a third time, a fourth time. In a year in Kronenberg I encountered only one owner of a private automobile, and not one refrigerator. Eggs were sold by the unit; who had money to invest in a dozen at a time, or a place to keep them fresh?

In our older boy's class, the sixth grade, in a school in our bourgeois, nonindustrial, county-seat town in a fertile valley, 10 per cent of the children were, eight years after the war, going to school without breakfast; the next 10 per cent had unspread bread; the next 10 per cent, bread with a nonfat spread; and only the top 30 per cent had any kind of milk or milk-substitute drink under their belts. Our younger boy, in the first grade, brought his new friend Bienet home with him and gave him a banana. Bienet ate the banana—and the skin.

And all this was in "recovery" Germany, West Germany, where the living standard had always been higher than it was in the East and was now, of course, very much higher. And in a small town surrounded by woods, in this "recovery" Germany, only kitchens were heated in winter for want of a few cents for kindling. My Nazi friend, young Schwenke, recommended to me a cigarette-rolling machine with a cloth, rather than a plastic, roller; I asked him why he himself used the machine with the plastic roller; it was because it cost two and a half cents less than the other.

Of course there were mink coats in Düsseldorf, the Rouge-et-Noir (as the Germans call it) was packed day and night at Baden-Baden, and there were block-long Mercedes limousines in Berlin. But, when the limousines had gone by, one might see the men, young men, middle-aged men, old men, going through the garbage cans (as if there were anything edible to be found in a German garbage can!). Nowhere was the assertion challenged that the spread between wealth and poverty in West Germany was much greater than it had been under the Nazis.

"Production is 150 per cent of prewar." But what is important is what is produced and where it goes. What was being produced in "recovery" Germany was not domestic consumer goods; machine tools are hard on the teeth. The soaring West German economy was an artifact, a political, cold-war, pump-priming operation like the soaring (if not so high) East German economy. To pile up the gold and dollar balance, tax concessions (paid ultimately by Michel, the standard chump of German comedy) were given exporters. Some of the units of the I.G. Farben chemical combine, broken up after the war, were bigger than ever; one typewriter manufacturer was exporting to one hundred and thirty-nine countries.

"Production is 150 per cent of prewar." But of Volkswagen's twenty thousand employees (including executives), only 2 per cent could afford to drive the cars they were making. In "150 per cent" 1953, the West German industrial wage was less than one-fourth of the American, the standard of living 15 per cent below that of armaments-saddled France, the per capita consumption of meat (which was unrationed) lower than austerity England's (which was rationed). The "150 per cent" was not going to the fifty million West Germans.

Since the end of the war, Germany, the only nation in Europe which did not enjoy the sovereign privilege of spending one-third to one-half its national budget on a military establishment, had constructed six times as many new housing units as "victorious" France; but it was still short four million units, and housing was still rationed to a maximum of one person per room. Unemployment figures, notoriously unreliable, ranged from a likely two million to an unlikely one million. There were no exact figures distinguishing part-time employment from employment and no exact figures on the ten million "expellees."

There were some simple distinctions which one might make—could not help making—by walking across the Potsdamer Platz in Berlin. In Communist East Berlin no worker was free—or unemployed; in Capitalist West Berlin one of every four workers was unemployed—but free. In Kronenberg, which had no heavy industry, unemployment of the normal working force (swelled by the "expellees") was 20 per cent in 1953, and an unemployed white-collar worker, with a family of four in one room, got a dole totaling $31.74 a month. He paid one-fourth our money price for rent, half our money price for food, and as much as we pay for all manufactured articles (including fuel and clothing). Our ten-cent bar of soap cost twenty-four cents in West Germany.

German men were coming down in money value as German materials went up; a shoemaker would work half an hour making repairs which did not require leather or rubber, and the bill would be twelve cents, but when he worked ten minutes putting on a pair of half-soles and heels, the bill was $2.50. The German people (not to be confused with German export and German industry) had not been rehabilitated. And they had not been rehabilitated by American aid. True, "they" had received three billion dollars in aid; true, too, they (without the quotation marks) had paid ten billion dollars in Occupation costs. And the aid, whatever forms it had taken and whichever persons it had reached, was, under the Marshall Plan and its successors, $28 per person in Germany, while it was $63 per person in England and $65 in France.

Whatever rehabilitation there was in Germany—the spectacular reconstruction not of the destroyed cities but *in* them—was the result of the back-breaking toil of seventy million German Michels. Tante Käthe, our housekeeper, was one of these Michels. "Work and save, Michel." Tante Käthe worked and saved. Twice she worked, and each time she saved close to $2,000, and each time, after 1918 and 1945, her $2,000 was inflated away. Tante Käthe, who reads and writes only the old German script, doesn't read or write much. She doesn't even know (any more than the shoemaker, whose materials are worth more than he is) that Marx is talking to her.

The German's acute property sense and his acute security sense have been at war within him during this whole second Thirty Years' War of 1914–45. The security sense is winning. The development of German anticapitalism was, at the turn of the century, phenomenal. In the first Reichstag, in 1871, the Social Democratic Party had two seats; in 1903, eighty-one; and before the first World War, with one hundred and ten seats, they were the strongest party in the country. In 1932 the anticapitalist forces held two-thirds of the Reichstag seats—the Left Center, the Social Democrats, the Communists, and the Nazis (the last receiving private support from German capital).

The dispossession of the German, especially of the middle class and most especially of the upper middle class, has been going on since the middle of the first World War, relentlessly, in "good" times and in "bad," moving toward completion. The propertyless Bürger does not cast his lot with the proletariat; but sooner or later his lot casts him. He lives (and, if he is old enough, dies) in his memories of *die goldene Zeit*, the golden time of the first Kaiserreich; but the grandchildren—it may be even the children—of this man have, without personal memory to sustain their illusions, lost them. When the situation has been bad enough long enough, there seems to be a neurotic incongruity, with only one entrance door for three families, in maintaining the hereditary doorplate with the family name engraved on it. So the grandson—or the son—takes it down. Marx is talking to him.

Marx doesn't care if, in this outbreak or that, or in this or that locality, he calls himself a Nazi, a Fascist, a Communist, a Nationalist, or an Odd Fellow. Marx is talking to the naked condition of his existence, not to the insignia in his lapel. "One hundred and fifty per cent of prewar" is the mumbo jumbo of dead financiers. Nothing costs money like war, whoever wins or loses. Nothing mass-produces proletarians like war, whoever wins or loses. Whoever wins or loses, Marx is talking to the man whose house and savings are gone, who has nothing to sell but his labor. Let the dead financiers talk of "150 per cent of prewar"; Marx knows that England and France, whose productive capacity, far from being destroyed, was scarcely touched, never recovered from the first World War. In the midst of the broken stones, the twisted steel, the burned-out shop, and the flooded mine stands the new proletarian: the German.

Remember—the Germans were rich once, by European standards, and now they are poor; so, subjectively, they are much worse off now than those who were always poor. They are approaching the point—no one knows where it is—where they will know that they are what they already are: proletarians. Between 1945 and 1955 it was costing Michel only

$155,000,000 a month to maintain the military forces that occupied his country; the minute he got his own military forces, that is, his "defense contribution" to "European defense," it would cost him $215,000,000 a month, just as a starter.

Michel hates Communism—*under that name*. But Hitler communized him, under National Socialism, and he never knew it. If this process of coming down in the world—not of *being* down but of *coming* down—continues, Michel will embrace some new, as yet unconceived "anti-Communism." But it will be Communism, just as National Socialism was, but more advanced in so far as materials, rising in value as men's value falls, are increasingly available only in collective form. And there is no reason, when the hatred of 1941–45 dies away, why this Communism (called, perhaps, "anti-Communism") should not be Russian, or Russian-German, a third Rapallo of the have-nots, who, like all have-nots, dream of being have-alls. There is, of course, the chance (on which Churchill bet and lost once) that the parties to the third Rapallo may destroy one another; but this chance is ever the rich man's dream.

Bourgeois pride, the title, the doorplate, the bow the higher *Beamte* receives from the lower, stand between Germany and Russia, but the pride, the title, the doorplate, and the bow are coming down. What the Germans did in Russia in the late war—and what the Russians did in Germany afterward—stands between them, too. The slogans of anti-Communism, pounded into the Germans by the Nazi Government and later by the American Occupation, these, too, will live for a while. But Frederick the Great and Bismarck, looking eastward, will outlive both the Nazis and the American Occupation. "Everyone knows," said the realistic Walter Lippmann late in 1954, "that the pull within Germany toward such a deal"—between West Germany and the Soviet Union—"is bound to be very strong, and to become all the stronger as Germany acquires great military power in her own right. The Russians," he went on, "hold big assets for a deal with the Germans: unification, withdrawal of the Army of Occupation, rectification of the frontiers, resettlement of the expelled refugees, trade, and great political influence in the destiny of Europe." The realist might have been even more realistic and added that Marx is talking to more Germans today than in 1914—or in 1939.

CHAPTER 34

The Uncalculated Risk

The way to relieve the pressure is to relieve the pressure. If, at whatever cost, the salvation of Germany, and therefore of Europe, and therefore of civilization, must be achieved, the test of every measure must be the test urged by the late Prime Minister of India: "Does it add to tension or not?" The Occidental who deplores the renunciation of both right *and* might implied here must narrow his eyes to an Oriental squint and keep them on the ball. If the Germans make the rest of the world suffer because they themselves suffer, and if they themselves suffer because they are under pressure, why, the first thing to do is to get the pressure off them. Niceties such as right and might must wait.

Take the pressure off them, and they might become insufferable. But they became insufferable with the pressure on them. Take the pressure off them, and they might claim that they won the last war. But that would be better than their claiming that they will win the next war. Take the pressure off them, and they might rearm. But they always have anyway. Take the pressure off them, and they might go Communist. But they did go Nazi.

The trouble is that the relief of the Germans would require something like the prior reconstruction of the world. To initiate—even to contemplate—a program of relief, there would have to be the kind of world that did not react to the proposal by asking, rhetorically, if the Germans are to be coddled for their crimes and paid off for losing the wars they started. It would have to be a world that could see beyond the end of its nose and turn that nose—together with the rest of its face—from the past to the future. It would have to be a world with—a *Weltanschauung*.

To say that this is not the kind of world we live in, or are soon likely to, would be to supererogate. A world that was disposed to relieve the Germans of pressure would have to be a world that itself was not under pressure, a world that breathed freely. So far are we from living in such a world that the two powers now dividing the world there is are both falling victim to the paranoid panic which brought Germany to its present pass, both of them sacrificing all other objectives to encircle their encirclers. In this one respect, at least, has Goebbels' perverse prediction been validated: "Even if we lose, we shall win, for our ideals will have penetrated the hearts of our enemies."

In such a world—the world we live in—such dreams as a United States of Europe are no further advanced in Europe than World Federalism is here. The Europa Union movement, in Germany as elsewhere, is widespread among, and only among, nongovernmental intellectuals, and especially among the young. At the University of Munich 88 per cent of the students, in a random sampling, favored "the unification of Europe" over "German sovereignty." But "the unification of Europe" means different things to different men —to some peace, to others war. And it is an ideal much more nebulous, and much more limited, than democracy. In the context of the world struggle, European Union means, first, military union of non-Communist Europe; second, economic union (presently supported by both the young idealists and the old cartelists); and last, if ever, political union. And

339

any union that left Germany divided would take place only on paper, if there.

There may be a possibility that the relief of the Germans would interest the Russians, who, after all, invented Russian roulette. As the Germans now are, the Russians are afraid of them, and with good reason. "It is now clear," said the London *Times* in 1954, "that neither Russia nor the West can agree to German unification on terms compatible with their national interests. The linch-pin of Western defense—West German cooperation—remains the hard core of Russian fears. And the main Western anxiety—Russian armies in the heart of Europe—is, in the Russian view, the indispensable condition of Soviet security. In the state of the world today, neither fear can be discounted as mere propaganda."

In such a state of such a world, it might be that the United States of America, by seizing the initiative and proposing German reunification on other than nonnegotiable terms, would have to sacrifice its immediate national interest in order to satisfy the Russians that their own interests would be served (or at least not disserved) by agreement. If such a thing has never before been done—if a nation has never sacrificed its immediate national interest in order to advance that of another—it might be done for the first time in history on the utopian basis that the relief of the Germans, at whatever sacrifice of immediate national interest, would create the possibility of saving civilization.

The cure of the Germans will not be free in any case, nor is it guaranteed by any prescription. If Germany is thought of—as it seems to be now, and mistakenly—as somebody's satellite, nobody will bother to do anything about it except to prepare it for war, including civil war. And war is not good for the Germans. Only if the interested great powers decide that ultimate self-interest is more interesting than immediate self-interest will they be interested in relieving the Germans of pressure. But it would not do at all to have the great powers undertake the relief themselves; the quick switch from exploitation disguised (unsuccessfully) as benevolence to a program of genuine benevolence would only mystify the Germans.

After many, many years of thinking it over, and at very close range, Mr. McCloy, the retired United States High Commissioner for the Occupation of Germany, came to the conclusion that it might have been helpful to have had neutrals sit on the bench at Nuremberg in 1946. There were those who, in 1946, suggested a neutral tribunal at Nuremberg, but they were not listened to, and it is now too late to listen to them. But it is not too late to listen to those who now suggest that neutrals sit on the border in Berlin.

The disadvantages to the West—or to the United States— of finding a way to reunite Germany would be immense. A unified Germany, although it would be anti-Communist, would be Socialist, because four-fifths of the East Germans are Social Democrats; and there are some Americans who do not like Socialism. In addition, the "abandonment" of Germany would mean loss of face for the United States, a prospect most obnoxious to Occidentals. Worst of all, it would mean the surrender of the whole present policy of containment by force—at least in Europe—and the whole present ambition of liberation by subversion and insurrection. It would mean that wherever and however Communist expansion would be stopped—assuming that such things are stoppable by military means—it would not be stopped by war on the Vistula, the Oder, the Elbe, or the Rhine. It would mean that Europe could not be "held."

But the alternative prospect of having to depend upon

the Germans to "hold" it is not attractive, either. The Germans have not been—and are not going to be, in the next six months or six years—transformed from first-class totalitarians to first-class freemen. When we remember what most of them so recently and habitually were, or at least did, it seems hardly worth the trouble, if the Germans must save us, to be saved from Communism.

In this lugubrious circumstance, a circumstance in which any program of real relief is, perhaps, so unrealistic as to be unworthy of consideration, there are, nevertheless, a few things that the United States could at least avoid doing without being accused of utopianism. On the eve of the German election of 1953, a *New York Times* headline said, "U.S. Scans Food Aid for East Germans. Weighs Plan To Ship Surplus Stocks To Help Adenauer and Embarrass Russians." Two weeks later Dean Heinrich Grüber of the Berlin Protestant Cathedral told his congregation: "When a charitable project is undertaken without the true spirit of love, the blessing turns into a curse. We will gladly co-operate with those who work to relieve hardship, provided only that they do so without mental reservations and without devious intentions. But we refuse to co-operate with those persons or powers who use works of charity to disguise their political and propaganda warfare."

No nation gorged with unmarketable surpluses in a starving world will ever relieve another by exploiting the other's hunger for a couple of weeks to win an election. And a nation which, as a matter of public policy, attempts to do so attempts to do what it shouldn't. Neither the *New York Times* headline nor Dean Grüber's sermon was broadcast by the "Voice of America"; it is not nearly so hard to find ways to take the pressure off the Germans as it is to want to.

The story is told—apocryphal, we may hope—that a friend

of John Dewey's encountered him on the street one day long ago in wet windy weather, with his little boy. The boy was standing, rubberless, in a puddle of water, and Dewey was watching him from the shore. "You'd better get that child out of that puddle," said the friend, "or he'll catch pneumonia." "I know," said the philosopher. "I'm doing it as fast as I can. I'm trying to figure out a way to get him to *want* to get out." It does not seem likely that the United States Government will take a chance on the Germans' catching pneumonia. It has their health—not to say its own —to consider. If our government cannot, for reasons of State, demonstrate democracy to the Germans, in the hope that the Germans will take to it some day, private agencies may still try. There is no law, German or American, to prevent the construction of, say, a *Vereinigte-Staaten-Haus* across the street from every *Amerika-Haus* in Germany. There are plenty of vacant lots. *Amerika-Haus* would advertise, FREE LECTURE, and *Vereinigte-Staaten-Haus* would advertise, FREE DEBATE.

Children misbehave under pressure. The greater the pressure, the worse the misbehavior. The affected child may be the quiet type, but one day he burns the whole house down. If we are his parents, we may relieve him by ignoring his minor depredations; by setting him a good example; and, if possible, by loving him. In so far as he recognizes the parental authority—but only in so far as he does so—he may be gently controlled. The Germans do not recognize our parental authority, however well behaved they may be, and the danger of acting on false analogy is considerable. What is more, their depredations are rarely minor, and it is not always easy to love them. But the cure is probably somewhat the same. At least, beating the Germans has had the same consequences as beating the child.

America has a great name in Germany; it used lovingly to be called "Little Germany" among the Germans, and every one of my ten Nazi friends had one or more relatives, no further removed than second cousin or uncle, who had emigrated to the United States. It may not be arrogant to assume that the Germans look to us, even now, for light. If they do, it would be nice if we Americans could manifest some of the compassion that relieves the compulsive child. It appears that the big things that ought to be done cannot, for reasons of State, be done, even if the failure to do them means the ruin of the State. It may be all the more urgent, then, to do the little things; and St. Francis' words, "I come to you in little things," may still be the clue to the cure of the Germans.

But maybe nothing can be done for the Germans, in which case, whatever anyone else does, we should let them alone. The proposition that anybody can do anything about anybody else is absolutely indemonstrable. Doctors of the body abound, but there are no doctors of the soul, or psyche. A great psychoanalyst once pointed proudly to a former patient and said: "He used to be the unhappiest rotter in town. Now he's the happiest." It may very well be impossible for one whole people, except by their example, to help another whole people transform their character; and that may be why, until 1945, it was never attempted. But a one-tenth-of-one-per-cent chance is one-tenth of one per cent better than no chance at all. It is risky to let people alone. But it is riskier still to press my ten Nazi friends—and their seventy million countrymen—to re-embrace militarist anti-Communism as a way of national life.

Acknowledgments

I am indebted to a very great many persons, none of whom may be charged with any responsibility for any of the things I have said in this book:

My friends who thought I might learn a little *something* in Germany, especially Robert M. Hutchins, then of the University of Chicago; Gilbert White and Douglas Steere, of Haverford College; A. J. Muste, of the Fellowship of Reconciliation; and Morris H. Rubin, editor of *The Progressive*.

My colleagues at the Institut für Sozialforschung, Frankfurt University, especially Professor Frederick Pollock, whose "baby" I was and who goaded and guided me, cried over me, prayed for me, and apologized for me from start to finish.

My two ardent assistants ("slaves" would be better) in Kronenberg, Frau Eva Hermann and Frau Martha Koch.

My three ardent friends in Kronenberg, Fräulein Dr. Gisela Prym, Dr. Leonora Balla Cayard, and Horstmar Stauber.

John K. Dickinson, of Cambridge, Massachusetts (and of Kronenberg), who, as I go through my notes, seems to have done all the research that went into this book; and the late Frederick Lewis Allen, of New York City, who, as I go through the manuscript, seems to have done all the writing

345

in the course of preparing sections of the book for serialization in *Harper's Magazine* in 1954.

Professor Robert H. Lowie, of the University of California, whose remarkable study, *The German People: A Social Portrait to 1914* (New York: Rinehart & Co., 1945), was the richest of the many treasures of other writers that I plundered.

My friends in Carmel and Monterey, California, Isabel Devine, Louise van Peski, Janet Farr, Marion Chamberlain, Liesel Wurzmann, Fritz Wurzmann, Charles Mohler, Harlan Watkins, Ephraim Doner, Francis Palms, Dr. Bruno Adriani, and the late R. Ellis Roberts.

Robert C. McNamara, Jr., of Chicago.

My daughter Julie, who set my fractured German, especially in Heine and the Talmud.

My mother, who thought I might learn a little something somewhere.

Mutti, my wife.

THE ARAB LOBBY

"In a pointed response to John Mearsheimer and Stephen Walt's equally scathing *The Israel Lobby and U.S. Foreign Policy* (2007), Bard goes full throttle in pursuit of what he sees as a more insidious, if less vociferous behind-the-scenes lobby by the masters of Gulf oil and foes of Israel."

—*Kirkus Reviews*

"A serious and timely look at a powerful and remarkably under-studied influence on U.S. foreign policy."

—*Tablet*

"Extraordinarily well-researched. . . . Bard has performed a valuable service with his book, which will be eye-opening to many, even among friends of Israel, who are not aware just how deep and long-lived is the historical animus not only to the actions of the Jewish state itself but also to the very idea of a Jewish state at all."

—*Commentary*

"A brilliant exposé of the powerful but inconspicuous interest group that for decades has persistently undermined U.S. foreign and national security interests."

—Efraim Karsh, Head of Middle East and Mediterranean Studies, King's College London, and author of *Palestine Betrayed* and *Empires of the Sand*

"After decades of hearing almost exclusively about the Israel lobby, Mitchell Bard finally provides the full story on the Arab lobby in this detailed, fast-moving, and fascinating study. He reveals the malign influence of an unpopular, hate-filled, but well-financed campaign that goes back, surprisingly, to the 1930s, and has been driven by Arab states, oil company executives, State Department Arabists, and assorted anti-Semites."

—Daniel Pipes, Director of the Middle East Forum and Taube Distinguished Visiting Fellow at the Hoover Institution, and author of numerous books, including *Militant Islam Reaches America*

"Mitchell Bard has written an extraordinarily important book vital to our nation's security. Meticulously documented, *The Arab Lobby* provides the most comprehensive account yet of the activities and influence of the Arab lobby in the media, Congress, think tanks, and even law enforcement."

—Steven Emerson, Executive Director of the Investigative Project on Terrorism and author of *American Jihad*

"Importing anti-Semitism, anti-Western ideas, historical inaccuracies, and pure fiction, the Arab lobby has had effects that are just now being felt, and this book will show us how. It is an extremely important work we all need to read."

—Gregg Rickman, State Department Special Envoy to Monitor and Combat Anti-Semitism, 2006–2009

THE

THE INVISIBLE ALLIANCE THAT UNDERMINES AMERICA'S INTERESTS IN THE MIDDLE EAST

ARAB

MITCHELL BARD

LOBBY

BROADSIDE BOOKS
An Imprint of HarperCollins*Publishers*
www.broadsidebooks.net

A hardcover edition of this book was published in 2010 by Harper, an imprint of HarperCollins Publishers.

FIRST BROADSIDE BOOKS PAPERBACK EDITION PUBLISHED 2011

Designed by William Ruoto

The Library of Congress has cataloged the hardcover edition as follows:

Bard, Mitchell.
     The Arab Lobby : the invisible alliance that undermines America's
interests in the Middle East / Mitchell Bard—1st ed.
        p.   cm.
     ISBN: 978-0-06-172601-9 (hardcover)
     1. Lobbying—United States. 2. Arab Americans—Politics and
government. 3. United States—Foreign relations—Middle East. 4. Middle
East—Foreign relations—United States. I. Title.
JK1118.B28   2010
324'.4089927073—dc22   2010011508

ISBN: 978-0-06-172597-5 (paperback)

11 12 13 14 15   OV/RRD   10 9 8 7 6 5 4 3 2 1

Many people provided invaluable assistance to me in the preparation of this book. I want to thank especially Allison Krant, who was an amazing researcher, without whom it is difficult to imagine how this work would have been completed. I'm also grateful to several people who slogged through early drafts and offered comments, including Geoffrey Green, Daniel Pipes, Bernard Reich, Abraham Ben-Zvi, and Howard Wachtel.

I am also thankful for the many people named and unnamed who agreed to speak to me. I would have liked to have interviewed many more, but many subjects declined requests for interviews. Fortunately, it was sometimes possible to find other interviews they had given on the record. For example, many former diplomats recorded interviews for the Association for Diplomatic Studies and Training Foreign Affairs Oral History Project. My preference was to rely on original documents. Because many government documents remain classified, however, those used here primarily cover the early history of the Arab lobby.

The book would not have been possible without the support and important contributions made by my editor, Adam Bellow. I also want to thank Miranda Ottewell for the terrific job she did as copy editor.

Last but not least, I want to thank my agent, Lynne Rabinoff, who always fights the good fight for her clients, and was unswerving in her commitment to the project and untiring in pushing it forward to completion.

CONTENTS

INTRODUCTION

During the 2008 presidential campaign, Barack Obama made clear that one component of his agenda would be to give a high priority to pursuing Arab-Israeli peace. Many Jews had some concerns about Obama, but his pro-Israel statements reassured them, and ultimately nearly 80 percent voted for him. Obama's appearance before the pro-Israel lobby, the American Israel Public Affairs Committee (AIPAC), and recitation of talking points from the Israeli lobby playbook were consistent with the popular view of a powerful lobby that demands the fealty of elected officials.

Within a few weeks of taking office as the nation's forty-fourth president, however, Obama seemed to pick a fight with the Israeli government over its settlements policy. He began to publicly demand that Israel freeze all settlement activity. When Israeli officials brought up the fact that certain understandings had been reached with Obama's predecessor regarding what the United States considered to be acceptable construction, Secretary of State Hillary Clinton denied any such agreements had been made.

In July 2009, Obama invited a group of Jewish leaders to the White House who were content to hear the president's views and asked only that he refrain from public criticism. Obama made clear he would do no such thing.

Israelis tried to steer the administration away from the settlement issue toward what they believed was the most urgent threat to their nation and the stability of the region, namely, the Iranian nuclear program. Obama's chief of staff, Rahm Emanuel, coincidentally a

Jew whose father is Israeli, said that the Israeli-Palestinian issue was the crux of solving the Iranian threat. Administration officials argued that the only way they could get Arab states to cooperate in the effort to stop the Iranian program was to solve the Palestinian issue.

Meanwhile, Obama's first interview as president was with an Arab publication, and his first trip to the Middle East omitted Israel and was highlighted by a speech in Cairo that was meant to reach out to the Muslim world. Ten months into his term, he still had not visited Israel, and the persistent public criticism by his administration had reduced the percentage of Israelis who considered him a friend of Israel to a shockingly low 4 percent.[1]

Thus, in less than a year, President Obama had created what appeared to be a crisis with his only democratic ally in the region while doing everything in his power to curry favor with the Arab and Muslim world. After eight years of feeling encumbered, the foreign policy establishment found an ally in the White House who shared their long-standing view that America's Middle East policy can best be served by cultivating relations with the Arabs and, concomitantly, distancing the United States from Israel.

The Obama policy, however, seems to fly in the face of the conspiracy theorists who have long believed in an all-powerful Jewish/ Israeli lobby that controls U.S. Middle East policy to the detriment of the national interest.

How can this be explained?

The following pages will show that U.S. policy is not controlled by an omnipotent Israeli lobby but rather heavily influenced by an equally potent—yet much less visible—Arab lobby that is driven by ideology, oil, and arms to support Middle Eastern regimes that often oppose American values and interests.

It is understandable if this statement is surprising, given that few books or articles examine the Arab lobby, while there is a long history of conspiracy theories suggesting that Jews control everything from the media to the U.S. Congress to the global financial system. *The Israel Lobby*, by Stephen Walt and John Mearsheimer, is the most recent screed to reinforce such beliefs.

Israel's detractors have embraced Walt and Mearsheimer's book because its argument fits in neatly with their fantasies about an all-powerful group of Jews who control U.S. foreign policy, but they should be offended by the racist, paternalistic tone of the book, which portrays the Arabs as impotent, unable to affect their own fate or influence U.S. actions. While the Israeli lobby is obsessively scrutinized, mischaracterized, and demonized, the role of the Arab lobby is denied, minimized, or ignored.

Why write a book about this subject now? One reason is the publicity given to the distorted portrayal of the Israeli lobby by Walt, Mearsheimer, and others. Also, this is a time when the Arab lobby has been engaged in an increasingly successful global campaign to delegitimize and ostracize Israel. Most important, though, it is a story that has never been told and must be exposed so the public understands the extent to which the Arab lobby seeks to manipulate American foreign policy. This book will illustrate that an Arab lobby does exist and that the Arab-Israeli conflict is fought in the Oval Office, Congress, the media, and campus quads and classrooms. This is not just a war of ideas but one that involves the security of the United States. Americans should understand what the Arab lobby is, how it operates, and why it is dangerous.

To be fair, Walt and Mearsheimer are not the only ones who give short shrift to the Arab lobby. For example, when DePaul professor Khalil Marrar contacted Arab American organizations to interview their representatives for his research on the subject, he was told, "There is no Arab lobby in Washington, DC."[2] Even one of the most prominent Arab Americans engaged in promoting the Palestinian cause, James Zogby, said in 1982, "There is no Arab lobby."[3] In the Foreign Affairs Oral History Project of the Association for Diplomatic Studies and Training, former State Department officials who dealt with Middle East affairs were repeatedly asked about the Israeli lobby, but the Arab lobby was never discussed.

Walt and Mearsheimer do not subject the Arab lobby to the same analysis they apply to the Israeli lobby; they simply dismiss its influence. Claiming that oil companies have not exerted influence, they conclude that their case is proven. They also suggest that if an influential Arab lobby did exist, it would try to distance the United States from Israel.[4] They are correct and this book will show this is one of the lobby's principal objectives. While they cite research I did more than twenty years ago for my PhD dissertation that showed the comparative advantage of the Israeli lobby, I have used the intervening years to study the Arab lobby and offer new evidence here of its influence.

Unlike many of the Israeli lobby's detractors, I do not suggest that Arab Americans or supporters of the Arab cause have no right to pursue their agenda. In a democracy, every group has the right to lobby and to make its case to the public and decision makers; the marketplace of ideas should decide which arguments have the most merit. The point of this study is to highlight how the debate may be distorted because of the vast financial resources of the Arab lobby, and to expose some of its efforts to manipulate public opinion and foreign policy, often beyond public view, in ways that have gone largely unnoticed and demand greater scrutiny. More specifically, I will demonstrate how the Arab lobby exerts a malign influence on U.S. policy that has led successive administrations to ignore fundamental American values in order to bolster repressive Arab regimes, in particular Saudi Arabia; how the lobby has undermined America's security through the support of terrorists and others acting contrary to U.S. interests; and most alarmingly, perhaps, how it has infiltrated the education system in an effort to create a distorted understanding of Islam and the Middle East and weaken support for the U.S.-Israel relationship.

This book also aims to expose how one foreign government, Saudi Arabia, seeks to influence U.S. Middle East policy. As in the case of Arab Americans, the Saudis have the right to do so; every country uses diplomacy, and sometimes American consultants and foreign agents, to advance its interests in Washington. But Saudi Arabia is notable for the magnitude of its campaign at every level, from primary school education to universities to the media to the Congress and White House. More important, the Saudi component of the Arab lobby consistently acts against U.S. interests and frequently undermines them. In particular, the Saudis are active sponsors of international terrorism, the main exporters of radical Islam, and the rulers of one of the world's most intolerant societies.

Though it is largely unknown to the public, the Arab lobby in the United States is at least as old as, and perhaps older than, the Israeli lobby. The first organization established to present an Arab perspective in the United States was the Arab National League of America in the 1930s. Other groups followed. In 1951, King Saud of Saudi Arabia asked U.S. officials to finance a pro-Arab lobby to counter the pro-Israel lobby, and the CIA obliged. Even before that, oil companies and sympathetic officials in the State Department, Pentagon, and intelligence agencies were trying to influence policy. When the chairman of the Joint Chiefs of Staff, General George Brown, launched an attack on the Jewish lobby and Jewish ownership of banks and newspapers in 1974, Senator Thomas McIntyre (D-NH), a member of the Armed Services Committee, acknowledged the influence of the Israeli lobby, which he said "reflects the will of a strong majority of *all* Americans." But what about the oil lobby? he asked. "The influence of Big Oil is far more insidious, and far more pervasive than the influence of the Jewish lobby, for oil and influence seep across ideological as well as party lines, *without* public approval or support." He added that "the Jewish lobby isn't in the same league with the General's *own* lobby—the Pentagon and the Defense establishment."[5]

McIntyre expressed a reality well known to Washington players, but alien to ivory tower denizens with no real-world political experience. Since the establishment of Israel in 1948, the Arab lobby—which is in large part, but not exclusively, an anti-Israel lobby—has grown to include defense contractors, former government officials employed by Arab states, corporations with business interests in the Middle East, NGOs (especially human rights organizations), the United Nations, academics (particularly from Middle East studies departments), Israel haters, a significant percentage of the media and cultural elite, non-evangelical Christian groups, European elites, hired guns, American Arabs and Muslims, and the leaders and diplomats from no fewer than twenty-one Arab governments (as well as from a number of non-Arab Islamic nations).

One of the most important distinguishing characteristics of the Arab lobby is that it has no popular support. While the Israeli lobby has hundreds of thousands of active grassroots members and public opinion polls consistently reveal a huge gap between support for Israel and the Arab nations/Palestinians, the Arab lobby has almost no foot soldiers or public sympathy. Its most powerful elements tend to be bureaucrats who represent only their personal views or what they believe are their institutional interests, and foreign governments that care only about their national interests, not those of the United States. What they lack in human capital, in terms of American advocates, they make up for with almost unlimited resources to try to buy what they usually cannot win on the merits of their arguments.

The heart of the Arab lobby has long been Saudi Arabia, its supporters within the U.S. government, and the various PR firms, lobbyists, and other hired guns employed on the kingdom's behalf to make its case to decision makers and the public. In the past, the Arab lobby was focused on keeping Saudi Arabia happy, preventing the spread of Soviet influence in the Middle East, and weakening America's relationship with Israel. Today, the Arab lobby in the United States is focused on feeding the American addiction to petroleum products, expanding economic ties between the United States and the Arab/Muslim Middle East, securing American political support in international forums, obtaining the most sophisticated weaponry, and trying to weaken the U.S.-Israel alliance.

Unlike critics of the Israeli lobby who suggest it has no redeeming qualities, I would acknowledge that some elements of the Arab lobby, usually those inside the U.S. government, do often take positions that are in the interest of the country and express valid concerns. For example, State Department officials were understandably concerned about Soviet penetration of the region during the Cold War and also have legitimate reasons to promote U.S. trade and the protection of American oil supplies. The problems arise when they abandon core American principles to support policies that are less clearly in the national interest.

The Arab lobby has demonstrated its power by ensuring that the

U.S. pays disproportionate attention to the interests of Arab states and supports countries that share none of our values and few of our interests. These states are all dictatorial regimes with abysmal human rights records that have been fawned over by every president, including Jimmy Carter, who made human rights the centerpiece of his foreign policy. While this may be partly attributable to Cold War realism, the U.S. was also constantly seeking better relations with Soviet clients such as Egypt and supporting the Saudis even as they threatened to turn to the Soviets and financed Soviet allies such as Syria. Worse, some of these nations, especially the Saudis, subvert American interests by supporting terrorism and promoting radical Islamic views on a global scale.

In a previous book, *The Water's Edge*, I defined the Arab lobby as *those formal and informal actors that attempt to influence U.S. foreign policy to support the interests of the Arab states in the Middle East.*[6] In truth, the lobby is more amorphous than its Israeli counterpart and is not centrally directed. Though defined similarly, the Israeli lobby does have one organization, AIPAC, which has effectively been deputized to lobby on behalf of Americans who believe that a strong U.S.-Israel alliance is in the interests of the United States. Supporters of Israel have the advantage of lobbying on behalf of a relationship with a single country, whereas the Arab lobby, at least in theory, has to reflect the interests of twenty-one Arab states and the Palestinians. Representatives of the Arab lobby rarely attempt to express the view of "the Arabs."

In some ways the term *Arab lobby* is a misnomer. Most lobbies focus on a single issue—abortion/choice, second amendment/gun control, Israel, Cuba, China—but the Arab lobby really has two issues, which occasionally overlap. One is pro-Saudi, based on oil, and is represented primarily by the Saudi government, Arabists, defense contractors, and other corporations with commercial interests in the kingdom. American companies are not interested in regional politics; they care only about profits, so their principal concern is expanding trade opportunities. The Pentagon also lobbies the arms dealers to sell weapons to the Arabs. The justification is typically the need for these countries, especially the oil-producing Gulf States, to defend themselves from external enemies, originally the USSR and now Iran. As we shall see, however, the weapons are more often sold for other reasons: to keep the Arab leaders happy, to prevent other nations from getting the business, or in response to blackmail. While many of these sales are justified by national security interests, they often have less to do with defending the Arabs than with the Pentagon's desire to lower the unit cost of systems it wants for U.S. forces and to extend the life of production lines.

Thus, the Arab lobby has had the petrodiplomatic complex led by Saudi Arabia at its heart from the beginning, but has incorporated a variety of other interested parties at different times. Some corporate executives may be hostile to Israel, but for the most part companies have been coaxed to join the lobby in specific instances where it satisfied their selfish business interests rather than because of a desire to weaken U.S.-Israel ties.

The other issue of concern to the Arab lobby is the Palestinian question. Though the first group sometimes gets involved in this, it is primarily Arab American groups, Christians, and Arabists who lobby on behalf of the Palestinians or, more often, against Israel.

"Arab lobby" is also misleading. It suggests that the principal members are Arabs and that their focus is on the Arab world; but, as we shall see, Arab Americans are only a small and mostly impotent part of the overall lobby that is being eclipsed by Islamic groups. Moreover, the lobby has no real interest in any other Arab nations or issues. The lobby does not campaign for human rights in any of these countries, does not defend Christians or other minorities, does not even try to get aid for Arab states. The only time any interest is shown in another country is if Israel is somehow involved, as in the case of Israel-Lebanon clashes, when suddenly the lobby expresses great concern for the people of Lebanon. Otherwise, the lobby never talks about such issues as the Syrian occupation, Hezbollah's takeover, the undermining of democracy, or the various massacres perpetrated by Lebanese factions against each other or Syrian assassinations of their opponents.

While detractors of Israel see a lobbyist, philanthropist, or other Jew behind each Middle East policy decision, they ignore all those non-Jews (and sometimes Jews!) who are agitating behind the scenes for the adoption of policies favorable to the Arabs and/or hostile toward Israel. Thus, while Louis Brandeis may have lobbied Woodrow Wilson for American support for the Balfour Declaration, the president's closest adviser, Colonel Edward House, was vigorously opposing it. Harry Truman's friend Eddie Jacobson asked for the president's support for Israel, while his secretary of state threatened not to vote for Truman if he recognized the newly established state. Similar examples can be found in every administration.

What's more, the critics of U.S. Middle East policy never can explain anomalies in their conspiracy theories; first and foremost, why American policy is so often at odds with the "powerful" Israeli lobby. The Israeli lobby, for example, failed for years to convince U.S. administrations to provide sophisticated arms to Israel, was unable to prevent Eisenhower from issuing dire threats that forced Israel's withdrawal from the Sinai after 1956, did not deter Ronald Reagan from imposing sanctions in the 1980s and George W. Bush from punishing Israel during his term, and cannot, even now, prevent dangerous arms sales to Arab countries or the adoption of critical resolutions at the United Nations. The reasons for the Israeli lobby's failures are sometimes complex—Cold War calculations, competition with allies, presidential lobbying, economic considerations—but the Arab lobby often plays a role.

One obstacle the Arab lobby faces is the negative image of Muslims and Arabs; consequently one of its principal objectives is to fight the stereotyping of Muslims and Arabs as terrorists. Members of the lobby complain, for example, about the portrayal of Muslims in films[7] as if they expect screenwriters to choose Norwegians or Swedes as villains rather than Arabs who have committed the types of atrocities reenacted in the movies. They have also tried to tar critics with the epithet Islamophobe, implying that anyone who dares suggest that radical Muslims may pose a danger to the United States is a racist. This is a conscious effort by the Arab lobby to imitate what it sees as the successful and cynical use by Jews of the term "anti-Semitism" to silence critics of Israel.

The problem is that terrorism continues, and many of the perpetrators *are* Muslims. Obviously, however, not all Muslims are radicals or terrorists, and Islam as a religion cannot be blamed for the actions of a few, so one justifiable role for the Arab lobby is to fight intolerance and prejudice.

While Walt/Mearsheimer and others may rage against a Middle East policy that they believe is counter to American interests, most Americans themselves disagree. The public believes that Israel is a reliable ally, and that support for Israel is in our interest. By contrast, little public support is demonstrable for closer ties with the Arab/Muslim world. Frustration with American public opinion also explains the Arab lobby's propaganda efforts in the media and, especially, in schools to try to change attitudes. Hundreds of millions of dollars have been invested in a long-term campaign to prettify the Arab world, especially Saudi Arabia, vilify Israel, sanitize radical Islam, and glorify the Palestinian struggle for independence. In the short run, the Saudis have taken a different tack from the Israeli lobby, focusing on a top-down rather than bottom-up approach to lobbying. As hired gun J. Crawford Cook wrote in laying out his proposed strategy for the kingdom, "Saudi Arabia has a need to influence the few that influence the many, rather than the need to influence the many to whom the few must respond."[8]

Though this lobbying effort has not yet shifted public attitudes, public support for Israel has not translated into automatic support for Israeli policies or the Israeli lobby's agenda. In fact, U.S. interests in the Middle East can be reduced to the following, in this order:

1. Assuring the supply of oil
2. Maximizing trade opportunities
3. Containing radical Islam/fighting terror
4. Ensuring Israel's security
5. Promoting democracy

Unlike those who see a global Jewish conspiracy in which an omnipotent Israeli lobby stands behind U.S. Middle East policy, I recognize that American policy is more nuanced, influenced not only by lobbies but also, first and foremost, by the ideology of the principal foreign policy decision maker, the president of the United States. For seventy years, the Arab lobby has persistently tried to influence policy, directly, by lobbying decision makers, and indirectly, by seeking to manipulate the media and propagandize the American educational system, often to the detriment of the national interest. The following chapters describe the key players in the lobby, their successes and failures, and the negative impact the Arab lobby has often had on American policy.

CHAPTER ONE

The Seeds of the Arab Lobby:
The Problem of "Palestine"

America's involvement in the Middle East began with nine-teenth-century missionaries who were interested in converting Muslims to Christianity and "rescue the land of the Bible from Moslem backwardness."[1] They failed miserably; the Muslims considered themselves the ones with faith and the Americans godless. This forced the missionaries to sublimate their overarching goal of conversion to a more practical and popular objective of providing education and social services to the Arabs.

This was also a period when the first Jewish pioneers began to move to Palestine in the hope of reestablishing a Jewish homeland. The missionaries had a natural antipathy toward Jews in general and the Jews of the Middle East in particular. They believed the Jews were Christ-killers who needed to be saved through conversion. To their dismay, however, the Christians found the Jews uninterested in their ministration and unwilling to convert. Paradoxically, the Christians would still feel affection for Muslim Arabs, who for the most part were equally uninterested in adopting Christianity. One of the earliest comments by a U.S. official came from the anti-Semitic consul in Jerusalem, Seth Merrill, who said in 1891 that "Palestine is not ready for the Jews . . . [and] the Jews are not ready for Palestine. . . . To pour into this impoverished country tens of thousands of Jews would be an unspeakable calamity both for the country and for the Jews themselves. . . . The quickest way to annihilate them would be to place them in Palestine with no restrictions or influences from any civilized government, and allow them to govern themselves; they would very soon destroy each other."[2]

The United States began its formal relationship with Zionism when President Woodrow Wilson was asked to support the Balfour Declaration, issued by the British in 1917, which called for the establishment of a Jewish homeland in Palestine. When Balfour issued his declaration, however, opposition quickly emerged. Much has been written about efforts by Jews such as Louis Brandeis to lobby Wilson to support Balfour, but much less has been said about those who opposed it, including Wilson confidant Colonel Edward House and Secretary of State Robert Lansing. House was not concerned about the Arabs so much as about the machinations of the English to secure their interests in India and Egypt; he feared the British were turning the region into "a breeding place for future war." He was, however, sympathetic to the Arabs as well, writing in his diary, "I have a kindly feeling for the Arabs and my influence will be thrown in their direction whenever they are right."[3]

Similarly, Lansing was more worried about Christian reaction than Arab/Muslim objections to the creation of a Jewish homeland. He did not support what he viewed as the theft of Turkish territory because he believed that Christians would "resent turning the Holy Land over to the absolute control of the race credited with the death of Christ." He also worried that the Muslims in the Middle East and North Africa would expect Wilson to support their self-determination, which conflicted with the president's commitment to Zionism.[4] America's ambassador to Great Britain also opposed the Balfour Declaration. William Yale, the State Department's representative to the British army in Syria and Palestine, was appalled by the arrogance of some Jews and predicted a global Muslim backlash and inevitable war if a Jewish state was established.[5]

The State Department exerted little influence over Wilson on the Palestine issue. In fact, Wilson and Lansing were barely on speaking terms. At the 1919 Paris Peace Conference, the department worked with Jewish anti-Zionists, the Arab delegation, Protestant missionaries, and the British Colonial Office to try to prevent the endorsement of the Balfour Declaration. But the views of Brandeis and other supporters of Zionism were more consistent with Wilson's messianic worldview, and their arguments were more persuasive. Wilson was "fascinated with the idea that a democratic Zionism might replace Ottoman despotism and create a haven for oppressed Jews in Palestine."[6] Ultimately, despite misgivings, particularly about the danger to Americans, Wilson did express support for the declaration. "The allied nations with the fullest concurrence of our government and people are agreed," he said, "that in Palestine shall be laid the foundations of a Jewish Commonwealth." To the consternation of Secretary of State Charles Evans Hughes, the U.S. Congress gave its endorsement to the Balfour Declaration in September 1922.[7]

The State Department afterward simply pretended that these congressional resolutions and presidential statements did not really reflect U.S. policy, discounting congressional statements as pandering for votes and suggesting that the president's positions were somehow ambiguous.

Americans working in the region vigorously opposed what they viewed as an abandonment of principle and a forfeiture of U.S. interests to the colonial ambitions of the Europeans. Missionaries held the Arabs in high esteem, and fell in love with the exotic qualities of the desert dwellers. They considered the Arabs intelligent and were drawn to their warmth and hospitality. As their affection for the Arabs grew, so did their enmity toward the colonial powers they believed were enslaving them and the Zionists, whom they viewed as encroaching on a noble people who wished to overcome their long oppression at the hands of the Turks and imperialists. These missionaries ultimately became an important component of the nascent Arab lobby.

While the missionaries were lobbying their government from outside, others who shared their views tried to influence policy from within the government. These officials, mostly diplomats in the State Department, with some allies in other agencies such as the CIA and the Defense Department, came to be known as Arabists.

The classic definition of Arabists recognized them as people who were fluent in Arabic and had spent a great deal of time living and working in the Arab world. Many had missionary parents and grew up in the region, or had family connections to the American universities in Beirut and Cairo. Others became enthralled by the region and took an academic interest. Over the years, however, the term took on a pejorative meaning, becoming associated with diplomats who "are assumed to be politically naïve, elitist and too deferential to exotic cultures."[8] Unlike the classic Arabists, those who became part of the Arab lobby often could not speak Arabic, and some had spent little or no time in the region. The quintessential Arabist, for example, was Loy Henderson, who headed the Near East Division but spoke no Arabic and had spent only two years in the region.

As America was asked to support the Zionists in Palestine, and later the state of Israel, the Arabists became vocal opponents. Some did so because of their own anti-Semitic views, while others believed they were making politically rational calculations of America's national interest, which sometimes appeared to outsiders as anti-Semitic because the diplomats' views were highly critical of Zionists or Israel and solicitous of the Arabs. These Arabists are often responsible professionals who have come to the conclusion that U.S. interests are best served by distancing the United States from Israel and working closely with Arab governments, often without regard for the internal affairs of those regimes. Others, however, are motivated by a self-righteous belief that they know what is best for America, and some maintain they also have Israel's interests at heart.

The principal U.S. interests in the 1920s were missionary endeavors, trade, and the protection of treaty rights established during the Ottoman period. Palestine was under British control, and diplomats believed Britain was responsible for dealing with the Zionists. Even when events in Palestine directly affected American citizens, the State Department would not fulfill its normal duty of assisting them. In 1929, for example, Arab riots at the Western Wall left eight American citizens dead. New York congressman Hamilton Fish Jr. called on the U.S. Navy to send ships to Palestine, and land marines if necessary, to protect Americans "endangered by fanatical and lawless mobs." The American consul general in Jerusalem, Paul Knabenshue, became perhaps the first State Department Arabist to make his presence felt on the Palestine issue when he responded by suggesting that the attacks "were precipitated by provocative acts of the Jews," and that raising the issue with the British would "undoubtedly create resentment against us here and in other Moslem countries."[9] Knabenshue was so blatantly anti-Semitic that American Jews called for his removal, and Secretary of State Henry Stimson transferred him to Baghdad.

Near Eastern Affairs chief G. Howland Shaw objected even to the idea of representing the dead Americans before the British commission investigating the riots. "Why," Shaw asked, "should the American Government assist in presenting either the Jewish or Arab side?"[10] One reason was that the U.S. government *had* endorsed the Jewish side reflected in the Balfour Declaration. Another reason was that Arab rioting provoked by the mufti of Jerusalem had caused the deaths of U.S. citizens.

After a series of Arab-instigated riots in 1936, the British asked William Peel to lead an investigation. He concluded the following year that the best solution to the competing claims of Jews and Arabs over the land of Palestine was to divide it (though not evenly) and create two separate states. The State Department Arabists vigorously opposed the Peel Commission's plan, insisting it would stimulate greater enmity toward the United States. Wallace Murray, an anti-Semite who headed the Near East Division for sixteen years (1929–45), said Jews should be sent far from the Middle East, suggesting they might find more hospitable homes in Angola, Cameroon, or Madagascar.[11]

The Arabs rejected the Peel Commission's plan and launched a nearly three-year revolt that again culminated in British reconsideration of the country's policy in Palestine. In 1939, Britain offered the Arabs a unitary state in all of Palestine. This so-called White Paper was a much better deal for the Arabs than the Peel plan, but the Arabs once again rejected the idea, largely because it allowed for continued Jewish immigration.

President Franklin Roosevelt told his secretary of state, Cordell Hull, that he would not support the British proposal, and the U.S. ambassador to Great Britain, Joseph Kennedy, was told to inform the British government of the president's disapproval. Kennedy privately let the Foreign Office know it did not have to take his message seriously, however. No doubt he understood that Roosevelt did not want to start a diplomatic row with America's closest ally at a time of international tension.

This would not be the last time that the State Department pursued a policy that was independent of the administration. Officials often promised Arab leaders that they would be consulted before any decisions were made on Palestine. Thus, while Hull told Kennedy to pass on Roosevelt's objections, he also instructed his officers to tell the Arabs that "while Washington did not give its approval to the White Paper, it did not give its disapproval, either."[12]

During the war, Secretary of State Hull and others were unwilling to support Jewish immigration to Palestine. They were not even helpful when it came to American Jews seeking to escape Hitler. Hull and the principal architect of the anti-Jewish policies during this period, Breckenridge Long, argued that Jews should not be treated differently than any other group. The fact that Hitler was singling them out for special treatment was no reason for the Americans to do so. The Department went so far as to oppose American Red Cross aid to refugees in Palestine because it might look as though the Jews were getting special treatment.[13]

As the plight of Jews in Europe grew more precarious, and reports of Hitler's actions filtered out, Jews in Palestine wanted to join the fight in Europe and lobbied the British government to allow them to do so. The State Department opposed this on the grounds that it would upset the Arabs and make it more difficult to use the Middle East as a base of operations.

As the magnitude of the Holocaust became clear, and tens of thousands of survivors clamored to move to their homeland, pressure increased on the United States to take a more active role on the Palestine issue. Murray and others at State also continued their campaign to reverse the Balfour Declaration, partly on the grounds that support for the Zionists was alienating the Arabs and endangering American troops in the Middle East. Their sympathy for the Arabs during the war was particularly ironic, given that only 9,000 Arabs enlisted in the British Army, and the leader of the Palestinians, Mufti Haj Amin al-Husseini, openly supported the Nazis. Meanwhile, 33,000 Jews (out of a much smaller population) signed up to fight the Germans even as they were being persecuted by the British within their homeland, and saw immigration strangled.

Some of the Arabists also held a view that would echo through the halls of the State Department for the next sixty years, namely that they knew what was best for the Jews and were actually trying to help them. One of the earliest manifestations of this attitude was undersecretary of state A. A. Berle's warning to American Zionist leader Emanuel Neumann that the Jews would suffer a horrible fate in Palestine if the Nazis conquered the area. He advised Neumann to cut a deal with ibn Saud of Saudi Arabia, renounce their claim to Palestine, and move most of the Jews to Kenya until the war ended. After the war, they would get a Vatican-like territory somewhere in Africa.[14]

Arabists also seized on any suggestion from Jews that statehood might not be such a good idea, as when the anti-Zionist rabbi Morris Lazaron publicly criticized the Zionist program. He was one of the first of many Jews who would also become involved in Arab lobby efforts to undermine the legitimacy of Israel. These Jews tended to speak either as individuals or as members of tiny organizations that, while making only marginal contributions to the debate, allowed diplomats and others to rationalize their position. Thus, Arabists such as Wallace Murray justified their opposition to Zionism by arguing they could not be expected to support a Jewish state when the Jews themselves were not unanimously behind the idea.

While the State Department was trying to promote the idea that Jews were disunited, it also sought to sabotage the organizations representing the Zionists. The department closely monitored the activities of the American Zionist Emergency Committee, the Zionist

Organization of America, and other Jewish and non-Jewish groups supporting the establishment of a Jewish state. Presaging efforts that would be made years later by the Arab lobby against AIPAC, the State Department hoped to find evidence that would require the AZEC to register as a foreign agent.[15]

Paradoxically, the State Department was largely responsible for the creation of the Israeli lobby and the methods Arabists would complain about for most of the succeeding sixty-odd years, which arose as a direct response to their obstructionism. In 1943, AZEC decided to try to force the State Department to adopt a more sympathetic policy by seeking congressional help. They succeeded in having resolutions introduced, calling for the repeal of the 1939 British White Paper limiting Jewish immigration to Palestine and support for the establishment of a Jewish state after the war. This set the precedent for the approach AIPAC would ultimately adopt of seeking congressional support for its agenda, using the legislative branch to influence, constrain, or obstruct executive branch policies.

This first effort during World War II was met with opposition from the secretary of war, who argued that the resolutions would upset the Arabs and might provoke a civil war in Palestine that could be exploited by the Axis. The Zionists, not aware of Henry Stimson's position, were given to believe they had the support of the administration. The British, however, had also weighed in against the legislation, and army chief of staff and future secretary of state George Marshall was called to testify in a secret session of the Foreign Relations Committee. Roosevelt also pressured several Zionist leaders to testify before the committee that delaying the measures would not adversely affect their goals. The resolutions subsequently were allowed to die. Most members of Congress supported the plan but would not vote on it because the administration maintained that doing so would upset the Arabs, and they were afraid to do anything that might undermine Allied war efforts.[16] This was similar to the rationale given for not doing more to rescue the Jews of Europe.

The AZEC tried to have passed resolutions in early 1944 calling for the United States to help facilitate Jewish immigration to Palestine for the purpose of ultimately establishing a Jewish state. The State Department once again succeeded in killing the legislation by arguing that "although not binding on the Executive, [the resolutions] might precipitate conflict in Palestine and other parts of the Arab world, endangering American troops and requiring the diversion of forces from Europe and other combat areas." If that wasn't sufficient, Hull piled on with the warning that "it might prejudice or shatter pending negotiations with ibn Saud for the construction of a pipeline across Saudi Arabia."

Another concern expressed by anti-Zionists was the fear of Jewish sympathy (and potential alignment) with the USSR. The Joint Chiefs of Staff summarized the view of many officials when they reported that the Zionist leadership "stems from the Soviet Union and its satellite states and has strong bonds of kinship in those regions, and ideologically is much closer to the Soviet Union than the United States."[17] The Defense Department under James Forrestal, who was an outspoken opponent of Zionist aims and a former lawyer for Texaco, worried about oil supplies, the possibility that the Arabs might ally with the Soviets if they were alienated by the West, and the prospect of sending troops to Palestine to enforce a settlement. Forrestal's principal Middle East adviser was Steven Penrose, an Arabist who served as the OSS intelligence head in Cairo and then chief of intelligence in Washington, D.C. Penrose used his official posts to fight the Zionists and refused requests for help in rescuing Holocaust refugees. Later, he became president of the American University of Beirut.[18]

The danger of Communist infiltration in the Middle East would become a recurring theme of the Arab lobby as it worked to prevent and later undermine U.S. support for a Jewish state. Harold Hoskins, who had been an emissary to the Middle East for Roosevelt, as an Aramco director in 1948 wrote to the State Department from Baghdad that American policy on Palestine was undermining the Truman Doctrine by making Soviet infiltration possible. Missionaries such as Bayard Dodge made apocalyptic predictions of the destruction of all the American institutions in the Middle East, which he believed would benefit the Russians, who were already planning to flood the Jewish state with Jewish Communists.[19]

This view was supported by the U.S. ambassador to Moscow, W. Averell Harriman, who argued that U.S. support for Zionism was provoking Arab anger and warned that the Soviets would try to exploit this resentment to gain influence in the region. When the Soviets later reversed their position and supported partition, anti-Zionists such as Kermit Roosevelt argued that the Russians were trying to secure a military foothold in the Middle East. Given the socialist leanings of the Jewish leadership, it was not totally unreasonable to fear that a Jewish state would be aligned with the Soviets, and it would not become obvious that the threat was exaggerated until the early 1950s.

Another theme that emerged during the war, which has remained a dominant one to this day, was that it was important that the United States make concessions to the Arabs to win their support or prevent them from siding with our enemies. During World War II, for example, the minister in Cairo, Alexander Kirk, became concerned that the Arabs were becoming too sympathetic to the Nazis and proposed that they could be won over to the Allies by a renunciation of support for Jewish statehood.[20] Later the Arabists warned that the Arabs would join the Soviet camp if the United States did not oppose the Zionists. Even after the United States became recognized as a superpower, it never occurred to them that America should insist that the Arab states back American interests to earn U.S. support.

The missionaries and their supporters at the State Department had long made the case that U.S. interests in the region were based on the presence of Americans in the Middle East and the importance of supporting their activities. Paradoxically, they saw no interest in Palestine despite the fact that 78 percent of all Americans (9,100 citizens, 84 percent of whom were Jews) in the Middle East lived there. More Americans were in that area than in all the others combined. In addition, $49 million was invested in Palestine, $41 million by American Jews, a sum larger than that invested in all the Arab countries combined, excluding Saudi Arabia. So purely on the basis of the need to protect American lives and investments, the case could be made that the United States should take a strong interest in Palestine and, especially, in Jewish settlement.[21]

The diplomats saw things differently, however, and insisted that interest in Palestine was politically driven by a small group pursuing their own narrow interests. The investments in Palestine were "artificial and chimerical," whereas the oil concessions in the Persian Gulf area represented real economic investments that advanced the national interest. Consequently, whenever American Zionists protested British restrictions in Palestine, the State Department dismissed them as matters for Great Britain to handle, but if American oil companies asked for diplomatic intervention, the State Department swiftly asserted the rights of American citizens.

America's main interest at this time shifted to Saudi Arabia, and the seeds for another major constituency of the Arab lobby were planted in the sand where engineers from Standard Oil of California (SoCal) received permission to search for oil on the Arabian peninsula. This was also the origin of the first lobbying efforts by the small Arab American community, who formed the Palestine National League to try to convince the U.S. government to pressure Great Britain to abandon the Balfour Declaration.

The Arab lobby expanded with the formation of the Arab League in March 1945, which created an umbrella organization for the Arab states to express their views. This was also a period when Arab Americans became more active, as did Christian groups. The Arab American community had grown from 200,000 in the 1920s to approximately 500,000 by World War II, and a number of organizations began to spring up across the United States to oppose Zionism and lobby the State Department. The inadequacy of these efforts, however, led the Arab governments meeting in Alexandria in October 1944 to establish an organization, the Arab Office, to counter the Zionists in Washington, London, and Jerusalem.

The oil companies also weighed in, with one executive suggesting that support for Jewish claims in Palestine might adversely affect U.S. interests in Saudi Arabia. He warned that American companies could even be expelled. The oil industry effectively joined the Arab lobby at this point. What makes this especially interesting is that it occurred at a time when the United States still had minimal interests in Saudi Arabia and had only recently struck oil. Actually, the companies warned the State Department from 1937 on that American support for Zionism might undermine American interests in the Middle East. One author noted that "by the late 1940s this point was so abundantly clear that no special advocates were required. . . . By 1947 all of the key people in State and Defense were aware of the strategic problem . . . there was little need for special lobbying."[22]

Still, some lobbying took place. James Terry Duce, then vice president in charge of Aramco operations, for example, met with officials at State on November 4, 1946, to complain about Truman's support for a Jewish state and issued dire warnings about the fate of the oil concession, going so far as to suggest that Aramco might have to "convert itself into a British corporation to save its investment."[23]

While the oil companies did present a pro-Arab view, they were mostly neutral on Zionism and admitted that King Saud was more dependent on the United States than America was on Saudi Arabia. Consequently, they were not seriously concerned that the Arabs could harm their interests. Abe Fortas, the undersecretary of the interior, told one of the pro-Zionist lobbyists that "even the oil companies hardly believe that strong American backing of Zionism would result in a permanent endangering of American interests."[24]

The Arabs were of course vigorously opposed to the Zionist enterprise, and no one was more adamant than the king of Saudi Arabia. Considering himself the leader of the Arabs and Muslims, King Saud felt compelled to speak out against Jewish aggression in Palestine. And it is important to note that he was speaking very explicitly about Jews. Today, especially, distinctions are sometimes drawn between Jews and Zionists; Israel's detractors suggest that they only oppose the actions of the Israeli government but have nothing against the Jewish religion. King Saud and his successors, however, made no secret of their hatred of Jews, as reflected in their statements and the long-standing practice of barring Jews and the practice of Judaism from the kingdom. For example, King Saud told British colonel H. R. P. Dickson on November 23, 1937, "Our hatred for the Jews dates from God's condemnation of them for their persecution and rejection of Isa (Jesus) and their subsequent rejection of His chosen Prophet." At one point in the mid-1940s, as the Palestine issue heated up, Saud threatened to execute any Jew who tried to enter the kingdom.[25]

One ongoing theme in discussions with the Saudis from this early point, as with many other U.S. Arab "allies," is the naive belief that they could be persuaded to either support America's pro-Zionist policies or at least minimize opposition to them. In May 1943, King Saud first made his views clear on the subject after viewing with alarm the Roosevelt administration's drift toward support for the establishment of a Jewish state. "Jews have no right to Palestine," he wrote the president. "God forbid . . . the Allies should, at the end of their struggle, crown their victory by evicting the Arabs from their home."[26]

The Saudis had not yet achieved the fabulous wealth they are now known for; in fact, they constantly needed American cash, and their oil reserves were not yet viewed as vital to American security, but government officials feared losing access to the oil fields and the prospect of another government, notably the British, gaining influence in the kingdom. The State Department subsequently backed the king's warnings by suggesting that support for the Zionists would undermine America's economic, commercial, cultural, and philanthropic interests throughout the Arab world.

Some diplomats held out hope that Saud's support for partition could be bought. In 1942, the British tried to arrange a deal where they would make him the leader of the Arab world (something the State Department would later try as well) if he worked out a deal with Chaim Weizmann, the Zionist leader, who would also arrange for Jewish funds to help him pay off his debts, which at that time were primarily owed to the British. Wallace Murray was convinced the only way Saud would accept such a deal would be if a single binational state was created that would effectively deny Jews the homeland promised by Balfour, so he hoped to set up a situation whereby the U.S. would get credit in the Arab world if Weizmann compromised and basically sold out the Zionist program and could blame the British if anything went wrong. Max Thornberg of SoCal, a consultant to the State Department at the time, favored the approach. He was convinced that ibn Saud was not really anti-Semitic, but was only saying what the British wanted him to.[27] Undersecretary of state Sumner Welles also believed the idea had a chance of success based on the precedent of meetings held between Weizmann and the Arab leader Emir Faisal after World War I. Roosevelt subsequently agreed to send Harold Hoskins as an emissary to ask ibn Saud whether he would be willing to meet with Weizmann or other representatives of the Jewish Agency to discuss a solution to the dispute.

The king's reaction was hostile. He told Hoskins that he was "prepared to talk to anyone, of any religion, except a Jew" and that he specifically disliked Weizmann because Saud claimed the Zionist leader had tried to bribe him. The State Department thought the entire exercise had been an embarrassing waste of time whose failure was predictable.[28]

Roosevelt decided to meet with Saud and discuss the issues face-to-face. Following his meeting with Stalin and Churchill at Yalta in February 1945, Roosevelt traveled to the Great Bitter Lake in the Suez Canal and met Saud, who was making his first trip outside his kingdom, aboard the U.S. cruiser *Quincy*. The translator for Roosevelt was William Eddy, the U.S. minister in Jidda and one of the pioneer Arabists in the State Department. (He later wrote a book about the meeting that was paid for in part by "the pro-Arab lobby and CIA-subsidized American Friends of the Middle East Inc."[29])

Roosevelt made plain his support for the Jewish survivors of what was not yet called the Holocaust. He also expressed his admiration for the Jews who fought against the Nazis and who had developed Palestine, and asked the king to support his idea of establishing in Palestine a free and democratic Jewish commonwealth. Saud would have none of it, arguing deceitfully that it was the Arabs and not the Jews who had fought against the Germans, and that it was the British and not the Jews who made the deserts bloom. The king was adamantly against allowing Jews to go to Palestine or establish their own state and suggested that they be given the homes of Germans instead. When Roosevelt said that three million Jews had been slaughtered in Poland alone, Saud replied that there must now be room there for three million more.[30]

Roosevelt was shocked by the vehemence of the king's reaction. He should not have been, given Saud's previous uncompromising statements, including his remark on the eve of the Yalta Conference that Palestine would be drenched in blood, and that the United States must choose between the Zionists and the Arabs.

Roosevelt argued that Palestine was such a small part of the Middle East that the Arabs would not be harmed by the creation of a Jewish state, and he was prepared to guarantee that "the Jews would not move into adjacent parts of the Near East from Palestine."[31] But he seemed to backtrack by the end of his meeting, promising the king that the United States would not take any position on Palestine without first consulting him and other Arab leaders, and would not do anything for the Jews at their expense. This was the promise he had made in May 1943, that "no decision altering the basic situation of Palestine should be reached without full consultation with both Arabs and Jews." He also pledged support for Syrian and Lebanese independence.

Afterward, Saud wrote a letter to Roosevelt in which he insisted that Palestine "has been an Arab country since the dawn of history and . . . was never inhabited by Jews for more than a period of time, during which their history in the land was full of murder and cruelty. . . . [There is] religious hostility . . . between the Muslims and the Jews from the beginning of Islam . . . which arose from the treacherous conduct of the Jews towards Islam and the Muslims and their prophet."[32]

While historian Michael Oren has called the meeting notable because "the leader of the world's most powerful democratic nation had in fact bowed to the dictates of an Arabian chieftain," he adds that Roosevelt saw it more as a "source of exotic entertainment" than a diplomatic landmark.[33] Nevertheless, it clearly had its effect. Roosevelt told a joint session of Congress on March 1, 1945, "I learned more about the whole problem, the Moslem problem, the Jewish problem, by talking with ibn Saud for five minutes than I could have learned in an exchange of two or three dozen letters." The Zionists were horrified, and feared he had reneged on his pledge of support for a Jewish state.

Privately, Roosevelt expressed conflicting opinions. He had told Hoskins that, given the size of the Arab population, a Jewish state "could be installed and maintained only by force." Before his meeting with Saud, however, he told undersecretary of state Edward Stettinius, "Palestine should be for the Jews and no Arabs should be in it." After his speech to Congress, Roosevelt wrote to reassure the American Jewish leader Stephen Wise that he supported unrestricted immigration to Palestine and a future Jewish state. Roosevelt told Wise he had arranged the meeting with Saud to make the Zionist case, but admitted, "I have never so completely failed to make an impact upon a man's mind as in his case." The Arabists, meanwhile, continued to reassure their friends in the Middle East that the United States would not act without consulting them, as Roosevelt had promised Saud. When the Arabs tried to suggest they had received a different commitment from Roosevelt, Wise released the letter from the president.[34]

Roosevelt was the consummate politician, telling partisans on both sides what they wanted to hear either directly or through his minions. As Jews would do after the war, Wise defended Roosevelt and excused his indiscretions as the result of being misled by "some supersubtle counselors in the State Department."[35] The president died before any decisions had to be made on the future of Palestine. Still, it is one of the great ironies of history that American Jews would revere him and developed a strong attachment to the Democratic Party as a result, despite the fact that Roosevelt failed to take steps before and during the war that could have saved thousands of European Jews, and that most of his actions with respect to the Zionist program were unhelpful.

CHAPTER TWO

The Arab Lobby Campaign
against a Jewish State

Six days after he assumed office as Roosevelt's successor, Secretary of State Stettinius warned President Truman of the likely pressure he would face from Zionists. Somewhat condescendingly, no doubt, he told the new president that Palestine was a complex issue (implying that only the Arabists could really understand it) and that it was necessary to handle it carefully (translation: reverse course on supporting Balfour) to avoid damaging U.S. interests in the region. In short, the Arabists tried to capitalize on Roosevelt's death by persuading Truman to abandon his policy of support for a Jewish state. Truman didn't take this well, and never really trusted most of the advice he received from the "striped-pants boys."[1]

The birth of the Arab lobby as a force in the United States coincided with the birth of the United Nations in April 1945. Five Arab states had official delegations in San Francisco and were joined by a number of pro-Arab organizations. An Arab Information Office was also opened in Washington, and pro-Arab speakers began to tour college campuses, recognizing that it was important to try to influence the views not only of current policy makers but of future ones as well.

When the UN convened, most of the delegations knew little or nothing of the Palestine issue. Churchill had announced prior to the meeting that the resolution of that matter would be postponed until the end of the war, but the Zionists still feared that the Arab lobby would attempt to undermine support for the Balfour Declaration and alter the form of the mandate. The Arabs had a significant advantage at the conference; five official government delegations—Egypt, Iraq, Saudi Arabia, Syria, and Lebanon—represented the second largest of the forty-nine delegations in San Francisco. As such, they were entitled to advance their interests with other delegations through normal diplomatic channels. They used informal approaches as well; for example, the oil companies paid for the Saudi delegation to take a group of leading American journalists on a tour of San Francisco Bay. As the Zionist representative Eliahu Elath noted, "The seagoing merriment was certainly not in keeping with traditional Wahhabi puritanism, but this did not seem to bother the Arabs aboard, who toasted the journalists drink for drink with something rather stronger than lemonade or Coca-Cola."[2] The Jewish representatives, meanwhile, had no official standing at the conference and had to make their case to delegates and journalists whenever they had an opportunity.

As the Zionists feared, the Arabs proposed that the UN Charter recognize the right of the Arab majority in Palestine to decide the political future of the country. The Zionists won the lobbying battle in the end, and the proposed changes received only the five votes of the Arab members.

From the outset, the Arab lobby had difficulty winning support because of its extremism. As one British diplomat observed, "The obstreperous activities of the Arab delegations have not . . . much improved their position against the Jews." Instead, he said their behavior had "boomeranged in favor of the Jews, [because of] the irritation which the reiterated and grandiloquent Arab claims produced amongst many of the other countries represented."[3] This summarizes one of the problematic features of the Arab lobby, which inhibits its effectiveness to this day.

To appease the Arabs, the British had placed restrictions on Jewish immigration to Palestine throughout the mandatory period. This policy continued after the war, provoking President Truman to issue a call for 100,000 Jews to be admitted. The Arabists were opposed, prompting Truman to remark that "the State Department continued to be more concerned about the Arab reaction than the sufferings of the Jews." He subsequently added that he believed a viable Jewish state should be created in Palestine to fulfill the promise of Balfour. The U.S. minister to Saudi Arabia, Colonel William Eddy, was so upset by Truman's pledge that he resigned in October 1947, telling Parker Hart privately that he believed his credibility with ibn Saud had been undermined, that he objected to the domestic influences he thought were responsible for the president's decision, and that Truman had betrayed Roosevelt's promise to ibn Saud.[4] In fact, the promise was kept: the United States consulted extensively with the Arabs but chose not to heed their opposition to Jewish immigration and, later, statehood.

King Saud also hoped to persuade President Truman of the importance of Saudi-American relations and discourage him from supporting the Zionists. Truman had tried to reassure the king of his commitment to Saudi Arabia while explaining his support for the creation of a Jewish national home in Palestine in a letter in October 1946. He added, "I do not consider that my urging of the admittance of a considerable number of displaced Jews into Palestine or my statements with regard to the solution to the problem of Palestine in any sense represent an action hostile to the Arab people."[5] The king was not mollified, however, and warned Truman that supporting a Jewish state would harm relations with the Arab world and that the Arabs "will lay siege to it until it dies of famine."[6]

Though Saud often made a show of his disdain for Jews and Zionists and his dissatisfaction with U.S. policy, he was far more concerned with other matters. As early as 1945, the tone was set for the U.S.-Saudi relationship, which would contradict the dire warnings of the Arabists for the last seventy years that America's support for Zionism and later Israel threatened ties with the Saudis. King Saud told Parker Hart that his disagreement with U.S. policy toward Palestine would have "no influence on his friendship with President Truman."[7] In fact, when Saud sent his son, Crown Prince Saud (who succeeded his father in 1953), to Washington two years later to oppose Zionism and communism and to "liberate US policy from the influence of local Jewish elements and Zionist propaganda," Saud's principal concern, besides a request for a $50 million loan for development, was to get reassurance that the U.S. would protect Saudi Arabia from not the Zionists but the Hashemites. This was the family that Saud had defeated and driven from Arabia, but which had won British favor because of their help in defeating the Turks in World War I. The British had rewarded the Hashemites by installing one member of the family as king of Iraq and creating Transjordan (later Jordan) for another member of the family to rule. King Saud feared that his old rivals might one day try to return to Saudi Arabia. This would remain a Saudi obsession until the Hashemite king in Iraq was deposed in a coup in 1958.

At the time partition was being debated, U.S. companies were building the Trans-Arabian Pipeline (Tapline) to carry Saudi oil to the Mediterranean for transshipment to Europe. Four days after the partition vote, on December 3, 1947, King Saud summoned U.S. representative J. Rives Childs and informed him that he would not try to change America's position on Palestine, but was more concerned with getting a commitment from the United States to protect him from his rivals in Transjordan and Iraq. Childs, nevertheless, reported to the department that the king might trade the relationship with the United States for an alliance with the British. Childs was either being disingenuous, putting his own spin on what he was being told, or completely misread the Saudi position. After getting instructions from Washington, Childs later told the king the United States would support Saudi Arabia through the UN, a response Saud did not find reassuring.[8]

Two weeks later, the Saudis' real interests became clearer when King Saud intimated that relations with the United States were dependent on obtaining military assistance. Loy Henderson recommended giving the Saudis what they wanted to forestall Saud from turning to the British, even as he was complaining about British support for the Hashemites. Saud expressed concern that his rivals might threaten the northern part of his kingdom, where the Tapline was being constructed. The king wanted the United States to equip and train 80,000 Saudis for mechanized warfare and provide fifty aircraft to defend the country against his rivals. "America," he insisted, "must help me at least as the British are helping the Hashemites."[9]

This was the first Saudi request for U.S. arms, but it would not be the last. Saud's request was turned down because of the arms embargo to the region. Forced to be consistent, the Truman administration had no choice but to tell him that the United States had decided not to export any weapons to Palestine or neighboring countries. The administration reassured him, however, that the United States remained committed to the territorial integrity and independence of Saudi Arabia. Saud was not mollified, however, and asked again for arms a few months later as well as proposing a formal defense treaty, ideas that were again rejected.[10]

Besides fearing the Communists and Hashemites, Saud had no money to modernize the country and considered it vital to secure loans and technical assistance from the United States. One of his top priorities was to build a railroad, and the State Department negotiated with Aramco to build and pay for it but allow the Saudis to own it.[11]

Ironically, at the time of the partition debate, the United States had great leverage over the Arabs. None of the Arab states, including the Saudis, had any great wealth or influence. U.S. investments outside Aramco were marginal. As one of two superpowers, the Arabs needed the United States much more than Americans needed the Arabs. Rather than pursuing the sycophantic line of the Arabists, the United States could have taken a tough stand that conditioned recognition and aid on support for the U.S. position on Palestine. In that case the Arabs might have been forced to accept the reality of a Jewish state and learned that they could not coerce the United States. Had that precedent been set early, U.S.-Arab relations, and the entire Middle East, might look very different today.

Arab opposition to the Zionist program was partly offset by the feeling that something should be done for the victims of Hitler, hundreds of thousands of whom remained stateless after the war and sought refuge in Palestine. The Arabists were unsympathetic to their plight, in part because of their own anti-Semitism and inability to identify with Jewish suffering. Many of them were conditioned by their upbringing at a time when anti-Semitism was still a powerful force in American life, particularly among the clubby northeastern establishment and schools that produced them, and many had little, if any, contact with Jews. Bill Stoltzfus Jr., who served in several Arab embassies, explained, "When the first photos and stories about the concentration camps appeared, I remember reading about it and being shocked, horrified. Sure, I felt sympathy for the Jews. But it was an abstract sympathy. Like the kind others feel when reading about the Cambodians or the Ethiopians. If you don't know people personally who have been affected, it's very hard to stay continually worked up over what has happened to them. The Jews were a distant, unreal world to us then, but the Palestinians were individuals we knew."[12]

Unlike the Arabists, Truman was sympathetic to the plight of the Jews, but even he often became frustrated, saying, for example, "Jesus Christ couldn't please them when he was on this earth, so how would anyone expect that I would have any luck?"[13] He was no less irritated by the Near East hands; according to him, they believed that "Great Britain has maintained her position in the area by cultivating the Arabs; now that she seems no longer able to hold this position, the United States must take over, and it must be done by exactly the same formula: if the Arabs are antagonized they will go over into the Soviet camp. I was never convinced by these arguments of the diplomats."[14]

In addition to the State Department Arabists, American Protestant missionaries were also agitating against the Zionist program. According to one British official involved in discussions about the future of Palestine, they "challenged the Zionist case with all the arguments of the most violently pro-Arab British Middle Eastern officials."[15] The reference to British officials, incidentally, is a reminder that the Arab lobby's activities are not limited to the United States.

The British Foreign Office, for example, had "gone native" long before American diplomats arrived on the scene.

After the British decided in February 1947 to turn the question of Palestine over to the UN, a special commission (UNSCOP) was appointed to determine the best course of action. The Arab Office collaborated with the Institute of Arab American Affairs to argue to UNSCOP against the partition plan, one of the final acts of the Arab League–funded effort to influence the Palestine debate. In December, the Arab Office closed its Washington headquarters after it was accused of being involved with anti-Semitic and pro-Nazi groups in the United States and violating the terms of the Foreign Registrations Act.[16]

The Arabists also tried to prevent a decision by UNSCOP in favor of partition. In a particularly ironic memo, William Eddy, still America's representative in Saudi Arabia, warned Secretary of State George Marshall that partition would be an endorsement of a "theocratic sovereign state characteristic of the Dark Ages."[17]

Once the commission's majority had concluded that dividing Palestine into a Jewish and an Arab state was the best solution, the Arabists lobbied within the administration to withhold support for the plan. They hoped to avoid the appearance that partition was an American plan because they feared it would provoke Arab anger. The Arabists also believed the proposal would not be adopted by the full UN General Assembly without vigorous backing from the United States. State succeeded in maintaining this policy for only about two weeks before it was foiled by the president, who instructed the State Department to issue a statement in support of partition.

After failing to prevent the endorsement of the UN majority report calling for partition, the Arabists tried to whittle away the borders of the Jewish state, proposing, for example, that the city of Jaffa be moved from the Jewish to the Arab side and that the eastern boundary of the Arab state be redrawn to include the holy Jewish city of Safed. The State Department also instructed ambassador to the UN Herschel Johnson to support the inclusion of the Negev—a region the Zionists viewed as critical for their state's future development, and which made up 60 percent of its area—in the Arab state. Chaim Weizmann met with Truman and convinced the president to oppose the change. Truman saw the potential of the area, which he compared in his memoir to the Tennessee River Basin. When Truman called General John Hilldring (the person he appointed in part to monitor what the State Department was doing) at the UN, and was told about the State Department's instruction, the president said that nothing should be done to "upset the apple-cart."[18]

Meanwhile, the Arab states made it clear that they would oppose partition by force. While King Saud was not willing to jeopardize his ties with the United States over the Palestine issue, he made no mistake about where he stood: "The dispute between the Arab and Jew will be violent and long-lasting and without doubt will lead to more shedding of blood. Even if it is supposed that the Jews will succeed in gaining support for the establishment of a small state by their oppressive and tyrannous means and their money, such a state must perish in a short time. The Arab will isolate such a state from the world and will lay siege to it until it dies by famine. Trade and possible prosperity of the state will be prevented; its end will be the same as that of those crusader states which were forced to relinquish coveted objects in Palestine."[19]

The Arabists, who had entertained doubts about Truman's understanding of foreign policy issues when he assumed office, were now convinced that the president was making a serious mistake. On November 24, 1947, Loy Henderson questioned the president's judgment: "The policy which we are following in New York at the present time is contrary to the interests of the United States and will eventually involve us in international difficulties of so grave a character that the reaction throughout the world, as well as in this country, will be very strong."[20]

The State Department did elicit an instruction from Truman not to coerce other delegations when it came time to vote for partition, but this was after the campaign to win support for the resolution was well under way. Early in October, Marshall had instructed the UN delegation not to persuade members of the General Assembly to support partition. Later in the month, however, he told Hilldring that the United States should "line up the vote" to support the American proposals for modification and implementation of the majority plan.[21] According to the Jewish Agency's David Horowitz, the U.S. posture changed. "As a result of instructions from the President," Horowitz observed, "the State Department now embarked on a helpful course of great importance to our own interest."[22]

The Arab lobby's campaign against partition has never been adequately addressed, but there is no doubt that pressure was exerted on delegations to oppose partition. While the State Department constantly carped about Zionist pressures, they rarely mentioned the lobbying by Arab delegations, which often took on threatening tones. Arab representatives warned they would ally with America's Soviet enemy if the United States did not support their position on Palestine. When the British foreign secretary complained about U.S. lobbying, Marshall noted, "The Arabs also had been bringing pressure to bear everywhere."[23] Loy Henderson suggested that the campaign to support partition was stimulated by "complaints reaching the White House that our delegates in New York were sitting on their hands while the Arabs and their friends were working."[24]

One example of Arab arm-twisting was the case of Chile. The Chilean president was sympathetic and instructed his delegation to vote for partition, but Arab groups in Chile used their own influence to persuade the government to change its position to an abstention. Greece was another country that acceded to Arab pressure. The Greek ambassador admitted that his country had cut a deal with the Muslim states: in return for Greece's vote against partition, they would support the country on issues before the UN.[25]

Even after Truman directed his administration to help secure the plan's approval, the State Department almost immediately began to try to sabotage the decision. Truman political adviser Clark Clifford (who, ironically, later worked for the Arab lobby) observed that "officials in the State Department had done everything in their power to prevent, thwart, or delay the President's Palestine policy in 1947 and 1948. Watching them find various ways to avoid carrying out

White House instructions, I sometimes felt they preferred to follow the views of the British Foreign Office rather than those of their President."[26]

Following the UN vote in favor of partition, the Arabs immediately made clear their intent to oppose its implementation by force. As violence escalated, and it became more obvious that outside intervention would be required if war was to be averted, the Arabists prevailed on Truman to consider what they described as a temporary interim measure to create a trusteeship for Palestine, to be administered by the United States, Britain, and France. The real goal was to sabotage the plan. In the words of one of its architects, Loy Henderson, the objective was to "decide once and for all" that the United States "will not permit itself" to be dominated by Zionism.[27]

Henderson, the son of a Methodist minister, succeeded Wallace Murray as director of Near Eastern Affairs in 1945. He was an anti-Zionist on practical grounds; he believed a Jewish state would be "economically unviable and militarily indefensible, requiring American intervention" and "a liability to American interests because it would alienate the Arab-Moslem world and would introduce into the conduct of foreign policy the presumably dangerous and inappropriate precedent of domestic ethnic politics."[28]

In Henderson's view, the national interest consisted of opposing the spread of Soviet influence, cultivating the goodwill of the Arabs, and preventing the UN from becoming too powerful and having the means to limit U.S. action. Support of the Zionist program undermined the first two interests, and he was determined to prevent his government from making such a mistake. One congressman said that Henderson had his own foreign policy, "based on such deep-seated prejudices and biases that he functions as a virtual propagandist for feudalism and imperialism in the Middle East." One of those prejudices was the conviction that international Jewry was supporting the Soviets.[29]

Henderson was also angry about the Zionist pressures exerted on the White House and had hoped to prevent the Jews from influencing the UN debate about Palestine. He was frustrated further by his limited access to the president. He was forced to report to Truman's pro-Zionist assistant David Niles on issues related to Palestine, which ensured that the president received carefully filtered information and that Niles could inform Truman of what his State Department was up to.

In an effort to prevent UN action, Henderson later suggested that the United States appoint a special adviser for Palestine and proposed the anti-Zionist Arabist ambassador to Iraq, George Wadsworth, for the post. Truman would later refer to Wadsworth as "so much a Jew-hater."[30] Niles got wind of Henderson's plan and told Truman that his policies were not being carried out at the UN and that he should appoint someone who was not known for his antagonism toward the Zionists. Truman accepted Niles's nomination of John Hilldring, a man who was not openly sympathetic to the Zionists but had developed an appreciation for their goals from his work with Jews displaced during the war. Journalist I. F. Stone observed that this decision prevented the State Department bureaucracy from sabotaging Truman's Palestine policy.[31]

In one remarkable memo, Henderson wrote to the secretary of state that despite expressing views that were contrary to administration policy, his office still intended to execute the secretary's decision "in a manner which will minimize as far as possible the damage to our relations and interests in the Near and Middle East"[32]—essentially telling his boss that the president had made a decision that was so bad, Henderson had to do damage control. Henderson then sent a top-secret memo to the secretary, arguing that it was his duty to "point out some of the considerations which cause the overwhelming majority of non-Jewish Americans who are intimately acquainted with the situation in the Near East to believe that it would not be the national interests of the United States for it to advocate any kind of a plan at this time for the partitioning of Palestine or for the setting up of a Jewish state in Palestine." His views, Henderson claimed, reflected those of "nearly every member of the Foreign Service or of the Department who has worked to any appreciable extent on Near Eastern problems."[33]

Though Niles managed to undercut one of Henderson's gambits to sabotage the UN debate, the diplomat continued to devise means for undermining the president's policy, starting with his proposal of an arms embargo on November 10, 1947. One of the few Arab lobby policies implemented, this probably succeeded because Truman was not consulted beforehand. The State Department prohibited the shipment of weapons to the Middle East on December 5, just days after the partition resolution was adopted, and after the Arabs had already begun to act on their threat to oppose it by force. Thereafter, the embargo was written into UN truce resolutions so Truman could not shift policy without appearing to undermine efforts to bring the fighting under control.[34]

In succeeding months, the Israeli lobby tried to convince Truman to end the embargo. Weizmann, who was so persuasive on other key issues, could not move the president; nor could Clifford, or even Eleanor Roosevelt. Why was Truman willing to resist pressure on this issue? The answer most likely is found in the president's desire to end bloodshed in Palestine and his naive belief that preventing the flow of American arms to the region would minimize the violence. War ensued despite his hopes for peace. The Arabs had multiple sources of arms, and the Jordanian Legion was led, trained, and armed by the British, creating the possibility of U.S. and British arms meeting on the battlefield. The embargo therefore took on even greater significance as a means of preserving the U.S.–Great Britain alliance. Although the Jews had to smuggle weapons, some from the United States, they acquired sufficient weapons to ultimately win the war.

The Arab lobby viewed the UN partition plan as a catastrophe. The Arab state component believed that the international community, but primarily the United States, had forced an alien entity upon them, and they were committed to destroying it. The missionaries saw decades of work cultivating the Arabs and building institutions going up in smoke. The Arabists in the U.S. government bureaucracy believed that Truman had provoked the wrath of the Arab world against America and sabotaged the prospects for expanding American political, cultural, and economic influence in the region. The

CIA showed the beginning of its traditional hostility toward Israel, along with inaccurate predictions about the Middle East, when it warned that partition could not be implemented and suggested that even Jews opposed the plan. The Defense Department also chimed in with dire warnings about the need to send U.S. troops to enforce partition.

Yet another reason given for reversing support for partition was the threat to oil supplies. First broached in 1948, this argument would become a staple of Arabist thinking. The oil industry in the region was still new and just beginning to expand. The Arab League threatened to deny pipeline rights to American companies if the government did not change its policy. Max Ball, director of the Oil and Gas Division of the Department of the Interior, sounded the alarm; American companies had to be sensitive to the Arabs' concerns, and failure to do so could lead to a shortage of gas for Americans. Secretary of Defense James Forrestal, a vigorous opponent of partition, warned that Americans would all have to drive four-cylinder cars without Middle Eastern oil.[35]

Much of the U.S. government bureaucracy, then, was convinced that the policy formulated by the president endangered American interests. Nearly all of their predictions proved to be wrong. Moreover, they did not take into account what would have happened if they had succeeded in preventing partition or convinced Truman to abandon his support for a Jewish state; the Zionists would not have given up their dreams, and undoubtedly would have continued to fight for independence.

Though today the American left is generally associated with critics of Israel, at that time the editor of the *Nation* was a supporter of partition. In May 1948, Freda Kirchwey wrote to Truman about Aramco's efforts to undermine his policy, informing him that the company's vice president for operations, James Terry Duce, had met in Cairo with Azzam Pasha, secretary general of the Arab League, to discuss alternatives to Jewish statehood. Duce was trying to convince policy makers that the creation of a Jewish state was not in America's interest, she said, in part because of the Jews' support for the Soviet

Union. Kirchwey quoted Duce saying, "Jewish Palestine will be organized as a communistic state."[36]

Shortly after Israel declared independence, Duce, "a fanatical anti-Zionist" who was in constant contact with Loy Henderson and served as a liaison between Aramco and the State Department, let Secretary Marshall know that ibn Saud had intimated he might be forced to impose sanctions on U.S. oil companies because of pressure from the Arab public, which objected to American policy. Though they were taken seriously at the time, these periodic references to Saudi public opinion were deceptive; Saudi Arabia was not a democracy, there were no surveys of public opinion, and the royal family paid no attention to the public. The reaction of Forrestal and the Arabists who feared a Saudi reprisal were also disingenuous, since a State Department study had found that only 6 percent of the world's oil supplies came from the Middle East, and that a cut in consumption "could be achieved without substantial hardship to any group of consumers."[37]

King Saud also made it clear that U.S. oil interests were not endangered. He called the U.S. decision "distasteful for the Arab world," but said in December 1947 that the issue was in the past, and though the Arabs would "take such measures as they deemed necessary for the defense of their interests . . . still we have our own mutual interests and friendship to safeguard." He expected to be pressured to support the general Arab position on Palestine, he said, but would not be "drawn into conflict with friendly western powers over this question." Indeed, when Iraq and Transjordan asked him to break relations with the United States and cancel oil concessions, Saud declined to do so, seeing no reason to take actions counter to Saudi Arabia's own interests. He went further: if pressed, he said, he would break relations with Iraq and Transjordan.[38]

This was not what the Arabists seeking to scuttle partition passed on to Truman. They also failed to point out that ibn Saud desperately needed American oil wealth to keep him solvent and U.S. military support to guarantee the country's independence, by which he really meant the Saud family's physical security.

Truman and the supporters of partition correctly deduced that the hysterical warnings of opponents were overblown attempts to change the administration's policy. Though similar threats would be issued for the next sixty years, the Arabs only tied the supply of oil to U.S. policy in the region successfully once. Equally valid today is Clark Clifford's response in 1948: "The fact of the matter is that the Arab states must have oil royalties or go broke. . . . Their need of the United States is greater than our need of them." Clifford made the case that the United States would only lose credibility by giving in to the threats of "a few nomadic desert tribes."[39]

The British minister to Saudi Arabia explained that the Saudis realized Israel was a reality and had "resigned themselves to its existence in practice while maintaining their formal hostility to Zionism." Ibn Saud rationalized his refusal to take action against the United States by claiming that oil royalties strengthened his country and thereby allowed it "better to assist her neighboring Arab states in resisting Jewish pretensions."[40] Desperately wanting to conclude a defense treaty with the United States, Saud used the British offer of an alliance to try to extort one from Truman. The president again demurred (the refusal to sign a formal defense agreement would be one of the few requests his successors would also reject).

Truman remained unconvinced by the anti-Zionist arguments made by even his most senior foreign policy advisers, Forrestal and Marshall, but was largely unaware that Henderson and his allies were still working against his policy. Their final gambit was to argue that the violence in Palestine after the UN decision made it impossible to implement the partition plan, and that a temporary trusteeship should be created instead.

Even though Truman had given instructions not to do anything at the UN that would suggest any change in America's position, and had privately promised Weizmann his continued support, Warren Austin, on instructions from the State Department, asked the Security Council to consider trusteeship for Palestine because the United States no longer believed partition was viable. The Arab states were jubilant, while the Zionists and their supporters were enraged.

Even more important, the president was furious. Upon reading in the newspaper on March 20, 1948, that the United States had reversed its policy, Truman recorded in his diary, "The State Department pulled the rug from under me today. . . . I am now in the position of a liar and a double-crosser. I've never felt so low in my life. There are people on the third and fourth levels of the State Department who have always wanted to cut my throat. They've succeeded in doing it."[41] Robert Silverberg says the incident turned Truman into a Zionist, and from that point on he no longer listened to "the appeasers of the Arabs, the worriers over oil, the frenetic anti-Communists, and the subtle anti-Semites in the Departments of State and Defense."[42]

Henderson, meanwhile, was gleeful, convinced that he had finally outmaneuvered the Zionists and repositioned administration policy in accord with his view of the national interest. To get a sense of how far Henderson had tilted to the Arab side, he tried to convince Azzam Pasha, the secretary general of the Arab League, to come to the United States to introduce a moderate voice into the debate on Palestine. This was the same Azzam Pasha who would declare a short time later, "This will be a war of extermination and a momentous massacre which will be spoken of like the Mongolian massacres and the Crusades."[43]

The overture to Azzam Pasha, who rejected the appeal, and another to Judah Magnes, a prominent Jewish leader who opposed partition, were examples of the more than two dozen State Department initiatives to prevent the implementation of partition before Britain's scheduled withdrawal on May 15, 1948. As time grew short, the diplomats grew more desperate. Austin tried to convince Weizmann to delay Israel's declaration of independence long enough for the State Department to find a way to prevent it (of course, this was not how he put it to Weizmann). On May 8, less than a week before the proclamation of statehood, Secretary Marshall tried to convince Moshe Shertok that the Jews' position was essentially hopeless because the Arabs held the strategic ground, had regular armies, and were better armed and trained (he proved to be wrong on all counts).

Meanwhile the Arabists continued to work behind the president's back to undermine his policy. According to Jorge Garcia Granados, Guatemala's representative to the UN Special Committee on Palestine, U.S. officials "exerted the strongest possible pressure on Jewish leaders in an effort to persuade them not to proclaim a state." Granados added that "veiled threats of possible American disfavor, even severe economic sanctions, were expressed."[44] In addition to the arms embargo, the officials also raised the specter of embargos on oil and dollars.

Lovett's last gasp was to threaten one of the American Jewish leaders on May 11 with exposure of the Zionists' pressure tactics. He warned that he would show the public that American Jews were more loyal to their homeland in the Middle East than to the United States, and opinion would turn against them. When the White House learned about Lovett's threats, Clifford made sure they were never carried out.

Though the Arab lobby maintained then, as now, that they represented the national interest and the will of the people, public opinion polls have consistently supported the Israeli lobby. As far back as December 1944, for example, a National Opinion Research Center poll reported that 36 percent of Americans favored a Jewish state, and only 19 percent opposed one. A December 1945 poll taken by the American Institute of Public Opinion (AIPO) found that 76 percent of Americans favored allowing the Jews to enter Palestine, while only 7 percent opposed it. Also, contrary to the misinformation put out by members of the Arab lobby, the vast majority of American Jews also backed partition.[45]

When it became clear that Israel intended to declare its independence, the president was faced with the question of whether to recognize the new state. Not surprisingly, the State Department opposed recognition on the grounds that it was unclear what type of state the Jews planned to create, and officials ominously warned of infiltration by Soviet agents. This was particularly mendacious, given their support for Arab regimes that did not share American values or interests.

Clifford made the case for recognizing Israel at a dramatic meeting in the Oval Office on May 12, 1948, arguing that "in an area as unstable as the Middle East, where there is not now and never has been any tradition of democratic government, it is important for the long-range security of our country, and indeed the world, that a nation committed to the democratic system be established there, one on which we can rely. The new Jewish state can be such a place. We should strengthen it in its infancy by prompt recognition."[46] Secretary Marshall responded that if the president took Clifford's advice, he would vote against Truman in the next election.[47] Despite the immense respect Truman had for Marshall, he did not take his advice on the Palestine issue. Eleven minutes after Israel declared its independence on May 14, 1948, Truman announced U.S. recognition of the new state. He wrote in his memoirs, "I was told that to some of the career men of the State Department the announcement came as a surprise. It should not have been if these men had faithfully supported my policy."[48]

The State Department did not take Truman's announcement as the final word, however. The Arabists still thought there was a good chance the Jewish state would not survive, especially after the five neighboring states invaded on the evening of its establishment. They also did what they could to facilitate Israel's demise by vigorously enforcing the arms embargo.

The uncertainty of the Jewish state's future was also used as a pretext to delay the formalization of diplomatic relations and appointment of an ambassador. The Arabists naturally wanted one of their own to be given the post, but Truman chose someone from outside the Foreign Service, James McDonald, who had served as the League of Nations high commissioner for refugees and had witnessed the State Department's indifference to the Holocaust firsthand. Undersecretary Lovett protested on procedural grounds, but his real complaint was that McDonald was pro-Zionist. Clifford made it clear that the president had made his decision, and it was Lovett's job to implement it.

The State Department's behavior reflected the Arabists' attitude toward politicians whom they viewed as ignorant about the Middle

East and captives of domestic influences. As President Truman put it, "The difficulty with many career officials in the government is that they regard themselves as the men who really make policy and run the government. They look upon elected officials as just temporary occupants."[49]

Contrary to those who maintain the omnipotence of the Israel lobby and the silencing of debate on issues related to Israel and Palestine, it is clear that a vigorous war of persuasion was engaged in by both sides, and the Arab lobby view did sometimes prevail. For example, while Clifford was ultimately successful in thwarting the Arabists from subverting partition, he failed to convince Truman to adopt more proactive policies. For example, his proposals to send arms to the Jews, create a volunteer international peacekeeping force, and have the UN brand the Arabs as aggressors were all rejected.[50] As would be the case for many future decisions, when the Israeli lobby's position was adopted, the result was a function of not only domestic politics but the national interest.

When the new state of Israel emerged as a democratic ally of the United States, it became clear, at least to most observers outside Foggy Bottom, that the Arabists had been wrong on almost every count. The Arabs had not been driven into the hands of either the Nazis or the Soviets by U.S. support for partition; the absorptive capacity of Palestine did not prevent the rapid growth of its population or lead to Israeli expansionism; the Arab states friendly to the United States (notably Saudi Arabia) did not turn against America; although the Soviets supported partition, Israel did not become a Soviet outpost; and the Jews were able to overcome the alleged military disadvantages Marshall had described and did not need outside intervention to win their war of independence. The only point the Arabists proved to be correct about in the short run, and this was one on which no one had expected otherwise, was that the Arabs would remain hostile toward Israel. Ultimately, this too was disproved when Egypt and Jordan signed peace treaties with Israel.

The Arabists undercut the president and hurt U.S. credibility with its allies and adversaries. By failing to stand squarely behind the Balfour Declaration and partition, the State Department gave the Arabs hope that they could prevent the establishment of a Jewish state. The doggedness with which the State Department fought White House policy toward Zionism and the new state of Israel was just a preview of what was to follow over the next six decades.

CHAPTER THREE

Cold War Competition:
Soviets, Suez, Sanction, and Saud

The establishment of Israel, its victory in the 1948 War of Independence, and U.S. recognition did little to dampen the hostility of the Arabists, who persistently tried to undo what they viewed as the mistakes of the Truman administration. In fact, career diplomat William Stoltzfus Jr. relates that "to a man, the American community in Syria and Lebanon remained opposed to the State of Israel, and some even crossed the line into anti-Semitism."[1]

The Arabists subsequently pursued a number of common themes:

- Support for Israel weakens America's ties with the Arab world.

- Israel, the Arab-Israeli conflict, and/or the Palestinian issue is the root of all problems in the Middle East.

- The United States should pursue an "evenhanded" policy; that is, shift away from support for Israel and give greater support to the Palestinians and Arab states.

- U.S. pressure can change Israeli policy, and such leverage should be used to force Israel to capitulate to Arab demands.

- The most important U.S. policy objective is to secure the supply of oil, and to do so, the Arabs must be placated.

- Support for Israel allows the Soviet Union (and, later, Muslim extremists) to gain influence in the region to the detriment of U.S. interests.

- Support for Israel provokes anti-U.S. sentiment among the peoples of the Middle East and is a cause of terror directed at Americans.
- Israelis don't know what is best for them, and the United States needs to save them from themselves by imposing policies that are really aimed at satisfying American interests in the Arab world.

The State Department's animus was reflected on the ground after the Israeli government declared Jerusalem its capital and moved its seat of government there in 1950. Refusing to recognize the city as Israel's capital, the United States established its embassy in Tel Aviv. The consulate in Jerusalem, which had been established in 1844, remained open, but only to deal with the Arabs in Jerusalem (and, after 1967, the Palestinians in the West Bank). A whole set of rules (e.g., not allowing official cars to fly the U.S. flag in the city, and marking the birthplace of Americans born in Jerusalem as Jerusalem rather than Israel) were then established to do everything possible to avoid the appearance of U.S. legitimation of Israel's capital. The United States not only refused to locate its embassy in Jerusalem, but also pressured others not to do so.[2]

The ambassador to Israel was considered a spy when the chiefs of mission in the Middle East got together. Ambassador Alfred Atherton recalled, "Very often you wondered whether the war between the Arabs and the Israelis was any more intense than the war between Embassies in Tel Aviv and Damascus, or Tel Aviv and Baghdad, or Tel Aviv and Amman." Relations eventually did improve between the U.S. ambassador in Tel Aviv and the consul general in Jerusalem, starting with ambassador Samuel Lewis in the late 1970s, but the Jerusalem consulate was a longtime bastion of anti-Semites.

Though some Arabists still hoped to somehow undo the establishment of Israel, most understood that having won its war of independence, Israel would likely survive at least until the next round of fighting. Thinking at the NEA therefore shifted in a new direction, one that has remained at the heart of the State Department's approach for six decades: to seek a peace agreement between Israel and the Arabs based on the premises that the Arabs will not compromise and that the United States should use Israel's dependence on American support as leverage to force it to make concessions acceptable to the Arabs. Implicit in this policy is the belief that the Arabs can be mollified. The director of NEA, G. Lewis Jones, put the department's view succinctly: "These ideas are based on the assumption that Israel needs peace more than do the Arab states, and that it would be Israel, not the Arabs, who would have to make concessions in order to obtain this peace, given the present Arab determination not to come to a settlement with Israel." Jones himself acknowledged this, writing, "We have no *assurance* that the steps, if taken would result in countersteps by the Arabs in the direction of better relations with Israel."[3]

The department adopted another policy that would become its standard operating procedure, namely to "discourage public comparisons between Israel and the Arab states prejudicial to the latter and at the same time work to achieve a balance between statements concerning Israel and statements concerning the Arab states. As the occasion arises, we should demonstrate to the American public, Israel and the Arab states that the policy of the United States Government is one of equal friendship and impartiality as between Israel and the Arab states."[4] What makes this policy unusual is that the Middle East is probably the only region where the United States considers a democracy, Israel, on an equal footing with totalitarian regimes.

One consequence of this policy during the 1950s was to deny Israel economic and military aid. The Arabists repeatedly argued that Israel should not receive "priority or exceptional treatment" because that would "contravene our established policy of impartiality" and "produce a most violent and hostile reaction in the Arab states." Another consequence was that Israel was prevented from joining the military alliances the United States was forming to defend interests the Israelis shared. They wanted, for example, to join NATO but were rebuffed.[5]

It did not take long for Israel's leaders, however, to align the country with the West and thereby provoke the enmity of the Soviets.

Instead, the Soviets seduced revolutionary and socialist regimes in Egypt, Iraq, Syria, and Libya—countries interested in building up their arsenals for the next round of fighting with Israel, unhappy with U.S. support for Israel, offended by American strings attached to U.S. aid, and generally opposed to American policies and Western capitalism—to become their allies. The United States wanted to be friends with everyone and keep the Soviets at bay, but the top priority remained securing oil supplies, and that meant keeping the Saudis happy.

When Israel sought $150 million in aid in 1951, General Hoyt Vandenberg, chief of staff of the U.S. Air Force, said the proposal would jeopardize relations with the Saudis and the use of the Dhahran air base. Relations with the Saudis were at an all-time low, he said, and would "go completely out of sight" if Israel got the aid. NEA director George McGhee agreed that aid to Israel would be "disastrous to our relations with the Arab states," but insisted that relations with the Saudis were excellent.[6]

The reference to Dhahran was especially interesting, given the fact that the air force had said it didn't need the base. Moreover, despite the warning about losing access to the base, the Saudis renewed the agreement that same year. The real issue for the Saudis was not Israel; it was the perception that they were not the masters of Dhahran.

In 1950, with the start of the Korean War, Truman agreed to provide military aid for the first time to Saudi Arabia. He justified the assistance based on Saudi Arabia's strategic location, the aid's importance to the defense of free nations, and the necessity of improving the kingdom's ability to defend itself. Truman's decision was part of the broader concern about the threat of communism to American interests in the Middle East. For the duration of the Cold War, the Saudis cleverly played on U.S. fears, warning of dire consequences if they did not get what they wanted: namely, that the Soviets would intrude and threaten the oil supplies. At other times, the monarchs would threaten to turn to the Soviets for help if the United States did not meet their needs.

Truman's successor, Dwight Eisenhower, did not share Truman's worldview or sympathy toward the Jewish people and Israel. Truman had wanted to do something for Jewish refugees after the Holocaust, redeem past promises for a homeland, and bring peace to the region. Though he had been moved by the plight of Jews during the war, and had seen firsthand the horrors of the concentration camps, Eisenhower believed that the creation of a Jewish state was impractical. He did not think it could survive without substantial U.S. military involvement that he feared would destabilize the region, open the door to Soviet infiltration, and threaten oil supplies. Seeing Israel as just one small piece on the global strategic chessboard, he would come to believe that Israel made his policies more difficult.

Eisenhower's secretary of state, John Foster Dulles, believed that Truman had "gone overboard in favor of Israel," so it was not surprising that when he returned from his first trip to the region, he reinforced the views of the Arabists in his department. In a radio address on June 1, 1953, Dulles talked about the need for the United States to "allay the deep resentment against it that has resulted from the creation of Israel." Given the overarching concern with the threat of international communism, the Eisenhower administration focused on bolstering the conservative Arab regimes to prevent the Russians from spreading their influence in the region.

The relationship with the Saudis at that time was viewed as mutually beneficial; the United States won access to a forward strategic military base, and the Saudis were placed under the American security umbrella. AIPAC was shocked to discover in 1956 that the United States had been selling arms to Saudi Arabia since 1952. The lobby found out only when eighteen tanks bound for Saudi Arabia were accidentally reported on a Brooklyn pier. Dulles later admitted that the United States had been sending military aircraft and other equipment to the Saudis for more than five years.[7] For the first time, when it learned of the plan to sell the Saudis M-41 tanks and B-26 bombers, AIPAC attempted to stop an arms sale, but it was ultimately overcome by the lobbying of the administration.

Henry Byroade, who was notorious for his antipathy toward the

Jews, wrote a personal message to President Eisenhower on February 23, 1956, suggesting that he go on television to talk about America's interests in the Middle East "in such a way as to practically break the back of Zionism as a political force."[8] Other Arabists subsequently blamed "Zionists" for Eisenhower's failure to build ties with Egypt. According to Edwin Wright, for example, after Dulles offered to build the Aswan Dam, Zionist opposition combined with that of southern cotton farmers led him to withdraw the offer. Dulles also irrationally blamed Israel. "We are in the present jam," he said, "because the past administration had always dealt with the Middle East from a political standpoint and had tried to meet the wishes of the Zionists in this country."[9] This was after the administration had already refused Israel's aid and arms requests, withheld the aid it did provide to force Israel to stop a hydroelectric project opposed by the Arabs, and rebuffed Israel's interest in joining the regional military alliance.

Dulles and the Arabists were looking for excuses for the failure of their policy, but the well-documented history of this period makes clear the dam project fell through as a result of Egyptian president Gamal Abdel Nasser. Parker Hart noted, for example, that Dulles was upset by Nasser's effort to play the United States off against the Soviet Union and the gratuitous anti-American statements emanating from Egypt. Nasser actually objected to the terms he was offered for building the dam, and further angered Washington by recognizing the People's Republic of China. Nasser also took the provocative step of nationalizing the Suez Canal on July 26, 1956.

Meanwhile, our good friends the Saudis were creating trouble for the British, the Hashemites in Iraq and Jordan, and the Baghdad Pact, while also trying to strengthen Arab opposition to Israel. King Saud also took a tough line in negotiations over the use of Dhahran, and U.S. officials feared he might turn to the Soviets for arms if a deal was not reached. This would become another consistent refrain in relations with the Saudis: even though they talked about how much they feared and detested the Communists, they always held out the threat of turning to them if they did not get what they wanted from the United States. At the same time, the Saudis remained anxious to avoid doing anything to endanger oil revenues from Aramco.[10]

Discussions over renewal of the basing rights at Dhahran were complicated when Senator Herbert Lehman introduced a resolution objecting to the exclusion of Jewish personnel from assignment to the base. The State Department responded, "It is fundamental that sovereign states have the right to control the internal order of their affairs in such manner as they deem to be in their best interests." Even more deceitfully, the department suggested that Jews might be embarrassed or endangered if sent to Saudi Arabia, so the exclusion was really looking out for their best interests. In testimony before the Senate Foreign Relations Council, Dulles admitted that American Jews could not be assigned to the American base at Dhahran. He explained that the Muslims had "a very particular animosity toward the Jews because they credited the assassination of Mohammad to a Jew." He said he disapproved of their discriminatory practices, but it was necessary to "accommodate ourselves to certain practices they have which we do not like."[11]

Relations with the Saudis were further complicated when Israel attacked Egypt in October 1956 as part of a campaign secretly agreed to by Britain and France to undermine Nasser. Eisenhower was personally offended; the attack took place a week before the presidential election, his allies didn't consult him, and the war had the potential to expand into a wider conflict that might have involved the Soviets. He was committed to aiding whoever was the victim of aggression, Eisenhower said, and he also believed that if force were permitted to settle a political dispute like Suez, then the future of the United Nations was in danger. After his reelection, he began immediately to pressure Israel to withdraw from the territory they had captured in the Sinai to avoid angering the Arabs, who might embargo oil. The flow of oil was interrupted anyway because the war had led to the closure of the Suez Canal, but after British and French troops landed in the Sinai, Saudi Arabia prohibited the offloading of any ships with oil destined for Britain or France. The United States wanted to make sure its allies could get oil, but was afraid to give the impression of collaborating in their military actions. On the other hand, allowing them to suffer shortages would let the Arabs know that their control of so much oil put them in a strong position.

Contrary to the common view that Eisenhower was taking a principled stand against aggression when he opposed the attacks, he was also motivated by security interests and the fear of an embargo. Subsequently, efforts were made to keep King Saud informed of U.S. actions to provide oil to Western Europe to make sure he wouldn't get "sore." The diplomats wanted to appease Saud by assuring him that the United States was concerned with his interests, and committed to pursuing regional peace and the withdrawal of all foreign forces from Egypt.

According to the popular image promoted by Walt/Mearsheimer and others, the State Department is under constant assault from the Israeli lobby; but in fact the government sometimes tries to mobilize support from lobbies for its position. In this instance, Eisenhower went on television to criticize Israel's failure to withdraw from the territory it had captured in the Sinai War, and warned that he would impose sanctions if it failed to comply. The Israeli lobby acted to blunt the impact of Eisenhower's threat by calling on the friends it had cultivated in Congress to oppose the administration's policy and to insist that Egypt be required to begin peace talks before Israel was forced to withdraw. Senate majority leader Lyndon Johnson told Eisenhower that Congress would not approve economic sanctions. To counter the Israeli lobby, Secretary Dulles tried to mobilize elements of the Arab lobby. For example, he asked the National Council of Churches to encourage its clergy to rally support for Eisenhower's policy from their pulpits. He also asked a group of non-Zionist Jews to persuade Israel to change its policy in what one newspaper described as "an arrogant intimidation of one group of American citizens."[12]

Dulles also made a number of remarks that could be interpreted as anti-Semitic. For example, in February 1957, he complained about "the terrific control that the Jews had over the news media" and lamented that Jewish influence "is completely dominating the scene," while the Israeli embassy was "dictating to the Congress."[13]

To pressure Israel to withdraw from the Sinai, Eisenhower escalated his threats to the point where he was prepared to cut off all economic aid, to lift the tax-exempt status of the United Jewish Appeal, and to apply sanctions on Israel. Members of Congress opposed the threats, and said they would prevent them from being enforced, but Israel could not risk a breach with its most important ally.

Arabists saw Eisenhower's success in forcing Israel's withdrawal as proof that America could impose terms on the Israelis consistent with U.S. interests in the region. This precedent gave the Arab lobby reason to believe that it was possible to pressure the United States to use its influence to force Israeli concessions. By refusing to heed the Israeli argument that he insist on a quid pro quo from the Egyptians, however, Eisenhower sowed the seeds of the next war. This lesson was not lost on Israel or its supporters.

Moreover, the Arab world did not become any more sympathetic to the United States. Nasser became more intransigent, and his prestige grew as a result of his humiliation of British, French, and Israeli troops. Perhaps more important was the failure of U.S. guarantees to ensure that Egypt would not engage in the actions that provoked the war in the first place.

Even after capitulating to U.S. pressure on Sinai, Israel was asked to make further concessions in the interest of U.S.-Saudi harmony. Israel had insisted on freedom of navigation in the Red Sea, as the blockade by Nasser had been a casus belli for the war, and the United States supported Israel's position. The Saudis were upset, however, because the king believed the Gulf of Aqaba was "one of the sacred areas of Islam" and a "closed Arab Gulf" that belonged to the Muslims. He rejected the idea that these were international waters; suggesting otherwise would be a "derogation of Saudi sovereignty and a threat to Saudi Arabia's territorial integrity." He was prepared to defend the area against the Jews who he believed threatened the "approaches to the Holy Places."[14]

The issue was a red herring, since only a tiny fraction of Muslim pilgrims came to Saudi Arabia via the Gulf, Israel did not interfere with their journey, and the Saudis' charges about Israel bombing

Saudi territory were fabrications. Nevertheless, the State Department pressured Israel to tie up its warships in Eilat, and NEA chief William Rountree wanted them removed from the Gulf altogether. Israel was prepared to assure the Saudis they would not interfere in the pilgrimage, but felt it had already done enough by sacrificing the legal right of its ships to transit the waterway. When the Israelis asked if complying with the American request would influence Saud's attitude, Rountree answered that he didn't believe it would alter the Saudi position at all. Nevertheless, he insisted that Israel's compliance would contribute to area stability.[15]

Meanwhile, the Communists were trying to wean the Saudis away from the United States. In 1955 the Soviet Union and China made overtures, with the former offering an unlimited supply of weapons. The Saudis informed the United States about these approaches and rejected them, deciding that America should be the sole arms supplier to the kingdom. King Saud hoped to get a large quantity of weapons to protect himself from his Arab enemies, especially Nasser. The Eisenhower administration, obsessed as it was with Soviet influence, was receptive to the idea. The United States provided a grant in 1957 to help develop a Saudi air force, build a new air base in Dhahran, and provide training to the Royal Guard at a cost of up to $50 million. In addition, the United States provided more than $100 million worth of weapons, including tanks and aircraft. That year, the Saudis also agreed to renew the Dhahran base agreement first signed in 1951.[16]

Nevertheless, the Saudis were unhappy with Eisenhower's unwillingness to meet all their arms requests. King Saud believed the British had refused to sell him arms in a deliberate effort to keep the Arabs weak. He felt ashamed by his weakness and claimed his people were demanding that he do something, a notion Eisenhower found unlikely, given that Saud was the absolute ruler of his country and was not influenced by public opinion. He told Saud that the idea that friendship should be measured by the amount of arms one country supplies another was a Communist concept. He also reminded Saud that he had taken special measures to expedite the delivery of weapons to Saudi Arabia. In response to Arab fears concerning Israel, Eisenhower reassured the king that the United States would prevent any effort by Israel to conquer an Arab country, as it had done earlier.

The openly anti-Semitic U.S. ambassador to Saudi Arabia, George Wadsworth, lauded Saud's subsequent letter to Eisenhower proposing a solution to the Arab-Israeli conflict. Eisenhower told Dulles the king had a "simple" and "unrealistic solution"—"the destruction of Israel."[17] Still, the consistent unhelpfulness of Saudi Arabia did not discourage the Eisenhower administration from viewing King Saud as its most important ally in the region.

Eisenhower began to see the implication of his shortsighted policy during the Sinai War as Nasser became more influential and worked to subvert American interests in the region. By 1957, Eisenhower became interested in trying to effect regime change in Egypt and hoped to elevate King Saud as an "Islamic pope" who would become the leader of the Arabs.[18] Eisenhower invited Saud to Washington in January 1957, the first official visit by an Arab head of state (no Israeli prime minister would be invited until 1964). Saud agreed to renew the lease on the Dhahran base for another five years, and the president agreed to provide the Saudis with additional arms and to help them create a navy.

It quickly became evident to the Americans, however, that Saud was not the man to lead the Arab world, and rather than oppose Nasser, the first thing the king did was to send his brother to meet with him. Initially, Saud supported the Eisenhower Doctrine and the effort to contain Nasser, but he began to backtrack by the end of 1957 when he was criticized by Egypt for being an American stooge. Then he denied supporting the Eisenhower Doctrine or receiving aid from the United States. Saud, supposedly the staunch anti-Communist, had also refused to censure the Soviet Union for its brutal suppression of the Hungarian uprising in 1956.

Meanwhile, Saud's position within Saudi Arabia became increasingly precarious, especially after he was accused by Syria in March 1958 of paying $5 million in bribes in a plot to kill Nasser. While this provoked the enmity of Nasser and his followers, Saud also stuck a finger in the eye of his American patrons by sending an emissary to Russia to discuss the purchase of arms and improving Saudi-Soviet ties. Saud also remained an outspoken enemy of Israel and said he would sacrifice ten million Arabs to exterminate Israel.[19]

Embarrassment over the revelation of the assassination plot as well as Saud's general incompetence, lavish and impious lifestyle, and declining health ultimately led the royal family to force him to relinquish power to his brother Faisal in 1958. Faisal immediately began to undermine U.S. interests by seeking a rapprochement with Nasser. He hoped to appease Nasser by promising not to renew the Dhahran lease and by withdrawing support from the pro-Western governments in Jordan and Lebanon.

By this time, Eisenhower had become disenchanted with the Saudis and concerned with the nationalist forces unleashed and stoked by Nasser in the region. The petrodiplomatic component of the Arab lobby also began to fray: the Arabists wanted American policy to be evenhanded, and to seek friends even among the revolutionary regimes, but the oil companies worried that the Nasserites would push for nationalization of their interests and supported the administration's greater emphasis on supporting anti-Communist regimes and leaders.

Israel benefited from the change in outlook. No longer viewed as an obstacle to U.S. policy, Israel came to be seen as a potential asset for the first time in July 1958, after the pro-Western government in Iraq was overthrown in a coup and nationalist forces were threatening the regimes in Lebanon and Jordan. Just two years after condemning the nation's allies for their intervention at Suez, Eisenhower sent U.S. troops into Lebanon to back the government there. He also agreed to ship to Jordan vital strategic materials, including petroleum, as part of a joint American-British airlift. Saudi Arabia, however, refused to allow either country to fly through its air space and even denied the U.S. access to the American airfield at Dhahran. Instead, the supplies were flown through Israel, which was happy to cooperate.

The Jordan crisis was the first demonstration of Israel's value as a strategic asset and helped bring about a nearly 180-degree shift in the administration's attitude. This was reflected in a memorandum submitted on August 19, 1958, to the National Security Council by the NSC Planning Board: "It is doubtful whether any likely US pressure on Israel would cause Israel to make concessions which would do much to satisfy Arab demands which—in the final analysis—may not be satisfied by anything short of the destruction of Israel. Moreover, if we choose to combat radical Arab nationalism and to hold Persian Gulf oil by force if necessary, then a logical corollary would be to support Israel as the only pro-West power left in the Near East."[20]

Walt and Mearsheimer devoted an entire chapter of their book to repudiating the idea that Israel has any strategic value to the United States (a view widely shared by the Arabists); not surprisingly, they skipped the Jordan crisis and all other cases that would disprove their thesis.

Eisenhower's record also destroys much of the case made by Walt and Mearsheimer. Eisenhower was (along with George H. W. Bush) the least pro-Israel president in history, but relations with much of the Arab world got worse rather than better. The Soviets gained a foothold in the region, Egypt joined the Soviet camp and was working to weaken America's allies, the Saudis failed to emerge as a reliable counterweight to promote U.S. interests, U.S. troops were forced to intervene to save pro-Western regimes in Lebanon and Jordan, and the pro-Western government of Iraq was overthrown. The Arabist policy of keeping Israel at arm's length to cultivate Arab support also proved a failure during this period.

Only one component of the Arab lobby was happy in the end— the oil companies—because of the administration's focus on securing oil supplies and bolstering the oil-producing regimes in Saudi Arabia and the Gulf. But trouble was on the horizon. George Kennan, the diplomat behind America's Cold War containment strategy, argued that the powers needed a coordinated policy "with a view to developing a collective Western bargaining power vis-à-vis these oil-producing countries which would permit us to take a stronger line with them."[21]

Anyone who asserts the omnipotence of the Israeli lobby has to ignore the 1950s, when Eisenhower said that he would make decisions "as though we didn't have a Jew in America" and Dulles said that he was determined to carry out foreign policy without seeking the approval of the Jews and characterized the Israelis as "millstones around our necks." The Arabist line that relations with the Arabs were related to U.S. policy toward Israel was proven completely wrong. Even after the United States had vigorously condemned Israel, and used all its political and economic leverage to force Israel to give up what it had won during the Sinai campaign, the Saudis were still unhappy, and the Egyptians and Syrians had still turned to the Soviets. Rather than change their preconceptions, however, the Arabists have stuck to them and, as we shall see, remained unmoved by the accumulation over the years of even more evidence of the fallacy of their position.

CHAPTER FOUR

War and Peace: The Futility of Evenhandedness

One area where the Arab lobby achieved success in the first decade and a half of Israel's independence was in preventing the United States from selling arms to the fledgling state. Despite the victory over Egypt in 1956, Israel remained concerned that a coalition of Arab states might again carry out their frequently expressed desire to throw the Jewish population into the sea. As the Soviet Union began to play out its confrontation with the United States around the globe, it sought to buy friends in the Arab world with weapons. Though they had periodic dalliances with socialism, the Arab states were not attracted to the ideology as much as the opportunity to build up their arsenals for the day when they could renew the battle with the Zionists. Several of the newly independent Arab states also viewed the United States as hostile because of its support for Israel.

This was precisely the situation the Arabists had warned about. Of course, these same states also had little in common with the United States, and it would not necessarily have changed their orientation if the country had abandoned Israel. Conversely, the more conservative Arab regimes, notably the Jordanians and Saudis, did not turn to the Soviets or against the United States despite their dissatisfaction with policy toward Israel.

Still, the State Department, this time backed by the Pentagon, opposed the sale of arms to Israel throughout the Eisenhower administration and the beginning of the Kennedy administration on the pretext that supporting Israel would hurt relations with the Arabs. Even the relatively hostile Eisenhower administration, however, encouraged its allies to provide Israel with some weapons, and directly supplied a limited amount of relatively trivial material (e.g., recoilless rifles). Kennedy overruled his advisers and sold the first major weapons—Hawk antiaircraft missiles—to Israel, but only after Egypt received long-range bombers from the Soviets.

Meanwhile, the Arabists were no less active during Kennedy's term in trying to undermine his policy. The ambassador to Lebanon, Armin Meyer, warned national security adviser McGeorge Bundy in 1962 that the election season would bring pressure to "do this or that for our little protégé, Israel." He then disseminated his case against strengthening ties with Israel to other officials who he feared might be influenced by the Israeli lobby.[1]

The Arabists also placed great faith in Nasser, whom they viewed as the key to stability in the region. Henry Byroade, who ran NEA and also served as ambassador to Egypt, said that until Israel's attack in 1956, Nasser was "the most sensible Arab leader on the subject of Israel," ignoring the fact that he had blockaded the Suez Canal to Israeli shipping and was instigating terror raids by Palestinians from the Gaza Strip.[2] Eisenhower saw him as pro-Soviet and untrustworthy and would not entertain Arabist ideas for improving relations after the Aswan Dam debacle. The election of Kennedy, however, brought a new opportunity, which the Arabists exploited by convincing the new president that Egypt might be weaned from the Soviet teat by U.S. aid and goodwill—an idea that Kennedy quickly discovered was mistaken, though the U.S. flirtation with Nasser continued up until the Six-Day War.[3]

Kennedy hoped to restrain the Egyptian firebrand's antagonism toward Israel and to convince him to focus on domestic issues rather than make trouble in the region. The main tool he had to encourage cooperation was foreign aid through the PL 480 Food for Peace program, which totaled during his term more than $500 million, compared to $254 million during the previous two administrations.

Nasser wrote to Kennedy to express his appreciation, and suggested the two countries could work together.[4]

The Saudis were upset by the prospect of a U.S.-Egyptian alliance. When King Saud met Kennedy on February 13, 1962, he insisted that Nasser was "a Communist who presents a real danger to the Arab world."[5] When Kennedy went ahead with aid to Egypt, the Saudis jealously complained that this reflected a weakening of the U.S. commitment to them.

The Arab and Israeli lobbies actually found common ground briefly in opposition to Kennedy's overtures. The Israelis feared that Kennedy was strengthening their strongest rival. The oil companies, meanwhile, were afraid that a strong Nasser would threaten Saudi Arabia. Nasser remained a threat for the next several years, but his influence was not enhanced by the United States, which, ultimately, gave up on him after it became clear foreign aid would not win him over.

The oil companies' basic philosophy has consistently been that "whatever was bad for Saudi Arabia's well-being was bad for America's economy." Instead of the oil companies lobbying Kennedy, however, it was Kennedy who recruited the former vice president of Aramco, Terry Duce, to meet with King Faisal on his behalf and reassure the Saudis of his support. Meanwhile, other oil executives lobbied the administration to recognize that Nasser was a threat to U.S. interests. Anger also grew, including at the White House, for the "be-nice-to-Nasser policy" advocated by the U.S. ambassador in Cairo, John Badeau.[6]

U.S.-Egyptian relations were another good example of the fallacy of Arabist thinking. Relations with Israel had nothing to do with the inability to build ties with Nasser. The Israeli lobby may not have been happy with Kennedy's flirtation, but he wasn't concerned about that. What ultimately doomed the effort was a combination of Nasser's behavior and the opposition of Saudi Arabia and the other conservative Arab regimes.

Egyptian-backed rebels overthrew Yemen, and Nasser began to send aid and troops to the new leaders, while the Saudis supported the ousted government. Nasser's direct involvement raised fears in Saudi Arabia that he was pursuing his revolutionary goal of overthrowing the conservative Arab regimes. The United States, already committed to the kingdom's integrity, was besieged by pleas from the monarchy to provide military assistance to protect them from the Egyptians.

On November 3, 1962, Saudi Arabia reported that several sites inside the nation had been bombed by Egyptian aircraft, and they needed assistance from the United States for air defense. Kennedy was reluctant to intervene, especially at a time when he was trying to woo Nasser, but it soon became clear that Egypt was not going to change its orientation, and that the United States could not afford to let Saudi Arabia come under attack, so Kennedy approved the deployment of a minimal air force—Operation Hard Surface—to deter the Egyptians from future attacks.

The Saudis, already sensitive about Egyptian criticism of the presence of Americans in the kingdom, were further embarrassed when Radio Cairo and the Voice of the Arabs reported that the Defense Department had assured Rep. Emmanuel Celler (D-NY) that American Jews were among the officers training the Saudis. Outraged, the Saudis said that no American military personnel would be allowed into the kingdom unless Celler's comments were denounced. In a rare display of defending American principles, which also proved that the United States could enforce them on the Saudis, Ambassador Parker Hart made it clear to Faisal that the States would not compromise on the principle of discrimination, and would pull its troops out if requested. The Saudis ultimately caved in when the Egyptians resumed bombing their territory, and Hard Surface went into effect.[7]

On July 10, 1963, the first of six U.S. aircraft arrived for Operation Hard Surface. The small unit was based eight hundred miles from Dhahran for the purpose of intercepting any Egyptian intruders. Naval forces were also deployed in the Red Sea. U.S. troops trained Saudi sailors and pilots, but the numbers were ridiculously small (seven pilots received combat training, and about eighty sailors were deployed on light patrol craft), reinforcing the obvious inability of the Saudis to defend themselves. Meanwhile, the chairman of the Joint Chiefs of Staff, Curtis LeMay, opposed the operation; he believed it served no purpose and diverted military resources needed elsewhere, an example of how State Department lobbying to pacify the Saudis was undermining America's broader security needs. Kennedy ultimately agreed, deciding to withdraw the Hard Surface unit by the end of January 1965, though he told Faisal it would return if needed.[8]

After Kennedy's death, Lyndon Johnson slowly began to shift policy away from the focus on Egypt. To the chagrin of the Arabists, Johnson also adopted a policy of overt support for Israel. Johnson saw Israel as the Alamo, surrounded by compassionless enemies, and Nasser as a reincarnated Santa Anna.[9] He sold the first American offensive weapons to Israel in 1965, and by the end of his term he had made the United States Israel's principal arms supplier and established the policy of maintaining Israel's qualitative edge over its neighbors.

The State Department, however, continued its mantra that the United States needed to maintain a balanced policy and could not become too close to Israel lest it destroy its relationship with the Arabs and push them into the arms of the Soviets.

While Kennedy had made an issue of Saudi intolerance and pressed for change, his successor was interested only in preserving and strengthening ties, which he did by almost immediately agreeing to sell the Saudis almost half a billion dollars' worth of weapons and installing a missile defense system. Secretary of state Dean Rusk ordered an end to "exhortations for reform," believing that the Saudis were "best qualified to judge [their] own best interests."

Johnson strictly adhered to a policy of balancing sales to Israel with comparable transfers to Arab countries until the end of his term, but this approach never applied to Saudi Arabia. From 1950 to 1964, the United States had provided the Saudis only $87 million worth of arms. In 1964 alone, however, sales totaled $341 million, and they continued to rise through Johnson's term.[10]

In 1965 the Saudis bought their first major offensive weapons,

Lightning fighter planes, from Great Britain. The Saudis had wanted to buy U.S. planes and focused on Lockheed F-104s, but the Pentagon, believing the planes too advanced for the Saudis to operate, sent a team of air force officers led by Chuck Yeager to persuade the Saudis to buy the less sophisticated F-5s instead. Yeager convinced everyone except the chief of the Saudi air force—who, as it turned out, was committed to the F-104 because Lockheed had paid him $100,000.

The State Department was so annoyed with Lockheed that Johnson's national security adviser, McGeorge Bundy, called chairman of the board Courtland Gross to ask him to stop pushing their plane to the Saudis. In his briefing points, Bundy was urged to tell Gross that the company should not be angling to make a few extra bucks when it was already making a lot of money on government contracts. Wanting something in return for sacrificing the F-104 sale, Gross asked for assistance in selling $15 million worth of C-130 transport planes to the Saudis.[11] This is a rare instance where the backroom wheeling and dealing of the defense contractors, Saudis, and State Department has come to light, and then only after thirty years, when the documents could be declassified.

Meanwhile, the United States wanted to sell more advanced F-111 fighters to the British, but the United Kingdom couldn't afford them, so a deal was struck whereby the British would sell the Saudis Lightnings and then use the proceeds to buy American planes. The United States, meanwhile, supplied the Saudis with Hawk ground-to-air missiles. Thus, "the Saudis in the end had been persuaded to buy British planes they did not want, to allow Britain to pay for American planes they could not afford."[12]

As the years passed, the Saudis made it a matter of national pride to have the best weapons available, and they had the wealth to buy whatever they wanted. As Hume Horan, former ambassador to Saudi Arabia, noted, "They desired end items that were very sophisticated and looked great on the mantelpiece, but they never had the manpower to operate or maintain it. They didn't even have high school graduates that could change the tires on these things."[13] And even as the Saudis fulminated about the Soviet Union, and Faisal was characterized as rabidly anti-Communist, Crown Prince Sultan was threatening to turn to the Soviets if the United States and Britain did not meet his country's arms requests. During the 1960s, the threats were not taken seriously.[14]

Another important element of these arms sales was secrecy. They were not debated in public or Congress, and therefore the statements and policies of the Saudis did not inhibit the administration's ability to arrange arms transfers. This was a good thing for the kingdom, given the views of King Faisal, a virulent anti-Semite who once told a congressman from San Francisco how much he liked the city, especially the signs in stores that said, "No dogs or Jews allowed." On a visit to Paris, he claimed that five children were murdered and their blood drained by Jews so they could use it to make Passover matzo. Faisal was also famous for giving visitors copies of the *Protocols of the Elders of Zion*. At the end of every meeting, according to Ambassador Horan, Faisal would say to his protocol assistant, "Have you given him THE BOOK? Get him THE BOOK!"

During a visit to Washington on June 22, 1966, Faisal made anti-Zionist remarks that prompted the mayor and governor of New York to cancel scheduled meetings. This was exactly the type of embarrassment the State Department had hoped to avoid. A public relations firm had worked for weeks prior to the visit to burnish the image of Saudi Arabia and its king.

A few months later, he declared that "either Zionism and Israel [must] renounce their project of creating a state in the bosom of the Arab nation, or the Arabs must have the necessary will and power to retake their fatherland by force."[15] This threat became more serious soon afterward when tensions escalated and Israel launched a preemptive strike on Egypt and Syria on June 5, 1967. While some revisionist historians argue that Israel could have avoided the war, Hermann Eilts suggested that the Arabists might have undercut the chance to prevent hostilities: the U.S. ambassador to Libya had proposed sending U.S. destroyers through the Straits of Tiran to reassure Israel it would honor the promise to keep the shipping lane open and send a message to Nasser that the States would stand up to his aggressive moves. The Arabists, Eilts said, opposed the idea out of fear of Egypt's reaction.[16]

The Arab lobby typically blames Israel for engaging in disproportionate force, or taking more extreme measures than necessary, but rarely asks the rhetorical question, What is the alternative? The Six-Day War was an example of Israel taking preemptive action that upset the Arabists, who believed Israel should have waited longer before attacking, and informed the United States of its plans. Secretary of State Rusk ultimately had to admit, however, that given the Arab mobilization and other hostile actions, "if the Israelis had waited for the Arabs to strike first, their situation could have been very grim."[17]

Moreover, Saudi oil minister Sheikh Ahmed Zaki Yamani told R. I. Brougham, the vice president of Aramco, on May 23, 1967, two weeks before Israel's preemptive strike, that a war was coming. Yamani warned that the United States should stay out of the crisis; if the States directly supported Israel, Aramco would be nationalized, "if not today, then tomorrow."[18] King Faisal told Brougham, in Saudi Arabia when the war broke out, that "one side or another must be defeated," and that if America became involved, it would suffer unspecified consequences. The same memo reported that the chairman of the board of the American University in Beirut, Calvin Plimpton, advised the United States not to support Israel because it would harm relations with the Arabs, claiming that "all of the important Christian professors on the University's faculty feel strongly to the same effect."[19]

After Israel's air strikes, initial reports disseminated throughout the Arab world suggested that Israel was finally about to be destroyed. The truth was very different, however, and Israel inflicted a humiliating defeat on the Arabs. The Saudis were furious with the Americans, and panicked oil executives evacuated their employees from the oil fields. Meanwhile, the French sought to take advantage of the anger toward the United States by embargoing arms to Israel (as did the United States, yet another example of the Israeli lobby's lack of influence) and offering to become the Saudis' arms supplier and to run Aramco.[20]

Saudi Arabia sent a brigade of three thousand soldiers to southern Jordan in a symbolic show of solidarity, but the troops did not fight. After their humiliating defeat within six days, all of the Arab leaders were under fire, but the Saudis were especially targeted for essentially sitting on the sidelines.

The Israeli victory also undermined Arabist arguments about the existence of Israel and the conflict with the Arabs as causes for Soviet encroachment in the Middle East. Israel, armed by the West, had humiliated the Soviet Union's two major clients, and the information provided before and during the war by the Soviets had further damaged their credibility. While the Soviet Union would continue to provide arms and assistance to its allies, the Communists' influence never spread further and slowly began to recede until its final collapse.

Faisal believed he had to persuade the administration to take a tough stand against Israel after the war to show that his friendship with the United States could benefit the Arabs. He also was convinced that the United States was responsible for Israel's existence and could pressure the Israelis to capitulate to Arab demands. He saw Eisenhower's ability to coerce Israel's withdrawal from the Sinai in 1957 as an indication of what the United States was capable of doing if it so desired.

Both Johnson and Faisal would be disappointed in their respective actions. Faisal was frustrated that the president would not force Israel to withdraw from the territories it had conquered, and Johnson was angry that Faisal had joined the other Arab leaders meeting in Khartoum in August 1967 in their "three noes" declaration: "No peace with Israel, no recognition of Israel, no negotiations with Israel." The United States should not have been surprised; Faisal had expressed the first two noes in a meeting with Ambassador Eilts in late June, even though the king would later claim he had been a force for moderation at the summit. Eilts continued to reassure Faisal that the United States expected Israel to withdraw from territory it captured, but he also pointed out that "withdrawal was hardly feasible when one party insisted it was still at war and refused to accept the right of the other party to exist as a state."[21]

Aramco also weighed in. Officials told Eilts they were "very disturbed" by the imbalance in U.S. policy. Eilts reported that they were "especially fearful that gradual deterioration of U.S.-Saudi relationships and confidence would increase Saudi pressures on the company and in the long run perhaps even lead to nationalization."[22]

The war also had indirect implications for Saudi-Israeli relations as the elimination of Nasser as a significant threat to both erased the one common interest of the Arab and Israeli lobbies. The destruction of the Egyptian army also forced Nasser to become dependent on the Saudis and the conservative monarchs in Libya and Kuwait. Still, one of the first steps taken by Johnson after the war was to approve a $15 million sale of C-130 aircraft to Saudi Arabia (the ones Lockheed wanted help selling in exchange for dropping their sales pitch for F-105s) and a nearly $10 million program for weapons maintenance and repair. The Saudis complained a few months later that a moratorium on the transfer of certain weapons was an indication they could not rely on the United States; the State Department, therefore, recommended sending them everything they wanted. Shortly thereafter the weapons were transferred.[23]

The U.S. experience of the 1960s reinforced the lesson of the 1950s, though it still would not sink into the consciousness of the Arabists: U.S. Middle East policy was derailed not by Israel, but by inter-Arab tensions.

The Saudis' principal concerns after the war were to finance Egypt, Jordan, and Syria and to pressure the United States to do something to force Israel out of the captured territories. Faisal was frustrated with the U.S. refusal to blame Israel for the war and its interpretation of UN Security Council Resolution 242 as not requiring a complete Israeli withdrawal to the prewar boundaries. Still, relations remained strong, in large measure because the Saudis wanted more American weapons. In the end the Saudis cared more about their own parochial interest, namely, the survival of the Saud dynasty, than about Israel or the Palestinians. This remains true today.

Israel's victory shook up the Middle East and also the Arabists' conception of the region. First, Israel had proven to be militarily powerful, which made it evident that the Arab states were unlikely to succeed in ever rolling back the clock. Second, the Soviets had lost prestige by misleading the Arabs about Israeli intentions and actions, and their weapons had proven inferior. Third, the magnitude of Israel's victory changed Israel in many officials' view from a strategic liability to a strategic asset.

The Arabists now argued that Israel's decisive victory proved it did not need more U.S. arms. That argument finally was overcome by a combination of forces that led Johnson to sell Israel its first major sophisticated offensive weapons, Phantom jets, and to establish the United States as Israel's principal arms supplier, guaranteeing the nation's qualitative edge rather than maintaining a balance of forces.

Arabist influence began to diminish with the crisis of 1967. One indication of how little respect NEA commanded by that time, even within the State Department, was the decision during June 1967 to bypass the region's experts and put the Bureau of International Affairs, run by Joseph Sisco, in charge of managing the crisis. "The impression people had," Alfred Atherton recalled, was "that this was building up to a life and death struggle for Israel. And therefore it was, I guess, viewed as perhaps not politic to have the bureau of the Department which was perceived to be more on the Arab than the Israeli side, running the crisis."[24]

From the Eisenhower administration through the Johnson years, according to U.S. ambassador Samuel Lewis, the dominant view was that America's overriding interest was in the Arab world, and Israel was a problem. Presidents starting with Kennedy became more directly involved in Middle East issues that State had previously handled; the voices within the administration were mixed, and included advocates for Israel. "Starting with Lyndon Johnson," Lewis added, "every president saw Israel as a military ally—an idea reinforced by the Six-Day War. From 1967 on, an unwritten alliance became more of a reality despite Arabist concerns."[25]

The decision in 1968 to sell Phantoms to Israel came as a great disappointment to the Arabists. They had hoped that once Johnson decided not to run for reelection, he would be free of the domestic pressure they believed was blocking the adoption of their preferred foreign policy. It was also about this time that the State Department first articulated its opposition to the building of Jewish settlements in the disputed territories and laid down the marker that has remained untouched for the last forty years, namely, that "nothing be done in the occupied areas which might prejudice the search for a peace settlement."[26]

Following the war, the United States found itself under pressure to distance its policy from Israel to avoid appearing to collaborate in the humiliation of the Arab world. Executives from Texaco and Mobil came to see the president in early July, hoping to elicit a statement in support of the Arab position that they could claim credit for. McGeorge Bundy also told the president, however, that "the moderate Arabs will always have a sore point as long as their fundamental grievance is that we are not directly arrayed against Israel." Bundy suggested the president refer to a poll showing American sympathy for Israel that pollster Louis Harris had called the most "sweeping and definite registration of overwhelming support for one side of a question" that he had ever seen.[27]

While the Arabists focused on how U.S. support for Israel might undermine the U.S.-Saudi relationship, something that did not occur, they showed no interest in how the Saudis' gradual involvement in sponsoring terrorism might affect American interests. Following the Six-Day War, the Saudis became financial supporters of the Palestine Liberation Organization (PLO).[28] The organization engaged in terrorist attacks, destabilized the region, threatened two American allies—Jordan and Israel—and later murdered American citizens. Meanwhile, changes were afoot in Washington. William Scranton, sent by Nixon as a special emissary to the region in 1968, promised the Arab states that the new administration would be more "even-handed." Secretary of state William Rogers subsequently unveiled a peace plan that reaffirmed U.S. support for Resolution 242, but clearly leaned on the Israelis to make territorial concessions, hoping to force them to return to the pre-1967 borders and to accept many Palestinian refugees.

The State Department knew the Rogers Plan was unacceptable to the Israelis, but the Arabists were more interested in responding to Saudi complaints about the U.S. failure to force Israel to withdraw. The Saudis for their part were less concerned about the Palestinians or the territories than that the United States was being blamed throughout the Arab world for Israel's "aggression," making the Saudis complicit because of their close ties with America.

As in the past, the State Department effort at appeasement utterly failed. Despite its tilt to the Arab position, both Nasser and his Soviet sponsors objected to the Rogers Plan. When Rogers tried to pressure Israel to make unilateral concessions and threatened to hold up the delivery of jet planes if they refused, Henry Kissinger—then national security adviser—intervened to reassure Israel.

Meanwhile Joseph Sisco was working to bring some balance to the NEA's approach to the region. Rather than trying to maintain the artificial separation of Middle East policy making from domestic politics that was an article of faith for the Arabists, Sisco understood that they were intertwined. He also realized that the Arabists were useful rapporteurs of Arab interests, but not as good about advocating the views of their own government. Sisco began to assign key posts in Arab countries to non-Arabists and sent the Arabists to posts farther from the main action, such as North Africa or the Mediterranean. The Arabists were never really blackballed—many did become ambassadors in important countries such as Lebanon and Syria—but they were generally excluded from decisions related to Israel and its neighbors, and were never promoted to higher ranks in Washington.

Sisco's balancing act was increasingly viewed as tilting in Israel's direction as larger and larger amounts of foreign aid and arms packages were approved. "There was a feeling that we were the only ones in Washington offering a balanced counterpart to the general atmosphere of pro-Israel partisanship," diplomat Michael Sterner complained.[29]

Sisco also ushered in a new era in which greater emphasis was placed on concluding a comprehensive peace between Israel and its neighbors. Previous administrations had all pursued initiatives to end the conflict, but the new breed of officials believed the Arab-Israeli conflict was fundamentally a political problem that had not been solved because none of their predecessors had been persistent or clever enough. Some of these "peace processors" had an almost messianic belief that they could bring peace to the region by devising the magic formula that eluded everyone else. After the Six-Day War of 1967, it was Sisco, Atherton, and National Security Council staffer, and later State Department official, Hal Saunders who took on this role; later it would be Jews such as Aaron Miller, Daniel Kurtzer, and Martin Indyk, and the ultimate peace processor, who spent more than a decade on "the problem," Dennis Ross.

The American plans throughout the last six decades have one thing in common—they have all failed. Francis Fukuyama, who worked on the State Department policy planning staff, explained that Arabists "have been more systematically wrong than any other area specialists in the diplomatic corps. This is because Arabists not only take on the cause of the Arabs, but also the Arabs' tendency for self-delusion."[30] The Arabist mind-set also sees the conflict as largely one-sided and therefore requires only Israel to compromise. Rather than recognizing that the parties themselves have to reach an agreement—as in the case of the treaties signed by Israel and Egypt and Jordan—the Arabists believe that peace should be imposed by the United States by coercing Israel. Richard Nixon's reaction to the Rogers Plan sums up the problem with this approach: "Do you fellows ever talk to the Israelis?"[31]

Nixon's cynicism about the State Department was also shared by Kissinger, who asserted control over foreign policy and marginalized not just the Arabists but the entire State Department bureaucracy. Kissinger was problematic for the Arabists because he was brilliant and had his own level of expertise on regional affairs. In Atherton's words, he was "his own desk officer." The Arabists may have also had reservations about the fact that Kissinger was Jewish, but those went unspoken. Kissinger also undermined the central argument of the Arabists by proving that "one could be friends with both the Arabs and the Jews at the same time."[32]

Kissinger saw American policy primarily through a Cold War prism, which meant that decisions were based more on their impact on the balance of power with the Soviets than on how they might be perceived by the Arabs. Thus, for example, when the Soviets moved SAM antiaircraft missiles into the Sinai in violation of the ceasefire terms of 1967, and Egypt continued to attack Israel in what became known as the War of Attrition (1967–70), a disagreement arose over how to respond to Israel's request for additional aircraft. As they had done consistently for two decades, the Arabists immediately objected that providing the Israelis with these planes would anger the Arabs. They were backed by Rogers, but opposed by the national security adviser. "Kissinger took the position that we should support our allies; the Israelis were our friends," Atherton explained. "And, as he put it, you can't let American arms be defeated by Soviet arms. And therefore if the Soviets are going to put in anti-aircraft missiles, we have to counter this with more aircraft for the Israelis."[33]

The Arabists' arguments had also grown weaker by the end of the 1960s, as it became apparent that relations with Israel and the Arab states were not the zero-sum game they claimed. Nothing the United States could do was likely to change the attitude of Nasser or the other revolutionary regimes, so improving ties with Israel couldn't make things worse. Meanwhile, the conservative monarchs of Jordan, Saudi Arabia, and the Gulf emirates needed American support and could not afford to get too upset about the developing U.S. bond with Israel.

Still, while some Arabists resigned themselves to America's special relationship with Israel, others acted as guerrillas in the bowels of the State Department or out in the field, where they sought to influence or sometimes sabotage policies they disliked beyond the immediate scrutiny of the media, Congress, or the Israeli lobby. Foreign minister Golda Meir once publicly complained that if not for the "low-level fanatics in the State Department," Israel's relations with the United States would be a lot better.[34]

Interestingly, from the time of Truman through the end of Nixon's first term, the Arab lobby's influence was exerted almost exclusively through the Arabists, Arab embassies, and oil companies. Arab Americans were uninvolved, and considered irrelevant. The vaunted Israeli lobby, AIPAC, meanwhile, was basically a one-man show that focused all its attention on Congress, specifically to counter the Arabists, and try to secure economic and military assistance for Israel. Following the Arab-Israeli War of 1973, those aid figures began to increase dramatically, but the balance of lobbying power also began to shift with the introduction of the oil weapon.

CHAPTER FIVE

The Petrodiplomatic Complex:
Do Saudis Really Have Us
Over a Barrel?

If the Middle East had no oil, the United States would pay no more attention to the Arab countries than it does to those in Africa. A State Department analyst referred in 1943 to the Saudi oil fields as "the greatest single prize in all history."[1] One of America's principal strategic interests is to guarantee the supply of oil. Rather than do so by force, successive administrations, in part because of Arabist influence, have allowed the Arab oil suppliers (and Iran) to increasingly dictate supply and demand for their interests at the expense of our own.

The Saudis have had us over a barrel from the moment of the first gusher. For the first fifteen to twenty years, Saudi Arabia was a poor desert kingdom with an image as an exotic land run by sheikhs who lived in tents in the desert and carried the nation's wealth in a treasure chest. From this earliest period, however, a pattern was established whereby the Saudis blackmailed the U.S. government to do their bidding. Within days of Barack Obama's inauguration, for example, Prince Turki al-Faisal—a member of the royal family, a former Saudi intelligence chief, and former ambassador to the United States—warned, "Unless the new U.S. administration takes forceful steps to prevent any further suffering and slaughter of Palestinians, the peace process, the U.S.-Saudi relationship and the stability of the region are at risk."[2] Responding like his predecessors, Obama waited less than twenty-four hours before calling Saudi king Abdullah to pledge fealty to the U.S.-Saudi relationship.

These threats have changed slightly through the years, but they have remained the underpinning of the relationship. Given Saudi Arabia's role in the oil market, this relationship may seem unexceptional, but when you consider the early decades, when the Saudis' economy and security were entirely dependent on American goodwill, its uniqueness is revealed.

One reason the Saudis have been so effective in manipulating U.S. officials may be simple American arrogance. Because the Saudis looked and acted like something out of the *Arabian Nights*, Americans underestimated their intelligence and skill in playing power politics. The ability to negotiate in the Arab bazaar, to exploit the weakness of their opponent, and more important, to outwit, destroy, or co-opt the constituent tribes of the kingdom, are skills the royal family has used to great effect in dealing with patronizing westerners.

In 1933, the country we know today as Saudi Arabia, dripping in oil and filled with princes of mind-boggling wealth, was little more than a pile of sand fought over by rival clans that still practiced slavery. The tribe that emerged victorious in the end was led by Saud Abd al-Aziz ibn Saud. He conquered the holy cities of Islam, Mecca, and Medina, and declared himself king of a new country named after himself. The United States was so uninterested in the new kingdom that it did not recognize it as a state or send an ambassador.

At that time the kingdom's wealth fluctuated with the number of Muslims who could afford to pay for the pilgrimage to Mecca. The trunk that served as a national treasury was nearly empty after the Great Depression dramatically reduced pilgrim revenues, so it was opportune for both parties when Standard Oil of California (SoCal; now Chevron) sought the rights to prospect for oil in the kingdom.

SoCal had discovered oil in Bahrain in 1932. Recognizing the potential for further discoveries, the company sent a representative to meet with King Saud and ask permission to explore the Saudi coastline opposite Bahrain. A coalition of companies known as the Iraq

Petroleum Company also sought the right to drill for oil. The Saudis, however, were wary of the imperialist powers, which had carved up the Ottoman Empire for themselves after World War I. Ibn Saud later explained he chose to work with the Americans because they were "good oil men"; they treated their Arab employees as equals (something that would not be true in Saudi Arabia); the United States is a big and powerful country more interested in business than gaining a political advantage; and, most important, he added, "You are very far away!"[3]

The agreement, signed on May 29, 1933, gave SoCal the exclusive rights for sixty years to explore an area of more than 360,000 square miles, and called for the company to provide a loan and royalty advance of about $175,000, a second loan of $100,000 to be made in eighteen months, and a final loan of $500,000 in gold upon discovery of oil. The deal was based on the concession system, whereby the oil company "contractually obtained rights from a sovereign to explore for, own, and produce oil in a given territory." The Saudis would later feel that they had been too generous to the Americans because of their relative weakness.[4]

SoCal created a subsidiary, the California-Arabian Standard Oil Company (Casoc), to handle its Saudi operations. In 1936 the Texas Company (later Texaco) bought half the subsidiary. Later, in 1944, the two partners renamed the company Aramco. For all the talk that would come later about a "clash of civilizations," from the founding of Casoc forward there has been what Daniel Yergin described as "an unlikely union—Bedouin Arabs and Texas oil men, a traditional Islamic autocracy allied with modern American capitalism."[5]

Oil was discovered in March 1938, and in April 1939 ibn Saud traveled across the desert to Dhahran to turn the valve that sent the first Saudi oil onto a SoCal tanker. Casoc subsequently paid an additional fee to secure the rights to explore a larger area. To win this new concession, as well as persuade the Saudis to reject offers it was receiving from other countries, such as Japan, Casoc had to provide more loans to ibn Saud.

To underscore that the U.S.-Saudi relationship is based on oil,

American diplomatic recognition was not granted until 1933, when SoCal obtained the petroleum concession in the kingdom. Even then, the United States did not see the country as important enough to warrant a resident diplomatic mission. SoCal lobbied the State Department to send a representative as the American oil community grew in size following the discovery of oil in 1938. Finally, in 1939, the U.S. ambassador to Egypt, Bert Fish, was assigned to visit occasionally until 1941, when a diplomatic presence was established in Jidda. The Saudis were initially reluctant to exchange diplomatic representatives because of the fear that U.S. diplomats would seek to liberate Saudi slaves, something the British had demanded. The United States, however, promised it would not interfere with this long-standing practice.

It took some time for the State Department to gain the confidence of the Saudis and supplant Aramco as America's interlocutors with the king. J. Rives Childs, who became the first ambassador (he was preceded by two foreign service officers who did not hold that rank), told the Saudis that Aramco was the proper address for oil matters, but that any political issues involving the United States were his responsibility. Aramco made this transition easier in the late 1940s when the issue of partitioning Palestine created angst in Saudi Arabia and the oil men decided it was best to let the Saudis vent their feelings to the State Department.

In 1943, Secretary of the Interior Harold Ickes, Roosevelt's confidant and director of the Petroleum Reserve Corporation, established to acquire oil outside of the United States, wanted to take over Aramco. One of Ickes's advisers was James Terry Duce, who was on temporary leave from his job as a Casoc executive (he later became president of Aramco). Ickes believed it was in the national interest to fully control the companies responsible for finding and supplying America's most vital resource. The Casoc partners wanted assistance, but did not want to be taken over by the government. Ickes finally agreed to a deal whereby the government would buy one-third of Casoc to protect the cash advances it anticipated making to finance the Ras Tanura refinery.

Ibn Saud apparently was not bothered by the idea that the U.S. government would own a controlling interest in the oil company, since this had also been the practice of the British and French. Instead, an objection came from the U.S minister in Saudi Arabia, Alexander Kirk, who anticipated the precise opposite reaction, expecting the king to object to America behaving like the imperialist Europeans. The agreement was scuttled, however, in the wake of a furious lobbying campaign by other American oil companies. Domestic producers did not want to compete with the government, which they feared would flood the market with cheap oil and put them out of business. Standard Oil of California and Texaco subsequently agreed to finance the refinery themselves.[6]

The lack of government involvement did benefit the United States in the short run; Aramco's independence allowed the Saudis, the oil company, and the U.S. government to subtly separate oil and politics. The oil companies could always say they had nothing to do with U.S. policies the Saudis disliked. Moreover, they wanted only to control oil production and distribution and had no desire to run the country. The companies elsewhere were suspect because of the imperial interests of their government owners.

At the outset of America's entry into World War II, Saudi Arabia was only the seventeenth-largest oil producer, and none of its oil was needed in the United States (some oil was imported from other Middle East countries). Nevertheless, the expectation that Saudi Arabian oil would become more important was an incentive to keep King Saud happy and in power. So long as he was content with the United States, and the sole authority for determining oil rights, the American position was secure. Consequently, U.S. policy was aimed at accomplishing both objectives. Thus, whenever Saud expressed displeasure over something, the State Department would do what it could to placate him by leaning on whichever party—Zionists, British, French—had offended him. This was true even when Saudi Arabia was still pumping little oil and had no wealth.

When the kingdom became strapped for cash because oil production came to a halt and pilgrimage traffic dried up, the king appealed to the United States for an emergency loan of $10 million. Oil executives supported the request, fearing an economic collapse would lead Saudi Arabia to look for help elsewhere. But the State Department remained convinced that the British and French should be responsible for the care and nurturing of the Arabs. This initial request for lend-lease aid to what the administration considered a "backward, corrupt and non-democratic society" was subsequently rejected. Instead, officials told the British that a condition of the loans they were getting from the United States was that they help the Saudis.

What most concerned the U.S. government at that time was ensuring that the supply of oil was controlled by American companies. Officials in Washington were worried about British designs on "their oil," and already could see the long-term importance of the Saudi oil fields.

In April 1945, NEA officers warned that the American oil concession was in danger of being lost if King Saud did not receive sufficient financial assistance. The Saudis wanted aid to cover the deficit for five years. There was no precedent, however, for the United States to provide the type of assistance they sought, and despite the recognition that Saudi Arabia had the largest oil reserves in the world, providing loans was considered a risk. NEA recommended a loan secured by future oil royalties.[7]

As we shall see, once the Saudis took control over their oil and began to accumulate wealth from the revenues, the United States treated them like an ATM whenever a foreign policy need arose that might not receive the political support of Congress. In the early days, however, the relationship was the reverse, with the Saudis treating the oil companies and, by extension, the U.S. government as their personal bank. Whenever a financial crisis arose in the kingdom, whether because of the king's extravagant spending, a decline in pilgrimage revenues, or a paroxysm of greed, the Saudis would turn to the oil companies and threaten to shut down operations if their demands were not met.[8]

After continued oil company lobbying, supplemented by oil company officials serving as advisers to the government, and a growing concern about the British getting a foothold in Saudi Arabia, Roosevelt authorized providing lend-lease assistance to the Saudis in February 1943, which continued to flow after it had ended to every other country. The United States also offered Saudi Arabia a $5 million development loan through the Export-Import Bank.[9]

The war also prompted the initiation of the U.S.-Saudi military relationship, as the Joint Chiefs of Staff concluded in March 1945 that construction of a U.S. airfield at Dhahran was needed to shorten the air route between Cairo and Karachi. King Saud was willing to allow the U.S. military to use the base for three years, and to give U.S. commercial airlines most-favored-nation status. The Saudis were extremely sensitive to suggestions that the king was "selling out his people to American imperialism and was bartering the traditions of the holiest of Moslem countries for American gold." They were also worried about rumors that American soldiers in Saudi Arabia were "the forerunners of the American military imperialism in the Near East."[10] This is one reason Dhahran was chosen as the site of the base; it was nearly a thousand miles from the holy cities.[11]

As the war wound down, however, the military value of the base diminished, and the War Department ultimately decided it was completely unnecessary. Still, the State Department was insistent that the field be built so King Saud would not think that U.S. policy toward Saudi Arabia was wavering. The State Department's desire to placate Saud won over the military's objection to wasting resources. In July 1945, the president approved construction of the base using existing War Department funds to evade congressional oversight. This became a precedent for keeping most of the U.S.-Saudi relationship secret, or at least beyond public scrutiny.

After the war, the Saudi monarchy continued to spend money faster than the oil company could earn it. The Saudis also were stuck with the agreement they had signed in 1933. When Venezuela forced the oil companies operating there to split profits in the mid-1940s, the oil companies in the Middle East came under greater pressure to renegotiate their deals. The Saudis became even unhappier when they realized how much money the United States was earning in taxes from Aramco compared to the royalties the company paid to them. In 1949, for example, Aramco paid $43 million in taxes and $39 million in royalties. The Saudis figured out that they could change the distribution of Aramco earnings by taxing the royalties.

To mollify the Saudis, as well as to provide them with indirect foreign assistance, the Treasury Department established a special oil tax credit that allows them to receive the oil companies' income tax payments and lets the oil companies pay little or no U.S. tax. The U.S. Treasury was the big loser, but the desire to keep the Saudis happy justified the cost. It had the added benefit of functioning as a foreign aid program for the Saudis without requiring the assent of Congress.

When Americans first went to Saudi Arabia, it was the oil companies that were largely responsible for developing the relationship. They had hundreds of employees in the country, while only a handful of diplomats were assigned there. Aramco had its own intelligence operation, ran a library, and was in constant contact with the royal family.

As late as the early 1950s, the State Department viewed Aramco as having greater expertise related to the country and allowed the oil company to operate with little interference. Aramco's involvement in Saudi society was all-encompassing, from providing maps of the country to resolving boundary disputes to paying for the crown prince to visit the United States to translating documents to building roads to controlling mosquitoes. For its part, the oil company was happy to divert Saudi anger over Israel to the diplomats. In fact, the oil company went so far as to bar the children of the American consulate general from attending the Aramco school, so as not to appear to be an arm of the U.S. government.[12]

In February 1951, the State Department sent a classified memo that raised questions about Aramco's policies and the need to monitor them more closely. "It can do a great deal to preserve American prestige and interests in the area and to combat communism," the memo read. "For example, Saudi Arabia's labor policy toward its 14,500 Arab workers is not only of nation-wide importance in Saudi

Arabia, but is a critical factor in the development of western orientation and democratic processes. The department should, therefore, encourage Aramco to pursue progressive and enlightened policies in connection with wages, housing for Arab employees, training and education, and to shift responsibilities to Saudi Arabians as fully and rapidly as possible."[13]

In fact, Aramco treated its American and foreign workers differently. The Americans stayed in their own compound, supplied with most of the modern conveniences that could be imported. The foreign workers were segregated and lived in primitive housing. A director of the company was asked in 1951 why the company had not planned family housing for the Saudi workers, and he replied, "Haven't you read your Bible? It says that Saudi Arabians are supposed to live in tents all their lives."[14]

Aramco also discriminated against American Jews. This was consistent with the general policy of the kingdom, which adopted the standard formula that no one whose "presence is considered undesirable" would be given a visa. As early as October 1944, after Saudi officials rejected his request for a visa for a Jewish reporter from *National Geographic*, Colonel Eddy informed the State Department: "It is recommended that all interested government agencies and private concerns planning to send personnel into Saudi Arabia be advised confidentially that the Saudi Arabian Government does not, at present, welcome Jews into the country."[15] Here, again, we see that instead of standing up for American values, the Arabist asks that U.S. principles be sacrificed to satisfy his client.

Aramco, meanwhile, was mounting a campaign to win support in the Arab world for Western investment. Eddy admitted that material was being "planted" with members of parliaments in Arab countries to illustrate "the tremendous development in Arab lands which can take place in the next few years by private capital." He even suggested how this would strengthen the Arabs' bargaining position with the West and aid their fight against Zionism. "The royalties and benefits to the Arabs . . . will arm them economically to withstand expanding Zionism, and give them a bargaining point with the Powers who

MUST have oil from the Near East and will therefore have to cooperate with the Arabs."[16] It was interesting that a State Department official was offering advice to Arab governments on how to undermine Zionists who had the backing of his government.

In 1946, TWA began regular flights between the United States and Saudi Arabia. In exchange for landing rights, the Saudis demanded that TWA help them create a national airline. The State Department wanted the Saudis to ease restrictions on air travel for Israel and to sign a long-term lease of the Dhahran air base.[17] Typically, the Saudis got what they wanted, but the United States did not.

Saudi intolerance was of no concern whatsoever in the 1950s. America's principal interest was in securing oil supplies. Thus, in 1950 Aramco completed the 753-mile Trans-Arabian Pipeline (Tapline), at the time the longest pipeline in the world. Tapline linked eastern Saudi Arabia to the Mediterranean, cutting the time and the cost of exports to Europe.

The main opponent of the U.S.-Saudi relationship was not the Israeli lobby; it was domestic oil producers who continued to be unhappy about the flow of cheap oil into the United States and lobbied the Eisenhower administration to impose quotas on imports. While the secretary of state argued that it was better to import oil to preserve domestic reserves, Eisenhower ultimately gave in to the lobbying of Texas oil interests and established a quota, which lasted for fourteen years.

Meanwhile, the State Department recognized that the Saudi monarchy in the 1950s was incapable of managing its money and that crises would recur if the Saudis did not put their financial house in order and stop treating the budget as a royal slush fund. The State Department hoped to convince the Saudis to enlist American advisers to teach them to manage their money and to encourage the royal family to invest more in developing their country.

The effort to reform and modernize Saudi Arabia was made nearly hopeless, however, by the profligacy of King Saud, who "could not say no to anyone—least of all himself, and continued to indulge his insatiable appetites for palaces and women."[18] Saud also precipitated a foreign policy crisis in the late 1950s, when the Syrians revealed that he had put out a million-dollar contract on Nasser. The key princes of the family essentially forced him to give up power to his rival and younger brother, Crown Prince Faisal ibn Abdul Aziz al-Saud, in 1958. Saud, it turned out, had spent about 60 percent of the country's oil revenues on himself and the royal family and had never created a budget for the kingdom. Faisal began to institute reforms, establishing some budgetary controls and reducing the total share appropriated for the family. Saud remained king, but became increasingly infirm.

When John Kennedy took office, he sent a letter to King Saud on May 11, 1961, which was designed to do little more than express his interest in maintaining good relations and beginning to discuss common interests as well as finding ways to address differences over the Arab-Israeli conflict. Kennedy was reportedly outraged when Saud responded with a letter criticizing U.S. support for Israel.

Typical of Saudi royal arrogance, when Saud came to the United States for medical treatment, he expected President Kennedy to come to see him. An elaborate diplomatic dance was performed that ultimately resulted in Kennedy going to his estate in Palm Beach while the king stayed in a nearby hotel. A meeting was arranged for February 13, 1962. Saud wanted to solicit a reaffirmation of American support for Saudi Arabia's independence and to seek economic aid for hospitals, schools, roads, and other development projects. Kennedy told him the World Bank could provide assistance for these projects, and that Saudi Arabia could also apply for loans for specific projects. Saud then resorted to his modus operandi of blackmail and suggested that it would be necessary to reduce the number of American military advisers training Saudi troops to save money. Kennedy called his bluff and said the number would stay the same, and that the United States was already paying most of the cost.[19]

Kennedy was much blunter when Crown Prince Faisal came to the White House in September 1962. The president gave him the reassurance he sought regarding America's devotion to Saudi independence and territorial integrity, but he also made clear that he expected the

Saudis to institute certain reforms, in particular the abolition of slavery. One of the little-publicized aspects of Saudi society, this was also one of the most dramatic examples of the difference in values. Slavery was an issue that was swept under the rug by the Arabists, who to this day show little concern for the human rights abuses of the Saudis. Kennedy was the only president who made this an issue, and his emphatic position was probably the reason that Faisal issued a proclamation outlawing slavery soon after he returned from Washington, and almost a century after the practice was abolished in the United States.

Here was evidence that a resolute U.S. president could impose change on the Saudis even if it was contrary to their tradition, religion, or values. No other president, before or since, would take such a principled stand against Saudi human rights abuses. Interestingly, though Kennedy helped put an end to slavery in Saudi Arabia, and various Jewish members of Congress helped reduce the level of discrimination toward Jews, no one has ever pressured the Saudis to change their discriminatory policies toward women.

In the meantime, paradoxically, it was the Aramco companies that began to threaten America's position in Saudi Arabia and access to oil. While the eventual nationalization of the oil companies occurred in the wake of the 1973 embargo and therefore was associated with U.S. support for Israel, the road to nationalization actually began in 1960, when the oil companies unilaterally reduced the price of oil without consulting the Saudi government. This angered the Saudis and provoked them to later join the other oil-producing states to form a cartel—the Organization of the Petroleum Exporting Countries (OPEC)—to defend the price of oil.

The creation of OPEC was a turning point toward the oil producers' taking control over their natural resources. The oil companies did not recognize this, however, and though they were prompted to apologize for the unilateral actions they'd taken, they did not see the organization as a serious threat to their dominance of the industry. Since the companies owned the concessions, they continued to believe they only had to negotiate better deals with their host countries.

Larger oil revenues also gave the Saudis an opportunity to develop the country, something of greater interest to Faisal, who had replaced Saud as king shortly after Kennedy was assassinated. One of the first projects was to contract with the U.S. Army Corps of Engineers to create a television network for Saudi Arabia. Previously, some Saudis had access to Aramco's TV station, which broadcast American programs that were censored by Saudi authorities to prevent anything offensive—such as references to alcohol, Israel, or Jews, or symbols of the Christian or Jewish religion—from being aired.[20] The contract for the corps was yet another opportunity for the United States to recycle petrodollars as well as to cement its role as the principal engine for developing a modern state in Saudi Arabia.

While most U.S. institutions were interested in Saudi Arabia primarily for the opportunity to make money, the Ford Foundation was a rarity in that it had the altruistic goal of helping to establish the structure of a functional government. Even some officials within the foundation found it uncomfortable to provide assistance to a country that, unlike others in the Third World, could pay for its own modernization. Nevertheless, from 1963 until about 1974, Ford provided advice and recommendations, some of which were accepted while many more were ignored. After the oil embargo and the sudden influx of wealth, the foundation found it harder to justify continued assistance, and believed the Saudis had made sufficient progress to continue development work on their own. The decision to leave was ultimately made for the foundation when the Saudis ordered it to cease operations because it was "an organization with Zionist aims."[21]

While various U.S. entities were assisting in Saudi development, tensions in the region were growing as a result of Nasser's efforts to unite the Arab world under his leadership with the backing of the Soviet Union. In January 1965 a group of oil executives from Aramco, Gulf, Socony Mobil, SoCal, and Standard Oil of New Jersey met with State Department officials to express their concern about U.S. policy toward Nasser, which they believed was upsetting the Arab oil producers. Ironically, they were accused of working with the Zionists on the Hill to lobby for legislation directed at Egypt, but they denied this.[22]

The CIA also believed that U.S. policy made the Arabs unhappy, but different groups were upset about different aspects of that policy. As a 1966 National Intelligence Estimate noted, "U.S. relations will remain troubled by the general Arab conviction that the US is basically pro-Israel, by the Arab radicals' belief that the US favors the conservatives [Arabs], and by the conservatives' feeling that the US should support them more than it does."[23]

The volatility of the region also became a concern for decision makers, who began to worry about the reliability of Middle East oil supplies. In 1963, for the first time since Harold Ickes had proposed a government takeover of Aramco, the Interior Department tried to play a role in oil policy. Secretary Stewart Udall told the press the president had put him "in charge of oil policy." In truth, Udall only had a say in domestic oil policy. He lost the bureaucratic battle to wrest control of broader policy from the State Department, thereby ensuring it would remain dominated by the Arabists.

Besides the strategic value of oil, policy makers were also conscious of its economic value to American business. A State Department assessment prepared in 1967, for example, made reference to the $2.75 billion invested in the area, of which $750 million in profits were returned to the United States. At that time about 93 percent of U.S. investment in the region was in the oil industry, and that figure did not include additional investments in tankers, terminals, refineries, and other downstream operations. Anticipating future problems, the report suggested "a crash program to obtain fuel energy from other petroleum areas and from other sources of energy (atomic power, coal, oil shale, tar sands)." A more feasible alternative, the report said, was to "play down our relations with Israel, and protect our fortunate access to the prolific oil resources in the area."[24]

Some of today's energy problems might have been avoided if the State Department and others had pushed the more difficult course of pursuing energy independence rather than hoping to prolong the existing energy policy by selling out Israel. As noted elsewhere, however, Israel was not an issue for the oil producers. A few weeks after the department's assessment, the NSC's Hal Saunders stated in a memo that Saudi Arabia's main concerns were "Nasser's foothold in Yemen and fear that he will expand this by moving into Saudi Arabia when the British pull out."[25]

Nasser, meanwhile, saw oil as a potential weapon. In his 1953 book *Philosophy of the Revolution*, Nasser wrote that oil was a "source of strength" for the Arabs against "imperialism." In 1956, Nasser tested the oil weapon by blocking the Suez Canal and persuading his Syrian allies to blow up oil pipelines. The actions had little impact, however, because the main oil producers did not embargo oil during the conflict.[26]

In 1956 Egypt was fighting alone, but in 1967 the entire Arab world was involved in the fight against Israel, and the oil producers, believing they had an obligation to use the one weapon at their command, imposed an embargo. According to then ambassador Hermann Eilts, King Faisal didn't want the embargo but felt pressured to do something by popular anger toward the United States due to its support for Israel, anger reflected in the bombing of a U.S. embassy building and Raytheon office in Jidda and mobs overrunning the Dhahran airfield and Aramco compound. Faisal ordered Aramco to implement the embargo, meaning that American oil companies were taking orders from a foreign government to act against U.S. interests.

At the time, approximately 80 percent of the kingdom's income came from oil, and rival oil producers were more than happy to fill the void created when the Saudis withdrew from the market, so they could not afford to stop selling their only real product. To save face, and their economy, the Saudis declared in early July 1967 that it was in the Arabs' interest to sell *more* oil to build up their economic strength, and there was no reason to continue the embargo, since they had learned that the United States and British had not helped Israel during the war. Saudi Arabia ended its embargo on September 2, and the other oil producers followed soon afterward.

Ironically, Saudi Arabia was the principal beneficiary of the Israeli victory; it had forced the withdrawal of Egyptian troops from Yemen and effectively ended Nasser's dominant role in Arab affairs. Faisal, with his delusional notions of a Communist-Zionist conspiracy, did not see it that way. In his mind, the Soviets had deliberately misled Nasser because they were really on the side of the Zionists.

The embargo lasted less than two weeks and was not strictly enforced. It was also ineffective; the United States still had sufficient unused spare capacity to make up the shortfall, at least domestically. Troops fighting in Vietnam had a problem, however, because 45 percent of the Defense Department's supply came from abroad, and 80 percent of its aviation fuel came from the Gulf. Not wanting to jeopardize his relations with President Johnson, Faisal agreed to provide fuel shipments during the embargo to American forces.

The embargo of 1967 backfired in a number of ways. First, it had no impact on Israel or its friends, in part because the war ended so quickly. The Arab states, especially Egypt, were also in desperate financial shape because of the war and needed money, which they could only get from the oil producers, but the Saudis could not afford to help if they didn't sell oil to make money. Aramco informed the Saudis that the continuation of the embargo would cost the kingdom $9 million per month, and they would lose another $1.5 million per month from continued stoppage of oil flowing through Tapline. The Saudis and others could therefore rationalize ending the embargo as a way to strengthen the Arab countries resisting Israeli "aggression."

Even though it had been ineffective, U.S. officials knew that a future embargo might have a greater impact. A secret interagency study of the issue prepared after the war presciently warned, "The danger exists that Western Europe and Japan would be willing to pay heavy political and economic prices to avert the loss of Arab oil." The report recommended that "given the inherent instability in the Arab world, it is important to seek and develop alternatives to Arab oil while recognizing that complete independence thereof is not likely to be achieved in the foreseeable future. As a tactical matter, to reduce Arab confidence that oil can be used as a political weapon, we should give maximum publicity to new developments. We should do this in a manner, however, which does not give unnecessary offense to the Arabs to whom we should stress that we welcome access to Arab oil so long as it is offered on reasonable terms."[27]

Rather than pursue the recommended policies, the Arab lobby focused on the traditional Arabist line that relations with Israel were threatening oil supplies. Beginning in 1967, major U.S. oil companies established a fund to help present the Arab side of the conflict with Israel and, on occasion, warned that oil supplies would be jeopardized by pro-Israel policies. Aramco also urged the United States to support a UN resolution to nullify Israel's unification of Jerusalem after the Six-Day War. The General Assembly approved the measure 90 to 0, with the United States abstaining.

In 1968, David Rockefeller, chairman of Chase Manhattan Bank, John J. McCloy, and a number of prominent oilmen met with president-elect Nixon to suggest he adopt a Middle East policy that was "more friendly to the Arabs."[28] Two years later, in May 1970, Aramco representatives met with assistant secretary of state Joseph Sisco and warned him that American military sales to Israel would hurt U.S.-Arab relations and jeopardize U.S. oil supplies. The former chairman of Aramco testified before Congress that the United States' pro-Israel policies were harming U.S. business interests. No evidence was offered to back this assertion.

Interestingly, while the Arabists saw the Israeli lobby as a nuisance sticking its nose where it didn't belong, the oil companies were seen as valued interlocutors. As we've seen, oil company officials actually held positions in the government at various times and have maintained steady contact with the State Department. William Rountree, a former head of NEA, said the oil companies "maintain an appropriate level of contact" and "exchange information of mutual interest." Unlike the one-sided pressure officials feel from the Israeli lobby, Rountree said relations with the oil companies were a two-way street that was beneficial to the State Department. In fact, he said, he couldn't recall any time when the oil companies lobbied the department to "take action or assume positions that would be inappropriate."[29]

U.S. policy did not change as a result of these Arab lobby interventions, and regional events worked against their interests. In September 1970, after Jordan's King Hussein decided to go to war to prevent the Syrian-backed effort by the PLO to take over his country, Israel was asked to prepare to intervene on the king's behalf. Ultimately, Hussein did not need Israel's help, but from that point on, Israel's stock as a strategic ally in the region began to rise and made Arab lobby arguments against strengthening U.S.-Israel ties far more difficult.

Still, the petrodiplomatic complex kept up the effort to influence policy. In 1972, at Kuwait's urging, Gulf Oil joined the Arab lobby campaign, providing $50,000 to create a public relations firm "to promote a more balanced view of Arab-Israel differences in the United States." More than half the money was used for an ad hoc organization that operated for only two years called International Affairs Consultants, Inc. It was run by several critics of Israel who used some of the money to fund a pro-Arab book and periodical. The money was also used to accuse Israel of human rights abuses in the disputed territories. Participation in the public relations campaign amounted to the price of doing business in the oil-producing nations.

The Gulf Oil example illustrated the danger the oil companies felt if they became too directly involved in the political debate, and helps explain why they have stayed largely in the background of the Arab lobby. Gulf's role in the Arab propaganda campaign became known when the company revealed its contribution during a May 16, 1975, Senate hearing. A boycott of Gulf was then organized by the Conference of Presidents of Major American Jewish Organizations. Gulf quickly apologized for the "improper" gift and essentially said it would never happen again. The Jewish boycott was then canceled. The Jewish reaction was exactly what the companies feared and has been the principal restraint on this type of direct political support for the Arab cause. Nevertheless, the oil companies have continued to be supporters of organizations that at a minimum are pro-Arab and sometimes also anti-Israel.

While the Arab lobby was focusing on Israel, unrelated events in the region again prompted a change in the security of America's oil supply. In 1971 Libya nationalized British Petroleum's holdings, and Iraq nationalized the Iraq Petroleum Company. The Saudis were reluctant to nationalize Aramco, fearing that it would cause political and economic instability, but they could not resist the trend for long after the other Arab countries had taken this step. In an effort to stave off full nationalization as long as possible, Aramco agreed in 1972 to give the Saudis a greater share of the company.

The implications of Saudi government control over a vital resource were clear to James Akins, who wrote a study for the State Department in 1971 in which he predicted that by 1975, if not earlier, it would be possible for oil producers to "create a supply crisis by cutting off oil supplies." He recommended policy changes to reduce consumption, increase domestic production, and seek more secure sources of oil.[30]

Akins's suggestions were ignored, and as he warned, the oil producers soon precipitated a crisis that continues to reverberate today.

CHAPTER SIX

The Lobby Realizes Its Power:
The Oil Weapon Is Unsheathed

The 1970s mark a turning point in the history of the Arab lobby. For most of the previous three decades the petrodiplomatic component of the lobby focused on ensuring access to Middle East oil by keeping Saudi Arabia (and to a lesser extent other oil producers) happy, preventing non-Americans and, especially, the Soviets from encroaching on the U.S. sphere of influence, and guaranteeing the security of the Saudis. The Saudis were almost totally dependent on the United States for their political and economic survival as well as the country's development. While they frequently expressed their displeasure with U.S. Middle East policy, primarily as it related to Israel, the Saudis used the threat of access to their oil to extort arms, economic assistance, and pledges to protect their regime from American administrations rather than to coerce policy changes. They also had no leverage on the international scene and did not try to influence international affairs. U.S. oil companies were starting to lose their grip over Aramco and would soon have to face a choice between protecting their company interests and those of the United States. Also, prior to the 1970s, there was no domestic Arab lobby to speak of. A few organizations came and went, but no serious group of Arab Americans had yet been formed with the specific goal of influencing U.S. policy. All of this changed in the 1970s as the Saudis took control of their oil and began to invest their newfound wealth in the United States and used their economic clout to demand changes in Middle East policy.

According to former CIA operative Raymond Close, Egyptian president Anwar Sadat sent a letter to King Faisal on April 17, 1973, informing him of his intention to attack Israel; "Sadat acknowledged unashamedly in this letter that he did not expect to win a war against Israel, but he explained that only by restoring Arab honor and displaying Arab courage on the battlefield could he hope to capture the attention of Washington and persuade Henry Kissinger to support a peace process." When Faisal sent his son to warn Nixon about the need to more vigorously pursue peace (on the Arabs' terms, of course) or face the inevitability of war and a likely oil embargo, Close said, "Washington had again failed through arrogance and ignorance to appreciate the significance of the term 'linkage.'"[1]

Instead of any new peace initiatives, the administration resorted to the now familiar tactic of trying to appease the Saudis with arms, proposing the sale of $1 billion worth of weapons, including Phantom jets, and a $600 million navy training program. The proposed sale prompted the Senate to amend the Military Sales Act, giving Congress the right to veto major arms sales. The proposal was killed later that year, but adopted in 1974, giving the Israeli lobby the opening to oppose future sales. Saudi arms purchases had been kept classified for many years. The debate over the new sale, however, resulted in the disclosure that between 1950 and 1972 they totaled at least $435 million. During the next three years that figure would more than double.[2]

While the Saudis were negotiating for more arms, they were also issuing new threats. In early May 1973, King Faisal told oil company executives that Zionists and Communists were "on the verge of having American interests thrown out of the area." Faisal expected the companies to try to change U.S. policy and suggested that "a simple disavowal of Israeli policies and actions" would help overcome anti-American feelings.[3]

The Saudis had always expected the oil companies to support their position, but had never demanded this as a condition of remaining in the country. This was the most assertive they had ever been in demanding allegiance to their anti-Israel policy. The change was partially due to their growing control over Aramco and the lessening of their dependence on the Americans to develop and market their resource. They also had learned from years of successful extortion that they could get what they wanted by threats.

On May 23, 1973, oil executives from Aramco, Standard Oil of California, Texaco, Exxon, and Mobil met in Geneva with the Saudi oil minister, Ahmed Zaki Yamani, to discuss the transfer of the ownership of Aramco to Saudi Arabia. A year earlier, the Aramco partners had agreed to sell 20 percent of their stake to the Saudi government, and they were going to have to give up more. The Americans were hoping to delay the inevitable as long as possible, and were therefore especially vulnerable to threats when King Faisal arrived and warned the Americans that if they did not take measures to inform the public and government officials as to America's "true interests" in the Middle East, they would lose their oil concession. "You will lose everything," Faisal said.[4]

A week later, executives from Texaco, Exxon, Mobil, Standard Oil, and Aramco flew to Washington for a series of lobbying appointments with officials in the White House, State Department, and Pentagon. They conveyed a simple message: if U.S. policy toward Israel did not change, "all American interests in the Arab world will suffer."

Here we have a very clear refutation of the assertions of Walt/Mearsheimer and others that an Arab lobby does not exist and that U.S. oil companies have not been engaged in efforts to influence U.S. Middle East policy. They made their case in terms of the national interest, but their actions were motivated primarily by self-interest.

On June 21, 1973, Mobil published its first advertisement/editorial relating to foreign affairs in the *New York Times*. Under the headline "U.S. Stake in Middle East Peace," Mobil explained how the American standard of living would in the future depend on the United States representing the interests of Saudi Arabia and Iran. Mobil called for the U.S. government to join the Soviet Union and "insist" on a peace agreement. Sheikh Yamani wrote to Mobil's president afterward expressing his appreciation for the ad and the expectation that this was "just a beginning."[5]

In July, SoCal's chairman sent out a letter to the company's 40,000 employees and 262,000 stockholders asking them to pressure Washington to support "the aspirations of the Arab people." He said there was a feeling in the Arab world that the United States was turning its back on the Arab people and it was important to work closely with Arab governments to improve relations and to give "more positive support of their efforts toward peace in the Middle East."

In response to the letter, Senator Alan Cranston (D-CA) wrote, "It is my understanding that Standard Oil is far more dependent on Arabian oil than is the United States. . . . I can understand your desire as chairman of the board to ensure the uninterrupted oil supplies for the good of Standard Oil, but I do not share your apparent inference that what is good for Standard Oil is necessarily good for the United States."[6]

A group of executives from ten oil companies returned to Washington in early August with John J. McCloy, a former government official and adviser to presidents going back to Roosevelt when he was in the war department and had opposed the bombing of Auschwitz and commuted the sentences of Nazi war criminals. Now a lobbyist working for a prestigious New York law firm, McCloy and his delegation warned undersecretary of state (later CIA director) William Casey and other top officials that America's position in the region was growing weaker.

Other briefings of key figures in government and the media sponsored by the oil companies followed, each stressing the theme that Israel was the main source of instability in the Middle East, a cause of the growing influence of the Soviet Union, and the principal reason for the deterioration of U.S. influence in the Arab world. Of course, this message dovetailed with what the Arabists had been saying for decades. Nevertheless, the lobbyists came away from their meetings feeling they had been unpersuasive.

The Arab lobby, which in addition to the petrodiplomatic components now included for the first time an Arab American organization, the National Association of Arab Americans, also failed to convince the media. The *Washington Post* and *Wall Street Journal*, for example, wrote warnings in April 1973 against giving in to Arab blackmail. The *Post* said, "It is to yield to hysteria to take such threats as Saudi Arabia's literally." Similarly, the *Journal* declared: "If the United States ever does suggest that it will bend its Middle East policy for the sake of oil, American policy would quickly find itself under intensified pressures and increasingly dangerous threats from all quarters."[7]

While the lobbying campaign against Israel was intensifying, so was Arab war planning. Sadat went to Riyadh to see Faisal on August 23, 1973, and informed him of his secret plan to go to war. Faisal agreed to provide financial aid and said he was prepared to use the oil weapon but was afraid that if the war ended too quickly, as in 1967, it would again fail to have an impact.

Normally press shy, King Faisal himself directly addressed the American people in a series of interviews with the media that he believed was controlled by unspecified forces hostile to Saudi Arabia. He said that Saudi Arabia had no wish to restrict oil exports to the United States, but suggested that it was difficult to continue to supply oil to a country supporting Zionism against the Arabs.

The United States did begin to show some signs of getting the king's message as President Nixon talked about the need for both sides in the Arab-Israeli conflict to negotiate, in part to reduce the threat of an oil embargo. The assistant secretary of state, Joseph Sisco, publicly said that U.S. and Israeli interests were not synonymous and that concerns in the United States over energy were a factor in determining American interests.[8] Because of the failure of the 1967 embargo, however, and the confidence in the existing supply of oil, policy makers did not take the Arab threats too seriously. Nevertheless, if U.S. officials had foreseen the ultimate impact of the embargo, perhaps they would have made a different calculation.

The truth was America's energy security had changed dramatically. World oil production grew from 8.7 million barrels per day in 1948 to 42 million in 1972. While U.S. production also increased (from 5.5 to 9.5 million barrels), America's share of production dropped from 64 percent to 22 percent as Middle East production grew an astronomical 1,500 percent (from 1.1 million barrels per day to 18.2 million). In addition, rapid economic growth after World War II stimulated an exponential increase in oil consumption, with U.S. consumption tripling between 1949 and 1972.[9]

The Saudis had not expected the United States to become so dependent on foreign oil so soon. America was expected to become more reliant on Gulf oil by the mid-1980s, but already in the early 1970s the Saudis had replaced Texas as the "swing producer" for the global market. The share of Saudi oil flowing onto the world market grew from 12.8 percent in 1970 to 21.4 percent in 1973. This increased demand for their oil, as well as that of the other OPEC members, convinced the Arab governments that they were now in a position to use their economic clout to advance their political aims, that the United States was vulnerable to a severe reduction in supply, and that America no longer had the excess capacity to make up for a shortfall for itself or its allies.[10]

Coincidentally, it was at this moment of growing Western dependency on Middle Eastern oil that the Arabs decided to strike. On October 6, 1973—the holiest day of the Jewish calendar, Yom Kippur—Egypt and Syria launched their surprise attack on Israel.

On October 11, 1973, Faisal wrote a letter to Nixon asking him to stop supporting Israel in the war. The following day the chairmen of Exxon, Mobil, Texaco, and SoCal sent President Nixon a memo warning of dire consequences if the United States continued to support the Israelis in the war. The same day, Israeli prime minister Golda Meir also sent an urgent letter to Nixon describing the setbacks the Israeli army had experienced and the desperate situation facing the country if the United States did not provide military supplies.[11]

The president's response to Faisal's letter isn't known; he did not respond to the oil executives' memo. He did react to Meir's, however, by approving a large-scale resupply of Israeli forces on October 14. Despite the months of lobbying and public relations, the oil companies had ultimately failed to change U.S. policy toward Israel. Here is another clear refutation of the Walt/Mearsheimer argument. An Arab lobby, notably led in this case by U.S. oil companies, aggressively asserted a position they claimed to be in the national interest. The president, however, came to a different conclusion and did so without any input from the Israeli lobby.

Meanwhile, the price of oil, which had risen from $2 to $3 in the twenty years preceding the war, spiked by more than 70 percent to $5.12 on October 16. This was an important difference from the situation in 1967; this time, the oil producers could afford to cut production as the skyrocketing price ensured their revenues would not fall. The same day, Faisal also sent another letter to Nixon expressing his dismay over the decision to airlift supplies to Israel and asking him to cease the resupply and demand an Israeli withdrawal.[12]

The following day, October 17, OPEC declared an embargo on oil shipments to unfriendly states, including the United States. The oil ministers said they would cut production 5 percent from the September level, and keep cutting by 5 percent each month until their demands were met. Oil supplies to "friendly" states would continue at previous levels.

The timing of the embargo and the declared rationale tied the action to U.S. support for Israel, but this was only the catalyst for the Saudis to act in their own self-interest and the culmination of an evolutionary process toward taking control of their own resources. As Yamani told members of OPEC on October 15, 1973, "This is a moment for which I have been waiting a long time. The moment has come. We are masters of our own commodity."[13]

Aramco enforced the embargo and thereby "became the instrument of a policy intended to undermine the economic security of the country in which its majority owners were based and most of their stockholders lived." Aramco was given strict instructions as to who would get oil and who would not. Their excuse was that they had no choice and that they were actually *helping* American interests by supplying oil to American allies.

Unlike 1967, when the Saudis made sure fuel reached U.S. military forces in Vietnam, this time Faisal ordered a cutoff of oil to the Sixth Fleet. Here was a dramatic example of the lobby acting diametrically opposed to American interests. The Saudi action prompted an irate William Clements, the undersecretary of defense, to call in senior Aramco executives and read them the riot act. "Find a way to get fuel to Vietnam. . . . Our kids are dying out there fighting Communists." When the message got back to Aramco president Frank Jungers in Saudi Arabia, he made sure Faisal understood the importance of keeping oil flowing to the U.S. military. Though it did little to mollify the anger of the United States, Faisal hoped to avoid a breakdown in relations with the United States by agreeing to allow oil to be sent to U.S. forces, but the exception was kept a secret.[14]

The behavior of both the Saudis and the oil companies was reminiscent in a way of the Nazis. The Saudi goal was to isolate the Jews from their supporters, and the Saudis used threats to attract collaborators. The Europeans (more echoes of the 1940s) were quick to appease the Arabs, criticizing U.S. support for Israel and adopting more pro-Arab views. Their excuse was that they were more dependent on Arab oil than the United States was.

Consider the irony of Saudi Arabia, which had a forty-year relationship with the United States based entirely on America's willingness to protect the ruling family, declaring economic war on its protector and going so far as to cut off the oil to the warships protecting it! American oil companies, meanwhile, were cutting not only the 10 percent the Saudis demanded on October 18, but even more to show where their loyalties lay. A second irony was that Prince (later king) Fahd bin Abdel Aziz al-Saud used the American resupply of Israel as an example of why the Saudis needed to have close relations with the United States. After showing his security officers evidence of the U.S. airlift, Fahd summarized the raison d'être of the relationship: "They are the only ones capable of saving us in this manner should we ever be at risk."[15]

A final irony was that the embargo was far more harmful to many of the Arabs' supporters than to the West. The appeasers in Western Europe and anti-Israeli countries of the Third World were hit far harder than the United States was.

Nixon was not intimidated by the Arab action. On October 19, he publicly called for $2.2 billion in emergency military aid for Israel, having warned friendly Arab countries earlier of his intention. The Saudis, and other Arab states that had so far only announced a cut in production, immediately retaliated by cutting off all shipments of oil to the United States.

Remarkably, an American official was advising U.S. businessmen how to support Arab efforts to blackmail the United States. The U.S. ambassador to Saudi Arabia, James Akins, telegrammed an Aramco official on October 25, 1973, urging the oil companies to "use their contacts at highest levels of government to hammer home point that oil restrictions are not going to be lifted unless political struggle is settled in manner satisfactory to Arabs. Industry leaders should be careful to deliver the message in a clear unequivocal way so that there could be no mistake about the industry position." It is no wonder Kissinger ultimately fired Akins for representing the Saudis rather than America, a decision that seemed even more justified after the former diplomat was free to express his personal views, which included the opinion that the Saudis should use their oil weapon to force the United States to change its policy.[16]

Unable to rely on his ambassador, Kissinger traveled to Riyadh in November 1973 to try to persuade Faisal to lift the embargo. The king not only refused, he lectured Kissinger on how Israel was helping the Communist advance in the Middle East. He said he would not end the embargo until the United States forced Israel to withdraw to the 1967 boundaries and the Palestinians established a homeland with Jerusalem as its capital. When Kissinger asked what would then become of the Wailing (Western) Wall, Israel's holiest shrine, Faisal replied that another wall could be built somewhere else where the Jews could wail. Faisal also declared his intention to stop the Jews' efforts to "run the world" with his "oil weapon."

The United States was furious at Faisal's refusal to immediately end the embargo, and Kissinger publicly threatened that steps would have to be taken against the oil producers if the embargo was not lifted. A variety of options were secretly explored, including seizing the oil fields, launching a food boycott against OPEC, and developing alternative fuel sources. The Saudis, meanwhile, countered with their own threat to blow up the oil fields.

Kissinger was doing what he did best, double-dealing. Publicly, he denied any connection between oil and the Arab-Israeli conflict, but privately, he talked about the need to pressure Israel. In November 1973 Nixon also talked about the possibility of going to the UN or applying other types of pressure on Israel to avert an oil shortage. In a December 1973 memo, Kissinger told Nixon that Israel needed to be prodded to attend the Geneva Conference to help mitigate the impact of the embargo. But he also told the Arabs that the United States would only use its leverage on Israel if they first ended the embargo.

In fact, however, Kissinger did begin to lean more on the Israelis to reach an agreement. He found an unexpected partner in Anwar Sadat, who, having achieved his principal objective of regaining Egyptian honor, was now prepared to engage in peace negotiations. In January 1974, the United States thought it had convinced the Saudis to lift the embargo, in part because Kissinger had negotiated a partial Israeli withdrawal from the Sinai. Syrian president Hafez al-Assad intervened, however, and persuaded Faisal to maintain the embargo until a disengagement agreement was reached for the Golan Heights. By this time, the impact of the embargo was already dissipating as oil seeped back into the market. Kissinger had been reluctant to try to negotiate with the Syrians and Israelis, but relented and convinced the Israelis to accept the idea of withdrawing from some of the territory Israel had captured. At the same time, he also offered the Saudis more aid and arms.

In mid-February 1974, Faisal met with Sadat and Assad. Sadat argued that the embargo was becoming a liability; the United States would be reluctant to continue to engage in negotiations under coercion. Assad wanted Faisal to hold out until Syria got what it wanted, but Faisal ultimately agreed to lift the embargo on March 18, after Kissinger reported progress in Israeli-Syrian talks. Notably, the embargo ended without any concessions regarding Palestinian demands.

The Arabs left open the possibility of reimposing the embargo if they were dissatisfied with American actions. That threat receded in the short run after Kissinger brokered the Syrian-Israeli disengagement agreement in early May; nevertheless, Faisal warned of a new embargo in September 1974 if Israel did not withdraw from all the territory it held before the end of the year.

If the various elements of the Arab lobby involved in supporting the embargo—the petrodiplomatic complex, the Saudis, and the nascent Arab American interests—expected the embargo to be blamed on Israel and American support for the Jewish state, they were mistaken. After the war, American sympathy for Israel reached a near-record high of 54 percent, compared to 8 percent who supported the Arabs. It was the oil companies that were the target of most of the nation's opprobrium. Congress was especially angry when it learned that Aramco and Gulf had been prevented from delivering oil to U.S. forces during the war, forcing the U.S. Sixth and Seventh fleets to curtail their operations. Members also learned that Aramco had provided the Saudis with information about indirect shipments of Saudi oil to the U.S. military, allowing the Saudis to reduce shipments to those suppliers.[17]

The executive branch's response was completely different. Even after Saudi Arabia declared economic war on the United States, the Nixon administration warmly embraced the Saudis and sought ways to exploit their newfound wealth. One month after the end of the embargo, for example, the United States announced a large sale of sophisticated weapons. One American military official said, "I do not know of anything that is non-nuclear that we would not give the Saudis. . . . We want to sell, and they want to buy the best." The new sales were part of a new strategy to defend the Persian Gulf; the "Two Pillar Policy" sought to avoid a buildup of U.S. troops by instead strengthening its two major allies, Iran and Saudi Arabia.[18]

After the embargo, the Saudis embarked on a massive spending spree, building roads, hospitals, airports, and entire cities; American companies were brought in to design, construct, and maintain many of these projects. The United States has even sold sand to the Saudis because the deserts of Saudi Arabia do not contain the type needed to make cement for construction. As a result of the petrodollar circle, U.S. trade with Saudi Arabia grew from $56.2 million in 1950 to roughly $68 billion in 2008.

One price of doing business with the Saudis was to comply with their boycott of Israel; another cost was paying bribes. The unspoken bargain with American business was that the Saudis would be happy to entertain their proposals and sign contracts in exchange for a commission of 5 percent or more to the Saudi middleman, usually a member of the royal family. Prince Bandar later admitted that as much as $50 billion of the $400 billion Saudi Arabia spent in three decades of nation-building was lost to corruption and mismanagement. "So what? We did not invent corruption," he told a PBS interviewer.[19]

So many contracts were negotiated with questionable payoffs to Saudis that in 1977 Congress adopted the Foreign Corrupt Practices Act to make it illegal to bribe foreign officials to obtain contracts. The law had little impact.

The consummate wheeler-dealer of the 1970s and '80s was Adnan Khashoggi, believed to be the middleman for 80 percent of U.S.-Saudi arms deals at the time. During congressional testimony in 1975, officials from the defense contractor Northrop admitted giving Khashoggi $450,000 to bribe two Saudi generals to buy their jet planes in 1972 and paying other kickbacks under pressure from defense minister Prince Sultan. Lockheed Aircraft Corporation's chairman, Daniel J. Haughton, later admitted during congressional testimony that his company had paid or committed $106 million in agents' fees to Saudi Arabia, most of which was paid to Khashoggi, who denied paying the bribes.[20]

The Saudis have grown accustomed to the idea that they can buy anything, including silence. When the British, for example, investigated and found evidence of approximately $2 billion in illegal payments to Prince Bandar by BAE Systems, Britain's largest weapons maker, in exchange for military contracts, the Saudis told the British government to back off or they would cancel a multibillion-dollar purchase of fighter planes, and that they would make it easier for terrorists to attack London. Bandar denied accepting "improper secret commissions," and the British killed the investigation. The Saudis subsequently signed an $8.7 billion order with BAE for seventy-two Eurofighter Typhoon warplanes. On April 10, 2008, the High Court in Britain ruled that officials investigating accusations of corruption in the deal acted unlawfully when they dropped the inquiry under pressure from British and Saudi authorities.[21] The wealth generated after the oil embargo also presented other U.S. corporations with an opportunity to enter an increasingly lucrative market for goods and services. One example was FMC Corporation. CEO Robert Mallott went on a tour of the Middle East sponsored by *Time* magazine in January 1975, came away impressed by the Saudis, and immediately began to speak about America's biased policy toward Israel and the need to be more evenhanded. Within the next ten years, FMC signed contracts worth more than $600 million to supply various goods to the Saudis and other Arab countries. Another company with heavy investments in Saudi Arabia was Bechtel, which received $3.4 billion in 1974 to build King Khalid International Airport in Riyadh and worked on the $40 billion petrochemical complex constructed in Jubail. The Justice Department accused the company of discriminatory practices, including refusing to employ Jews, which led Bechtel to sign a consent decree agreeing not to engage in such behavior.[22]

The U.S. oil companies were the biggest winners from the Arab-Israeli War of 1973, with Standard Oil and Exxon posting profit increases exceeding 50 percent. Exxon, in fact, earned an all-time record for any corporation, when it made $2.5 billion. At the time, the Saudis still owned only 60 percent of Aramco, but the reality was that the Saudi government controlled the company. In 1972, OPEC had negotiated an agreement to gradually increase their stakes in the Western companies pumping their oil. The final takeover took effect in 1980, and the company was renamed the Saudi Arabian Oil Company (Saudi Aramco) in 1988.[23]

While individual companies benefited from the lifting of the embargo, the overall impact on the U.S. economy was devastating. The price of oil increased 600 percent; inflation was at the post–World

War II high of 10 percent, with unemployment at 8.5 percent, the highest since 1941. Industrial production fell for twenty-one consecutive months.[24]

Treasury secretary William Simon saw that the government's budget deficit was getting out of control, and the economy was sinking under the weight of escalating oil prices caused by panic over the embargo. The U.S. economy could not grow if it could not generate sufficient foreign exchange to pay its oil import bill. Simon concluded that the way to finance the debt was to convince the OPEC nations to invest their earnings in the United States. Secretly, he negotiated a deal allowing the Saudi national bank to buy U.S. Treasury securities outside of the normal auction.

The Saudis deposited $1 billion in a special Treasury Department account to pay for all of the American technical assistance. A Joint Economic Commission (JECOR) was also formed to facilitate contacts and to create a vehicle for justifying U.S. technical assistance and feasibility studies. It was established by executive order and paid for by the Saudis, which allowed the Nixon administration to side-step Congress.

The commission proved to be a moneymaker for the Treasury, collecting more than $500 million by 1981 from Saudi-funded feasibility studies.[25] By the fourth quarter of 1977, Saudi Arabia held 20 percent of all Treasury notes and bonds purchased by foreign central banks.

While the Arab investments helped ameliorate America's short-term debt crisis, they also increased the Arab countries' potential to use them for political leverage, something they did after 9/11. Meanwhile, successive administrations refused to provide Congress with information about the Arab investments and told the Saudis the information would never be disclosed. The Saudis, in turn, threatened that they would transfer their money elsewhere if OPEC investment data were made public.

Thanks to the rapid increase in oil prices, from $1.80 per barrel in 1970 to $39 in 1980, the oil producers were making money faster than they could possibly spend it. In 1970, Saudi Arabia alone earned $2.3 billion from the sale of oil. By 1980 the figure was more than

$110 billion. The profit windfall gave it international clout on financial markets and the ability to invest worldwide in Western economies. Foreign investment is not unusual, and the Saudis are not even the largest investors in the United States (so far as we know), but what distinguishes the Saudi investments is that they are made by the government, members of the royal family, and those whose fortunes derive from their ties to the monarchy. And these investments are not made solely on the basis of profit, as is the case for other foreign investors; the broader goal is to influence U.S. policy.

Arab oil producers began to purchase significant interests in banks (such as Citibank), media (such as Warner Brothers), real estate (such as Toll Brothers), and other industries. Federal regulations require that corporations disclose investments that exceed 5 percent of a public company's stock, so Arab investors have usually kept their purchases below the threshold. Nevertheless, a House Banking Subcommittee study found that even a 1 or 2 percent stake "can gain tremendous influence over a company's policies and operations."[26]

Though worrisome, the prospect of Arab governments buying controlling interests in key industries is unlikely; the government must approve the acquisition of U.S. companies in certain sectors, such as defense. Nevertheless, as reporter Tad Szulc noted, "there is no way of knowing how much money is invested anonymously in companies operating in these sensitive areas by OPEC Arabs working through 'fronts.'" One report found that in 1981 Kuwait alone had spent $7 billion to buy up to 4 percent of the stock in dozens of different American companies, including thirty-six utilities, twenty oil companies, seventeen banks and finance companies, and eight chemical companies.[27] Szulc argued that Arab threats to pull their money out of the United States if their investments were disclosed were probably empty in part because "the United States is considered the safest repository for surplus foreign sums" and because the value of their assets would suffer.[28] Nevertheless, when Congress began to investigate, the Saudis and Kuwaitis threatened to provoke an economic crisis by withdrawing their funds if their investments were disclosed to the public.

Prior to the embargo, the Saudis had no international clout; they could only blackmail the United States. By the late 1970s, however, they were able to coerce other countries. For example, most sub-Saharan countries severed diplomatic ties with Israel after the war because they were promised cheap oil and financial aid and because they were afraid to defy the Organization of African Unity resolution, sponsored by Egypt, calling for the severing of relations with Israel.

The Saudis also undermined U.S. interests at the UN, where they used financial incentives to African and other nations to win votes on resolutions opposed by the Nixon and Ford administrations, such as the call for Palestinian self-determination, the invitation of the PLO to participate in UN General Assembly debates on Palestine, the granting of observer status to the PLO, and the equating of Zionism with racism.

The Saudis likewise warned other countries against moving their embassies to Jerusalem. When Canada announced it would move its embassy in 1979, Saudi Arabia and Kuwait canceled more than $400 million worth of contracts with Canadian firms and threatened to withdraw their deposits from Canadian banks. The value of the Canadian dollar sank, and the country faced a potential economic crisis. The government subsequently decided to postpone the embassy move. Two decades later, it still sits in Tel Aviv. Similar threats directly against the United States have never been made public, but it is not difficult to imagine they have been made privately, especially after Congress voted to relocate the U.S. embassy in 1980; each president since then has used a national security waiver in the legislation to avoid the move.

In 1978, the Senate Foreign Relations Committee prepared to issue a report criticizing the Aramco-Saudi relationship. Before the report was made public, the Saudis let it be known that it would jeopardize the future of Saudi investments in the United States and would eliminate any incentive to reconsider supporting the Israel-Egypt peace agreement (something they had no intention of doing under any circumstances). The report was subsequently sanitized and cleared with the Saudis before its release; not surprisingly, it did not contain any embarrassing disclosures. The Saudis later made similar threats to successfully quash a Justice Department antitrust investigation of Aramco. During a December 1979 visit, Saudi oil minister Sheikh Yamani reportedly pounded his fist on the table and pointedly told treasury secretary William Miller that he expected the probe to be dropped. The NSC joined the State Department in lobbying Justice to scotch the investigation.[29]

Fast forward to 2002, when relatives of nine hundred people who were killed on 9/11 filed a $116 trillion lawsuit alleging that Saudi money had "for years been funneled to encourage radical anti-Americanism as well as to fund the al-Qaeda terrorists." The suit named three members of the Saudi royal family, including the defense minister. Afterward, the *Telegraph* reported that the kingdom's richest investors threatened to pull billions of dollars out of America. The Bush administration sided with the Saudis against the American terror victims. A stated reason was the principle of opposing lawsuits against foreign leaders and governments out of fear that the U.S. government and American leaders would then be sued in foreign countries. It is reasonable to assume the Saudi threats may have also played a role in the decision. The case was eventually dismissed by the district court in 2005 after the court ruled the main defendants to have foreign sovereign immunity. The victims lost their appeal and petitioned the U.S. Supreme Court to consider the case. In May 2009, the Obama Justice Department filed a brief supporting the lower court ruling. The filing came less than a week before President Obama was scheduled to meet in Saudi Arabia with King Abdullah as part of his initiative to reach out to the Muslim world. A few weeks later, the Supreme Court decided not to overturn the federal appeals court's ruling.[30]

After the embargo, American decision makers had to take into account the possibility that angering the Arabs could result in an act of economic war against the United States, and future policy would be calibrated accordingly. Moreover, for some of the radical Muslims, economic warfare is part of their vision of jihad. On September 28, 2001, after the attacks on the United States, Osama bin Laden called on jihadists "to look for [and strike] the key pillars of the U.S. economy."

The idea of using their economic clout to influence U.S. Middle East policy has been expressed by more mainstream Saudis, such as Prince Alwaleed bin Talal, who has stakes in banks (Citigroup), the media (News Corporation) and resorts (Four Seasons Hotels), and also made huge donations to Georgetown and Harvard as well as the Carter Center. In May 2002, bin Talal said that if the Arabs "unite through economic interests," they would achieve influence over the U.S. decision makers.[31]

The ability of the Saudis and other oil producers to threaten the United States diminished as they gradually lost control of oil prices. After the price spikes of the 1970s, demand took control, and October 1981 was the last time the OPEC price rose for a decade. OPEC's control was further weakened as production from non-OPEC countries such as the Soviet Union grew. The United States also took steps to protect itself when Congress authorized the creation of the Strategic Petroleum Reserve (SPR), which was designed to hold enough crude oil to replace imports for ninety days.[32]

The Arab oil producers lost their stranglehold over the energy market when the New York Mercantile Exchange (NYMEX) introduced futures in crude oil in 1983. From that point on traders and speculators would determine "spot" prices—oil for immediate delivery—and prices for "futures"—oil to be delivered in a month or later—and reap much of the benefits. Saudi Arabia and the other OPEC members decided to focus on maintaining market share instead, and have tried to control supply by setting production levels.

Meanwhile, Saudi earnings steadily declined from a high of $119 billion in 1981 to $26 billion in 1985. The Saudis continued to spend, however, as though they would earn ever-growing revenues, and soon found themselves running a large budget deficit. As their fortune declined, they worried about their waning political power.

In fact, as Aramco was celebrating its seventy-fifth anniversary in 2008, and enjoying the windfall from record high prices, the Saudis found themselves in much the same position as in the earliest days of oil production. After years of trying to buy off potential unrest by providing citizens with free health care and education, the kingdom is beginning to face the prospect of serious domestic problems that it cannot afford to address.

These domestic concerns explain why fears of a future cutoff of oil are exaggerated. While one Saudi monarch famously said that if they had no more oil, they'd simply go back to living in tents, while the United States would have serious trouble, the Saudis know that a precipitous decline in their income might lead their subjects to bury them in their tents, especially if the United States lost interest in keeping them in power.

The Saudis remain in the energy driver's seat, however, because they sit on 22 percent of the world's proven reserves, an estimated 260 billion barrels, a figure that has grown over the years as more oil has been discovered than produced. Saudi oil is also the cheapest to extract. Furthermore, the Saudis control half the world's surplus production capacity—2–3 million barrels a day—which provides a cushion to preserve market stability. A shift from oil will not eliminate the nation's influence, as Saudi Arabia also sits on the fourth-largest reserves of natural gas.[33]

For the first forty years of the relationship, the principal fear of the United States was that the oil concession would be lost. After the Saudis nationalized Aramco completely in 1980, that threat was no longer on the table. Similarly, after the 1973 embargo, OPEC never used the oil weapon again, even after Israel invaded Lebanon and fought uprisings with the Palestinians. Now, changes in the energy market, as well as preventive measures taken by the United States, such as filling the Strategic Petroleum Reserve, make it unlikely that another embargo would be effective. Still, the petrodiplomatic component of the Arab lobby has remained as solicitous over the last thirty-five years as in the first four decades because of their conviction that protecting the royal family is crucial to assuring the supply of oil. And these lobbyists continue to actively make their case at the highest level. As former CIA operative Robert Baer observed, "I'd seen, too, how some midlevel oil exec could pick up the telephone and get a meeting with the National Security Council as fast as Bandar could get one with the president."[34]

Thus, Saudi Arabia continues to extort American concessions even though it now accounts for only about 8 percent of U.S. crude oil consumption and 16 percent of petroleum imports. It is the Far East that now depends most heavily on Saudi oil, importing about half of all Saudi crude. This suggests that the United States does not need Saudi oil, or at least not enough to kowtow to its demands.

Moreover, Saudi officials have their own concerns, one of which is that al-Qaeda seeks support by claiming that the United States is exploiting Muslim resources. Ayman Zawahiri, the organization's number-two official, said in December 2005, for example, "I call to concentrate efforts on the stolen oil of Muslims, whose main profit goes to the enemies of Islam, while the remainder is stolen by the thieves that control those countries."[35] This echoes the themes of Arab nationalists of the 1950s who similarly accused the Saudis of being American puppets.

The Saudis also fear that if oil prices rise too high or too fast, the world will be more motivated to develop new energy sources. Richard Murphy explained in a nutshell the rationale for the Saudi oil policy: "Saudi policy makers believe, for Saudi Arabia's own self-interest, that their wisest policy is to maintain predictable prices of oil, avoiding spikes which stimulate research on alternative energies and which inevitably collapse, upsetting rational plans for the country's development." Or, as former oil minister Sheikh Yamani once noted, "The Stone Age did not end for lack of stone."[36]

The Saudis understand this better than anyone, which is precisely why they have been the "moderating" force within OPEC. It is not, as their apologists would have you believe, because they are friends of the United States, but because they recognize that it is in their interest to keep Americans dependent on oil; and they are willing to forgo short-term profits from higher prices that might provoke a radical change in U.S. policy.

A vivid example of the Saudis' lack of interest in American concerns occurred in May 2008, a time when the U.S. economy was reeling from the subprime mortgage meltdown and record high oil prices around $100 a barrel, American troops remained mired in Iraq, international sanctions aimed at stopping Iran's drive for a nuclear bomb were failing, and the president was trying to push the Palestinians and Israelis to reach an agreement before he left office. President George W. Bush traveled to Saudi Arabia to meet with King Abdullah to seek his help and personally lobby the king to increase production and lower oil prices. The country advertised as our closest Arab ally rebuffed the president on every issue. Abdullah had already publicly criticized America's "illegitimate foreign occupation of Iraq" and was not interested in doing anything to help achieve the U.S. objectives there.[37] The king also made a point of criticizing the president for going to Israel earlier and making a pro-Israel speech in the Knesset. The Saudi oil minister said the kingdom had no intention of pumping more to bring down the price of oil and would adjust output only "when the market justifies it."

Nevertheless, U.S. policy remained consistent. The Bush administration continued to find new ways to boost the regime, including plans for a multibillion-dollar arms sale and an agreement for cooperation in the field of nuclear energy. The nuclear deal was viewed by the administration as a means of helping the Saudis diversify their energy resources, but the Saudis were clearly interested in developing a counter to the Iranian nuclear weapons program.[38]

It has become more popular today to argue for an energy policy that will free the United States from its dependence on foreign oil. The enthusiasm waxes and wanes with the price at the gas pump. Prince Turki al-Faisal, the former Saudi ambassador to the United States, ridiculed this idea as "demagoguery." He called talk of energy independence "political posturing at its worst—a concept that is unrealistic, misguided, and ultimately harmful to energy-producing and consuming countries alike." He added, "There is no technology on the horizon that can completely replace oil as the fuel for the United States' massive manufacturing, transportation, and military needs."[39] There is little question, however, that multiple American interests would be served by finding alternative energy sources. The

Saudis and other oil producers would lose all their leverage over us, along with the justification for providing them a security umbrella. The United States would then be free to base its relations on common values and interests rather than submit to the scare tactics and blackmail that have too often led us to sacrifice our principles.

CHAPTER SEVEN

Jimmy Carter's Conversion:
From Peacemaker to Provocateur

President Jimmy Carter owed his narrow 1976 election victory, in part, to the support of Jewish voters. Almost immediately upon taking office, however, he began to waffle on his campaign promise to support strong legislation against the Arab boycott of Israel and reversed his predecessor's position on an important Israeli arms sale. Even as he helped bring about a long-dreamed-of peace agreement between Israel and Egypt, he pursued policies that undermined his main objective of a comprehensive peace. Carter sometimes intentionally, and other times inadvertently, made statements and adopted policies that alienated his Jewish supporters and reflected the outlook of the Arab lobby. By the time he ran for reelection, Carter's policies were viewed as a threat to Israel's security, and he was so reviled in the Jewish community that he received the smallest proportion of the Jewish vote of any Democratic candidate since 1924.[1]

Carter was also the one president who made human rights the cornerstone of his foreign policy; yet now he is one of the leading apologists for the apartheid Saudi regime, which also happened to provide significant funding to the Carter Center. Carter's current views are even more ironic, given that it was the Saudis who played a major role in undermining his greatest accomplishment as president, the mediation of the Israeli-Egyptian peace treaty. Yet Carter remains a popular international figure and is now perhaps the most prominent member of the Arab lobby.

During the 1976 presidential campaign, Carter, like most candidates, said what the Israeli lobby wanted to hear. The one concern that some Jews had was that as a born-again Christian he might harbor some views on church-state relations that would create differences on domestic issues. This was a time before the emergence of a strong Christian Zionist political movement, but the general assumption of many Jews was that someone who talked so much about the Bible and his Christian beliefs could not help but be pro-Israel. As Menachem Begin told a group of American Jews before his first meeting with the president, "Jimmy Carter knows the Bible, and that will make it easier for him to know whose land this is."[2]

In fact, Carter was not a Christian Zionist. While he continued to give politically correct speeches throughout his term expressing support for Israel, his anti-Zionist beliefs were exposed in his post-presidency writings. Unlike Christian Zionists who believe the Jews were meant to be restored to Zion, Carter adopts replacement theology, which says the church has inherited the promises God made to the Jews, and then shares this inheritance with the Muslims. Few other American Christians share his view that Judaism and Islam have anything approaching equal moral validity, but this outlook shapes Carter's attitudes today and probably influenced his policies as president as well.[3]

Carter actually started out as president by supporting the effort to make it illegal for U.S. companies to comply with the Arab boycott against Israel. The battle over the adoption of that legislation is a textbook example of the war between the Israeli and Arab lobbies. The story begins more than thirty years before Carter took office.

The Arab boycott was formally declared by the newly formed Arab League Council on December 2, 1945: "Jewish products and manufactured goods shall be considered undesirable to the Arab countries," and all Arab "institutions, organizations, merchants, commission agents, and individuals" were called upon "to refuse to deal in, distribute, or consume Zionist products or manufactured goods."[4] The boycott consists of a primary, secondary, and tertiary boycott. The primary boycott is the refusal of Arab states to trade with Israel. Beginning in April 1950, the boycott was extended to include the refusal by Arab states to trade with third parties—non-Israelis—which are thought to contribute to Israel's military and economic power. Companies doing business with Israel were put on a blacklist and were supposed to be barred from commercial activities with Arab countries. This is the secondary boycott. The tertiary boycott prohibits trade of goods containing components made by blacklisted firms.

The objective was to isolate Israel from its neighbors and the international community, as well as to deny it trade that might be used to augment its military and economic strength. The Arab states selectively adhere to the boycott, making exceptions whenever it suits their interests.

The State Department policy reflected the Arabist bent. A statement in 1956 said, "[We] are obliged to recognize that any attempt by this country to force our views on a foreign national would be considered intervention in the domestic affairs of that nation and therefore greatly resented."[5] In 1961, after New York and California state legislatures adopted resolutions calling for action against the Arab boycott, the State Department declared that the Arab states were "entitled to establish rules and regulations that proscribe dealings with any individuals or firms in accordance with what they deem to be the interests of their national security." The department also inaccurately reported that the boycott was not directed against Jews, but only against those doing business with Israel.[6]

Congress, spurred by the Israeli lobby, periodically condemned discrimination against Americans in resolutions that were routinely tacked onto foreign aid legislation, but no serious effort to combat the boycott was taken until 1965. AIPAC began to lobby for legislation opposing restrictive trade practices, but the Johnson administration objected that this approach might backfire and provoke the Arabs to intensify their boycott practices. President Johnson also feared that taking a stand against the boycott would incite opposition to U.S. embargoes against Cuba, China, Vietnam, and Korea. Nevertheless, an amendment to the Export Control Act was adopted after the administration forced a compromise whereby the president was given the discretion to decide whether to prohibit boycott compliance. Efforts to make the antiboycott provisions mandatory failed in the next five congresses.

PRIOR TO 1973, THE ARAB boycott was considered a "toothless and gutless" propaganda ploy. After the oil embargo, however, it was viewed as a tool to force the United States to reduce its support of Israel. The Arab world had become America's fastest-growing export market, and Arab investments began pouring into the United States. In June 1974, Kissinger signed an economic cooperation agreement with the Saudis to assist in "the realization of Saudi aspirations," which meant channeling billions of dollars of new business into the kingdom. This new business, however, was conducted on Saudi terms, which meant "exclusion of hundreds of blacklisted U.S. companies plus discrimination against American Jews."[7]

Also in 1974, the chief executives of seven blacklisted firms, including RCA, Ford, and Coca-Cola, urged Kissinger to use his "best efforts to persuade the Arab nations that the new role of the United States and the Middle East and the new climate of diplomatic accommodation in the region would be well served by an end to these discriminatory barriers." A few months later, Senator Frank Church made public for the first time a list of fifteen hundred American firms on the 1970 Saudi blacklist, which made the public aware of the scope of the boycott. Even more disturbing, however, were revelations of U.S. government complicity in the boycott. The public would never learn many of the details of that collusion, but representatives of the Army Corps of Engineers admitted that Jewish soldiers and civilian employees were excluded from projects the corps managed in Saudi Arabia.[8]

After the U.S. policy was publicized, the secretary of defense announced that Jews would not be screened out of projects and President Ford declared on February 26, 1975, that "such discrimination is totally contrary to the American tradition and repugnant to American principles. It has no place in the free practice of commerce and in the world."⁹ The declaration was immediately undercut by the disclosure of a Pentagon contract to train Saudi national guardsmen that contained a discriminatory clause

As in so many other cases, it never seemed to occur to anyone in the government to take the stand Kennedy did against Saudi slavery or say to the Saudis, If you don't end your discriminatory practices, we will stop selling you arms and remove our defense umbrella. The State Department could have taken a lesson from Hilton Hotels, which planned to build a hotel in Tel Aviv in 1961 and was warned about the Arab boycott by the American-Arab Association for Commerce and Industry: "Should Hilton Hotels persist in going ahead with its contract in Israel, it will mean the loss of your holdings in Cairo and the end of any plans you might have for Tunis, Baghdad, Jerusalem [part of which was then in Jordanian hands] or anywhere else in all Arab countries." Hilton fired back a response that the company would adhere to "the principles of Americanism as set out by our Founding Fathers and of the principles for which America has stood since its founding." Hilton built its hotel in Tel Aviv; others were built in Jerusalem and throughout the Arab world.

As the Ford administration began to wind down, the pressure for antiboycott legislation escalated. Ford tried to forestall legislation by issuing an executive order strengthening the Commerce Department's reporting requirements and proposing a package to prevent discrimination against Americans, but the Israeli lobby saw these as merely cosmetic changes that failed "to come to grips with the full scope of Arab boycott operations in the United States." As the House prepared to vote, Mobil Oil ran ads warning against passing the bill, and Exxon adopted "one of the strongest stands it has ever taken on a controversial public issue." The National Association of Arab Americans (NAAA), which had originally taken no position, also took out ads opposing the legislation. The Saudi foreign minister, Prince Saud al-Faisal, spoke with the president and lobbied members of Congress.¹⁰ Treasury secretary William Simon also weighed in, using the argument that administrations would later use in arms sales debates, that the Arabs would go elsewhere if the law was passed: "In the administration's view, heavy-handed measures which could result in confrontation with the Arab world will not work."[11]

Neither the administration nor the Arab lobby was convincing, and the House voted 318–63 on September 22, 1976, in favor of a ban on boycott-related activities. A less restrictive measure was passed by the Senate, 65–13. The victory was only temporary, however, as the Export Administration Act containing the antiboycott provisions expired before the competing bills could be reconciled.

Meanwhile, candidate Jimmy Carter was making the boycott a campaign issue. In the foreign policy debate on October 6, 1976, he said, "The boycott of American business by the Arab countries because those businesses trade with Israel or because they have American Jews who are owners or directors in the company is an absolute disgrace." He promised to "do everything I can as President to stop the boycott of American business by the Arab countries."[12]

As Carter prepared to take office and, presumably, fulfill his campaign pledge, the Arab lobby created a boycott task force—Full Employment in America Through Trade, Inc. (FEATT)—at a meeting convened on November 11, 1976, by the NAAA. FEATT hoped to defeat the legislation by scaring legislators with the prospect of massive job losses—800,000 to 1 million over a five-year period; however, Congress did not take these warnings seriously, especially after organized labor backed the legislation.

Despite the legislative momentum at the end of Ford's term, widespread public support, and candidate Carter's own campaign promises, President Carter began to retreat from his support for antiboycott legislation. Carter feared the legislation would upset the Arabs and thereby endanger both American oil supplies and his peace agenda.

Though Carter proposed much weaker restrictions than Congress had adopted months earlier, Aramco chairman Frank Jungers warned that business would shift away from the United States to other countries, and that "as an American citizen and as a businessman, I find that I must condemn any laws that are opposed to American interests." The notion that the man who justified and helped manage the oil embargo against his own country should be the arbiter of American interests was laughable.

Jungers also argued that the Arab boycott was okay because it had been around for twenty-five years, and was in his view no different from the American boycott of China, Cuba, and North Korea. Jungers proclaimed that the whole issue had arisen because "Zionist elements" were trying to force the United States to take sides in the Arab-Israeli conflict. "I'll do my best," he added, "to ensure that American legislators realize that anti-boycott laws will not end the Arab-Israeli dispute but will intensify it."[13]

Unlike Jungers, most business leaders hoped to avoid a fight with either the administration or the Israeli lobby. Carter stayed above the fray until April 1977, when his top political adviser, Stuart Eizenstat, told Jewish leaders and corporate executives he wanted them to work out a deal. Ultimately, a compromise was worked out between the Israeli lobby and the forty-two-member policy committee of the Business Roundtable. Even Exxon's chairman, Clifton Garvin, went along after being personally lobbied by secretary of state Cyrus Vance, Eizenstat, and other business leaders.

Congress adopted the antiboycott bill by overwhelming margins in both chambers, and Carter signed it into law. The Arab League responded in typically bombastic fashion, threatening to take a decisive stand against the law and to buy their goods elsewhere. Contrary to the claims of opponents who said American trade to the region would suffer, the volume of exports actually increased substantially. Broader diplomatic and cultural relations with Arab states also improved.

Egypt was the first country to officially end its boycott after signing a peace treaty with Israel. It took about fifteen more years before the six Gulf Cooperation Council states announced on September 30, 1994, that they would no longer support the secondary boycott barring trade with companies doing business with Israel. Since the signing of peace agreements between Israel and the PLO and Jordan, the boycott has gradually crumbled. The primary boycott—prohibiting direct relations between Arab countries and Israel—has slowly cracked as nations such as Qatar, Oman, and Morocco have negotiated deals with Israel. Furthermore, few countries outside the Middle East comply anymore with the boycott.

The boycott is still technically in force, and Saudi Arabia remains one of its most vigorous proponents. In 2005, Saudi Arabia was required to cease its boycott of Israel as a condition of joining the World Trade Organization. In June 2006, the Saudi ambassador admitted that his country still enforced the boycott, in violation of promises made earlier to the Bush administration, and the Saudis participated in the 2007 boycott conference. Saudi officials continue to reiterate their intention to enforce the boycott.

The boycott debate was just a sideshow in Carter's first year in office; his main concern was pursuing peace. He believed that he could bring about world peace by ending the conflict. "There is an increasing realization," he said in May 1977, "that peace in the region means to a great degree a possibility of peace throughout the world."[14] Carter apparently believed that he could convince all the parties to end their decades-long conflict if he could get them all in a room together in Geneva. As political scientist Steven Spiegel put it, Carter had an "almost mystical belief in face-to-face contact with other leaders, an attitude perhaps influenced by his religious tradition of personal witness."[15]

Most Arab leaders, however, had little interest in making peace under any conditions except Israel's complete capitulation to their demands, and the Israelis were not anxious to get in a room where their enemies would gang up on them. They were especially alarmed by a number of statements by Carter and his advisers that left them wary of the president's commitment to their security.

Carter sent a message almost immediately to the Israelis that his administration would take a different tack than did its predecessor. One of his first acts in office was to reverse Kissinger's approval of a sale of Israeli-built Kfir planes to Ecuador that not only cost Israel the value of that sale but also killed any chance for similar sales to other Latin American countries. Carter also canceled the sale of U.S. concussion bombs to Israel. These decisions were supposed to reflect the new president's desire to curtail arms sales and to end the practice of using weapons transfers as a foreign policy instrument; however, Carter almost immediately approved the first of a number of arms sales to Saudi Arabia.

Carter also adopted a position long advocated by the Arabists that Israeli settlements were illegal and an obstacle to peace. This was at a time when there were still only a handful of settlements in the territories, and the Jewish population there was about 6,000. This immediately set him on a collision course with Prime Minister Begin, who was committed for ideological reasons to expansion of the Jewish presence in the territories. Carter's public condemnation of Israel also riled the Israeli lobby. Carter further angered both Israelis and their American supporters by beginning what would be a nearly four-year flirtation with the PLO. The Arabists believed the PLO was the representative of the Palestinian people and therefore would have to be part of any negotiations over their future. Henry Kissinger had made a commitment to Israel, however, that the United States would not negotiate with the PLO unless the group accepted Israel's right to exist *and* UN Resolution 242. Carter was willing to talk to the PLO if they met at least one of the conditions, and repeatedly tried to cajole them to do so. He failed, but the effort cost him support in the pro-Israel community.

Anwar Sadat was also concerned with Carter's policy. Having regained Egyptian honor in the Arab-Israeli War of 1973, he was now prepared to make peace if he could recover the territory Israel had captured in the Sinai. It soon became apparent, however, that Carter's policies were jeopardizing his goal. In particular, he did not want his national interest held hostage by the more radical Syrians whom Carter wanted to entice to participate in an international conference. Sadat knew they would not agree to peace with Israel and would do everything possible to sabotage his own plans.

Carter's dalliance with the Syrians offers one of the most vivid examples of his naïveté. When the presidents met in Damascus to discuss his plan for a peace conference, Carter found Assad "very constructive," "somewhat flexible," and "willing to cooperate." After his presidency he wrote in his memoir, "This was the man who would soon sabotage the Geneva peace talks . . . and who would . . . do everything possible to prevent the Camp David Accords from being fulfilled."

As journalist Morton Kondracke later wrote, it was Carter's "freshman-year ineptitude that scared Sadat into dramatic independent action." When Sadat made the dramatic decision to go to Jerusalem to address the people of Israel directly, Carter's team was shocked, and the president's agenda was thrown into chaos. Rather than seeing Sadat's bold gesture as the psychological breakthrough that it was, national security adviser Zbigniew Brzezinski was furious. "Sadat's upsetting our careful plans for trying to bring everyone together for the Middle East," NEA's Nicholas Veliotes quoted him as saying.[16]

When Israeli prime minister Begin, considered a hard-liner uninterested in peace, showed that he too was open to an agreement, Carter ultimately realized the opportunity to mediate negotiations that could lead to a historic result. The Israeli lobby was unreserved in its praise for Sadat, but the Arab lobby objected to the administration's support for Sadat's initiative. In the only reference to the Arab lobby contained in any of the memoirs of the Carter administration, Carter wrote that he was under pressure from the American Arab community and its friends: "They [Arab Americans] have given all the staff, Brzezinski, Warren Christopher, and others, a hard time."[17]

Most of Carter's people did not have to be pushed. Robert Strauss, who served as Carter's Middle East envoy, said that most of the officials in the Middle East section of the State Department were anti-Israel, and he "didn't trust them as far as I could throw them."[18] These Arabists had a powerful ally in the "realist" national security adviser, Zbigniew Brzezinski, who shared their view that it was important to solve the "Palestinian problem" to protect American interests in the Persian Gulf. Brzezinski agreed with the Arabists that the United States should use its leverage to force Israel to withdraw from the territories with the goal of creating a Palestinian state, which he expected to be dominated by the PLO. Unlike the more knowledgeable Arabists, he had a naive view of that state peacefully coexisting with Israel.[19]

Acting on the views of Brzezinski and others who believed that the Arabs were ready for peace, Carter became the first president to declare support for a Palestinian state in March 1977. When asked about the decision, he said it was "consistent with our policy in the UN for decades." In fact, when asked, Nicholas Veliotes had told the White House that the United States had never supported a Palestinian homeland at the UN. More significantly, Carter had essentially made a concession at Israel's expense that undermined his own peace agenda. As Veliotes noted, "He gave it away for nothing. We could have bartered that for something we wanted from the Palestinians, maybe recognition of Israel."[20]

Once Israel and Egypt reached an agreement, Carter was concerned about the reaction of the Arab world. It came swiftly and was universally negative. Still, Sadat believed the key to winning an endorsement for the accords and possibly even broadening the process to include Syria and others was the backing of Jordan and Saudi Arabia. Carter assured him that he could deliver their support.

The Saudis led Carter to believe they would help marshal support for the peace process, but instead they joined the other Arab states in denouncing the agreements, in part because they objected to Egypt signing a separate peace that left the Syrians and, especially, the Palestinians out in the cold.

Interestingly, for all their public declarations of fealty to the Palestinian cause, the Saudis have never used oil as a weapon on their behalf. In fact, although Carter said that all the Arab leaders were vigorous public supporters of the Palestinians, privately, they were not as committed to a Palestinian state. "Really, it would be a very great surprise to me," Carter told reporters in 1979, "for Crown Prince Fahd to send through our Ambassador, John West, to me a message: 'If you don't expedite the resolution of the Palestinian question, we will cut off your oil.'"[21] This unprecedented admission that, contrary to the view of the Arabists, the Palestinian issue was not the most important factor in U.S. relations with the Arabs belies the policies that Carter and his successors nevertheless persisted in following.

Camp David actually created a golden opportunity for the Palestinians to move closer to the objective of statehood. Begin had offered them only a limited form of autonomy, but they refused to even negotiate over the proposal, which Yasser Arafat referred to as "garbage." Had they accepted this plan, it would have been difficult for Israel to prevent the Palestinians from gradually taking complete control over their affairs. Rather than see this possibility, the domestic Arab lobby joined the PLO in rejecting it out of hand.

Carter made excuses for the Saudis, saying that they would only support the treaty privately and that the Arab criticism would have been worse if not for the Saudis exercising restraint. The truth was that Carter had sent a private letter to King Khalid seeking his support and been rebuffed. Sadat had warned that there would be problems if the Saudis didn't support the Camp David Accords, and Hermann Eilts, the former ambassador to Saudi Arabia, told Carter the Saudis would never accept the agreement. Displaying the messianic conviction that had led him to believe he could persuade the Arabs to make peace by the force of his personality, Carter said, "Hermann, don't you worry about the Saudis, I'll take care of them." Eilts was left thinking that Carter must know something he didn't. It turned out that Eilts was correct, and Carter subsequently "felt [Crown Prince] Fahd had betrayed him."[22] From Eilts's point of view, this was a case of the Arabist experts being ignored to the detriment of America's foreign policy interests. Meanwhile, of course, it was Saudi subsidies that were helping to finance the radical parties that were bent on sabotaging the agreement, such as the PLO and Syria.

In another example of Carter's unearned sympathy for the Saudis, he blamed Begin for the Saudis' opposition to Camp David. He said that Begin had promised to freeze settlements for the duration of autonomy talks, which were expected to take months, if not years. Begin, however, insisted he had agreed only to a three-month freeze while the peace treaty was negotiated—and the evidence supports his position. Nevertheless, Carter insisted that Begin reneged on his commitment and maintained that this alienated both the Saudis and Jordanians.[23] It would also be a source of lasting bitterness for Carter.

Despite the opposition of the Saudis and others, the Arab lobby did not prevent Israel and Egypt from making peace. Moreover, despite tensions between Carter and Begin, the United States became more intimately tied to Israel. As late as 1973, Israel had received less than $500 million in total aid, but from 1980 on, aid to Israel averaged $3 billion annually. Egypt also benefited, becoming the second-largest aid recipient after Israel, which, ironically, has been supported primarily by the Israeli lobby and Egyptian government and not any other part of the Arab lobby.

The fact that the Saudis tried to sabotage Carter's most important foreign policy initiative did not deter him from offering to sell them $1.5 billion worth of weapons within weeks of their rebuff of Camp David (Carter would sell the Saudis arms worth $5.1 billion in 1979). How can this be explained? It is most likely a result of the usual Saudi policy of bribery. In this case, the kingdom announced a temporary increase in oil production. Carter's spokesman denied any linkage, but Sheikh Yamani offered another possible clue when he told *Newsweek* that he was warning the West that the PLO could threaten tankers in the Persian Gulf.

Carter's sycophancy toward the Saudis was evident throughout his term, and particularly embarrassing when he praised them for pursuing a "responsible and unselfish" oil policy and producing more oil than "perhaps was best for them." According to Carter, "between ourselves and Saudi Arabia there are no disturbing differences at all." Contrary to Carter's rosy portrayal, the Saudis actually made a strategic decision to join the Arab rejectionists, and rather than acting "unselfishly," they cut oil production and triggered a panic in the world oil market after promising they would not do so.[24]

Carter was still embroiled in the antiboycott bill debate, and already over his head in machinations to organize a peace conference in Geneva, when he decided to sell F-15 fighter planes to Saudi Arabia. The Ford administration had earlier promised to replace the Saudis' obsolete planes with any aircraft they wanted. The Saudis chose our best at the time, the F-15. Though it was clear they did not need the most sophisticated plane (according to a report by the comptroller general of the United States, the Saudis had difficulty operating and maintaining the older F-5 planes, and new planes would only exacerbate the situation), the Pentagon wanted to make the sale to keep U.S. procurement on schedule and lower production costs for our air force. When Carter visited Riyadh after the election, he was reminded of Ford's promise and was told that if the United States did not sell them the planes, the Saudis would turn to the French. Some of Carter's advisers suggested that the Saudis should either get less sophisticated planes or join peace negotiations before receiving them. The Saudis rejected any changes to their shopping list.

During the 1970s, the Israeli lobby had formulated a policy that it would oppose arms sales to states at war with Israel, since there was a legitimate concern American weapons could be used against Israel in a future conflict. Many members of Congress shared the concerns of Carter's advisers and the Israeli lobby about the sale; nevertheless, Carter saw an opportunity to overcome the opposition when Sadat traveled to Jerusalem in November 1977. Carter wanted to reward Sadat for his courage by offering Egypt fifty F-5E aircraft, and also compensate Israel with seventy-five F-16s. In an effort to circumvent opposition to the planes for Saudi Arabia, he packaged the sale of sixty F-15s to the Saudis with the Egyptian and Israeli planes. He hoped to hold the jets for Israel hostage in an effort to ensure that Saudi Arabia and Egypt received arms. The Israeli lobby was willing to accept the sale to help Sadat, but the Saudis were viewed as a potential military threat.

The sale's opponents faced an uphill battle; Congress had never vetoed an arms sale before, and Carter was coming off a major legislative victory—the ratification of the Panama Canal Treaty. In addition, the Arab lobby made a dramatic appearance in Washington. As a congressional aide told journalist Hoag Levins,

> The Arabs just suddenly appeared in Washington in 1978. It was that quick. Boom! . . . The progress they made was in-

credible. Four years before, the Arab lobby was a joke. You had maybe two people here who knew what they were doing. . . . They didn't even understand the theory of the system, let alone how it works here on the Hill on a day-to-day basis. And then, Wham! Arabs are everywhere; know exactly what they are doing; are very slick about doing it. It was amazing.[25]

One change was the Arabs' investment in foreign agents. There were twenty-five agents lobbying on the Saudis' behalf for the F-15 sale. For example, the South Carolina consulting firm Cook, Reuf, Span and Weiser received a $65,000 contract from the Saudis to lobby for the F-15 sale, and another $100,000 as a down payment to implement a long-term strategy to enhance the kingdom's image. The choice of a South Carolina firm may seem odd, but two of the opponents of the sale were the state's senators, Ernest Hollings and Strom Thurmond. The head of the firm, J. Crawford Cook, had worked for Hollings and was well connected on the Hill. When Thurmond abruptly canceled a press conference to announce his opposition to the sale the day of the vote and instead voted for it, the senator's change of heart was attributed to Cook's lobbying. Cook's efforts were later rewarded with an increase in the size of his contract with the Saudis to $470,000 annually.[26]

The Washington savvy of these agents complemented the charm of Saudi royals and diplomats, who made a positive case that they should be sold the planes while simultaneously threatening to go elsewhere if they did not get their way. Prince Bandar even succeeded in obtaining an endorsement from California governor Ronald Reagan. Once again it was the defense industry component of the lobby that played a critical role as Bandar contacted the CEO of Northrop, Tom Jones, whose company made F-5 planes purchased by the Saudis. Jones, a member of Reagan's Kitchen Cabinet, agreed to set up a meeting. The governor was interested in Bandar's answers to only two questions: "Are you friends of ours? Are you anticommunist? When I said yes to both, he said, 'I will support it.'"[27]

While the Israeli lobby was accustomed to having allies in the

White House, in the Carter administration they faced a formidable enemy, national security adviser Zbigniew Brzezinski, who was seen as the architect of the arms package. Brzezinski was advocating a number of positions in the Middle East that were anathema to the Israeli lobby, such as talking to the PLO and coercing Israel to withdraw to the pre-1967 borders. He reportedly said that the F-15 vote would "break the back of the Israeli lobby."[28]

Carter also adopted the position that he was acting in Israel's best interest. For example, Carter claimed that Israeli prime minister Menachem Begin didn't object to the sale, but when Begin publicly criticized the sale, Carter emphasized the importance of the United States fulfilling its commitment to its friend, saying, "I believe that it's best for Israel to have this good, firm, solid, mutually trustful, friendly relationship with the moderate Arab leaders."[29] This attitude was largely to blame for the deterioration of his ties with Israel's supporters. Carter also undermined his own policy by his heavy-handed approach toward Begin, which drove Americans who disagreed with Begin's policies to defend him against what they viewed as the president's unfair attacks.

Carter and supporters of the F-15 sale argued that the planes were only for self-defense and that the Saudis would not transfer the planes to a third nation without U.S. permission. King Khalid wrote a letter to Carter reminding him of the kingdom's long friendship with the United States and its proven mutual benefits. He also emphasized the need for the F-15s to blunt "Communist expansion in the area."

The NAAA argued the sale was necessary to give the United States the leverage to play peacemaker. Administration officials also suggested that the sale would positively influence Saudi oil policy, even though Saudi oil minister Sheikh Yamani specifically said that "linking the F-15 with oil sales is not justified," and, shortly before the vote on the sale, announced a reduction in oil production to prevent a decline in prices.

A few members of Congress were willing to call the Saudis' bluff to buy arms from France. Senator Jacob Javits asked rhetorically, "Do you think they are going to lean on France for their security for the next five years? They are not crazy, believe me." Others pointed out that the Saudis were likely to buy weapons from France regardless, but the planes would not be as good and would not lead to pressure to follow up the sale with a request for radar planes such as AWACS. Senator Daniel Patrick Moynihan summed up the sale as "a rationalization of American nervelessness in the area of international economic policy as well as political and military policy."[30]

Henry Kissinger suggested sweetening the arms package for the Israelis and placing some restrictions on the use of the F-15s for the Saudis. The administration adopted the idea, pledging not to sell fuel tanks that would allow the Saudi planes to reach Israel, or bomb racks or air-to-air missiles that could give the F-15s offensive capabilities. The administration also got a commitment from the Saudis not to base the planes within striking distance of Israel, and promised not to sell AWACS or any other systems that would enhance the F-15s' ground-attack capability. The concessions allowed him to pick up some additional support, though the Israeli lobby remained determined to block the sale. The White House then began to frame the issue as a test of who would determine U.S. foreign policy: the prime minister of Israel and the Israeli lobby, or the president.

The Senate voted 54–44 against the resolution to block the sale on May 16, 1978. Afterward, Saudi Arabia's state radio proclaimed that "the Jewish lobby in the United States is weakening."[31] The NAAA also declared victory: "The political conclusion to be drawn from the vote is that the Israeli lobby lost its major fight and its apparent veto over American policy toward the Arab world. . . . The vote confirmed that the Israeli lobby is subject to political limits. This reality opens the door to a more constructive and balanced American approach to the Middle East."[32]

Thirty years later, Walt, Mearsheimer, Carter, and others would still be claiming that the lobby was all-powerful.

Israeli media, meanwhile, were reporting that White House aides Hamilton Jordan and Jody Powell had told journalists they had broken the back of the Israeli lobby and were now free to make policy without its interference. Both denied they had made the remarks, though several sources said they had heard them. The net effect was to worsen the already deteriorating relations between Israel and its supporters and the administration.

Though the Israeli lobby succeeded in extracting a number of concessions and a promise of even more planes for Israel, the bottom line was that the Saudis got the planes. Moreover, within a few years, all of Carter's promises were broken as the Reagan administration sold the Saudis most of the equipment that had been withheld in addition to AWACS radar planes. It is now clear that the F-15 battle was the beginning of the end of the Israeli lobby's efforts to prevent arms sales to the Arabs.

From the Saudi perspective, nothing was ever enough, no matter what guarantees they were given for their security or how many weapons they were permitted to buy. At the time Carter asked them to support the peace process, the Saudis were miffed by congressional action, ultimately supported by Carter, to end the boycott and by other congressional efforts to force disclosure of their investments in the United States. They were also angered by the leak of an intelligence report suggesting that Crown Prince Fahd's power was waning. They took out their anger on Carter in part by subverting his greatest diplomatic achievement, by supporting the Arab League's decision to ostracize Egypt, and by declining Carter's request that they pick up the $525 million cost of new jet fighters he wanted to sell Egypt as a reward for making peace with Israel. They also expelled the CIA station chief from Riyadh. Even after all Carter did for the Saudis, Crown Prince Fahd told *Al-Hawadess* in 1980, "We are not compelled to be friends of the Americans. There are many doors wide open to us, be it on the military, technological or economic level. . . . We can easily replace the Americans."[33]

Meanwhile, Carter completely absolved the Saudis of any responsibility to conform to his professed commitment to human rights. He made no effort to pressure the Saudis to change their apartheid policies toward women or to stop their export of radical Islamic teachings. Carter also undermined a second centerpiece of his foreign policy related to arms transfers. In May 1977, Carter had said that his administration would "henceforth view arms transfers as an exceptional foreign policy implement, to be used only in instances where it can be clearly demonstrated that the transfer contributes to our national security interests." Some of his advisers had suggested that the F-15 sale would subvert this policy; nevertheless, Carter went ahead and sold not only the fighter planes, but additional arms worth billions of dollars.

After the fall of the shah of Iran and the Soviet invasion of Afghanistan in 1979, U.S. priorities shifted from Carter's emphasis on Arab-Israeli peace and human rights to regional security. On January 23, 1980, Carter enunciated a new strategic doctrine that put Saudi Arabia and the other Gulf states at the forefront of American defense planning: "Any attempt by an outside force to gain control of the Persian Gulf region will be regarded as an assault on the vital interests of the United States of America, and such an assault will be repelled by any means necessary, including military force."

The Carter Doctrine satisfied the Saudis' persistent need for reassurance, which this time was provoked by Carter's failure to do more to support the shah, who was originally viewed as the stronger of the pillars in the "twin pillar" policy (the other being Saudi Arabia). The Saudis, however, were not interested in doing anything to support the new doctrine and rejected American requests, as they had done throughout the Carter years, for establishing American bases in the kingdom.

Meanwhile, the Saudis were actively trying to prevent the United States from taking measures to protect itself from oil supply disruptions and price fluctuations. In response to the Arab oil embargo, the United States had created a Strategic Petroleum Reserve (SPR) in 1975 to create a stockpile of oil in event of an emergency. In March 1980, the Saudis threatened to cut oil production by one million barrels a day if the Carter administration bought oil for the SPR.[34] "We don't like to see any building of that strategic stockpile," Saudi oil minister Ahmed Zaki Yamani reportedly said. "We don't think it is necessary." Columnist Hobart Rowen responded, "The Saudis now seem to be making decisions of the highest strategic order for this country and there is not a peep out of President Carter." The *Los Angeles Times* observed that the Arab petroleum-producing nations wanted the United States to remain vulnerable to the oil weapon: "The strategic petroleum reserve is too important to be stalled indefinitely out of deference to the Saudis."[35]

Ultimately, the Saudis, who raised oil prices 60 percent in 1979, helped drag down the U.S. economy and contributed to Carter's reelection defeat. The Saudis, of course, continued to rake in profits; and while the overall American economy suffered, the defense industrial component of the Arab lobby did not. For example, between 1976 and 1980, 22 to 44 percent of Northrop's total sales were to Saudi Arabia.[36]

The instability in the region was magnified in September 1980, when Iran and Iraq started what would become a ten-year war of attrition. Panic over the possible interruption of oil supplies sent the price skyrocketing to a then record high of $42 per barrel and precipitated a recession in the United States.

Meanwhile, the potential for the Iran-Iraq War to spill over to Saudi Arabia prompted the Carter administration to immediately approve additional weapons for the Saudis. When Carter was defeated for reelection, he recommended that the new Reagan administration provide more arms to the kingdom.

Near the end of his term, Carter's pro-Palestinian UN ambassador, Donald McHenry, argued that the United States should vote in favor of a Security Council resolution condemning Israeli settlements. The administration naively hoped that by voting for the Arab-sponsored rebuke, it would attract support for the Camp David Accords. Carter, as noted above, was convinced the settlements were obstructing his grand design for Middle East peace. He was willing to go along with his advisers and reverse their previous policy of abstaining on such resolutions so long as references to Jerusalem were removed, since he had promised Begin that issues related to Jerusalem would be resolved during future peace negotiations. The State Department told Carter that the references had been removed, and the president authorized a yes vote. But the resolution that was adopted called for Israel to dismantle its existing settlements and freeze construction in the territories, "including Jerusalem." Israel and its supporters were outraged. Carter, embarrassed, subsequently admitted that the United States had made a mistake.

By the time Carter ran for reelection, he had alienated much of the pro-Israel community; as noted earlier, he received the lowest proportion of the Jewish vote—45 percent—of any Democratic presidential candidate in more than half a century. The feeling that Jews had cost him the election may have provoked him to become one of the most outspoken detractors of Israel. Carter also seems to have never gotten over the feeling that Begin lied to him about freezing settlements, and held him responsible for his failure to achieve his dream of Middle East peace. As ex-president, Carter repeatedly attacked Begin for his decisions to destroy Iraq's nuclear reactor, deploy Israeli troops to Lebanon, and annex the Golan Heights. While the Reagan administration's legal adviser had rejected Carter's portrayal of settlements as a violation of international law, Carter continued to say otherwise. Carter has also remained frustrated that the Israelis never accepted his vision for a comprehensive peace (although the Arabs, including his "blood brother" Sadat, did not accept it, either).

In retirement, Carter gradually became a beloved figure whose postpresidential legacy has eclipsed his presidential accomplishments, a popularity based largely on his charitable work for groups such as Habitat for Humanity and his efforts to promote democracy and the end of conflict in mostly Third World countries. He also retained his messianic zeal for bringing peace to the Middle East, believing that he was serving Christ, and that that was more important than the views of his own government. Consequently, the "Saint Paul of conflict resolution" conducted his own private foreign policy and offered unsolicited advice to his successors. For example, in October 1981, Carter, along with Gerald Ford, called for the Reagan administration to begin talks with the PLO. Reagan responded that the United States had long been prepared to do so once the terrorist group satisfied the long-standing condition that it recognize the right of Israel to exist, which the PLO refused to do.

Carter also periodically lobbied members of Congress to support Arab positions on arms sales, and opposed recognizing Jerusalem as Israel's capital. Carter also accused Israel of human rights violations and would rely on his PLO friends for documentation of abuses. When he complained about the treatment of Palestinians in 1987, for example, prime minister Yitzhak Rabin replied that all of the Palestinians Carter referred to were involved in a "network of coordinated terror aimed at totally disrupting peaceful daily existence, causing loss of life to innocent victims." Not surprisingly, Carter's public attacks on Israel won plaudits from Arab leaders.

Another familiar Carter theme is that Israeli settlements are the obstacle to peace. This is easily disproved by the fact that the Arabs were not willing to make peace prior to the establishment of settlements in the territories, and Palestinian terror has continued after Israel's disengagement from Gaza. But Carter has little concern for terror committed against Israelis. In one of the rare references to Palestinian terrorism in his book *Palestine: Peace Not Apartheid*, Carter mentions two suicide bombings in March 1996. However, he seemed less bothered by the atrocities than by the fact that the attacks allowed the "hawkish" Benjamin Netanyahu to defeat Shimon Peres in Israel's election. He also leaves out the fact that it was Netanyahu who agreed to give up Israeli control of Hebron, the most sensitive city in the entire disputed territories, and accepted the Clinton administration's proposal to withdraw from an additional 13 percent of the West Bank.

Carter also advised foreign leaders. In 1990, for example, in an effort to reshape the terrorist's image, Carter helped Yasser Arafat draft a speech to the UN and praised him for doing everything he could to promote peace. Two days earlier, Arafat had stood beside Saddam Hussein and said he would fight Israel "with stones, with rifles, and with al-Abed," an Iraqi missile.[37] This pattern would be repeated numerous times as the person Carter called a man of peace called for a jihad or was caught involved directly in terrorism.

By contrast, Carter routinely asserts that Israel does not want peace, is stealing Palestinian land, and refuses to trade land for peace.

Yet he admitted in *Palestine: Peace Not Apartheid* that on his first visit to Israel in 1973, Israeli leaders wanted to trade land for peace. Later, he acknowledged that Prime Minister Rabin concluded an agreement with Jordan, announced his willingness to negotiate with Syria, and concluded an agreement with Yasser Arafat on Gaza and Jericho. Still, he insists that Israel puts "confiscation of Palestinian land ahead of peace," despite the fact that Israel has withdrawn from 94 percent of the territory it captured in 1967.

Carter has also actively worked to undermine his own government. As U.S. forces prepared to invade Iraq, Carter secretly wrote to the presidents of Saudi Arabia, Egypt, and Syria, urging them not to support the war against Saddam Hussein because it might "postpone indefinitely any efforts to resolve the Palestine issue."[38] The Bush administration later learned that Carter had written to all the Security Council members, asking them to oppose his own government's position to give Saddam Hussein an ultimatum to withdraw from Kuwait. Once the war began, Arafat was Iraq's principal cheerleader, but this did not seem to bother Carter. It did, however, enrage the Saudis, prompting Arafat to ask Carter to fly to Riyadh and appeal to the king to forgive him and restore Saudi funding to the PLO. Carter's freelance foreign policy initiatives led members of at least two administrations with little else in common—Bush Sr. and Clinton—to view his actions as bordering on treason.[39]

Carter also has shown no hesitancy about violating the unwritten rule of American foreign policy: you should never say anything abroad that might undercut the sitting president. In 1987, for example, while praising the autocratic leaders of Egypt and Jordan, he excoriated the Reagan administration.[40]

But it is in his books and articles that Carter has most fully demonstrated his conversion to the Arab perspective. In his various writings, Carter has established a pattern of historical revisionism, inaccurate and naive descriptions of the region and its history, and a penchant for blaming Israel and absolving the Arabs of all responsibility for the absence of peace. In his much-reviled book *Palestine: Peace Not Apartheid*, he provided aid and comfort to the new anti-

Semites, whose goal since the 2001 UN World Conference against Racism, Racial Discrimination, Xenophobia and Related Intolerance in Durban, South Africa, has been to link Israel to apartheid-era South Africa. He has also become an apologist for Saudi Arabia. In a fawning section about the Saudis in his book, Carter talks about the "impressive closeness" of the monarchy to the subjects while ignoring the discriminatory aspects of Saudi society. He says nothing about the Saudis' crude anti-Semitism and their hostility toward Israel. Carter praises the 2002 Saudi peace proposal without examining the various elements that made it a nonstarter, not to mention the Saudi rejection of directly negotiating with Israel. He talks about how Saudi Arabia "can be a crucial and beneficial force in the Middle East," but ignores that it is a sponsor of terrorism and the principal funder of schools that teach the most radical views on Islam.

Following the publication of Carter's book, Kenneth Stein, the first executive director of the Carter Center, stepped down from his position at the center. Stein had firsthand experience with the president and personal knowledge of events Carter related in his book, and was so appalled that he wrote in his resignation letter that the book's title was "too inflammatory to even print, is not based on un-varnished analyses; it is replete with factual errors, copied materials not cited, superficialities, glaring omissions, and simply invented seg-ments."[41] Soon after, fourteen members of the Carter Center's two-hundred-person Board of Councilors also resigned to protest Carter's anti-Israel screed. "You have clearly abandoned your historic role of broker in favor of becoming an advocate for one side," they wrote in their letter of resignation. "It seems that you have turned to a world of advocacy, including even malicious advocacy," they added. "We can no longer endorse your strident and uncompromising position. This is not the Carter Center or Jimmy Carter we came to respect and support." In 1982 Carter and his wife, Rosalynn, founded the Carter Center at Emory University. Though its formal mission is "advancing human rights and alleviating unnecessary human suffering," Carter has used it also as a platform for continuing his unfinished pursuit of Middle East peace. Though supposedly "nonpartisan" and "neutral in dispute-resolution activities," Carter has been nothing of the sort. In fact, Carter's desire to be a peacemaker has led him to invite African warlords and Latin American despots to Atlanta for consultations. Since founding the center, Carter has been involved in a variety of initiatives, from election monitoring to interceding in hostage negotiations. For example, in 1996 Carter led a Carter Center delegation that monitored the Palestinian Authority elections, which he said were "well organized, open and fair." Former CIA director Jim Woolsey said of the same election, "Arafat was essentially 'elected' the same way Stalin was, but not nearly as democratically as Hitler, who at least had actual opponents."[42]

In the same 2002 op-ed extolling the virtues of the Palestinian election, Carter excoriated Ariel Sharon as anti-peace and offered a remarkable defense of suicide bombers, saying that Arafat "may well see the suicide attacks as one of the few ways to retaliate against his tormentors, to dramatize the suffering of his people, or as a means for him, vicariously, to be a martyr." He concluded with a prescription for peace based on the Saudi peace plan and the need for the United States to place demands "on both sides." He then proceeded to argue for one-sided pressure on Israel.[43]

In 2006, Carter again monitored Palestinian elections and declared them "completely honest, completely fair, completely safe and without violence." Despite the victory of Hamas, he said, the United States and others should financially support the new government. President George W. Bush had already said that Hamas could not be a partner for Middle East peacemaking without renouncing violence and recognizing Israel's right to exist. Still, Carter expressed the hope that Hamas would act "responsibly."[44] Over the next three years, however, Hamas launched more than 10,000 rockets and mortars into Israel and provoked a war. This did not stop Carter from literally embracing Hamas during his many freelance peace missions to the region. For example, in April 2008, Carter laid a wreath at the grave of Arafat and then met and hugged Hamas politician Nasser Shaer. To the displeasure of the Bush administration, Carter volunteered to serve as a conduit between the group and the U.S. and Israeli governments, and said that isolating Hamas is counterproductive. Carter subsequently went to Syria to meet Hamas's exiled leader, Khaled Mashaal.[45]

In 2009, Carter again met with Mashaal and Hamas leaders in Gaza. Carter frequently comes out of these meetings claiming that the Palestinians were committed to peace and prepared to change their policies. In June 2009, for example, Carter said after meeting with Hamas officials, "They made several statements, and showed readiness to join the peace [process] and move towards establishing a just and independent Palestinian state." The very next day, however, Ahmed Yousef, the deputy Hamas foreign minister, declared, "The visit has not led to a significant change. Hamas finds the conditions unacceptable. Recognizing Israel is completely unacceptable."[46]

Carter has consistently accepted whatever Arab leaders tell him in private, no matter how many times they make a fool of him by their subsequent statements and actions. He has never acknowledged that his one-sided attacks on Israel might undermine his avowed goal of convincing Israelis to make peace.

Carter has also maintained his popularity in the Muslim world by his apologetics for radical Islam. This reached an extreme when he criticized Salman Rushdie for mocking the Koran after Iran's Ayatollah Khomeini had called for his execution.[47]

Even more odd have been his attacks on Israel's treatment of Christians and silence on their condition elsewhere in the Middle East. In *Palestine: Peace Not Apartheid*, he repeatedly refers to "Christians and Muslims" in an effort to suggest that Israeli actions are harming Christians and not just Muslims or Arabs. On a visit to Jerusalem in 1990, he said he met with a variety of Christian leaders who he said complained of various abuses, and ascribes the "surprising exodus of Christians from the Holy Land" to the intolerance of Israeli religious authorities. Actually, while Christians are unwelcome in Islamic states such as Saudi Arabia, and have for the most part been driven out of their longtime homes in Lebanon, Christians continue to be welcome in Israel. In fact, it is the Palestinians whose religious extremism has victimized Christians. According to a report by the Foundation for the Defense of Democracies, "the Palestinian Authority has adopted Islam as its official religion, used shari'a Islamic codes, and allowed even officially appointed clerics to brand Christians (and Jews) as infidels in their mosques."[48] Vatican Radio correspondent Graziano Motta said after Arafat's death that Christians "have been continually exposed to pressures by Muslim activists, and have been forced to profess fidelity to the intifada." Motta added, "Frequently, there are cases in which the Muslims expropriate houses and lands belonging to Catholics, and often the intervention of the authorities has been lacking in addressing acts of violence against young women, or offenses against the Christian faith."[49] Samir Qumsiyeh, a journalist from Beit Sahur, told the Italian newspaper *Corriere della Sera* that Christians were being subjected to rape, kidnapping, extortion, and expropriation of land and property. Qumsiyeh compiled a list of ninety-three cases of anti-Christian violence between 2000 and 2004. He added that "almost all 140 cases of expropriation of land in the last three years were committed by militant Islamic groups and members of the Palestinian police" and that the Christian population of Bethlehem has dropped from 75 percent in 1950 to 12 percent today. "If the situation continues," Qumsiyeh warned, "we won't be here anymore in 20 years."[50]

The former president has reaped financial rewards for his views, notably including millions of dollars in donations to the Carter Center from Saudi Arabia and other Arab sources. *Investor's Business Daily* listed a number of "founders" of the center, including "the king of Saudi Arabia (who pledged $1 million during Carter's 1983 visit to Saudi Arabia), BCCI scandal banker Agha Hasan Abedi (who gave $500,000 to the center and $10 million to other Carter projects), and Arafat pal Hasib Sabbagh." Sabbagh, whose construction firm became a subcontractor to Bechtel, served as a conduit between Arafat and Carter. He was also one of a number of wealthy Palestinians who supported the center. In 1990, Carter visited Rafiq Hariri, then president of Lebanon, who was married to a Palestinian. He came home with $250,000 for the Carter Center.

The Saudis have been especially generous to the center. Saudi arms merchant Adnan Khashoggi picked up the $50,000 tab for a center fundraiser in October 1983, just six months after Carter extolled Saudi Arabia's virtues at a Saudi trade conference in Atlanta.[51] In 1993, King Fahd of Saudi Arabia donated $7.6 million to the center. As of 2005, the king's nephew, Prince Alwaleed bin Talal (whose post-9/11 offer of $10 million to New York City was rejected by then-mayor Rudolph Giuliani because it was accompanied by the suggestion that America should cut back its support of Israel), has given at least $5 million to the Carter Center. In 2000, ten of Osama bin Laden's brothers jointly pledged $1 million, as did Sultan Qaboos bin Said of Oman in 1998. The Saudi Fund for Development has been another major contributor, as have the Kuwait Fund for Arab Economic Development and the OPEC development fund.

In 2001, Carter received the $500,000 Zayed International Prize for the Environment from the Abu Dhabi–based Zayed Center, which had also hosted Holocaust deniers and suggested a Jewish conspiracy behind 9/11 and a general *Elders of Zion*–type effort by Jews to dominate the world. Sheikh Zayed bin Sultan al-Nahayan is the donor whose anti-Semitic history eventually led Harvard to return his multimillion-dollar donation to its Divinity School.[52]

Alan Dershowitz observed that "despite the Saudi Arabian government's myriad human rights abuses, the Carter Center's Human Rights program has no activity whatever in Saudi Arabia." It does, however, list an office in the nonexistent state of "Palestine." Dershowitz also notes that Carter has criticized Jewish influence in American foreign policy, suggesting that politicians and others who receive Jewish money cannot formulate objective opinions. Dershowitz concludes that, using Carter's own standards, "it would be almost economically 'suicidal' for Carter 'to espouse a balanced position between Israel and Palestine,'" and that his views "must be deemed to have been influenced by the vast sums of Arab money he has received."[53]

While this kind of financial incentive cannot be ruled out, it seems more likely that Carter's views were already in sync with those of the Arabs, though he appears to have grown more strident and inflexible since his presidency. As indicated earlier, Carter's anti-Zionism was implicit in his strain of fundamentalist faith and has led him to read the Bible in peculiar ways as granting equal claims to both Jews and Palestinians. An element of wounded vanity and resentment of uncooperative Israeli leaders may also figure into it. But whatever the source of his views, Carter has become a formidable foe of Israel and, in effect, an Arab lobby unto himself.

CHAPTER EIGHT

Arms Sales Fights: The Arab Lobby
Knocks Out Its Opponent

For roughly thirty years, the effort to influence U.S. Middle East policy was conducted primarily behind the scenes in the executive branch. The Arab lobby did not have a formal base such as AIPAC for most of that time, and therefore engaged in very little traditional lobbying activity with the legislative branch. AIPAC, in contrast, made Congress its principal focus, and, beginning in the 1960s, started trying to influence policy through legislation aimed sometimes at constraining and other times at encouraging the executive branch's Middle East decision making.

Until the boycott debate, the Arab and Israeli lobbies rarely confronted each other directly, but this changed in the early 1970s, when AIPAC became stronger and more assertive and adopted the position that it would oppose the sale of sophisticated U.S. weapons to Israel's enemies. Congress had given itself the power to veto arms sales, and the pro-Israel lobby was emboldened after it successfully lobbied members in 1975 to prevent the sale of mobile Hawk antiaircraft missiles to Jordan. Though Jordan ultimately got the missiles, albeit a smaller number with a variety of restrictions, AIPAC believed it had won a great victory and now had the power to prevent the Arab lobby from obtaining whatever arms it sought from the White House. Shortly after the "victory" on the Hawks, however, the battle over the sale of F-15s to the Saudis proved the Arab lobby was no paper tiger. Still, AIPAC had again forced modifications to the sale and remained committed to the principle that states refusing to make peace with Israel should not be rewarded with arms.

The true extent of the Israeli lobby's influence on arms transfers had yet to be tested, but it would soon discover the limit of its power in a direct confrontation with the Arab lobby, backed by the most powerful Middle East lobbyist of all.

One of the key compromises President Carter made to secure support from Congress for the F-15 sale to the Saudis in 1978 was to strip them of some components that would threaten Israel and improve the Saudis' offensive capability. The Saudis were furious, and the American ambassador subsequently warned about the possibility of another oil embargo.[1] Shortly after Reagan assumed office in 1981, however, his administration said it was reneging on Carter's earlier commitment because of the instability of the region and the risk of Soviet penetration. Though Israel was again compensated with additional aid and planes, the Israeli lobby was shocked and angered when the press revealed that the president had decided to add airborne warning and control system (AWACS) radar planes to the new deal. For the Israeli lobby, the proposal set a dangerous precedent by offering an Arab state a weapons system superior to anything provided to Israel.

The decision to sell AWACS was made at a National Security Council meeting on April 2, 1981, while Reagan was recovering from wounds suffered in an assassination attempt. General David C. Jones, chairman of the Joint Chiefs of Staff, had apparently pushed the decision for economic as well as strategic reasons: "a sack of cash from the Saudis for the AWACS would hold down the cost of producing the radar planes for the U.S. Air Force."[2] When asked why the president had reversed a campaign pledge, national security adviser Dick Allen replied, "That was the campaign, this is the White House."[3]

The decision came just after Prince Fahd said in an interview that if Israel agreed to total withdrawal from the disputed territories, Saudi Arabia would bring other Arab states and the Palestinians to negotiate peace. The Fahd Plan was a nonstarter for negotiations, but making noises about a peace agreement was a clever lobbying tactic to win support for the arms sales. It allowed the administration to paint the Saudis as moderates. Eight months later, after winning the AWACS battle, the Saudis hosted an Islamic conference that denounced the Camp David Accords, rejected Resolution 242, and called for a jihad against Israel. When Secretary of State Alexander Haig visited Riyadh to press the Saudis to join the strategic consensus he was trying to build against the Soviets, the Saudis went out of their way to say that the only threat to the region was Israel.[4]

Congress reacted immediately, with more than a hundred members of the House coming out against the AWACS sale, and only twenty senators expressing support. Promises that the planes would be used only to protect the oil fields and would have other limitations placed on them did nothing to mollify the critics, who were backed by the public by a margin of 59 to 28 percent.

The Israeli lobby mounted a full-court press against the sale. The timing was not propitious, as Israel was being condemned for bombing Beirut and taking out the Iraqi nuclear reactor, which provoked international outrage and strained ties with the new administration. Nevertheless, AIPAC succeeded in securing support in both chambers to reject the sale. The Arab lobby was equally active, as investigative journalist Steven Emerson documented:

> The Saudi lobbying campaign resulted in one of the most successful manipulations of American business and American foreign policy ever attempted by a foreign power. Saudi Arabia demanded and received the aggressive support of the most powerful corporations in America. Scores of other business interests joined the campaign in order to protect existing petrodollar contracts or to obtain new ones. Still thousands of others were indirectly induced to join by pressure from their own domestic suppliers, purchasers, or business partners. And many others with no commercial stake in the sale, or even in Saudi Arabia, jumped into the lobbying fray because they were prevailed upon to believe that not upsetting the Saudis was vital to the U.S. economy.[5]

The offensive was led by Prince Bandar, who became Saudi Arabia's ambassador to the United States in 1983 and served for the next twenty-two years. He exemplified the personal touch involved in lobbying and the way the Arab lobby, as represented by the Saudis, influenced policy through direct access to the president and his top advisers. Bandar was not just a diplomat but the tennis partner of secretary of state George Shultz and racquetball opponent of the chairman of the Joint Chiefs of Staff, General David Jones. Colin Powell developed such a close relationship with Bandar over more than two decades that he referred to him as a brother. Powell said Bandar was such a frequent visitor to top officials in the Reagan administration that he acted as if he were a member of the Cabinet. Senate majority leader Howard Baker provided Bandar with a Senate office to coordinate the Arab lobby activities on the Hill, which included arranging meetings with forty senators.[6]

The oil industry engaged in its most extensive campaign on behalf of the Arab lobby, with Mobil spending more than half a million dollars on full-page advertisements extolling the virtues of the economic partnership between the United States and Saudi Arabia. No mention was made in the ads of the AWACS, only the $35 billion in business for American firms and the hundreds of thousands of jobs created by Saudi contracts.

In fact, when lobbying for the AWACS began, more than seven hundred corporations in forty-two states had contracts with Saudi Arabia. Each of these, in turn, had hundreds of subcontractors, all of whom shared the principals' interest in keeping the Saudis happy. Boeing, the main contractor for the AWACS, and United Technologies, which had $100 million at stake, orchestrated the largest campaign in support of the sale, with the presidents of the two companies sending out more than 6,500 telegrams to subsidiaries, vendors, and suppliers all over the country. When asked if the Saudis had pressured UT, a spokesperson told Emerson, "They didn't have to. It was a matter of pure economic self-interest."[7]

As Emerson noted, however, American business was mobilized in an unprecedented way, and companies not previously associated with

the Arab lobby and with seemingly little interest in the sale, s̲
the Florists Insurance Companies and Fisher-Price Toys, lobbied in ι̲
favor. Although he never took a formal position, the president of the
U.S. Chamber of Commerce, Richard Lesher, wrote to every senator
the day before the AWACS vote. That same month, the chamber held
a reception for the Saudi minister of commerce, Soliman Sulaim, who
took the opportunity to lobby the businesspeople in attendance. In addition, the 860,000 recipients of the chamber's newsletter were advised
of the adverse consequences for U.S. trade if the sale was not approved.

The Saudis' chief lobbyist, Fred Dutton, was the single most
effective spokesman during the campaign. He sent a sixteen-page
booklet, *Why Saudi Arabia Needs AWACS*, to every member of Congress. He also arranged for Saudi officials to appear on news shows
and brief the press. Most important, he cleverly framed the debate as
a fight between the prime minister of Israel and the president of the
United States, telling the *New York Times* that senators who opposed
the sale would have to explain "how they will run foreign policy now
that they have chosen Begin over Reagan." "If I had my way," he told
the *Washington Post*, "I'd have bumper stickers plastered all over town
that say 'Reagan or Begin.'"[8]

Dutton was not the only lobbyist on the case. He also worked
with J. Crawford Cook and Stephen Conner, and the three were collectively paid $1 million for their services in 1981.[9] One of Conner's
contributions was to set up a meeting between Bandar and former
president Gerald Ford. The following month Ford began to lobby for
the sale. In addition, at the request of President Reagan, both Jimmy
Carter and Richard Nixon joined the lobbying effort.

Opposition remained strong, however, because of fears that the
sale could lead to the compromise of American technology, would
reward Saudi Arabia for its refusal to join the Camp David peace
process and its financial assistance to the PLO, and would contradict
earlier assurances that the capabilities of the Saudi F-15s would not
be enhanced. Secretary of State Haig argued, however, that the sale
was vital to the administration strategy to protect American interests
from the Soviet Union and its proxies.

Opponents were unconvinced, given that the Saudis had been longtime supporters of Soviet proxies such as the PLO, Syria, and Iraq. They also recalled Kissinger's comment during the F-15 debate that you couldn't say the weapons would allow the Saudis to defend themselves against the Soviets and then claim they were no danger to Israel. Besides, in the midst of the debate, Defense Minister Khalid warned that if the United States did not sell AWACS, they would go to the Soviet Union for radar planes! Just the year before, Crown Prince Fahd had said that a meeting of Islamic foreign ministers was going to plan a jihad to "liberate Jerusalem and the occupied Arab lands."

Now, however, the Saudis were trying to overcome their image as opponents of peace by floating their own plan. But neither Israel nor the United States viewed it as workable, and it was dropped into the dustbin, only to be retrieved, dusted off, and cosmetically improved after 9/11.

Meanwhile, in an effort to buy off Israeli opposition, during Prime Minster Begin's visit to Washington the administration offered the first-ever strategic cooperation agreement with Israel. The hope that this would silence Israeli opposition to the AWACS sale quickly proved illusory as Begin continued to angrily denounce it. This provoked Reagan into getting personally involved, and at a press conference on October 1, 1981, he directly challenged the Israeli lobby: "American security interests must remain our internal responsibility," he said, adding, "It is not the business of other nations to make American foreign policy." Once the president painted Israel and the Israeli lobby as potentially undermining the national interest, the opponents realized that "If we lose, we lose; if we win, we lose."[10]

The NAAA, which at the time had one lobbyist, a staff of eight, and no grassroots support, lobbied for the sale, arguing that it would not threaten other countries and that the Saudis were a force for price moderation within OPEC and were playing a positive role in peace-making. AIPAC effectively rebutted these points and won an overwhelming victory in the House, which rejected the sale by a vote of 301–111.

It appeared as if AIPAC was on the verge of preventing a sale for the first time, as reports indicated at least fifty senators on the lobby's side. The day before the Senate vote, however, Roger Jepsen, one of the original sponsors of the resolution of disapproval, reversed his position. This shocking twist, along with the eleventh-hour decisions of several others to change their positions, resulted in a stinging defeat for the Israeli lobby and a game-changing victory for the Arab lobby. According to Hoag Levins, "That AWACS vote represented nothing less than a revolution within the Capitol's established order. . . . The Arab lobby had established itself as a major force in American politics and was continuing to consolidate and strengthen its position."[11]

Levins can be forgiven for jumping to this conclusion, but in fact the domestic Arab lobby did not become a major force on Capitol Hill. One of the main reasons the Arab lobby was successful in 1981 was the unprecedented involvement of business groups in lobbying activities. Not only did the business component of the lobby take a more visible role, but there was also a successful campaign to build a coalition of businesses normally uninvolved or uninterested in Middle East politics. Minnesota Republican David Durenberger, who withstood the pressure and voted against the sale, said, "It's not Reagan vs. Begin, it's oil vs. the Jews." Alabama Democrat Howell Heflin, for example, received a delegation of twenty-six businessmen from his state who had contracts with the Saudis and conveyed the message that defeating the sale would cost a lot of people, including Heflin, their jobs. Mobil Oil's president called Arkansas Democrat David Pryor to lobby for the sale. Boeing naturally leaned on the senators from its base in Washington.[12]

The Israeli lobby did influence the outcome by winning some assurances from the administration regarding the use of the AWACS and securing a commitment for additional military aid and planes. The closeness of the vote also discouraged the administration from proposing new arms sales to the Saudis, but only for a short time. Ultimately, the loss did break the Israeli lobby's back, as Brzezinski had hoped in 1978, at least with regard to arms sales. Never again would AIPAC make a serious effort to stop an arms transfer to an Arab ally of the United States.

The main lesson of the AWACS fight was that the president is *the* foreign policy lobbyist, and that when issues are cast in security terms, it would take extraordinary circumstances for a lobby to defeat him. AIPAC's executive director, Tom Dine, agreed that it was President Reagan rather than the Arab lobby who had snatched victory from the jaws of defeat. After September, Reagan met with twenty-two Republican senators, fourteen of whom voted with him, and twenty-two Democrats, swaying ten. Dine called the sale "a vote of confidence in President Reagan himself," and a response to the president's "appeal that if the sale were defeated, his effectiveness would be impaired."[13] This was reflected also in the statements by many senators, such as Jepsen, who said he'd gotten a classified briefing from the president to ease his fears and that he considered a vote for the sale "a vote for my president and his successful conduct of foreign policy."[14] Another switcher was William Cohen, the future defense secretary and defense industry consultant. After being convinced by the president to vote for the sale, he told his colleagues he was only trying to help Israel. Everyone in the Senate dining room laughed. "Come on, Bill," one senator replied, "just say you sold out. But don't give me that stuff about saving Israel."[15]

A key to persuading uncommitted senators to support the sale, and opponents to switch, was a letter Reagan wrote to Congress promising that before delivering the AWACS to Saudi Arabia, he would "certify" to the Senate that he had obtained agreements from the Saudis that would prevent the use of the planes against Israel or the compromise of its technology. The letter also appeared to commit the president to obtaining "substantial assistance" from Saudi Arabia in advancing Middle East peace. As in the past, however, the United States had missed an opportunity to use its leverage to obtain a quid pro quo from the Saudis, which at that time would have been support for the Camp David peace process.

Instead, the Saudis soon turned on Reagan and started to sabotage his initiatives, as they had done before with Carter after they got the arms they wanted from him. Just one day after the Senate approved the AWACS sale, OPEC raised the price of oil $2 per barrel, and the following day Saudi Arabia announced a production cut-back. A few weeks later, Saudi Arabia gave the PLO $28 million. In November 1981, Saudi Arabia denounced Oman for participating in a U.S. military exercise and offered money to the emirate if it canceled an agreement allowing American access to its military facilities. Saudi Arabia also undermined U.S. interests in peace by punishing countries that improved relations with Israel. In 1982, for example, the Saudis broke ties with Zaire when that country restored its ties with Israel. Relations were also severed with Costa Rica when it moved its embassy to Jerusalem.[16]

Over the next five years, the Saudis also opposed U.S. policy in Lebanon after Israel's invasion (during which Israel discovered PLO fighters had M-16s they'd gotten from the Saudis), opposed the re-integration of Egypt into the Arab world and its application for a seat at the Security Council, threatened to impose sanctions on King Hussein if Jordan negotiated with Israel, and continued to bankroll the PLO and Syrians against American wishes. Just as the United States was trying to isolate the Qaddafi regime after terrorist attacks attributed to the Libyans at the El Al counters in the Rome and Vienna airports, the Saudis declared their support for Muammar Qaddafi and condemned the United States for its April 1986 air strike on Libya.

Even after winning the AWACS battle, and signing an agreement to create a U.S.-Saudi military committee to hold annual consultations (similar to one created for Israel), the Saudis again resorted to their familiar pattern when President Reagan decided in 1984 to withdraw the planned sale of Stinger missiles to the kingdom. The missiles, which could pose a serious threat to aviation if they fell into the hands of terrorists, were of little use for defending the Saudis from external threats and had provoked vigorous opposition from members of Congress. This time Ambassador Bandar implied that unless they got the weapons they wanted, they would go to the Soviet Union. This was particularly galling, since a major argument for the AWACS sale was that the Saudis needed to protect themselves from the Soviets. A few weeks after withdrawing notice of the sale,

Reagan used a "national security" waiver to bypass Congress and sold four hundred Stingers to the Saudis.

The Saudis were not used to having their requests questioned, delayed, or denied. Growing tired of fighting with Congress and the Israeli lobby, they decided to reduce their reliance on U.S. hardware and diversify their suppliers. Bandar again played a key role, negotiating a deal in 1985 with Britain. Rather than a bruising lobbying battle in which the kingdom was dragged through the mud, he was able to reach an agreement with Prime Minister Margaret Thatcher in less than half an hour that turned out to be the largest arms deal in British history, worth $86 billion. The al-Yamamah deal allowed the Saudis to augment their inventory of U.S. aircraft with seventy-two top-of-the-line planes as well as a variety of other weapons and services. The Saudis paid for the purchase with oil and, best of all, from their perspective, faced none of the humiliating and onerous restrictions the Israeli lobby had forced them to accept in the United States. As Bandar told a group of McDonnell Douglas executives after the rejection of Saudi Arabia's request for additional F-15s and missiles in 1985, "My friends, let me tell you, we are not masochists; we don't like to spend billions of dollars and get insulted in the process." By contrast, the British government squelched all discussion of the deal and suppressed an audit report on grounds of national interest.

As in the case of the AWACS sale, the Saudi stick was accompanied by a carrot, an agreement by Bandar to provide $1 million a month to the Contras in Nicaragua (the total ultimately reached $32 million). The Saudis also reportedly agreed to build a network of naval and air bases that American forces could use to protect the region. They also responded to a request from CIA director William Casey to contribute $10 million to a campaign to help Italy's Christian Democratic Party against Italian Communists and to supply funds for anti-Communist groups in other parts of the world.[17]

In addition, the Saudis underwrote "Charlie Wilson's War" in Afghanistan by paying for Soviet arms that were captured from the PLO in Lebanon by the Israelis and sent to the Afghan rebels. Saudi involvement actually began during Carter's term, when the Saudis agreed to an arrangement cooked up by Zbigniew Brzezinski whereby the United States agreed to match Saudi contributions to the Afghan resistance. By 1981, the Saudi share was $5.5 billion.

The Saudis also provided funding to the leaders of Zaire and Somalia to fight pro-Soviet rebels in Angola and Somalia. At one point in 1981 Bandar boasted, "If you knew what we were really doing for America, you wouldn't just give us AWACS, you would give us nuclear weapons."[18]

The exchange of U.S. arms for Saudi favors in covert operations continued throughout the 1980s. In early 1986, Reagan proposed selling the Saudis $354 million worth of weapons, including 2,500 Stinger, Harpoon, and Sidewinder missiles. For the first time, majorities of the House and Senate voted to disapprove the sale, but Reagan vetoed the measure, and the sixty-six senators who tried to kill the transfer could not win any additional converts, so the sale went ahead.

Bandar was almost a one-man Arab lobby during much of this period. In addition to negotiating arms sales and encouraging his government to support America's covert programs, he also tried to influence the inner workings of the administration. In 1983, for example, Reagan was trying to decide whether to appoint Robert McFarlane or Jeane Kirkpatrick as his new national security adviser. Kirkpatrick was an outspoken supporter of Israel as ambassador to the UN who had had no contact with Bandar, while McFarlane had become a close friend to Bandar while serving as a special Middle East envoy. Bandar reportedly spoke to Nancy Reagan and suggested that McFarlane was the better choice. He ultimately got the job. On another occasion, Bandar learned from Nancy that the president was unhappy with George Shultz and planned to get rid of him. Bandar, who believed the Shultz State Department was too pro-Israel, suggested to the first lady that Secretary of Defense Caspar Weinberger, one of the Saudis' staunchest allies and Israel's harshest critics in the administration, be appointed in his place. He didn't get his wish for that position.[19]

A year later, in March 1987, when the USS *Stark* came under attack by Iraqi aircraft, the Saudis ignored a U.S. request to intercept the plane, and thirty-seven sailors were killed. Reagan's reaction? A proposal to sell $360 million worth of missiles to the kingdom. This time congressional resistance was sufficiently strong to prompt the administration to withdraw the sale in June 1987. About the same time, the *Washington Post* leaked news that the administration had asked for Saudi help in defending the Gulf, but was told its American-made AWACS would only be deployed after U.S.-flagged Kuwaiti tankers passed the Straits of Hormuz. Meanwhile, the Saudis denied U.S. aircraft and aircraft carriers landing rights.

Once again, the administration was apparently unconcerned by the lack of Saudi support, and in October 1987 it proposed yet another arms package, this time worth $1.4 billion. Congress opposed the package and forced the administration into a compromise that removed 1,600 Maverick missiles from the deal but still provided the Saudis with twelve F-15s and lots of other materiel.

Saudi duplicity reached its zenith when U.S. intelligence detected missile sites in the Saudi desert in 1988. American officials subsequently learned that the kingdom had made a secret deal to buy medium-range Silkworm ballistic missiles from China. The purchase of the Chinese missiles was upsetting to American policy makers on a number of levels. The deal was reportedly negotiated by Bandar, making the sense of betrayal even more acute. Officials were furious that Bandar had gone behind their backs, especially to the Communists. They were also upset that Saudi Arabia would purchase a weapon that had a range of nearly two thousand miles, which would allow it to hit any of its neighbors, including Israel.

Hume Horan was instructed to communicate America's displeasure to King Fahd and to tell him the United States wanted all work on the missile sites suspended. Bandar apparently got wind of this and convinced his White House friends to rescind the rebuke. Horan thought that Bandar's main interest was in collecting his commission on the missile sale. Regardless, Horan's message that the deployment was unacceptable was countermanded by a new message telling the king the issue should be discussed, and intimating it would not be a problem.

The State Department sent a delegation to Riyadh, led by Philip Habib, who told the king that the United States wanted to confirm that the missiles were nonnuclear and that construction on them had stopped. The Saudis rejected the U.S. demand to inspect the missiles, and the king blew up in anger, blaming Horan for creating a problem between the two governments. The king also made a reference to Horan's "Iranian blood"—his father was Persian—which Horan took as a slur. The bottom line was that Horan could no longer be effective after he'd alienated the king, but Horan also suspected that the Saudis did not like the fact that he spoke Arabic and could speak to people independent of the normal channels used by his predecessors. Fahd made clear that Horan was persona non grata, and the State Department quickly replaced him with the non-Arabic-speaking Walter Cutler.

Horan's departure was less surprising than the fact that he had ever been posted in Saudi Arabia in the first place. The Saudis were determined to ensure that whoever was posted to Riyadh would be their man, and were accustomed to U.S. ambassadors serving effectively as their lobbyists within the U.S. government. Horan had the heretical view that his job was "to represent the values and interests of the United States" and "not just the State Department but the U.S. Congress and the White House, too."[20]

Secretary of State George Shultz visited Riyadh shortly after the quarrel over the Chinese missiles and persuaded the Saudis to sign the Nuclear Non-Proliferation Treaty, which was supposed to reassure critics that the missiles would not be armed with nuclear warheads. U.S. arms sales then resumed with the 1993 sale of seventy F-15s.

King Fahd's reaction to the battle over arms sales was to declare Saudi independence—and thereby confirm the belief of political realists that nations always act in their self-interest. "The Kingdom of Saudi Arabia is not tied to anyone and does not take part in any pact that forces upon it any sort of obligations. . . . If things become complicated with a certain country we will find other countries, regardless of whether they are Eastern or Western. . . . We are buying weapons, not principles."[21] No clearer statement has ever been made to illustrate that the Saudis share neither our values nor our interests.

Of course, it did not take long for the Saudis to come back to the United States for more arms. In 1989 they wanted tanks, and were entertaining bids from British, French, German, and Brazilian companies. General Dynamics made the better tank, but congressional opposition was a potential obstacle. Chas Freeman, U.S. ambassador in Riyadh, convinced General Dynamics to adopt the strategy of studying "the economic impact of the deal on every congressional district in the country, so that each congressperson was provided, in his home district, with an indication of the number of jobs that would be generated if the sale were to go through, or, conversely, the number of people would be laid off if the sale did not."[22] The Saudis ultimately bought the U.S. tanks.

Saudi Arabia's posture toward America did not change the fact that the United States had grown dependent on Saudi oil and remained committed to protecting the royal family in the belief that this was the best way to ensure an uninterrupted supply. Thus, when Saddam Hussein began to threaten his neighbors and ultimately invaded Kuwait in August 1990, the United States decided it had to defend the kingdom.

Before the invasion, Saudi misinformation had imperiled U.S. interests. In 1990, for example, after Saddam Hussein threatened to attack Israel, Bandar flew to Iraq to meet with the Iraqi dictator, who assured him he had no intention of attacking Israel, a message dutifully repeated to administration officials a few months before he would launch Scud missiles against Tel Aviv in the midst of the First Gulf War. On July 27, 1990, Bandar assured the administration that Saddam would not invade Kuwait. Less than a week later, on August 2, Iraqi troops entered Kuwait.

Hussein had massed his troops along the Saudi border and was in position to quickly capture the largely undefended Saudi oil fields. The UN condemned Iraq's aggression, imposed a trade embargo, and called for an immediate withdrawal of Iraqi troops, but Hussein was unmoved. Prince Abdullah tried to suggest that Hussein's actions were misdirected, and that Iraq should instead be fighting beside the Saudis to "restore the legitimate rights in Palestine."[23]

The United States was in no position to stop the Iraqis because, as we saw earlier, the Saudis had refused to allow the United States to base a large force in the country. Instead of launching an immediate attack, however, Hussein kept most of his troops poised on the Iraqi side of the border and gave President George H. W. Bush time to persuade the Saudis to allow American troops onto their soil. The king was given U.S. intelligence showing that Iraqi armor had crossed into Saudi Arabia, but Fahd remained reluctant to allow the deployment of American forces, even after Bush promised they would go home when asked. Fahd sought the opinion of religious authorities and secured a ruling that the nonbelievers were permitted to enter the kingdom because they were coming to defend Islam. The United States then launched Operation Desert Shield to get sufficient troops into Saudi Arabia to deter Saddam from attacking the Saudis.

Bush did not want to fight Iraq alone, however, and set out to build an international coalition to blunt the opposition to war in the United States and placate Arab leaders who were hypersensitive to Western interference in their affairs. Over the course of five months, Bush succeeded in building a coalition of three dozen nations, which contributed a combined 670,000 troops (roughly 75 percent American, the bulk of the rest British and French).

Besides defending the oil fields, the primary concern of the Saudis was that the Americans live by Muslim rules. The Saudi commander said nothing would be tolerated that "clashed with our Muslim customs, national traditions, religious practices and beliefs."[24]

For example, the troops were not allowed to have alcohol, even on their bases; chaplains had to remove or conceal their crosses; women could not wear T-shirts or jog, and when they left their base, they had to wear traditional head-to-toe *abayas*, be accompanied by a man, and ride in the backseat of vehicles. Jews were permitted to defend the kingdom, but not to pray there, so Powell had to arrange for them to be taken by helicopter to ships in the Persian Gulf if they wanted to worship. When President Bush came to visit troops at Thanksgiving, the leader of the free world and defender of the kingdom was told not to say grace before dinner with the troops for fear of upsetting the religious authorities.

The Bush administration, like all of its predecessors and successors, completely misunderstood the nature of the Islamic extremists who were seeking to reestablish the caliphate and subjugate the Western infidels. The effort to appease the radicals was futile, and it should not have been surprising that they would use the American presence as a pretext to attract followers who disliked both the corrupt Saudi monarchy and the United States.

From the beginning of the crisis, one of the critical elements was how to prevent the conflict from engulfing Israel. The Bush administration was convinced that the Arab states would not support a war against Iraq if Israel were involved; consequently, the president urged the Israelis to stay out, even if provoked or attacked. Israel's decision to accede to Bush's request was an extremely painful one, however, because it meant that Israel would have to absorb a first strike and almost certainly suffer casualties that might be avoided by preemptive action. On January 19, 1991, Iraq fired its first Scud missiles at Israel; the nation would be hit by thirty-nine altogether during the war, causing billions of dollars of damage to property and the economy and dozens of casualties. Israel desperately wanted to respond, but Bush pressured Prime Minister Yitzhak Shamir to let the coalition forces handle the problem.

In the run-up to the war, the Israeli lobby and the Saudis were on the same side. Bandar even met with Jewish leaders to solicit their support for going to war against Saddam. Though most Jews are liberal Democrats, and many did not support the use of force, the Israeli lobby supported the war because Saddam was viewed as an implacable enemy of the United States and Israel. The Arab lobby was less unified, as usual, because the PLO had chosen to side with Iraq, putting Arab American organizations in a bind. The informal alliance between the Israeli lobby and the Saudi faction of the Arab lobby did not last beyond the war as the Saudis immediately reverted to their traditional anti-Israel position and Jews who had met with

Bandar accused him of breaking promises he had made to recognize Israel in exchange for the Israeli lobby's support.

After just forty-three days of fighting, the First Gulf War ended on February 28, 1991. The Saudis were only too happy to pay the bill when secretary of state James Baker asked, since they knew the U.S.-led forces had saved them. Ironically, the U.S. ambassador in Riyadh, Chas Freeman, suggested the Saudis might not be able to afford the cost of the war, but Baker dismissed his concerns as "a classic case of clientitis."[25]

The Iraqi invasion had another important consequence for the Saudis, and the Arab lobby generally, and that was to open the floodgates for weapons sales. No one was prepared to challenge transfers in the run-up to the war, so President Bush took advantage by waiving congressional bans on the sale of weapons such as F-15s, which Congress had denied to Saudi Arabia in 1985. More than $10 billion worth of arms were approved between August and December 1991. This was followed by the sale of an additional seventy-two F-15s in 1992 and a $9 billion package approved by President Bill Clinton in 1993.[26]

The arms sales continued despite the fact that the war of 1990–91 had shown that billions of dollars of sales to the Saudis had done nothing for Saudi security; they were still entirely dependent on the U.S. umbrella. The sales were also made despite the knowledge that the Saudis didn't need the weapons they were getting and couldn't adequately operate or maintain them. Meanwhile, when a former government official alleged that the Saudis had transferred sensitive U.S. technology from Patriot missiles to China, the administration looked the other way.[27] The defense industry component of the Arab lobby really didn't care. As one consultant put it, "All defense companies have powerful lobbyists to keep arms sales on track. It's just an exchange of money. Oil for equipment which sits in the desert, which they don't fly and can't maintain."[28] In fact, one of the principal arguments used to quiet Israel's friends was that the Saudis were too incompetent to pose a threat. Two of the most absurd examples were offered by a former diplomat in Riyadh who recalled that the U.S.

Military and Training Mission had difficulty getting the 30,000-man National Guard to appear where they were supposed to or carry out maneuvers effectively. He said Saudi naval war vessels "could not be pried from their port berths," and that during exercises with the U.S. Navy the commanders would refuse to allow their ships to go out of sight of land and required that the crews be able to return before dark.[29]

The Saudis also proved typically uncooperative in promoting peace between the Israelis and Arabs. When the Saudis were desperate for U.S. help to defend them from Saddam, Prince Bandar made the rounds on Capitol Hill, promising that his kingdom would lead peace efforts once Saddam was defeated. Following the war, however, when the Bush administration decided to organize an international peace conference to jump-start negotiations, the Saudis insisted they would not participate. Secretary of State Baker angrily told the Saudi foreign minister, "I guess that it was okay to be partners in war, but not in peace."[30] Under heavy pressure from the administration, and facing furious criticism from members of Congress, the Saudis ultimately agreed to come to the conference in Madrid as "observers" rather than participants. Much of the pressure on the Saudis was really meant to coerce Israeli prime minister Yitzhak Shamir to give up his reservations about the conference.

Though no Arabist himself, chief negotiator Dennis Ross largely bought into the Arabist view that the Saudis were the linchpin in a comprehensive peace and spent more than a decade imploring them to help advance the American agenda. Ross said the Saudis promised all sorts of concessions, such as ending the boycott if Israel stopped settlement construction, and normalizing relations if an agreement was reached between Israel and Syria. The Saudis kept these assurances private, rendering them of dubious value; in any case, they proved moot, as the Syrians remained uninterested in a peace agreement, while the Israelis saw no point in compromising when they were getting nothing in return from the Arabs. Even when the Saudis went through the motions of trying to be helpful, it became clear that their influence was limited primarily to obstructionism, and they had little clout for any positive steps. This became evident when Bandar lobbied Yasser Arafat to accept the dramatic offer Israeli prime minister Ehud Barak made in 2000 to withdraw from 97 percent of the West Bank, dismantle most settlements, and establish a Palestinian state with East Jerusalem as its capital. Arafat said no, a decision that Bandar considered a betrayal and a crime against the Palestinian people.

Even though most troops left after the war ended, the Saudis became increasingly uncomfortable with any American presence as the monarchy came under attack from religious authorities and other conservative elements in the kingdom. In 1993, just a year after the end of the Gulf War, the king rejected the Clinton administration's request to permit an armored brigade to be based in Saudi Arabia. The administration's Gulf security plan envisioned using American-built bases and facilities in the kingdom to pre-position equipment and to engage in joint training exercises, but the Saudis rejected the plan, and the Pentagon was forced to refocus its strategy on the other Gulf states.

In 1998–99, the Saudis allowed restricted access to air bases when the U.S. requested their use for air operations over Iraq. In 2001, however, U.S.-led forces launched an air raid from Saudi Arabia without asking permission and were subsequently forbidden to conduct offensive operations against Iraq. The Saudi refusal to allow use of their bases after 9/11 for the war against Afghanistan led the United States to use Qatar as its principal base of operations in the region. This did not stop American presidents from satisfying the Saudis' thirst for arms (and U.S. contractors' interest in profits), with sales totaling more than $9 billion between 1998 and 2005.

Clinton continued to supply the Saudis with the arms they requested, even though they were in dire financial straits and unable to pay billions of dollars in debt to U.S. defense contractors. Bandar was in the embarrassing position of having to negotiate payment schedules, which the arms makers could not afford to turn down. Meanwhile, Bandar's influence in Washington waned. His close ties with the previous Republican administrations rankled some of Clinton's advisers, who decided he should no longer be given the special treatment that allowed him almost unfettered access to presidents and their top advisers. Bandar's influence within Saudi Arabia also waned when Crown Prince Abdullah became the effective ruler after King Fahd became too ill to govern. He was finally recalled in 2005 and replaced by Prince Turki al-Faisal.

In 1995 the Saudis were avidly courted by the president of France and the prime minister of Great Britain when they announced plans to place a large order for new commercial aircraft for the national airline. Bill Clinton wanted the sale for the American competitor, Boeing, and persuaded King Fahd to buy American planes and engines worth more than $7 billion. Presidents are usually accused of pandering to the Israeli lobby for political benefit, but mega business deals such as this and the AWACS sales also provided political windfalls. Clinton, for example, could now claim responsibility for creating an estimated 100,000 jobs in Boeing's home base of Washington, at the McDonnell Douglas plant in California, at Pratt & Whitney's Connecticut plant, at General Electric's Ohio facility, and in various other locations. The states benefiting from the deal were worth 122 electoral votes in the forthcoming election. In the 1992 election against Clinton, Bush had touted the fact that the sale of F-15s he approved for the Saudis had created 40,000 jobs.

The Saudis said they chose the U.S. bid over those of other countries to show gratitude for saving them from Saddam. The only trouble was that the Saudis were essentially bankrupt, and could not pay the bill. Clinton intervened by getting the U.S. Export-Import Bank to guarantee loans to cover the entire cost.

The national interests of the United States proved of little consequence to the Saudis once America had served their needs. As one former State Department official put it, "The Saudis are good at showing indispensability—they were anti-Nasser, then anti-Communist. They do just enough to look like they are, but they're not. They did what they did for their own interests, not for the good of the U.S."[31]

CHAPTER NINE

The Lobby Cover-up:
The Saudi-Funded War on America

As we have seen, the United States has developed a pathological relationship with Saudi Arabia over the last seven decades. America's political leaders have allowed themselves to be blackmailed by the Saudi monarchy because of their belief that capitulation to Saudi demands is necessary to ensure the continued flow of oil on which the American economy depends. Successive administrations have sold the kingdom billions of dollars' worth of arms they don't need and can't use to keep the Saudis happy and to recoup part of the cost of the oil. Beyond this compact, which offers the monarchs economic and personal security, the Saudis are only willing to support American interests either if their lives literally depend on it, as in the Gulf War, or if they can do so without risking criticism from their public or other Arabs, as when they provide funds for U.S. covert programs. U.S. officials were content with this relationship until the 1990s, when they began to realize that the Saudis were engaged in a widespread campaign to promote radical Islamists committed to America's destruction.

Just as the United States seeks to export its Western values around the world, Saudi Arabia uses economic and diplomatic means to spread its vision of Islam. The Saudis budget more than $4 billion annually for Islamic activities, a total greater than the Soviet Union spent on subversion during the Cold War.[1] Some Saudi funding is directed to propagating extremism through Islamic schools, and thereby indirectly fosters terrorism and threats to American security. The government and individuals also subsidize "martyrs" and directly support terrorist groups that have attacked Americans, threatened our allies, destabilized the Middle East, and damaged our interests.

Long before 9/11, Saudi Arabia was a major funder of terrorist organizations, in particular the PLO at the height of its international terror campaign. The United States looked the other way, as it has with regard to most other Saudi behaviors that have undermined our values and interests. The public did not become fully aware of the extent of the Saudi role in terrorism, of course, until 9/11, when it was revealed that fifteen of the nineteen hijackers were Saudis.

The 9/11 Commission "found no evidence that the Saudi government as an institution or senior Saudi officials individually funded [al-Qaeda]," but said Saudi Arabia "was a place where Al Qaeda raised money directly from individuals and through charities . . . with significant Saudi government sponsorship."[2] Twenty-eight pages of the 900-page report were redacted, however, and people such as Senator Pat Roberts (R-KS), chairman of the Senate Select Committee on Intelligence, have suggested that this was done to protect Saudi Arabia.[3]

While the Saudis felt exonerated by the report, subsequent investigations and statements by U.S. government officials made it clear that Saudi Arabia is intimately involved in terrorism. For example, in 2002, the Council on Foreign Relations (CFR) issued a report on terrorist financing that concluded, "For years, individuals and charities based in Saudi Arabia have been the most important source of funds for Al Qaeda. And for years, Saudi officials have turned a blind eye to this problem." That same year Jean-Charles Brisard presented a report to the United Nations on terror financing that concluded that Saudi bankers and businessmen had transferred as much as half a billion dollars to al-Qaeda in one decade. That same year, intelligence sources in the United States confirmed that Saudi Arabia had violated its commitment to stop funding al-Qaeda.[4]

"The Saudis are active at every level of the terror chain, from planners to financiers, from cadre to foot soldier, from ideologist to cheerleader," Rand Corporation analyst Laurent Murawiec told the Defense Policy Board on July 10, 2002. Publication of his remark provoked a firestorm, and Murawiec came under attack from the Saudis' allies and official spokesmen. The secretaries of state and defense, as well as President Bush himself, all proved to be the best press agents for the Saudis as they repudiated Murawiec's briefing, praised the relationship between the two countries, and reassured Saudi leaders that nothing had changed.[5]

The Arabists' attitude is typified by Richard Murphy, the former NEA director who, as a senior fellow at the Council on Foreign Relations, testified before Congress that the Saudis had been cooperative in establishing controls on charitable groups funding terrorism. He excused their failure to do more because this was so difficult, as evidenced, he said, by the seven years it took the FBI to close down the Texas-based Holy Land Foundation for funneling money to Hamas. This is an absurd comparison, given the FBI's need to carefully gather evidence that meets the rigorous American legal standards, compared to the royal family's ability to immediately shut down any charity at any time with or without evidence. Moreover, while the Saudis often claim to have no control over the activities of their citizens, charitable Muslim causes based in the kingdom must receive authorization from the interior ministry to collect money.[6]

The U.S. government certainly knew about the Saudi connection to terror. Nevertheless, just months before 9/11, the American embassy in Riyadh streamlined its screening procedures and agreed to grant a visa to any Saudi, without even requiring them to personally appear. In this way fifteen unemployed Saudis obtained visas, flew to the United States, and ultimately crashed airplanes into the World Trade Center and the Pentagon. In 2003, the State Department finally began to scrutinize who was being given diplomatic visas; on discovering that Saudi religious scholars, clerics, and professors had gained entrance to the United States this way, they started to issue visas only to legitimate officials.

Meanwhile, the Saudis continue to work to spread their extreme views around the world, often with tragic consequences. In 1962 the

Muslim World League (MWL) was created as a nongovernmental organization to spread Wahhabism in part through mosque construction in the United States. In a two-year period in the 1980s, for example, MWL spent $10 million on building new mosques.[7] Though not officially part of the government, its secretary general is required to be a Saudi, and funding for offices in more than 120 countries is provided by generous Saudi donors.

The U.S. Treasury Department froze the assets of some of the MWL's organizations because of suspected connections to terrorist activities. Agents raided the group's U.S. offices in Falls Church, Virginia, in 2002, along with those of a branch of the league, the International Islamic Relief Organization (IIRO), as part of an investigation into groups with alleged ties to terrorism. The IIRO contributed $1,000 to the families of Palestinian "martyrs" during the intifada and was believed to be connected to al-Qaeda.[8] The MWL office was raided again in 2006, and the director of the group, Abdullah Alnoshan, was arrested and deported to Saudi Arabia for using fake documents to enter and live in the United States.

The Saudi-based Al-Haramain Islamic Foundation opened 1,100 mosques, schools, and Islamic centers and, in 2000 alone, printed 13 million Islamic books. The U.S. Treasury Department froze the assets of Al-Haramain, because of suspicions that money was being diverted to terrorists. In April 2010, the investigation of the group was dealt a blow by a federal court's decision that the wiretaps the feds used to gather evidence on the group were improper.[9]

After 9/11, the Saudis were pressured to crack down on charities supporting terror, such as Al-Haramain. The Saudis took some steps to control charities, such as prohibiting them from sending funds outside of the kingdom. They have also worked with the FBI to identify and prosecute individuals involved in terrorist financing. In October 2007, the most senior Wahhabi cleric in Saudi Arabia, Sheikh Abdel-Aziz al-Asheikh, issued a *fatwa* (religious edict) against engaging in jihad outside the country. This was especially aimed at Saudis who were going to fight in Iraq and was notable because "the Saudis are generally reluctant to concede either that there is Saudi-based financial support for terrorism or that Saudi counterterrorism efforts are inadequate." The Saudi Arabian Monetary Agency (SAMA) said, however, that it would not monitor private bank accounts, and that no accounts had been frozen in connection with terror funding.

A related organization directed specifically at younger Muslims is the World Assembly of Muslim Youth (WAMY). Founded in 1972, WAMY is based in Riyadh and has 450 branches in thirty-four countries. Its goal is to "serve the true Islamic ideology," namely, the Wahhabi brand, and to coordinate the activities of Muslim youth around the world. WAMY provides millions of dollars in aid for students and the establishment of mosques. The group also has been suspected of connections to terrorists, including Hamas, allegations the group denies. WAMY was directed by Abdullah bin Laden (Osama's brother), and another bin Laden brother, Omar, was on the board. The president of WAMY in 2002 was Saleh al-Asheikh, the Saudi minister of Islamic affairs. One of WAMY's employees was Sheikh Saad al-Buraik, who in 2001 called for enslaving Jewish women and killing their children. Al-Buraik was also the religious adviser to Prince Abdul-Aziz bin Fahd, the king's son.

"WAMY was involved in terrorist support activity. There is no doubt about it," according to a former Bush administration official.[10] The FBI and military intelligence officials said they were prevented for political reasons from investigating WAMY and bin Laden's relatives who had links to the group. "There were always constraints on investigating the Saudis," intelligence sources told the *Guardian* in November 2001; and, they said, these grew worse after Bush took office. The sources were told to "back off" from investigating the bin Laden family, Saudi royals, and possible Saudi links to Pakistan's nuclear program.[11]

This is one reason the Israelis seem to know much more about Saudi activities than the United States does. The CIA does not conduct intelligence operations inside Saudi Arabia; the station chief acts primarily as a liaison with the head of Saudi intelligence.

One area where intelligence was lacking for many years was in mosques around the world where Saudi-trained and -funded preachers teach intolerance. In London, for example, British film-makers went undercover at the London Central Mosque, considered one of the most prestigious in Britain, to see if they preached some-thing different privately from the moderate image they projected in public. The documentary reportedly exposed imams "teaching the faithful that God orders them to kill homosexuals and apostates; that they should curtail the freedom of women; and that they should view non-Muslims in a derogatory manner and limit contact with them."[12]

Similarly, in the United States, Saudi Arabia has directly invested in the establishment of at least sixteen Islamic and cultural centers in California, Missouri, Michigan, Illinois, New Jersey, New York, Ohio, Virginia, and Maryland. At its peak, in addition to the diplo-mats engaged in political activity, the Islamic affairs department at the Saudi embassy in Washington had thirty-five to forty diplomats and an annual budget of $8 million. Many of the department's of-ficials were engaged in proselytizing rather than diplomacy, but had entered the country with diplomatic visas. In 2003, the department was dissolved, and the embassy stopped distributing the Koran in the United States.[13]

Interestingly, the Saudi investment in the United States began "as a bulwark against the spread into American mosques of radical Shiism, which surged after Khomeini deposed the shah of Iran."[14] Instead, the Saudis seek to indoctrinate American Muslims with their Wahhabi beliefs and the conviction that Islam "is the superior religion and must always be so." Perhaps as many as 80 percent of America's 1,200 mosques are run by Wahhabi imams.[15]

In addition to mosques, the Saudis are also trying to infiltrate the United States and spread Wahhabism through Muslim chaplains hired by the U.S. military and federal prisons. Prison conversions have been one reason for the rapid growth of Islam in the United States. Approximately 350,000 inmates in federal, state, and local prisons identify themselves as Muslims, which is 15 to 20 percent of the total prison population.

In June 2003, web sites for navy and air force chaplains had links to Islamworld.net, a Wahhabi site that in turn had links to lectures that advocated jihad against the United States and denigrated Judaism and Christianity. The links were removed after their extremist ties were disclosed.

The Saudis insist they are not sponsors but victims of terror. On November 13, 1995, a car bomb exploded outside the Saudi National Guard building in Riyadh. Among the sixty-seven casualties were five Americans. The Saudis later arrested four suspects, who publicly confessed and then were beheaded. The United States wanted to investigate the bombing, but the Saudis would not allow it, and never permitted the FBI to interrogate the suspects before they were put to death.

That same year, U.S. intelligence informed Saudi officials that the mastermind of the 1983 Beirut bombing that killed 241 U.S. Marines was on a flight from Khartoum to Beirut that was scheduled to stop in Jidda. The FBI sent agents to arrest the terrorist, Imad Mughniyeh, and Clinton's national security adviser Anthony Lake believed he had the cooperation of the Saudis. When the plane was about to land, however, the Saudi government intervened and prevented it from doing so, allowing Mughniyeh to escape.[16]

The Saudis continued to impede American efforts to fight terrorism after a truck bomb exploded on June 25, 1996, at Khobar Towers, an eight-story building housing U.S. Air Force personnel in the city of Khobar, near Saudi Aramco's Dhahran headquarters. A total of 19 American soldiers were killed, and 373 other people were wounded. Again, no Saudis were hurt, making it clear that the terrorists were not striking against the government but targeting Americans. As in the 1995 case, the Saudis were totally uncooperative when the FBI tried to investigate the attack.

After 9/11 the Saudis have publicized operations that they claim have broken up terrorist plots and cells in the kingdom, and tried to create the perception that they are fighting with us in the war on terror. Former Rand defense analyst Laurent Murawiec makes an interesting observation, however, about the nature of terror allegedly directed against the monarchy. "Bombs have indeed gone off in Saudi Arabia, but no one has attacked the royal family or its henchmen, its symbols, or its foundations. Television, radio, and the newspapers are intact. The countless royal palaces, ministries, and princely properties have never been touched. King, princes, princelings, and courtiers all peacefully go about their business. The soft targets supposedly represented by the palaces, villas, and manor houses in Marbella, Geneva, Paris, Aspen, Surrey, and London have not even had a stone thrown at them. For an evil genius able to destroy the Twin Towers, this is negligent." Murawiec notes that the attacks inside Saudi Arabia have been directed against English and American targets. The explanation for the anomaly, he suggests, on the basis of unconfirmed information he received from an Arab foreign minister, is that the Saudis agreed not to bother Osama bin Laden, and to pay him $200 million, if he agreed not to act against the kingdom.

Other sources confirmed that members of the royal family were supporting bin Laden. "We've got information about who's backing bin Laden, and in a lot of cases it goes back to the royal family," said Dick Ganon, former head of the State Department's Office of Counterterrorism. NSA intercepts obtained by journalist Seymour Hersh revealed that "by 1996 Saudi money was supporting Osama bin Laden's Al-Qaeda and other extremist groups in Afghanistan, Lebanon, Yemen, and Central Asia and throughout the Persian Gulf region."[17] Another Clinton official said the Saudis were believed to have begun paying off bin Laden in 1995, the year the National Guard headquarters was attacked. "The deal was, they would turn a blind eye to what he was doing elsewhere. 'You don't conduct operations here, and we won't disrupt them elsewhere.'" By 1998, Dore Gold concluded, bin Laden was using Saudi Arabia as "a base of operations against American targets, but no longer attacked Saudi Arabia itself."[18]

As former secretary of state George Shultz put it, this relationship with terrorists is "a grotesque protection racket."[19] According to the *Sunday Times*, the Saudis paid at least $300 million in "protection money" to al-Qaeda and the Taliban.[20] According to former CIA director James Woolsey, the Saudis had impeded investigations into the Riyadh and Khobar Tower bombings; refused to participate in an FAA-run program that tells U.S. officials who is arriving in America from abroad; refused to take bin Laden into custody in 1996, when the Sudanese offered to deliver him there; and refused to let the United States arrest Hezbollah's Imad Mughniyeh, who was implicated in the bombing of the U.S. Marine barracks in Beirut and the murder of a U.S. Navy diver. Woolsey also complained that American business, especially the oil companies, had for too long been allowed to "cloud thinking" and to shape U.S. policy.[21]

After 9/11, the Saudis also tried to distance themselves from the hijackers and to portray themselves as allies in the war on terrorism. Yet at the very time Crown Prince Abdullah was visiting President Bush at his ranch in Crawford on April 25, 2002, the Israeli army discovered extensive documentation demonstrating the funding of Palestinian terrorism by Saudi Arabia.

In fact, just two weeks earlier, the Saudis sponsored a telethon for "Palestinian martyrs." While the Saudis denied that they were supporting terrorists, suggesting that the funds were for humanitarian assistance, the documents Israel captured during operations against terrorists in the West Bank showed that hundreds of thousands of dollars were being distributed to the families of terrorists by the Saudi Committee for Support of the Al-Quds Intifada, which had been created by the minister of the interior, Prince Nayef, at the suggestion of Crown Prince Abdullah, who had said the fund would contribute to "the children of the Palestinian martyrs."

The Israelis also found Saudi government accounting schedules showing how much was paid to each Palestinian or his family, with the names of suicide bombers and others who carried out terror attacks highlighted. A table listing payments by the Saudi committee had the names of more than three hundred Palestinians who had died in the uprising, including many who attacked Israeli citizens. The Israelis later released a Saudi spreadsheet from the committee that recorded a payment to the suicide bomber who blew up a bus in Jerusalem on August 21, 1995, killing a U.S. citizen.[22]

The International Islamic Relief Organization (IIRO) also funneled money to Islamic committees in the territories associated with Hamas. An IIRO report captured by the Israelis said that Saudi money had been earmarked for the families of victims as well as Hamas-affiliated groups. Money was given, for example, to families whose sons had committed terror attacks such as the bombing of a Tel Aviv disco where twenty-three Israeli teenagers were killed and more than one hundred wounded, and a shooting at a bus station that killed three civilians and injured fourteen. An angry letter from the Saudis was found that complained about the revelation of the secret Saudi involvement in terror financing in a Palestinian newspaper report that thanked the kingdom for helping the families of terrorists.[23]

Ironically, Mahmoud Abbas, then a deputy to Yasser Arafat and now the president of the Palestinian Authority, complained to the Saudis that money from Prince Nayef's committee was being given to his rivals in Hamas. Previously, the Saudis had been supportive of Arafat because his principal rivals were pro-Marxist Palestinian factions. The Israelis reported that the Saudis now, "for their own reasons (apprehension [about] PA corruption, hostility to Arafat, ideological proximity to Hamas) preferred to transfer the money to Hamas."[24] In 2003, it was estimated that up to 60 percent of the Hamas budget was supplied from Saudi Arabia, some from government sources, and the rest from individuals and organizations whose activities are permitted by the government or protected by the Saudis. Israel also arrested a Hamas operative who admitted he was on his way to Saudi Arabia to discuss the development of Qassam rockets and seek additional funding for their development.[25]

The revelations about Saudi support for terror were not surprising given the kingdom's long history as a sponsor of violence, from its early financing of the PLO to its more recent policy of underwriting suicide bombers under the guise of a welfare program for the families of "martyrs." On October 20, 2000, for example, Crown Prince Abdullah recommended that $200 million be allocated for this purpose. Ultimately, more than $250 million was committed for the year 2000 alone. Another $109 million was raised in the April 2002 terrorthon hosted by Sheikh Saad al-Buraik, who was known to have referred to Jews as "monkeys" and called for a jihad.[26] These

Saudi subsidies helped fuel the Palestinian war from 2000 to 2005, which killed more than a thousand Israelis, but the U.S. government remained silent while the Saudis portrayed themselves as interested in peace while simultaneously undermining American efforts to end the Arab-Israeli conflict.

The Saudis' actions actually highlighted an important change in the nature of that conflict from one between the Arab states and Israel to one between radical Islam and Israel. Egypt and Jordan have signed peace agreements with Israel, and several Gulf and North African Arab countries have had varying levels of contact with the Israelis and have shown a willingness to normalize relations. It is the radical Muslim terrorists, as well as their sponsors, led by the Saudis and the Iranians, who have transformed the Arab-Israeli dispute, which was largely political and geographical and therefore solvable, into an Islamic-Israeli conflict based on theology that is irreconcilable.

Following the disclosures that Saudi Arabia was providing funding for terrorists in the West Bank and Gaza Strip, Saudi public relations agent Michael Petruzzello tried to dismiss the evidence: "It is complete and utter nonsense that the Saudi government has been giving money to the families of suicide bombers."[27] Prince Bandar launched into a fit of righteous indignation, accusing the Israelis of a shameful and counterproductive effort to discredit the "leading voice for peace." He said that the charge that Saudi Arabia was paying suicide bombers was "totally baseless and false."[28]

Apparently Bandar didn't read his own embassy press releases, which included one from January 2001 describing the Saudi Committee for Support of the Al-Quds Intifada run by Saudi interior minister Prince Nayef. The document boasted that the committee had distributed $33 million to the "families of 2,281 prisoners and 358 martyrs," with martyrs often referring to those who engaged in attacks against Israel. A March press release referred to a $50 million donation to a pan-Arab fund to supplement the $5,333 Prince Nayef's committee offered to each family that "suffered from martyrdom." A month later, the embassy boasted how Nayef's committee had disbursed $40 million to Palestinians, including "families of those martyred."

Saudi funding for terror during the Clinton and Bush administrations strengthened those trying to subvert negotiations. Their support of Hamas facilitated the group's eventual takeover of Gaza and the escalation of violence against Israel, undermining U.S. efforts to isolate the radicals and promote moderate Palestinian leaders.

The public was generally unaware of Saudi Arabia's historic involvement in terrorism or its efforts to infiltrate and subvert American institutions. That all changed on September 11, 2001. Following the attacks on the Pentagon and the World Trade Center, the Saudis had a severe image problem. The fact that fifteen of the nineteen hijackers had come from Saudi Arabia created an immediate need to reassure Americans that the terrorists were not "real Saudis." An added embarrassment was the revelation that the wife of the Saudi ambassador to the United States, Prince Bandar, had transferred to a Saudi student $130,000 that unknowingly ended up in the pockets of the hijackers. Moreover, the claims of Prince Sultan, the minister of defense, and his brother, Prince Nayef, the interior minister, that the Mossad was really behind the attacks, only reinforced their image as rabid anti-Semites.

The Saudis were largely unaccustomed to the type of negative publicity that surrounded the involvement of Saudi nationals in the attacks. The Saudis were convinced, moreover, that the criticism they received was attributable to the worldwide Jewish conspiracy, the Zionist lobby, and the Jewish-controlled media. "The people of the kingdom have not been affected by what certain newspapers publish and you know who is behind this media," Crown Prince Abdullah told a reporter. This view was echoed by one of the anti-Semitic imams who regularly preached hateful sermons to his followers. In a February 2002 sermon at the Grand Mosque in Mecca, Sheikh Abd al-Rahman al-Sudais was quoted as saying, "The mask of the Western media has now been removed. It is quite evident that most of the news agencies and satellite television channels are controlled by Zionist organizations, and are dummies in the hands of the Zionist lobby."[29]

Prior to the debate over the oil boycott in the 1970s, the Saudis had managed to stay mostly under the radar and not attract much criticism in the United States. They had retained the public relations firm of Hill & Knowlton in the 1960s, but spent so little that the firm convinced Aramco that the oil conglomerate could do an adequate job speaking for the government.

One of the Saudis' early PR efforts occurred at the end of 1974, in the wake of the embargo, when Charter Corporation proposed a $7.7 million campaign to produce newspaper and magazine supplements, fund professorships, and organize a tour for Saudi princes to appear throughout the country. A fawning portrait of the royal family was also published in the Sunday newspaper supplement *Family Weekly*, which was partly controlled by Charter.[30]

Parade magazine in 1976 found that "the Arab nations have mobilized a vast network of influential lawyers, Washington lobbyists, public relations experts, political consultants and a host of other highly paid specialists" to implement a secret plan that called for the expenditure of $15 million annually on propaganda. The plan, prepared by Martin Ryan Haley and Associates, had targeted six vulnerable senators in the 1974 election campaign that it viewed as adversaries, and another five viewed as friends who needed help. It also called for providing various campaign services and money to friendly candidates. "American citizens of Arab extraction," Haley's document said, "would have to carry the burden in the political field because 'United States law is very clear about prohibiting other nations from playing a part in U.S. election campaigns.'" In addition, former senator J. William Fulbright's law firm received $25,000 per year from the United Arab Emirates; former defense secretary Clark Clifford's firm received $150,000 a year from Algeria; Nixon's former attorney general, Richard Kleindienst, was paid $120,000 annually by Algeria; Frederick Dutton, an adviser to Robert Kennedy, got $100,000 a year from the Saudis; and the polling firm headed by Patrick Cadell, Jimmy Carter's pollster, received $80,000 from the Saudis to survey American attitudes toward Saudi Arabia.[31]

In 1975, just as the boycott debate was heating up, the Saudis hired Doremus A.G., a new company whose majority stakeholder was Samir Khashoggi (the daughter of Saudi Arabia's first Western-educated physician, who served as doctor and adviser to the monarchy); its minority owner was a respected firm with extensive ties to Wall Street as well as the international market.[32]

Unlike Arab American and Muslim groups that operate on shoe-string budgets, the Saudis and other Arab states have almost un-limited resources to invest in image building, damage control, and promoting their cause. In 1976, for example, according to *Near East Report*, the Arab League mounted a five-year, $30 million propaganda campaign to "sell the American people on the idea that the Palestinian and Jerusalem issues—and not the Arabs' rejection of Israel's right to exist—are the crux of the Middle East conflict." The funds were allocated for propaganda committees in key cities, under-writing books, a television show to be broadcast in the United States, western Europe, and Latin America, polling, cultural exhibits, and other activities aimed at improving the image of the Arabs. Funds were also distributed to college campuses to revive moribund activist organizations such as the Organization of Arab Students.[33]

Another distinction between the lobbying efforts of the Arab states and domestic organizations is that the former devote most of their activity to promoting relations between Arab governments and the United States, whereas the latter are more focused on the Palestinian issue and anti-Israel activity. Still, the Arab states, and the Saudis in particular, sometimes lead the chorus of Israel bashing. This was the case, for example, after Israel's 1982 inva-sion of Lebanon. The Arab Women's Council hired the PR firm of Robert Keith Gray, a former associate of Ronald Reagan, to organize events highlighting the impact of Israel's military opera-tions on the people of Lebanon. The council was organized by the wife of the Saudi ambassador, Nouha Alhegelen, together with the wife of the Arab League's observer to the UN, Hala Maksoud, to stop the "genocide in Lebanon." To get an idea of Alhegelen's views, she was asked if the West Bank was the rightful homeland of the Palestinians and responded, "Well, the rightful home for a long time has been the whole of Palestine—what is Israel today, what is the West Bank."[34]

Robert Keith Gray was paid more than $300,000 for a two-week PR blitz to "undermine American support of Israel." In addition to Saudi Arabia, the group received money from the UAE, Kuwait, Qatar, Tunisia, Bahrain, Oman, Algeria, Sudan, Jordan, Morocco, and Mauritania. A number of different organizations emerged to join the council's efforts, creating the impression of widespread opposition to Israel. Many turned out to be front organizations, however, funded by the council itself. For example, Peace Corps for Middle East Understanding sent letters to eighty thousand Peace Corps alumni, asking them to lobby Congress to cut off aid to Israel. The council secretly funded the campaign, and the mailing was traced to the Saudi embassy.[35]

While bashing Israel on one front during 1982, the Saudis also launched a PR offensive to polish their own image. A three-part puff piece on the kingdom that aired on PBS suggested the Arab-Israeli conflict was the major issue for the Saudis, rather than a variety of inter-Arab conflicts that had nothing whatsoever to do with Israel. The same year, the Saudis put up $4 million for a pavilion at the World's Fair in Knoxville, Tennessee. Billionaire Sheikh Mohammed S. A. al-Fassi, the brother-in-law of a Saudi prince best known for painting garish colors on the genitalia of nude statues at his Beverly Hills mansion, came to visit Washington and gave D.C. mayor Marion Barry $50,000 to help the city's summer jobs program for youth. A week later, the Saudi ambassador arranged to underwrite the $100,000 cost of transporting an outdoor theater from Dubai to Wolf Trap, the performing-arts center just outside Washington, to temporarily replace the structure burned in a fire. The chairman of Wolf Trap at the time was Robert Keith Gray.[36]

In 1989 the Saudis launched a national propaganda exhibition, *Saudi Arabia: Yesterday and Today*, to celebrate the U.S.-Saudi friendship. The exhibit extolled the virtues of King Fahd and his role in promoting peace. The Saudis, meanwhile, routinely voted to expel Israel from the UN and other agencies, voted for the UN resolution equating Zionism with racism (and voted against the resolution's repeal in 1991), and supported other one-sided resolutions condemning Israel. Speaking of the UN, the Saudis have also historically opposed American positions there more than 90 percent of the time and, paradoxically, voted 100 percent with the Soviets, whom they claimed to despise.

The Saudis' image problem was infinitely worse after 9/11, however, and they hired Qorvis Communications to design and manage a public relations campaign on their behalf. Michael Petruzzello, the firm's managing partner, said the Saudis had two things in their favor. "The first is the Bush Administration, which has placed the Saudis off limits from criticism. And the second is Bandar, the un-Saudi Saudi." These assets would not be enough, however, to offset the Saudi connection to terror.[37]

The Saudi government paid a $200,000-a-month retainer to Qorvis. Three of the founding partners of Qorvis were so angry, however, that they quit. Associates commented that "their departure reflects a deep discomfort in representing the government of Saudi Arabia against accusations that Saudi leaders have turned a blind eye to terrorism."[38] As we shall see, the discomfort didn't last.

In addition to PR, the Saudis also sought out a bipartisan team of high-powered lobbyists. Patton Boggs received $100,000, for example, to "educate" members of Congress. The firm, which owned a 15 percent stake in Qorvis, was founded by Thomas Hale Boggs Jr., a former government official whose father, Hale Boggs, was the House majority leader, and whose sister is journalist Cokie Roberts. In addition to Patton Boggs on the Democratic side, they also contracted with Akin Gump Strauss Hauer & Feld, which was founded by longtime Democratic insider Robert Strauss, the former head of the Democratic National Committee. In addition, Frederick Dutton was paid $536,000 to help manage the kingdom's public relations effort.

On the Republican side, the Saudis offered a $720,000-a-year retainer to the law firm of Loeffler Jonas & Tuggey. Tom Loeffler was a former Texas congressman who was the finance cochair of George W. Bush's presidential campaign and later national finance cochair of the 2008 McCain presidential campaign. Michael Daniels, a former aide to congressman Lamar Smith, and Susan Nelson, ex–finance director of the Republican Governors Association, also worked on the account. The Saudis also hired James P. Gallagher, a former aide to New Hampshire senator Judd Gregg, and the media-buying firm of Sandler-Innocenzi. To add firepower to the PR effort, the Saudis paid Burson-Marsteller $2.7 million to place ads in the American press extolling the Saudis as allies.[39]

Overall, in the last decade, Saudi Arabia has recruited more than two dozen U.S. firms as foreign agents, and spent nearly $100 million on American lobbyists, consultants, and public relations firms. These hired guns have attempted to rebrand the Saudis as allies in the war on terror, rather than as the leading purveyors of radical Islamic views through schools in the United States and around the world. Here is a partial list of firms that reported their incomes from the kingdom:

Akin Gump Strauss Hauer & Feld LLP	$220,770
Boland & Madigan, Inc.	$420,000
Burson-Marsteller	$3,619,286.85
Cambridge Associates, Ltd.	$8,505
Cassidy & Associates, Inc.	$720,000.00
DNX Partners, LLC	$225,000.00
Dutton & Dutton, PC	$3,694,350.00
Fleishman-Hillard	$6,400,000[40]
Gallagher Group, LLC	$612,337.37
Iler Interests, LP	$388,231.14
Loeffler Group, LLP	$10,349,999.99
Loeffler Tuggey Pauerstein Rosenthal, LLP	$2,350,457.12
Loeffler, Jonas & Tuggey, LLP	$1,260,000.00
MPD Consultants, LLP	$1,447,267.13
Patton Boggs, LLP	$3,098,000.00
Powell Tate, Inc.	$900,732.77
Qorvis Communications, LLC	$60,314,803.80
Sandler-Innocenzi, Inc.	$8,885,722.65

These firms have been engaged to facilitate meetings between the Saudis and members of Congress, congressional staff, and officials in the executive branch and have lobbied to support bilateral U.S.-Saudi relations, Saudi cooperation on the global war on terrorism, oil- and energy-related issues, economic development and the Saudi role in the World Trade Organization, Saudi reform efforts, the role of women, the Arab Peace Plan, and terrorism financing.

These are just contracts between the Saudi government and foreign agents. Individual companies also have relations with various American PR companies and agents. For example, in 2002 Hill & Knowlton, which has an office in Jidda, signed a deal with Saudi Basic Industries. Hill & Knowlton was directed by the former head of the Clinton White House's office of Legislative Affairs, Howard Paster.

In addition to the American agents, the Saudis deployed the man a former State Department official called "the Michael Jordan of Saudi Arabian diplomacy," Adel al-Jubeir, Crown Prince Abdullah's thirty-nine-year-old American-educated foreign policy adviser. Jubeir spoke perfect English, was comfortable in front of a camera, and presented a moderate, reasonable voice for the kingdom. Always speaking in a calm, measured tone, Jubeir insisted that his country was a friend of the United States and denied any connections to terrorism. Previously, Jubeir had made contacts in the Jewish community and even invited Jewish leaders for extraordinary visits to Saudi Arabia in an effort to co-opt them and show Saudi tolerance to officials in Washington.[41]

One of the first projects of Qorvis was to launch a multimillion-dollar media blitz of thirty-second television ads and sixty-second radio spots aimed at promoting the image of the Saudis as friends of the United States and allies against terrorism. At the time, even the pro-Arab pollster John Zogby found that 58 percent of Americans had an unfavorable view of Saudi Arabia, and only 24 percent had a favorable one.[42]

One series of radio ads produced by Qorvis in 2002 ran in thirty U.S. cities on behalf of a group of Arab American organizations it referred to as the Alliance for Peace and Justice. The spots called for an end to the Israeli "occupation." They also praised the Arab League's "fair plan" for a Middle East peace settlement. This was the plan originally formulated by Saudi crown prince Abdullah. *Time* reported that the ads were actually financed by a "bridge loan" of $679,000 from the Saudi embassy, which was repaid with funds solicited by al-Jubeir from businesses associated with the Chambers of Commerce in Saudi Arabia and believed to be close to the Saudi government. In 2004, the FBI raided three of Qorvis's offices and delivered subpoenas to a fourth as part of an investigation into whether the alliance, which ceased to exist after the ad campaign, was designed to avoid violating the Foreign Agents Registration Act, which requires "political" or "informational" messages to be clearly labeled with a statement that they are sponsored by a foreign government. The Justice Department also revealed that Saudi Arabia paid Qorvis $14.6 million over a six-month period, ending in December 2002, "to promote public awareness" of the kingdom's "commitment in the war against terrorism and to peace in the Middle East." No further publicity was given to the investigation.[43]

The Qorvis ad campaign provoked controversy inside Patton Boggs. A source from the firm told the *Forward*, "The ads were extremely scurrilous. . . . The suggestion that Israel was starting the violence and with no reference to Palestinian terrorism or to the history of the conflict—it angered people. . . . The term 'occupation' really set people off." The source said some partners in the firm wanted to sever ties with Qorvis. Whatever uneasiness members of the firm may have felt, they were apparently sufficiently soothed by the size of the contract to keep the Saudis as clients, though one lawyer quit in protest.

Meanwhile the Saudis engaged in a parallel anti-American campaign in their own press as partial retaliation for the perceived media bias against the kingdom. Saudi media reported on the detainment of Saudi citizens after 9/11, and later repeated the accusations from some of them that they had been mistreated. The Saudis also upset American investigators when they paid hundreds of thousands of dollars to provide lawyers and bail for Saudis detained or questioned in connection with terror investigations.

In 2004, Qorvis set up one-on-one interviews with media stars such as NBC's Tim Russert, CNN's Wolf Blitzer, and Fox News' Tony Snow. Kingdom officials were also sent to make appearances in major cities such as Los Angeles, Dallas, and Chicago. A few months later, Adel al-Jubeir was sent to meet with more than a hundred reporters, including those at the top newspapers, to report on the progress the Saudis claimed to be making in fighting extremism.[44]

Qorvis also deployed a variety of experts to lend a veneer of academic respectability to its PR campaign. As the director of the Middle East Forum, Daniel Pipes, has observed, "A range of public figures—former ambassadors, university professors, think tank experts—routinely opine in America about the Kingdom of Saudi Arabia while quietly taking Saudi funds. . . . They learnedly discuss Arabian affairs on television, radio, in public lectures, and university classrooms. Having no visible connection to Saudi money, they speak with the authority of disinterested U.S. experts, enjoying more credibility than, say, another billionaire prince from the royal family."[45]

By far the most effective PR move made by the Saudis occurred when Crown Prince Abdullah invited *New York Times* columnist Thomas Friedman to dinner in Riyadh and suggested that the Arabs would be prepared to normalize relations with Israel in exchange for Israel's complete withdrawal from the disputed territories. When Friedman reported the conversation in his column of February 17, 2002, it caused a sensation. The "Abdullah Plan" suddenly became the focus of American and international diplomacy. Arabists in particular saw a potential breakthrough in the long-stalled peace process. The effect, as the Saudis must have intended, was to divert attention in the United States from their connection to 9/11 and to shift them from "the box of states supporting terrorism to the box of peacemakers."[46]

As it turned out, the seemingly forthcoming ideas that Friedman had publicized were substantially modified when the Arab League met to discuss them. When the "Arab Peace Initiative" was announced on

March 28, 2002, the plan no longer offered normalization of relations with Israel and added a number of prerequisites that were nonstarters for the Israelis, such as the requirement that Palestinian refugees be given the "right of return" to homes lost in the 1948 war. Israeli prime minister Ehud Olmert called Abdullah's bluff and offered to negotiate on the basis of the Arab Peace Plan, but when it became clear that Abdullah would never invite Olmert to Riyadh or travel to Jerusalem, Abdullah's sincerity was called into question.

When George W. Bush came to power in early 2001, the Saudis were ecstatic. Yet almost from the outset the Saudis had been surprised and frustrated by Bush's Middle East policy. George H. W. Bush had been considered the most pro-Arab and anti-Israel president in history, and everyone, including the Israeli lobby, expected the son to follow in the father's footsteps. It came as a shock when Bush demonstrated early in his term that he was not interested in becoming enmeshed in peace negotiations between the Israelis and Palestinians, which he saw as having little chance of success after Clinton's failure to achieve an agreement before leaving office. Bush also quickly developed a close relationship with Israeli prime minister Ariel Sharon, who was reviled in the Arab world for his hawkish views and controversial history as a military commander and defense minister. The Saudis were further outraged by Bush's unwillingness to condemn Israel for its measures in response to Palestinian terrorism that had begun in September 2000. They decided to adopt their usual modus operandi of threatening the United States, which came in the form of a message conveyed by Bandar to Condoleezza Rice on August 27, 2001, which angrily denounced America's biased policy and proclaimed the kingdom's intention of protecting its interests "regardless of where America's interests lie in the region." Crown Prince Abdullah was so upset that he took the unprecedented step of refusing an invitation to the White House. George H. W. Bush subsequently called Abdullah to reassure him that his son's "heart is in the right place," and he was "going to do the right thing."[47]

A month before 9/11, however, after Bush criticized Arafat and defended Israel's refusal to negotiate under terrorist threat, Abdullah wrote an angry twenty-five-page letter complaining about U.S. policy toward Israel and making vague threats about the possibility of unsheathing the oil weapon. Bandar was more specific, saying that Saudi Arabia would cut oil production by one million barrels a day and also suggesting that the Saudis would stop cooperating with the CIA and the FBI, refuse use of their air bases, and call an emergency Arab summit to declare a freeze in relations with the United States. By now, an oil embargo should no longer have been viewed as a serious threat; more than half of the oil exports to the United States were being shipped to refineries and gas stations owned by Saudi Aramco, so a cutoff would do significant harm to Saudi investments. Nevertheless, Saudi anger prompted Bush to write a letter to Abdullah outlining views far more sympathetic to the Saudi position than what he said publicly. Bush assured him of his concern for the Palestinians and made his first commitment to a Palestinian state, something no previous president had done before. The Saudis considered the letter "groundbreaking," and it "transformed Bush's reputation in the small circle of Saudis who run their country."[48] Abdullah reportedly showed off the correspondence to fellow Arab leaders and hoped to press Bush to follow through on his positive statements. Bush was considering a meeting with Arafat and a major speech that would reflect policies very similar to those of Bill Clinton. Bandar was invited to discuss matters—on September 13. Everything changed, however, when Saudi terrorists flew airplanes into the World Trade Center.

A slightly different version of this story appeared in the *New York Times*, which said that Bush had not mollified Abdullah, because the specter of the oil weapon was raised again a few months later as Bush prepared to meet the crown prince in what the *New York Times'* Patrick Tyler described as "undeniable brinksmanship."[49] The threats did not seem to have much impact on Bush, who declared after meeting Abdullah on April 25, 2002, that Saudi Arabia would not use oil as a weapon. The only change in policy Abdullah appeared to extract was pressure on Israel to end its siege of Yasser Arafat's compound in Ramallah. For once, a president had called the Saudis' bluff. In fact, Bush announced his own vision of peace in a June 24, 2002, speech that was markedly different from Abdullah's, placing the onus for peace on the Arabs and Palestinians rather than on Israel. While reiterating his support for the creation of a Palestinian state, he also called for the ouster of Arafat as head of the Palestinian Authority, demanded an end to Palestinian terror, and asked the Arab states to build closer diplomatic and commercial ties with Israel that would result in full normalization of relations. The Saudi peace plan was subsequently shelved in 2003 in favor of the "road map for peace" drawn up by the Quartet—that is, the United States, the European Union, Russia, and the United Nations—which required the Palestinians to stop terror and take a number of other steps toward peace, while also placing obligations on the Israelis and the Arab states. In June 2003, when Bush tried to relaunch the peace process in a meeting with Crown Prince Abdullah and other Arab leaders at Sharm al-Sheikh, he asked the Saudis to sign a joint statement supporting normalization with Israel, and Abdullah refused.[50]

Reporter David Ottaway links Saudi anger over Bush's Middle East policy to the decision a few months later to cut American oil companies out of a huge deal to explore for gas in the kingdom. American companies lost their long-standing monopoly on development of energy resources to companies from Europe, Russia, and China. He also notes the irony that Bush was unable to help secure a deal for U.S. companies despite the widespread perception that he was a tool of the oil industry and had a special relationship with the Saudis.[51]

The U.S. military was also losing its position in the kingdom. About the same time the peace initiatives were being launched, the Saudis were telling the administration that the U.S. presence had become too conspicuous. They had been angered right after Bush took office when U.S. planes attacked Iraqi targets from Saudi bases in February 2001 and thereby drew attention to their continuing presence in the kingdom. This was also around the time the Defense Department built a command center in Saudi Arabia to manage operations in the theater, and about the time the United States was gearing up for attacks on Iraq and Afghanistan. The Saudis were not happy about the subsequent war, but did allow American forces to operate from their bases. After the United States declared "victory," however, the Pentagon withdrew the troops and relocated its command structure elsewhere in the Gulf.

While Bush began to pay more attention to the peace process, his priority was the war on terror, and Saudi involvement in supporting Muslim radicals remained a major concern. The Saudis themselves finally became more concerned with the threat to their regime posed by terror when three compounds housing foreigners in Riyadh were bombed by al-Qaeda in May 2003, killing thirty-five people, including nine Americans. One of the targets belonged to the Vinnell Corporation, a U.S. company training the Saudi National Guard. U.S. ambassador Robert Jordan had complained just days before that the Saudis were not providing sufficient protection for the Americans living in Riyadh. Jordan's public criticism, combined with remarks he had made suggesting it was time for the ailing King Fahd to be replaced, resulted in his departure after less than two years in the post. The attack on the American compound came the same month that a Saudi scholar, Sheikh Nasir bin Hamid al-Fahd, issued a *fatwa* that justified the use of weapons of mass destruction against the United States.[52]

The views expressed by Saudis such as Sheikh al-Fahd, along with continuing attacks on Americans in the kingdom, exacerbated the Saudis' image problem. Qorvis was again enlisted for damage control. A multimillion-dollar television ad campaign with the theme "The Values We Share" was broadcast in twenty major cities. The PR effort also sought to portray the Saudis as fighters against terrorism by promoting the first international counterterrorism conference in Riyadh in February 2005.

Meanwhile, Saudi religious leaders have continued to attack the United States. A statement by 126 Islamic scholars in June 2008, for example, labeled the Bush administration "a first class sponsor of international terrorism" and, in a clear reference to Bush's state of the Union speech calling Iran, North Korea, and Iraq an "axis of evil," said the United States and Israel "form an axis of terrorism and evil in the world."[53] This was just after President Bush had promised to sell the Saudis yet more weapons. Shortly thereafter, the *Financial Times* reported the Saudis had withdrawn as much as $200 billion of their estimated $700 billion to $1 trillion in U.S. investments.[54]

Still, the Saudis tried to promote an image of tolerance as well as present their perspective on Islam and Middle East affairs. The former has been done through high profile activities, such as the July 2008 interfaith conference sponsored by King Abdullah, and the latter through its investments in the American educational system. The interfaith conference won the king the positive press he sought in part because the media did not scrutinize the substance of the meeting or, more important, the location—Madrid rather than Riyadh. It would have been unconscionable for the Custodian of the Two Mosques to invite nonbelievers onto holy Islamic soil to discuss their religious beliefs.

Similarly, the Saudis sponsored a UN meeting on religious tolerance in November 2008. This meeting was held in New York and was ridiculed by a Shiite Muslim dissident from Saudi Arabia who said, "It's like apartheid South Africa having a conference at the UN on racial harmony."[55] Nevertheless, the conference attracted President George W. Bush and other world leaders, which unquestionably gave the Saudis the propaganda victory they sought and continued a campaign to promote an image of the Saudis as tolerant, peace-loving Muslims. The State Department tried to assist in this fiction by reporting that King Abdullah spoke to Israeli president Shimon Peres at the meeting. This was too much for the Saudis, however, who demanded that the State Department retract the claim by Undersecretary William Burns and "offer an explanation and clarification of the reasons behind this falsehood that does not serve relations between the two friendly countries." Peres had been invited by the UN, not the Saudis, who also had made a point of denying a report that they had invited Israel to participate.[56]

The Saudi PR offensive has not changed the view of experts regarding the Saudi role in terrorism. In June 2003, David Aufhauser, general counsel for the Treasury Department, told the Senate

Judiciary Committee that Saudi Arabia is the "epicenter" of terrorist financing. Two years later, a Treasury Department official would still lament that "private Saudi donors may be a significant source of terrorist funding, including for the insurgency in Iraq." On the sixth anniversary of the 9/11 attacks, undersecretary of the treasury for terrorism and financial intelligence Stuart Levey said, "If I could somehow snap my fingers and cut off the funding from one country, it would be Saudi Arabia," and in April 2008, he reiterated that Saudi Arabia remained the world's leading source of money for al-Qaeda and other extremist networks. In July 2009, treasury secretary Timothy Geithner praised more recent Saudi efforts to combat terrorist financing, but U.S. special envoy to Pakistan and Afghanistan, Richard Holbrooke, said that the Taliban was continuing to receive funding from Saudis. In addition, the group accused of the 2008 terror attacks in Mumbai, LET, operates in Saudi Arabia.[57]

If you think the influence of the Arabists has waned, and that our diplomats in Saudi Arabia now represent our government rather than theirs, consider the comments of the U.S. ambassador to Saudi Arabia from 2007 to 2009, Ford Fraker, in the context of the information above. According to Fraker, the U.S.-Saudi partnership is "the most productive counterterrorism partnership we have in the world, especially when you couple it with the fact that King Abdullah clearly is winning the minds and hearts battle with the populace."[58] It is hard to imagine how he could suggest that Saudi Arabia is a "more productive counterterrorism" partner than, say, Great Britain or Israel, or how Abdullah has grown more popular, when polls show huge majorities supporting bin Laden. The State Department also has limited faith in the Saudis' counterterrorism efforts; it has prohibited family members from living with foreign service officers in recent years because of ongoing security concerns.

It was a testament to the power of the Arab lobby that despite the mountains of evidence for Saudi involvement, the Bush administration refused to place Saudi Arabia on the list of countries that sponsor terrorism. In fact, Bush exercised a personal waiver to the legislation banning support for the Saudis, and certified to Congress that the Saudis were cooperating with efforts to combat terrorism. Paradoxically, a few months later, the Treasury Department froze the assets of the Saudi headquarters of the Al-Haramain Islamic Foundation following similar actions against other branches of the charity because of its support for al-Qaeda.

The lack of cooperation in the war on terror did not discourage the administration from continuing to provide the Saudis with some of America's most sophisticated weapons. In 2007, the administration agreed to sell $1.4 billion worth of arms, which included satellite-guided bombs. The inclusion of these high-tech weapons provoked a rare effort by the Israeli lobby to have the munitions stripped from the sale, but it did not mount a major campaign, especially after the Israeli government did not make it an issue, and once again, the president got what he wanted. The Saudis, however, were no longer interested in giving the United States preferential treatment in the expansion of their arsenal and signed a new $40 billion agreement with BAE, the company accused of bribing Bandar and other royals, to purchase Europe's Typhoon fighter plane.

Still, the United States was called on to train the Saudi National Guard, and a new agreement was signed in 2008 to train and supply a 35,000-man force to protect the kingdom's energy infrastructure. Ambassador Fraker described it as the biggest initiative in the relationship, worth tens of billions of dollars. Largely in response to the Iranian threat, the United States also signed a cooperation agreement to combat nuclear terrorism and to help the Saudis develop a peaceful nuclear industry, something the world's largest oil producer does not need any more than the Iranians do. The United States also announced plans in August 2009 to help the Saudis establish a war college.

As the clock ticked down on the Bush administration, officials became more desperate to curry favor with the Saudis in hopes of getting some cooperation in the war on terror, as well as curbing rising oil prices that threatened to undermine the U.S. economy during the presidential campaign, convincing them to rally Arab support for U.S. policies in Iraq and Afghanistan and for taking steps to prevent

Iran from acquiring a nuclear weapon. Abdullah was uncooperative on every issue. The Bush administration had learned nothing
from the long history of U.S.-Saudi relations. Part of the problem
was that the president had appointed Condoleezza Rice as secretary
of state, and she was almost immediately co-opted by the Arabists.
A Sovietologist, Rice, like most of her predecessors, did not know
enough about the region to recognize the folly of the Arabists' advice.
Thus, she attempted to appease the Saudis with offers of arms and
a commitment to midwife a Palestinian state. The Saudis, meanwhile, did everything they could to undermine the administration's
broader agenda. Bush wanted to isolate Syria and Iran, for example,
and Abdullah met with the leaders of both countries against the
president's wishes. The United States was trying to stabilize Iraq, and
Abdullah denounced the American presence as "an illegal foreign occupation." The *Washington Post* subsequently noted that "attempting
to achieve U.S. strategic ends through partnerships with Arab autocracies yields mixed results, at best, in the short term and is cancerous
in the longer run."[59]

Abdullah continued to harp on the Palestinian issue and express
anger over Bush's continuing support for Ariel Sharon. In March
2008, the king told Vice President Dick Cheney to pressure Israel
to make a deal before Bush left office. Hoping to mollify Abdullah, Bush launched an eleventh-hour push for an agreement, sending
Secretary of State Rice to the region. The Saudis undercut their pur-
ported interest in helping the Palestinians, however, by strengthening Hamas at the expense of the more "moderate" Fatah leaders that
America backed. Since both the United States and Israel refused to
deal with Hamas until it met the minimal conditions of recognizing Israel, renouncing terror, and agreeing to fulfill past agreements,
Saudi interference virtually guaranteed the last year of shuttle diplomacy Rice pursued would fail.

When three years of Hamas rocket attacks finally provoked Israel
to invade Gaza in December 2008, Bush supported Israel's defensive
action, but the fighting produced new images of Palestinian suffering
that further stoked Abdullah's anger. American support for Israel's

operation also reflected the failure of the Arab lobby to exert influence outside of Washington. Indeed, it is the failure to win public support for their cause that has placed the greatest limits on the lobby's power. Ambassador Fraker observed that for thirty years the Saudis had been "ineffective putting their own case across to the American public despite the money spent."[60] This is borne out by the fact that despite the $100 million post-9/11 Saudi PR campaign, Americans have developed a strong dislike for Saudi Arabia. According to Gallup polls, in August 1991, after the Saudis allowed U.S. forces to fight Iraq from their territory, 56 percent of Americans had a favorable opinion of the kingdom. A decade later, the figure had dropped to 47 percent. After 9/11, in February 2002, attitudes dramatically changed, and 64 percent of Americans held unfavorable views of the Saudis. Dislike of the kingdom peaked at 66 percent in 2004, and today 60 percent still have mostly or very unfavorable opinions of Saudi Arabia (compared to 63 percent with favorable views of Israel).

Saudis don't like Americans either. The Saudi intelligence service found that 95 percent of educated Saudis between the ages of twenty-five and forty-one supported bin Laden in October 2001. Saudis who are not directly benefiting from the kickbacks enjoyed by members of the royal family from their relations with the United States feel little or no loyalty to America. Nearly a year after 9/11, the people from their hometowns considered "the Fifteen," as the hijackers are called, heroes who were protecting Islam.

Saudis also remained heavily involved in terror activities. Hundreds of Saudis were fighting alongside the Taliban against American forces in Afghanistan (a secret Saudi opinion poll found that preachers in 6,000 of 11,200 mosques supported the Taliban). Nearly one-third of the insurgents fighting in Lebanon were Saudis. Between twenty and thirty Saudis intending to be suicide bombers cross into Iraq each day. More than a thousand Saudis were training in an al-Qaeda camp in Syria, while others trained in camps in Pakistan, Afghanistan, and Iran. At least seven hundred Saudis were in jail in Iraq and another hundred in Jordan on terrorism charges. More than one-third of the 350 hard-core fighters being held at Guantanamo

Bay in 2002 were Saudi nationals, and at least 14 of those released and sent home to Saudi Arabia have rejoined terror groups after going through a Saudi rehabilitation program for former jihadists.[61] Documents gathered by lawyers for the families of 9/11 victims have found new evidence of Saudi financing for terrorism, but this information may never become public because of the successful effort by the U.S. and Saudi governments to block the lawsuit against members of the Saudi royal family.

In addition, throughout the kingdom, imams were condemning the United States at prayers every Friday. In 2003, Ambassador Robert Jordan said, "We have noticed lately in influential mosques the imam has condemned terrorism and preached in favor of tolerance, then closed the sermon with 'O God, please destroy the Jews, the infidels, and all who support them.'"[62]

These are our friends and allies.

CHAPTER TEN

The Lobby Takes Root:
The Day of the Arab American

Strangely enough, the domestic Arab lobby did not originate with Arab Americans organizing to support the Arab world or oppose Israel. The first organizations were mostly created by Arab states or non-Arabs in the United States. In fact, after Israel's establishment, the first lobbying organization was a product of the machinations of State Department Arabists backed by CIA funding.

Arab Americans did not become actively involved until the 1970s, and even today, because of a mixture of demographic and cultural factors, they remain largely inactive in politics. Even as Arab American groups began to engage in lobbying, they suffered a number of disadvantages relative to the rival Israeli lobby. One of these is the differing priorities of the various Arab states, which has prevented most of the organizations from developing a positive agenda in support of Arab interests. Instead, the Arab lobby groups have consistently maintained a largely negative agenda aimed at undermining the U.S.-Israel relationship, which has been notably unsuccessful. Their greatest success has been to raise the profile of the Palestinian issue, even though a tiny fraction of Arab Americans are of Palestinian descent or support their cause. Moreover, despite their relatively small numbers, politicians have increasingly viewed Arab Americans as a constituency they must take into account. In addition, American Muslims have also become more politically active, using the counterterror measures taken after 9/11 as a rallying point for asserting their rights, fighting perceived discrimination, and gaining access to the political system to also lobby on Middle East issues. Still, all these groups face the daunting task of overcoming the widespread American sympathy for Israel, the general recognition that the United States shares values and interests with only one Middle Eastern country, and the advocacy efforts of the Israeli lobby.

Unlike the broader Arab lobby, which is interested principally in oil and commerce, the domestic Arab lobby groups are driven primarily by the Palestinian issue. These groups believe that, as the director of the American-Arab Relations Committee put it in 1980, "The road to the liberation of Palestine is through Washington."[1]

Unlike foreign governments attempting to influence the policy of the United States, or other elements of the Arab lobby that operate outside the democratic process, such as the Arabists, the individuals and groups discussed in this chapter are exercising their constitutional right to petition their government. While there may be issues regarding foreign funding of some organizations, and the connection of others to terrorism, the principal groups are engaged in legitimate activities to promote their agendas. However, for the most part these groups do not act in America's interest and have remained relatively weak because of their inability to raise money, cultivate membership, or develop persuasive arguments for changing U.S. policy.

The domestic Arab lobby has remained fragmented, with little institutional memory beyond a handful of omnipresent figures such as James Zogby. While pro-Israel organizations have been around for decades, many of the Arab American groups have been one-person fly-by-night operations or weak coalitions that coalesce at the time of a particular event, such as the Lebanon War or intifada, and then disappear after doing little more than placing some anti-Israel ads in the press and protesting Israeli behavior.

Moreover, the Arab American component of the Arab lobby often relied on foreign individuals and governments that "compromised their political independence."[2] Paradoxically, the Arab states themselves do not see these groups as playing an important role in representing their interests. Though some minimal financial support is offered to a few organizations, the governments prefer to lobby themselves or hire prominent consulting firms. Arab governments such as Saudi Arabia's don't trust Arab Americans to represent their interests and fear that their case will be hurt by the negative image of Arabs and Muslims; consequently, they prefer to hire well-known, politically connected American public relations and lobbying firms.[3] This also has put the Arab lobby at a disadvantage; the targets of these hired guns know that they do not share Jews' passion for the issues. "It's not a cause, it's an account for foreign agents," AIPAC's longtime director Tom Dine notes, and they "could just as easily lobby the opposite side if the money was better."[4]

In the interwar period, Arab lobbying efforts were initially focused on London, where the mandatory government was based. In the mid-1930s, following a series of visits by Arab delegations seeking to undo the Balfour Declaration, the Palestine Information Center was created. About the same time, Arab Americans organized the first group to defend Arab rights in Palestine, known as the Palestine National League or Palestine Anti-Zionism Society, which later became the Arab National League. The group was organized prior to World War II by journalist Habib Katibah and scholar and physician George Khairallah and led by New York surgeon Fuad Shatara. A non-Arab group, the American Friends of the Arabs, led by Elihu Grant, was also formed around this time. The league met with State Department officials as early as 1938, and became "well known" to the Division of Near Eastern Affairs, telling them that relations with the Arabs would suffer if the United States supported the Zionists. The British Colonial Office viewed the league's involvement as proof that there were "pro-Arabs in the United States."[5]

The Arab Americans were depicted as selfless because they were not asking for anything for the Arabs; they only wanted the United States not to back the Zionists. Rather than selfless, however, the league set the precedent that would be followed by all of its successors, namely, an emphasis on the negative, opposition to Zionism (later Israel) rather than advocating for something positive on behalf of the Arabs. The league was ineffective, and disbanded after Pearl Harbor because of its Nazi sympathies.

A few other organizations emerged during the war, such as the League of American-Arabs Committee for Democracy, which was established in 1943 in Flint, Michigan. The Institute of Arab American Affairs was founded in New York in 1944 as an educational organization that also engaged in anti-Zionist propaganda. It was essentially a replacement for the Arab National League.

By the end of World War II, the Arab American community had grown from around 200,000 in the 1920s to about 500,000. As a Zionist report in 1945 said, "Where formerly Arab propaganda activities were limited and sporadic, within the past 12 months, well coordinated Arab American organizations, apparently well-financed have sprung up with branches in the major cities."[6]

American diplomats encouraged pro-Arab Americans to form the Committee for Justice and Peace in the Holy Land in 1948 to try to rescind the partition resolution, arguing that anti-Semitism would increase if the resolution was implemented. Failing to achieve their goal, the group disbanded. Several ad hoc pro-Arab groups came and went, often lasting for less than a year—the Institute of Arab American Affairs (1945–50), the League for Peace with Justice in Palestine (1946–48), the Holy Land Christian Committee (1949), and the Holy Land Emergency Liaison Program (1949). These and a handful of other small operations published occasional materials representing the Arab point of view but did not attract much support or attention, and disappeared without a trace within a short time of their founding.

In October 1944, a meeting of Arab leaders concluded that they needed to organize a propaganda office to respond to the Zionists. The Iraqi government put up $400,000 after the war to open offices in Washington, London, and Latin America. The pro-Western Iraqi government's involvement rankled the Egyptians, who subsequently viewed the office as "little better than British agents." The first head of the "Arab Office" was Ahmad Shuqeiri, a Lebanese who later was a Saudi diplomat and the first chairman of the PLO. The office's most significant activity was lobbying participants at the founding UN conference in San Francisco in 1945 to oppose the creation of a Jewish state in Palestine. Like the lobbyists and consultants the Saudis would hire decades later, the people running the Arab Office understood how the political game in Washington was played and were instructed to, for example, "entertain lavishly" and do everything in a "first class" manner and establish "official and social" contacts with "politicians, journalists and government officials." Thus, from the outset, the Arab lobby believed it could essentially go over the head of the American people directly to decision makers to persuade them of the merits of their case, and at the time they had the advantage of the support of much of the administration. The Arab leadership was also convinced that the United States supported the Zionists because of their propaganda, and that they could counter this with their own to show that American policy "would lead to disaster." Consequently, they never understood the depth of Americans' feeling for the justness of the Zionist cause and underestimated what would be required to influence policy.[7]

The Arab Office was not established by Arab Americans, but worked with them prior to 1948, cooperating in particular with the Institute of Arab American Affairs, including preparing a rebuttal to the UNSCOP partition proposals in 1947. The Zionists were alarmed by the Arab Office's "large-scale anti-Zionist propaganda . . . tremendous financial means [and] American publicity agents," but they need not have worried; the group was shut down shortly after the partition vote because of the "complete and arrogant disregard for Arab rights, Arab interests and Arab feelings."[8]

Following the UN partition resolution, a group of prominent Americans, who were not of Arab origin, organized the Committee for Justice and Peace in the Holy Land to lobby the Truman administration to abandon its support of the Jewish state. That group was led by Dr. Virginia Gildersleeve, dean emeritus of Barnard College; Kermit Roosevelt, the grandson of Theodore and a militant anti-Zionist who worked for the OSS and, later, Gulf Oil; and the Reverend Garland Evans Hopkins, a preacher from Virginia. The group argued that U.S. support for Israel threatened oil supplies and U.S.-Arab relations, and would cause a backlash of anti-Semitism against American Jews. When Truman recognized Israel and made it clear that he would not reverse course, the committee disbanded.

The triumvirate behind the committee soon was back in business, thanks to funding from Aramco, which helped underwrite a new Holy Land Emergency Liaison Program (HELP). The first director was Colonel William Eddy. He was replaced by Alfred Lilienthal, the Jewish anti-Zionist. This group, too, was short-lived.

In 1951, King Saud asked U.S. diplomats to finance a pro-Arab lobby to counter the American Zionist Committee for Public Affairs (later the American Israel Public Affairs Committee—AIPAC). Rather than emerging from the Arab American community, the lobby was actually a creation of the Arabists. U.S. diplomat Cornelius Van Engert corresponded with Allen Dulles, then CIA director of plans, who helped arrange a secret subvention through the Dearborn Foundation in Chicago to establish the American Friends of the Middle East (AFME).

The group was initially led by journalist Dorothy Thompson, who set out to present "the other side" of the Middle East story. The group's primary mission was to blunt the spread of communism in the Middle East through cultural and educational programs, but it was also hostile toward Israel. That Thompson would lead what became an Aramco-sponsored arm of the Arab lobby was shocking; she had been an outspoken supporter of Zionism in the 1940s, even speaking to a Madison Square Garden throng in 1944 to accuse opponents of Zionism of hypocrisy. It was more understandable when Harold Minor, a former State Department official who opposed the Zionists during the partition debate and became an Aramco consultant, became executive secretary in the late 1950s and early 1960s. Though the group did engage in activities to promote a positive image of the Arab world, and provided beneficial aid to the region, it often strayed into extreme anti-Israel positions, as voiced by Elmo Hutchison, a former UN official, who joined AFME because he wanted to be a part of the group's fight against Zionism, and who declared that

Israel was "fascist, intolerant, defiant, aggressive, expansionist" and would not last. The chairman of AFME's National Council during the 1950s was Edward Elson, a Presbyterian minister who served as a pastor to President Eisenhower and Secretary of State John Foster Dulles. He lobbied Dulles to adopt AFME's positions, but ironically, Dulles dismissed AFME as a "partisan Arab group" even though it was supported by his brother and funded by the CIA.[9]

AIPAC's Sy Kenen questioned the propriety of U.S. taxpayers funding such an organization. Myer Feldman, an aide to President Kennedy, didn't know about the CIA funding, but investigated and learned that Kenen was right. Feldman told him in 1962 that the CIA no longer supported AFME, but funding was only reduced and did not cease until 1967. At the group's peak, the U.S. government was providing $400,000 a year to "wage a propaganda offensive against Israel," while AIPAC's budget was less than $100,000.

AFME's director of information services, Joan Borum, gave an example in 1974 of the group's position when she called U.S. support for the creation of Israel "a big mistake" and said, "We don't think Israel will ever be a viable entity in the Middle East."[10]

For a number of years, AFME was the principal pro–Arab American organization, but it was led by non-Arabs. AFME's board was typically filled by prominent anti-Zionists of the time, such as Elmer Berger, Aramco's Terry Duce, and Gulf Oil's Kermit Roosevelt. The group received funding from oil companies and other corporations as well as the Ford Foundation, the State Department, and the Saudi national airline. Gradually, the group became less active in anti-Israel propaganda and focused more on Arab medical, educational, and economic progress, later changing its name to America-Mideast Educational and Training Services (AMIDEAST). Two of the group's four board members today are former heads of NEA.

About the same time AFME was formed, the Organization of Arab Students (OAS) was established in the United States and Canada. The group limited its activities to propaganda on campus and had its heyday in the 1960s, when it aligned with the New Left, Black Power, and other Third World movements. The group hoped to influence young Americans to oppose Israel, especially after the Six-Day War of 1967, but it never had a measurable impact on or off campus.

In the early 1960s, the only pro-Arab organization registered to lobby Congress was the Citizens Committee on American Policy in the Near East (CitCom), which was organized by Hopkins and others and represented by Harold Minor. "The basic difference between AIPAC and the Citizens Committee," AIPAC's Kenen wrote, "is that AIPAC urges strong public support for the traditional U.S. commitment to resist aggression in the Near East and to move forward towards a peace settlement, while CitCom's proposals studiously avoid any reaffirmation of that commitment or the need for peace negotiations." This group also came and went without fanfare or impact.[11]

Aramco and individual oil companies have been funders of a number of Arab American organizations that are critical of Israel, but focus more on humanitarian groups such as American Near East Refugee Aid (ANERA). In fact, one complaint of Arab Americans was that the oil industry was not sufficiently generous because companies were afraid of possible repercussions from the Israeli lobby. Still, Gulf Oil contributed $2.2 million after the Arab-Israeli War of 1973, a significant increase from the $10,000–$15,000 it had donated in the past. According to their Web site, the organization still receives funding from Saudi Aramco (listed as donating $100,000 or above) and Exxon Mobil ($25,000–$49,999). ANERA was created in 1968 as a national coordinating agency for the relief and rehabilitation of Palestinian refugees, but it also frequently engaged in anti-Israel propaganda. Its chairman, John Davis, was a former commissioner general of the United Nations Relief and Works Agency (UNRWA); the *New York Times* called him "probably the best-known American who is an outspoken supporter of the Arab cause." He was also a well-known critic of Israel who questioned Israel's right to exist. In a 1974 interview, ANERA's president John Richardson admitted his organization had little influence on the American public, blaming American Zionists for deluding the public with "one-sided" information.[12]

Today, the organization is the largest American NGO operating in the territories. It receives significant U.S. government funding, so it behooves the organization to avoid political controversy that might upset members of Congress. Now the principal complaint against ANERA is that it fails to place recent events in context, discussing Palestinian hardships, for example, without explaining that many of the difficulties they describe are a direct or indirect consequence of terrorist attacks on Israel.

After the Six-Day War of 1967, the ratio of nine Christians to one Muslim Arab among immigrants to the United States steadily declined, and the newcomers of this generation were less prone to assimilation and intermarriage. These Arab Americans took greater pride in their ethnic identity and also began to react to a sense of persecution as a result of the Arab oil embargo; the U.S. government's refusal to recognize the PLO; the 1978 FBI Abscam sting operation in which FBI agents posing as Middle Eastern businessmen offered government officials money in exchange for political favors to a nonexistent sheikh; the Israeli invasions of Lebanon in 1978 and, especially, 1982, when they saw the impact of Israeli military attacks on Palestinians in Lebanon on television; and the intifada of the late 1980s, which presented stark images of Palestinian rock-throwing Davids facing off against the tanks and guns of the Israeli Goliath.

One of the changes in the Arab lobby approach, particularly on college campuses, after the Six-Day War was an outgrowth of the Palestinian national consciousness that was emerging as Palestinians realized the Arab states could not defeat Israel for them. Similar feelings began to stir in America as well, and advocates changed their emphasis from defending Arab governments to supporting Palestinian liberation movements and trying to label Israel as the "embodiment of racism, colonialism and imperialism."

In the late 1960s and early 1970s, the lobby tried to draw parallels between Israel and Vietnam, portraying Israel as "the brutal suppressor of Arab aspirations, as the capitalist 'giant' exploiting a people yearning to be free."[13] This meshed with the growing popularity at that time of liberation theology. During this time, the Arab lobby formed informal and fleeting alliances with radical blacks and the New Left. Israel was cast as another Western villain whose treatment of Arabs compared with America's discrimination toward blacks. MIT linguistics professor and longtime Israel critic Noam Chomsky went so far as to compare Israel to the Nazis. The Jewish community was seen as an oppressive part of the establishment, and since Israel is "the darling of the Jewish community," attacking Israel "shakes up the establishment."[14] These organizations were large in number and made a lot of noise, but actually represented few people. Moreover, by consistently aligning with the far left in a desperate search for allies, the Arab lobby made a monumental strategic miscalculation that prevented it from gaining mainstream public support.

Today, Arab Americans remain a small, fractious minority divided by a variety of issues. According to the 2000 U.S. census, 1.2 million Americans were of Arab descent. It is impossible for Arab Americans to represent "the Arabs" because, unlike the Israeli lobby, which can stand up for the strengthening of America's relationship with a single nation, Americans of Arab descent come from no fewer than twenty-one countries, which have conflicting interests and are often at war with each other. As Jawad George, the executive secretary of the Palestine Congress of North America, said, "The same things that divide the Arab world divide the Arab American world."[15]

American Jews also feel a greater urgency to support Israel than do Arab Americans to their homelands. As Malcolm Hoenlein, executive vice chairman of the Conference of Presidents of Major American Jewish Organizations, described the Jewish motivation, "If we're not there, they won't be there." He adds that another source of the strength of the pro-Israel community is that "Jews in the Israeli lobby are also involved in a lot of other issues, so they can build coalitions with groups that know the Jews are not indifferent to their interests. That is not the case for Arab Americans." In fact, AIPAC sometimes even went to bat for Arab countries, lobbying *for* arms for a Maghreb country, for example, and supporting aid to Egypt and Jordan.[16]

One distinction is between Arab Americans with a nationalist view, who are critical of U.S. policy and supportive of the Palestinian cause, and those who have a regional or religious outlook and are apathetic or even hostile toward the Arab lobby. For example, Lebanese Christians, who comprise more than one-third of all Arab Americans (some estimates have placed their proportion as high as 80 percent), have very different attitudes toward Middle East issues than do most other Arabs because of their experience with Muslim and Palestinian organizations in Lebanon. Many Lebanese-American Maronites, for example, support the anti-Palestinian American Lebanese League (ALL), which for years believed U.S. policy should take a tougher stand against the PLO and Syria. "How the hell can NAAA [National Association of Arab Americans] have a constituency among the Lebanese," ALL chairman Robert Basil asked at the time the PLO had created a state within Lebanon, "when they support Syria, which is shelling Lebanese villages, and Saudi Arabia and Kuwait, which fund the PLO?"[17]

The one issue that does unite most of the Arab world, at least rhetorically, is the Palestinian issue. That is one reason it has been a principal focus of the Arab lobby even though only 6 percent of Arab Americans, about 70,000 people, are Palestinians. Palestinians receive more per capita aid than any other group in the world. Even as hundreds of thousands of people die in Darfur, it is the Palestinians who get the world's sympathy and donations of billions of dollars. And Palestinians get support from the U.S. government despite the fact that Americans have little sympathy for them. Gallup polls since 1967 show that an average of 47 percent of Americans support Israel (63 percent in the latest poll), while only 12 percent sympathize with the Arabs/Palestinians (15 percent in the recent poll). The Palestinian Authority is also disliked by an overwhelming majority of Americans, ranking just above Iran and North Korea.

This lack of support may be attributable in part to negative stereotypes about Arabs, but it is also a result of the association of Arabs with terrorism. Arab American groups have also been handicapped in the battle for public support because of their frequent unwillingness to unambiguously condemn terrorism. Even before 9/11, hundreds of Americans had been victims of Palestinian and Islamic terrorist groups, and Americans have little tolerance for apologetics and moral equivalence. For years the Arab lobby could not bring itself to criticize terrorists at all. With the adoption of a more moderate tone in recent years, the lobby has been more willing to speak out after spasms of violence, but they are very careful to avoid offending Palestinians engaged in "resistance." If they say anything critical, it will be directed at both sides, to suggest a moral and substantive equivalence. Even this concession is typically accompanied by suggestions that radical Islam either does not exist or is not really a threat. In the post-9/11 era of the war on terrorism, moreover, the lobby's opposition to laws designed to protect Americans, such as the Patriot Act, has placed it further from the mainstream.

Even though they have moderated their rhetoric, the Arab lobby organizations' agenda is consistent with that of the Palestinian organizations in the Middle East they support. For example, the logo of the Islamic Association of Palestine (IAP),[18] like that of Fatah, showed all of Israel incorporated into "Palestine." IAP distributed Hamas literature and was called a "Hamas front" by former FBI counterterrorism chief Oliver Revell. IAP president Amer al-Shawa has admitted that his group shares many ideals with Hamas and acknowledged that speakers at its events sometimes take anti-American and anti-Jewish positions.

Israel celebrated its sixtieth anniversary in 2008. On the occasion of its fiftieth birthday, most of the major organizations—ADC, NAAA, AAUG, AAI—cosponsored a tour highlighting villages they claimed Israel destroyed in 1948. The tour's logo also showed Israel's pre-1967 borders, along with the disputed territories, under the caption "Palestine: 50 Years of Dispossession: 1948–1998." The implication of this argument, like the Palestinians' celebration of the *nakba* (catastrophe), which they date to 1948, is that the Arab lobby does not accept the existence of Israel; otherwise, their protest would be focused on contemporary Israeli policies or on the territories disputed since 1967. By questioning Israel's right to exist within even the pre-1967 borders, it is clear they have not reconciled themselves to a two-state solution, once again placing their position outside the American consensus.

Arab American involvement in the Arab lobby grew out of the oil embargo. "The day of the Arab American is here," boasted Richard Shadyac; "the reason is oil."[19] Arab Americans also took pride in the fact that for the first time Arab armies had performed well and erased the shame of 1967. They became more confident that the American public would grow sympathetic to their demands that Israel withdraw from the disputed territories as they felt the pain of rising oil prices.

Shadyac founded the first formal Arab American lobby organization in 1972, the National Association of Arab Americans (NAAA), which is consciously patterned after its pro-Israel counterpart, AIPAC. In fact, the NAAA even duplicated AIPAC's stationery, changing only the name, and even more brazenly, asked the Israeli lobby for help. Both AIPAC's former executive and legislative directors told the story of being outside a hearing room on Capitol Hill and having NAAA director David Saad come over and say, "How would you guys like to earn some extra money? Train my staff." Tom Dine said he told Saad, "'We do it for the love of the cause, not for money.' That moment said more about them than us."[20]

Shadyac believed the power and wealth of the Arab countries, stemming from their oil reserves, would allow the Arab lobby to take advantage of the political process in the same way Arabs thought Jews had done. Like AIPAC, the NAAA made its case on the basis of U.S. national interests, arguing that a pro-Israel policy harmed those interests. The lobbying agenda, however, was almost entirely negative and focused largely on trying to drive a wedge between the United States and Israel and reduce American aid to Israel. "Arab American groups are clumsy," AIPAC's former legislative director Douglas Bloomfield observed. "Their position was always, 'This is what I want you to do to Israel, never anything positive we can do for the Palestinians.'"[21] This was clear from the earliest days of the NAAA's activity on Capitol Hill, when the group joined eighteen other pro-Arab organizations in lobbying Congress to oppose arms and emergency aid for Israel to defend itself in the Arab-Israeli War of 1973. Peter Tanous, head of the NAAA, told members, "If we are cold this winter it will be because we have turned our backs on the Arabs' plea for peace with justice in the Middle East." He also defended the oil companies' economic war on his country: "We must respect the right of Arab producers to exercise leverage in behalf of their own interests."[22]

In 1984, the NAAA supported an amendment introduced by Rep. Nick Joe Rahall (D-WV), one of only a handful of Arab Americans to serve in Congress, to prevent Israel from using U.S. military aid for the production of its Lavi fighter plane. The Reagan administration and a large majority of Congress opposed the amendment. The fact that it received forty votes, however, was considered a victory by the NAAA. This was typical of the domestic lobby's "victories," which consist primarily of getting an issue on the agenda or winning a few votes, rather than having its legislation adopted or effecting changes in U.S. policy.

The highlight of the NAAA's early efforts was a meeting between President Ford and twelve NAAA officials in 1975. Afterward, the NAAA participated in meetings with each president and obtained access to top government officials. In 1977, for example, after Sadat's historic visit to Jerusalem, the Arab lobby made its displeasure over U.S. support for the initiative known to President Carter, who complained about Arab Americans giving his staff "a hard time."[23] Still, even at its peak, when the organization dubiously claimed more than 200,000 members (even today AIPAC has only half this number), NAAA leaders admitted they had "not been effective in changing Congressional sentiment on Middle East policy."[24]

One obstacle, particularly in the 1980s, was the strong support for Israel of the Reagan administration, the evolution of Israel's strategic relationship with the United States, and the perception that Israel was a democratic bulwark against Communist intervention in the region (a complete reversal from the Arabist/Dulles/Eisenhower conception of the 1950s). At that time, most Israelis still opposed the creation of a Palestinian state, as did the United States, so there was also little support for Palestinian independence and an unwillingness to speak with the PLO, the "sole legitimate representatives" of the Palestinian people, to whom most of the Arab American groups swore their allegiance.

Despite some success, the NAAA had little financial support; its staff dwindled from twenty to three, and it never succeeded in creating the organizational structure and grassroots membership of its rival. Its director, Khalil Jahshan, attributed the group's downfall to its controversial policy of ambivalence toward the Gulf War, supporting it while expressing discomfort, which satisfied neither supporters nor opponents of the war, and the general suspicion he said Arab Americans held about lobbying, which involves "compromises and corruption" and which the Israeli lobby was "better at anyway."[25]

The NAAA merged in 2000 with the American-Arab Anti-Discrimination Committee (ADC), which describes itself as a grassroots civil rights organization committed to defending the rights of people of Arab descent and promoting their rich cultural heritage. The focus was also pragmatic; antidiscrimination was more of a consensus issue for Arab Americans than the controversial Middle East questions, making it easier to attract followers. ADC was founded in 1980 by former U.S. senator James Abourezk, the first Arab American to serve in the Senate, and one of the members most critical of Israel.

ADC was patterned after the Anti-Defamation League, but a comparison of their budgets gives an indication of their relative clout. In 2006, ADC had a budget of $2.4 million, while the ADL's was $60 million. Like the ADL, ADC engages in work related to discrimination and also wades into Middle East issues. While the NAAA was associated with the Republican Party, wealthy Arab Americans, and corporations, ADC was connected to the Democrats, liberal progressives, and lower- and middle-income Arab Americans. Like other Arab lobby groups that claim to represent Arab Americans, ADC received substantial funding from non-Americans, in particular Saudi prince Alwaleed bin Talal, who in 2005 donated $2.6 million toward the purchase of the organization's national headquarters in Washington, D.C.[26]

A look at ADC's 2008–9 resolutions gives a good indication of its disposition. The board principally targeted Israel and ignored discrimination against Arabs by anyone other than Israel or the United States. Instead, they called for the U.S. government to force Israel out of the territories and to freeze settlements; to halt military aid; to allow assistance to Gaza; to dismantle the security fence that dramatically reduced Palestinian terrorism from the West Bank; to adopt an "even-handed" Middle East policy (a code word suggesting policy is too pro-Israel and should be more pro-Arab); and to impose a boycott and other sanctions on Israel. The only pro-Arab resolution relating to the Middle East called for the creation of a Palestinian state and endorsed the "right of return of Palestinian refugees."

ADC has been active in trying to weaken laws designed to improve security after 9/11 because of concerns that Arabs and Muslims are unfairly profiled. The Arab American concern with what they perceive as assaults on their civil liberties as a result of counterterror operations did not begin after 9/11. As early as 1972, when Palestinian terrorists hijacked a Lufthansa plane, eleven Arab American organizations protested the "singling out of people of Arab origin . . . as targets of surveillance, investigation and interrogation."[27]

ADC also has tried to alter the portrayal of Arabs in films where they are too often depicted as "brute murderers, sleazy rapists, religious fanatics, oil-rich dimwits, and abusers of women."[28] The group also tries to dissuade writers and filmmakers from portraying Arabs as terrorists. In 1986, for example, ADC tried to persuade NBC to modify the film *Under Siege* because the group objected to the plot, which envisioned Arab terrorist attacks paralyzing the United States. The group sent a letter to the writers that said FBI reports showed Puerto Ricans and Jews committed more attacks in the United States than Arab groups, apparently implying that these groups would make more realistic villains.

The principal lobby for Palestinian issues today is the American Task Force on Palestine (ATFP), which was founded in 2003. It exemplifies some of the changes in the Arab lobby as it has shifted from militant radicalism that turned off all but the most hard-core partisans to a more moderate-sounding advocate that has taken the unusual step of criticizing some Palestinian actions, especially what it views as counterproductive terror attacks by Hamas. According to its mission statement, "ATFP is strictly opposed to all acts of violence against civilians no matter the cause and no matter who the victims or perpetrators may be. The Task Force advocates the development of a Palestinian state that is democratic, pluralistic, non-militarized and neutral in armed conflicts."

By taking a more temperate public tone, ATFP has succeeded in winning a modicum of access to decision makers. At its inaugural gala dinner in 2006, for example, Condoleezza Rice gave the keynote speech. The following year, undersecretary of state for political affairs Nicholas Burns spoke about his Palestinian sister-in-law and how he learned from her family about the refugees' plight. The organization also has tried to work with marginal Jewish organizations to lobby for an increase in financial aid to the Palestinian Authority. ATFP founder Ziad Asali is unusually clear-eyed and blunt in his assessment of the Palestinians' situation, reflecting an understanding or at least an honesty that most of their advocates lack. For example, in March 2009, he wrote about how politically weak the PA was and that "Hamas offers only bloody resistance that appeals to the Palestinian and Arab sense of dignity, while also piling up a record of deaths, injuries and destruction."[29]

Tom Dine, the former AIPAC director who now works for Search for Common Ground, says that Asali is the most effective member of the domestic Arab lobby today. "He's effective as an individual. He has respect. He's a low-key American. He gets calls constantly from Abu Mazen [Palestinian Authority president Mahmoud Abbas] to find out what's going on in Washington."[30] (As is often the case with leaders of the Arab lobby, however, their moderation is frequently superficial. I had some personal experience with Asali on a panel during which I raised the issue of incitement in the Palestinian media and textbooks, and his moderate response to all criticism of the Palestinian Authority was simply to ignore the facts and call me a racist.)

Even a moderate tone adopted for the clear strategic purpose of appealing to mainstream America, however, provokes opposition from hard-liners in the Arab lobby. During the early 1990s, for example, James Zogby came under attack for making favorable remarks about Clinton appointees such as Martin Indyk, a Jew from the pro-Israel Washington Institute for Near East Policy. After Zogby endorsed the Oslo Accords and began to cooperate with some American Jews interested in economic development in the Palestinian Authority, he was denounced as a "collaborator" and vilified by the head of the ADC as well as by Edward Said. In the case of ATFP, the ire of militant activists was provoked because it supports a two-state solution (rather than the replacement of Israel with a Palestinian state) and recognizes that the Palestinian refugees will have to accept less than an unequivocal right to return to their homes. It is remarkable and unprecedented for an Arab lobby organization to face stronger criticism from its fellow Arabs than from supporters of Israel. The attacks were so serious that the group published a ten-page response to its critics. Dine, who praised Asali's effectiveness, still concluded the Arab lobby remains weak. "The grassroots has gone from no place to nowhere."[31]

It remains to be seen if ATFP will have any greater influence or staying power than the many other pro-Palestinian groups that have come and gone. Its 2008 tax return showed a budget of less than $875,000 (compared to nearly $70 million for AIPAC). In 2008, ATFP had only five employees and fired its number-two official, Rafi Dajani, a prominent spokesman on Palestinian affairs, after tens of thousands of dollars disappeared in what ATFP described as an "apparent breach of his fiduciary responsibilities."[32]

Another active group is the Arab American Institute (AAI). Its founder-president is James Zogby, a cofounder, with Senator Abourezk, of the ADC (James's brother, political pollster John Zogby, also serves on the AAI board). Zogby started the group in 1985 and was particularly involved in encouraging Arab Americans to become active in Democratic Party politics. AAI board chairman George Salem was similarly active in promoting Arab American participation in Republican Party activities. Salem was solicitor of the U.S. Department of Labor during the second Reagan administration, and played key roles in the Bush-Quayle and Bush-Cheney campaigns. Like ATFP and the other domestic groups, AAI has a relatively small budget, about $1.3 million in 2007.

The Association of Arab-American University Graduates (AAUG) was founded by Palestinian professors such as Edward Said and Hisham Sharabi. It advertised itself as an educational and cultural organization, but was one of the most fervently anti-Israel groups. The group received funding from Arab governments and Aramco, but has withered and appears to have now died. One member looked back on the organization fondly and offers a good analysis of the way members of the Arab lobby once saw themselves:

> We were never under the illusion that we could create a counter to the pro-Israel lobby in this country. Some Arab Americans suffered from this illusion and sought the largesse of Saudi Arabia and some of the Gulf countries trying to convince them that they can in fact produce a lobby that could neutralize the influence of pro-Israel groups. We were not convinced of the value of this approach for several reasons. One was that our community was relatively small and our numbers of politically aware individuals tiny by comparison to those of American Jews. . . . A second factor is that the alleged power of the pro-Israel lobby derives from the fact that it agrees fundamentally with and enhances that of the official American position on the Middle East. By contrast, we saw ourselves as oppositional to the manner in which American foreign policy was conducted in the region. Many of us felt that our voice would be severely marginalized no matter how much money we spent. In the third place, we did not see ourselves as mouthpieces for corrupt and dictatorial Arab governments which had hitched their stars to the rising American empire in the region.[33]

A number of other organizations can also be associated with the Arab lobby. One is the Foundation for Middle East Peace (FMEP), a nonprofit organization that "promotes peace between Israel and Palestine, via two states, that meets the fundamental needs of both peoples." Today, the group devotes most of its energy to criticizing Israeli settlement policy. The Middle East Research and Information Project was formed in 1971 to provide a critical perspective on the region, but it has also historically devoted its *MERIP Reports* to criticism of Israel. Other groups include the Middle East Affairs Council and the American Palestine Committee.

The Arab lobby has also occasionally been aided by groups founded by Jews, such as Rabbi Elmer Berger, who was one of the leaders of the American Council for Judaism (ACJ). This group, founded by Reform rabbis in 1943 who opposed the Zionist program, was a fringe organization that was sometimes used by opponents of Jewish statehood to show that Jews were also against creating Israel. Berger later created another group, American Jewish Alternatives to Zionism, and published materials critical of Israel used by various anti-Israel organizations.

Other far-left Jewish organizations, such as New Jewish Agenda and Breira, came and went because of limited followings and never influenced U.S. policy; however, these groups and individuals were valuable pawns in the Arab lobby campaign that allowed Israel's detractors to say that even Jews agreed with them, counting on the fact that most Americans would have no idea that these particular Jews were marginal figures who were unrepresentative of the wider community's views. After the Six-Day War, the anti-Zionist Jews all but disappeared. Today, the most visible group is the ultra-Orthodox Neturei Karta, a small sect that is so extreme its members went to Tehran to attend a Holocaust-denial conference. Less extreme but marginal groups on the far left of the pro-Israel spectrum, such as Americans for Peace Now and J Street, have now become occasional allies of the Arab lobby, finding common cause in their opposition to settlements and belief that the U.S. government should force Israel to withdraw from the West Bank.

While all of the Arab American groups advertise themselves as supporters of peace, most toed the PLO's intransigent line throughout the period when Yasser Arafat was the group's leader and the principal spokesman for the Palestinian cause. Thus, for example, while most of the world regarded the Egyptian-Israeli peace treaty as a triumph for U.S. Middle East diplomacy, the Arab lobby viewed it as a betrayal. Rather than attempt to influence the Arab world to support and, ideally, expand the peace agreement, the lobby was driven more by criticism of the PLO, which viewed the Camp David autonomy proposals as unacceptable, and by the Arab League, which objected to any of its members breaking ranks and making peace with the "Zionist entity." Rather than seizing on the opportunity to build on the autonomy offer, the pro-Palestinian groups followed the PLO line in condemning the idea and became more active in agitating for what they viewed as the neglect of Palestinian rights.

So long as the PLO remained beyond the pale of official U.S. diplomatic efforts in the Middle East, the close association of the Arab American groups with the terror organization ensured they would remain outside the political establishment. The Arab lobby remained helpless to change this reality until the PLO itself won recognition first from the U.S. government and later from the Israelis.

CHAPTER ELEVEN

From Mavericks to Mainstream: Arab and Muslim Americans Gain Recognition

Though some individuals were active in the Arab lobby during the 1960s and '70s, the overwhelming majority of Arab Americans remained apathetic and uninvolved. This began to change with Israel's bombing of the Iraqi nuclear reactor in June 1981 and what Arabs considered to be increasingly repressive Israeli measures in the territories. The most important catalyst, however, was Israel's invasion of Lebanon in June 1982 to root out the PLO terrorists who were threatening Israel's citizens in the north. Many previously uninvolved members of the community became motivated to speak out by what they viewed as Israeli aggression against Lebanon and the Palestinians living there. Hussein Ibish, a senior fellow at the American Task Force on Palestine, believes this was also a turning point because it gave the Arab lobby the opportunity to show the destructive impact of Israel's "occupation of Arab lands."

During the 1982 Lebanon War, for example, the NAAA (ignoring decades of Lebanese history, including a civil war in the 1970s) declared that "without the creation of Israel and its subsequent crimes against the Palestinian people, there would be no trouble in Lebanon today." Gray & Company proposed a $2 million telethon to raise funds "to benefit the survivors of the Holocaust in Lebanon," and to "alter American attitudes on the Middle East" with the goal of creating an image of Israel as an "aggressor nation."[1] The NAAA did not think the campaign was sufficiently forceful, and Gray dropped the NAAA as a client.

As noted earlier, one of the unique aspects of the Arab lobby is that rather than try to centralize its message in one organization, as the Israeli lobby has effectively done through AIPAC, it often creates a variety of ad hoc organizations as events occur. Thus, during the 1982 Lebanon War there were groups such as the "Concerned Americans for Peace," "Americans for Peace" (which was traced to the director of the PLO's Washington office), and the Ad Hoc Committee in Defense of the Palestinian and Lebanese People (which was traced to the wife of Edward Said, the Columbia professor who served on the PLO's Palestine National Council).[2] Full-page ads appeared in the *New York Times* and other major papers accusing Israel of war crimes, but the groups behind them were often mysterious.

These groups exploited the horrors of war to paint Israelis as murderers who were undermining U.S. interests. A basic theme was to suggest that American taxpayers should not underwrite Israel's military campaign. "We feel the United States is a persuadable entity," said Clovis Maksoud, the Arab League's ambassador to the United States—and a ubiquitous figure on television. "For a time the Israelis had a monopoly on image-making. Now I think we have hit a responsive chord."[3] Support for the Arabs did reach its all-time high (28 percent) and sympathy for Israel its low (32 percent) in June 1982 after disclosure of the massacre of Palestinian refugees by Christian Phalangists at Sabra and Shatila, but six months later, public attitudes returned to more traditional levels, with only 12 percent sympathizing with the Arabs compared to 49 percent for Israel.

Furthermore, the enthusiasm and cooperation of many Arab Americans dissipated soon after the war, when it became clear that the principal objectives—cutting aid and ending arms sales to Israel, generating greater support for the Palestinians, driving a wedge between the United States and Israel, and shifting public opinion—had not been achieved.

As early as 1983, there was a recognition that the Arab lobby was changing its approach and becoming more sophisticated. Angry spokesmen who would rant and rave about Israel's sins, challenge its right to exist, and justify terror against it were being replaced by attractive young men and women who appeared to be voices of reason, suggesting that all of America's troubles in the Middle East would vanish if it would just pressure Israel to accept the legitimate and just demands of the Palestinians for independence. While pro-Israel spokespeople delivered complex history lessons, the Arab lobby reduced its argument to three words, "End the occupation."

The Arab lobby also adopted the terminology of the Israeli lobby and turned it against Israel. For example, Palestinians, like Jews, now live in the "Diaspora." Israelis are compared to Nazis, and their actions are characterized as "pogroms," "ethnic cleansing," and "genocide." Israel is accused also of creating "ghettoes" and engaging in a "holocaust." The lobby has succeeded in turning the disputed territories into the "occupied West Bank and Gaza." A new term was also invented, "Islamophobia," which is presented as a corollary to anti-Semitism, and is used to accuse anyone critical of radical Islam or Muslims of bigotry.

The ability of the tiny minority of Palestinian Americans and their supporters to put their concerns front and center on the Middle East policy agenda has been the domestic Arab lobby's greatest success. Much of its propaganda has now become accepted in regular discourse about the conflict. It is now almost unthinkable for the media to report on the issue without including a representative of the Arab lobby's point of view.

Of course, old habits die hard. In 1985, ADC and the NAAA launched an ad campaign attacking aid to Israel. What was striking about their approach was that rather than pursue their stated goal of defending the rights and promoting the heritage of Arab Americans, the groups focused on convincing Americans that their economic hardships were due in part to America's financial assistance to Israelis.

The campaign against aid to Israel has been the most obvious example of the Arab lobby's failure. Though cutting or conditioning aid to Israel has been a top priority of Arab American organizations since their inception, assistance to Israel continued to grow, and the terms of that aid became more generous. In 1996, Israel voluntarily agreed to phase out economic aid as it became unnecessary, but the United States agreed simultaneously to increase military aid and, in 2008, reached a new agreement to provide Israel $30 billion in military aid over the next ten years. The decision was negotiated between the governments and not influenced by partisan lobbying, but the Israeli lobby easily lined up the votes in Congress to support the deal, which represented a major defeat for the Arab lobby.

Interestingly, the Arab American groups played no appreciable role in the major battles between the Israeli and Arab lobbies in the 1970s and '80s over the sale of arms to Arab states still at war with Israel. One reason was that the NAAA initially was ambivalent about supporting arms sales. Another is that the principal lobbyists were those who would most benefit from the sales—the Arab governments seeking the arms, the Pentagon, and the defense contractors. Even during the high-profile AWACS fight in 1981, domestic organizations played little role, though the NAAA claimed to have helped coordinate the activities of Arab governments and businesses lobbying for the sale.

Arab Americans became more politically active following the AWACS battle. As AIPAC grew in stature, size, and funding, Arab lobby groups became increasingly agitated over the strengthening of the U.S.-Israel relationship. Fouad Moughrabi recalled a meeting where Hisham Sharabi came with a group of Arab American businessmen to propose the formation of an umbrella organization to mimic the pro-Israel community's Conference of Presidents of Major American Jewish Organizations.[4] Sharabi said Saudi Arabia was willing to invest in the idea, but Moughrabi said, "We will not allow ourselves to become pimps for the Saudis." Many Arab Americans did not like the idea of Arab states, especially the Saudis, interfering in their affairs, but the Saudis got their way, and the National Council of Presidents of Arab-American Organizations was established in 1983 with seventeen groups. Not surprisingly, however, it never achieved the type of consensus or influence of the Jewish organization, and faded away.

Another period of ferment for the domestic Arab lobby was the first intifada in the late 1980s. As during the Lebanon War, numerous ad hoc groups were established to criticize Israel, but again, they were not unified and could not sustain their level of activity as the intifada turned into an *intra*fada where more Palestinians were killed by their fellow Palestinians than died in clashes with Israel, and tensions in the Persian Gulf turned Americans' attention toward Iraq. The groups also minimized their opportunity to win sympathy for the Palestinians' plight by supporting the violence against Israelis. Nevertheless, Arab American leaders believe this period was, in the words of the NAAA's Khalil Jahshan, "the father and mother of the peace process, a single event that convinced all in the West that we need the two-state solution."[5]

Jahshan is partially right, as the two-state idea did gain traction, but that was largely because a growing number of Israelis were willing to accept the idea. The Arab lobby had no influence on U.S. policy, which remained staunchly pro-Israel, and supported the Israeli conception of a Palestinian state. In Congress, "American policymakers did not offer the Palestinians any respite outside of calling Israel to show restraint."[6] And while AAI demanded in 1988, "PALESTINE STATEHOOD NOW!" more than twenty years have passed with little progress toward the establishment of that state.

Whatever gains the lobby might have made during the intifada by portraying Israel as a ruthless Goliath were largely erased with the onset of the First Gulf War. The Arab lobby was typically divided, with some organizations that were "heavily dependent on Gulf connections"—the NAAA and AAI—publicly supporting the Bush administration, and others—ADC, Palestine Aid Society, Palestine Solidarity Committee—joining the PLO in backing Saddam Hussein and opposing American intervention. During the First Gulf War, Kuwait expelled 300,000 Palestinians, but no criticism was heard from the Arab lobby, whereas Israel's expulsion of a handful of Palestinian terrorists would spark a national campaign. The explanation is partly related to the fact that the Arab American groups were heavily dependent on support from the Gulf States backing America's war on Saddam Hussein. The behavior of Palestinians in the territories also undermined the lobby's efforts and reinforced their image as pro-terror and anti-American when Arafat publicly sided with Iraq and Palestinian marchers cheered Scud missile attacks on Israel.

The lobby got another chance to make its case following the war when President Bush organized the Madrid peace conference. Once again, however, Arab Americans were divided, even as the Bush administration took an increasingly hostile line toward Israel.

More important, however, was the end of the Cold War, which the Arab lobby believed had put them at a disadvantage since Israel was viewed as staunchly anti-Communist while the Palestinians and much of the Arab world were supported by the Soviets. ADC president Mary Rose Oakar observed that after the Cold War, the Palestinians and Arab Americans "would be viewed on their own merits" rather than "as pawns in an ideological rivalry." The Palestinian struggle also was no longer "construed as a rebellion against an anti-Soviet ally."[7]

The period following the signing of the Oslo Accords caused schisms among Palestinians in the Middle East and also in the United States. AAI's Zogby called the agreement "a great and historic moment," and the NAAA said it heralded "a new era of peace and understanding" and "wholeheartedly" supported it. ADC did not endorse the agreement and declared it would "continue putting daily pressure" on Israel to make concessions. Several of the elder statesmen of the cause in America, however, became disillusioned with the direction in which their former hero, Yasser Arafat, was taking the PLO. Hisham Sharabi, who had become a professor at Georgetown, abandoned his earlier support and began to warn that Arafat was seeking to establish a dictatorship and that radical Islamists were threatening prospects for a Palestinian democracy. Edward Said, a Columbia professor and longtime member of the Palestine National Council, had almost the polar opposite reaction, calling the Oslo Accords "capitulation."

AAI's Helen Samhan still believed Oslo was a milestone because the Arab lobby position was validated. She and other Arab American leaders participated in the signing ceremony on the White House lawn, where they were treated on a par with representatives of the Israeli lobby. "We were given equal billing when, for so long, we used to be so unwelcome. After the Oslo peace process we were actually invited to weigh in on issues having to do with the Palestinians and American foreign policy."[8]

Paradoxically, Oslo severely weakened the Arab lobby. One reason was that the agreement meant giving up the dream of a state in all of Palestine. Moreover, the perception that the conflict was moving toward resolution resulted in a decline in membership and support for many of the Arab lobby groups. For a brief period, the groups that did support Oslo found common cause with some pro-Israel organizations, as the Israeli lobby dropped its opposition to the PLO and joint efforts were made to promote the Palestinian economy. Violence soon escalated, however, and the euphoria that accompanied the early agreements evaporated along with the goodwill between the lobbies. By 1995, Zogby and others who supported Oslo had returned to demonizing Israel, calling for U.S. pressure, opposing monitoring of PLO compliance with its agreements, and objecting to congressional efforts to move the U.S. embassy to Jerusalem.

When Israelis elected Benjamin Netanyahu as prime minister in May 1996, the Arab lobby's rhetoric again became extreme. Indeed, its positions remained so far outside the American mainstream that Arab American groups returned to the margins of political debate.

This is particularly evident when Israel defends itself against terrorists. Typically, the Arab lobby goes into full attack mode, justifying attacks on Israeli citizens while castigating Israeli forces for responding. After reacting to provocations from Hezbollah in Lebanon in 1996, for example, AAI, ADC, NAAA—the whole Arab lobby alphabet soup—used terms such as *aggression, state terrorism, disproportionate, inhumane, atrocities,* and *massacre* to describe Israel's actions.

In December 1998, after Arafat and Netanyahu signed the Wye agreement, in which Israel committed to withdraw from an additional 13 percent of the West Bank, secretary of state Madeleine Albright met with American Jewish and Arab leaders to encourage them to "build a constituency for peace." While the Israeli lobby endorsed the meeting, ADC, NAAA, and AAI all criticized various aspects of the negotiations and cosponsored a *Washington Post* ad that scurrilously accused Israel of ethnic cleansing.[9]

The hostility of the Arab lobby reinforced the notion that the Arabs really had no interest in peace. When Arafat rejected the Israeli offer in 2000 of a Palestinian state with 97 percent of the West Bank and East Jerusalem as its capital, the Palestinians were seen once again as a people who never missed an opportunity to miss an opportunity. Every Arab leader who offered peace and security, and could implement his promise, got peace and territory from Israel. The Palestinians, however, remained unwilling to end the conflict, and the American public and policy makers recognized their irredentism as the obstacle to peace.

During the Second Intifada from 2000 to 2005, and Israel's war with Hezbollah in 2006, the Arab lobby simply reverted to its habit of bashing Israel and seeking to drive a wedge between the United States and its ally. The same tactics and messages were employed that were used during the First Intifada of 1987–93 and the Lebanon War of 1982, accusing Israel of atrocities and disproportionate force and calling on the government to condemn and sanction Israel. Unlike his father, however, President George W. Bush was a staunch defender of Israel, and viewed most of Israel's actions as reasonable responses to the terror attacks. Congress was even more supportive; rather than imposing sanctions on Israel as the lobby wanted, members voted to give Israel additional aid and to place restrictions on financial aid for the Palestinians. The president did come out in favor of creating a Palestinian state and provided large amounts of aid to the Palestinian Authority over the objections of Congress, but these decisions were made without regard to the lobby. They were principally a response to the international consensus that the Palestinian economy had to be bolstered to increase the prospects for peace.

By 2008, the Arab lobby was concerned with a number of legislative issues. Several were related to Iran, and all opposed the tough measures favored by the Bush administration and most of the international community. In particular, the lobby opposed sanctions and a possible blockade, but supported unconditional negotiations and a requirement that Congress consent to any military action against Iran. The lobby also supported legislation asking the secretary of state to try to convince Israel to lift its restrictions on Gaza while opposing resolutions congratulating Israel on the fortieth anniversary of the reunification of Jerusalem, condemning Hamas as a terrorist organization, proposing sanctions against the Palestinian Authority, and seeking cooperation from Arab states in the peace process.

While the Arab American organizations were mostly spinning their wheels, changes in the community were afoot. In the Middle East, radical Islam became more appealing to many Palestinians and other Arabs, and groups such as Hamas, Hezbollah, and Islamic Jihad became more powerful. This move from ideology to religion was mirrored in the United States as many American Muslims began to shift their allegiance from Arab American to Muslim American political organizations.

This trend also occurred on college campuses, where young Arab Muslims turned away from the AAUG and joined Muslim student groups such as the Muslim Students Association, a group founded in 1962–63 by members of the Muslim Brotherhood at the University of Illinois at Champaign-Urbana whose goal was to spread their militant brand of Islam to students.

One common feature of most of the Muslim groups associated with the Arab lobby, as distinct from the more sophisticated Palestinian organizations, is that they do not even pretend to have an interest in Middle East peace. These groups condemned the Oslo peace process, and their leaders regularly criticize Israel and have suggested that an Islamic state replace Israel.

The Muslim organizations, in particular, have credibility problems resulting from the discovery of officials with connections to terrorism and other legal problems. For example, the former president of the Islamic Association of Palestine was indicted for naturalization fraud in January 2008; he failed to disclose that he was a member of "an organization that sought to raise funds for Hamas."[10]

The Saudis also consciously created a "Wahhabi lobby" in the United States "to create a secure base for planning terrorist operations in Israel, to amass funds and recruits, and finally to control all discussion of Islam and Muslim societies in American media and government." The lobby exploits American values while seeking to undermine them. "They wanted all the benefits and guarantees of American society while, at the same time, rejecting the foundation of American religious liberty: tolerance of differences."[11]

The strictures of Wahhabism are ill suited to life in the United States, so it has found relatively few adherents here. One group that represents a Wahhabi point of view is the Muslim Public Affairs Council (MPAC), which was founded in 1988 and bills itself as "a public service agency working for the civil rights of American Muslims, for the integration of Islam into American pluralism, and for a positive, constructive relationship between American Muslims and their representatives."[12] One of its advisers, Maher Hathout, exemplified how these values are applied when he said that Arab governments that meet with Israelis would be "flushed down in the cesspools of history of treason," labeled Israel an "apartheid state," and said that Arabs have to "throw a bomb in a market or send somebody to suicide" because they don't have the "ability to target real targets in Israel."[13] The group also has often been an apologist for terror attacks, as in 2001, when a suicide bomber blew up a Jerusalem pizzeria and MPAC blamed Israeli policy, or when it referred to the 1983 bombing of the U.S. Marine barracks in Beirut by Hezbollah terrorists as a "military operation."[14]

One of MPAC's recent legislative efforts, along with ADC, was to try to block a proposed House resolution calling for greater transparency by the UN Relief and Works Agency to ensure it is not "providing funding, employment or other support to terrorists." The legislation was prompted by revelations about UNRWA's behavior and association with terrorism in the Gaza Strip. It is difficult to understand the justification for opposing the idea that an organization whose largest donor is the United States be held accountable for how it spends taxpayer money and not be involved in facilitating terrorism, unless the Arab lobby is afraid such scrutiny will interfere with supporting terrorist groups they endorse, such as Hamas. ADC and other Arab lobby groups also opposed legislation condemning the biased and inaccurate report produced for the UN Human Rights Council about the 2008–9 war in Gaza. That legislation nevertheless passed the House by a vote of 344–36.[15]

Like ADC, MPAC has little interest in abuses against Muslims outside of the United States and Israel. One case that was so egregious that it provoked MPAC to make an exception occurred in 2007, when the victim of a gang rape in Saudi Arabia was sentenced to two hundred lashes and six months in jail. MPAC called for the sentence to be overturned. The same day, ADC was condemning the "collective punishment of Gaza students."

The vast majority of American Muslims are exercising their democratic right to participate in the political process, but some are engaged in support for terrorists abroad and have been involved in domestic plots. A number of cases have been in the news the last few years of individuals and organizations with alleged and proven connections to terrorists. The FBI was investigating at least twenty groups with suspected links to terrorists. While Muslim groups see this as a form of persecution, one Justice Department official explained, "We have a problem with Islamic terrorism. . . . If we had a problem with Latvian terrorism, we'd focus on Latvians."[16]

One of the most high-profile cases involved the Holy Land Foundation, which was named as a Specially Designated Global Terrorist Organization and indicted on charges of providing material support to Hamas. In November 2008, a jury convicted five former foundation officials of conspiracy to provide material support to terrorists. Other charges included money laundering and tax fraud. The charity itself was convicted on thirty-two counts, including funding schools and social welfare programs controlled by Hamas. One of the founders, Shukri Abu Baker, was sentenced to sixty-five years in prison.[17]

Legitimate Muslim organizations are outraged by the behavior of radical groups such as the Holy Land Foundation, which perpetuate negative stereotypes of Muslims as anti-American and supporters of terrorism. This is why M. Zuhdi Jasser, founder of the American Islamic Forum for Democracy, applauded the convictions in the Holy Land Foundation trial.

The most visible of the Muslim organizations is the Council on American-Islamic Relations (CAIR). In 1993, Hamas members and sympathizers met in Philadelphia to discuss ways to undermine the newly signed Oslo Accords, including the creation of a new organization in Washington. The following year, CAIR was established. CAIR immediately condemned the Oslo peace accords and declared that "Palestine is an Islamic and Arabic land which no one has the right to trade, sell, or give up." Since then, CAIR has been an active critic of Israel, routinely condemning Israeli actions, calling for a cut in U.S. aid, and advocating the creation of a Palestinian state. During Israel's war with Hamas in December 2008–January 2009, for example, CAIR did not criticize the indiscriminate rocket attacks by Hamas on Israeli cities (which had been going on for more than three years), but instead organized anti-Israel rallies and demanded that the U.S. government take steps to stop Israel's military operation.

CAIR views itself as a "Muslim NAACP." When President George W. Bush visited the Islamic Center of Washington several days after September 11, 2001, to signal that he would not tolerate a backlash against Muslims, he invited CAIR's executive director, Nihad Awad, to join him at the podium. Two months later, when secretary of state Colin Powell hosted a Ramadan dinner, he too called upon CAIR as a representative of Islam in America. When the State Department seeks out Muslims to welcome foreign dignitaries, journalists, and academics, it calls upon CAIR. The organization came under a cloud of suspicion, however, when it was named an unindicted coconspirator in the trial of the Holy Land Foundation. Responding to a congressional inquiry, Assistant Attorney General Ronald Weich said that trial transcripts and exhibits "demonstrated a relationship among CAIR, individual CAIR founders, and the Palestine Committee. Evidence was also introduced that demonstrated a relationship between the Palestine Committee and Hamas, which was designated as a terrorist organization in 1995." In another case, federal prosecutors wrote, "From its founding by Muslim Brotherhood leaders, CAIR conspired with other affiliates of the Muslim Brotherhood to support terrorists."[18]

Awad has said he supports Hamas and has protested the use of the word *Israel* in an American Muslim magazine, chastising the editors for not referring to it as "Occupied Palestine." He also suggested that there was evidence that the Mossad and Egyptian intelligence were involved in the 1993 World Trade Center bombing. CAIR's communications director, Ibrahim Hooper, could not bring himself to condemn Osama bin Laden when interviewed shortly after 9/11. In 2003, the *Cleveland Plain Dealer* reported, "While the Islamic council says it has denounced suicide bombings against Israeli civilians, spokesman Ibrahim Hooper yesterday would not criticize suicide attacks against Israeli soldiers. Instead, he spoke of Palestinians exercising 'the right to resist military occupation.'"[19] As recently as 2008, when Hooper and CAIR's legislative director Corey Saylor were asked to specifically condemn Hamas or Hezbollah, they stuck to formulations such as "CAIR condemns terrorist acts, whoever commits them, wherever they commit them, whenever they commit them," but frustrated their interviewers by never directly answering their questions.[20]

More recently, however, CAIR marked the fifth anniversary of the terrorist attacks in Madrid by repudiating terror. "Our position is clear. We unequivocally condemn all acts of terrorism whether carried out by al-Qaida, the Real IRA, FARC, Hamas, ETA, or any other group designated by the U.S. Department of State as a 'Foreign Terrorist Organization.'"[21] CAIR also trumpets its cooperation with law enforcement. It produced a guide for police that explains how officers should behave to show respect to Muslims, but says nothing about how they might identify extremists in the community. Meanwhile, the group opposed the creation of a National Commission on Terrorism and has campaigned against other measures adopted to protect American security on the grounds that they discriminate against, or lead to the persecution of, Muslims. In 2008, the FBI cut off contacts with CAIR because of questions about the group's association with Hamas, a move praised in a letter from senators Jon Kyl (R-AZ), Tom Coburn (R-OK), and Charles Schumer (D-NY) to FBI director Robert Mueller, which called for the policy to be adopted government-wide.[22]

Unlike the other major domestic organizations lobbying on Middle East issues, CAIR has received significant financial support from foreign sources. Though it initially denied receiving foreign funds, CAIR now says it is "proud to receive support . . . from foreign nationals . . . as long as there are no 'strings' attached." Contributors include Saudi Arabia, which gave the organization $250,000 to purchase a plot for its Washington headquarters; the ruler of Dubai's foundation, which provided nearly $1 million for the building; and the Bank of Kuwait, which lent the organization $2.1 million. Saudi prince Alwaleed bin Talal donated $500,000 to the group. In 2007, Saudi prince Abdullah bin Mosa'ad wired the group $112,000. CAIR also reportedly received financial support from the World Assembly of Muslim Youth, a Saudi-sponsored group associated with the spread of radical Islamic views, which announced in 1999 support for CAIR's plan to construct a new headquarters building in Washington. In 2002, the two groups planned a million-dollar PR campaign. CAIR's acceptance of funds from abroad and activities to further the contributors' interests have prompted calls to require CAIR to register as a foreign agent.[23]

Though muted, some Muslims have questioned the wisdom of accepting money from Saudi Arabia, in particular, because they believe it prevents them from criticizing what they view as the kingdom's misrepresentation of Islam.

In 2006, CAIR announced plans for a $50 million media campaign to improve the image of Islam and Muslims. The plan, Awad announced, was to spend $10 million annually for five years on materials for television, radio, and newspapers.

CAIR monitors the treatment of Muslims in the United States and often labels criminal investigations of Muslims as acts of discrimination. By accusing those who criticize or investigate Muslims as guilty of bias or "Islamophobia," CAIR "encourages Muslims to feel angry and non-Muslims to feel guilty" and "tends to intimidate or silence even the most sensible critics."[24]

The group has also been very successful in promoting the idea that American Muslims are frequent victims of hate crimes and that 9/11 provoked widespread attacks against them. Any crimes or discrimination against Muslims on the basis of their faith is unacceptable, but FBI crime statistics show that the number of incidents has been consistent in recent years and declined significantly after 2001. Moreover, hate crimes committed against Muslims are a small fraction of the number reported against Jews.[25]

Like the ADC, CAIR has also been involved in trying to discourage Hollywood from portraying Arabs and Muslims as terrorists. Its most notable success occurred in 2002 when pressure from the organization persuaded filmmakers adapting the Tom Clancy best seller *The Sum of All Fears* to replace the novel's Arab terrorists with neo-Nazis. The film's director wrote to CAIR, "I hope you will be reassured that I have no intention of portraying negative images of Arabs or Muslims."[26] CAIR has been less successful in convincing the writers of Fox's hit show *24* not to regularly use Muslim and Arab villains, though more sympathetic characters have been introduced in recent seasons. Season 8 found hero Jack Bauer preventing the assassination of a Muslim leader interested in peace, but the plot still focused on radical Muslims from a country similar to Iran attempting to obtain nuclear weapons and explode a dirty bomb in New York.

CAIR has also actively defended Arab Americans accused of involvement in terrorism. One of the most celebrated cases involved University of South Florida professor Sami Al-Arian, who was originally found not guilty of several major charges and the jury deadlocked on others. After the trial, the *St. Petersburg Times* wrote:

> Even though Al-Arian was not convicted of supporting terrorist acts, he stands exposed for what he is—a carrier of hate. He is not just an innocent academic with unpopular views about the Israeli-Palestinian conflict, as he has so often claimed, or a "prisoner of conscience." The trial demonstrated

that Al-Arian was deeply connected to the PIJ [Palestinian Islmic Jihad], which is believed responsible for more than 100 deaths in the Middle East. He was described by his own lawyers as a fundraiser for the "charitable arm of the PIJ." And Al-Arian was not blind to the group's monstrous tactics, as he was the regular recipient of faxes announcing the group's suicide bombings. . . . In a 1994 fax, Al-Arian wrote to PIJ headquarters after a suicide bombing, that "pride and glory overwhelm us." . . . The trial has laid bare Al-Arian's involvement in one of the most violent groups in the Middle East. He may now claim an acquittal, but he can never again claim moral innocence.[27]

In 2006, after denying his involvement for more than a decade, Al-Arian pleaded guilty to conspiracy to provide support to the terror group Palestinian Islamic Jihad and was sentenced to fifty-seven months in prison. The Justice Department believed Al-Arian was the main North American organizer for the group and charged him with criminal contempt after he served his sentence because he failed to testify, as required in his plea agreement, as to the alleged connection between the International Institute of Islamic Thought and terrorist organizations. Al-Arian refused to testify, despite a grant of immunity, and staged a highly publicized hunger strike while appealing a contempt citation, an appeal he ultimately lost.

CAIR and others tried to portray Al-Arian as a victim of persecution by government officials seeking to silence him because of his outspoken support for the Palestinian cause. Rather than as a "political prisoner," however, the judge who sentenced Al-Arian saw him very differently: "But when it came to blowing up women and children on buses, did you leap into action then? Did you offer to form a committee to protect the innocent? Did you call your fellow directors and enlist their aid in stopping the bombing or even stop the targeting of the innocent? No. You lifted not one finger, made not one phone call. To the contrary, you laughed when you heard about the bombings, what you euphemistically call 'operations.' You even pleaded for donations to pay for more such actions. Your only connection to widows and orphans is that you create them, even among Palestinians."[28]

The former chief of the FBI's counterterrorism division, Steve Pomerantz, said, "CAIR has defended individuals involved in terrorist violence, including Hamas leader Mousa Abu Marzook. . . . The modus operandi has been to falsely tar as 'anti-Muslim' the U.S. government, counter-terror officials, writers, journalists and others who have investigated or exposed the threat of Middle East-based terrorism. . . . Unfortunately CAIR is but one of the new generation of new groups in the United States that hide under a veneer of 'civil rights' or 'academic' status but in fact are tethered to a platform that supports terrorism."[29]

CAIR has been remarkably successful in presenting itself as the representative of American Muslims. In fact, CAIR, like other Arab lobby groups, has a small constituency that has reportedly been shrinking. According to a report by the *Washington Times*, the group's membership declined by more than 90 percent since 9/11, from more than 29,000 to 1,700 in 2006. M. Zuhdi Jasser, director of the American Islamic Forum for Democracy, said it was a "myth that CAIR represents the American Muslim population" and that "post 9/11, they have marginalized themselves by their tired exploitation of the media attention for victimization issues at the expense of representing the priorities of the American Muslim population."[30]

Another Muslim organization that has gained credibility is the American Muslim Council (AMC), which was founded in 1990 to "provide a national structure within which American Muslims may express and act upon their shared concerns, promote, encourage and foster better understanding, in the United States, of Muslim culture, values and history and enhance, encourage and foster the common good and general welfare of the people of the United States."[31]

While condemning terrorism in general, AMC has refused to denounce specific groups such as Hamas and Islamic Jihad. It described antiterrorism policies as "anti-Muslim and anti-Arab" and suggested they were the product of Jewish pressure. AMC opposed loan guarantees, called for an end to aid to Israel, and charged Israel in May 1996 with committing "genocide" in Lebanon. That same year, the media began to scrutinize the activities of AMC and criticize it for expressing sympathy for terrorists. A number of individuals and groups, particularly Christian organizations, came to its defense, denouncing critics for engaging in "Muslim bashing." The American Friends Service Committee, the National Conference of Catholic Bishops, the National Council of the Churches of Christ, and the Presbyterian Church wrote a letter of protest and endorsed the AMC as "the premier, mainstream Muslim group in Washington."[32]

Meanwhile, AMC's founder, Abdurahman Alamoudi, met with both Clintons in the White House and joined George W. Bush at a prayer service dedicated to victims of the 9/11 attacks. He arranged a Ramadan fast-breaking dinner for congressional leaders, lectured on behalf of the State Department, and founded an organization to provide Muslim chaplains for the Department of Defense.

This was the same man who was described as an "expert in the art of deception" in a report by *Newsweek* journalists Mark Hosenball and Michael Isikoff, for expressing moderate, pro-American sympathies in his lobbying and public relations work with Americans, but then being caught on camera expressing support for Hamas and Hezbollah at an Islamist rally. For example, at a pro-Palestinian rally outside the White House in 2000, he told the crowd, "We are all supporters of Hamas. . . . I am also a supporter of Hezbollah." Later he was photographed in Beirut at a conference attended by representatives of al-Qaeda, Islamic Jihad, Hamas, and Hezbollah. Wiretapped conversations also recorded him praising the 1994 bombing of the Jewish community center in Buenos Aires, Argentina, where eighty-six people died. Alamoudi called it "a worthy operation."[33]

When the government began to investigate Alamoudi for possible ties to terrorism, James Zogby and others defended him as the victim of "a shameful hysteria campaign of McCarthyism." On July 30, 2004, he pleaded guilty to three charges of illegal dealings with Libya, after admitting that he participated in a plot to murder Saudi crown prince Abdullah for Muammar Qaddafi and accepted hundreds of thousands of dollars from top Libyan officials, in addition to tax and immigration violations. He was sentenced to twenty-three years in jail.

Few Muslims are willing to speak out against the extremist organizations in the Arab lobby. One of the rare critiques came from Mustafa Elhussein, secretary of the Ibn Khaldun Society, who said, "[These] self-appointed leaders who spew hatred toward America and the West and yet claim to be legitimate spokespersons for the American Muslim community . . . [should] not only be kept at arm's length from the political process, they should be actively opposed as extremists."[34]

Supporters of Israel became alarmed when they read reports of a rapidly expanding Muslim American population that was growing increasingly active in politics and was expected to be hostile to Israel. These fears were fanned by Muslim organizations that claimed huge memberships and spoke about a constituency of 8 million that had the potential to form a larger voting bloc than the Jews, whose total population is only about 5 million. As it turns out, the influence and numbers of American Muslims have been greatly exaggerated. Rather than 8 million Muslims, for example, the Pew Research Center estimated the population at less than one-third that figure—2.35 million. Another study found the number could be as high as 2.8 million, but was more likely closer to 1.9 million.

In addition, the American Muslim community is multiethnic, with about 30 percent African American, 33 percent of Asian origin, and only 25 percent of Arab descent, which means that not all Muslims are focused on Middle East issues or share the views of the Arab lobby. Iranians, for example, have a very different outlook from Muslims from Arab countries. Indo-Pakistanis are active and well organized and mostly uninterested in Middle East issues, focusing instead on matters directly related to the conflict between India and Pakistan, such as the disputed region of Kashmir. African Americans, meanwhile, are focused primarily on domestic issues and those affecting African nations.

While the Muslim organizations express opinions on the Arab-

Israeli conflict, their principal influence has been exerted through the education system and the media, where they have tried to portray Islam in its most benign form and to convince Americans that radical Muslims do not exist, act contrary to Islam, or are only hostile to the United States because of American policy in the Middle East. They have had limited success because of the reality that Americans (and others) continue to be attacked by Islamists. Thus, for example, a *Washington Post*/ABC News poll in 2009 found that 48 percent of Americans have an unfavorable view of Islam, the highest figure since late 2001, and 29 percent believe mainstream Islam advocates violence against non-Muslims (58 percent said it is a peaceful religion).

This is similar to the problem Arab American groups have had in portraying the Palestinians as peace-loving, while the media report that Hamas and other Palestinians continue to reject Israel's existence and engage in terror. The Muslim organizations' other priority, to weaken domestic counterterrorism laws, has been unsuccessful because most Americans have accepted the tradeoff of some civil liberties for the need to protect the nation from terrorists. In fact, a Cornell University study found in 2004 that 44 percent of Americans believe the U.S. government should restrict the civil liberties of Muslim Americans; about 27 percent said that all Muslim Americans should be required to register their location with the federal government; 26 percent said they think that mosques should be closely monitored by U.S. law enforcement agencies; 29 percent agreed that undercover law enforcement agents should infiltrate Muslim civic and volunteer organizations to keep tabs on their activities and fund-raising; and about 22 percent said the federal government should profile citizens as potential threats based on the fact that they are Muslim or have Middle Eastern heritage.[35]

Another reason the domestic Arab lobby has had limited influence is that in contrast to the pro-Israel community, Arab Americans and Muslims have played a trivial role in electoral politics. American Jews vote and participate in all aspects of campaign politics in disproportionate numbers. While their overall influence on election outcomes is debatable, there is no question that their involvement forces politicians to pay attention to their concerns. Moreover, the lack of comparable Arab involvement means that candidates have no incentive to take positions that might be viewed as hostile to Israel, as that would lose them Israeli lobby support and win little or nothing in return. As Harry Truman said in 1948, "In all of my political experience I don't ever recall the Arab vote swinging a close election."[36]

This attitude naturally carries over to when a candidate is elected. He or she will need votes and money to be reelected and is unlikely to attract either by taking positions hostile to Israel. That is why the Arab lobby considers it a victory if anyone puts one of their issues on the agenda or votes against the Israeli lobby.

About half of the Arab population is concentrated in five states—California, Florida, Michigan, New Jersey, and New York—that are all key to the electoral college. Still, the Arab population is dwarfed by that of the Jews in every one of these states except Michigan.

JEWISH AND ARAB POPULATIONS IN KEY STATES

State	Arab Population	Arabs as % of Total State	Jewish Population	Jews as % of Total State
CA	142,805	.48	999,000	2.9
FL	49,206	.38	628,000	3.9
MI	76,504	.82	110,000	1.1
NJ	46,381	.60	485,000	5.7
NY	94,319	.52	1,657,000	8.7

The Arab lobby did not take an active and visible role in campaigns until the 1984 election. The lobby then targeted Maryland Democrat Clarence Long, the chairman of the House Appropriations Subcommittee on Foreign Operations and a driving force behind increasing aid to Israel. He was chosen "to serve notice to members of Congress that the Arab lobby is ready and able to make life uncomfortable for Israel's friends on Capitol Hill." The NAAA took credit for Long's defeat, but the loss had less to do with the effort of the Arab lobby than the facts that redistricting took away a large percentage of his constituency and that, after a narrow victory in 1982, he became a high-priority target of the Republican National Committee.[37]

The 1984 presidential election was the first time that Arab Americans participated as an organized community in a national political campaign. A small group backed Jesse Jackson, who had a record of sympathy for the Palestinian cause and had made controversial remarks that Jews felt were anti-Semitic, and James Zogby gave one of the nominating speeches for Jackson at the Democratic convention. Ironically, Arab Americans also actively supported the very pro-Israel Ronald Reagan. The reason was that the Republican Party made a concerted effort to court their vote, whereas the Democrats did not. Moreover, Arab Americans were upset that Democrats were pressuring Reagan to move the U.S. embassy from Tel Aviv to Jerusalem.

Zogby and other Arab Americans subsequently became regulars at the Democratic National Convention and began to try to affect the party's platform at the state and national level by introducing language that would give greater recognition to the Palestinian cause. In 1988–89, for example, the AAI managed to secure passage of platform planks favoring a Palestinian state at eight Democratic Party conventions. These campaigns provoked a response from the Israeli lobby, which persuaded the party to remain committed to its long-standing support for a strong U.S.-Israel relationship, and pro-Israel forces became more vigilant in fighting and defeating Arab lobby efforts to shape party platforms.

In 2000, Zogby claimed another milestone when both Al Gore and George W. Bush became the first presidential candidates to meet with Arab Americans to solicit their support. This was also the first election in which Muslim Americans played an active role in a campaign.

Muslim involvement in the 2000 election can be traced to the efforts of Grover Norquist, president of Americans for Tax Reform, and a well-known conservative Republican activist. In 1998 Norquist founded the Islamic Free Market Institute (IFMI) to promote his conservative agenda among American Muslims and increase American Muslim participation in the political process. The organization also seeks to "introduce traditional American values to the Muslim community and traditional Islamic teachings and values to decision-makers" and to "promote an Islamic perspective on domestic issues (social and fiscal) to help enhance the Muslim community's input in the decision-making process."[38]

The institute's main supporter has been Qatar, from which it has received hundreds of thousands of dollars. Other funders have included Saudis and the government of Kuwait. Most of the institute's contributions come from foreign governments, companies, and individuals writing checks on foreign banks. Other funders, such as the Safa Trust and the International Institute of Islamic Thought, have been raided by federal authorities as part of an investigation into suspected terrorist financial networks.[39]

One of Norquist's funders was Abdurahman Alamoudi, the head of the American Muslim Council who made multiple visits to the Clinton White House and met with then-candidate George W. Bush in Austin in July 2000, offering to support his bid for the White House in exchange for Bush's commitment to repeal certain antiterrorist laws. (As discussed earlier, Alamoudi was sentenced in 2004 to twenty-three years in prison for a variety of offenses, including a plot to kill Saudi crown prince Abdullah.) Khaled Saffuri, the director of IFMI, also enlisted Sami Al-Arian to attract Muslim voters in Florida.

One of Norquist's main objectives on behalf of the Arab lobby was to try to persuade the presidential candidates in the 2000 election to weaken the pre-9/11 policy regarding investigating suspected illegal immigrants. Norquist subsequently took credit for George W. Bush's statement in a nationally televised debate on October 11, 2000, "Arab Americans are racially profiled in what's called secret evidence. . . . We've got to do something about that." Bush's remarks won the support of more than twenty Arab American groups.[40]

A year later, leaders of a half dozen Arab American and Muslim organizations were scheduled to meet with President Bush at 3:00 p.m. on September 11, "to discuss their desire to end ethnic profiling, as well as the policy of 'secret evidence' that allows American law enforcement officials to detain non-U.S. citizens based on evidence they are not compelled to share."[41] Instead, after 9/11, Bush championed even more vigorous use of secret evidence and profiling and provoked widespread anger in the Arab-American and Muslim community.

Despite the Muslim outreach efforts of Norquist, Bush lost the state of Michigan, the only state with a large enough Arab/Muslim population to make even a marginal difference in an election. Also in that election, the only Arab American in the Senate, Spencer Abraham, lost his bid for reelection (President Bush later named him secretary of energy).

Nevertheless, since the 2000 election was so close, every constituency can claim to have influenced the outcome. Arab Americans are no different. After Bush's narrow victory in Florida, most attention was focused on elderly Jewish voters who, believing they had voted for Gore, had accidentally cast ballots for Pat Buchanan. Meanwhile, the Tampa Bay Islamic Center claimed that 50,000 Muslims in Florida voted, and an exit poll conducted by the American Muslim Alliance showed Bush won 88 percent of the Muslim vote, compared to 8 percent for Ralph Nader and 1 percent for Al Gore. This allowed Norquist to claim that Bush was elected as a result of the Muslim vote. The lopsided outcome was due partly to the expectation that George W. would be at least as pro-Arab as his father, and also undoubtedly partly to the fact that Gore's running mate, Joe Lieberman, was Jewish and unabashedly pro-Israel.

Gore actually was viewed as having taken the Muslim vote for granted. Not until two weeks before the election did the campaign consider sending his wife to a Muslim-American convention in Chicago, but the idea was apparently shot down because of concerns about Jewish voters' reactions.

In 2004, the major Muslim organizations tried to unite to form a Muslim-American voting bloc. A coalition comprised of the American Muslim Alliance (AMA); the Council on American-Islamic Relations (CAIR); the Islamic Circle of North America (ICNA); the Islamic Society of North America (ISNA); the Muslim Alliance of

North America (MANA); the Muslim American Society (MAS); the Muslim Public Affairs Council (MPAC); the Muslim Students Association-National (MSA-N); the Muslim Ummah of North America (MUNA); Project Islamic Hope (PIH); and United Muslims of America (UMA), which represented most mosques in the United States, established the American Muslim Taskforce on Civil Rights and Elections—Political Action Committee (AMT-PAC) to protest "oppressive laws" against Muslims and support John Kerry. The Arab lobby was disenchanted with Bush because of the post-9/11 security measures they viewed as discriminatory, and because of his unexpectedly strong support for Israel. Overwhelming Muslim support did not change the outcome, however, as Kerry lost.

In the 2008 election, John McCain's pro-Israel credentials were well established from his record in the Senate and outspoken support of Israel during the campaign, so he was never likely to get the votes of many Arab Americans. Other components of the lobby, notably the petromilitary elements, were likely to support McCain because of his support for oil drilling and a robust military.

The candidacy of Barack Obama presented a bit of a conundrum for the Arab lobby. On one hand, some people believed he was a Muslim, which attracted support, but the fact that he was not, and emphasized his Christian beliefs, made him problematic for some Muslims. James Abourezk, for example, complained after the election that Obama "wanted nothing to do with Arabs, either Christian or Muslim" and that his staff "prevented Muslim women with head scarves from sitting behind him in view of the television cameras during his campaign rallies." While Obama visited churches and synagogues, Abourezk said he "refused to visit even one mosque during the campaign."[42]

In addition, Obama's policy positions related to Israel were virtually identical to McCain's, which were not to the lobby's liking, but his desire to withdraw troops from Iraq and negotiate with Iran were more positive signs, as were his friendship with Columbia professor Rashid Khalidi, a vitriolic critic of Israel and former PLO spokesman, not to mention the statement by Jesse Jackson that Obama would decrease the influence of "Zionists who have controlled American policy for decades" (Jackson claimed later to have been misquoted).[43] Obama was also determined to radically change course from what was viewed as a rabidly pro-Israel Bush administration. Several of his advisers were critics of Israel; he spoke about becoming more engaged in the peace process, which was interpreted as opening the possibility for pressuring Israel; he was committed to opening diplomatic channels to countries such as Syria and Iran and, unlike McCain, did not emphasize the war on terror or the danger of radical Islam. The Arab lobby hoped to receive a more sympathetic hearing for their concerns, and that they would have an opportunity to pressure President Obama to pursue an "evenhanded policy," which focused on the Palestinians. The lobby also hoped to silence discussion that might cast any aspersions on Islam and roll back security measures used to investigate Muslims and Arabs.

On the positive side for the lobby, at least initially, Obama appointed a national coordinator for Muslim American affairs. The person chosen, Chicago lawyer Mazen Asbahi, lasted less than a month, resigning after questions were raised about his participation on the board of a subsidiary of the Saudi-funded North American Islamic Trust, which promotes Wahhabi Islam and owns title to many mosques. Asbahi was also described by the *Wall Street Journal* as frequently speaking before groups associated with the Muslim Brotherhood. Before Asbahi joined the campaign in late July, Obama did not have a Muslim-outreach coordinator, which had provoked complaints by Muslims who felt this was unfair, since Obama did have outreach staff for Catholics, evangelical Christians, and Jews.[44]

In 2008 the American Muslim Taskforce on Civil Rights and Elections reported that 89 percent of Muslims voted for Obama, while only 2 percent voted for McCain (only 4 percent identified themselves as Republicans). As for most voters in 2008, by far the most important issue for Muslim voters (63 percent) was the economy, followed by the wars in Iraq and Afghanistan (16 percent).

Ironically, while Obama received the overwhelming support of Arab Americans, Palestinians in the Middle East viewed him with great suspicion. One journalist described his "phobic reaction to any-thing and everything Islamic," and other Palestinians were appalled by his statements of support for Israel at the AIPAC conference in June 2008 and during his one-day stopover in Israel in July. The forty-five-minute visit Obama paid to Mahmoud Abbas in Ramallah and his expression of support for a Palestinian state were viewed as insufficient. A poll of Palestinians found that 34 percent actually fa-vored McCain, who never visited the West Bank, while only 28 per-cent supported Obama. Pollster Nabil Kukali explained, "People had high expectations for Obama, but his statements to AIPAC indicated that he does not understand Palestinian suffering." The Palestinians were also disenchanted with the Arab American groups, which they believed failed to promote their concerns.[45]

One of the most surprising aspects of the Arab lobby, which per-haps partially explains its minimal influence in electoral politics, is the paltry amount of money given to political campaigns. As in much of its strategy, the idea was to match the electoral involvement of the Israeli lobby and create political action committees that could reward sympathetic candidates and punish those who were too pro-Israel. The NAAA formed the first Arab American PAC—NAAA-PAC—in 1984. It gave out a paltry $20,000, split among twenty-two Democrats and twenty-four Republicans. The same year, more than seventy pro-Israel PACs distributed more than $4 million.

In 2003, Arab Americans in Virginia formed the New Dominion PAC. Since then, it has distributed more than $126,000, $34,000 of that in the 2008 campaign (nothing was given to Republicans).

"Traditionally, Arab Americans participated as individuals" in elections, according to then director of AAI, Jean Abi Nader, but in 2004, Nader said, they realized they could be more influential by contributing to PACs and predicted that AAI's PAC alone would raise $200,000.[46] In fact, in that election cycle, AAI raised half that amount, and the rest of the pro-Arab PACs contributed only about $50,000 more, a total of $150,000, which paled in comparison to the $3.1 million donated by pro-Israel PACs (nearly $3 million more was donated by individuals).

In 2008, three Arab American PACs (Americans for a Palestinian State, Arab American Leadership PAC, and NAAA-ADC) contributed a total of just over $60,000 to candidates. Ten Muslim PACs existed at one time, but only three were active in 2008, and only two contributed a total of about $15,000 to candidates. These data are misleading because the Center for Responsive Politics does not include all PACs that are part of the Arab lobby. The New Dominion PAC, for example, is missing from their data. By comparison, thirty-one pro-Israel PACs had contributed nearly $3.1 million (on a broader comparison, the top PAC contributor, the National Association of Realtors, gave $4 million). If anything, disclosure of Arab campaign contributions alarms the Israeli lobby, and it responds with even more money to more than compensate for the Arab lobby's donations.

Khaled Saffuri, executive director of the Islamic Institute in Washington, has argued that the PAC donations are misleading, as most major donors do not contribute to PACs and therefore do not show up in studies of campaign financing: "There is lots of money giving on a personal level and most of the donors do not tie in on Arab and Muslim issues. They do so on personal interest rather than community interest." Though he had no evidence to back the claim, Saffuri said Arab American and Muslim donors had given a minimum of $2 million to the Bush campaign.[47]

When Arab Americans and Muslims make contributions to candidates, they often provoke controversy. For example, when Hillary Clinton was running for the Senate in 1998, she received a $50,000 donation from the American Muslim Alliance, which presumably was pleased by her endorsement of a Palestinian state, but her campaign returned the money after it was alerted to offensive material on the group's Web site. Still, Zogby claims that questions raised about campaign donations actually work in the lobby's favor because "we get copy for the next three days about that issue." He says it is "the best money we never had to spend."[48]

The Israeli lobby is often accused of directing money to pro-Israel political candidates, but it typically does not have to give donors formal instructions; the candidates who are supportive are generally well known, and to the extent advice is needed, it may be on the order of which races are close enough that additional contributions may affect the outcome. The same holds for the Arab lobby. Very few members of Congress have not supported Israel over the years, and an even smaller number have been identifiably hostile. Since these members stand out as a minority, it is easy for the Arab lobby to know whom to support. Nevertheless, some direction may be given, as occurred in the notorious 1982 election involving Paul Findley. Findley called himself "Yasser Arafat's best friend in Congress" and later compared the terrorist leader to Gandhi and Martin Luther King Jr. He blamed his defeat on the Israeli lobby, but never mentioned the support he received from the Arab lobby. For example, the Saudi newspaper *Al-Jazirah* reported "All Findley needs now is $150,000 to $200,000. Is this amount too much for companies [with contracts in the Arab world] to contribute through political action committees . . . ?"[49] Ultimately, Findley was defeated because his district suffered from a high unemployment rate, and his district was gerrymandered to his disadvantage.

In fact, in 1982 and in subsequent elections, the corporate component of the Arab lobby did not support pro-Arab candidates. The *Boston Globe*, for example, examined the donations of the oil industry and found little correlation with candidates' positions on Middle East issues. This finding reinforces the point that corporations do not consistently support the lobby's agenda, mostly participating only when their immediate interests are at stake.

This should not be surprising, as oil and other companies are focused on their bottom lines, which are affected by a range of issues beyond the Arab-Israeli conflict; moreover, donors tend to prefer incumbents because they have a higher probability of victory, are known quantities, and have seniority on key committees. Since members of Congress have been overwhelmingly supportive of Israel, this increases the likelihood that this will remain true. To change the balance of opinion in Congress would require the Arab lobby to target often powerful, well-funded incumbents. Given their limited involvement in campaigns, both as participants and funders, it is easy to see why members of the Arab lobby have not been able to weaken congressional support for Israel.

Though Congress has long been supportive of Israel, only in the last twenty years or so have a disproportionate number of Jews been elected to serve. These Jewish members, combined with sympathetic non-Jews, have ensured a comfortable majority in support of most legislation favored by the Israeli lobby. Few Arab Americans have served in Congress, but those who have typically became Israel's principal critics in Congress. This was the case in the early 1970s, when South Dakota Democrat James Abourezk became the first Arab American elected to the Senate. He joined representatives Toby Moffett, Abraham Kazen Jr., and James Abdnor in an informal Arab lobby alliance in Congress. As a leading pro-Arab or, more typically, anti-Israel voice in Congress, Abourezk became a popular speaker for Arab American groups, and when he left Congress, he cofounded the ADC.

Keith Ellison (D-MN) became the first Muslim member of Congress in 2006 and was soon followed by Andre Carson (D-IN). As the groundbreaker, Ellison came under particular scrutiny. Although he has not shied away from speaking to the Arab lobby, he has also made a concerted effort to show the Israeli lobby that he is a friend of Israel. Carson, after participating in a town hall meeting sponsored by CAIR, apparently began to have second thoughts about appearing at the group's events. CAIR spokesman Hooper advised CAIR chapters not to publicly invite Carson, for fear he would turn them down and critics could then say, "Oh, a Muslim member of Congress won't even be seen with CAIR."[50] Meanwhile, on AIPAC's top priority, foreign aid, both voted with the pro-Israel lobby in 2009.

The weakness of the Arab American groups can be seen every time a major conflict occurs between Israel and its neighbors. The Israeli military operation Cast Lead, designed to stop Hamas rocket fire in December 2008–January 2009, is a good example. After exercising restraint for three years and absorbing nearly 10,000 mortar and rocket attacks fired by terrorists in the Gaza Strip at the civilian population in southern Israel, the Israel Defense Forces launched a large-scale counterterrorism operation in Gaza. Despite extraordinary efforts to avoid civilian casualties, which included dropping leaflets and making phone calls to warn bystanders to stay away from the terrorists, many innocent Palestinians were killed, and destruction was widespread. The international press pilloried Israel, its often distorted and inaccurate reports conveying an image of Israel as a brutal aggressor that created a humanitarian disaster. The Arab lobby immediately organized protests and called for the government to stop the Israeli onslaught and condemn its actions. To the chagrin of the groups described here, however, the Bush administration backed the Israeli operation as a legitimate act of self-defense, and the House voted overwhelmingly (390–5), and the Senate unanimously, to support Israel's actions. Months later, the UN Human Rights Council established a fact-finding mission headed by Richard Goldstone that resulted in a highly controversial and widely criticized report accusing Israel of war crimes. The Arab lobby strongly supported the report, but the House of Representatives voted 344 to 36 to condemn it.

In part because the Arab lobby has been so unsuccessful in making its case at the national level, it has often tried to win points at the local level by promoting anti-Israel measures it hopes will snowball into a national campaign that undermines the U.S.-Israel relationship. These efforts are often the product of ad hoc groups that also are formed in a community, usually an especially liberal one. Though practically meaningless in terms of foreign policy, these groups seek to delegitimize Israel through symbolic acts such as using the divestment campaign employed against South Africa. Thus, as early as 1984, Taxpayers for Peace in the Middle East sought to put a measure on the ballot in Berkeley, California, that called for foreign aid to be reduced by the amount Israel spends on settlements. The measure was defeated overwhelmingly, but attracted publicity and sparked similar movements in several other communities. In 2004, anti-Israel activists in Somerville, Massachusetts, sought to divest its $137.4 million pension fund from Israeli bonds and companies that sell military equipment to Israel. The resolution was defeated 10–0. More recently, anti-Israel activists tried to make Seattle the first major American city to divest from companies that provide material support to Israel. That effort also failed when a court ruled the proposed ballot initiative invalid. While ineffective to this point, such activities represent another component of the Arab lobby's persistent campaign at all levels of society to weaken the U.S.-Israel alliance.

More than twenty years ago, James Zogby boasted about the strength of the Arab lobby in comparison to the Israeli lobby. "They control the Hill, but we've got a lot of the positions around the Hill. We have a lot more allies than we ever had before." He acknowledged the need to have greater impact on elections, but concluded, "We're on the track towards power."[51]

The truth is different, however, as his colleague Hussein Ibish admitted. Ibish, a longtime activist and staff member of different Arab lobby groups, told an audience in Bahrain that organizations such as the ADC and AAI had not changed in size since the 1990s. Ibish said numerous Arab-Muslim organizations have been created, but "none of these organizations are particularly strong or effective representatives of the Arab American community."[52]

CHAPTER TWELVE

God Takes a Side:
Christian Anti-Zionists Join the Lobby

Though much is written about the support for Israel today among the estimated 75 million evangelicals in the United States, approximately 200 million American Christians are not evangelical and, historically, the most active Christian organizations have been hostile toward Israel and more sympathetic to the Arabs. This is ironic, given that a substantial proportion of Arab Americans are Christians, but generally unsupportive of the Arab lobby.

The roots of anti-Israel sentiment in the Christian community can be traced to anti-Semitic theology as well as years of Vatican hostility based, in part, on concern that a Jewish state would jeopardize Catholic attachment to the Holy Land. Later, when liberation theology emerged as an influential strain of Christian ideology, the idea was introduced that Israel was part of the Western imperialist effort to oppress the downtrodden Palestinians. When these ideas lost favor within the church, they were superseded by a Palestinian version that attempts to wipe Israel and the Jews from the Bible and deny the Jews' historical ties to their homeland.

Much of the focus of the Christians in the Arab lobby is on Jerusalem and the objection to its control by Jews. They also rail against real and imagined offenses against Christians committed by Israel while remaining mute in the face of discriminatory policies of the Palestinians and the Arab and Muslim states. Christian groups have given the Arab lobby moral cover and helped create the impression that the case against Israel is based on human rights and justice rather than politics, religion, psychology, history, geography, and, ultimately, Arab irredentism. Besides this halo effect, the Christian groups have helped keep criticism of Israeli human rights at the forefront of discussions about the Middle East and poisoned the minds of many of the faithful in the denominations that have joined the Arab lobby.

Today it is common to hear evangelical Christian leaders talk about the consistency of their faith with the strengthening of Israel, but other Christians have a very different view rooted in their theology. "The central issue between Judaism and Christianity," wrote Millar Burrows in *Christian Century*, "lies in their answer to the question: What do you think of Christ? . . . The present resurgence of Jewish nationalism is a repetition of the same fatal error that caused Israel's rejection of Jesus. It is the focal point at which Christian opinion, in all brotherly love, should make clear and emphatic its disagreement with the dominant trend in contemporary Judaism. For the authentic, dominating, just now apparently all-conquering devotees of political Zionism we would feel the sorrow that Jesus felt when he wept over Jerusalem. . . . The Christians' final attitude may be that of Paul: 'Brethren, my heart's desire for Israel is that they may be saved.'"[1]

The U.S. Presbyterian Church takes a different position and separates the discussion of Israel from the Bible. In its view, "the State of Israel is a geopolitical entity and is not to be validated theologically." The Presbyterians have been perhaps the most committed denomination on the Palestinian issue, and one of the first to call for the United States to "end its unqualified commitment to Israel" and "deny further aid to Israel until . . . [Israel] ends its West Bank and Gaza settlements policy."[2]

The influence of Christians dates back to the beginning of America's involvement with the Middle East, as the first Americans to live in the region were missionaries. The Presbyterians, for example, have been involved in the region for more than 160 years. Many of the organizations and individuals who became vocal critics of Israel had institutional commitments in the Arab Middle East.

Meanwhile, the Catholic Church made clear its position on

Zionism as early as 1904, when Theodor Herzl went to Rome to meet Pope Pius X to solicit his support for the Jewish homeland. The pope's position was unambiguous: "The soil of Jerusalem is sacred in the life of Jesus Christ. As head of the Church, I cannot say otherwise. The Jews did not acknowledge our Lord and thus we cannot recognize the Jewish people. Hence, if you go to Palestine and if the Jewish people settle there, our churches and our priests will be ready to baptize you all."[3] At this point, the Zionist movement was not significant enough to have generated the pope's political concern, so the response to Herzl was more likely an expression of the replacement theology that dominated church thinking; that is, the view that Christianity had replaced Judaism, that Jews are no longer God's chosen people, and that God does not have specific future plans for the nation of Israel. It was therefore not surprising that the Vatican later refused to endorse the Balfour Declaration's call for the establishment of a Jewish homeland in Palestine.

As the debate over the idea of creating a Jewish state became more intense in the 1940s, so did the arguments among non-Jews. Eminent theologians such as Reinhold Niebuhr were vigorous supporters of the Zionists, but others were hostile, sometimes relying on their interpretations of the Bible and other times expressing anti-Semitic attitudes. The *Christian Century*, the magazine of U.S. mainline Protestantism, for example, trumpeted the notion of Jewish disloyalty, insisting that Jews decide "whether they are an integral part of the nation in which they live, or members of a Levantine nation dwelling in exile." The Baptist *Watchman-Examiner* adopted a more theological critique, arguing that "Israel cannot be restored except in the divine plan and purpose. If Israel is now being restored, then, as we interpret the Bible, history is rapidly approaching its climax."[4]

In June 1943, the apostolic delegate in Washington wrote to Myron Taylor, the American representative to the Vatican, "If the greater part of Palestine is given to the Jewish People, this would be a severe blow to the religious attachment of Catholics to this land. To have the Jewish People in the majority would be to interfere with the peaceful exercise of these rights in the Holy Land already vested in Catholics [*sic*]. . . . If a 'Hebrew Home' is desired, it would not be too difficult to find a more fitting territory than Palestine. With an increase in the Jewish population there, grave, new, international problems would arise."[5]

The debate over the future of Palestine was also conducted in the aftermath of the Holocaust and the shadow of the church's general silence during that catastrophe. It would be many years later, however, before the controversy over the role of Pope Pius XII during the war would generate tension between Catholics and Jews. While the church did engage in some efforts to rescue Jews, it was explicitly opposed to taking measures that would bring any to Palestine. In May 1943, for example, the Vatican's secretary of state, Cardinal Luigi Maglioni, gave as one of the reasons for the pope's refusal to rescue two thousand Jewish children from Slovakia the fear that an influx of Jews into Palestine would threaten Christian interests.[6]

The Vatican believed it should have a say in determining the future of the Holy Land. Its representatives were primarily concerned about Jerusalem, and lobbied the State Department to support internationalization as the only way to preserve the holy places. The Zionists argued that they had every intention of protecting the holy places of all faiths; moreover, they maintained that Jews had a connection to Jerusalem dating back nearly three thousand years, and that it should be their capital.

As the debate on the future of Palestine headed toward its denouement, the Arab lobby now included the petrodiplomatic complex, a few domestic organizations, the Arab states, and the Catholic Church. They were all aligned against partition at the UN, but the Zionists had some faint hope that the Vatican might yet support a Jewish state and use its influence with some countries, particularly in Latin America, where Catholic influence was particularly strong. That did not occur. The Zionists were actually fortunate that the Vatican did not lobby more actively *against* the resolution. Israel's future prime minister, Moshe Sharett, believed that the Vatican did not actively oppose partition because it did not want to declare war on the Jewish people, who it hoped would join the international front against communism, and because it saw the partition resolution's internationalization of Jerusalem as effectively giving Christians control over the city. Still, the church left no doubt where it stood when the Vatican's semiofficial newspaper, *L'Osservatore Romano*, proclaimed the day before Israel announced its independence that "modern Zionism is not the true heir of biblical Israel. . . . Therefore the Holy Land and its sacred sites belong to Christianity, which is the true Israel."[7]

When it became clear that the partition resolution would not be implemented and that war would decide the fate of the Holy Land, the Vatican remained silent. Israelis believe this was because the Vatican expected the Jews to lose the war and was hoping to find a way to get along with the Arabs and still assume a dominant position in Jerusalem. The silence ended when reports of Jewish soldiers damaging and defiling Christian holy sites were disseminated. While some incidents did indeed occur, the Israelis felt they were being exaggerated for propaganda purposes by various parties interested in generating hostility toward the new state. Prime Minister David Ben-Gurion understood the danger the negative publicity could cause and ordered Israeli troops to protect all holy sites, going so far as to tell commanders to make "merciless use of machine guns against any Jews, and in particular any Jewish soldier, who tries to loot or defile a Christian or Muslim Holy Place."[8]

The Vatican represented Catholics, but other denominations had their own views of Zionism. Many mainline Protestants, in particular, were hostile because of their historic missionary activities in the Middle East, which they believed were threatened by the establishment of a Jewish state. One influential leader of the anti-Zionists was Virginia Gildersleeve, the president of Barnard College and a member of the board of the American University of Beirut, who argued that Zionism would "plunge much of the region into war, sow longstanding hatred and make the Arabs consider America not the best-liked and trusted of the nations of the West . . . but the most disliked and distrusted."[9] In 1948, she was a founder of the Committee for Justice and Peace in the Holy Land (CJPHL), which later merged with the American Friends of the Middle East (AFME), and her organization became a vigorous member of the Arab lobby, supported by Aramco and the CIA. At the time of the partition debate, CJPHL and other prominent Protestants, such as Dorothy Thompson, Harry Emerson Fosdick, and Henry Sloane Coffin, were lobbying the Truman administration to prevent Jewish statehood.

A few months after Israel declared independence, another player joined the Arab lobby. On August 22, 1948, the World Council of Churches (WCC) was established and has grown to include hundreds of churches in the East and West. Individual Christians pay little heed to the WCC; however, political leaders sometimes accept WCC declarations as a reflection of the opinion of "the Christians." As Israel was fighting for its life, the WCC would not take a position on its survival, but urged the international community to see it as "a moral and spiritual question" rather than a political, economic, or strategic one. The WCC hinted, however, that the creation of a Jewish state might provoke anti-Semitism: "The establishment of the state of 'Israel' adds a political dimension to the Christian approach to the Jews and threatens to complicate anti-Semitism with political fears and enmities."[10]

After the end of Israel's War of Independence, relations with Christians did become more complex. Thousands of Palestinian Christians fled their homes or were expelled and were not allowed to return; Jews now controlled Christian holy sites; Christians elsewhere in the Middle East were separated from their shrines and the community remaining in the Holy Land; and Israeli Jews feared missionary activities by Christians in Israel.

The Mennonites and Quakers began relief work among the Palestinians after the 1948 Arab-Israeli War and were for some time the only Christian denominations lobbying on Middle East issues through Washington-based advocacy offices. They have been persistent critics of Israel, joining the general Arab lobby campaign of condemnation and delegitimization. The Mennonite Central Committee, for example, routinely portrays Israel's existence as the cause of the Arab-Israeli conflict and calls for a one-state solution. The group also sponsors "Christian Peacemaker Teams" that are sent to the West Bank to confront Israeli soldiers, but like other such "peace" groups, they do nothing to challenge Palestinian terrorists. These groups have undoubtedly influenced their membership, but there is no indication they have had any influence on policy. They maintain a consistent presence in the Middle East and Washington, and the Friends Committee on National Legislation remains active.

Like some U.S. State Department officials, the Vatican feared the new state might turn Communist and resisted entreaties to establish formal diplomatic relations with Israel. In fact, when the U.S. ambassador to Israel suggested that the pope meet with Chaim Weizmann, the Holy See rejected the idea and complained that the United States had recognized Israel but not the Vatican. The pope also reiterated that he would never accept Israeli sovereignty over the Holy Land. In April 1949, Pius XII issued an encyclical on Palestine that made specific demands on Israel. Israel had no problem with his call for freedom of access to holy places and worship, which were guaranteed in Israel's declaration of independence, but the pope's support for the return of the Palestinian refugees and the internationalization of Jerusalem were considered dangerous because the refugees were seen as a potential fifth column that would undermine Israel from within, and internationalization of Jerusalem threatened Israel's claim to its capital.

While in 1947 the Vatican did not weigh in on the partition resolution, it shifted policy after the 1948 Arab-Israeli War when Israel and Jordan gained control over the Christian holy places. The Vatican successfully lobbied the UN General Assembly to reaffirm the recommendation to internationalize Jerusalem, even though events and facts on the ground had made that aspect of the resolution unworkable. The Vatican also focused its criticism on Israel, even though Jordan (then Transjordan) controlled the eastern half of Jerusalem, including the Old City, where many of the Christian shrines were located. The Vatican would also remain silent for the next nineteen years when Israeli Christians were denied access to their holy places, and Jews were barred from the Western Wall.

The church's anti-Israel position became clear when it tried to prevent the UN from granting membership to Israel. Delegations were told not to vote for Israel's admission unless an agreement was reached on the internationalization of Jerusalem. Cardinal Francis Spellman, the most influential American Roman Catholic leader, lobbied Truman to oppose Israel's admission to the UN and then hoped to reverse the president's decision after the United States joined the majority approving Israel's membership.[11] This is not part of the history of the period you will find in the books asserting the omnipotence of the Israeli lobby, which leave out all the countervailing pressures to create an image of American political leaders pandering to Jewish voters rather than statesmen choosing between competing arguments by domestic and foreign interests.

It is an overstatement to suggest, as Uri Bialer does in *Cross on the Star of David*, that the pope was the "most dangerous challenge to Israeli control over West Jerusalem and, indirectly, to all of Israel's gains in the 1948 war," but he is undoubtedly correct when he says that the hostility of the church became one of the political obstacles Israel would have to confront as it sought to legitimate its borders and international standing.[12] Catholic leaders and spokespeople repeatedly attacked Israel for ruining shrines, for defying UN resolutions, and for its "illegal" claim to jurisdiction over any part of Jerusalem. Given the Vatican's position, it should not be surprising that Catholic institutions outside Rome and other Christian groups might adopt antagonistic attitudes toward Israel.

Israel felt less threatened by the Vatican's position by the mid-1950s, when it perceived its status in Jerusalem to be more secure. Though not only the Vatican but the United States and other nations had protested when Israel began to move the institutions of government from Tel Aviv to the capital in Jerusalem, the realization set in that Israel was not going to be dislodged from the city. Furthermore, the Jordanians had been no less adamant in staking their claim to the half of the city they controlled. In fact, though only two nations recognized Jordan's occupation of the territory it captured in 1948, the international community gradually accepted that the partition resolution was dead. After annual votes reaffirming the General Assembly's commitment to the internationalization of Jerusalem, the idea was dropped in the early 1950s, and the level of tension with the Vatican declined.

Israel still had little success in improving relations with the Vatican or gaining recognition, in large measure because of the opposition of the church's secretary of state, Cardinal Domenico Tardini, who remained committed to the internationalization of Jerusalem and, like his counterparts in Washington, feared that an improvement in Israeli-Vatican relations would adversely affect ties with the Arabs. Like the Arabists of the early part of the century, Tardini also worried that Catholics in the region might be endangered by acceptance of a Jewish state in the Islamic heartland. But Tardini was similar to some American Arabists, who made the case against ties with Israel on policy grounds but were also motivated by personal beliefs. Tardini's view was expressed, for example, in a discussion with a fellow cardinal during which he said, "There is no possibility of contact or negotiations with the killers of God."[13]

Not only the Catholics feared the reaction of Arabs. At the WCC's Second World Assembly in 1954, a group of theologians proposed a statement that Israel was one of the recent signs of hope. The proposal was narrowly defeated after a Lebanese Christian political leader, Charles Malik, argued that the group should not take positions that might alienate Arab Christians.

Following the Suez War in 1956, it was the State Department that contacted the Christian community in an effort to elicit support for its policy of pressuring Israel to withdraw from the Sinai. Secretary of State Dulles contacted Dr. Roswell Barnes, the associate general secretary of the National Council of Churches (NCC), and told him that the "Jews and those very much influenced by Jews" were the only ones speaking out, and they were critical of Eisenhower's stand. The NCC is composed of thirty-two Protestant denominations, including virtually all major church bodies, and has historically been critical of Israel. At the time, Dulles was frustrated that no one else was taking an interest in the Sinai issue, and he ultimately got little from Barnes beyond the statement that he had been working on some comments to include in sermons and a promise to try to convince the president of the NCC to do something.[14] The NCC's involvement was not necessary, as Eisenhower's pressure was sufficient to force Israel to withdraw.

The church's relations with Israel and the Jews also grew more complicated in the 1960s, as more and more research was conducted on the Holocaust. While the Vatican was unhappy with Israeli policies relating to Jerusalem and the treatment of Catholics, Jews became increasingly angry over the revelations of what had happened during the war and the pope's failure to do more to save European Jews or speak out against Hitler. Pope Paul VI did little to endear himself to Jews or Israelis when he visited Israel for eleven hours, refused to meet the chief rabbis or government officials, and avoided the use of the word *Israel* during his stay.

Sometimes the anti-Israel Christians exert the greatest influence within their own ecumenical bodies. They are frequently more active and vocal than other Christians and therefore can have a disproportional impact. For example, in 1963, the Reverend Gustave Weigel said that a statement condemning anti-Semitism was prepared for the Ecumenical Council in Rome and had the support of a majority of the 2,500 bishops. It was never introduced, Weigel said, "because the Arab states would understand it as backing up Israel and therefore chiding and rebuffing the Arab states." He added that his colleagues were also hesitant because of concern about the fate of Christians in Arab lands and the presence of Arab bishops.[15]

Still, a watershed in Jewish-Christian relations occurred the following year, when the Second Vatican Council adopted the Declaration on the Relation of the Church with Non-Christian Religions (*Nostra Aetate*), which, among other things, officially absolved the Jews of responsibility for the death of Jesus. This resolved, at least on an official level, one of the theological bases for centuries of Christian anti-Semitism.

The reaction of Muslims to *Nostra Aetate* was anger; it represented, they feared, a change in the church's view toward not only Jews but Zionism. How could Christians be counted on to oppose the Jewish state if they no longer were expected to hate Jews for killing their savior? The Vatican tried to minimize the damage in the Middle East by explaining that "the measure was being enacted largely to stabilize the Jewish communities outside Israel, especially those in Catholic countries (e.g., France and Latin America), in an attempt to insure that they would never again be driven by some new Christian persecution to mass emigration to the Zionist state."[16]

Theology gave way to politics as Christians in the Arab lobby found new reasons for hostility toward Israel during the crisis in June 1967 and the aftermath of the Six-Day War. For weeks, Nasser and other Arab leaders made bellicose statements about their intention to annihilate Israel. Egypt mobilized its troops in the Sinai and block-aded the Straits of Tiran. Like the rest of the Arab lobby, the National Council of Churches and other Christian groups said nothing. Immediately after Israel's victory, however, the NCC suddenly spoke up, announcing that it could not "condone by silence territorial expansion by armed force." From that point on the NCC, along with the WCC, has adopted the Arab lobby's rhetoric and blamed Israel for the ills of the region, accusing it of starting the succeeding wars to acquire more territory and to "incorporate innocent and abject Arab populations."[17]

Most of the world was impressed by the stunning Israeli victory over the Arabs. Much of the church, however, was appalled by the outcome, and especially angry over Israel's reunification of Jerusa-lem and assertion of sovereignty over the entire city. James Kelso of the United Presbyterian Church condemned Israel's "crimes against Arab Christians and Arab Muslims." The WCC rejected Israel's claim to its capital.

Jewish leaders were dismayed by the Christian reaction. Many had long been engaged in interfaith dialogue and were shocked by the silence of the Protestant and Catholic establishments. Rabbi Marc Tannenbaum criticized "the failure of the 'diplomatic' institu-tions of Christendom to speak an unequivocal word in defense of the preservation of the Jewish people." This was the principal source of Jewish anger. "Jews did not expect unanimous Christian support for every policy decision of the State of Israel," Judith Banki, a major player in Jewish-Christian dialogue for the American Jewish Committee, noted. "What they did expect was an outpouring of protest at the threats to annihilate human beings—the Jews of Israel—and an affirmation of the right to defend themselves and their nation. The relative silence of the churches on this matter, combined with later remonstrances regarding Israel's 'territorial expansion,' was inexplicable to Jews, particularly when it seemed clear that the overwhelming majority of Americans supported Israel's position."[18]

The Quakers became one of the most persistent critics of Israel after the war. Typically, the group's spokespeople and publications expressed what they undoubtedly viewed as impartiality by suggesting that both sides were equally to blame for the war and subsequent ceasefire violations. Ultimately, however, they placed the burden of making peace on Israel, which they maintained must "recognize the obligations as military victor in past combats to make the first move toward peace" and "give forthright assurances on eventual withdrawal from occupied territories and on rejection of future expansionist aims."[19] As is the case in general with the Arab lobby, the Arabs are not viewed as having any responsibility for provoking war or any obligation to make concessions to facilitate peace.

While the Johnson administration was considering the sale of Phantom jets to Israel, the Friends Committee on National Legislation (the Quakers) sent Congress a 20,000-word memo criticizing Israel's demand for direct negotiations and preoccupation with "security" as opposed to "justice" for the Arabs. The memo called for all the occupied territories except the Jewish part of the Old City of Jerusalem to be placed under a UN trusteeship. The Protestant journal *Christianity and Crisis* also began to reflect the more critical view of the movement's leadership as founder Reinhold Niebuhr, a staunch supporter of Israel, was eclipsed by younger rivals. That publication, founded in 1941 to encourage American participation in the war against Germany, had become so hostile toward Israel by 1972 that Niebuhr's widow demanded that his name be removed from the masthead.[20]

Franklin Littell, a Methodist minister and renowned Holocaust scholar, also noted that some Christians, particularly after Israel's victory in 1967, had difficulty seeing Jews as anything but victims. "The thing the nineteenth-century Liberal Protestant, the Christian humanitarian, cannot grasp is the Jew who is a winner, a citizen soldier of liberty and dignity, who does not have to beg protection of a patron or toleration of a so-called Christian nation, who can take the Golan Heights in six hours if necessary. This is precisely the reason why Israel is a stone of stumbling, and why also the generally covert anti-Semitism of liberal Protestantism can be just as dangerous as the overt anti-Semitism of the radical right."[21]

From 1967 on, many Christian groups became among the most vociferous members of the Arab lobby as they focused on what they perceived as human rights abuses regarding the Palestinians while typically ignoring Israel's security dilemma, which neither interested them nor fit into their newly developed "liberation theology." Though originating in Europe, this mind-set became particularly prevalent in Latin America, where the West in general, and the United States in particular, were viewed as oppressors trying to impose Western culture and merciless capitalism on Third World peoples. Father Daniel Berrigan, a leading spokesperson for the liberationist viewpoint as regards Israel, condemned the nation as a "criminal Jewish community" and "settler state" seeking "Biblical justification for crimes against humanity."[22]

As Soviet support of anti-Western guerrilla movements waned, and the Catholic Church formally condemned liberation theologians, the movement withered. This created an intellectual vacuum that was filled by Palestinian Christians, who developed their own theology, casting the war against Zionism as part of the larger struggle against capitalism, imperialism, and Eurocentrism.

Ironically, because there are so few Palestinian Christians, Palestinian liberation theology is more popular among Western, especially Protestant, churches, which have had a longtime presence in the region. It is appealing because it makes the case for the Palestinians based on an "ideology of resistance of injustice" and the claim that God has "an overriding concern with the poor and the oppressed." One of the goals of these Christians is to reinterpret biblical references that both Christian and Jewish Zionists see as supporting the religious claim to Israel. In the process, notes Adam Gregerman of the Institute for Christian and Jewish Studies, they have begun to reintroduce "some of the ancient anti-Jewish teachings that Western Christians have been working for decades to discard or alter."[23]

Oddly, the groups that advertise themselves as peace organizations were unsupportive of the first negotiated treaty between Israel and an Arab state. The NCC, for example, denounced the agreement for ignoring the national ambitions of the Palestinians.[24]

The NCC has taken consistently anti-Israel stands. During the Arab-Israeli War of 1973, when Israel was attacked by Arab armies on Yom Kippur, the NCC, unwilling to blame Egypt and Syria for starting the hostilities, held a meeting that was punctuated by anti-Semitic speeches. A resolution was adopted that was meant to be evenhanded but did not criticize Egypt and Syria's actions. As early as 1980, the group called for the creation of a PLO state. In the 1980s, Aramco subsidized a special Middle East newsletter critical of Israel called *SWASIA (Southwest Asia)*, which was distributed by the NCC. Besides passing anti-Israel resolutions, the NCC puts on seminars, radio shows, and conferences. In recent years, Presbyterians have been at the forefront of efforts to divest from Israel. The Reverend Isaac Rottenberg wrote in the *New York Times* on May 24, 1978, that "a persistent anti-Israel propaganda campaign" was waged in the council, and that "every NCC Governing Board meeting has been preceded by internal bureaucratic power plays aimed at criticizing Israel." Rottenberg added that whenever "concerns were raised in the Council about anti-Semitism, the Holocaust or the emergence of neo-Nazi movements, attempts have been made to trivialize or neutralize them."[25]

For many Christian groups, the treatment of the Palestinians by the Israelis was less a matter of a new theology than of simply pursuing justice and supporting the oppressed. Following the intifada (1987–91), however, Palestinian Christians did turn their activism into what they referred to as a Palestinian theology for national liberation. In their view, Israel does not exist in the Bible, and the Christians who believe in the restoration of the Jewish people to their homeland have been victims of a "manipulation of the Bible by the Jews." In the Palestinian conception, Jesus was a revolutionary, the founder of the intifada, and the Holy Land is the homeland of the Palestinians who lived there from time immemorial. The Bible used by Palestinian Christians has been mutilated. "All the passages considered unacceptable to Muslims have been eliminated from the Arab version. Entire generations of Palestinian Christians have grown up ignoring God's alliance with Israel and the Jewishness of Jesus, of the Madonna, of the Apostles. To them, they were all Arabs!"[26]

While these Christian theologians of liberation have been used to support Palestinian propaganda, their position has nevertheless become more precarious. The percentage of Christians in the Palestinian territories has declined precipitously, from 15 percent in 1950 to less than 2 percent today. Christians have also become increasingly concerned about the Islamization of life under Palestinian Muslim rule, especially in Gaza, where Hamas has begun to apply sharia law.

THE VATICAN'S EFFORTS TO CURB liberation theology had nothing to do with Israel, and its own policy remained largely unfriendly toward Israel and, in the view of Israelis, hypocritical. The most outrageous incident occurred in September 1982, after Israel invaded Lebanon to stop the PLO from menacing its northern border. After much bloodshed provoked by Yasser Arafat's terrorist organization, a deal was struck by which Arafat and his henchmen were to be expelled from Lebanon and exiled in Tunisia. Shockingly, the pope, who had been silent throughout the years of Lebanon's civil war, during which the Christian community had been devastated, invited Arafat to an audience in Rome. Israeli foreign minister Yitzhak

Shamir denounced the decision: "If the Pope is going to meet Arafat, it shows something about the moral standards of the Church." The Vatican responded harshly and, six years later, invited Arafat for another visit. In the interim, the pope declared that the Palestinians had "the natural right in justice to find once more a homeland and to be able to live in peace and tranquility with the other peoples in the area."[27]

While the Vatican had diplomatic relations with most of the Arab world, it continued to withhold recognition of Israel. Not until 1993 was an agreement signed for mutual recognition. It took several more years to fully implement the agreement. Finally, the Vatican also accepted Israel's control of Jerusalem in exchange for assurances that the holy places would be safeguarded.

In 2000, Pope John Paul II made a pilgrimage to Israel that contrasted sharply with the brief tour of John VI. The pope was warmly received throughout his visit, was greeted upon arrival by the chief rabbis and many of Israel's top public officials, and made highly publicized trips to Yad Vashem and the Western Wall. The goodwill generated by the trip had almost been undone before it started, when the pope met once again with Arafat a few weeks earlier and signed an agreement with the PLO supporting the Palestinian opposition to Israeli policies in Jerusalem. Ironically, when the pope visited Jerusalem, he was free to pray at Christian and Jewish shrines, but was prohibited by the mufti of Jerusalem from praying on the Temple Mount.

Pope Benedict visited Israel in 2009, but that visit was viewed more ambivalently. The government saw the visit as a step toward stronger ties, but the pope upset many Israelis by his failure to apologize on behalf of the Catholic Church or express remorse about the Holocaust, by his pointed criticism of Israel's security barrier, and by his calls for an end to restrictions placed on the Gaza Strip as a result of Hamas terror attacks and for international pressure to establish a Palestinian state.

While liberation theology has fallen out of favor with the Vatican, groups committed to Palestinian "liberation" have remained vocal.

One of the most active Christian organizations on behalf of the Arab cause today is the Sabeel Ecumenical Liberation Theology Center. Founded in 1989 and led by Naim Ateek, Sabeel is an Arab Christian nongovernmental organization based in Jerusalem that "strives to empower the Palestinian community as a whole and to develop the internal strengths needed for participation in building a better world for all." The organization is also outspoken in its criticism of Israel and its government. It has been one of the main coordinators for anti-Israeli advocacy among U.S. churches and a leading proponent of divestment from Israel. Several Protestant church groups that have expressed support for divesting from Israel, such as the World Council of Churches, the Anglican Church of Britain, and the Presbyterian Church, quote Sabeel publications in their divestment statements.

Sabeel also supports a "one state solution, two nations and three religions," meaning that it advocates the dismantling of Israel as a Jewish state. "Indeed," claims its publication *Cornerstone*, "the ideal and best solution has always been to envisage ultimately a bi-national state in Palestine-Israel where people are free and equal."

Sabeel considers Christian Zionists heretics: "We categorically reject Christian Zionist doctrines as a false teaching that undermines the biblical message of love, mercy and justice." While Sabeel presents itself as a pro-peace Christian group invested in the Palestinian cause, its publications, conferences, and Web site are platforms for extremist anti-Israel views.

Another organization that agitates against Israel is Churches for Middle East Peace (CMEP), a coalition of twenty-two Orthodox, Protestant, Anglican, and Catholic church bodies. The group includes mainline churches and groups such as the Presbyterian Church, the United Methodist Church, the American Friends Service Committee (AFSC), and the National Council of Churches. CMEP consistently engages in one-sided advocacy, eschewing criticism of Arab behavior and ignoring the treatment of Christians in Arab lands. In fact, the group went so far as to suggest that Islamist groups have not been a problem for Palestinian Christians, and that Christian-Muslim relations are congenial despite the fact that Hamas was driving Christians out of Gaza and that even the more "moderate" Muslims in the West Bank persecuted Christians.

CMEP routinely criticizes Israel and calls for punishment for building settlements, opposes loan guarantees for the absorption of immigrants, objects to the unification of Jerusalem, and favors cutting aid to Israel. CMEP has been especially critical of Israeli policy in Jerusalem; it advocates international guarantees of access (which Israel already ensures) and calls for the city to be shared by Israel and the Palestinians. On the eve of Secretary of State Hillary Clinton's first trip to Israel in March 2009, CMEP sent a letter to Clinton that mentions the need to hold both sides "accountable for their obligations," but focuses only on Israel and the group's insistence that Israel freeze all settlement activity.[28]

The 1993 Oslo Accords and subsequent peace negotiations reinvigorated support from moderate Christian leaders for the Palestinians. In 1995, for example, the president of the National Council of Catholic Bishops, William Keeler, outlined a series of issues he said would undermine the peace process that focused on Israel and U.S. support for Israeli positions: "Israel's expropriation of Palestinian land; Israel's plans for 'Greater Jerusalem'; Israelis' implicit claim to exclusive sovereignty over Jerusalem; recent U.S. hedging over the issue of East Jerusalem, which previous administrations have considered occupied territory subject to UN Security Council Resolution 242 and total Israeli withdrawal; and the failure of U.S. policy to recognize and support Palestinian rights and interests in Jerusalem."[29]

The bottom line for Christians in the Arab lobby since at least 1967 has been that recognition of Israel's sovereignty is contingent on first settling the Palestinian refugee problem, complete Israeli withdrawal from the territories captured in 1967, and the establishment of a Palestinian state in the West Bank and Gaza with Jerusalem as its capital. The Israeli lobby position is precisely the reverse: the Arab states must first recognize Israel's right to exist within secure and defensible borders before Israel makes seemingly irrevocable and dangerous territorial concessions.

One tactic adopted by Christian groups to punish Israel and try to coerce a change in policy is to support boycotts, divestment, and sanctions. In 2004 the Presbyterian Church voted to begin divesting from companies it said were benefiting from Israeli "occupation." This was followed by similar moves by the Episcopal Church, the United Methodist Church, and the World Council of Churches. In July 2005 the United Church of Christ voted for a more limited proposal calling for "multiple, non-violent strategies, including economic leverage, to promote peace in the Middle East." Meanwhile, no such coercive measures are proposed to pressure the Palestinians or Arab states to recognize Israel or offer concessions for peace.

Ultimately, while the divestment issue continues to be raised by anti-Israel members of the church groups in an effort to embarrass, isolate, and delegitimize Israel, the majority of the membership has opposed the move. For example, in May 2008, Methodists overwhelmingly defeated proposals for divestment. Meanwhile, none of the U.S. churches have actually carried out any significant divestment; in 2006 the Presbyterians rescinded their divestment plan, and they rejected calls in 2008 to readopt it. In 2009 the Episcopal Church held its annual convention and a one-sided resolution was introduced that called for the dismantling of the security barrier, a just resolution to the Palestinian refugee issue, and an end to a variety of Israeli policies. The House of Bishops rejected the resolution by a narrow vote as opponents insisted on a more balanced approach.

Mainstream Presbyterians tried to mend fences with the Jewish community in 2008 when they drafted a document, "Vigilance against Anti-Jewish Ideas and Bias," that outlined many of the church's troublesome actions and writings, such as the 2004 overture "Confronting Christian Zionism," which suggested that "the Jewish people are no longer in covenant with God" and repeated the medieval Christian notion that Jews were responsible for the crucifixion of Christ. The document admitted that the church sometimes misrepresented the Zionist movement and that its analysis of the Israeli-Palestinian conflict sometimes "employs language or draws on sources that have anti-Jewish overtones, or clearly makes use of classic Christian anti-Jewish ideas" that "cloud complicated issues with the rhetoric of ignorance."

Jewish organizations applauded the statement, but it was subsequently revised and "infused with the very bias that the original statement condemned." The document was changed, for example, to suggest that the biblical promise of the land of Israel to the Jewish people was actually a promise made to the Jews "and to all the descendants of Abraham," including Palestinian Arabs.[30]

Many of these groups continue to seek ways to promote the Arab cause at Israel's expense, and often seem intent on provoking the Jewish community and Israel. A good example occurred on September 25, 2008, when the Mennonite Central Committee, the Quakers, the World Council of Churches, Religions for Peace, and the American Friends Service Committee sponsored a meeting with Iranian president Mahmoud Ahmadinejad. This occurred at the height of protests against his appearance at the UN and amid renewed efforts by the international community to impose sanctions on Iran for its refusal to comply with previous Security Council resolutions and ongoing pursuit of nuclear weapons. Ahmadinejad had already earned a reputation for being perhaps the world's most anti-Israel leader after threatening to destroy Israel and repeatedly denying the Holocaust. Iran under the ayatollahs has also become known for its persecution of religious minorities. Despite the record, these groups, which ordinarily oppose nuclear weapons and advocate religious freedom, chose to give their imprimatur to the Iranian leader.

A World Council of Churches official said the event "demonstrated both the power and potential of religious leaders contributing to peace." By contrast, in a rare instance of siding with the Israeli lobby, NCC head Michael Kinnamon released a statement saying, "President Ahmadinejad's hateful language, denying the Holocaust and apparently calling for Israel to be 'wiped off the map,' must be persistently and forcefully denounced by all who value peace."

The hallmark of the Christian component of the Arab lobby is hypocrisy. Like Arab American groups, Christian elements of the Arab lobby, despite their flowery rhetoric about peace and justice, have difficulty making simple declarative statements condemning Palestinian terrorism. When terrorists were hijacking planes or killing Israeli athletes, or more recently, when suicide bombers and Qassam rockets killed Israeli civilians, the Christian groups were usually silent, yet they would not hesitate to condemn Israel for both real and imagined sins against Arabs as well as any Israeli actions to defend their citizens.

In 2006, the WCC Executive Committee launched a one-sided attack on Israeli policy that it said was consistent with six decades of policy toward the conflict. This was shortly after Palestinian elections brought the terrorist group Hamas to power, which the WCC called "legitimately elected leaders."[31] Rather than celebrate Israel's sixtieth anniversary in 2008, the WCC organized "a collective public witness for peace" on five continents and highlighted the "disintegration of Palestinian society and dispersal of some 750,000 Palestinians as refugees."

The Christians of the Arab lobby do not even speak out on behalf of their coreligionists. In addition to Lebanon, where the sizable Christian minority has gradually lost power as the population has fled to escape Muslim persecution and the oppression of first the PLO, then the Syrians, and now Hezbollah, smaller Christian communities that are even more vulnerable have not gained any more sympathy. The Arab lobby even refuses to condemn abuses in countries such as Saudi Arabia, which have never allowed Christians to practice their faith. The AFSC, which received financial support from Aramco, was quick to express concern for Palestinian refugees but uninterested in slavery in Saudi Arabia or the discriminatory treatment of Aramco's Saudi employees.

The attitudes of the anti-Israel Christians stand in stark contrast to the vigorous support for Israel expressed by Christian Zionists, especially among the evangelical community. Professor Paul Merkley offers the following explanation for the dramatic difference in views:

> The history of the relations between the Church and Israel has been shaped by the fact that, somewhere along the line since the war for Israel's independence in 1948–49, most official spokesmen of most of the churches reworked the moral

arithmetic and came to find more "justice" in the claims of the Palestinian Arabs and less in the cause of Israel than they saw in 1947. In contrast, most Christians who define themselves as theologically conservative have remained constant in their preference for Israel's claims. That is because for "Christian Zionists" the case for the Restoration of the Jews in the first place, even though it was manifestly defensible in terms of "justice," actually stood upon a firmer ground: namely, that it was predicted and ordained by scripture.[32]

The Christian anti-Zionists believe that the use of theology to justify the existence of Israel by evangelical supporters of Israel is nothing short of "heresy."

One of the leading representatives of this school of thought is Jimmy Carter. When he was running for office, and later as president, Carter would often cite the Bible and his Christian beliefs as a basis for his sympathy for Israel and the Jewish people. He was never a Christian Zionist, however, and Merkley argues that at least since 1985 he has become "*a champion of Christian anti-Zionism.*"[33] In particular, he adopted the equivalence of the Jewish and Arab narratives and accepted the historically specious claim popularized by the Middle East Council of Churches that the Palestinians are descendants of the Canaanites and the other original peoples of Palestine.

Despite the large numbers of evangelicals, and the widespread perception of the disproportionate influence of Jews in electoral politics, Rabbi Gary Greenebaum, director of Interreligious Affairs for the American Jewish Committee, notes that "the mainline churches are still important because they have elected all but four presidents, including Obama, who is from a UCC background, and a disproportionate number of members of Congress." These groups disseminate publications around the world and put on a tremendous number of programs. So many Palestinians visit and speak at mainline churches, churchgoers are inevitably influenced by the anti-Israel rhetoric they hear.

Joseph Stalin once dismissively asked, "How many divisions does the Pope have?" Israel and its supporters have been far more respectful in their assessment of the overall Christian challenge to the state's legitimacy and policies. Though by no means a monolith, many elements of the Christian world remain uncomfortable with the idea of a Jewish state and disturbed by Israeli actions that are acceptable (or at least tolerated) when carried out by other states but unreasonable when undertaken by Jews. By often siding with Israel's most vociferous critics, some clergy have created a halo around many individuals and organizations that apply double standards to Israel's behavior, demonize the Jewish state, and attempt to delegitimize it.

CHAPTER THIRTEEN

The Diplomatic Alumni Network: The Lobby's Revolving Door

One of the Arab lobby's strengths is that many of its members work inside the government, whereas the Israeli lobby must typically exert influence from outside. Moreover, when these people retire, they use their contacts and the cachet of their former positions to continue to do the work of the lobby, and do so with an added veneer of credibility. Arab lobbyists in the private sector are well compensated; they can get lucrative positions in lobbying firms, land prestigious jobs at think tanks and universities, and become regulars on the lecture circuit and as media pundits. They can also exploit their expertise to set up commercial interests in the Arab world, serve on corporate and nonprofit boards of companies and organizations related to the Middle East, and find high-paying jobs in oil, defense, and other industries with interests in the region. Given the potential of these post-retirement opportunities, it would not be surprising if officials adopted positions while in government to make themselves marketable to the Arab lobby.

Undersecretary of state George Ball made the case during hearings on foreign lobbying in 1963 that the State Department benefits from lobbying. "American lobbyists for foreign interests were in a better position than their clients or policy makers, he believed, to call attention to the impact of legislation on their clients' countries and thus on U.S. foreign relations." On the other hand, as Deborah Levy, a lawyer for Wilmer, Cutler & Pickering, also notes, "foreign interests, by hiring former officials, may gain an advantage they ought not to enjoy . . . and, even more troubling, incumbent officials, knowing that they may be for sale to the highest foreign bidder after they leave office, may not aggressively protect U.S. interests when dealing with foreigners." Senator David Boren (D-OK) was even more explicit, declaring that Washington lobbyists hired by foreign interests present "a real threat to our national security and interests in trade, defense, and foreign policy."[1]

Diplomats naturally think about what they might do after leaving government, and they have learned that their former clients can become generous employers. Saudi ambassador Bandar put it bluntly: "If the reputation then builds that the Saudis take care of friends when they leave office," he said, "you'd be surprised how much better friends you have who are just coming into office."[2]

The Saudis have applied this philosophy to presidents and presidential candidates as well as bureaucrats. Jimmy Carter is by no means the only president to be rewarded by the kingdom. For example, the Saudis contributed $1.5 million to charities affiliated with George H. W. Bush, including his high school, Phillips Academy. They contributed $1 million to George H. W. Bush's presidential library (Kuwait, Oman, and the United Arab Emirates also contributed) and pledged $1 million to George W. Bush's eventual presidential library. At the suggestion of Ambassador Bandar, King Fahd also kicked in $1 million for Barbara Bush's campaign against illiteracy (he had earlier donated a similar amount to Nancy Reagan's campaign against drugs). Bush Sr. also received money for his library from Kuwait, Oman, and the United Arab Emirates.[3]

The Saudis did not get all they bargained for, however, when they approved Bill Clinton's 1991 request to create a Middle East studies program at the University of Arkansas. Clinton had been seeking funding from the Saudis since 1989 without success. After he was elected president, the university received $3 million as "a gesture of respect" for the Arkansas governor. Two weeks after his inauguration, the university received another $20 million. When he became president, Clinton turned out to be the most pro-Israel president in history. Though that may have rankled the Saudis, he still succeeded, contrary to Arabist opinion, in maintaining good ties with the Saudis and other Arabs. They were sufficiently happy with his presidency— or hopeful of winning favor in the event that Hillary reached the White House—that Clinton's $165 million presidential library received donations of approximately $10 million from the Saudi royal family. The governments of Dubai, Kuwait, the United Arab Emirates, and Qatar also contributed. Middle Eastern business executives and officials who gave at least $1 million include Saudi businessmen Abdullah al-Dabbagh, Nasser al-Rashid, and Walid Juffali, as well as Issam Fares, the former deputy prime minister of Lebanon. The William J. Clinton Foundation has also benefited from the largesse of the Saudis. The kingdom was listed as donating between $10 and $25 million. Oman, Qatar, the ruling family of Abu Dhabi and the Dubai Foundation (both based in the United Arab Emirates), and the Friends of Saudi Arabia, founded by a Saudi prince, all gave more than $1 million.[4]

The employment of former government officials serves the Arab lobby in a number of ways. These officials have valuable experience and can offer advice to their clients on how to manipulate the levers of power, provide insight into U.S. policy and policy makers, and use the contacts they've developed in their government careers to gain access to decision makers. They are also effective propagandists; the media call on them as former officials to comment on Middle East affairs and usually treat them as nonpartisan experts rather than paid spokespeople for Arab interests.

The revolving-door problem is certainly not unique to foreign policy; government officials from regulatory agencies, for example, frequently go to work for the industries they once regulated. The difference is that those relationships rarely affect U.S. national security. Charles Lewis, executive director of the Center for Public Integrity, a Washington-based government watchdog group, observed that the cozy relations between former officials and the Saudis have helped to quiet criticism of the kingdom's role in terrorism. "The chances to cash in and the amount you can cash in for are starting to become absolutely astronomical," Lewis said. "Who wants to look like the Boy Scout complaining about it and potentially jeopardize their own post-employment prospects?"[5]

Consider the case of Michael Deaver, former Reagan White House deputy chief of staff. Deaver earned $70,200 as one of the president's top advisers. A *Time* magazine story on Washington lobbyists disclosed that when he left the White House, he earned $400,000 as a public affairs consultant. After the story was published, the Saudis signed Deaver's firm as one of its agents with a $500,000 annual retainer.[6]

Former defense secretary William Cohen is a case study of the revolving door from government official to well-compensated special interest lobbyist. The *Washington Post* reported how he was saddled with credit card debt for more than thirty years in politics; but "within weeks of leaving office, he was living in a $3.5 million McLean mansion with a swimming pool, a cabana and a carriage house."[7] Cohen formed a consulting and lobbying firm, the Cohen Group, to work for some of the largest defense contractors, among other clients. Other members of the firm include Joseph Ralston, former vice chairman of the Joint Chiefs of Staff; James Loy, former deputy secretary of homeland security; and Marc Grossman, a former undersecretary of state. On the company's Web site, they list the Middle East as an area of expertise with a photo of Cohen shaking hands with the king of Saudi Arabia. The site states that "as Congressman, Senator, and Secretary of Defense, Secretary Cohen visited the region on numerous occasions and established close and enduring relationships with the region's key leaders." It also touts the diplomatic credentials of other former government officials working for the firm.[8]

According to lobbyist disclosure documents, the Cohen Group represents Lockheed Martin, Pratt & Whitney, Sikorsky Aircraft, Rolls-Royce North America, and General Dynamics. Given Cohen's connections, it was not surprising that he would tell participants at the Herzliya Conference in April 2008 that Israel should not be worried if the United States made large arms sales to Arab states. "President Bush has proposed a $20 billion armaments package to the Gulf. I think we should go through with this package because if we fail to, other nations like China, Russia, and France, won't hesitate to do so in our place. If we, the U.S. do it, we can assure the security of Israel, as well as other interests, much more so than if not." One of the most controversial components of the proposed sale were JDAMs, highly accurate smart bombs that are supplied by Lockheed Martin, which is represented by the Cohen Group, a fact he did not disclose to his audience.[9]

Many other top officials have provided their services to the Arab lobby. One of the most ironic twists was that Clark Clifford, the political adviser who played perhaps the most important role in influencing President Truman to support partition and recognize Israel, later became a consultant to various Arab governments and investors. Another irony is that the former director of the FBI, Louis Freeh, who complained about Saudi stonewalling of terror investigations, is now being paid to defend Prince Bandar against the $2 billion corruption charges he faces in connection with his role in arms dealing.[10]

While State Department Arabists have been the most common government officials to go through the revolving door, a number of top Treasury Department officials have also joined the Arab lobby. For example, former treasury secretary William Simon, who negotiated the secret deal with the Saudis to conceal their investments, became a consultant and later chairman of Crescent Diversified, Ltd., the American investment company started by Saudi billionaire Suliman S. Olayan.[11] Simon was succeeded at Crescent by Carter's treasury secretary, Michael Blumenthal, who was one of the key figures in the discussions about the sale of F-15s to the Saudis. In addition to Crescent, he also was chairman of another of Olayan's investment companies, Gentrol. Simon's assistant for monetary affairs, Gerald Parsky, who helped set up the Joint Saudi Economic Commission, went to work for Gibson Dunn & Crutcher, where he was hired as a foreign agent for Saudi Arabia and the UAE. The firm later opened an office in Riyadh and picked up the Saudi Public Transportation Company and the University of Riyadh as clients.

Another former Treasury secretary from the Nixon era, John Connally, became a consultant and also invested money with wealthy Saudis to purchase a controlling interest in the Main Bank in Houston. When he decided to run for president, Connally proposed a Middle East peace plan that linked Israeli concessions to stabilizing oil prices and parroted Arab lobby calls for Israeli withdrawal from the disputed territories, creation of a Palestinian state, and dismantling of settlements.

The revolving door ensures that the Saudis will always have some of America's most politically astute and well-connected individuals working for them outside of government and attuned to their interests while serving in the government. Brent Scowcroft, for example, the former national security adviser under George H. W. Bush, runs a firm that analyzes oil and energy companies, and was on the board of Pennzoil–Quaker State. Scowcroft frequently comments on Middle East affairs and is not considered a friend of Israel. He is, however, a booster for the Saudis. Scowcroft told an interviewer in October 2001 that Osama bin Laden was probably more dangerous to the Saudis than to the United States, and that he saw no "problem with Wahhabism, as long as it is not engaged in terrorism." Rand analyst Laurent Murawiec calls him the "honorary chairman of the Saudi lobby in Washington."[12]

Former CIA officials also have spun through the revolving door into lucrative deals with the Saudis. One of the most interesting is Raymond Close, the former station chief in Riyadh, who started a business relationship with Saudi intelligence chief Kamal Adham. "On the day he retired from the CIA, Ray walked across the street and joined Kamal Adham in a business relationship," according to another former CIA officer, Duane Clarridge. "To many officers in the CIA this seemed untoward because, as a government official, he had an official relationship with Kamal Adham. Now he was in a commercial relationship which over the years reportedly made Close a very wealthy man." In addition to setting up a consulting firm to do business with Saudi Arabia, Close also worked with the Faisal Foundation, the royal family's fund for medical research and philanthropy. Close's son Kenneth is also a registered agent for Saudi Arabia. Close has been a frequent critic of Israel, accusing the Israelis, for example, of disproportionate retaliation to "resistance" by the Palestinians for more than half a century. Given his background, it was not too surprising to learn that when Close served as an adviser to the Baker-Hamilton commission tasked in 2006 with making recommendations regarding Iraq, he called for "significant modifications" in Israel's position and suggested that the United States might have to "put pressure on Israel to make territorial concessions in the Golan."[13]

Michael Scheuer spent twenty-two years at the CIA and has become a frequent critic of Israel since his retirement. In June 2009, Scheuer told Glenn Beck, "The only chance we have as a country right now is for Osama bin Laden to deploy and detonate a major weapon in the United States." He became a senior fellow at the Jamestown Foundation, but said he was forced out because of his anti-Israel views.[14] Another former CIA officer, Philip Giraldi, became famous for claiming in 2005 that the United States was preparing plans to attack Iran with nuclear weapons in response to a terrorist attack against the United States. He has also become an outspoken critic of Israel, claiming, for example, that Israel is trying to convince the United States to attack Iran, and that the Israeli-occupied media are abetting them. He is presently a partner in an international security consultancy, Cannistraro Associates.[15]

Some of the figures involved in the Iran-Contra scandal apparently recognized that Saudi largesse could benefit not only foreign guerrillas but also their own careers. Charles Tyson, a member of the National Security Council, for example, went to work for Saudi arms merchant Adnan Khashoggi. Oliver North's supervisor at the NSC, Robert Lilac, cashed in his position as director for political military affairs for a job consulting for Saudi ambassador Bandar. The former deputy assistant secretary of defense, Richard Secord, who played a key role in negotiating and lobbying for the AWACS sale, reportedly became an arms broker for the Saudis and the Contras.[16]

One of the most influential facilitators for the Arab lobby is the Carlyle Group, which helped Prince Talal grab a $590 million stake in Citicorp, making him the largest individual shareholder. In addition to founder David Rubenstein, a former Carter domestic policy adviser, and longtime chairman Frank Carlucci, a former defense secretary, the investment company boasts the former budget director, Richard Darman, and secretary of state, James Baker, in the George H. W. Bush administration, as partner and special adviser, respectively. Bush himself has served as a conduit between the company and Arab leaders and investors. Bush, Baker, and former British prime minister John Major went to Saudi Arabia on behalf of Carlyle to drum up business, for example, and a source told the *Financial Times* that when the two leaders who "saved the Saudis' ass in the Gulf War" came in, the companies they were representing "are going to have it pretty good."[17]

Not surprisingly, Carlyle benefited from investments from individual Saudis as well as government contracts to companies owned by the group. Vinnell, for example, received a $163 million contract to modernize the Saudi National Guard, and Vought Aircraft, makers of tail sections of aircraft, received a portion of the $6 billion contract for fifty commercial aircraft. Carlyle had a controlling stake in BDM International, which received $50 million annually in the 1990s to provide training and logistical services to the Saudi National Guard. For some years the Carlyle Group advised the Saudis on an "economic offset program," whereby U.S. arms manufacturers selling weapons to the Saudis had to give back a portion of their revenues in the form of contracts to Saudi companies that inevitably were owned or somehow connected to the royal family. Because Carlyle is a private company, the public does not know how much of its money comes from Saudi or other foreign investors.[18]

The investments flow in both directions, as Prince Bandar and his father, Prince Sultan, the Saudi defense minister, have put money into Carlyle. Another investor became more of an embarrassment after 9/11, however, when it was disclosed that the bin Laden family had put at least $2 million into the company. After the attacks, Carlyle severed its ties with the bin Laden Group.

Another former government official we met earlier, Robert Gray served in the Eisenhower administration before becoming the chief lobbyist for Hill & Knowlton and later starting his own lobbying firm. In 1986, Gray's firm merged with JTW Group and its Hill & Knowlton subsidary, which Gray chaired. Gray hired a number of former officials and became involved early on with the Kuwait Petroleum Company after questions were raised about its purchase of an American company that owned a nuclear technology subsidiary. He was subsequently hired by the group organized by the wife of the Saudi ambassador to conduct the campaign condemning Israel's 1982 military operation in Lebanon. He used the high profile of that anti-Israel effort to solicit other Arab lobby clients, such as the NAAA, with the pitch that he could help weaken public support for Israel. Gray did some work for the NAAA before ending his relationship with the group because he found them "too strident." Gray then reportedly met with the Israeli ambassador to the United States, Moshe Arens, and assured him he held no animus toward Israel and wouldn't engage in any more anti-Israel campaigns. He said this even as he was circulating another proposal to the Arabs, "A Strategy to Improve Perceptions of Arabs in the United States," which suggested that a Jewish conspiracy controlled U.S. policy and that he could develop a campaign to improve the Arabs' standing in the United States. In 1982, he received a $100,000 contract from Prince Talal Abdul Aziz ibn Saud. He later received another six-figure payment to help the League of Arab States. In 1984, Gray stopped working on projects related to the Arab-Israeli conflict.

Gray's lobbying firm is typical of many that seem to be interested primarily in their clients' ability to pay and not in their politics. They are not necessarily anti-Israel, just hired guns. Thus, for example, while Gray was representing the staunchly anti-Communist Saudis, he was also lobbying on behalf of the widely reviled Marxist government of Angola.

Qorvis, the firm that does most of the Saudis' PR work, also has its share of officials with government connections. The account was handled, for example, by Jack Deschauer, a former legislative counsel for the U.S. Navy during the George H. W. Bush administration, and Ed Newbury, a former aide to Rep. Frank Wolf (R-VA). In 2006, Qorvis retained the services of Les Janka, a former member of the NSC staff, special assistant to Henry Kissinger, deputy press secretary under Reagan, and deputy assistant secretary of defense.

One of the best known pro-Arab lobbyists was Fred Dutton, a former assistant secretary for legislative affairs and special assistant to President Kennedy, and an adviser to Robert and Edward Kennedy. He also worked on the presidential campaigns of Hubert Humphrey and George McGovern. Dutton's wife did legal work for the Saudi embassy. He advised Mobil Oil in the early 1970s to buy an ad on newspaper op-ed pages to argue a single topic, which frequently related to Middle East affairs, and thus gave birth to the corporate advertorial.

Senator J. William Fulbright, a persistent critic of Israel in the Senate, where he chaired the Foreign Relations Committee, first suggested to Dutton that he consider representing the Saudis, who needed help with their image after the oil embargo. The oil companies also were looking to disentangle themselves from the job of advising the Saudis on political matters. The Saudis had approached several well-known Washington operatives, but none wanted the job. Dutton reportedly was hesitant out of fear it would hurt his relations with pro-Israel Democrats, but he went ahead anyway and provided the Saudis in 1974 with a "Public Affairs Program for the Arab World," which outlined a strategy for "manipulating American public opinion, the press and the political process." The program called for an effort to defeat six senators viewed as hostile to the Saudis and an advertising campaign in major media outlets to promote the Saudis' agenda.

A year later, Dutton registered as a foreign agent of Saudi Arabia. One of his first assignments was to arrange meetings for Saudi officials to lobby against the antiboycott legislation. Later, he spearheaded the AWACS campaign and conceived the "Reagan vs. Begin" angle. He arranged for Saudis to appear on the major television networks and meet with newspaper editors and performed similar public relations tasks, as well as crisis management, for more than thirty years, earning the moniker "Fred of Arabia." During that time he collected millions of dollars in fees from the Saudis without any serious impact on his broader political ties.

After being defeated for reelection, Dutton's patron, Senator Fulbright, was hired by the Washington law firm of Hogan and Hartson and soon became an agent for the UAE and the Saudis. The Saudis paid Fulbright a $50,000 annual retainer to personally provide "counsel and guidance in connection with the laws and policies of the United States, possible Congressional or other action affecting these, as well as commercial and other ventures, and what steps might be appropriate and proper for us to consider from time to time."[19]

Fulbright is one of many former members of Congress and their staffs who have joined former executive-branch officials as lobbyists and consultants. A number of these officials, such as James Abourezk and Mary Rose Oakar, have started or joined Arab American organizations.

Another former member of Congress who became actively involved in the Arab lobby, though he is not of Arab descent, is Paul Findley. A Democrat from Illinois, Findley was considered one of the most unfriendly members by the Israeli lobby, and an effort was made to defeat him when he ran for reelection in 1982. As previously explained, Findley's district suffered from a high unemployment rate, and had been gerrymandered to his disadvantage, but he blamed the Israeli lobby when he was defeated. Along with another disgruntled pro-Arab former congressman, Paul McCloskey, he then established the Council for the National Interest (CNI), which is devoted to undermining the U.S.-Israel relationship and promoting the Arab lobby agenda. The current president of CNI is Eugene Bird, a twenty-three-year State Department veteran who served as counselor in the U.S. embassy in Saudi Arabia, among other Middle East posts. The description of CNI begins with the following statement from Findley: "The United States provides the support without which Israel could not maintain its repression of human rights and its territorial expansion. This collusive relationship severely damages the U.S. influence and credibility worldwide. It has led our government into a disgraceful practice of turning a blind eye to Israeli violations of both international and U.S. law, a habit widely noted by foreign leaders." The group's mission, to "repair the damage being done to our political institutions by the over-zealous tactics of Israel's lobby," has made CNI one of the most visible of Israel's detractors.[20]

Not surprisingly, after leaving the Foreign Service, many Arabists became advocates for the Arab cause. Many were true believers who remained convinced that American interests were best served by close ties to the Arab world and undermined by the special relationship with Israel. Some were bitter about how they were treated, especially when the Arabists began to lose influence to pro-Israel political appointees and peace processors. Others were outraged by what they claimed was the disproportionate and nefarious influence of domestic politics on foreign policy making and, especially, the role of AIPAC. Still others found it profitable to become part of the Arab lobby because they could receive handsome paychecks from Arab governments and companies doing business in the Middle East. They could also count on finding positions at prestigious scholarly and quasi-academic think tanks interested in promoting a pro-Arab point of view and being invited to join the lecture circuit to rail against Israel on college campuses and at events hosted by Arab lobby organizations. In some cases, officials embodied all of these elements.

William Eddy resigned over Truman's decision to support partition and, subsequently, became a consultant to Aramco in charge of organizing its anti-Zionist lobby. About the same time, two other men with close government connections also became involved with Aramco. One was Halford Hoskins, a Lebanese-educated American who had been a Middle East envoy for Roosevelt. Another was Samuel Kopper, a deputy director of NEA who resigned in 1951 because of Truman's Palestine policy. He became the chief aide to the chairman of Aramco and worked as an observer at the UN.

Marshall Wiley was a product of the American University of Beirut. A rarity among Arabists, he served in Israel in the mid-1950s but did not come away with a positive view of the Israelis. When he went to the AUB, he learned "the other side" of the story of the conflict and became more sympathetic to the Palestinians. He also became convinced of the harmful influence of the Israeli lobby. His personal experience further embittered him when he learned that Israel had bombed an Egyptian military base during the War of Attrition that was close to the school his children attended. Wiley retired from the Foreign Service in 1981 in large measure because he believed the incoming Reagan administration was too pro-Israel. He subsequently organized the U.S.-Iraq Business Forum with the help of Iraq's ambassador to the United States, Nizar Hamdoon. The forum charged major American corporations annual dues of $2,500 to $5,000 with the implicit purpose of opening doors to Saddam Hussein's Iraq. The forum became a "revolving door" for retired Arabists, and Wiley became an apologist for Saddam after his invasion of Kuwait.

Today, one of the advisers to Palestinian president Mahmoud Abbas is the former U.S. consul general for Jerusalem, Edward Abbington. One of Abbington's predecessors in Jerusalem, Philip Wilcox, is president of the anti-Israel NGO Foundation for Middle East Peace.

John West served as governor of South Carolina before becoming the first noncareer Foreign Service diplomat to be appointed ambassador to Saudi Arabia. West was in Riyadh at the critical time of the Camp David negotiations when the support of the Saudis, which had been promised to President Carter, might have changed the history of the region by giving other Arab countries cover to join in talks with the Israelis and move toward a comprehensive peace. Instead, West had difficulty answering the question he said the Saudis asked him as to how they would benefit from supporting the peace process. He also was extremely critical of Egyptian president Anwar Sadat, the leader Carter idolized. Hermann Eilts, then ambassador to Egypt, complained that West was operating a "public relations firm for the Saudis." Toward that end, West became an apologist for the kingdom's human rights abuses as well as oil price hikes. After leaving the State Department, he established a consulting firm to help American companies do business with Saudi Arabia and created a foundation whose contributors included the head of the Saudi intelligence service, Prince Turki. He also became a prominent critic of Israel, accusing the Israelis in Lebanon, for example, of behaving toward the PLO the way Hitler treated the Jews.

Henry Byroade, one of the most vitriolic opponents of Israel among the Arabists, retired when Carter came into office after having served as ambassador to six countries. He became vice president for Saudi Arabia of Northrop and was based in Riyadh for two years.

Talcott Seelye was an Arabist fixture at the State Department for more than three decades, during which time he served in Jordan, Kuwait, Saudi Arabia, Lebanon, Tunisia, Syria, and the NEA. He retired in 1981, but had not even left the embassy before telling the press his personal views on what the U.S. government should have been doing, notably replacing the Camp David process and establishing a relationship with the PLO, which at that time had not fulfilled the minimal steps the United States expected before opening a dialogue. He retired, according to the *Washington Post*, because the Reagan administration would not offer him a good position, and he blamed the Israeli lobby for sabotaging his chances by arguing he was too sympathetic to the Arabs. Not surprisingly, in his postretirement career Seelye became a leading figure in the Arabist alumni component of the Arab lobby and a frequent critic of Israel. He also became consultant to Rezayat America Inc., a Saudi-owned company that coordinated service contracts between American firms and the kingdom.

Chas Freeman served as ambassador to Saudi Arabia and fit the mold of the Arabist afflicted, as James Baker said, with "clientitis." He admitted, for example, that he spent a lot of time trying to resolve disputes over the failure of Saudis, especially members of the royal family, to meet contractual obligations to Americans. He blamed Jews for complicating U.S.-Saudi relations by alerting members of Congress to the Saudis' behavior. Of course, it was Freeman's job to support those Americans, but he viewed his role as avoiding irritants to the relationship. Thus, he also objected to the Bush administration's insistence that the Saudis pay a share of the costs of the 1991 Gulf War, in which U.S. troops likely saved them from being overrun by the Iraqis, because the demand was a "huge irritant" in his relationship with the monarchy.

Freeman became the president of the Saudi-supported Middle East Policy Council. He frequently speaks out on the Arab-Israeli conflict and makes ignorant claims such as "Israel's democracy denies full rights of citizenship to one-fifth of its inhabitants and any rights at all to the millions it rules in the occupied territories."[21] Freeman blamed right-wing Israeli governments, rather than the persistence of Palestinian terrorism, for undoing the Oslo Accords. Freeman also implicitly blamed Israel for 9/11, saying in 2006, "Americans need to be clear about the consequences of continuing our current counterproductive approaches to security in the Middle East. . . . We have paid heavily and often in treasure in the past for our unflinching support and unstinting subsidies of Israel's approach to managing its relations with the Arabs. Five years ago we began to pay with the blood of our citizens here at home. We are now paying with the lives of our soldiers, sailors, airmen and marines on battlefields in several regions of the realm of Islam." Freeman denies he was blaming Israel for 9/11, but says Israel's actions toward the Palestinians have "helped to create an atmosphere first in the Arab world and now through all of Islam, in which anti-Americanism flourishes."[22]

Freeman's comments and business interests caught up to him in 2009, when he was appointed chair of the National Intelligence Council and, not surprisingly, provoked opposition from a wide range of people, including several members of Congress, who called for a review of Freeman's ties to foreign governments. While his defenders argued that he was being targeted because he had the courage to speak out against Israel, one of his harshest critics, Rep. Frank Wolf (R-VA), did not even mention Israel in explaining why he opposed Freeman's appointment. Wolf and Speaker of the House Nancy Pelosi were far more concerned with his statements and activities related to China. Freeman served on the advisory board of the government-owned Chinese National Offshore Oil Co. This affiliation and controversial comments he made regarding the Tiananmen Square massacre are what elicited the most serious objections to his appointment.

Freeman was quick to blame the Israeli lobby for derailing his appointment, a charge the *Washington Post* called a "grotesque libel." In fact, the American Israel Public Affairs Committee never took a formal position on Freeman's appointment, and numerous members of Congress, both Republicans and Democrats, questioned whether someone who "headed a Saudi-funded Middle East advocacy group in Washington and served on the advisory board of a state-owned Chinese oil company" was the right choice to the chairmanship responsible for reviewing intelligence agencies' analysis and preparing intelligence reports for the new administration.[23]

The *Washington Post* rejected Freeman's contention that American policy is somehow dictated by Israeli leaders. "That will certainly be news to Israel's 'ruling faction,' which in the past few years alone has seen the U.S. government promote a Palestinian election that it opposed; refuse it weapons it might have used for an attack on Iran's nuclear facilities; and adopt a policy of direct negotiations with a regime that denies the Holocaust and that promises to wipe Israel off the map. Two Israeli governments have been forced from office since the early 1990s after open clashes with Washington over matters such as settlement construction in the occupied territories." The *Post* noted that Freeman and "like-minded conspiracy theorists" ignore such facts. The paper also rejected Freeman's claim that Americans cannot discuss "Israel's nefarious influence," noting that "several of his allies have made themselves famous (and advanced their careers) by making such charges—and no doubt Mr. Freeman himself will now win plenty of admiring attention. Crackpot tirades such as his have always had an eager audience here and around the world." Freeman had been president of the Middle East Policy Council (MEPC) and was replaced by William Nash, the former chief of the Near East and South Asia division of the CIA. MEPC traces its origins to a group of former Foreign Service officers who served in Arab countries and who founded the American Arab Affairs Council. Its advisory committee included eleven American ambassadors, most of them prominent Arabists such as Andrew Killgore, Lucius Battle, Parker Hart, and Talcott Seelye. The group was subsidized by major corporations with business interests in the Middle East. That group is now the Middle East Policy Council, which publishes a journal, *Middle East Policy*, and has had on its board former defense secretary Frank Carlucci and Fuad Rihani, research and development director of the Saudi bin Laden Group.

MEPC is just one of a number of quasi-academic institutions and think tanks supported by Arab lobby interests seeking to buy credibility and influence policy makers through conferences, publications, lectures, media interviews, and trips to the region. These nonprofit organizations often claim to be nonpartisan, or as MEPC's mission statement says, "to ensure that a full range of U.S. interests and views are considered by policy makers." The full range, however, rarely includes the Israeli point of view. These groups are largely populated by former government officials, and many Arabists have found comfortable homes from which to advocate pro-Arab and, often, anti-Israel policies that were either ineffective or rejected by their bosses when they actually had the power to implement them.

One of the best known of these organizations is the Washington-based Middle East Institute (MEI), nicknamed "the chorus of the friends of Aramco." Founded in 1946 to promote understanding of the Arab world, the institute has received substantial support from Saudi Arabia, Aramco, and the oil industry and has had numerous former government officials and Arabists among its board members and directors. A current member is Michael Petruzzello, the CEO of Qorvis Communications, the Saudis' PR firm.[24]

MEI tends to have more balanced programs and publications than some Arab lobby–affiliated groups, but it is not known for having members with pro-Israel sympathies. On the contrary, it has historically been home to detractors. The organization has benefited from Saudi support, and the organization's directors, such as Ray Hare, who was succeeded by Parker Hart, have often served as ambassadors to the kingdom. Other directors, such as Lucius Battle, who used the MEI platform to criticize the press for its "sanctimonious and absolutely emotional" criticism of the oil embargo, were secretaries or undersecretaries of NEA.

Wyche Fowler Jr., a former congressman and ambassador to Saudi Arabia, is chairman of the MEI board. To get a sense of his views, when asked on CNN about the requirement that American women adhere to the Saudi dress code, Fowler replied, "They wear what my mother and sister always wore on Wednesday and Friday night. They wear what amounts to a choir robe."[25]

Edward Walker Jr., a former assistant secretary of state for NEA and ambassador to Egypt and Israel, served as president of MEI and is another apologist for Saudi Arabia; after 9/11, for example, he said, "We cannot condemn an entire people for the actions of a few of its citizens. . . . Saudi Arabia is far from the worst in comparison to the rest of the world." Near the height of Palestinian suicide bombings in Israel, Walker also defended the right of Palestinians to "resist occupation," though he opposed killing innocent civilians. "I do not think anyone considers the fights between the Israeli army and Palestinian fighters in occupied territories terrorism," he told the Arab newspaper *Jerusalem Times*. When he was asked whether it was legitimate to attack settlers, Walker said, "I believe women and children are not appropriate targets"—leaving open the question of whether men are.[26]

One person who had a particular animus toward Israel and never got over what he viewed as the mistakes of the State Department was Andrew Killgore. He spent more than three years doing "highly paid consulting" to help American companies doing business in the Gulf and to assist U.S. oil companies that did not yet have interests there get a foot in the door. He also organized the American Citizens Overseas Political Action Committee, and raised money from Americans living in Saudi Arabia to fund pro-Arab candidates running for Congress. Killgore and other former State Department officials and businesspeople created the American Educational Trust in 1982 as a means of expressing their views on the Middle East with a frequent anti-Israel emphasis. Killgore and Richard Curtiss, a former International Communications Agency and U.S. Information Agency official, put out the AET publication *Washington Report on Middle East Affairs*, which they dedicated to ensuring that "no Zionist statement go unchallenged." The publication often publishes attacks on the Israeli lobby, Zionism, and Israeli leaders and policies. It views Zionism as racism, supporters of Israel "collaborators" and "fifth-columnists," Congress as "Israeli occupied territory," and the media as dominated by Jews.[27]

After he retired, former Saudi ambassador James Akins became a popular spokesman for the Arab cause, regularly condemning Israel and repeatedly making dire predictions about the future of U.S. Middle East relations if more pro-Arab policies were not adopted, as when he said in 1979 that the Camp David Accords would likely spark a war in the region. A few years later, at the time of the AWACS debate, Akins appeared at an energy conference in which he claimed that the Saudis had responded positively to American requests to produce more oil, hold down oil prices, and defend the dollar. He also suggested that the Saudis would link oil production to the sale of AWACS. The suggestion that failure to appease the Saudis would have severe consequences would not have been an unusual position for an Arabist to take if not for the fact that the Saudi oil minister had spoken just before him and specifically said the arms sale was not tied to oil policy. In 1989, Akins and others asked the Federal Election Commission (FEC) to regulate the American Israel Public Affairs Committee (AIPAC) as a political committee. When the FEC rejected the request, Akins became the lead plaintiff in a lawsuit against the FEC, which went all the way to the U.S. Supreme Court, which ruled that the FEC had the authority to decide how to treat AIPAC.

The National Council on U.S.-Arab Relations was established in 1983 to improve American knowledge and understanding of the Arab world. Founder John Duke Anthony has also been involved in a number of other pro-Arab organizations and is a leading apologist for the Arab states. In a July 2007 interview with NPR, for example, he was asked about putting conditions on the sale of weapons to Saudi Arabia until they become more cooperative with American efforts in Iraq and stopping Saudis from going to fight against U.S. troops. Anthony said the number of Saudis fighting was "tinier than minuscule," they came from Syria and not Saudi Arabia, and were understandably fighting because they "rightly" believed their relatives and fellow tribal members were besieged. When asked to react to another guest's statement that after purchasing $117 billion worth of arms, the Saudis had not done anything to contribute to stability, Anthony gave the implausible answer that the Saudis had helped end the Iran-Iraq War, prevented the expansion of the Iranian revolution, and brought the Red Army to its knees in Afghanistan.[28] It's not surprising that he would defend the Saudis and the sale of arms to them, looking at the list of sponsors for the 2008 Arab-U.S. Policymakers Conference Anthony's group sponsored, which included Halliburton, Shell, Chevron, General Dynamics, BAE, Boeing, ExxonMobil, Raytheon, General Dynamics, Northrop Grumman, ConocoPhillips, and Aramco.

Another non-Arab organization that has spent the last four decades attacking Israel is Americans for Middle East Understanding (AMEU), which was created in 1968 by Aramco and has had on its board prominent Arabists such as James Akins and critics of Israel such as Paul Findley. The group has also received money from Prince Khalid bin Sultan, the Olayan Charitable Trust, and the World Muslim League. Its publication, the *Link*, routinely criticizes Israel.

For all of the effort and money spent, it is difficult to determine what real impact former government officials have had on U.S. policy. Clearly, the detractors of Israel have had no success to date in driving a wedge between the United States and Israel. Outside of promoting relations with the Gulf States in general, and the Saudis in particular, they have also done little to promote ties with the Arabs. Most, in fact, have no real interest in the rest of the Arab world, which is mostly poor and unable to pay for their services.

Unlike the Arab American and Muslim groups, this component of the lobby is less interested in the Palestinian issue. It is discussed more in the context of the traditional Arabist view that the persistence of the "Palestinian question" undermines American interests in the broader Arab world. Even in the case of lobbying on behalf of the Saudis, the alumni's interest is more complementary than determinative, as they are typically pushing through open doors to officials who are already sympathetic to the idea, for example, of expanding commercial and defense ties with the Saudis. Still, as in the case of the broad public support for Israel, the Arab lobby helps to create a supportive atmosphere in which policies affecting the Arab world are debated.

CHAPTER FOURTEEN

The Abuse of Academic Freedom: The Lobby Infiltrates the Classroom

The Arab lobby has devoted a great deal of money to trying to shape the views of the next generation of Americans and, especially, future decision makers. For more than fifty years, the Arab lobby has invested in creating centers and chairs at universities to propagate its views. The lobby succeeded in hijacking the field of Middle East studies and now has faculty across the country who use their positions to advance a political agenda. In recent years, the lobby has begun to extend its reach into precollegiate education as well. The lobby clearly understands the potential to influence Americans across a wide spectrum of professions. Aramco's magazine observed that courses "once tailored for diplomats and missionaries now draw students who plan careers in banking, business, law, public health, education and urban studies," and "university 'outreach' programs are developing and providing courses on the Middle East for both high school [actually K-12] and adult-education programs."[1]

The Arab lobby's takeover of the classrooms has been slow and quiet, and perhaps more successful than any other campaign it has conducted in the United States. At the same time, the lobby has long been active in trying to influence student opinion outside the classroom, an effort that provoked a vigorous response from the Israeli lobby that has helped to counter the impact of Israel's detractors on the campus green.

The study of the Middle East is important, and there is no doubt that insufficient attention has been given to instruction in Arabic and the history, politics, and theology of Muslims. These topics have become even more important because of the rise of Islamism, the threat of Muslim terrorism, the denial of human rights in Arab/Muslim countries, and efforts by radical Muslims and some Middle Eastern governments (including our putative allies) to undermine American values and interests. The Arab lobby, however, is determined to minimize these dangers and suppress discussion of them.

The first Arab lobby group on campus was the Organization of Arab Students (OAS), which was formed in 1952 by the American Friends of the Middle East. Prior to 1967, the group was dominated by the Egyptian point of view as Nasser's influence in the region spread to the Arab American community. After the humiliation of Nasser's forces and those of the other Arab states, however, the students began to identify more with liberation movements and sought to build alliances with the antiwar American left and radical blacks. Whereas the group had kept its distance in the past from the Communists, in the postwar period OAS openly sided with Communist and Third World states that supported the Arab position.

With the ascendancy of the PLO, the General Union of Palestinian Students (GUPS), a student arm of the PLO's Palestinian National Council, became the principal Arab lobby organization on American campuses, sponsoring speaking tours by anti-Israel speakers and organizing protests and other activities, though it is no longer active.

The principal agent of the Arab lobby among college students today is the Muslim Students Association (MSA), an organization created in 1963 with close links to the Muslim World League. The organization has chapters across the country and is frequently the source of much anti-Israel student activity. There is some variation from campus to campus, and occasionally the leadership on a particular campus will be moderate enough to engage in dialogue with pro-Israel students. My own experience with the MSA in the early 1980s included visiting their table in Sproul Plaza at Berkeley, where they would post a sign that said Zionism Is Racism and hand out highlights of the *Protocols of the Elders of Zion*, the notorious Russian forgery accusing Jews of a conspiracy to control the world.

Little has changed.

For example, according to Leila Beckwith, the Muslim Student Union and Society of Arab Students at the University of California–Irvine since 2001 has sponsored speakers and programs that "used classic anti-Semitic themes, and demonized Israel and Jews with Nazi comparisons. Some Jewish students were harassed and intimidated. When they asked for help from the administration, it was not given."[2] The MSU put on weeklong hate fests at UCI with titles such as "Anti-Oppression Week," "Holocaust in the Holy Land," and "Tragedy in the Holy Land Week," which featured one speaker who compared Zionists to Nazis and said that the Mossad destroyed the Twin Towers. In October 2004, the Zionist Organization of America sued UCI under Title VI of the 1964 Civil Rights Law provision prohibiting discrimination based on race, color, or national origin. It was the first time a complaint of university anti-Semitism was investigated by the Office for Civil Rights of the Department of Education. No formal action was taken against UCI, but partly as a result of the lawsuit and the furor raised by it, the U.S. Commission on Civil Rights initiated a public education campaign to end campus anti-Semitism.

The Jewish community and Israelis, especially, have an image of American campuses as hotbeds of anti-Semitism because of incidents of swastikas painted on walls, the annual parade of anti-Israel speakers, and various efforts to demonize Israel through divestment petitions and other symbolic measures. However, according to the Anti-Defamation League, in 2007 only eighty-one anti-Jewish incidents were reported across the country, and these were primarily instances of graffiti. Most anti-Israel student activities have gone on for decades and had little or no impact, but are frequently blown up into major incidents. Israel's detractors regularly engage in guerrilla theater such as "die-ins," mock checkpoints, and "apartheid walls." They hold "Palestine Weeks" and "Israel Apartheid Weeks," which cause consternation for the pro-Israel students, but rarely attract the attention of students who are not already disposed to the anti-Israel point of view. For the generally apathetic students of today, especially, these anti-Israel activities are irrelevant or just a nuisance.

One example of the disproportionate attention given to some of these student activities was a debate held at Yale between students and *Israel Lobby* author John Mearsheimer. The *Jerusalem Post* published the story under the headline "Yale Students 'End' US-Israel Relations." Actually, forty-four students—less than one half of one percent of the Yale student body—voted to end America's "special relationship" with Israel. One might argue that one of those forty-four may be the future president, but it's probably more likely that one of the twenty-five who voted against the resolution will have a political future. Regardless of such speculation, the fact is that no one cares what those handful of students think, and it has no impact whatsoever on U.S. policy.[3]

The Arab lobby may have had limited impact on the campus quad, but it is not for lack of trying. Over the years many different organizations have come and gone, coalescing around particular issues of the day, but having in common a hatred of Israel. As in the case of the lobbyists in Washington, the campus branches of the Arab lobby rarely focus on any positive agenda for promoting democracy or human rights in the Arab world or ending terror. To the contrary, their focus is primarily on demonizing Israel and propagating Palestinian victimhood. A good example was the Palestine Solidarity Movement (PSM), which put on conferences for five consecutive years with the goals of ending the Israeli "occupation of Palestine"; promoting equality under the law for Palestinians living in Israel; demanding the "right of return" for Palestinian refugees; opposing oppression; and endorsing divestment as "our tactic of resistance."[4]

Pro-Israel students called the bluff of organizers at the PSM conference held at Duke in 2004 when they asked them to sign an innocuous statement before the event calling for a civil debate that would "condemn the murder of innocent civilians," "support a two-state solution," and "recognize the difference between disagreement and hate speech." The organizers refused to sign the statement. By hosting a group that could not bring itself to object to the murder of Jews, Duke gave their views legitimacy, as did the other universities—Berkeley, Wisconsin, Ohio State, and Georgetown—that blackened their reputations by allowing the event on their campus.

The PSM conferences featured professors exhibiting their animus for Israel as well as a rogue's gallery of activists with nefarious intentions, such as instructing students how they could infiltrate birthright trips to Israel (free trips for Jews who have never been to Israel) and then sneak off to engage in protests in the West Bank, and ways to insinuate their propaganda into public schools (one example is to offer a teacher a Jewish and Palestinian speaker to provide a balanced presentation without letting on that the Jew actually shares the Palestinians' views). In the end, the PSM lost its momentum. Only a few hundred students would come to the conferences, and they did not successfully attract students who were not already on their side. The last conference was in 2006, and like many other Arab lobby groups, PSM faded away.

For the most part, the Jewish community accepts that anti-Israel speakers and conferences are a matter of free speech and is afraid to do anything that might suggest an effort to stifle what is actually hate speech. In 1983 AIPAC published a booklet, *The Campaign to Discredit Israel*, with information about speakers who regularly appeared on campus to express hostile views. ADL published a similar book. Both were vilified for producing a "blacklist" and never revised the publications. More recently Daniel Pipes started "Campus Watch," which at first published "dossiers" on faculty engaged in dubious research; he, too, was accused of McCarthyism. This has become a rallying cry for the Arab lobby, which protests what it claims are efforts to silence critics of Israel by using their own McCarthyite tactics to intimidate, silence, and defame anyone audacious enough to scrutinize their advocates.

Certain activities have now become regular features on many college campuses, such as demonstrations on the anniversary of the UN partition decision and "Israel Apartheid" Week. Perhaps the best example of a concerted campaign waged by the Arab lobby against Israel is the effort to convince universities to divest from Israel.

Divestment proponents hope to tar Israel with an association with apartheid South Africa, an offensive comparison that ignores the fact that all Israeli citizens are equal under the law. Moreover, the divestment campaign against South Africa was specifically directed at companies that were using that country's racist laws to their advantage. In Israel, no such racist laws exist; moreover, companies doing business there adhere to the same standards of equal working rights that are applied in the United States.

The calls for divestment began to intensify in 2002, after British academics launched an effort to boycott Israel. This came on the heels of the 2001 Israel-bashing UN conference in Durban, South Africa, which launched the strategy of delegitimization represented by these movements. By October 2002, more than fifty campuses were circulating divestment petitions. "Profoundly anti-Israel views are increasingly finding support in progressive intellectual communities," said Harvard president Lawrence Summers. "Serious and thoughtful people are advocating and taking actions that are anti-Semitic in their effect, if not their intent."[5]

Only one campus has voted for divestment, and the anti-Israel campaign has probably been most effective in provoking greater sympathy for Israel.[6] Though beaten back in 2002, proponents were reenergized by opposition to Israel's war with Hamas in Gaza in 2008–9 and renewed their calls for divestment.

In January 2009, faculty detractors also called for an academic and cultural boycott of Israel. Given the strong opposition to boycotts in the United States, it is unlikely American professors will be as successful as their British counterparts in mobilizing support. In 2007, nearly three hundred university presidents denounced the British boycott in a statement that said, "In seeking to quarantine Israeli universities and scholars, this vote threatens every university committed to fostering scholarly and cultural exchanges that lead to enlightenment, empathy, and a much-needed international marketplace of ideas." Alan Dershowitz noted that "many of the people who want boycotts claim that Israel is inflicting collective punishment on the Palestinians, but a boycott is essentially punishing every Israeli academic without regard for what their views may be." The British boycott was more enlightened, as it exempted "Israeli academics and intellectuals who oppose the colonial and racist policy of their state."[7] As of February 2009, fewer than two hundred American professors had signed the boycott petition.

These faculty-initiated attacks on Israel have served as a wake-up call to the Israeli lobby, whose attention had been diverted by student activities on campus quads.

The Arab lobby was meanwhile quietly building a formidable army of pro-Arab and, more often, anti-Israel faculty, who assumed dominant roles in Middle East studies departments throughout the country. These professors, along with like-minded faculty in other disciplines, habitually abuse their academic freedom and have turned their classrooms into bully pulpits to advance the Arab lobby agenda.

From the Arab lobby perspective, there was a need to counter what they saw as the overwhelming Jewish influence on campuses. Jews, after all, had funded Jewish studies departments and Holocaust chairs throughout the country, and it was also no secret that a disproportionate number of faculty were Jewish. Most Jews also believed that their interests were being advanced on campus, and assumed that courses on Israel were being taught and that faculty was speaking out on Israel's behalf.

In fact, a study of the top seventeen political science departments found that six had no tenured or tenure track faculty members with a specialty in the Middle East, and only five had a faculty member whose principal specialization was the Middle East. Five of the seventeen departments offered no courses on the Middle East, and no department offered more than four courses. The situation is even worse when you look more specifically at courses related to Israel across all departments. A study in 2006 found that 53 percent of the major universities offered *zero courses* on Israel, and 77 percent offered zero or one.[8] Moreover, few of those Jewish professors who were assumed to be pro-Israel actually were politically engaged, and those who were tended to be unsympathetic.

Universities were not always anti-Israel propaganda machines.

Originally, Middle East scholars, or orientalists, as they were often called, were dispassionate scholars who immersed themselves in the history and culture of the region and studied original texts written in the languages of the region. These scholars also were not usually of Arab descent. In fact, two of the earliest and most prestigious Middle East centers were established at Harvard and UCLA by a British and German scholar, respectively, Sir Hamilton Gibb and Gustave E. von Grunebaum.[9] Another center was at the University of Chicago, which was directed by a virulent opponent of Zionism in the 1940s, John Wilson. One of the few prominent Arab orientalists was Lebanese historian Philip Hitti, another anti-Zionist scholar, who created a center at Princeton.[10]

In his study of the decline of Middle East studies, *Ivory Towers on Sand: The Failure of Middle Eastern Studies in America*, Martin Kramer points to George Hourani's 1968 presidential address to the Middle Eastern Studies Association as the origin of the anti-Israel era in Middle Eastern studies: Hourani declared that "the Arabs' claim to a state [in Palestine] is . . . based on indisputable facts," while "the claims of the Jews to live in and have a state in a part of Palestine . . . present a serious ethical problem." Hourani rejected Jewish historical and religious claims to the land of Israel and characterized early Zionist settlement as immoral. He would not even acknowledge the legitimacy of the necessity of Jews finding a haven in Palestine from the Nazis, since "it cannot be assumed that if Palestine had not been available all other gates out of central Europe would have been closed to these individuals." Hourani believed that the Jews should have recognized that their desire for a state would cause suffering for the Arabs and abandoned the Zionist enterprise. This was a watershed in Middle East studies that marked the end of the tradition of keeping personal views out of the classroom and academic writing and introducing partisanship to the discipline; scholarship subsequently became secondary to the advancement of a political agenda.[11]

Kramer cites a survey of major articles and books on the history of the Middle East published between 1962 and 1985, showing that more than a third dealt with some aspect of the Arab-Israeli

conflict—a disproportionate amount of attention paid to a single issue in a region riddled with wars, religious upheaval, and political
and social instability. This attention, Kramer concludes, "came at the
expense of other countries and subjects, many of which suffered from
relative neglect."

The shift in perspective, not surprisingly, coincides with the
growth in the number of professors from the Middle East. A little
more than a decade after Hourani's address, more than two thousand
professors with "an intimate knowledge of their own language, history and civilization" were teaching on campuses across the country.[12]

In addition to an obsession with Israel and the Palestinians, the
faculty now commonly associated with Middle East studies have little
interest in history and original texts and express subjective opinions
based on anti-Western, anticolonial, anti-imperial, and anti-American attitudes. They tend to view Arabs as victims, deny the existence
of radical Islamists or minimize their influence, and apologize for
terrorism. The range of opinions tends to vary from the left (Israel
must capitulate to Arab demands) to the far left (a Jewish state is illegitimate).

Anti-Israel sentiment became the springboard for a dramatic expansion of scholars' political activism in 1978, when the virulently
anti-Israel professor Edward Said, who taught English literature at
Columbia University, published *Orientalism*. Said turned the tradition of the orientalists on its head by arguing that westerners speaking about the Orient were by his definition ethnocentric racists and
imperialists. Said delegitimized Western scholarship on the East,
arguing that all of its practitioners were, consciously or not, tainted
by prejudice and the desire to keep the Arab peoples in a state of submission. Essentially, only Muslims were capable of studying Islam or
the Muslim world.

The popularity of Said's conception dramatically shifted the political orientation of Middle Eastern scholarship. Orientalism made it
acceptable for scholars "to spell out their own political commitments
as a preface to anything they wrote or did," and enshrined "an acceptable hierarchy of political commitments, with Palestine at the top,

followed by the Arab nation and the Islamic world." As a member of the Palestine National Council, Said could hardly be considered an objective scholar. Still, Said's influence cannot be overstated, as his book has become omnipresent on syllabi. As one Barnard graduate put it, "I had to read Said in every class except maybe math."

One consequence of the Saidian influence has been to largely ignore the phenomenon of Arab and, especially, Muslim violence. American academics were quick to point out that focusing on it would only reinforce stereotypes. Consequently, in the 1990s, few Middle East scholars paid any attention to radical Islam. Even after fundamentalist groups began to engage in widespread terror, most Middle East "experts" were unwilling to acknowledge that a problem existed. The most often quoted professors on the Arab world, such as Georgetown's John Esposito (whose institute was funded by the Saudis), only see moderate Islam and consistently try to minimize the threat of radical Muslims. Just before 9/11, for example, Esposito was criticizing antiterrorism legislation because of its disproportionate impact on Muslims and wrote: "Bin Laden is the best thing to come along, if you are an intelligence officer, if you are an authoritarian regime, or if you want to paint Islamist activism as a threat. There's a danger in making Bin Laden the poster boy of global terrorism."[13] Even after 9/11, he has suggested that Hamas, Hezbollah, and the Muslim Brotherhood are legitimate organizations while making artificial distinctions between their military and political wings. Consistent with these views, Esposito defended Professor Sami Al-Arian, who had pleaded guilty in 2006 to conspiring to provide goods and services to the Palestinian Islamic Jihad and was later jailed a second time for contempt, as "an extraordinarily bright, articulate scholar and intellectual-activist, a man of conscience with a strong commitment to peace and social justice" in a July 2, 2008, letter to U.S. district judge Leonie Brinkema. A few weeks later, Esposito spoke in Dallas for a Council on American-Islamic Relations fund raiser "to show solidarity not only with the Holy Land Fund [*sic*; Holy Land Foundation], but also with CAIR." Ultimately, the Holy Land Foundation was convicted for its connections to terrorists, and CAIR has come under increasing scrutiny for its alleged ties to extremists.[14]

When a Saudi Arabian court sentenced a nineteen-year-old rape victim to two hundred lashes and six months in prison, and the Justice Ministry suggested that the woman invited the attack because she was in a parked car with a man who was not her relative, Esposito and his colleague John Voll were mostly concerned that the case would allow "Islamophobes" to "blur the distinction between the barbaric acts of Muslim extremists and terrorists and the religion of Islam." The trouble, of course, was that the sentence was carried out in the name of Islam not by extremists, but by the government Esposito and Voll routinely defend.[15]

Nevertheless, as director of a center funded by Saudi Arabia, Esposito can influence diplomats because Georgetown boasts the oldest and largest school of international affairs in the United States and is one of the principal training centers for the foreign service (and also has a campus in Qatar). As a former president of the Middle East Studies Association and author of numerous books and articles, he is automatically assumed to be an authority on the Arab and Islamic world. Moreover, his books are widely read and assigned in courses on the basis of his reputation. He is also invited to offer his views to decision makers and to comment on the news in the media.

One example of misleading information disseminated by Esposito is found in a study he coauthored titled *Who Speaks for Islam? What a Billion Muslims Really Think*. In it, Esposito and Dalia Mogahed, executive director of the Gallup Center for Muslim Studies, argued that most Muslims are just like ordinary Americans. The book claimed to represent the views of more than 90 percent of the world's 1.3 billion Muslims and concluded that only 7 percent are radicals, whom they defined as people who believed that the September 11 attacks were "completely" justified and held unfavorable opinions of the United States. The West, therefore, has nothing to fear from the overwhelming majority of Muslims, and the minority, they said, may change their minds if the United States shows them more respect.

The authors glossed over the fact that the minority that holds hos-

tile opinions of the United States totals 91 million Muslims, a significant number, especially considering the fact that it took only nineteen
to carry out the 9/11 attacks. The situation is actually worse; the
authors vastly underestimated the number of Muslims whose views
might concern Americans. Robert Satloff noted that rather than
7 percent of the sample expressing a "radical" view, the actual figure
was 13.5 percent. Another 23.1 percent said the 9/11 attacks were in
some way justified, which means that the number of Muslims with
troubling views exceeds 400 million! "Amazing as it sounds," wrote
Satloff, "according to Esposito and Mogahed, the proper term for a
Muslim who hates America, wants to impose Sharia law, supports
suicide bombing, and opposes equal rights for women but does not
'completely' justify 9/11 is . . . 'moderate.'"[16]

Perhaps the most renowned Middle East scholar today, Princeton's Bernard Lewis, observed that Middle East studies programs
have been distorted by "a degree of thought control and limitations
of freedom of expression without parallel in the Western world since
the 18th century." He added, "It seems to me it's a very dangerous
situation because it makes any kind of scholarly discussion of Islam,
to say the least, dangerous. Islam and Islamic values now have a level
of immunity from comment and criticism in the Western world that
Christianity has lost and Judaism never had."[17]

The principal representatives of the danger Lewis speaks about
can be found among the 3,000-member Middle East Studies Association (MESA). Interestingly, then MESA president Joel Beinin
said the association did not discuss the Six-Day War of 1967 and had
a long-established "gentleman's agreement" that "discussion of the
Arab-Israeli conflict would be avoided because it would generate too
much controversy and undermine the collegiality of the organization" as well as "the claim of Middle East studies to objective and scientific knowledge."[18] As Beinin acknowledged, however, things have
dramatically changed, though he did not acknowledge that a major
reason is the growing influence of the followers of Edward Said.

Beinin himself is an outspoken critic of Israel who, for example,
initiated a petition in 2002 that charged Israel with plotting the "eth-

nic cleansing" of Palestinians under cover of the approaching war in Iraq and predicted that Ariel Sharon would use the war as an opportunity to push the Palestinians into Jordan.

MESA is not monolithic, but a sense of its priorities can be gleaned from the topics at its annual conferences. Prior to 1992, the general tenor reflected the popular support for the PLO and Arafat. The end of the Cold War injected some measure of realism, though the typical anti-Western, anti-Israel feelings remained latent. The signing of the Oslo Accords in 1993 temporarily threw the group into chaos. By the following year, however, the tenor began shifting back toward the usual hostility toward Israel, with an added undercurrent of anger toward Arafat for what some perceived as selling out the Palestinian cause. As the reality of Oslo's failure set in over the next several years, the broad animus toward Israel returned.

"There's been a lot of lamenting about the political correctness that's taken over MESA," Tristan Mabry, a visiting assistant professor of government at Georgetown University, told the *Wall Street Journal*. "The A-No.1 issue that dominates MESA is always Israel, and even if you're not interested in Israel [Mr. Mabry's research focuses on Pakistan, India, and Bangladesh], where you stand on Israel is always a litmus test."[19] Richard Bulliet, professor of Middle East history at Columbia, agreed: "You have a big chunk of the [Middle Eastern history] specialist community that starts every sentence with the word Palestine. And they have successfully from 1967 onwards, partly through the extraordinary skills of Yasser Arafat, to turn [*sic*] this side-show into a great world concern so that it's given in many, many quarters in the Arab world that all problems stem from the Palestine question. That's a great sell. Certainly it's succeeded on this campus."[20]

Franck Salameh, assistant professor of Near Eastern studies at Boston College, highlights the myopic view of the Middle East promulgated by the MESA leadership, which ignores all the non-Israel-related rivalries, such as Turkish versus Kurdish, Islamist zealots versus modernist secularists, nationalists versus Islamist dictators, and Sunnis versus Shiites. "Heaven forbid one should dare advocate for

Middle Eastern Jews, Christians, and non-Arabs and give airtime to *their* story and *their* epics of suffering, dispossession, triumph and renewal! According to the official line laid down by MESA's leaders, after all, they are not indigenous to the Middle East, but relics of the odious eleventh century Western colonialist enterprise." Salameh also observes the power that the MESAns can wield. "Grants, appointments, promotions, publications, and one's general workplace atmosphere are all affected by whether or not one is willing to submit to exponents of select historical perceptions and attitudes regarding the Middle East and its allegedly monolithic peoples and cultures."[21]

The centrality of the Palestine issue is apparent at MESA conferences. In a study of the three-year period following 9/11, Martin Kramer found that 1,900 papers were presented:

> For MESAns, the Palestinians are the chosen people, and more so now than ever. More papers are devoted to Palestine than to any other country. There are ten times as many Egyptians as there are Palestinians, but they get less attention; there are ten times as many Iranians, but Iran gets less than half the attention. Even Iraq, America's project in the Middle East, still inspires only half the papers that Palestine does. Papers dealing with Israel are only half as numerous as those on Palestine, and only three of these are about Israel per se, apart from the Arab-Israeli conflict. More than half of the Israel-related papers actually overlap the Palestine category.[22]

The situation has only marginally improved. In 2007, eleven panels were devoted solely to Palestinian grievances. In 2008, a few panels addressed Israel in a scholarly way and included Zionist Israelis. The preliminary program for 2009 listed six panels related to Israel, and only one, on Turkish-Israeli relations, did not have some tie to the Palestinian issue.

What concerns MESA, however, is "academic vigilantism on campuses to watch, report, and if necessary to intimidate scholars who present 'biased,' 'anti-Israel,' 'pro-Islamic' or 'pro-Palestinian' views in their class lectures, in public statements outside their institutions, or in their writings." MESA president (2005) Ali Banuazizi said these "smear tactics and confrontations have begun to threaten the rights of free speech and inquiry and, if not contained, could potentially undermine the integrity of academic institutions."[23] This suggests Banuazizi supports freedom of speech for those with whom he agrees, but is less tolerant of the rights of critics.

IT IS NOT SURPRISING THAT many members of MESA would be anti-American and anti-Israel, given that their funding often comes from Arab sources, and their research depends on access to countries that hold similar views.

The Saudis and other Arabs have a great appreciation for American education and recognize that it is a route to knowledge, influence, and power. King Faisal sent seven of his eight sons to prep schools in the United States (the Hun School of Princeton or Lawrenceville in New Jersey) and universities in the United States or England.[24] Given this appreciation for American education, it is reasonable to ask why anyone should care whether the Saudis and other Arab governments donate money to institutions where students *should* learn to speak Arabic, understand Islam, and analyze Middle East affairs. The problem with Arab investments, especially from the Saudis, is what they would like Americans (and others) to learn. Consider some of the lessons from Saudi-produced textbooks used inside and outside the kingdom:

- "The Jews and Christians are enemies of the believers, and they cannot approve of Muslims."
- "The clash between this [Muslim] nation and the Jews and Christians has endured, and it will continue as long as God wills."
- "The punishment for homosexuality is death. . . . Ibn Qudamah said, 'The companions of the Prophet were unanimous on killing, although they differed in the description,

that is, in the manner of killing. Some of the companions of the Prophet stated that [a homosexual] is to be burned with fire. It has also been said that he should be stoned, or thrown from a high place."

- "In Islamic law, however, [jihad] has two uses: One usage is specific. It means to exert effort to wage war against the unbelievers and tyrants."

- "In its general usage, 'jihad' is divided into the following categories: . . . —Wrestling with the infidels by calling them to the faith and battling against them."

- "In these verses is a call for jihad, which is the pinnacle of Islam. In (jihad) is life for the body; thus it is one of the most important causes of outward life. Only through force and victory over the enemies is there security and repose. Within martyrdom in the path of God (exalted and glorified is He) is a type of noble life-force that is not diminished by fear or poverty."

- "As cited in Ibn Abbas: The apes are Jews, the people of the Sabbath; while the swine are Christians, the infidels of the communion of Jesus."

- "The decisive proof of the veracity of the Protocols [of the Elders of Zion] and the infernal Jewish plans they contain is that the plans, plots, and conspiracies they list have been carried out. Whoever reads the protocols—and they emerged in the 19th century—will realize today how much of what they described has been implemented."

- "You can hardly find an example of sedition in which the Jews have not played a role."[25]

The Center for Religious Freedom's report on Saudi textbooks notes that "Wahhabi teachings . . . are murderously intolerant toward the Shi'a, Jews, Baha'i, Ahmadiyya, homosexuals, apostates and 'unbelievers' of all kinds, and horribly repressive with respect to everyone else, especially women. The ultimate Wahhabi objective is quite clear from a wide range of their writings—the establishment of a worldwide theocratic dictatorship, the caliphate. These are essentially the same basic beliefs as those expressed by al Qaeda."[26] Even the State Department conceded that the Saudi textbooks "contain some overtly intolerant statements against Jews and Christians and subtly intolerant statements against Shi'a and other religious groups."[27]

Given these beliefs, it is a matter of grave concern that Saudi Arabia is spending an estimated $4 billion per year globally on education and outreach programs.[28] "The rulers of the Arab oil states are neither simple philanthropists nor disinterested patrons," former English diplomat John Kelly observed. "They expect a return upon their donations to institutions of learning and their subsidies to publishing houses; whether it be in the form of subtle propaganda on behalf of Arab or Islamic causes, or the preferential admission of their nationals, however unqualified . . . or the publication of the kind of sycophantic flim-flam about themselves and their countries which now clutters sections of the Western press and even respectable periodical literature."[29]

The Arab lobby understood from the beginning that it was important to use American universities for its own purposes, namely to train specialists who would appreciate the Arab point of view and who could work directly and indirectly on its behalf. Colonel William Eddy, the intelligence operative, Aramco adviser, and State Department representative to Saudi Arabia, reported that Aramco began funding programs as early as the 1950s. In 1956, he wrote to his son, "ARAMCO contributes to institutions like Princeton, the Middle East Institute, at [sic] Washington, and the American University of Beirut not only because these centers prepare future employees, but because they also equip men to come out to the Near East in the Foreign Service, or in teaching or in other capacities, which strengthens the small band of Americans who know the Arabs and understand them."[30]

In 1969, tiny Ricker College in Houlton, Maine, which closed in the mid-1970s, received funding from King Faisal of Saudi Arabia, the government of Kuwait, and Aramco to support the first undergraduate program on the Muslim world in the United States, and offered academic credit to students spending their junior year abroad at a college in a Muslim country.[31]

Starting as early as 1976, Arab governments and individuals began to make large gifts to universities to create chairs and centers in Arab, Middle Eastern, and Islamic studies. More than ninety universities sought assistance from the Saudis, but the first endowment was created at USC, with $1 million. Though universities usually jealously guard their prerogatives to choose their faculty and normally refuse to allow donors a say in hiring, even when the donor's name is on the position, Saudis were given the right to approve the appointment of the King Faisal Chair in Islamic Studies. Their first choice was Willard Beling, an international relations professor who had worked for Aramco. Investigative journalist Steven Emerson suggested that the choice of USC as the first recipient of Saudi aid might have been related to the fact that many Saudis attended the school, including the ministers of industry, commerce, and planning. USC president John Hubbard, whose office had a photo of him with Saudi king Khalid, actually claimed in a 1978 interview that the Saudis had moderated their oil policy "because of the USC connection."[32]

Three years later, the Saudis gave $200,000 to Duke for a program in Arabian and Islamic studies (which was doubled to $400,000 three years later); Libya donated $750,000 for a chair in Arab culture at Georgetown; and the UAE gave Georgetown another $250,000 for a visiting professorship in Arab history.[33]

Few universities have the courage to reject multimillion-dollar offers from donors. Harvard's Divinity School, for example, took $2.5 million in 2000 from Sheikh Zayed bin Sultan al-Nahayan, the dictatorial ruler of Abu Dhabi. Besides presiding over a country condemned for its human rights abuses, Zayed established a think tank that promoted Holocaust denial, anti-Semitism, and anti-American conspiracy theories. Rachel Fish, a graduate student at Harvard, began to raise questions in 2002 about the propriety of accepting money from a source that promoted hatred of Jews. She also produced the terms of the gift agreement, which said a liaison officer would "advise the U.A.E. on procedures relating to application and admission to the University." Though she received little assistance from other students or Harvard faculty, Fish persisted in arguing for more than a year, continuing even after she graduated, that the gift should be returned. In 2003, Harvard put the funds on hold and said it would reassess the gift. When it became clear Harvard was likely to return the money, Zayed asked for his money back.[34]

More recently Temple University turned down a $1.5 million chair in Islamic studies after trustees raised questions about the donor, the International Institute of Islamic Thought (IIIT), a nonprofit organization that was under scrutiny as part of a government investigation into the funding of terrorists. IIIT found a more welcoming reception from Shenandoah University, which agreed to cooperate in "course development, educational programs, and research with a goal of promoting an understanding of Islam and Muslims in America, and Islamic civilization and culture," based on "the principles of equality and reciprocal benefit."[35]

Though it has the oldest visiting Israel scholar program in the United States and today has a growing program in Jewish civilization that hosts very good scholars of Israel, Georgetown has long been viewed as sympathetic toward the Saudis and other Arab governments. In 1978, for example, the university issued a press release quoting visiting lecturer Clovis Maksoud, the chief spokesman for the Arab League, criticizing Israel's military operation in Lebanon in response to a PLO attack on a civilian bus in Tel Aviv. Maksoud also had called for replacing the "egocentric" Jewish state of Israel with a Palestinian state. He said that the destruction of "Zionism is a precursor to any dialogue of consequence" and called "Palestinian resistance . . . the healthiest expression of the Arab people in the aftermath of the 1967 defeat."[36] Columnist Art Buchwald said afterward, "I don't see why the PLO has to have a PR organization when Georgetown is doing all their work for them."[37] Maksoud was later hired by American University as a professor of international relations and director of the Center for the Global South.

When Georgetown received a $750,000 donation from Libya for an endowed chair in 1977, Buchwald chastised the university for accepting "blood money from one of the most notorious regimes in the world today" and suggested the university also consider establishing a "Brezhnev Studies Program in Human Rights or an Idi Amin Chair in Genocide." Center director Michael Hudson's response was that "the Libyans say they are just as anti-terrorist as anyone else."[38]

The person who led Georgetown's fund-raising effort in Libya and defended the grant was Peter Krogh, dean of Georgetown's School of Foreign Service and founder of the Center for Contemporary Arab Studies, whose sympathies were apparent in 1980 when he joined a coalition of groups trying to cut U.S. aid to Israel by $150 million. Krogh actually had solicited all the Arab embassies and missions in Washington with the goal of getting half the money needed to start the center from Arab governments. "I went to all of them," Krogh said, "whether they had diplomatic relations with the United States or not, whether they were moderate or radical, whatever their stripe." Before he got money from Libya, donations came in from Oman, the UAE, Egypt, and Saudi Arabia. Later, Jordan, Qatar, and Iraq sent contributions.[39]

After nearly five years of defending the decision to accept the "blood money," university president Rev. Timothy Healy returned the money to Libya with interest because of its support of terrorism. The person who was supposed to hold the chair (he still got one under a different endowment), Hisham Sharabi, responded by calling Healy a "Jesuit Zionist."[40] Sharabi, incidentally, in addition to being a professor of European intellectual history at Georgetown and one of the founders of its Center for Contemporary Arab Studies, also was a founder of the Institute for Palestine Studies (which received Aramco funding), "the unofficial academic wing of the PLO," which publishes the *Journal of Palestine Studies*; and he was a founder and president of the National Association of Arab Americans. Sharabi also ran the Arab American Cultural Foundation, which was supported by grants from Saudi Arabia, Kuwait, and other Arab sources. One of the foundation's projects was to fund an anti-Israel propaganda film, *Days of Rage*, which PBS aired without knowing the producer had received funds from a group with a political interest in the outcome.[41]

In 1975, Saudi Arabia was asked to finance a $5.5 million teacher-training program, but a number of schools, including Harvard, would not participate after the Saudis banned Jewish faculty from participating. MIT also lost a $2 million contract to train Saudi teachers because it insisted that Jewish faculty be allowed to participate.[42]

In the late 1970s, Saudi arms merchant Adnan Khashoggi offered $600,000 to establish a Middle East studies program at Swarthmore, Haverford, and Bryn Mawr, but the deal fell through after revelations about his alleged involvement in passing bribes on behalf of Northrop. After that firestorm blew over, he offered $5 million to American University in Washington, D.C., where he served on the board of trustees from 1983 to 1989. His 1984 contribution was for construction of the Adnan Khashoggi Sports and Convocation Center. Ironically, the center was also to be named after a local Jewish family. After criminal charges surfaced, the issue of keeping the building's name was debated. Khashoggi was eventually acquitted of all charges, but in 1986 he admitted to advancing $5 million toward the shipment of arms in the Iran-Contra scandal, and the university came under pressure to remove Khashoggi's name from the center. In the middle of the night, his name was apparently surreptitiously removed, which was later attributed to his failure to pay his financial pledge.[43]

The Midwest Universities Consortium for International Activities (Illinois, Indiana, Wisconsin, Michigan State, and Minnesota) won a contract to give curricular advice to the University of Riyadh but withdrew after four Jewish professors were denied visas to enter the country. In a rare example of a university standing on principle, the dean of international studies at Wisconsin, David Johnson, said, "We are not really dependent on an infusion of Arabian funds. Even if we were, this organization is not going to prostitute itself for oil money."[44]

The Saudis and other Arab donors did not have to worry; many other universities were happy to do so.

Georgetown and Harvard, for example, accepted $20 million gifts in 2005 from Saudi Prince Alwaleed bin Talal, whose offer of money to victims of 9/11 was rejected by then mayor Giuliani because of the prince's suggestion that America rethink its support of Israel. Georgetown's funding was used to support a center for Muslim-Christian understanding, which was subsequently renamed the Prince Alwaleed bin Talal Center for Muslim-Christian Understanding (the center was originally created in 1993 with $6.5 million from a foundation of Arab businessmen led by an Arab Christian, Hasib Sabbagh).[45] Prospective Jewish donors to Georgetown might ask why it is not a center for Muslim-Christian-*Jewish* understanding, but Jews aside, other donors might wonder why a Jesuit university is accepting funding for such a center from a government that does not allow the practice of Christianity. A good indication of the center's posture was a 2007 symposium it hosted on "Islamophobia and the Challenge of Pluralism" that was organized by CAIR with $300,000 from the Organization of the Islamic Conference.

Rep. Frank Wolf (R-VA) asked in February 2008 whether "the center has produced any analysis critical of the Kingdom of Saudi Arabia, for example in the fields of human rights, religious freedom, freedom of expression, women's rights, minority rights, protection for foreign workers, due process and the rule of law." He also wanted to know if the center "has examined Saudi links to extremism and terrorism" or produced any critical study of the "controversial religious textbooks produced by the government of Saudi Arabia that have been cited by the State Department, the U.S. Commission on International Religious Freedom and non-governmental groups for propagating extreme intolerance."

Georgetown president John DeGioia responded by extolling the virtues of Prince Talal as "a global business leader and philanthropist" whose investments in Citicorp were helping the company address its financial distress from the subprime mortgage situation. Without answering Wolf's questions directly, DeGioia simply pointed out that the center had experts who had written about the extremism of Wahhabism and human rights issues. He also lauded the center's director, John Esposito.

To bolster the credibility of the center, DeGioia actually revealed the real reason for the Saudis' interest in Georgetown, and the ultimate threat it poses: "Our scholars have been called upon not only by the State Department, as you note, but also by Defense, Homeland Security and FBI officials as well as governments and their agencies in Europe and Asia. In fact, a number of high ranking U.S. military officials, prior to assuming roles with the Multi-National Force in Iraq, have sought out faculty with the Center for their expertise on the region."[46]

The Harvard and Georgetown donations were just pocket change to the Saudi prince, the nineteenth-richest person in the world on the 2008 Forbes list (net worth $21 billion), who has also given millions to other universities in the United States and abroad. In fact, the director-general of MI5 said in 2008 that Saudi contributions to British universities had caused a "dangerous increase in the spread of extremism in leading university campuses."[47]

The prince's donation was not the first dip into the petrodollar trough for these universities. Harvard, for example, received its first donation from the Saudis in 1977, $300,000 to establish a chair in Islamic law. In 1982, the Saudi royal family gave $600,000 to preserve photographs of Middle Eastern life at the Semitic Museum. That same year, a Saudi businessman made a contribution that was believed to be conditional on the hiring of a faculty member with ties to the PLO, a charge that was never proven. In 2001 Saudi businessman Khalid Alturki added $500,000 to the $1.5 million he had already given to establish the contemporary Arab studies program at Harvard. The university also received $5 million for the King Fahd Chair for Islamic Studies in 1993, and hosts the H. E. Sheikh Ahmed Zaki Yamani (the former head of OPEC, who led the campaign to turn the oil weapon against the West) Islamic Legal Studies Fund and the Bakr M. Binladin [Osama's brother] Visiting Scholars Fund, and the government of Kuwait endowed the only chair in the world in the history of Islamic science. The commemorative book published on the fiftieth anniversary of the establishment of Harvard's Center for Middle Eastern Studies noted that the center's outreach program was funded by the federal government, Harvard, and Aramco.[48]

Georgetown received $100,000 from the sultan of Oman to develop Arab studies programs and $250,000 from the UAE to support a visiting professorship of Arab civilization, and two-thirds of the funding for its Center for Contemporary Arab Studies came from Arab countries (its board of advisers included representatives from Egypt, Jordan, Libya, Qatar, Oman, Saudi Arabia, and the UAE).[49]

According to the U.S. Department of Education, between 1986 and 2007, donors from Arab countries made more than 100 contributions, worth in excess of $320 million, to American universities. This report does not include Saudi Arabia's $20 million gifts to Harvard and Georgetown.[50] Nearly half of the gifts in the report came from Saudi sources. Counting the recent gifts, Saudi Arabia has invested more than $130 million in American universities; Qatar, $150 million; the UAE, $52 million; Kuwait, $12 million; and Oman, $9 million. By far the largest donation on the Department of Education list, nearly $85 million, came from Qatar, to Carnegie-Mellon for a council for information and technology. The government of Saudi Arabia gave $29 million to the University of Virginia, and King Fahd donated $18 million to the University of Arkansas. Qatar gave $17 million to Georgetown and another $10 million to Cornell. The UAE gave nearly $15 million to Harvard.

College presidents, whose jobs depend more on their ability to raise money than their ability to educate students, see dollar signs when they look to the Middle East and have taken to prospecting for petrodollars. Columbia, for instance, happily (some might say greedily) took money from the United Arab Emirates, among others, to endow a chair in Middle East studies named after Edward Said (whose field was literature, not Middle East studies), thereby institutionalizing an anti-Israel faculty position on the campus. Predictably, the chair was filled by an outspoken critic of Israel, former PLO spokesman Rashid Khalidi.[51] For many months, efforts were made to learn where the estimated $4 million had come from to endow the chair, but the university refused to disclose the information until bad publicity forced the publication of the names of the donors. Actually, the university, which stonewalled requests for the information, was legally obligated to provide the information; foreign gifts of $250,000 or more must be disclosed to the U.S. Department of Education, though the department does little to enforce the law, which has no penalty for noncompliance. In New York State, a similar disclosure law applies to amounts of $100,000 or more.[52]

Interestingly, MESA has "consistently called for open and full disclosure of funding sources for research, conferences and teaching programs, since MESA has been concerned about restrictions on academic freedom that can be imposed—explicitly or implicitly—by funders, whether American or foreign." MESA certainly has never complained about Arab funding in the United States, though "the Board of Directors has warned against blanket accusations that funding by Middle East governments necessarily means that those governments control the academic content of the programs and the hiring of faculty, this issue is also one that should be of particular and continuing concern for us." No, the group's real concern is with funding from U.S. government agencies, namely the CIA and Department of Defense, which seek academic support for the benefit of America's national security because such connections create "'dangers for students and scholars by fostering the perception [abroad] of [their] involvement in military or intelligence activities.'"[53]

Columbia has become one of the symbols of the politicization of Middle East studies. Since the Khalidi appointment, the university also hired Timothy Mitchell, a politics professor from New York University, to head its graduate studies program in Middle East studies. Mitchell is married to another controversial Columbia professor, Lila Abu-Lughod, and both signed an open letter in 2004 supporting an academic boycott of Israel.[54]

As the Department of Education list of foreign donors below indicates, the Arab lobby has focused on elite universities. Berkeley, for example, received two large gifts from the Saudis in the 1990s. The Alireza family donated $2 million for a program to promote understanding of Muslims and technology transfer to the Muslim world, especially Saudi Arabia. The Sultan bin Abdul Aziz Charity Foundation gave $5 million to broaden understanding of the Arab and Islamic worlds.[55]

The following list is just a sample of the universities that have received large donations from the Saudis and others interested in politicizing the academy:

Arkansas	$20,000,000	Saudi Arabia—King Fahd Center for Middle East and Islamic Studies
Cornell	$11,000,000	Saudi Arabia
Rutgers	$5,000,000	Saudi Arabia
George Washington	$3,300,000	Kuwait Foundation
Harvard	$2,000,000	Saudi Arabia—Prince Khalid al-Turki
Harvard	$2,500,000	Saudi Arabia
Harvard Law	$5,000,000	Saudi Arabia—King Fahd Chair for Islamic Shariah Studies
Princeton	$1,000,000	Saudi Arabia
UC Berkeley	$5,000,000	Saudi Arabia—two Saudi sheiks
Georgetown	$8,100,000	Saudi Arabia—scholarship from Prince Alwaleed bin Talal
Texas A&M	$1,500,000	Saudi Arabia
MIT	$5,000,000	Saudi Arabia
UCLA		Saudi Arabia
Columbia	$2,000,000	UAE and other donors—Edward Said Chair
UC Santa Barbara		Saudi Arabia—King Abdul Aziz ibn Saud Chair in Islamic Studies
Johns Hopkins		Saudi Arabia
Rice University		Saudi Arabia
American University		Saudi Arabia
Chicago		Saudi Arabia
Syracuse University		Saudi Arabia
USC		Saudi Arabia
Duke University		Saudi Arabia
Howard University		Saudi Arabia

UC Berkeley	$5,000,000	Saudi Arabia—Sultan bin Abdulaziz al Saud Foundation and Sheikh Salahuddin Yusuf Hamza Abdeljawad
Harvard	$2,000,000	Sheikh Khalid al-Turki
Georgetown	$20,000,000	Saudi Arabia—Prince Alwaleed bin Talal
Harvard	$20,000,000	Saudi Arabia—Prince Alwaleed bin Talal
USC	$1,000,000	Saudi government—King Faisal Chair for Arab and Islamic Studies
Duke University	$200,000	Saudi Arabia—program in Islamic and Arabian development studies
Georgetown	$750,000	Libyan government—Al-Mukhtar Chair of Arab Culture
Georgetown	$250,000	United Arab Emirates—visiting professor in Arab civilization
American University	$5,000,000	Saudi arms dealer Adnan Khashoggi
Phillips Academy	$500,000	Prince Alwaleed bin Talal
Cornell	$10,000,000	Prince Alwaleed bin Talal

The totals for the highest-grossing universities:

- Carnegie Mellon—nearly $111 million from Qatar
- Georgetown—more than $60 million from Qatar, Saudi Arabia, and Oman
- Harvard—more than $42 million from the UAE, Saudi Arabia, Lebanon, Kuwait, and Oman
- University of Virginia—more than $29 million from Saudi Arabia

- The Colorado School of Mines in Golden—more than $19 million from the UAE
- Cornell—nearly $11 million from Qatar
- George Washington University—nearly $20 million from Saudi Arabia and Kuwait

Given the lack of effort by the Department of Education in enforcing the disclosure law, it is likely that this list only represents a sample of the total Arab investments in American universities. For example, Saudi Aramco has also donated tens of thousands of dollars to universities such as Columbia, Georgetown, Arizona, and Utah for "outreach" and trips for educators to Saudi Arabia. In fact, while it is difficult for most Americans to visit Saudi Arabia unless they are invited for business purposes, Aramco funds their Educators to Saudi Arabia Program through the Institute of International Education "to provide a professional development opportunity to U.S. educators with the goal of increasing their knowledge and understanding of Saudi Arabia, its culture, and values." Another program aimed at promoting understanding of Saudi Arabia in the wake of 9/11 was founded by Prince Faisal F. Al Saud and Dr. J. Gregory Payne. The Saudi Global Exchange (SGE) has held more than a thousand events in the United States and sponsored at least a hundred trips to Saudi Arabia for academics, professionals, and citizens.[56]

In addition to fishing for money in the Gulf and offering to set up new departments of Middle East, Arab, and Islamic studies if given the resources, universities are also increasingly seeking lucrative deals with Gulf states to fund branches of their campuses in the Middle East. This is not entirely new, since the American University in Beirut was established in 1866, but in just the last few years more than a dozen colleges have established campuses in Qatar, the UAE, and Dubai. As in the case of the offers of endowments, few schools are willing to turn down the opportunity to reap a windfall from the eager Gulf donors. One exception is Yale, which decided in 2008 to forgo a planned arts institute in Abu Dhabi because Yale was not willing to offer degrees at the campus.

On the other extreme is the president of NYU, John Sexton, who was referred to as the "Emir of NYU" in a *New York* magazine article about accepting a "blank check" to become the first university to open an American liberal arts college that will function as an equal with the home campus on the desert island. According to the article, Abu Dhabi has already committed $50 million to the program and agreed to finance the Middle East campus as well as parts of the New York campus. Some critics of the deal have raised questions about the wisdom of collaborating with a nation that has a record of human rights abuses and anti-Semitism. Sexton seemed unconcerned about potential problems that might arise for gay students (homosexuality is illegal) or Jews (Abu Dhabi was home to a think tank that denied the Holocaust) or Israeli scholars (Israelis are barred from the country). He would only grant that anyone on the NYU Abu Dhabi campus would have to accept the norms of the society. The coordinator of the program from the Abu Dhabi government was more blunt. "NYU was aware of our local culture and rules and guidelines," said Mubarak Al Shamesi, "and our policies on Israelis or homosexuality were clearly not a concern for them."[57]

NYU is not alone in taking the money. Among the institutions that have overseas branches are American University, Carnegie Mellon, Cornell Medical School, George Mason, Georgetown, Johns Hopkins, Michigan State, MIT, Northwestern, Rochester Institute of Technology, Texas A&M, and Virginia Commonwealth.[58] As in the case of donations, a few universities do stand on principle and reject the easy money offered by the sheikhdoms. The University of Nevada at Las Vegas, for example, turned down Dubai's offer to open a campus because of concerns about human rights.[59]

In addition, Jewish donors have discovered, to their chagrin, that they have little control over how their money is spent. A Bay Area donor, for example, gave $5 million to Berkeley to endow a visiting Israel scholar position, and the Middle East studies department chose one of the Israeli academics most critical of his country's policies.

Arab donors know, however, that the positions they fund will be given to academics who share their worldview and who invariably are anti-Israel and content to present a one-sided, sanitized version of Islamic and Middle Eastern history. This is what the Saudis expect as they hope "to encourage and develop communication between Islamic culture and other cultures, to encourage greater understanding of the true nature of Islam by clearly explaining the beliefs of Muslims and correcting false conceptions and caricatures, and to show that Islam welcomes knowledge with enthusiasm."[60]

The allure of Arab money can influence universities in other ways as well. For example, Texas A&M University effectively censored the PBS station it managed by canceling the broadcast of *Death of a Princess*, a film the Saudis were desperate to keep off the airwaves because of its unsympathetic portrayal of the kingdom. University president Jarvis Miller explained that his university didn't want to "risk damaging international relations by showing a movie that reportedly relies on sensationalism and shock value to attack a culture and religion that is foreign to us. As a university we are attempting at this very time to establish significant new ties with the people who are most offended by this movie."

The University of Houston also prevented the film from being shown on its station. A press release explained that the university wanted to "avoid exacerbating the situation" in the Middle East. Several years earlier the university had signed a lucrative contract to provide instruction for a Saudi princess in Riyadh, and the university received a significant percentage of its donations from oil companies.[61]

In addition to funding from Arab sources, the U.S. government unwittingly helps to support the Arab lobby by providing financial support. In addition to the Edward Said Chair at Columbia, for example, Rashid Khalidi was named the director of Columbia's Middle East Institute, which was expected to receive about $1 million in federal subsidies over the following three years under Title VI of the 1958 National Defense Education Act.

Faculty bitterly complain when any "outsiders" try to hold them accountable for their scholarship or their behavior inside or outside the classroom. Columbia offers a case study where the university did nothing when made aware of problems until it was publicly embarrassed by a film documenting abuses by professors. Middle East and Asian Languages and Cultures Department (MEALAC) professor Dan Miron told the press that faculty abuse of students is a long-existing problem, and that students came to his office at least once a week to complain of being "humiliated" in the classroom. A pro-Israel organization, the David Project, produced a film in 2004, *Columbia Unbecoming*, which interviewed students who complained about bias in the classroom. The video documented that two students met with Columbia dean Kathryn Yatrakis to complain about Professor George Saliba. Their complaints were ignored and they were told their Jewish upbringing may have affected their reaction to the professor's behavior. This reinforced the argument of students who said they were unable to file complaints because of fears that they would be discriminated against by the department chair or other professors.

In one of the more notorious incidents, an Israeli student (and former IDF member) asked Professor Joseph Massad a question at a public lecture, and Massad responded by demanding, "How many Palestinians did you kill?" A student of Massad's later told the *Jerusalem Post* (December 31, 2004) that Massad shouted at her, "If you're going to deny the atrocities being committed against the Palestinian people then you can get out of my classroom!" This same professor has written that Israel is a racist, colonialist state and that Zionists are Nazis, and proposed a one-state solution to the Middle East conflict.[62] The film also reported that on April 17, 2002, Israel's Independence Day, an anti-Israel rally was scheduled to compete with a pro-Israel celebration. Massad addressed the rally, proclaiming that Israel is "a Jewish supremacist and racist state," and that "every racist state should be threatened." Nicholas De Genova, a professor of Latino studies, told the crowd, "The heritage of the victims of the Holocaust belongs to the Palestinian people. The state of Israel has no [legitimate] claim to the heritage of the Holocaust." Hamid Dabashi and George Saliba, two MEALAC instructors, canceled their classes to attend the demonstration and encouraged students to attend.[63]

In the spring of 2003, Columbia president Lee Bollinger appointed a faculty committee to investigate bias in the MEALAC Department. The committee did not submit a written report, only an oral one, which concluded that they had "not found claims of bias or indoctrination." The committee was read a portion of the *Columbia Unbecoming* transcript and was offered a copy of the video, but declined to view it.

In December 2004, Bollinger appointed a new committee to investigate the charges made in the film. The investigative committee itself reflected the need for such outside monitoring because all too often giving universities exclusive power to police themselves is like the proverbial fox guarding the henhouse.

In this case the committee was comprised of some of Israel's harshest critics on the faculty. The members were selected by vice president for arts and sciences Nicholas Dirks, who had signed a petition the previous year calling on Columbia to divest its holdings from companies selling hardware to Israel. Professor Dirks's wife, a professor in the MEALAC department, was coteaching with one of the professors accused of bias. Another member, Lisa Anderson, dean of the School of International Affairs, had traveled to Saudi Arabia on an Aramco-financed junket just months before and had served as a dissertation adviser to Joseph Massad. Committee member Mark Mazower, program director of the Center for International History, "compared Israel's 'occupation' of the 'West Bank' to the Nazis' occupation of Eastern Europe," according to Scholars for Peace in the Middle East. The last two members of the committee, Jean Howard, vice provost for diversity initiatives, and comparative literature professor Farah Jasmine Griffin, also signed the divestment petition. The chair of the committee, Ira Katznelson, professor of political science and history, presided over some of the committee sessions during which students claimed their academic freedom had been denied in some of the Middle East studies classes. Columnist Nat Hentoff pointed out that 106 faculty members signed the divestment petition, while 360-plus faculty members opposed that petition in writing. "How come President Bollinger appointed not a single one of those 360-plus to the committee?" Hentoff asked. "Or any others from Columbia's 3,224 full-time faculty?"[64]

The report the committee produced focused less on the substance of the students' allegations than on maligning those who raised concerns. The *New York Times* (which received an advance copy of the report, allegedly with the condition that no comments be solicited from students) trumpeted the committee's findings clearing the faculty of charges of anti-Semitism, allegations that were actually not made.[65] The committee said the faculty had the obligation to "assess the quality of the research and teaching of their colleagues," but then said it was beyond its purview to investigate complaints about the content of the courses and criticized professors for encouraging students to report on what goes on in other classrooms. The report itself had anti-Semitic overtones, criticizing throughout outside agitators—all Jews—who were trying to defend students, monitor the faculty, and assess their scholarship.

At this book's writing, Professor Massad was being considered for tenure. Reportedly, the review committee voted to deny it, but, in an extraordinary decision, Bollinger permitted Dirks to authorize a second tenure review and now will ask Columbia's trustees, in "an almost-unheard-of trustee intervention that would infuriate a good part of the faculty," to make the final decision. The university was in a delicate situation; it knew that the failure to grant tenure would provoke a storm of criticism from Massad and his supporters, describing the decision as politically motivated. In the current atmosphere of political correctness, and given the Arab lobby's ability to intimidate administrators, the expectation was that Massad would indeed be granted tenure despite serious reservations about whether it was merited on the basis of his scholarship. At last report, Massad had been granted tenure, but the school had not announced it. Fourteen Columbia professors subsequently protested to provost Claude Steele that Massad's tenure approval—after his previous bid was reportedly denied—violated procedural policy. They raised questions as to whether Massad had shown the evidence of "substantial scholarly growth" required of faculty reapplying for tenure.

Prominent Jewish donors angered by the disclosures about MEALAC agreed to provide more than $3 million to fund a chair in Israel studies. They foolishly handed their money over to the university, which then appointed two notoriously anti-Israel professors (Rashid Khalidi and Lila Abu-Lughod) to the search committee, which ultimately chose an Israeli whose scholarly reputation and attitudes would probably not have made him a candidate for an Israel studies chair at a school with a more unbiased search committee. Meanwhile, in 2009, 139 professors signed a letter to Bollinger calling on him to condemn Israel and support academic freedom of Palestinians.

Unlike Arab governments, Israel does not fund chairs or centers in the United States. Some pro-Israel philanthropists do invest in academic positions, but the emphasis is on academic scholarship and credibility rather than politics, and visiting Israeli professors are the first to say they are not interested in being advocates for Israel. Even those who chafe at the politicization of the campus and oppose the demonization of Israel prefer to cling to an ivory tower standard of scholarly detachment. Ilan Troen, the director of the Schusterman Center for Israel Studies at Brandeis, for example, dismisses the idea that he is fighting a war between pro- and anti-Israel faculty. "I don't agree with the notion of combat," he told *Moment* magazine. "We assume that knowledge can dissipate baseless animosity. To that extent, we're there to combat ignorance, not advocate a particular line."[66] Alan Dowty, who held a chair in Israel studies at the University of Calgary, echoed Troen's views: "Our objective is not to do something equally politicized on the other side," he said. "Our idea is to go back to the academic ideal of scholarly research."[67]

This is the academic equivalent of a boxer adhering to the Marquess of Queensberry rules in a street fight with a bully carrying a crowbar and a broken beer bottle. For example, in January 2009, a program on Israel's Gaza operation was cosponsored by three Rice University student organizations: the Muslim Students Association, Student Forum on Israeli-Arab Affairs, and Houston Hillel. Rice Hillel student president Laura Shepherd said Hillel agreed to cosponsor the program based on the presumption that it would be balanced and would have academic merit. The program was presented as an opportunity for Rice students and Houstonians "to express our shared desires for peace"; however, much of the discussion was devoted to attacking Israel with the alleged crimes of "racism," "ethnic cleansing," "apartheid," and "60 years" of illegitimacy and "occupation."

Most of the anti-Israel pronouncements were made by Ussama Makdisi, the nephew of Edward Said, who holds the Arab American Educational Foundation chair of Arab studies at Rice and is known for "promoting anti-Israel advocacy on the Rice campus, both in the classroom, according to students interviewed by the JH-V [*Jewish Herald-Voice*], and through history department-sponsored lecture series, attended and documented in the JH-V by this reporter over the past three years."[68]

Makdisi's presentation was expected to be counterbalanced by Ranan Kuperman, the Joan and Stanford Alexander Visiting Israeli Professor at Rice; however, "Kuperman's nuanced and dispassionate analysis contrasted greatly with the bluntness, tone and loaded language employed by the other panelists," reporter Michael Duke observed. "Whereas Makdisi and Cohen, at times, instructed the audience to agree with their positions and interpretations of data, Kuperman simply offered his remarks and invited others to decide for themselves. As one audience member commented after the program, 'It was like bringing a stack of spreadsheets to a gunfight.'"

ONE UNIQUE ASPECT OF THE bias related to Israel is the tendency for faculty in courses and disciplines completely unrelated to the history and politics of the conflict to inject their anti-Israel views into their classes. By contrast, pro-Israel faculty rarely expose their biases inside or outside the classroom, in part out of fear of the impact on their image on campus and within their fields. In fact, those scholars (Jews and non-Jews) who do teach about the Middle East typically go out of their way to declare their commitment to scholarship and forswear advocacy.

Here are just a few examples of the politicization of the university:

- Prior to the U.S. invasion of Iraq, 1,500 academics signed a petition warning of a possible impending "crime against humanity"—that Israel would expel large numbers of Palestinians during the fog of the Iraq War.
- Columbia hosted a faculty panel discussion titled "60 Years of Nakba: The Catastrophe of Palestine, 1948–2008." Panelist Lila Abu-Lughod told the audience that the Palestinian homeland was "buried, erased and rewritten by Israel." She then told a colorful story about her father's return to Israel and his inability to find his way because he couldn't read Hebrew, neglecting to mention the fact that Arabic is an official language in Israel, and road signs are in Hebrew, Arabic, and English.
- At American University, an anthropology professor used a comic book in the vein of *Der Stürmer* as a text. Another professor crossed out the word *Israel* on a student's exam and wrote in the margin, "Zionist entity." Another handed out maps of the Middle East without Israel on them.
- Berkeley offered a course titled The Politics and Poetics of Palestinian Resistance, which the instructor said would explore how Israel "systematically displaced, killed, and maimed millions of Palestinian people."
- At Clemson University, a philosophy professor taught a Humanities course titled Living under Occupation.
- Princeton offered a course titled Society under Occupation: Contemporary Palestinian Politics, Culture and Identity.
- More than one thousand academics signed a petition written by the Faculty for Israeli-Palestinian Peace, which criticizes Israel's security fence and presence in the territories and calls for protecting accessibility to educational institutions in the West Bank and Gaza Strip. The group also sponsors a conference called "An End to Occupation,

A Just Peace in Israel-Palestine," aimed at "mobilizing the Academia worldwide to promote an end of the Israeli occupation."

- At the University of Chicago, a doctoral student in the Middle East Studies program was discouraged by faculty from studying militant Islamic ideologies and told that this topic was created by a "sensationalist media" and advances "Zionist" interests.

The problem is even more serious on many campuses where whole departments legitimate the radical views of the Arab lobby professors. At UC Santa Cruz, for example, an academic conference on Zionism was sponsored and funded by eight university departments in March 2007. UCSC lecturer Tammi Rossman-Benjamin noted, "Each of the speakers concluded that Zionism was an illegitimate ideology and Israel a racist state, each professed to being an anti-Israel activist, and one speaker even urged members of the audience to join in the movement demanding that businesses and universities divest from Israel."[69]

As noted above, the attacks on Israel often occur in academic forums that are totally unrelated to the Arab-Israeli conflict or Middle East studies. For example, in 2009, the Modern Language Association approved a resolution accusing Israel of stifling education and calling for the endorsement of "teaching and scholarship about Palestinian culture" and supporting members "who come under attack for pursuing such work" and expressing "solidarity with scholars of Palestinian culture."[70]

Few people have noticed the bias in academia because students rarely complain. They are too afraid it will negatively impact their grades and their career. Thus, the misinformation produced by professors such as Walt and Mearsheimer can be part of courses around the country without anyone being aware of it. Usually faculty bias is only exposed when professors publish their outrageous views in mainstream media. Then they immediately retreat behind the shield of academic freedom and castigate their critics as McCarthyites.

Criticism of pseudo-scholars has sometimes produced a backlash, as these professors have won sympathy as victims of "smear campaigns." Yet no one has silenced any of these professors. Many are tenured and received lifetime employment despite controversies surrounding their work. Moreover, academic critics of Israel are routinely invited to lecture at campuses around the world, and no one prevents them from speaking. Hypocritically, however, many of these same professors are the ones calling for the silencing of pro-Israeli colleagues and the boycotting of Israeli universities.

In fact, it is the study of Israel that has been marginalized, delegitimized, and demonized, and it is to the detriment of everyone. As Gary Schiff put it nearly thirty years ago: "The tendency to deny Israel and the Hebrew language their fair share of attention and resources in the universities should be recognized and resisted, not only by the federal government and the universities themselves, but also by anyone concerned to preserve peace in the Middle East and, perhaps, in the world."[71]

CHAPTER FIFTEEN

Brainwashing the Children:
The Lobby Goes After the Next
Generation

The Arab lobby is no longer content to try to influence college students. An increasing effort is being made to shape the views of Americans from an early age through creative programs and educational resources. This is no doubt partly a result of the failure to significantly shift public opinion or policy away from Israel or toward the Arab/Muslim world with prior strategies. The new emphasis on younger Americans is also a function of the challenge and opportunity created by 9/11. On one hand, the terror attacks prompted great fear and some misunderstanding about Muslims and Islam. The knee-jerk pull of political correctness, however, also gave the lobby the chance to present its sanitized version of events that seeks to downplay Arab/Muslim distinctions, ignore differences in values or interests, and dismiss links between Islam and terror. Many of the lobby's efforts in this regard are actually underwritten by U.S. taxpayers through government-funded programs that have largely escaped scrutiny and allowed the lobby to insinuate its views into the American educational system.

The effort to influence future generations extends beyond college to grade schools. The collegiate Middle East programs are often the propagators of knowledge to the precollegiate level. Under Title VI of the Higher Education Act, the federal government provides funding to Middle East Studies centers to conduct public outreach. The reviewers of grant applications have typically been Middle East studies professors who naturally reject any proposals related to Israel and fund the work of like-minded colleagues at centers often funded by the Saudis. Stanley Kurtz, a senior fellow at the Ethics and Public Policy Center, summarizes the impact:

> The United States government gives money—and a federal seal of approval—to a university Middle East Studies center. That center offers a government-approved K-12 Middle East studies curriculum to America's teachers. But in fact, that curriculum has been bought and paid for by the Saudis, who may even have trained the personnel who operate the university's outreach program. Meanwhile, the American government is asleep at the wheel—paying scant attention to how its federally mandated public outreach programs actually work. So without ever realizing it, America's taxpayers end up subsidizing—and providing official federal approval for—K-12 educational materials on the Middle East that have been created under Saudi auspices. Game, set, match: Saudis.[1]

The program began when Congress passed Title VI of the 1958 National Defense Education Act to fund the establishment of institutes to teach foreign languages of strategically important areas unavailable elsewhere. The first Middle East centers were set up at Michigan, Princeton, and Harvard. Others were later established at Texas, Utah, UCLA, NYU, Penn, Berkeley, Georgetown, Ohio State, Arizona, Chicago, UC Santa Barbara, Washington, and Emory. Today, the U.S. Department of Education provides funding for seventeen Middle East centers and nearly one hundred student fellowships (at a cost of $4 million per year).[2]

These centers, which do not have scholars on Israel and are primarily inhabited by faculty hostile to Israel, are training centers for future leaders and housed at the most elite universities. They are also viewed as credible and respected sources of information about the

Arab/Muslim world and have an exponential impact because they reach tens of thousands of Americans through their appearances in the media, consultations with policy makers, publications, lectures and conferences, and teacher training. They have all been in particular demand since 9/11. The Texas center, for example, went from receiving dozens of calls to hundreds. Professors and graduate students were dispatched to speak to schools, businesses, churches, and other groups, reaching 20,000 people in the four months following the attack on the World Trade Center. The Arizona center met several times with the local congressman, Jim Kolbe, to discuss issues related to the 9/11 attack and its aftermath. The Texas center has also published more than sixty books that are marketed around the world.[3]

In 1981, the University of Arizona distributed a "Media Briefing Packet" produced by its Near Eastern Center, filled with inaccuracies and featuring a cover map of Middle Eastern countries in which Israel was the only one with no designated capital. The center also sent materials to public schools that included exhibits on Saudi Arabia and films glorifying Islam and the Arab world, without mentioning Israel. A fact-finding report to the university president later documented that the program received funding from Aramco, Exxon, the Mobil Foundation, and Standard Oil of California.[4] Also in 1981, the Middle East Outreach Council, the association of coordinators of federally funded outreach activities at the centers, held a conference on expanding public understanding of the Middle East that was cosponsored by the Mobil Foundation and Exxon Corporation.

In 1981, not all the centers had become politicized. In fact, Columbia was noted for its "objective, scholarly and apolitical" approach despite receiving small amounts of funding from corporations such as Exxon and Texaco. At the time, "no major Middle East government was clamoring to endow chairs at Columbia." The center's reputation for evenhandedness was attributed to the director, J. C. Hurewitz, coincidentally a Jewish scholar with impeccable scholarly credentials, a far cry from the former PLO spokesman who now runs the center.[5]

At that time, the University of Pennsylvania and UCLA had more problematic programs. Penn's center was run by an Arab American,

Thomas Naff, who became involved in several controversies related to the involvement and funding of programs by Arab governments. The center established cooperation and exchange programs with seven Middle Eastern universities, but none in Israel. The imbalance provoked pro-Israel faculty to create the Penn-Israel exchange program, which upset Naff, who saw it as interfering with his program. UCLA's center had flourished under the leadership of founder Gustave E. von Grunebaum, a distinguished historian of Islam, but began a steady decline when he was replaced by Malcolm Kerr, a pro-Arab partisan who would later become president of the American University of Beirut and die at the hands of Muslim terrorists. Nearly thirty years later, both centers, ironically, at very philo-Semitic universities, are considered hostile to Israel.

At Penn, for example, here are the resources offered to K-12 schools to learn about the Middle East:

- Teaching Resources about Islam and Muslims
- Tapestry of Travel: Contributions of Arab/Muslim Civilization to Geography and World Exploration
- The Arabic Language
- Who Are the Arabs?
- The Contributions of Arab Civilization to Mathematics and Science
- Educational System in Saudi Arabia and Various Booklets on Saudi Arabia

The first publication comes from the very problematic Council for Islamic Education (see below); the publications on Saudi Arabia are products of the Saudi Arabian Cultural Mission, and the rest of the materials are from the Saudi-funded Center for Contemporary Arab Studies at Georgetown University. Nothing is offered related to Israel.

UCLA's federally subsidized Center for Near Eastern Studies (CNES) staged a public symposium titled "Gaza and Human Rights" that featured four outspoken critics of Israel. CNES director Susan

Slyomovics opened the session by telling the audience they would learn the "truth" about Gaza that had been hidden or distorted by the media. UCLA historian Gabriel Piterberg compared Zionist policy since 1900 to European colonialism that led to the extermination and enslavement of the indigenous peoples. UCSB's Lisa Hajjar, who chairs the Law and Society Program, accused Israel of war crimes. Richard Falk, who taught international law at Princeton before being named UN special rapporteur on human rights in the Palestinian territories, compared the Israeli treatment of Palestinians to the Nazi extermination of Jews, insisted that Hamas and its missiles posed no security threat to Israel, and labeled Israeli action in Gaza as a "savagely criminal operation." The fourth speaker, UCLA English literature professor Saree Makdisi, said that it was Israel's "premeditated state policy" to kill Gazans and stunt the growth of their children. The event was later referred to as an "academic lynching," a "one-sided witch hunt of Israel," a "Hamas recruiting rally," or at the very least "a degradation of academic standards." UCLA chancellor Block responded to the controversy by restating UCLA's commitment to the "free exchange of ideas . . . as a core value of academic freedom" and praised UCLA as one of the most invigorating intellectual campuses in the world.

The event may have violated the congressional mandate that federally supported outreach programs promote intellectual diversity and balanced debate. When asked if CNES would plan any events to present an alternative point of view, the center's director, Susan Slyomovics, reportedly said no. Sondra Hale defended the one-sided panel and said it was necessary to criticize the "state policies that have led to this calamity." In another example of the fox guarding the henhouse, Hale, chair of the center's faculty advisory committee, is an organizer of the academic boycott of Israel.

The Jewish Telegraphic Agency reported on another outreach program put on by the center at Georgetown:

> Chairs are lined up in neat rows. Coffee is brewing, muffins arrayed. The table is thick with handouts. One of them

is Saudi Aramco World, a magazine published by Aramco, the Saudi government-owned outfit that is the largest oil company in the world. "The Arab World in the Classroom," published by Georgetown University, thanks Saudi Aramco on its back cover. Alongside it is the brochure of The Mosaic Foundation, an organization of spouses of Arab ambassadors in America, whose chairwoman and president of the board of trustees is Her Royal Highness Princess Haifa Al-Faisal of the Royal Embassy of Saudi Arabia. If you think this is a meeting of Saudi oil executives or Middle Eastern exporters or Saudi government officials, you are wrong: It's a social studies training seminar for American elementary and secondary teachers, held last year at Georgetown University. It's paid for by U.S. tax dollars, as the organizer points out in her introduction.[6]

Indeed, the program was underwritten with Title VI funds.

Georgetown also sponsors symposiums on "Palestine." The Center for Contemporary Arab Studies Web site says it has had a particular interest in Palestine since its establishment in 1975, which begs the question of why the experts in charge of the center are seemingly unaware that no such place has existed during that time period. In 2009, nevertheless, the center sponsored a program titled "Palestine and the Palestinians Today," which featured some of the most vitriolic critics of Israel (including three of the four participants from the UCLA program on Gaza) and post-Zionist Israeli professors.

An extraordinary example of a Title VI–funded center is the Palestinian American Research Center (PARC), the first and I believe only "academic" center focusing on "Palestine" and Palestinian studies. PARC was established in 1998 and has raised more than $550,000 since 2002 to "improve scholarship about Palestinian affairs, expand the pool of experts knowledgeable about the Palestinians, and strengthen linkages among Palestinian, American, and foreign research institutions and scholars."[7] Professors associated with PARC include several well-known academic critics of Israel, such as

Stanford's Joel Beinin, Columbia's Rashid Khalidi, NYU's Zachary Lockman, and Penn's Ian Lustick, so it should not be surprising that the work produced under its auspices "glorifies Palestinian 'resistance' against Israel and vilifies the Jewish state."[8]

PARC originally operated out of Randolph Macon College, but no longer has any university affiliation. It is an independent non-profit organization with no academic credentials whatsoever. The president, Philip Mattar, was previously the director of the Institute for Palestine Studies and editor of its journal.

PARC has awarded more than 120 fellowships to researchers from thirteen countries since 2000. Funding has come from grants from the Ford, Rockefeller, Tananbaum, and Earhart foundations and the U.S. Department of Education. Foreign funding has come in from a member of the London School of Economics Students' Union, a professor from An-Najah National University in the West Bank, and other sources in the U.K., Lebanon, Greece, the West Bank, East Jerusalem, and the Gaza Strip.[9] PARC also receives support from the U.S. Department of State and "nearly 20 leading U.S. universities" that have institutional memberships.

The conclusions of the American Jewish Committee's 1981 study of Middle East centers are shockingly still valid today. The study found:

- The omission of Israel or its minimalization in some of the centers' own literature
- The virtual absence of federal funding for the study or teaching of Hebrew
- The general absence of courses on Zionism in the curricula of the Middle East centers
- The expanding pattern of funding by Arab governments or pro-Arab corporations of chairs, programs and other activities related to the Middle East
- The entire scope of federally mandated and funded outreach programs, which, while not excluding Israel in every case, in many curriculum development and evaluation

projects, evince a determination to improve the image of
the Arab world or, as in the case of business-oriented outreach programs, project decidedly entrepreneurial orientation, geared almost exclusively towards the Arab Middle
East[10]

It is not just the university Middle East centers that are trying
to shape the minds of young Americans. The Arab lobby is actively
engaged in developing, monitoring and shaping the materials used
in K-12 schools. Since at least the early 1990s, publishers have been
pressured to revise textbooks to better reflect multicultural values. In
1993, I reviewed eighteen of the most widely used world and American history texts, which were filled with egregious factual errors and
specious analyses. The mistakes invariably were to the detriment of
the Jews or Israel, raising questions about the predisposition of authors and publishers. The anti-Israel bias was usually a result of factual inaccuracy, oversimplification, omission, and distortion. Common errors included getting dates of events wrong, blaming Israel
for wars that were a result of Arab provocation, perpetuating the
myth of Islamic tolerance of Jews, minimizing the Jewish aspect of
the Holocaust, apologizing for Arab autocrats, refusing to label violence against civilians as terrorism, and suggesting that Israel is the
obstacle to peace. Some of the most flagrant examples that occur in
more than one book are the failure to mention that Syria and Egypt
launched a surprise attack in 1973 on Israel's holiest day, Yom Kippur, and that Iraq fired SCUD missiles at Israel during the 1990–91
Gulf War. The books in this study were so poorly written that all but
one required major revisions.[11]

To be fair, writing textbooks that satisfy everyone is probably impossible. Most have multiple authors and are therefore unevenly written. The authors rarely have a background in Middle East or Jewish
history. Moreover, in eight-hundred-page tomes designed to cover all
of world and American history, events must be condensed. In the case
of U.S. history texts, space devoted to Jews, Israel, and the Middle
East is of necessity limited. Still, given the extent of media coverage

on the Middle East and the level of U.S. aid provided to Israel, one might expect greater efforts would be made to explain the basis of the U.S.-Israel alliance.

Two newer studies have documented remaining distortions in history textbooks now being used by public schools. For example, they tend to whitewash the meaning of jihad, make no distinction between sharia and Western law, downplay discrimination against women, and ignore radical Islam. No effort is made to explain Muslim involvement in terrorism or the animus toward the United States and Israel.

In a study of twenty-eight public school textbooks by Gary Tobin and Dennis Ybarra, the authors found five hundred problematic passages about Judaism, Christianity, Islam, Israel, and the Middle East. Among the problems they identified were:

- Negative stereotypes of Jews
- Misrepresenting the relationship between Christians and Jews
- Denying the Jewish connection to the land of Israel
- Blaming Israel for all the wars in the Middle East
- Glorifying Islam compared to Christianity and Judaism
- Making excuses for Arab and Muslim terrorism

The authors conclude:

> Discovering in our schools a pervasive set of erroneous beliefs about such a vital topic should alarm every taxpayer, every parent, and every school official. To allow biased textbooks and outright propaganda in supplemental materials into the schools is to pervert the very purpose of public education and a misuse of our democratic system.[12]

The subject of distortions in textbooks alone could fill an entire volume. I will just cite one other example of how the Arab lobby is trying to propagandize through the public schools. The textbook

History Alive! The Medieval World and Beyond was piloted in Scottsdale, Arizona, and provoked protests from parents. According to William J. Bennetta of the Textbook League, the book, produced by the Teachers' Curriculum Institute (TCI), is unfit for public schools because it presents Muslim religious tales and religious beliefs as matters of historical fact, strives to induce students to embrace Islam, and sometimes exhibits contempt for Judaism and Christianity. TCI also appears to have a relationship with the Islamic Networks Group (ING), a nonprofit dedicated to educating the public about Islam. The ING endorses TCI's products, but no other textbooks.[13]

Curiously, the vaunted Israeli lobby has been largely silent with regard to textbooks, leaving the field to the Arab lobby to demand that publishers "whitewash and glorify all things Islamic and promote Islam as a religion" and "promote a pro-Arab, pro-Palestinian agenda."[14] Textbook publishers now openly court and try to appease Muslim organizations. The Council on Islamic Education (CIE), for example, has been particularly active in trying to shape the coverage of Islam in textbooks and has had members serve as academic reviewers. According to the group's Web site, CIE is interested in empowering students to understand the world and "not engage in or support 'censoring,' 'sanitizing,' or 'vetting' instructional content." However, according to the American Textbook Council's Gilbert Sewall, starting in the 1990s, publishers "allowed Islamic organizations—notably the Council on Islamic Education—to strong-arm them and in effect act as censors."[15]

The dissemination, often at no charge, of distorted textbooks and other materials is one of the principal means by which the Saudis and others are attempting to propagandize K-12 education about the Middle East. Following 9/11, educators concluded that a need existed to better explain Islam so students would have a better understanding of the beliefs of 1.3 billion people who were now a greater focus of American attention. Almost immediately, however, parents began to complain when they saw what some of the lessons contained and when the source of the materials became known. According to Sandra Stotsky, a former member of the Massachusetts Department of

Education who was in charge of the Center for Teaching and Learning and is now a research scholar at Northeastern University, "most of these materials have been prepared and/or funded by Islamic sources here and abroad, and are distributed or sold directly to schools or individual teachers, thereby bypassing public scrutiny."

For example, as part of its post-9/11 PR offensive, the Saudi government sent thousands of schools copies of a PBS report, *Islam: Empire of Faith*, and Karen Armstrong's book *Islam: A Short History*. "This book," Stotsky notes, "attributes the failure of the Muslim world to modernize to Western 'colonization' rather than to self-imposed intellectual isolation from the revolutionary political, religious, social, economic, and scientific ideas arising in Europe from the 1500s on."[16]

In 2002, the Massachusetts Department of Education made Islamic history a priority for its summer institutes because of the recognition that few history teachers knew much about the topic. The program was developed for teachers by someone from the Education Cooperative in Wellesley, Massachusetts, and the outreach coordinator for Harvard's Center for Middle Eastern Studies. For the final assignment, teachers were asked to propose classroom lessons or curricular units. Stotsky noted that the proposals were "academically weak and contained little history." The focus was on early Islamic history, and few covered anything after 1500. None of the proposals, she said, would have helped students understand Islamic fundamentalism and terrorism; the lack of democracy in the Muslim world; the lack of a free press in most of the Muslim world; the history of slavery in Muslim countries; the lack of basic legal and political rights for women in most of the Muslim world; or a number of other contemporary topics.

Stotsky was particularly shocked that some teachers believed the best way to teach tolerance of Muslims was to study and even act out their religious practices in a way that would be totally unacceptable with regard to lessons on other religions:

> If any teacher asked students to write down and memorize
> the Ten Commandments, listen to the Torah being chanted,

study the religious practices of Hasidic Jews, and prepare a public presentation dressed in men's Sabbath garb or women's Sabbath dress and wig, People for the American Way, Americans United for Separation of Church and State, and the A.C.L.U. would descend upon them like Furies. One can only imagine the public uproar if middle school students, dressed and shaven as Buddhist monks or as Hari Krishnas, began soliciting donations in the neighborhoods surrounding their school or chanting "ommmmm" for the purpose of gaining the "other's" perspective.[17]

One source of materials for schools and teachers is Berkeley-based Arab World and Islamic Resources (AWAIR), which offers free workshops designed to provide teachers a pro-Islamic view, and produces and distributes a number of publications (with the Middle East Policy Council), such as *The Arab World Studies Notebook, The Arab World Notebook: For the Secondary School Level, The Arabs: Activities for the Elementary and Middle School,* and *A Medieval Banquet in the Alhambra Palace.* The director of AWAIR and author of the *Notebook,* Audrey Shabbas, claims that that publication alone has been distributed to 10,000 teachers. She told the *Daily Star* of Lebanon, "If each notebook teaches 250 students a year over 10 years, then you've reached 25 million students." Between 2000 and 2006, AWAIR conducted 208 teacher workshops in thirty-nine states, the District of Columbia, and the British Virgin Islands. It's no wonder *California Catholic Daily* said Shabbas "may be America's most effective educator in guiding public students to embrace a radically pro-Islamic world view."[18]

A review of the *Notebook* by the American Jewish Committee concluded that while "attempting to redress a perceived deficit in sympathetic views of the Arabs and Muslim religion in the American classroom, veers in the opposite direction—toward historical distortion as well as uncritical praise, whitewashing and practically proselytizing." The result "is a text that appears largely designed to advance the anti-Israel and propagandistic views of the *Notebook's* sponsors, the Middle East Policy Council (MEPC, formerly the Arab American Affairs Council) and Arab World and Islamic Resources (AWAIR), to an audience of teachers who may not have the resources and knowledge to assess this text critically."[19] The teachers are undoubtedly further confused by the fact that the Middle East Studies Association has endorsed the work of AWAIR.

William Bennett, president of the Textbook League, a resource for middle school and high school educators, notes in his review of the *Notebook* that it "is a vehicle for disseminating disinformation, including a multitude of false, distorted or utterly absurd claims that are presented as historical facts. I infer that the Notebook has three principal purposes: inducing teachers to embrace Islamic religious beliefs; inducing teachers to embrace political views that are favored by the MEPC and AWAIR; and impelling teachers to disseminate those religious beliefs and political views in schools." He adds that "the promotion of Islam in the *Notebook* is unrestrained, and the religious-indoctrination material that the *Notebook* dispenses is virulent. . . . Shabbas wants to turn teachers into agents who, in their classrooms, will present Muslim myths as 'history,' will endorse Muslim religious claims, and will propagate Islamic fundamentalism. In a public-school setting, the religious-indoctrination work which Shabbas wants teachers to perform would clearly be illegal."[20]

Another organization, Dar al Islam, based in Abiquiu, New Mexico, has used Saudi funding to sponsor workshops in 175 cities in forty-three states, reaching more than 16,000 educators. The organization produces both Wahhabi Korans and curriculum guides for Title VI workshops. Its curriculum "reveals a not-so-subtle package of anti-American and anti-Israeli biases." For example, one guide asks, "Why was America attacked on September 11, 2001?" The answer supplied: "Because of its support for Israel."[21]

In addition to seeding classrooms with propaganda, the Arab lobby is also filling public libraries with materials aimed at propagating its view of the Middle East. In 2002, Prince Alwaleed bin Talal gave CAIR $500,000 to stock American libraries with books and tapes about Islam. The books included a version of the Koran that was eventually banned by the Los Angeles school system because of its anti-Semitic commentaries, which included: "The Jews in their arrogance claimed that all wisdom and all knowledge of Allah were enclosed in their hearts. . . . Their claim was not only arrogance but blasphemy"; "A trick of the Jews was to twist words and expressions, so as to ridicule the most solemn teachings of the faith"; and "The Jews blaspheme and mock, and because of their jealousy, the more they are taught, the more obstinate they become in their rebellion. . . . Their selfishness and spite sow quarrels among themselves, which will not be healed until the Day of Judgment."[22]

While it is well known that the Saudis are bankrolling madrassas around the world to propagate the militant Wahhabi version of Islam, it may come as a shock to learn that the Saudis are doing the same thing in the United States. At the Islamic Saudi Academy (ISA) in Fairfax, Virginia, for example, maps of the Middle East were missing one country. Students were taught that the "Jews conspired against Islam," and an eleventh-grade textbook said that on the Day of Judgment, the trees will say, "Oh Muslim, Oh servant of God, here is a Jew hiding behind me. Come here and kill him." Students told a *Washington Post* reporter that in Islamic studies they were taught that they should shun or dislike Christians, Jews, and Shiite Muslims. One teenager said that some instructors "teach students that whoever is kuffar [non-Muslim], it is okay for you to hurt or steal from that person." Two years later, even Muslim groups complained that first-graders at the school were being taught an extreme version of Islam that fosters contempt for other religions. For example, a twelfth-grade Islamic studies textbook quoted a Koranic verse: "It is said: The apes are the people of the Sabbath, the Jews. The swine are the unbelievers of Jesus' table, the Christians." A revised textbook called jihad "the pinnacle of Islam" and extolled the virtues of martyrdom. It should not be surprising to learn that these views are promulgated in a Saudi-sponsored school. In Saudi Arabia, students are programmed to believe that "anyone who is not a Muslim is our enemy, and that the West means enfeeblement, licentiousness, lack of values."[23]

In an effort to quell criticism, the school revised the textbooks and deleted some of the most controversial passages. Ali al-Ahmed, director of the Institute for Gulf Affairs in Washington, reviewed the books for the Associated Press and acknowledged improvements in the tone of the books, but he said that Wahhabism remained the basis for what ISA was teaching. "It shows they have no intention of real reform," al-Ahmed said.[24]

The school has not been tied to any illegal acts, but the values it teaches are alarming, and at least three graduates have been connected to terrorism. The academy's 1999 valedictorian, Ahmed Omar Abu Ali, was convicted in 2005 and sentenced to thirty years in prison for conspiracy to assassinate the president, conspiracy to hijack aircraft, and providing support to al-Qaeda. A federal appeals court ruled the sentence should have been more severe, and he was subsequently sentenced to life in prison. In December 2001, two former ISA students were denied entry into Israel when authorities discovered one was carrying what the FBI believed was a suicide note linked to a planned terror attack. In 2008, the school's then-director, Abdala al-Shabnan, was convicted for failing to report a suspected case of child abuse.

The students at the school are not only teens. The U.S. army also sends soldiers to the school's "Arabic as a Second Language" program, where they are taught about "Middle Eastern culture and traditions."[25]

In 2002, the academy withdrew its membership from a respected association of private schools in Virginia and lost its accreditation with the group after the organization asked questions about how the academy was funded and governed. The U.S. Commission on International Religious Freedom (USCIRF) reported in 2008 that it had serious concerns that the academy was promoting religious intolerance that could pose a threat to the United States. Earlier the USCIRF had recommended that the State Department close the school until it proves that it does not teach religious intolerance or promote terrorism. The State Department refused to interfere on the grounds that the school is private and not part of a diplomatic mission. In fact, the Saudi ambassador is the chairman of the board, the school receives funding from the Saudi embassy, the embassy owns one of the school's properties and leases the other from the county (the lease was renewed in 2008 for $2.2 million, and in 2009 the academy was granted a zoning exemption to expand at its thirty-four-acre campus),[26] and when questions were raised about the school's curriculum, a reporter was referred to the Saudi embassy for comment. In fact, until the USCIRF raised the issue and this reference was removed, the ISA Web site stated that its Arabic-language and Islamic studies curriculum was "based on the Curriculum of the Saudi Ministry of Education."

The USCIRF maintains that the U.S. government has a right to intervene because the Foreign Missions Act empowers the secretary of state to regulate the activities of foreign missions and to take action if the interests of the United States are adversely affected. A number of members of Congress have also demanded that action be taken against the school, but the State Department has stonewalled them with promises that reforms were being made even as the school refused to give the members access to the textbooks.

This appears to be yet another example of the State Department's persistent fear of offending the Saudis. The USCIRF concluded:

> It is deeply troubling that high school students at a foreign government-operated school in the United States are discussing when and under what circumstances killing an "unbeliever" would be acceptable. The U.S. government must ensure that the Saudi government thoroughly reviews and, as necessary, revises the books it has distributed globally. In both the UN Human Rights Council and UN General Assembly, Saudi Arabia has co-sponsored and supported repeated resolutions urging UN member states to "take resolute action to prohibit the dissemination . . . of racist and xenophobic ideas and material aimed at any religion or its followers that constitute incitement to racial and religious hatred, hostility or violence" and to "ensure that all public officials, including . . .

educators, in the course of their official duties, respect different religions and beliefs and do not discriminate against persons on the grounds of their religion or belief." The U.S. government should insist that the Saudi government meet these commitments fully as a member in good standing of the international community.[27]

USCIRF also pointed out that Saudi Arabia agreed in 2006 to revise its textbooks within two years, and the secretary of state subsequently waived taking action against the kingdom required under the International Religious Freedom Act. "Whether this will prove to be an historic turning point," the Center for Religious Freedom concluded, "or simply a public relations maneuver by Saudi Arabia remains to be seen."[28]

There is nothing comparable to this orchestrated Arab lobby effort to introduce a political agenda into the educational system. One of the most shocking results is that American students are becoming more radical than the Arabs in the region. Khaled Abu Toameh, an Israeli Arab who is the Palestinian affairs correspondent for the *Jerusalem Post*, returned from a speaking tour on college campuses and reported that "there is more sympathy for Hamas there than there is in Ramallah. Listening to some students and professors on these campuses, for a moment I thought I was sitting opposite a Hamas spokesman or a would-be suicide bomber." Despite being known for his honest reporting, which often criticizes the Palestinian leaders, Abu Toameh said he never felt intimidated on a Palestinian campus, but he said he needed police protection while speaking in the United States. He added that he found many Palestinian Authority and Hamas figures more pragmatic than their supporters in the United States. "The so-called pro-Palestinian 'junta' on the campuses has nothing to offer other than hatred and de-legitimization of Israel. If these folks really cared about the Palestinians, they would be campaigning for good government and for the promotion of values of democracy and freedom in the West Bank and Gaza Strip."[29]

The problem is not unique to the United States. In fact, the director-general of MI5 in Great Britain, Jonathan Evans, said in 2008 that the Saudi government's multimillion-dollar investments in British universities have led to a "dangerous increase in the spread of extremism in leading university campuses."[30] Abu Toameh believes the situation is equally serious in the United States. "What is happening on these campuses is not in the frame of freedom of speech," he concluded. "Instead, it is the freedom to disseminate hatred and violence. As such, we should not be surprised if the next generation of jihadists comes not from the Gaza Strip or the mountains and mosques of Pakistan and Afghanistan, but from university campuses across the U.S."[31]

The Arab Lobby's Nefarious
Influence

We can now see that, contrary to the propaganda put out by Stephen Walt, John Mearsheimer, and others, a vigorous Arab lobby does exist, at times exerts great influence, and has consistently acted to undermine U.S. values (freedom, democracy, human rights) and security interests (stability, Arab-Israeli peace, economic growth). The Arab lobby is a many-headed hydra that is less easily defined and less visible than its counterpart. It has no central address comparable to AIPAC and few consensus positions. Unlike AIPAC and the Israeli lobby, which operate primarily in the open and are transparent, much of the Arab lobby works behind the scenes, and its machinations are often difficult, if not impossible, to trace. While the Israeli lobby is principally extragovernmental, a significant component of the Arab lobby is actually part of the governing power structure. The Arabists, in particular, have been a force whose actions are usually not revealed for the twenty-five years it takes before the State Department declassifies its cables, and even then, we do not know how much of their activity is kept secret for national security reasons, concealed to avoid embarrassment, destroyed purposely or inadvertently, or simply omitted because historians can only publish a tiny fraction of the correspondence produced each year.

Israel's detractors, however, prefer to believe the conspiracy theory woven by Walt and Mearsheimer in their book *The Israel Lobby*. If someone didn't know the pedigree of the authors, they would never believe *The Israel Lobby* was written by academics. The book has been widely panned and was derisively reviewed in publications such as *Foreign Affairs*, the *New York Times*, the *New Republic*, and the *New Yorker*.

The authors selectively quote from my work when it suits them, but ignore an entire book's worth of evidence I produced that disproves their thesis. They spend a long time, for example, on the lobby's influence and conclude that it has an "almost unchallenged hold on Congress." As evidence, they mention letters written in support of Israel by members, but they ignore actual policy and the fact that letters reflect more of the lobby's weakness than its power.

Walt and Mearsheimer insist that the lobby doesn't accept that the United States and Israel may have different interests. On the contrary, supporters of Israel understand quite well that the United States has multiple interests, such as maintaining good relations with Arab states and often arming them with weapons that directly threaten Israel. The authors argue that Jews put Israel's interest above those of the United States, but provide no evidence of lobby actions that have undermined U.S. interests. It is true that the lobby may sometimes disagree with the president or other officials, but this is true of all lobbies and individual citizens as well. What they seem to say is that if the lobby disagrees with a president, it is disloyal and acting contrary to American interests. Why can't the lobby express a different view on the national interest? As critics of the Iraq War, Walt and Mearsheimer wouldn't admit that they are acting contrary to the national interest by opposing the president's policies, although a case could be made that they are doing just that.

It is particularly shocking that two academics associated with the "realist" school have such a naive understanding of the fundamentals of U.S. Middle East policy. They ignore the principal U.S. interest in the region, namely oil. Without oil, Americans would not care at all about Arabs. Since this is the most vital U.S. interest in the Middle East, the hypothesis that the lobby is harming American security ought to show that policy toward Israel has somehow affected the flow of oil. With the exception of the embargo in the 1970s, however, no such evidence exists, and even then, OPEC's action was a matter more of self-interest than of fealty to the Palestinians.

As realists, perhaps Walt and Mearsheimer don't like the fact that America also has interests in freedom and democracy in the Middle East, and that Israel is the only country in the region where those values are respected. In the book, they try to show that Israel does not share American values, but the imperfection of Israeli society hardly disqualifies it as a free, democratic society that most Americans recognize as far more like our own than the Arab/Muslim states.

In fact, the Arab lobby, hypocritically, supports the Palestinian Authority and Arab states that do not believe in values Americans take for granted and actively seek to undermine them. The Arab lobby is completely unconcerned with the fact that these entities deny their people freedom of the press, assembly, speech, and religion, discriminate against women and homosexuals, and would curtail our liberties if they had the chance (and do when Americans are within their borders).

Ultimately Walt and Mearsheimer are forced to admit that the Israeli lobby simply does what all lobbies do, but is more effective than most. One of the strengths of our vibrant democracy is the freedom it offers to individuals and groups with different points of view to wage a battle of ideas for the hearts and minds of the public and decision makers. An Israeli official once observed, "The Almighty placed massive oil deposits under Arab soil, and the Arab states have exploited their good fortunes for political ends during the past half century. It is our good fortune that God placed five million Jews in America. And we have no less a right to benefit from their influence with the United States Government to help us survive and to prosper."[1]

Arab and Muslim Americans have every right to pursue their interests through the political process, but there is still a need to be vigilant to ensure that advocates are playing by the rules and that they are not endangering the United States by directly or indirectly supporting radical Islamists or terrorist organizations.

While asserting its right to express its views, members of the Arab lobby do not see the supporters of Israel as having the same freedom. Israel's detractors complain constantly about the Israeli lobby "silencing debate," but the reality is that their point of view is highly publicized, and its spokesmen have been invited to lecture around the world and express their views through the world's major media outlets. It is the Arab lobby that calls for boycotts and has tried, and sometimes succeeded, in silencing critics. Moreover, unlike the Israeli lobby, which might complain about its detractors, supporters of the Arab cause will sue and sometimes threaten those it believes are overly critical or in some way slight Islam.

One tactic that has been adopted to silence critics has been dubbed "libel tourism," whereby lawsuits are filed in the United Kingdom, where it is much easier to win judgments against authors accused of defamation. Unlike the United States, where it has to be proven that what was written was not only untrue but published maliciously and recklessly, English law requires authors to prove that what they wrote is true and can hold them responsible regardless of their intent. This tactic has been especially used against writers who have written about terrorism. For example, journalist Rachel Ehrenfeld was sued by Saudis mentioned in her book, *Funding Evil*, who she said provided financial support to terrorists. Ehrenfeld chose not to defend herself and was ordered by a British court to pay $225,000 to each plaintiff plus costs, apologize for false allegations, and destroy existing copies of her book.[2]

The effort to quiet anyone who raises the alarm about radical Islam has even extended to key departments of the government. For example, in 2008, Stephen Coughlin, the Pentagon's expert on Islamic law and Islamist extremism, was fired because a key aide to deputy defense secretary Gordon England, Hasham Islam, objected to Coughlin's work. At one point Islam accused Coughlin of being a Christian zealot and tried to get him to soften his views on Islamism.[3]

The Arab lobby is more complex than the Israeli lobby, which is most visibly represented by AIPAC. As we've seen, the Arab lobby also is really almost two separate groups of actors whose interests

only occasionally overlap. The homegrown Arab American component is comprised of Arab Americans and Muslim Americans who
are only loosely organized, whose focus is singly on the Palestinian
issue, and whose approach is primarily negative, that is, aimed at
criticizing Israel in an effort to drive a wedge between the U.S. and
its ally. Though Arab Americans have tried to emulate AIPAC, no
single organization or group of organizations has succeeded in fash-
ioning a sustainable grassroots-based lobbying operation.

These pro-Palestinian groups are backed by Christian anti-Zionists and occasionally the other elements of the lobby, such as Arabists
who argue that the Palestinian issue must be resolved for the sake of
U.S.-Arab relations. The domestic Arab lobby has grown more active and sophisticated over the years, eschewing much of the strident
rhetoric of the past and gamely trying to present itself as a moderate
advocate for peace.

Other allies of the lobby that have not been discussed here are
international actors such as the United Nations, which has long been
a one-sided forum for promoting the Palestinian cause and denigrat-
ing Israel, and nongovernmental organizations such as Amnesty International and Human Rights Watch, which have used their image
as neutral observers to present frequently distorted and ill-informed
reports castigating Israeli policies that are used in Arab lobby efforts
to delegitimize Israel and paint it as a human rights abuser rather
than (pace Alan Dershowitz) "the only nation in the Mideast that
operates under the rule of law."[4]

The more powerful part of the Arab lobby is represented almost
exclusively by Saudi Arabia and the corporate (especially oil company) and diplomatic interests that view its well-being as paramount
to U.S. economic and security concerns. No other Arab state has any
representatives with even marginal clout; in fact, AIPAC often is the
most effective lobbyist for its peace partners Jordan and Egypt. Other
countries, such as Syria, don't even try, and smaller states are of little
interest. The Saudis, in particular, have engaged in an unprecedented
effort to influence U.S. policy through politics, economics, and academics. Like all governments, they put their own interests first, and

in the case of the Saudis, those interests include the denial of human rights, the weakening of Israel, the perpetuation of the world's oil addiction, the spread of militant Islam, and the support of international terror.

The Saudis and other Arab states do much of their lobbying on a personal level, leader to leader, but because of their unpopularity, especially after 9/11, the Saudis have spent tens of millions of dollars on hired American guns to help them make their case to Congress and the public and try to improve their image. For some time Prince Bandar was almost a one-man lobby, with unprecedented access and influence, but the close ties with the Saudis were developed long before he arrived on the scene and have continued since his retirement. As we've seen, that relationship has been based less on national interest than on the Saudi ability to blackmail successive administrations into ignoring their human rights abuses and providing them arms and a security umbrella in exchange for oil. As Dick Cheney pithily observed, "The good Lord didn't see fit to put oil and gas only where there are democratically elected regimes friendly to the United States."[5]

Arms sales are one area where there is a mutuality of interests between the Saudis and the United States. The United States wants to protect its oil reserves, at least in theory, by arming its ally, recoup some of the money Americans spend on petroleum through Saudi arms purchases, and lower the unit cost of weapons systems and keep production lines open. The Saudis want to create a dependent relationship between the U.S. defense industry and the kingdom, portray themselves as capable of defending U.S. interests while ensuring that America guarantees its security, and enrich individual royals who serve as middlemen in all contracts.

American arms makers and government officials rationalize sales to the Saudis in terms of competition with other nations; that is, if the United States doesn't sell to them, others will. The reality is that after the boom in oil revenues in the 1970s, the Saudis could afford to buy whatever they wanted from the United States and other suppliers. The Saudis purchased from the French, the British, and even their supposed archenemies, the Communists. Over the last half century, they have bought approximately $100 billion worth of American arms alone.[6] The Saudis spend approximately 10 percent of their GDP on arms, the third-highest per-capita total in the world, and Saudi defense spending does not take into account that their security is really provided by U.S. forces that are paid for by American taxpayers. The Saudis have perhaps the best-equipped army outside of NATO and have not fought a real war in more than seventy years, but the more important expenditures are directed toward the monarchy's personal security. As former CIA operative Robert Baer put it, "About one in every five or six times you pull up to the pump you're contributing something like a dollar toward keeping Saudi royal heads attached to their necks."[7]

Certainly the U.S. defense industry has benefited from this relationship, but America's broader economic interests are also served by U.S.-Israel ties. In fact, despite its small size, Israel is a better market for America. In 2008 the United States imported nearly $55 billion worth of goods from Saudi Arabia, almost entirely petroleum and related products. U.S. exports to the kingdom were a fraction of that total, about $12.4 billion. By comparison, the United States imported more than $22 billion in goods (nearly half of that being diamonds, and another 13 percent medical/pharmaceuticals) from Israel and exported nearly $14.5 billion.

Still, the financial resources of the Saudis are incomparable. "American businesses and the American financial sector will not be able to ignore Saudi Arabia to the extent that they did in the immediate aftermath of 9/11," ambassador Chas Freeman observed. "So I think there are some natural corrections that will take place. Money is an attractive force and the Kingdom will have more money in the future, and that will result in more realistic attitudes on the part of many Americans than we have seen."[8]

So far Freeman's prediction has not come true with regard to the general public; Congress, however, is more responsive. Though it is overwhelmingly supportive of Israel, Congress continues to go along with the Saudi agenda in part because doing business, especially arms sales, is good for its members' constituents in the arms industry, and because trade also benefits state and local economies. Congress also remains committed to the tradition of deferring to the president on national security matters, and so as long as the president takes a pro-Saudi or broader pro-Arab position on national security grounds, it is likely to go along. The Israeli lobby can sometimes persuade Congress to place limits on a president's freedom of action, for example, by making it difficult for him to impose severe sanctions on Israel, but a president intent on pressuring or punishing Israel can do so, as exemplified by the sanctions imposed by Eisenhower and the penalties implemented by George W. Bush.[9]

Critics of President Bush suggested that he was somehow in the pocket of the Saudis because of his family involvement in the oil business, and that this explained his pro-Saudi policy. The Bush family, especially George H. W., does indeed have an extraordinarily close relationship with the royal family; however, every president, Republican and Democrat, has allowed the Saudis to manipulate his policies.

From the early days of America's involvement in the Middle East, when the United States had the maximum leverage over the poor, weak, newly independent Arab states, the Arab lobby prevented the government from pressuring them. It never occurred to the Arabists, for example, that the United States might use arms sales, foreign aid, diplomatic backing, and the American security umbrella as levers to pressure the Saudis or other Arab states to support American policies in the Middle East, especially those related to the peace process. In the absence of any U.S. pressure, the level of Saudi cooperation is best summed up by Ambassador Hume Horan: "The Saudis are masters of inactivity. Anything they didn't want to do, you felt you were walking into a mountain of warm cotton candy. You would never get a flat 'No,' just nothing would ever happen. In some areas they'd help. But if it ever meant Saudi Arabia getting out in front or even getting alongside other regional powers, you could forget it."[10] Rarely did the Saudis take any measures that enhanced American security. In fact, one of the remarkable aspects of U.S. Middle East policy is that through all the changes in the region and at the State Department, the ties with Saudi Arabia have remained consistent. It did not matter whether the Saudis actively opposed our interests or subtly undermined them. This remains true today as President Obama continues this solicitous policy, even as the Saudis reject all his overtures to assist him in advancing the peace process.

When it comes to PR exercises, such as the Fahd or Abdullah peace plans, where the Saudis get to set an agenda that is unthreatening to them because it is consistent with the uncompromising Arab consensus, they are prepared to engage in the process. Otherwise, when the United States is setting the agenda, as in the Madrid or Annapolis conferences, they have to be dragged kicking and screaming. Ambassador Horan observed that the Saudis never want to get involved because they believe they are already in an ideal position. "We get the arms; you get the oil. Your weapons shops keep producing, and at lower unit costs. From time to time we'll denounce al-Kiyaan al-Sahyouni, the Zionist entity, but everyone knows we are not a factor in the Arab-Israeli conflict. You ought to leave well enough alone."[11]

The Arabists try to steer U.S. policy; journalist Joseph Kraft astutely observed, however, they do not get their way in a confrontation over policy with the president or other executive officials, but "in an atmosphere of unconfrontation, when nobody knows what to do, when one policy is exhausted and another needs to be tried, they come into their own."[12] The Arabists found fertile ground for this reason upon the inauguration of Barack Obama. After eight years of what they considered a failure to sufficiently engage in Middle East diplomacy, the Arabists felt unshackled by Bush's departure and immediately pressed the new administration to jump into the Arab-Israeli conflict.

The key to influencing policy is to make arguments that most closely fit the worldview of the president. In the case of Obama, the Arabist case was consistent with his foreign policy vision of improving ties with the Arab/Muslim world, resolving regional conflicts through diplomacy, adopting a more balanced approach to the Arab-Israeli conflict, and not tolerating Israeli policies, in particular settlements, that might interfere with the other aspects of his agenda. He might have pursued similar policies regardless of the views of the Arab lobby, but his initial foray into Middle East affairs was certainly harmonious with its agenda.

The resurgent Arabists also urged Obama to pressure Israel to make concessions rather than use his clout to push the Arabs to take steps for peace. By taking a tough public line calling for a total settlement freeze, Obama sought to demonstrate that he was not going to be Israel's lawyer, as Bush was perceived to be, and would not hesitate to pressure Israel. He may have believed Israel would be forced to cave in to his demands because of his popularity and Israel's dependency on the United States, or that Israeli obstinacy would cause such a severe strain in the relationship that Israelis would seek a change in leadership, as they did when George H. W. Bush's antagonism toward Yitzhak Shamir appeared to threaten U.S.-Israel ties. Mahmoud Abbas was so confident of this result, he told the *Washington Post* after meeting the president, he was prepared to wait for years until that happened.[13]

The administration apparently was banking on the majority of Israelis who favor dismantling most settlements and withdrawing from 90 percent or more of the West Bank to support its position. The strategy backfired, however, when the Obama administration criticized Israeli construction in Jerusalem, uniting much of the country behind Prime Minister Netanyahu's position that the United States had no right to tell Israelis they could not live or build homes in their capital. Obama further alienated the Israeli public by his apparent determination to appease the Arab world at their expense. By refusing to go to Israel and to speak directly to the people there, he sowed so much distrust that polls showed only 4 percent of Israelis believed him to be a friend of Israel.

Meanwhile, the Arab states were not moved by Obama's stance; they believed Obama was not willing to put sufficient pressure on the Israelis, and apparently they hoped that if they stood firm, he might yet do so. Thus, when Obama suggested in May 2009 that the Arab League modify its peace plan to make it more palatable to Israel, the

Arab leaders flatly refused and continued to present it as a take-it-or-leave-it proposition. "There is no change to the Arab Peace Initiative, and there is no need to amend it. Any talk about amending it is baseless," King Abdullah of Jordan said.[14] Prince Turki al-Faisal said that King Abdullah of Saudi Arabia would never follow in the footsteps of Anwar Sadat and visit Jerusalem. A few weeks later, Saudi foreign minister Saud al-Faisal expressed the general view of the Arab world that "the U.S. has the means to persuade the Israelis to work for a peaceful settlement," and suggested that all aid to Israel be cut off.[15]

In subsequent meetings with Arab foreign ministers, the administration was continually rebuffed. Out of desperation to win any concession from the Arabs that they might present to the Israelis as a sign of the benefits to compromise, officials sought agreement from Arab states to allow Israel the right to fly over their countries. It is hard to imagine why anyone at the State Department believed that Israelis would risk territorial compromises that put their capital and major cities in rocket range in exchange for the promise that their planes could fly 30,000 feet above the Gulf states. The idea immediately became moot when the Arab states rejected it.

In every administration a point comes when the secretary of state will either take charge and define U.S. Middle East policy or allow the Arabists in the State Department to seize the agenda. The test came early in the Obama administration, and Hillary Clinton failed by adopting the illogical view that the Palestinian issue must be solved, or the Arab world will not cooperate in the effort to prevent Iran from obtaining a nuclear weapon.

This is just the latest incarnation of the general Arabist view that all problems in the region stem from the Israeli-Palestinian conflict. A simple thought experiment, however, proves the fallacy of the premise that the world would be a better place without Israel, or if its conflict with its neighbors were solved tomorrow. Would any of the inter-Arab border disputes go away? Would Shiites and Sunnis in Iraq stop killing each other? Would Islamists lose interest in world domination and using terror against infidels?

Clinton's statement that Arab officials "believe that Israel's willingness to reenter into discussions with the Palestinian Authority strengthens them in being able to deal with Iran" was prompted by misleading reports from Israel that Prime Minister Netanyahu was going to insist that the Iranian issue be resolved before he would pursue peace talks with the Palestinians. In fact, Netanyahu made clear that he was prepared to negotiate with Palestinian Authority leader Mahmoud Abbas, but that the Iranian threat was the overarching concern for his government (meanwhile, Abbas refused to enter talks with Netanyahu).

Clinton's declaration on Iran expressed the well-worn, and long-discredited, view of State Department Arabists who believe that the Arab states care more about the Palestinians than their own self-interest, and that U.S. support for Israel undermines U.S.-Arab relations. Even Jimmy Carter revealed in 1979, "I have never met an Arab leader that in private professed the desire for an independent Palestinian state."[16] Arab leaders are far more concerned with their survival, and that is threatened by Iran.

Iran's Arab neighbors accused Tehran of threatening the sovereignty and independence of the kingdom of Bahrain and territories of the United Arab Emirates. Egypt was fulminating after discovering Iranian-backed Hezbollah agents in the country, planning attacks on Israel. Morocco broke diplomatic ties with Iran after accusing the Iranian diplomatic mission of interfering in the internal affairs of the kingdom and attempting to spread Shia Islam in a nation where 99 percent of the population is Sunni Muslims. Note that these disputes are unrelated to the Palestinian issue.

Fear of Iran has grown, especially as Arab states have become more skeptical that the international community will prevent Iran from developing nuclear weapons. One indication of regional anxiety is that at least twelve countries have either announced plans to explore atomic energy or signed nuclear cooperation agreements. Only the naive would believe that they all suddenly decided they need to generate nuclear power.

Our Arab allies desperately want us to take measures to stop Iran's drive for regional hegemony. Unlike the Arabists at State, they are clear-eyed enough to recognize that the Palestinian issue will not be solved before the danger from Iran reaches critical mass.

Clinton was apparently so anxious to show fealty to her department, however, that she fed the obsession with the Palestinian issue at the expense of broader U.S. interests. In doing so, she repeated the missteps of her predecessor, Condoleezza Rice, who caved in to the Arabists and persisted in a quixotic last-minute quest for peace that predictably achieved the same result as the prior sixty years of State Department–inspired peace initiatives—failure. A major consequence was to convince the Arab states that George W. Bush had lost his nerve and was unwilling to confront Iran.

Nevertheless, in an effort to prove that this was not the Bush administration, and in the naive belief that the people in the region would swoon over President Obama in the way the Europeans and American voters had, they engaged in a rush to diplomacy. Officials chose to ignore the realities on the ground, which made it clear progress would be impossible because the Palestinians were deeply divided and could not speak with one voice. Furthermore, the Israeli public was weary, having endured in nine years three wars and persistent rocket attacks directed at them from territories they had given up in the hope of peace. Only after nearly ten months of futile diplomacy and fruitless Middle East trips by George Mitchell did the administration show signs of recognizing the fallacy of its policy and begin to accept the idea that the time was not ripe for negotiations and that the parties, especially the Palestinians, would have to change their attitudes before meaningful talks could resume. The Arab lobby, meanwhile, grew increasingly frustrated by what was viewed as Obama's inability to deliver Israel.

By making his first Middle East trip to Cairo in June 2009, Obama also reinforced the widespread view in the region that America is not interested in human rights in Arab countries. This was a policy that was supposed to have changed during the Bush administration when, in December 2002, State Department director of policy and planning Richard Haas finally called for an end to what he called the "democratic exception," that is, the American policy of promoting democracy virtually everywhere in the world except in Muslim countries. He announced the administration's intention to "be more actively engaged in supporting democratic trends in the Muslim world than ever before."[17] The State Department launched a variety of initiatives aimed at promoting democracy, but it was quickly evident that little effort would be made to encourage reform in pro-Western autocracies such as Egypt, Jordan, and Saudi Arabia.

It is time to acknowledge, after more than seventy years of failure, miscalculation, and misreading, that the Arabist and pseudo-realist approaches to Middle East policy have failed to advance American interests. America has lost respect inside and outside the region with its appeasement of autocrats who abuse human rights, and has weakened itself by allowing oil pushers to addict us to their products and to persuade decision makers to protect the dealers. America has endangered itself and the Western world by turning a blind eye to its erstwhile allies' support for terrorism. America has also betrayed its principles by failing to stand for freedom and democracy. Instead of changing our relationship with the only democracy in the region, Israel, as these groups demand, it is time to consider a new approach to relations with the Arab world. The policy of appeasement and indulgence of the Saudis and other Arabs has clearly not convinced them to support our policies. Moreover, the Arab lobby has been consistently wrong in suggesting that the U.S.-Israel alliance complicates efforts to reach a peace agreement. To the contrary, it is the close ties between these countries that forced the Arabs to realize that America would never allow them to destroy Israel, and that they would therefore have to coexist with the Jewish state. Furthermore, the two countries that did sign peace treaties with Israel received rewards in the form of economic, political, and military support that have strengthened their countries and the ruling autocratic regimes. It is better to make clear U.S. support for Israel and to use our leverage to demand that the Arab states make peace with Israel if they want to continue to receive arms, aid, and a security umbrella.

Arabists see the Saudis as wise exotic rulers, but if not for oil they would be dismissed as anti-Semitic, paranoid crackpots of the ilk of

Idi Amin and Qaddafi. The Arab lobbyists argue, of course, that oil trumps everything. "America could remain secure without Israel," notes David Dumke, a former legislative director for Rep. John Dingell (D-MI) and now a principal of MidAmr Group, an organization that promotes U.S.-Arab understanding, "but would suffer greatly should Arab oil cease to flow."[18] This is the straw man on which much of the Arabist argument is built. Why would Arab oil stop flowing? Where would it go? How would the oil producers support their economies and ensure their physical security and their personal profligacy? If nothing else, the last sixty years have shown that the United States does not have to play the Arab lobby's zero-sum game of choosing between relations with Israel and the Arabs.

And what would happen if the Saudi monarchy fell as a result of our insisting on democratization, or if the United States failed to protect the regime from its opponents? Dennis Ross says that the fear is that things would be worse, and that is why interests trump values. But what is the worst case? If Saudi Arabia became an Islamic republic like Iran, the new leaders might raise oil prices, they might withhold supplies, but they need the revenue to keep the country afloat, so they would sell their oil. Would a different regime promote radicalism and terror? Perhaps, but so does the royal family. What matters to the United States is Saudi Arabia's oil, not who sells it. After all, when the shah fell, Iran continued to export its oil to the West. Bin Laden and all the other Saudis understand that whatever power they have is derived from the sale of their oil, so while some American interests might be harmed by a change of regime in Saudi Arabia, the danger to our oil supplies is low. Oil prices might be raised, but the new regime would likely come to the same conclusion as the Saud family: that it is in their interest to moderate prices to avoid provoking America to invest more in conservation and alternative fuels. Any radical regime that attempted to seriously threaten U.S. oil supplies should also understand that we are not likely to stand by and let it happen; the plans Nixon had drawn up in the 1970s to seize the oil fields could be updated.

While the Arab lobby insists that America's relationship with Israel has damaged our image in the Arab world, it is in fact our relationship with Saudi Arabia's corrupt tyrants that has tarnished our image. And if there was any doubt as to Saudi views of the United States, they should have been dispelled when Crown Prince Abdullah said in 2002, "From now on, we will protect our national interest, without regard for American interests in the region."[19] Of course, this was always the policy of the kingdom.

Moreover, today, the primary threat to the United States is radical Islam and the terror it supports. Rather than an ally combating this threat, the Saudis are the principal funders behind it. Walt, Mearsheimer, and other critics of Israel blame U.S.-Israel relations for Muslim hatred of Americans and Osama bin Laden's terror campaign, when it is the close U.S.-Saudi ties that have provoked the radicals. Bin Laden wants the United States out of Saudi Arabia, not Israel. Meanwhile, bin Laden wants to undermine the Saudi monarchy even though it is perhaps the world's most active supporter of the extreme version of Islam adhered to by al-Qaeda.

Thus, the war on terror requires the Arab lobby's fundamental premise to be turned on its head: the best way to prevent terror and fight the Islamists would be to place restrictions on relations with the totalitarian, terrorist-sponsoring, and violence-provoking Saudis, and strengthen ties with the democratic, terror-fighting Israelis.

Administrations have never hesitated to criticize and sometimes punish Israel for its failings, but this has rarely been true of our policy toward the Saudis, who for too long have been shielded by the Arab lobby and its allies. By forcing the Saudis to abolish slavery, President Kennedy proved that a determined president can demand that the Saudis adhere to Western moral and ethical standards. Such leadership has been lacking for far too long. It is time for a change.

The Arab lobby, especially the Arabists, prefer, however, to stress the importance of evenhandedness, as though the United States should not distinguish between allies and enemies, democracies and dictatorships. It was the Arabs who threatened to drive Israelis into the sea, not the other way around, so why should the two sides be treated the same? Israel is a pro-American democracy; none of the

Arab states are democracies, and most were historically anti-American, and yet our policy toward all is supposed to be "balanced." Israel is fighting terror; the Saudis are sponsoring terror; and yet the Arab lobby wants to reward the terror promoter and punish the victim. It made no sense in the past, and it still makes none.

It is understandably frustrating for the Arab lobbyists to fail so frequently to advance the anti-Israel elements of their agenda, and far easier to blame a mythological Jewish cabal than to accept the possibility that their arguments are unpersuasive and have therefore been rejected by the majority of Americans. Besides the merits of the respective cases, Americans can see a clear distinction, for example, between oil companies "lobbying to secure investments and the flow of profits" and the Israeli lobby seeking to "secure the survival of a people who were almost wiped out in the Nazi Holocaust, and who have been subjected to terror and siege ever since."[20]

The Saudi element of the Arab lobby has had great success in achieving its principal objective with the United States, namely, ensuring the survival of the monarchy, but it has not succeeded in fooling the American people into believing that the Saudis are friends or allies. While the detractors of the Israeli lobby may not like its agenda or degree of influence, no one can dispute that it represents the views of a significant number of Americans. By contrast, the Saudi lobby has no base of popular support inside the United States; it is solely a product of the interests of the royal family, which is for the purposes of lobbying a monolith with almost unlimited financial resources.

Another big difference between the lobbies is the level of commitment of pro-Israel Americans to Israel versus Arab Americans' commitment to "Palestine" or other Arab countries. Pro-Israel groups contribute hundreds of millions of dollars to support Israel, independent of U.S. government assistance. In addition, hundreds of volunteers have gone to fight for Israel during its wars, and thousands more have emigrated. By contrast, few Arab Americans emigrate to the region; they contribute little money and have been unwilling to put their lives on the line for the cause they rhetorically support. As Khaled Abu Toameh has written, instead of demonizing Israel, Palestinian sympathizers could send teachers to the territories to teach Palestinians English, or monitors to record human rights violations by Hamas or help Palestinian women being harassed by Muslim fundamentalists: "Shouting anti-Israel slogans or organizing Israel Apartheid Week in the U.S. and Canada does not necessarily make a person 'pro-Palestinian,' but promoting good government and reform in the Palestinian territories does make one 'pro-Palestinian.'"[21]

While the Israeli lobby is entirely funded by Americans, the domestic Arab lobby receives significant support from foreign governments and individuals, which raises questions about its commitment to America's national interests. Ironically, the part of the Arab lobby that should have the greatest legitimacy, the Arab Americans, is its weakest component.

Overall, then, the Israeli lobby is more effective than the domestic Arab lobby because it enjoys advantages in every area considered relevant to interest-group influence. It has a large and vocal membership, members who enjoy high status and legitimacy, a high degree of electoral participation (voting and financing), effective leadership, and a high degree of access to decision makers and public support.

Arab American lobby groups have helped ensure that the Palestinian issue receives attention disproportionate to its importance in U.S. foreign policy, but even without these groups, it is likely that the emphasis placed on the Palestinians, albeit dishonestly, by Arab states communicated through the Arabists would keep the matter on the diplomatic front burner.

Pressure to pursue a solution to the "Palestinian question" is also exerted by another important component of the Arab lobby that has gone unmentioned here, and that is the European nations. The lobbying for Arab interests in Europe and by Europe is too big a topic to tackle here, but suffice it to say the European nations have long held views similar to those of the Arabists and believe their economic well-being would be endangered if they did not support the political agenda of the Arab states and Palestinians. They do not even make a pretense of caring about the values America seeks to uphold, fecklessly seeking to curry favor with the Arab states. Consequently, these nations routinely vote with the Arabs against Israel and the United States at the UN, and European leaders attempt to pressure their American counterparts to force Israeli concessions. They have also long sought to be more directly involved in negotiations, but have been shunned by both sides—the Israelis view them as too pro-Arab, and the Arabs recognize that Europe does not have sufficient clout to force Israel to capitulate to their demands. Still, the Europeans contribute to the Arab lobby's drumbeat of criticism of Israel and pressure on the United States to reduce its support for Israel.[22]

The place where this pressure is most intensely felt is the United Nations, which, since playing midwife to the birth of Israel, has become an ally and tool of the Arab lobby. UN secretary general Kofi Annan has admitted that Israel is often unfairly judged at the United Nations: "On one side, supporters of Israel feel that it is harshly judged by standards that are not applied to its enemies," he said. "And too often this is true, particularly in some UN bodies."[23]

Starting in the mid-1970s, an Arab–Soviet–Third World bloc joined to form what amounted to a pro-PLO lobby at the United Nations. This was particularly true in the General Assembly, where these countries—nearly all dictatorships or autocracies—frequently voted together to pass resolutions attacking Israel and supporting the Palestinians. In 1975, the Arab lobby was the instigator of Resolution 3379, which slandered Zionism by branding it a form of racism. This was a watershed event that gave an international imprimatur to the Arab lobby's campaign to delegitimize Israel. Though this calumny was rescinded in 1991 by a vote of 111–25, no Arab country voted for repeal. The Arabs "voted once again to impugn the very birthright of the Jewish State," the *New York Times* noted. "That even now most Arab states cling to a demeaning and vicious doctrine mars an otherwise belated triumph for sense and conscience."[24]

The Arab lobby also succeeded in securing the establishment of the Committee on the Inalienable Rights of the Palestinian People in 1975. This committee and several others receive millions of dollars in funding to issue stamps, organize meetings, prepare films, and draft resolutions in support of Palestinian "rights." November 29—

the day the UN voted to partition Palestine in 1947—was declared an "International Day of Solidarity with the Palestinian People," and ever since has been observed at the UN with anti-Israel speeches, films, and exhibits. During one of these events, a map of the Middle East was exhibited that did not have the UN member state of Israel. Instead it was replaced by "Palestine." During the 2007 celebration, which coincided with the sixtieth anniversary of the partition resolution, the day was marked by speeches from all UN leaders in a room adorned with just two flags, the UN flag and a Palestinian flag.[25]

The Arab lobby has had less success in the Security Council, where the United States veto has so far ensured that no serious measures can be taken against Israel, such as imposing sanctions, but the idea that U.S. support is automatic or influenced by the Israeli lobby is a myth. The United States did not cast its first veto until 1972, and it has used it only forty-three times since, while the Security Council has adopted more than 150 resolutions on the Middle East, most critical of Israel. The Bush administration took a particularly hard line against UN bodies unfairly targeting Israel, insisting, for example, that resolutions condemn Palestinian terror and name Hamas, Islamic Jihad, and other groups responsible for attacks as a condition for support.

The Arab lobby has been even more successful at politicizing the subject of human rights. The original UN Commission on Human Rights became such a travesty that it was disbanded and replaced by the Human Rights Council (HRC) in 2006. This body has been equally bad, focusing nearly all its attention on allegations brought against Israel while ignoring the genocide in Darfur and the actions of repressive governments such as China and Cuba, which happen to hold seats on the council. The Arab League contingent on the council has been reinforced by members of the Organization of the Islamic Conference and nonaligned governments that do not recognize Israel. Even countries that have improved their ties with Israel in recent years, such as Russia and China, continue to join the lynch mob against Israel because they, like most other countries, see no benefit to voting with Israel and angering dozens of Muslim and

Arab countries. Politically, it makes more sense to irk Israel and appease the Arab lobby, which they may need on votes affecting them, in addition to wanting to remain on good terms with their principal suppliers of oil.

The HRC went even further in 2009 by appointing a commission to investigate alleged war crimes committed during the war with Hamas in December 2008–January 2009. The four-person panel, led by South African jurist Richard Goldstone, included Christine Chinkin, who had accused Israel of war crimes even before the investigation began.[26] The commission based virtually all of its 575-page report on unverified accounts by Palestinians and NGOs. The Israeli government did not cooperate with the commission because of its one-sided mandate.

Following the report's release, Susan Rice, the U.S. ambassador to the United Nations, said, "The mandate was unbalanced, one-sided and unacceptable. . . . The weight of the report is something like 85% oriented towards very specific and harsh condemnation and conclusions related to Israel and very lightly treats without great specificity Hamas' terrorism and its own atrocities."[27] Similarly, the U.S. House of Representatives overwhelmingly approved a resolution condemning the UN report as "irredeemably biased" against Israel.[28]

Despite the U.S. response, the report has given new ammunition to the Arab lobby to attack Israel's morality and its legitimacy. By not holding Hamas accountable for targeting Israeli civilians, the report essentially legitimizes terrorism and criminalizes self-defense. It allows the lobby to cast Israel as a human rights abuser and to try to shake the support, especially, of liberal Americans.

The Arab lobby is hampered, however, by the incredibility of some of its arguments. When the Arab lobby restricts its case to the evils of the "occupation," the argument is compelling; however, critics insist on attacking Israel on multiple levels when it is viewed as a reliable ally that shares U.S. interests and values, unlike the Palestinians or the Arab states. Furthermore, the lobby often resorts to outright fabrications and specious arguments, as when they repeat claims about alleged Israeli massacres or label Israel an "apartheid" state.

The international campaign to delegitimize Israel gained momentum after the UN World Conference against Racism in Durban, South Africa, in 2001, which turned into an Israel-bashing festival and helped the lobby's effort to isolate Israel. This effort has borne fruit in international forums and, especially UN bodies. The Goldstone Report has taken the delegitimization of Israel to a new level.

While the Arab lobby may view these impressionistic trends as indicators of its effectiveness and raise the hope that it may yet achieve its long-term goals, by objective measures the U.S.-Israel relationship remains strong. The web of relations between the people of Israel and the United States is extensive and involves billions of dollars of commercial trade; cooperative research in a range of fields from health to agriculture to energy; joint military programs, such as weapons development and combat exercises; academic exchanges; and much more. In fact, the only country that might be comparable to Israel in terms of the extent of our ties is Great Britain. It is unlikely such relations could ever be developed between Americans and Arabs.

These people-to-people interactions, as well as the understanding that Israel, unlike the Arab states, does share our values and interests, help explain the popular support Israel continues to enjoy. According to Gallup polls dating to 1967, the average sympathy for the Arabs is 12 percent. In February 2010, support for Israel was a near-record 63 percent, while sympathy for the Palestinians was 15 percent. It is a testament to the Arab lobby that the Palestinians get any support whatsoever, given that Palestinians comprise only 0.42 percent of the U.S. population, and Palestinians make up only 6 percent of Arab Americans. The data indicate very clearly, however, that contrary to Arab lobby claims, U.S. policy reflects the wishes of the American people, and it is Walt, Mearsheimer, and their fellow travelers in the Arab lobby whose views are out of sync.

The "national interest" is not some Platonic abstraction. It is a calculation based on the needs and desires of the American people. Lobbies often compete to try to influence American interests not only in the Middle East but elsewhere around the world. For too long, however, the Arab lobby has been allowed to operate behind the scenes, beyond public scrutiny, to guide American policy in directions counter to the views of the public and to the nation's detriment. This book has pulled back the veil on the lobby's activities so its advocates can no longer pretend it does not exist, or that a mythical Israeli lobby somehow controls U.S. policy. Now that it has been exposed, it is time to shake off the influence of the Arab lobby and to bolster ties with countries that do share our values and interests.

INTRODUCTION

1. Gil Hoffman, "4% of Israeli Jews: Obama Pro-Israel," *Jerusalem Post*, August 27, 2009.

2. Khalil M. Marrar, "Lobbying Public Opinion: The Pro-Arab Lobby and the Two-State Solution" (paper presented at the Annual National Conference of the International Studies Association, March 26–29, 2008).

3. Curtis Wilkie, "Arab Lobbyists Find More Sympathy for Their Cause," *Boston Globe*, August 8, 1982.

4. John Mearsheimer and Stephen Walt, *The Israel Lobby* (New York: Farrar, Straus and Giroux, 2007), 140–46.

5. *Near East Report*, February 5, 1975 (emphasis in original).

6. Mitchell Geoffrey Bard, *The Water's Edge and Beyond: Defining the Limits to Domestic Influence on United States Middle East Policy* (New Brunswick, N.J.: Transaction, 1991), 7 (emphasis in original).

7. See, for example, Jack G. Shaheen, "Reel Bad Arabs: How Hollywood Vilifies a People," *Annals of the American Academy of Political and Social Science*, July 2003.

8. William Simpson, *The Prince* (New York: Regan, 2006), 325.

CHAPTER 1: THE SEEDS OF THE ARAB LOBBY

1. Robert D. Kaplan, *The Arabists: The Romance of an American Elite* (New York: Free Press, 1995), 19.

2. Peter Grose, *Israel in the Mind of America* (New York: Knopf, 1983), 41; Phillip Baram, *The Department of State in the Middle East, 1919–1945* (Philadelphia: University of Pennsylvania Press, 1978), 47n.

3. Michael Oren, *Power, Faith, and Fantasy: America in the Middle East, 1776 to the Present* (New York: W. W. Norton, 2007), 360, 373.

4. Warren Bass, *Support Any Friend* (New York: Oxford University Press, 2003), 17–18; Grose, *Israel*, 70. A year later Lansing tried to get Wilson to reject a request for a Zionist medical unit to visit Palestine and was rebuffed.

5. Grose, *Israel*, 82–83, 89–90; Baram, *Department of State*, 269n.

6. Steven L. Spiegel, *The Other Arab-Israeli Conflict* (Chicago: University of Chicago Press, 1985), 11.

7. *New York Times*, March 3, 1919; *The Letters and Papers of Chaim Weizmann: Series B, Papers 1931–1952* (New Brunswick, N.J.: Transaction, 1984), 557; Baram, *Department of State*, 247.

8. Kaplan, *Arabists*, 7.

9. Baram, *Department of State*, 249, 270n; Oren, *Power, Faith, and Fantasy*, 425.

10. Baram, *Department of State*, 248.

11. Oren, *Power, Faith, and Fantasy*, 428.

12. Baram, *Department of State*, 280.

13. Mitchell G. Bard, *Forgotten Victims: The Abandonment of Americans in Hitler's Camps* (Boulder, Colo.: Westview Press, 1994); Baram, *Department of State*, 261.

14. Melvin Urofsky, *We Are One* (New York: Anchor, 1978), 54.

15. Baram, *Department of State*, 288.

16. Urofsky, *We Are One*, 56–57.

17. Grose, *Israel*, 135, 259; Joint Chiefs review from March 16, 1948.

18. Robert Vitalis, *America's Kingdom* (Stanford, Calif.: Stanford University Press, 2007), 65; e-mail from Professor Shlomo Aronson and his book *Hitler, the Allies, and the Jews* (Cambridge: Cambridge University Press, 2004), 98.

19. Michael Cohen, "William A. Eddy, the Oil Lobby and the Palestine Problem," *Middle Eastern Studies*, January 1994; Kaplan, *Arabists*, 80.

20. Grose, *Israel*, 137.

21. Baram, *Department of State*, 254.

22. Cohen, "William A. Eddy."

23. Ibid.

24. Bard, *Water's Edge*, 132.

25. Official British document, Foreign Office file no. 371/20822 E 7201/22/31; Elie Kedourie, *Islam in the Modern World* (London: Mansell, 1980), 70–74; Grose, *Israel*, 151.

26. Oren, *Power, Faith, and Fantasy*, 469.

27. Baram, *Department of State*, 277, 307–8n.

28. Eliahu Elath, *Zionism at the U.N.* (Philadelphia: Jewish Publication Society, 1976), 316n; Parker T. Hart, *Saudi Arabia and the United States* (Bloomington: Indiana University Press, 1998), 38; Baram, *Department of State*, 278–79, 307–8n.

29. Cohen, "William A. Eddy."

30. Grose, *Israel*, 153; Oren, *Power, Faith, and Fantasy*, 471.

31. FDR plan told to Stettinius on January 2, 1945, cited in Grose, *Israel*, 149.

32. Benny Morris, *1948* (New Haven, Conn.: Yale University Press, 2008), 393.

33. Oren, *Power, Faith, and Fantasy*, 473.

34. Grose, *Israel*, 147; Baram, *Department of State*, 295; Urofsky, *We Are One*, 63.

35. Urofsky, *We Are One*, 62–63.

CHAPTER 2: THE ARAB LOBBY CAMPAIGN AGAINST A JEWISH STATE

1. Grose, *Israel*, 190; Baram, *Department of State*, 316n.

2. Elath, *Zionism at the U.N.*, 258.

3. Grose, *Israel*, 212–13.

4. Harry S. Truman, *Memoirs*, vol. 2, *Years of Trial and Hope* (New York: Doubleday, 1956), 140. Eddy subsequently got a job as an Aramco consultant with the job of organizing the company's anti-Zionist lobby in Washington and met with the Joint Chiefs of Staff on December 10, 1947, to warn that "the Jews of Palestine were about to be soundly beaten, if not massacred, in the first Arab-Israeli war." Cohen, "William A. Eddy"; Vitalis, *America's Kingdom*, 79; Hart, *Saudi Arabia*, 40–41.

5. "President Truman to the King of Saudi Arabia Concerning Palestine," October 25,

1946, in U.S. Department of State, *Foreign Relations of the United States* (henceforth cited as *FRUS*), 1946, vol. 8, 716–17.

6. Daniel Yergin, *The Prize* (New York: Free Press, 1991), 425.

7. Hart, *Saudi Arabia*, 42.

8. Minister (Childs) in Saudi Arabia to secretary of state, January 13, 1948, in *FRUS*, 1948, vol. 5, 209; Dore Gold, *Hatred's Kingdom* (Washington, D.C.: Regnery, 2003), 66–67; Thomas W. Lippman, *Inside the Mirage* (Boulder, Colo.: Westview Press, 2004), 273.

9. Memorandum by the director of the Office of Near Eastern and African Affairs (Henderson) to the secretary of state, January 26, 1948, in *FRUS*, 1948, vol. 5, 218; minister (Childs) in Saudi Arabia to the secretary of state, April 24, 1948, in *FRUS*, 1948, vol. 5, 235–37.

10. Hart, *Saudi Arabia*, 43; *FRUS*, 1947, vol. 5, 1336–40; Nadav Safran, *Saudi Arabia: The Ceaseless Quest for Security* (New York: Cornell University Press, 1985), 64.

11. *FRUS*, 1947, vol. 5, 1330–33.

12. Kaplan, *Arabists*, 4.

13. Oren, *Power, Faith, and Fantasy*, 487–88.

14. Ibid., 489; Truman, *Years of Trial*, 162.

15. Kaplan, *Arabists*, 81.

16. Rory Miller, "More Sinned Against Than Sinning? The Case of the Arab Office, Washington, 1945–1948," *Diplomacy and Statecraft* 15 (June 2004): 311–19.

17. Cohen, "William A. Eddy."

18. Memorandum prepared in the Department of State, September 30, 1947, in *FRUS*, 1947, vol. 5, 1167; memorandum for the file by Mr. Robert M. McClintock, November 19, 1947, in *FRUS*, 1947, vol. 5, 1271–72; Frank J. Adler, "Review Essay," *American Jewish Historical Quarterly* 62 (June 1973): 418; Truman, *Years of Trial*, 156.

19. King Abdul Aziz ibn Saud to President Truman, October 30, 1947, in *FRUS*, 1947, vol. 5, 1212.

20. Memorandum from the director of the Office of Near Eastern and African Affairs (Henderson) to undersecretary of state (Lovett), November 24, 1947, in *FRUS*, 1947, vol. 5, 1281; Adler, "Review Essay," 418.

21. Memorandum from secretary of state to acting United States representative at the United Nations (Johnson), October 22, 1947, in *FRUS*, 1947, vol. 5, 1199.

22. Grose, *Israel*, 250–51; memorandum of telephone conversation by the acting secretary of state, in *FRUS*, 1947, vol. 5, 1284. See also *FRUS*, 1947, vol. 5, 1173–74, 1198–99, 1248; Bard, *Water's Edge*, 151.

23. British memorandum of conversations, December 17, 1947, in *FRUS*, 1947, vol. 5, 1313.

24. Interview with Loy W. Henderson, June 14 and July 5, 1973, transcript, Harry S. Truman Library and Museum.

25. Acting secretary of state to the embassy in Chile, November 28, 1947, in *FRUS*, 1947, vol. 5, 1290 n. 1; memorandum by the acting secretary of state to President Truman, December 10, 1947, in *FRUS*, 1947, vol. 5, 1307 n. 4.

26. Clark Clifford with Richard Holbrooke, "President Truman's Decision to Recognize Israel," Institute for Contemporary Affairs, May 1, 2008; www.jcpa.org.

27. Oren, *Power, Faith, and Fantasy*, 494.

28. Baram, *Department of State*, 78.

29. Grose, *Israel*, 225; Kaplan, *Arabists*, 90.

30. *Near East Report*, January 12, 1977, 6.

31. *Near East Report*, January 30, 1974, 19; Adler, "Review Essay," 417.

32. The consul general at Jerusalem (Macatee) to the secretary of state, June 23, 1947, in *FRUS*, 1947, vol. 5, 1158 n. 1.

33. The director of the Office of Near Eastern and African Affairs (Henderson) to the secretary of state, September 22, 1947, in *FRUS*, 1947, vol. 5, 1153–54.

34. Shlomo Slonim, "The 1948 American Embargo on Arms to Palestine," *Political Science Quarterly* 94 (Fall 1979): 497–98.

35. James Forrestal, *The Forrestal Diaries* (New York: Viking Press, 1951), 347.

36. Ronald and Allis Radosh, "Righteous among the Editors: When the Left Loved Israel," *World Affairs*, Summer 2008.

37. Elath, *Zionism at the U.N.*, 309; Yergin, *Prize*, 426.

38. The minister in Saudi Arabia (Childs) to the secretary of state, December 4, 1947, in *FRUS*, 1947, vol. 5, 1336; minister in Saudi Arabia (Childs) to the secretary of state, December 15, 1947, in *FRUS*, 1947, vol. 5, 1341.

39. Grose, *Israel*, 270.

40. Quoted in Yergin, *Prize*, 426.

41. Margaret Truman, *Harry S. Truman* (New York: Quill, 1972), 388; Grose, *Israel*, 276.

42. Robert Silverberg, *If I Forget Thee O Jerusalem: American Jews and the State of Israel* (New York: William Morrow, 1970), 392–94.

43. Howard Sachar, *A History of Israel from the Rise of Zionism to Our Time* (New York: Alfred A. Knopf, 2000), 333.

44. Silverberg, *If I Forget Thee*, 400–401.

45. Bard, *Water's Edge*, 141.

46. Clifford with Holbrooke, "President Truman's Decision."

47. Memorandum of conversation by secretary of state, May 12, 1948, in *FRUS*, 1948, vol. 5, 972–77; Herbert Druks, *The U.S. and Israel* (New York: Robert Speller & Sons, 1979), 30–31; Grose, *Israel*, 293.

48. Truman, *Years of Trial*, 164.

49. Ibid., 165.

50. Memorandum by the president's special counsel (Clifford), March 6, 1948, in *FRUS*, 1948, vol. 5, 687–96.

CHAPTER 3: COLD WAR COMPETITION

1. Kaplan, *Arabists*, 7.

2. In 1959, for example, Israel complained that two countries (Liberia was one) moved their embassies from Jerusalem to Tel Aviv in response to U.S. pressure. In 2002, Congress passed a law that said that American citizens who wished to do so could have "Israel" listed as their birthplace on U.S. passports. The State Department, however, refused to do so. The parents of Menachem Binyamin Zivotofsky, an American citizen born in Jerusalem, sued the State Department to force the government to enforce the law. The case was dismissed by the district court on the grounds that it raised a political question the court could not resolve. That decision was upheld in 2009 by the D.C. Court of Appeals, which agreed that the determination of Israel's sovereignty over Jerusalem was a political question. "Dismayed: U.S. Court Refuses to Enforce U.S. Law Granting Jerusalem-Born U.S. Citizens Right to Have

'Israel' Listed On Official Documents," Zionist Organization of America, July 15, 2009, www.zoa.org/sitedocuments/pressrelease_view.asp?pressreleaseID=1669; instruction from the Department of State to all diplomatic posts, February 20, 1959, in *FRUS*, 1958–60, vol. 13, 147; memorandum of conversation, March 9, 1959, in *FRUS*, 1958–60, vol. 13, 151–52.

3. Memorandum by the director of the Office of Near Eastern Affairs (Jones) to the assistant secretary for Near Eastern, South Asian, and African Affairs (McGee), January 3, 1951, in *FRUS*, 1951, vol. 5, 559–60 (italics in original).

4. Department of State policy statement, February 6, 1951, in *FRUS*, 1951, vol. 5, 572.

5. Memorandum by the deputy assistant secretary of state for Near Eastern, South Asian, and African Affairs (Berry) to the secretary of state, March 15, 1951, in *FRUS*, 1951, vol. 5, 596; Nadav Safran, *Israel: The Embattled Ally* (Cambridge, Mass.: Belknap Press, 1981), 167.

6. State Department draft minutes of discussions at the State–Joint Chiefs of Staff meeting, May 2, 1951, in *FRUS*, 1951, vol. 5, 655–56.

7. I. L. Kenen, *Israel's Defense Line* (Buffalo, N.Y.: Prometheus, 1981), 127–28.

8. Byroade once recalled telling Israeli prime minister David Ben-Gurion to make peace. "If you go ahead and do it," Byroade said, "your people are so capable, they'll be running every bank in the Middle East in 50 years." Abraham Ben-Zvi, *The United States and Israel: The Limits of the Special Relationship* (New York: Columbia University Press, 1993), 52; interview with Henry Byroade, September 19, 1988, Association for Diplomatic Studies and Training Foreign Affairs Oral History Project [henceforth ADST].

9. Oral history interview with Edwin M. Wright, July 26, 1974, transcript, Harry S. Truman Library and Museum; Spiegel, *Other Arab-Israeli Conflict*, 66–67.

10. "Special National Intelligence Estimate," July 31, 1956, in *FRUS*, 1955–57, vol. 16, 89.

11. Lippman, *Inside the Mirage*, 215; Kenen, *Israel's Defense Line*, 128.

12. Urofsky, *We Are One*, 316.

13. Ben-Zvi, *The United States and Israel*, 72–73.

14. Memorandum of a conversation, February 7, 1957, 101–2; editorial note, in *FRUS*, 1957, vol. XVII, p. 17 (Arab-Israeli Dispute), 498.

15. Memorandum of a conversation, April 4, 1958, in *FRUS*, 1958–60, vol. 13, 36–38.

16. Hart, *Saudi Arabia*, 65, 68–69; David Long, *The United States and Saudi Arabia: Ambivalent Allies* (Boulder, Colo.: Westview Press, 1985), 39.

17. Memorandum of conversation, Department of State, December 5, 1957, in *FRUS*, 1957, vol. 17, 17 (Arab-Israeli Dispute), 843n.

18. Oren, *Power, Faith, and Fantasy*, 514.

19. The head of the Syrian security service, Abdel Hamid Sarraj, announced at a press conference on March 5, 1958, that Saud had tried to pay him to kill Nasser to abort the Egyptian-Syrian merger. Vitalis, *America's Kingdom*, 191–93; Safran, *Saudi Arabia*, 85–87; Rachel Bronson, *Thicker Than Oil* (New York: Oxford University Press, 2006), 79; *Near East Report*, May 1, 1961.

20. "Factors Affecting US Policy toward the Near East," quoted in Abraham Ben-Zvi, *The Origins of the American-Israeli Alliance: The Jordanian Factor* (New York: Columbia University Press, 1998), 31–53.

21. *Near East Report*, August 17, 1959.

CHAPTER 4: WAR AND PEACE

1. Bass, *Support Any Friend*, 56–57.
2. Interview with Henry Byroade, September 19, 1988, transcript, ADST.
3. Joseph Kraft, "Those Arabists in the State Department," *New York Times*, November 7, 1971.
4. Arthur M. Schlesinger Jr., *A Thousand Days* (New York: Fawcett Premier Books, 1985), 522–23.
5. Bass, *Support Any Friend*, 88.
6. Ibid., 114–15.
7. Hart, *Saudi Arabia*, 194–201; interview with Parker T. Hart, August 12, 1988, transcript, ADST.
8. Hart, *Saudi Arabia*, 210–28.
9. Oren, *Power, Faith, and Fantasy*, 523.
10. Bronson, *Thicker Than Oil*, 90, 91 n. 55, 94.
11. Talcott W. Seelye, September 15, 1993, transcript, ADST. See also *FRUS*, 1964–68, vol. 21, entries for January 30, 1964, February 5, 1964, April 3, 1964, March 23, 1965, and April 19, 1965.
12. Bronson, *Thicker Than Oil*, 95–96.
13. Lippman, *Inside the Mirage*, 297.
14. See for example, telegram from the embassy in Saudi Arabia to the Department of State, February 20, 1967, in *FRUS*, 1964–68, vol. 21.
15. *Near East Report*, October 4, 1966.
16. Kaplan, *Arabists*, 143.
17. Paul Merkley, *American Presidents, Religion, and Israel* (Westport, Conn.: Praeger, 2004), 60.
18. Memorandum for the record, May 24, 1967, in *FRUS*, 1964–68, vol. 34.
19. John J. McCloy to Secretary of State Rusk, June 5, 1967, in *FRUS*, 1964–68, vol. 34.
20. Kaplan, *Arabists*, 134.
21. Telegram from the embassy in Saudi Arabia to the Department of State, June 23, 1967, in *FRUS*, 1964–68, vol. 21; telegram from the embassy in Saudi Arabia to the Department of State, August 27, 1967, in *FRUS*, 1964–68, vol. 21.
22. Telegram from the Department of State to the embassy in Saudi Arabia, October 24, 1968, in *FRUS*, 1964–68, vol. 21.
23. Telegram from the Department of State to the embassy in Saudi Arabia, October 24, 1967; memorandum from Secretary of State Rusk to President Johnson, January 19, 1968, in *FRUS*, 1964–68, vol. 21.
24. Alfred Leroy Atherton Jr., Summer 1990, transcript, ADST.
25. Interview with Samuel Lewis.
26. Airgram from the Department of State to the embassy in Israel, April, 8, 1968, in *FRUS*, 1964–68, vol. 20, 268–69.
27. When asked who they sympathized with more, 47 percent of Americans said Israel; only 1 percent, the Arabs. Harris poll, June 1967. Memorandum from the executive secretary of the National Security Council Special Committee on the Middle East Crisis (Bundy) to President Johnson, July 10, 1967, in *FRUS*, 1964–68, vol. 34.
28. Gold, *Hatred's Kingdom*, 82–83.
29. Kaplan, *Arabists*, 167.
30. Ibid., 7–8.

31. Barry Rubin, *Secrets of State: The State Department and the Struggle over U.S. Foreign Policy* (New York: Oxford University Press, 1985), 163.

32. Richard B. Parker, "'The Arabists': A Review Essay," *Journal of Palestine Studies*, Autumn 1994, 71–72.

33. Alfred Leroy Atherton Jr., Summer 1990, transcript, ADST.

34. Andrew Killgore, "Other Hostages: The State Department Arabists," *Washington Report on Middle East Affairs*, August 12, 1985.

CHAPTER 5: THE PETRODIPLOMATIC COMPLEX

1. Vitalis, *America's Kingdom*, 64.

2. "Saudi Prince Says US Ties at Risk over Mideast," Reuters, January 23, 2009.

3. "A Beginner's Guide to Saudi Aramco," *Saudi Aramco World*, May/June 2008, 8; Hart, *Saudi Arabia*, 38.

4. Yergin, *Prize*, 291, concession quote, 583; Robert Baer, *Sleeping with the Devil* (New York: Three Rivers Press, 2003), 76–77; Oren, *Power, Faith, and Fantasy*, 414; Baram, *Department of State*, 35.

5. Yergin, *Prize*, 428.

6. Vitalis, *America's Kingdom*, 77; Yergin, *Prize*, 398; Hart, *Saudi Arabia*, 32–33.

7. Memorandum by the Director of Financial and Development Policy (Collado) to the President of the Export-Import Bank of Washington (Taylor), October 19, 1945, in *FRUS*, 1945, vol. 8, 960–61; Memorandum by the Assistant Secretary of State (Clayton) to the Assistant Secretary of State (Dunn), April 7, 1945, in *FRUS*, vol. 8, 869.

8. Yergin, *Prize*, 445.

9. The minister in Saudi Arabia (Eddy) to the secretary of state, October 2, 1945, in *FRUS*, vol. 8, 959; Baram, *Department of State*, 211, 236; Bronson, *Thicker Than Oil*, 40.

10. Memorandum of conversation by the director of the Office of Near Eastern and African Affairs (Henderson), July 31, 1945, in *FRUS*, vol. 8, 1003.

11. The minister in Saudi Arabia (Eddy) to the secretary of state, July 8, 1945, in *FRUS*, vol. 8, 925. Already in mid-1945, the United States offered to train Saudi pilots. See Department of State to the British embassy, July 6, 1945, in *FRUS*, vol. 8, 922–23.

12. Morris Draper, February 27, 1991, transcript, ADST.

13. Lippman, *Inside the Mirage*, 46–48.

14. Vitalis, *America's Kingdom*, 119, 142.

15. Ibid., 82–83.

16. Letter from Eddy to his wife, in ibid., pp. 124–25 (emphasis in original).

17. Lippman, *Inside the Mirage*, 125–27.

18. Ibid., 102–3.

19. Ibid., 104.

20. Vitalis, *America's Kingdom*, 184.

21. Lippman, *Inside the Mirage*, 148–53.

22. Memorandum of conversation, January 13, 1965, in *FRUS*, 1964–68, vol. 21.

23. National intelligence estimate, February 17, 1966, in ibid.

24. "Near East Oil: How Important Is It?" February 8, 1967, in ibid.

25. Memorandum from Harold H. Saunders of the National Security Council Staff to the president's special assistant (Rostow), May 16, 1967, in ibid.

26. *Near East Report*, August 17, 1959, 22.

27. "Western Interests in Arab Oil," December 27, 1967, in *FRUS*, 1964–68, vol. 21.

28. Terrence Prittie and Walter Henry Nelson, *The Economic War against the Jews* (London: Corgi, 1977), 124.

29. William M. Rountree, December 22, 1989, transcript, ADST.

30. "The International Oil Industry through 1980," Department of State, December 1971, quoted in Yergin, *Prize*, 591.

CHAPTER 6: THE LOBBY REALIZES ITS POWER

1. Raymond Close, "Intelligence and Policy Formulation, Implementation and Linkage: A Personal Perspective," remarks at the Thirteenth Annual Arab-US Policymakers Conference, Washington, D.C., September 13, 2004.

2. Military sales credits added another $257 million. Between 1973 and 1976, U.S. military commitments would grow to $1.042 billion. Kenen, *Israel's Defense Line*, 292–93; *Near East Report*, May 9, 1973, 73, June 6, 1973, 89, and June 13, 1973, 94; Safran, *Saudi Arabia*, 155.

3. Yergin, *Prize*, 595–96.

4. Steven Emerson, *The American House of Saud* (New York: Franklin Watts, 1985), 23, 28.

5. Kenneth C. Crowe, *America for Sale* (New York: Anchor, 1980), 152–53.

6. Letter from O. N. Miller, July 26, 1973, cited in full in *Near East Report*, August 8, 1973, as is Cranston's response; Crowe, *America for Sale*, 153.

7. "The Saudi Oil Threat," *Washington Post*, April 20, 1973; *Wall Street Journal*, April 26, 1973.

8. Yergin, *Prize*, 598.

9. Ibid., 499–500, 541–42. In 1966, 71 percent of the oil used by OECD nations came from the Middle East and North Africa, while 12.9 percent came from Saudi Arabia. By 1972, the figures were 76 and 21.6 percent, respectively. Safran, *Saudi Arabia*, 161.

10. Emerson, *American House of Saud*, 28; Yergin, *Prize*, 594.

11. It was unusual for the oil companies to put anything in writing; they preferred to communicate their views orally. Safran, *Saudi Arabia*, 156; Yergin, *Prize*, 605; Crowe, *America for Sale*, 153.

12. Yergin, *Prize*, 615; Safran, *Saudi Arabia*, 156.

13. Josh Pollack, "Saudi Arabia and the United States," *Middle East Review of International Affairs*, September 2002.

14. Bronson, *Thicker Than Oil*, 119–20; Lippman, *Inside the Mirage*, 157.

15. Bronson, *Thicker Than Oil*, 118.

16. *Near East Report*, August 21, 1974, 183; Kaplan, *Arabists*, 176–77.

17. Kenen, *Israel's Defense Line*, 321–22.

18. *Near East Report*, September 18, 1974; Long, *Ambivalent Allies*, 55.

19. Robert G. Kaiser and David Ottaway, "Oil for Security Fueled Close Ties; But Major Differences Led to Tensions," *Washington Post*, February 11, 2002.

20. Gerald L. Posner, *Secrets of the Kingdom: The Inside Story of the Secret Saudi-U.S. Connection* (New York: Random House, 2005), 70; Baer, *Sleeping with the Devil*, 41; *Near East Report*, September 17, 1975. In 2008, Lockheed paid $4 million to the federal government to settle charges that the company did not obtain proper clearances for a proposed missile sale to the UAE and had revealed classified information. Stephen Manning, "Lockheed to Pay $4 Million to Settle Missile Sale Charge," *Washington Post*, August 9, 2008.

21. Julia Werdigier and Alan Cowell, "Court Faults Britain for Halting Arms Deal Inquiry," *New York Times*, April 11, 2008. Bandar was not the only one accused of taking bribes. Prince Turki bin Nasser, the Saudis' contact with BAE, also allegedly received about $32 million worth of perks, including a three-month summer vacation, a wedding video for his daughter, and a Rolls-Royce for his wife's birthday. John R. Bradley, *Saudi Arabia Exposed* (New York: Palgrave, 2005), 141. A U.S. pension fund has also sued BAE, accusing current and former directors and executives of breaching their fiduciary duties and wasting corporate assets by allegedly allowing illegal bribes and kickbacks. The plaintiff's case was dismissed by an appeals court, but may be appealed to the Supreme Court. The U.S. Justice Department did not respond to the paper's inquiries regarding the investigation it opened in 2007 into BAE's activities. "BAE Suit Could Go to U.S. Supreme Court," Reuters, January 1, 2010.

22. Emerson, *American House of Saud*, 43–44, 49; Posner, *Secrets of the Kingdom*, 59.

23. Yergin, *Prize*, 651–52.

24. Emerson, *American House of Saud*, 56.

25. JECOR was shut down in 2000. According to Chas Freeman, the Saudis gradually became virtually bankrupt in the 1990s following the 1991 Gulf War and simply could not afford to support the commission. Chas W. Freeman Jr., "What Are the Prospects for Democracy in Saudi Arabia?" remarks made at the Center for American Progress panel, June 15, 2004.

26. Crowe, *America for Sale*, 192.

27. Emerson, *American House of Saud*, 329.

28. Tad Szulc, "Recycling Petrodollars: The $100 Billion Understanding," *New York Times*, September 20, 1981.

29. Posner, *Secrets of the Kingdom*, 87–88; *Near East Report*, December 19, 1979, 221–22.

30. Simon English, "Saudi Threat to Withdraw Billions in US Investments," *Telegraph*, August 19, 2002; Terence J. Kivlan, "$1 Trillion 9/11 Case against Saudis Is Languishing," *Staten Island Advance*, June 25, 2006; Eric Lichtblau, "Justice Dept. Backs Saudi Royal Family on 9/11 Lawsuit," *New York Times*, May 30, 2009; Chris Mondics, "Solicitor General Asked to Weigh In on 9/11 Suit," *Philadelphia Inquirer*, February 24, 2009; Chris Mondics, "Phila. Firm Files Brief on Behalf of 9/11 Victims," *Philadelphia Inquirer*, June 11, 2009; "Court Won't Hear Sept. 11 Claims vs. Saudi Arabia," Associated Press, June 29, 2009.

31. According to *Forbes* ("The World's Billionaires," March 5, 2008), "Alwaleed joined the Singapore government investment arm and several other investors in a $12.5 billion capital injection for Citigroup in January 2008; the size of his investment is undisclosed. In the early 1990s, Alwaleed made a risky bet on Citigroup that paid off hugely; in recent years it accounted for nearly half his fortune." That investment, incidentally, was arranged by the Carlyle Group, whose chairman is former defense secretary Frank Carlucci. In December 2007, the Abu Dhabi Investment Fund invested $7.5 billion in convertible bonds of Citigroup, which increased the Gulf oil producers' influence at the bank. Shmuel Even, "Strategic Implications of the Global Oil Market," in *The Middle East Strategic Balance 2007–2008*, ed. Mark Heller (Tel Aviv: Institute for National Security Studies, 2008), 105. Talal quote in Lachlan Carmichael, "Arab Boycott Campaign Worries US Business," *Arab News*, May 1, 2002.

32. Yergin, *Prize*, 714; Robert Bamberger, *The Strategic Petroleum Reserve: History, Perspectives, and Issues* (Washington, D.C.: Congressional Research Service, 2008), 2.

33. Even, "Strategic Implications," 98; Baer, *Sleeping with the Devil*, xxvi; "A Beginner's Guide to Saudi Aramco," *Saudi Aramco World*, May/June 2008, 7.

34. Baer, *Sleeping with the Devil*, 187.

35. Even, "Strategic Implications," 104.

36. Statement of Richard W. Murphy before the House Armed Services Committee Special Oversight Panel on Terrorism, May 23, 2002; "How to Break the Tyranny of Oil," *Economist*, October 23, 2003.

37. Peter Kenyon, "Saudi King Criticizes U.S. for 'Illegitimate' Occupation," NPR, February 10, 2009.

38. Michael Abramowitz, "Oil Efforts Are Best Possible, Saudis Say," *Washington Post*, May 17, 2008; "US Unveils Deals with Saudi on Nuclear Power, Oil Protection," Agent France-Presse, May 16, 2008.

39. "Turki Slams US Policy on Energy," *Saudi Gazette*, August 27, 2009.

CHAPTER 7: JIMMY CARTER'S CONVERSION

1. In 1976, Carter received 76 percent of the Jewish vote; in 1980, the figure declined to 45 percent. Carter's unpopularity was not entirely based on his Middle East policy. Like many Americans, Jews also were disturbed by his handling of the Soviet invasion of Afghanistan and the hostage crisis in Iran as well as the U.S. economy.

2. Merkley, *American Presidents*, 139.

3. Ibid., 141, 143, 147–48.

4. Prittie and Nelson, *Economic War*, 20.

5. Dan Chill, *The Arab Boycott of Israel* (New York: Praeger, 1976), 47.

6. *Near East Report*, May 15, 1961, 97.

7. Prittie and Nelson, *Economic War*, 37; Kennan L. Teslik, *Congress, the Executive Branch, and Special Interests: The American Response to the Arab Boycott of Israel* (Westport, Conn.: Greenwood Press, 1982), 69; Sol Stern, "On and Off the Arabs' List," *New Republic*, March 27, 1976; Robert J. Samuelson, "As the Oil Flows, So Flows the Trade," *National Journal*, January 29, 1977, 162.

8. Teslik, *American Response*, 5, 71; Prittie and Nelson, *Economic War*, 80; Will Maslow, "The Struggle against the Arab Boycott," *Midstream*, August–September 1977, 12.

9. Prittie and Nelson, *Economic War*, 82.

10. "More Oil Firms Warn of Impact on U.S. of Antiboycott Laws," *Wall Street Journal*, September 30, 1976; Teslik, *American Response*, 105, 146–47.

11. Teslik, *American Response*, 131; Prittie and Nelson, *Economic War*, 200; Paul Lewis, "Administration Is Boycotting Anti-Arab Boycott Bills," *National Journal*, June 19, 1976, 858.

12. "Carter Moves Cautiously on Antiboycott Proposals," *Weekly Report Congressional Quarterly*, March 12, 1977, 437.

13. Prittie and Nelson, *Economic War*, 204–5.

14. Visit of Crown Prince Fahd of Saudi Arabia—Toasts of the President and the Crown Prince at a Dinner Honoring His Royal Highness, May 24, 1977.

15. Spiegel, *Other Arab-Israeli Conflict*, 325.

16. Interview with Nicholas A. Veliotes, January 29, 1990, transcript, ADST, 110.

17. Jimmy Carter, *Keeping Faith* (New York: Bantam, 1982), 299.

18. Robert S. Strauss, October 25, 2002, transcript, ADST.

19. Spiegel, *Other Arab-Israeli Conflict*, 320, 322.

20. Interview with Chas W. Freeman Jr., May 24, 1984, transcript, ADST; interview with Veliotes, January 29, 1990.

21. Jimmy Carter, "Tampa Florida Question-and-Answer Session with Florida Newspaper Editors," August 30, 1979.

22. Interview with Hermann Eilts, August 12, 1988, transcript, ADST.

23. Spiegel, *Other Arab-Israeli Conflict*, 362. Confirmed in an e-mail to the author by former Israel High Court chief justice Aharon Barak, who took notes at the meeting where Begin made his pledge.

24. Visit of Crown Prince Fahd of Saudi Arabia—Remarks to Reporters on the Crown Prince's Departure, May 25, 1977; Safran, *Saudi Arabia*, 230.

25. Hoag Levins, *Arab Reach* (New York: Doubleday, 1983), 10–11.

26. Emerson, *American House of Saud*, 102–4.

27. David B. Ottaway, *The King's Messenger* (New York: Walker, 2008), 33; Simpson, *The Prince*, 56.

28. Rehavia Yakovee, "Arms for Oil/Oil for Arms: An Analysis of President Carter's 1978 Planes 'Package Deal' Sale to Egypt, Israel and Saudi Arabia," Claremont, Ph.D. diss., 1983, pp. 60–61 from the *Los Angeles Times*, May 19, 1978; *Jerusalem Post*, December 21–27, 1980.

29. Carter, "Question-and-Answer Session."

30. Congressional Quarterly, *Congressional Quarterly Almanac* (Washington, D.C.: Congressional Quarterly Press, 1978), 410–11.

31. *Near East Report*, May 17, 1978, 85.

32. *The Washington Lobby* (Washington, D.C.: Congressional Quarterly Press, 1979), 150.

33. *Near East Report*, August 21, 1989.

34. *Near East Report*, March 5, 1980.

35. *Los Angeles Times,* March 5, 17, 1980; *Near East Report*, March 26, 1980.

36. Long, *Ambivalent Allies*, 56.

37. Douglas Brinkley, *The Unfinished Presidency: Jimmy Carter's Journey to the Nobel Peace Prize* (New York: Viking Penguin, 1998), 330.

38. Merkley, *American Presidents*, 182–83; Brinkley, *Unfinished Presidency*, 339–43.

39. Jay Nordlinger, "There He Goes Again," *National Review*, May 20, 2002; George Bush and Brent Scowcroft, *A World Transformed* (New York: Alfred A. Knopf, 1998), 413–14; Brinkley, *Unfinished Presidency*, 339–40, 378.

40. "Reagan Is Faulted on Mideast," Associated Press, March 20, 1987.

41. Kenneth W. Stein, "Resignation from Carter Center," text of Stein's e-mail to friends and former students, December 5, 2006, www.ismi.emory.edu/Articles/resignationltr.html.

42. Jimmy Carter, "America Can Persuade Israel to Make a Just Peace," *New York Times*, April 21, 2002; Jay Nordlinger, "There He Goes Again," *National Review*, May 20, 2002.

43. Carter, "Just Peace." For more on the Saudi peace plan, see "Analysis of the Arab League 'Peace Plan,'" www.jewishvirtuallibrary.org/jsource/Peace/arabplan1.html.

44. Etgar Lefkovits, "Carter Calls for Funding Palestinians," *Jerusalem Post*, January 26, 2006.

45. Dalia Nammari, "Jimmy Carter Embraces Hamas Official," Associated Press, April 15, 2008.

46. Erin Cunningham, "Why Israel and Hamas Are Meeting with Jimmy Carter," *Christian Science Monitor*, June 16, 2009; "Hamas Rejects Carter Plea to Recognize Israel,"

Associated Press, June 17, 2009; Howard Schneider, "Defiant Abbas Reiterates Conditions before Talks," *Washington Post*, October 12, 2009.

47. Brinkley, *Unfinished Presidency*, 253.
48. Jonathan Adelman and Agota Kuperman, "The Christian Exodus from the Middle East," Foundation for Defense of Democracies, December 18, 2001, http://defend democracy.org/index.php?option=com_content&task=view&id=11782108.
49. "Christians in Palestine Concerned about Their Future," Zenit News Agency, November 14, 2004.
50. Khaled Abu Toameh, "Away from the Manger—A Christian-Muslim Divide," *Jerusalem Post*, October 21, 2005; Harry de Quetteville, " 'Islamic Mafia' Accused of Persecuting Holy Land Christians," *Telegraph*, September 9, 2005.
51. Brinkley, *Unfinished Presidency*, 78, 111, 224, 239, 329; Baer, *Sleeping with the Devil*, 64. See also Emerson, *American House of Saud*, 407–8.
52. Lloyd Greif, "To See Jimmy Carter's True Allegiances, Just Follow the Money," *New York Daily News*, April 27, 2008; See also "Donors with Cumulative Lifetime Giving of $1 Million or More," Carter Center Annual Report, 2007–8.
53. Alan M. Dershowitz, "The Real Jimmy Carter," FrontPageMagazine.com, April 30, 2007, www.frontpagemagazine.com/Articles/Read.aspx?GUID=14F14A6C-2BBE-439E-929A-425288DA09E4; Carter Center, IRS Form 990, 2006.

Chapter 8: Arms Sales Fights

1. Interview with Samuel W. Lewis, August 9, 1998, transcript, ADST.
2. George J. Church, "AWACS: He Does It Again," *Time*, November 9, 1981, 16.
3. Confidential interview with defense industry consultant.
4. Fahd interview, *Washington Post*, May 25, 1980. Islamic conference was held January 14–30, 1981, and Haig visit was April 7–8, 1981. Safran, *Saudi Arabia*, 326, 328.
5. Steven Emerson, "The Petrodollar Connection," *New Republic*, February 17, 1982; see also Emerson, *American House of Saud*.
6. Levins, *Arab Reach*, 17; Emerson, *American House of Saud*, 187; *New York Times*, October 1, 1981; Craig Unger, *House of Bush, House of Saud* (New York: Scribner, 2004), 130; Simpson, *The Prince*, 361.
7. Levins, *Arab Reach*, 19; Emerson, *American House of Saud*, 213.
8. *New York Times*, September 18, 1981; *Near East Report*, September 25, 1981, 178; Edward Tivnan, *The Lobby* (New York: Simon and Schuster, 1987), 143; Emerson, *American House of Saud*, 187–88.
9. John Rourke, *Congress and the Presidency in U.S. Foreign Policymaking* (Boulder, Colo.: Westview Press, 1983), 260; Emerson, *American House of Saud*, 188–89.
10. Richard Cohen, "Even If He Wins on Saudi Arms Sale, Reagan May Find It a Hollow Victory," *National Journal*, September 12, 1981, 1621.
11. Levins, *Arab Reach*, 3.
12. In his meeting with Reagan, the president told the Roman Catholic Durenberger that the pope would vote for AWACS. Walter Isaacson, "The Man with the Golden Arm," *Time*, November 9, 1981.
13. *Near East Report*, November 6, 1981, 203.
14. Isaacson, "Man with the Golden Arm," 25; George J. Church, "AWACS: He Does It Again," *Time*, November 9, 1981, 13.
15. *New York Times*, October 29, 1981; Isaacson, "Man with the Golden Arm," 26.

16. *Near East Report*, December 11, 1981, and June 11, 1982. Only two countries had the courage to open embassies in Jerusalem—Costa Rica and El Salvador. In 2008, both countries moved them to Tel Aviv.

17. Unger, *House of Bush*, 60–64; Robert G. Kaiser and David Ottaway, "Oil for Security Fueled Close Ties; But Major Differences Led to Tensions," *Washington Post*, February 11, 2002; Baer, *Sleeping with the Devil*, 63–64.

18. Posner, *Secrets of the Kingdom*, 115–16.

19. Ottaway, *King's Messenger*, 65; Simpson, *The Prince*, 103, 131–32.

20. Kaplan, *Arabists*, 230–31.

21. Pollack, "Saudi Arabia and the United States."

22. Interview with Chas W. Freeman Jr., April 14, 1995, transcript, ADST.

23. Saudi TV, August 22, 1990.

24. Lippman, *Inside the Mirage*, 304–5.

25. Bronson, *Thicker Than Oil*, 198; Lippman, *Inside the Mirage*, 311.

26. Bronson, *Thicker Than Oil*, 202.

27. Interview with David Wurmser. According to Wurmser, the Saudis have engaged in a lot of technology transfers without any government reaction. By contrast, allegations of technology transfers by Israel have prompted public rebukes and sanctions.

28. Confidential interview with defense industry consultant.

29. Timothy N. Hunter, "Appeasing the Saudis," *Middle East Quarterly*, March 1996.

30. Dennis Ross, *The Missing Peace: The Inside Story of the Fight for Middle East Peace* (New York: Farrar, Straus and Giroux, 2004), 72–75, 218.

31. Interview with David Wurmser.

CHAPTER 9: THE LOBBY COVER-UP

1. Laurent Murawiec, *Princes of Darkness: The Saudi Assault on the West* (Lanham, Md.: Rowman and Littlefield, 2003), 96–99.

2. Alfred Prados and Christopher Blanchard, *Saudi Arabia: Terrorist Financing Issues* (Washington, D.C.: Congressional Research Service, 2007).

3. Simpson, *The Prince*, 318–20.

4. Council on Foreign Relations, *Terrorist Financing*, report of an independent task force, October 2002, 1, www.cfr.org/pdf/Terrorist_Financing_TF.pdf; Jean-Charles Brisard, "Terrorism Financing," report prepared for the president of the Security Council, United Nations, December 19, 2002; Murawiec, *Princes of Darkness*, 100–101.

5. Murawiec, *Princes of Darkness*, xiii–xv; Thomas E. Ricks, "Briefing Depicted Saudis as Enemies," *Washington Post*, August 6, 2002.

6. U.S. Congress, Hearings of the House Armed Services Committee Special Oversight Panel on Terrorism, May 23, 2002.

7. Blaine Harden, "Saudis Seek U.S. Muslims for Their Sect," *New York Times*, October 20, 2001.

8. Murawiec, *Princes of Darkness*, 45.

9. Action was first taken against branches of the charity in 2002, and then all its assets in the United States were frozen in 2008. "US Moves Against Saudi-Based Charity," Associated Press, June 20, 2008; Stephen I. Landman, "Federal Court's Ruling Poses Threat to Terror-Finance Investigation," IPT News, April 1, 2010. See also "Designated Charities and Potential Fundraising Front Organizations for FTOs [Foreign

Terrorist Organizations]," U.S. Department of the Treasury, www.ustreas.gov/offices/enforcement/key-issues/protecting/fto.shtml (accessed April 8, 2010).

10. Unger, *House of Bush,* 179; Schwartz, *The Two Faces of Islam* (New York: Anchor Books, 2002), 268; "Anti-Semitic Books Distributed by Saudi Embassy in Washington Will Be Displayed," Saudi Information Agency, August 26, 2002; "Saudis Spread Hate Speech in U.S.," FrontPageMagazine.com, September 16, 2002; Jerry Markon, "U.S. Raids N. Va. Office of Saudi-Based Charity," *Washington Post,* June 2, 2004; Dore Gold, "Saudi Arabia's Dubious Denials of Involvement in International Terrorism," Jerusalem Center for Public Affairs, October 1, 2003.

11. Greg Palast and David Pallister, "Officials Told to 'Back Off' on Saudis before September 11," *Guardian,* November 7, 2001.

12. Jack Fairweather, "Saudi-Backed Hate Propaganda Exposed," *Washington Post,* September 3, 2008.

13. David Ottaway, "U.S. Eyes Money Trails of Saudi-Backed Charities," *Washington Post,* August 19, 2004; Ottaway, *King's Messenger,* 185, 197.

14. Ottaway, "U.S. Eyes Money."

15. Stephen Schwartz, *Two Faces of Islam,* 259; Blaine Harden, "Saudis Seek U.S. Muslims for Their Sect."

16. Mughniyeh evaded capture for more than a decade before he was murdered in Damascus by unknown assassin(s) on February 12, 2008.

17. Seymour M. Hersh, "King's Ransom," *The New Yorker,* October 22, 2001.

18. Gold, *Hatred's Kingdom,* 181.

19. Speech George Shultz delivered as the recipient of the Ralph Bunche Award for Diplomatic Excellence from the ADST in Washington, D.C., January 25, 2002.

20. Quoted in "Report: Members of Saudi Royal Family Paid Osama bin Laden Not to Attack Targets in Kingdom," *Al Bawaba,* August 25, 2002.

21. Charles M. Sennott, "Doubts Are Cast on the Viability of Saudi Monarchy for Long Term," *Boston Globe,* March 5, 2002; U.S. Congress, "The Future of U.S.-Saudi Relations," Hearing Before the Subcommittee on the Middle East and South Asia of the Committee on International Relations of the House of Representatives, One Hundred Seventh Congress, Second Session, May 22, 2002.

22. David Tell, "The Saudi Terror Subsidy," *Weekly Standard,* May 20, 2002.

23. Gold, *Hatred's Kingdom,* 202; Kenneth R. Timmerman, "Documents Detail Saudi Terror Links: Saudi-Government Accounting Schedules Showing Payments to Families of Suicide Bombers Are Among Records Israel Seized from Palestinian Terrorist Cells," Insight on the News, June 10, 2002, http://findarticles.com/p/articles/mi_m1571/is_21_18/ai_87460065/.

24. Gold, *Hatred's Kingdom,* 199–200; Schwartz, *Two Faces of Islam,* 238.

25. Jean-Charles Brisard. "Terrorism Financing," Report prepared for the President of the Security Council, United Nations, December 19, 2002; Mathew Levitt, "Who Pays for Palestinian Terror?" *Weekly Standard,* August 25, 2003.

26. Schwartz, *Two Faces of Islam,* 238, 276–77.

27. Timmerman, "Documents Detail Saudi Terror Links."

28. Ben Barber. "Saudi Millions Finance Terror Against Israel; Officials Say Papers Prove It," *Washington Times,* May 7, 2002.

29. Quoted in Pollack, "Saudi Arabia and the United States"; Simpson, *The Prince,* 326.

30. *Near East Report,* January 1, 1975.

31. *Near East Report*, June 23, 1976, 109.

32. Crowe, *America for Sale*, 136–47.

33. *Near East Report*, June 9, 1976.

34. *Near East Report*, June 11, 1982.

35. Amy Kaufman Goot and Steven J. Rosen, eds., *The Campaign to Discredit Israel* (Washington, D.C.: AIPAC, 1983), 29, 62–63; *Wall Street Journal*, August 10, 1982; Posner, *Secrets of the Kingdom*, 114.

36. *Near East Report*, May 28, 1982.

37. Simpson, *The Prince*, 335.

38. The three departing partners were Bernie Merritt, Jim Weber, and Judy Smith. Philip Shenon, "Threats and Responses: Publicists; 3 Partners Quit Firm Handling Saudis' P.R.," *New York Times*, December 6, 2002; Judy Sarasohn, "Saudi Arabia a 'Fascinating Client' for Qorvis," *Washington Post*, March 21, 2002.

39. "Saudis Spend $5.4M At Loeffler Group," O'Dwyerpr.com, August 9, 2006. Loeffler resigned from the McCain campaign after it banned lobbyists from working for the candidate, "Saudi Arabia's Lobbyist Resigns Team McCain," O'Dwyerpr.com, May 19, 2008; Christopher Marquis, "Worried Saudis Pay Millions to Improve Image in the U.S.," *New York Times*, August 29, 2002; Baer, *Sleeping with the Devil*, 55; Gold, *Hatred's Kingdom*, 193; Schwartz says the figure was $2.5 million: *Two Faces of Islam*, 290–91.

40. "F-H Collects $6.4M from Saudis," O'Dwyerpr.com, January 3, 2008.

41. Janine Zacharia, "'Michael Jordan of Saudi Diplomacy' Leading PR Full-Court Press," *Jerusalem Post*, November 11, 2001.

42. Bob Deans, "Crisis in the Middle East: Saudi Arabia; Media, Diplomacy Enlisted to Improve Kingdom's Image," *Atlanta Journal-Constitution*, April 27, 2002.

43. Sari Horwitz and Dan Eggen, "FBI Searches Saudi Arabia's PR Firm," *Washington Post*, December 9, 2004.

44. "Saudis Spend $7.3M at Qorvis," O'Dwyerpr.com, December 3, 2004; "Just Say No to Terror, Saudis Told," O'Dwyerpr.com, March 7, 2005.

45. Daniel Pipes, "The Saudis' Covert P.R. Campaign," *New York Sun*, August 10, 2004.

46. Thomas L. Friedman, "An Intriguing Signal from the Saudi Crown Prince," *New York Times*, February 17, 2002; Gold, *Hatred's Kingdom*, 197.

47. Jane Perlez, "Bush Senior, on His Son's Behalf, Reassures Saudi Leader," *New York Times*, July 15, 2001.

48. Ottaway, *King's Messenger*, 152–53, 269; David Ottaway and Robert Kaiser, "Saudi Leader's Anger Revealed Shaky Ties," *Washington Post*, February 10, 2002; Ross, *Missing Peace*, 786.

49. Patrick E. Tyler, "Mideast Turmoil: Arab Politics; Saudi to Warn Bush of Rupture over Israel Policy," *New York Times*, April 25, 2002.

50. See "The Middle East Road Map," www.jewishvirtuallibrary.org/jsource/Peace/roadtoc.html.

51. Ottaway, *King's Messenger*, 218–20.

52. Jordan resigned to give the impression he was not being expelled. Ibid., 181–82, 204–5; Simpson, *The Prince*, 322.

53. Gold, *Hatred's Kingdom*, 204.

54. Matt Welch, "Shilling for the House of Saud," *National Post*, June 16, 2008.

55. Neil MacFarquhar, "Saudi Arabia Seeks U.N. Platform to Promote Pluralism Abroad," *New York Times*, November 12, 2008.

56. "U.S.-Saudi Relations in a World without Equilibrium," address by William J. Burns to the New America Foundation, April 27, 2009; "King Abdullah Did Not Meet Peres in New York," *Arab News*, May 1, 2009; "Saudi Ambassador Denies Inviting Israel to Inter-Faith Meet," Agence France-Presse, November 7, 2008.

57. Prados and Blanchard, *Saudi Arabia*; Michael Abramowitz, "Oil Efforts Are Best Possible, Saudis Say," *Washington Post*, May 17, 2008; Michael Jacobson, "Saudi Efforts to Combat Terrorist Financing," *PolicyWatch* #1555, Washington Institute for Near East Policy, July 21, 2009; "US Demands More Saudi Action on Terror Finance," *Kuwait Times*, October 1, 2009.

58. "A Conversation with Ambassador Ford Fraker," pt. 3, Saudi–U.S. Relations Information Service, www.susris.com (henceforth cited as SUSRIS), December 1, 2008.

59. "The Limits of Bad Policy: The Bush Administration Relearns the Fact That Saudi Arabia Is Not a 'Moderate' State," *Washington Post*, April 1, 2007.

60. "Conversation with Ambassador Fraker."

61. Youssef Ibrahim, "The Saudi Reign of Terror," *New York Sun*, September 14, 2007; Andrew O. Selsky, "U.S. Defends Transfers as Ex-Detainees Vow Terror," *Washington Post*, January 27, 2009; Robert F. Worth, "Saudis Issue List of 85 Terrorism Suspects," *New York Times*, February 4, 2009.

62. Gold, *Hatred's Kingdom*, 230.

Chapter 10: The Lobby Takes Root

1. Goot and Rosen, *Campaign to Discredit Israel*, 3; Zogby said the same in 1997, Mehdi in 1993; Michael Lewis, "Israel's American Detractors—Back Again," *Middle East Quarterly,* December 1997.

2. Yossi Shain, "Arab-Americans at a Crossroads," *Journal of Palestine Studies* 99 (Spring 1996): 49.

3. Alexander Gainem, "Is There a Muslim Lobby in the US?" *Journal of Turkish Weekly*, May 1, 2007.

4. Interview with Tom Dine.

5. Miller, "Case of the Arab Office," 303–4.

6. Ibid., 305–6.

7. Kenen, *Israel's Defense Line*, 121; Miller, "Case of the Arab Office," 307–8.

8. Miller, "Case of the Arab Office," 308–11, 313, 318.

9. *Near East Report*, October 1964; Hugh Wilford, Friends of the Princeton University Library, July 2009, www.princeton.edu/rbsc/fellowships/2009-10/wilford.html.

10. *Near East Report*, August 28, 1974.

11. *Near East Report*, August 25, 1964, and October 1964.

12. *Near East Report*, September 4, 1974; Kenen, *Israel's Defense Line*, 118.

13. *Near East Report*, October 29, 1969.

14. Urofsky, *We Are One*, 370–71; *Near East Report*, October 29, 1969.

15. Goot and Rosen, *Campaign to Discredit Israel*, 6.

16. Interviews with Malcolm Hoenlein and Douglas Bloomfield.

17. Richard Parker, April 21, 1989, transcript, ADST; Nabeel A. Khoury, "The Arab Lobby: Problems and Prospects," *Middle East Journal* (Summer 1987): 386; Goot and Rosen, *Campaign to Discredit Israel*, 7; see also C. L. Gates, "The Lebanese Lobby in the U.S.," *MERIP Reports*, December 1978, 19.

18. IAP went out of business in 2005, and some of its staff and founders essentially replaced it with the Council on American-Islamic Relations (CAIR). In 2004, a federal judge in Chicago ruled that the IAP (along with the Holy Land Foundation) was liable for a $156 million lawsuit for aiding and abetting the terror group Hamas in the death of the seventeen-year-old David Boim, an American citizen. In 2007, the United States Court of Appeals for the Seventh Circuit overturned the judge's ruling, holding that plaintiffs failed to prove that financial contributions to Hamas played a direct role in Boim's slaying (Darryl Fears, "Ruling against Muslim Group Is Overturned; Former Charity, Others Not Liable in Teen's Death," *Washington Post*, December 29, 2007).

19. Congressional Quarterly, *The Washington Lobby*, 17.

20. Interviews with Tom Dine and Douglas Bloomfield.

21. Interview with Douglas Bloomfield.

22. Kenen, *Israel's Defense Line*, 308.

23. Carter, *Keeping Faith*, 299.

24. Marrar, "Lobbying Public Opinion," 11.

25. Ibid., 23.

26. Khoury, 383; ADC press release, May 12, 2008.

27. *Near East Report*, November 1, 1972.

28. Shaheen, "Reel Bad Arabs," 172.

29. ATFP press release, March 24, 2009.

30. Interview with Tom Dine.

31. Interview with Tom Dine.

32. Nathan Guttman, "Top Pro-Palestinian Lobbyist Ousted," *Forward*, March 2, 2008.

33. Fouad Moughrabi, "Remembering the AAUG (Association of Arab-American University Graduates," *Arab Studies Quarterly* (Summer–Fall 2007).

CHAPTER 11: FROM MAVERICKS TO MAINSTREAM

1. Goot and Rosen, *Campaign to Discredit Israel*, 32, 35.

2. Ibid., 31.

3. Wilkie, "Arab Lobbyists." Maksoud's wife, along with the Saudi ambassador's wife, also led a coordinated PR effort to have women tell horror stories about the Israeli campaign in Lebanon (see chapter 20).

4. The Conference of Presidents was actually created at the instigation of the State Department, which tired of being approached by representatives of different organizations and wanted to deal with one representative group.

5. Marrar, "Lobbying Public Opinion," 17.

6. Ibid., 20.

7. Ibid., 27.

8. Ibid., 31.

9. *Near East Report*, December 14, 1998.

10. *IPT News*, January 30, 2008.

11. Schwartz, *Two Faces of Islam*, 246–47.

12. Muslim Public Affairs Council, www.mpac.org/index.php.

13. Speech in Lafayette Park, October 28, 2000; Capitol Hill Panel Discussion, June 18, 1998.

14. Steven Emerson, *American Jihad: The Terrorists Living among Us* (New York: Free Press, 2002), 232–33.

15. "Speak Up: Call on House Foreign Relations Committee to Reject Proposed Resolution to Block U.N. Aid to Palestinians," MPAC, February 4, 2009, www.mpac.org/article .php?id=780; "Action Alert: URGENT: Act Now to Defend UNRWA in Gaza," ADC, n.d., http://capwiz.com/adc/issues/alert/?alertid=12585311; "ADC Thanks 36 House Representatives Who Opposed H.RES 867," ADC, www.adc.org/index.php?id=3517.

16. John Mintz and Michael Grunwald, "FBI Terror Probes Focus on U.S. Muslims; Expanded Investigations, New Tactics Stir Allegations of Persecution," *Washington Post*, October 31, 1998.

17. "US Man gets 65 Years for Funding Hamas," Associated Press, May 27, 2009.

18. Letter from Assistant Attorney General Ronald Weich to Rep. Sue Myrick, February 12, 2010; "Brief for the United States," *United States of America v. Sabri Benkahla*, On Appeal from the United States District Court for the Eastern District of Virginia in the United States Court of Appeals for the Fourth Circuit.

19. Stephen Koff, "Kucinich Now Plans to Return Hamas Supporter's Gift," *Cleveland Plain Dealer*, October 3, 2003.

20. Corey Saylor, interview by David Lee Miller, "Where Are the Moderate Muslims in America?" Fox News Live Desk, Fox News, August 8, 2008; Jim Popkin, "Obama Concedes Mistake over Muslim Outreach Meeting," MSNBC News, October 9, 2008.

21. CAIR press release, March 11, 2009, www.cair.com/ArticleDetails.aspx?ArticleID =25775.

22. "Schumer, Kyl Inquire About Recent FBI Decision to Sever Ties with Islamic Group," Press Release, Office of Senator Jon Kyl, February 24, 2009; "FBI Explains Its CAIR Cut Off," IPT News, May 7, 2009; Gaubatz and Sperry, *Muslim Mafia*, 83–91.

23. Associated Press Online, "U.S. Muslims Split over Saudi Donations," December 2, 2002; Steven Emerson, "Funding Ties with HLF and Foreign Donors Show CAIR's True Agenda," *IPT News*, March 25, 2008, www.investigativeproject.org; Schwartz, *Two Faces of Islam*, 262; David Gaubatz and Paul Sperry, *Muslim Mafia* (Los Angeles: WND Books, 2009), 126, 166–72; "CAIR and the Foreign Agents Registration Act," CAIR Observatory, http://cairunmasked.org/.

24. John Leo, "Pushing the Bias Button," *U.S. News & World Report*, June 9, 2003.

25. Hate crimes against Muslims peaked at 481 in 2001 (26 percent of all religious hate crimes compared to 57 percent committed against Jews), but have averaged 141 since then. The latest report (2008) found 1,013 offenses directed against Jews (66 percent of all those attributable to religion) compared to 105 against Muslims (8 percent of the total). "Hate Crime Statistics, 2001–2008," FBI, http://www.fbi.gov/ucr/ucr .htm.

26. Reihan Salam, "The Sum of All PC," *Slate*, May 28, 2002.

27. "The Al-Arian Verdict," *St. Petersburg Times*, December 7, 2005.

28. *United States of America vs. Sami Amin Al-Arian*, Transcript of Proceedings, United States District Court Middle District of Florida, Tampa Division, May 1, 2006.

29. Emerson, *American Jihad*, 222.

30. Audrey Hudson, "CAIR Membership Falls 90% since 9/11," *Washington Times*, June 12, 2007. CAIR internal records showed a membership of 5,133 rather than the 50,000 the group claimed. Gaubatz and Sperry, *Muslim Mafia*, 125.

31. AMC Web site, www.amcnational.org/new/amcdetails.asp?PageName=aboutamc.

32. Ira Stoll, "Bye Alamoudi," *American Spectator,* October 23, 2003; Schwartz, *Two Faces of Islam,* 252–53.

33. "The Brotherhood," PBS, www.pbs.org/weta/crossroads/about/show_the_brotherhood .html; "Declaration in Support of Detention," in the United States District Court for the Eastern District of Virginia, Alexandria Division, *United States of America v. Abdurahman Muhammad Alamoudi,* September 2003.

34. Mustafa Elhussein, "Commentary: Misjudged Muslims," *Washington Times,* December 17, 2000.

35. Erik C. Nisbet and James Shanahan, "Restrictions on Civil Liberties, Views of Islam, and Muslim Americans," Cornell University, December 2004, www.news.cornell .edu/releases/Dec04/Muslim.Poll.bpf.html.

36. Francis O. Wilcox, *Congress, the Executive, and Foreign Policy* (New York: Harper and Row, 1971), 138.

37. Ira Mehlman, "Arab American Lobby Takes on Rep. Long, Other Israel Allies," *Jewish World,* January 20–26, 1984, 37; David J. Sadd and G. Neal Lendenmann, "Arab American Grievances," *Foreign Policy,* Autumn 1985, 23–24.

38. Islamic Free Market Institute, www.islamicinstitute.org (site no longer working).

39. Mary Jacoby, "Friends in High Places," *St. Petersburg Times,* March 11, 2003.

40. Tom Hamburger and Glenn R. Simpson, "In Difficult Times, Muslims Count on Unlikely Advocate," *Wall Street Journal,* June 11, 2003; Frank J Gaffney Jr., "A Troubling Influence," FrontPageMagazine.com, December 9, 2003.

41. Jake Tapper, "Setback for Arab-Americans," *Salon,* September 17, 2001.

42. James G. Abourezk, "How to Vote against Your Own Interests," *Counterpunch,* November 11, 2008, www.counterpunch.org/abourezk11122008.html.

43. Amir Taheri, "The O Jesse Knows," *New York Post,* October 14, 2008.

44. Glenn Simpson and Amy Chozick, "Obama's Muslim-Outreach Adviser Resigns," *Wall Street Journal,* August 6, 2008.

45. Jihan Abdalla, "An Irrelevant Race," *Jerusalem Report,* October 27, 2008, 24–28.

46. Elizabeth Kelleher, "Arab-Americans, American Muslims Pump Up Political Influence," America.gov, September 2, 2004, www.america.gov/st/washfile-english/2004/ September/20040902164910cpataruk0.2117426.html.

47. Ghada Elnajjar, "Arab Americans in Virginia Form Political Action Committee," Office of International Information Programs, U.S. Department of State, February 25, 2003, http://usinfo.state.gov.

48. Unger, *House of Bush,* 209; Jim Zogby and Joe Stork, "They Control the Hill, but We've Got a Lot of Positions Around the Hill," *MERIP,* May–June 1987, 25.

49. Jeffrey Goldberg, "Real Insiders," *New Yorker,* July 4, 2005; Goot and Rosen, *Campaign to Discredit Israel,* 10.

50. Gaubatz and Sperry, *Muslim Mafia,* 207.

51. Zogby and Stork, "They Control the Hill," 27.

52. Lecture by Hussein Ibish, October 27, 2008, Bahrain Center for Studies and Research, www.bcsr.gov.bh/BCSR/En/News/2008/2ndnov2008news.htm.

Chapter 12: God Takes a Side

1. Urofsky, *We Are One,* 124.

2. Duncan L. Clarke and Eric Flohr, "Christian Churches and the Palestine Question," *Journal of Palestine Studies* (Summer 1992): 69, 72.

3. Uri Bialer, *Cross on the Star of David* (Bloomington: Indiana University Press, 2008), 3; Paul Merkley, *Christian Attitudes towards the State of Israel* (Montreal: McGill-Queen's University Press, 2001), 136–38.

4. Grose, *Israel*, 215–16.

5. Baram, *Department of State*, 309n.

6. Bialer, *Cross on the Star*, 4.

7. Ibid., 4; Merkley, *Christian Attitudes*, 140.

8. Bialer, *Cross on the Star*, 7–8.

9. Merkley, *Christian Attitudes*, 6–7.

10. Ibid., 35, 45.

11. Bialer, *Cross on the Star*, 23; Merkley, *Christian Attitudes*, 141–42.

12. Bialer, *Cross on the Star*, 23.

13. Ibid., 63.

14. Memorandum of a telephone conversation between the secretary of state in Washington and Dr. Roswell Barnes in New York, February 22, 1957, in *FRUS*, 1957, vol. 17 (Arab-Israeli Dispute), 239–40.

15. *Near East Report*, July 2, 1963.

16. Merkley, *Christian Attitudes*, 149.

17. Ibid., 162; Judith Hershcopf Banki, *Christian Reactions to the Middle East Crisis*, pamphlet (New York: American Jewish Committee, 1967), 3.

18. Banki, *Christian Reactions*, 17. A July 1967 poll indicated that 82 percent of Americans believed Israel's existence should be accepted by the Arab states, and 79 percent opposed UN condemnation of Israel as the aggressor in the war.

19. *Near East Report*, March 4, 1970.

20. *Near East Report*, May 3, 1972.

21. Urofsky, *We Are One*, 364–65.

22. Judith Hershcopf Banki, *Anti-Israel Influence in American Churches* (New York: American Jewish Committee, 1979), 4.

23. Adam Gregerman, "Old Wine in New Bottles: Liberation Theology and the Israeli-Palestinian Conflict," *Journal of Ecumenical Studies* (Summer–Fall 2004).

24. Merkley, *Christian Attitudes*, 162.

25. Urofsky, *We Are One*, 433; Emerson, *American House of Saud*, 280; Banki, *Anti-Israel Influence*, 12–13.

26. Merkley, *Christian Attitudes*, 77–79.

27. Ibid., 152.

28. Letter from James Fine, board chair, and Warren Clark, executive director, CMEP, to Secretary of State Hillary Clinton, March 2, 2009.

29. Marrar, "Lobbying Public Opinion," 34.

30. "Vigilance against Anti-Jewish Ideas and Bias," Presbyterian Church (USA) Office of Interfaith Relations, May 2008. Joint statement signed by the American Jewish Committee, American Jewish Congress, B'nai B'rith International, the Central Conference of American Rabbis, Hadassah, Jewish Council for Public Affairs, Jewish Reconstructionist Federation, the Rabbinical Assembly, United Synagogue of Conservative Judaism, Union for Reform Judaism, Women's League for Conservative Judaism, and Women of Reform Judaism, June 2008.

31. "Executive Committee Statement on Israel/Palestine: The Time Is Ripe to Do What Is Right," World Council of Churches, May 16–19, 2006.

32. Merkley, *Christian Attitudes*, 217–18.
33. Merkley, *American Presidents*, 140 (italics in original).

CHAPTER 13: THE DIPLOMATIC ALUMNI NETWORK

1. Deborah M. Levy, "Advice for Sale," *Foreign Policy*, Summer 1987, 64–76.
2. Unger, *House of Bush*, 153.
3. Ibid., 199–200.
4. Ibid., 175–76n; Peter Baker and Charlie Savage, "In Clinton List, a Veil Is Lifted on Foundation," *New York Times*, December 18, 2008; Susan Schmidt, Margaret Coker, and Jay Solomon, "Clinton Reveals Donors," *Wall Street Journal*, December 19, 2008; John Solomon and Jeffrey H. Birnbaum, "Clinton Library Got Funds from Abroad," *Washington Post*, December 15, 2007. The list of donors also includes prominent supporters of Israel, but there is a difference between American citizens offering support and foreign governments.
5. Jonathan Wells, Jack Meyers, and Maggie Mulvihill, "Bush Advisers Cashed In on Saudi Gravy Train," *Boston Herald*, December 11, 2001.
6. Evan Thomas, "Peddling Influence," *Time*, March 3, 1986; *Near East Report*, March 31, 1986, p. 51.
7. David S. Hilzenrath, "From Public Life to Private Business," *Washington Post*, May 28, 2006.
8. The Cohen Group, www.cohengroup.net/expertise/middle_east.cfm.
9. Address by William Cohen to Eighth Herzliya Conference, April 2008; Eric Rosenberg, "William Cohen Pushes Mideast Arms Deal," Muckety.com, January 3, 2008, http://news.muckety.com/2008/01/03/william-cohen-pushes-foreign-arms-deal/271.
10. Posner, *Secrets of the Kingdom*, 84; Tom Hamburger and Josh Meyer, "Former FBI Director Defends Saudi Prince from Bribery Allegations," *Chicago Tribune*, April 7, 2009. Freeh complained that the Saudis would not allow the FBI to interview suspects in the 1996 Khobar Towers bombing and blamed President Clinton for not pressuring the Saudis to cooperate. He later praised Prince Bandar for his cooperation. Louis J. Freeh, "Remember Khobar Towers," *Wall Street Journal*, May 20, 2003.
11. Emerson, *American House of Saud*, 114-115.
12. Interview with Brent Scowcroft, *Frontline*, October 2001; Murawiec, *Princes of Darkness*.
13. Eli Lake, "Baker Panel Aide Expects Israel Will Be Pressed," *New York Sun*, November 29, 2006; Ed Lasky, "Will James Baker Stay True to Form?" *American Thinker*, November 13, 2006.
14. Scheuer on Glenn Beck, Fox News, June 30, 2009; Michael Scheuer, "Lobby? What Lobby?" antiwar.com, February 10, 2009.
15. Philip Giraldi, "America's Israeli-Occupied Media," antiwar.com, August 12, 2008, www.antiwar.com/orig/giraldi.php?articleid=13288; Giraldi, "Attack on Iran: Preemptive Nuclear War," *Global Research* (August 2, 2005).
16. Emerson, *American House of Saud*, 260; Ed Magnuson, "Pursuing the Money Connections," *Time*, January 26, 2007.
17. Quoted in Unger, *House of Bush*, 167.
18. Ibid., 168–69; Baer, 49; Jonathan Wells, Jack Meyers, and Maggie Mulvihill, "Bush Advisers Cashed In"; *Near East Report*, February 12, 1975.

19. Crowe, *America for Sale*, 145–46; Emerson, *American House of Saud*, 100.

20. Council for the National Interest, www.cnionline.org/. The quotations were on the site as recently as June 2008, but have been removed from CNI's newer site.

21. Chas W. Freeman Jr., "Remarks to the MIT Security Studies Program," February 11, 2008.

22. Larry Cohler-Esses, "Freeman, Straight, No Chaser, as Critic of Israel," *Forward*, March 25, 2009.

23. "Blame 'the Lobby,'" *Washington Post*, March 12, 2009.

24. Murawiec, *Princes of Darkness*, 51–52, 123. The largest donors to MEI, contributors of $25,000 or more, are part of the "President's Circle." The 2007 members of the circle were: Chevron, Conoco-Phillips Corporation, ExxonMobil, Raytheon, Saudi Aramco and Shell Oil Company. Middle East Institute, www.mideasti.org/membership/supporters, August 2, 2008.

25. Matt Welch, "Shilling for the House of Saud," *National Post*, June 16, 2008.

26. Murawiec, *Princes of Darkness*, 129–30; Seth Lipsky, "Ned Walker's Wrong Turn," *Wall Street Journal*, November 28, 2001.

27. Interview with Andrew I. Killgore, ADST, June 15, 1988; Emerson, *American House of Saud*, 257; Kaplan, *Arabists*, 253, quoting *Saudi Report*, September 6, 1982; *Near East Report*, July 27, 1998.

28. Interview with John Duke Anthony, "To the Point," NPR, July 31, 2007.

Chapter 14: The Abuse of Academic Freedom

1. "Arabic, Arabists and Academic," *Saudi Aramco World*, May/June 1979.

2. Leila Beckwith, "Anti-Zionism/Anti-Semitism at the University of California–Irvine," in *Academics against Israel and the Jews*, ed. Manfred Gerstenfeld (Jerusalem: Jerusalem Center for Public Affairs, 2007), 115.

3. Allison Hoffman, "Yale Students 'End' US-Israel Relations," *Jerusalem Post*, September 13, 2008.

4. Palestine Solidarity Movement, www.palestinesolidaritymovement.org/pointsofunity.htm (August 15, 2007). Site no longer available.

5. Richard Lacayo, "A Campus War over Israel," *Time*, October 7, 2002; address at morning prayers, Memorial Church, Cambridge, Massachusetts, September 17, 2002, Office of the President, Harvard University.

6. Hampshire College's Students for Justice in Palestine group accused six companies that the college invested school assets in of profiting from or supporting Israel's occupation of the Palestinian territories. The board of trustees held a review of the companies in which it invested funds and found that two hundred of the companies violated the college's standards for social responsibility (unfair labor practices, environmental abuse, military weapons manufacturing, etc.). The board approved a proposal to divest school assets from those companies. Three of the companies had been previously named by the pro-Palestinian group, which then released a statement claiming that Hampshire was the first American college to divest from Israel. School officials said that their decision had nothing to with Israel, but that the three companies had failed a screen for socially responsible investing because of their sales of military equipment and their employee safety record. The college leadership released a statement that insisted that the "decision expressly did not pertain to a political movement or single out businesses active in a specific region or country." "Statement of Clarification Re-

garding Trustees' Actions on College Investments," Hampshire College, 2009.

7. "Israel Boycott Movement Comes to U.S.," *Inside Higher Ed*, January 26, 2009; Raphael Ahren, "For First Time, U.S. Professors Call for Academic and Cultural Boycott of Israel," *Haaretz*, January 29, 2009; Erin Sheley, "War of Silence," *Weekly Standard*, March 20, 2009.

8. Joel Beinin, "Middle East Studies after September 11," 2002 MESA presidential address, *MESA Bulletin*, Summer 2003; *In Search of Israel Studies: A Survey of Israel Studies on American College Campuses* (Washington, D.C.: Israel on Campus Coalition, 2006).

9. "A Scattering of Scholars," *Saudi Aramco World*, May/June 1979.

10. Elath, *Zionism at the U.N.*, 167.

11. Martin Kramer, *Ivory Towers on Sand* (Washington, D.C.: Washington Institute for Near East Policy, 2001), 16; Marla Braverman, "The Arabist Predicament," *Azure* 15 (Summer 2003): 176–84.

12. "A Scattering of Scholars," *Saudi Aramco World*, May/June 1979.

13. John. L. Esposito, "The Future of Islam," *Fletcher Forum* (Summer 2001): 32.

14. Letter from John L. Esposito to Judge Leonie Brinkema, July 2, 2008; Daniel Pipes, "John Esposito and Me," September 10, 2007, updated October 2, 2008, www .danielpipes.org/blog/2007/09/john-esposito-and-me.

15. Scott Jaschik, "Campus Watch in the Media: Professor John L. Esposito: A Profile," *Muslim Weekly*, March 21, 2005; John L. Esposito and John O. Voll, "Sudan and Saudi Arabia: Who Speaks for Islam?" *Washington Post*, November 30, 2007; Nigel Duara, "A Perspective on Islam: Prof. Esposito Explains Reasons for Modern Views, Policies," *Missourian*, April 11, 2005.

16. Robert Satloff, "Just Like Us! Really?" *Weekly Standard*, May 12, 2008; John L. Esposito and Dalia Mogahed, *Who Speaks for Islam? What a Billion Muslims Really Think* (New York: Gallup Press, 2007).

17. Matt Corrade, "Lack of Openness Makes Scholarly Discussion of Islam Dangerous, Says Bernard Lewis," *Congressional Quarterly's Homeland Security News and Analysis*, April 27, 2008.

18. Beinin, "Middle East Studies."

19. Charlotte Allen, "Taste: Bernard Lewis Takes on Political Correctness in Middle East Studies," *Wall Street Journal*, May 2, 2008.

20. Katie Reedy, "The Rationale of Richard Bulliet," *Bwog*, September 27, 2007, http:// bwog.net/2007/09/27/the-rationale-of-richard-bulliet.

21. Franck Salameh, "Seeking True Diversity in Middle East Studies," FrontPageMagazine.com, January 16, 2008 (emphasis in original).

22. Martin Kramer, "MESA: The Academic Intifada," November 21, 2005, www .geocities.com/martinkramerorg/2005_11_21.htm.

23. Ali Banuazizi, "In These Times . . . ," *MESA Newsletter*, May 2005. See also Lisa Anderson, "Scholarship, Policy Debate and Conflict: Why We Study the Middle East and Why It Matters," 2003 MESA presidential address, *MESA Bulletin*, Summer 2004.

24. Katrina Thomas, "America as Alma Mater," *Saudi Aramco World*, May/June 1979.

25. Quoted from textbooks in Center for Religious Freedom of Hudson Institute, *2008 Update: Saudi Arabia's Curriculum of Intolerance* (Washington, D.C.: Hudson Institute, 2008).

26. Center for Religious Freedom of Hudson Institute, *2008 Update*.

27. "Saudi Arabia," International Religious Freedom Report 2009, U.S. Department of State, October 26, 2009. See also Neil MacFarquhar, "A Nation Challenged: Education; Anti-Western and Extremist Views Pervade Saudi Schools," *New York Times*, October 19, 2001.

28. Jack Fairweather, "Saudi-Backed Hate Propaganda Exposed," WashingtonPost.com, September 3, 2008, http://newsweek.washingtonpost.com/postglobal/islamsadvance/2008/09/saudi-backed_hate_propaganda_e.html.

29. Murawiec, *Princes of Darkness*, 51.

30. Vitalis, *America's Kingdom*, 145.

31. Philip Harsham and Robert Azzi, "Arabs in America," *Saudi Aramco World*, May/June 1979.

32. Emerson, *American House of Saud*, 294–95.

33. Julia Duin, "Saudis Give Big to U.S. Colleges," *Washington Times*, December 10, 2007.

34. Jonathan Jaffit, "Fighting Sheikh Zayed's Funding of Islamic Studies at Harvard Divinity School: A Case Study," Jerusalem Center for Public Affairs, November 17, 2005, www.jcpa.org/phas/phas-jaffit-05.htm.

35. Kathy Boccella, "Temple University Rejects IIIT Funding for Islamic Chair Honoring Mahmoud Ayoub Citing Concerns about Terror Ties," *Philadelphia Inquirer*, January 5, 2008; IIIT Web site, www.iiit.org/ (September 2, 2008), accessed September 23, 2008.

36. *Near East Report*, January 9, 1974.

37. Emerson, *American House of Saud*, 303.

38. Hudson's expertise on Libya is revealed in his book *Arab Politics*, which fawningly talks about one of the world's most autocratic leaders and leading supporters of terrorism. He calls Qaddafi "handsome," "youthful," and heroic," and observes that "he frequently threatens to retire completely and never tires of insisting that Libyans must learn to govern themselves rather than relying on a particular leader." More than thirty years later, Qaddafi remains in power. Seth Cropsey, "Arab Money and the Universities," *Commentary* (April 1979).

39. Krogh said he lobbied members of Congress "in a personal capacity." *Near East Report*, April 9, 1980, 73; Paul Findley, *They Dare to Speak Out* (Westport, Conn.: Lawrence Hill, 1985), 195–200.

40. Emerson, *American House of Saud*, 304; Lawrence Feinberg, "GU's Agile Leader," *Washington Post*, December 30, 1980.

41. *Near East Report*, September 11, 1989, 158; Murawiec, *Princes of Darkness*, 123.

42. Prittie and Nelson, *Economic War*, 186–87.

43. Chris Cottrell, "Indiana University Considers Removing Segregationist's Name from Building," *Eagle*, April 30, 2007; Baer, *Sleeping with the Devil*, 42; Paul Findley, *They Dare to Speak Out*, 189–95.

44. Prittie and Nelson, *Economic War*, 187.

45. John L. Esposito, "A Man and His Vision," in *Hasib Sabbagh: From Palestinian Refugee to Citizen of the World*, ed. Mary-Jane Deeb and Mary E. King (Lanham, Md.: University Press of America, 1996), 71–82; Aileen Vincent-Barwood, "Georgetown's Bridge of Faith," *Saudi Aramco World*, May/June 1998.

46. Details of Wolf letter in Steven Emerson, "Wolf to Georgetown: Detail Use of Saudi Millions," *IPT News*, February 15, 2008, and DeGioia's February 22, 2008, response

can be found at the Investigative Project, www.investigativeproject.org/documents/misc/104.pdf.

47. Catherine Philip, "West Turns Blind Eye to Friend It Dare Not Offend," *London Times*, March 26, 2009. Prince Alaweed bin Talal also gave £16 million to Cambridge and Edinburgh universities to set up research centers to promote a better understanding of Islam. The agreement was signed at Buckingham Palace and attended by the Duke of Edinburgh. Richard Garner, "Saudi Prince Gives Universities £16 million for Study of Islam," *Independent*, May 8, 2008. King Fahd gave another £20 million to establish the Oxford Centre for Islamic Studies. These are just the latest investments by the Arab lobby in the UK. According to the Brunel University Centre for Intelligence and Security Studies, eight British universities received more than £233.5 million from Saudi and Muslim sources since 1995, the largest source of external funding. The center's director, Anthony Glees, says that the universities engage in anti-Western propaganda and a one-sided presentation of Islam and the Middle East. He reported, for example, that 70 percent of the politics lecturers at St. Anthony's College, Oxford, were "implacably hostile" to the West and Israel, a charge Oxford denied (Ben Leach, "'Extremism' Fear over Islam Studies Donations," *Telegraph*, April 14, 2008. See also Melanie Phillips, "The Jihad Against Britain's Jews," *Spectator*, February 10, 2009.

48. Giuliana Vetrano, "No Strings Attached?" *Harvard Crimson*, March 8, 2006; Arthur Clark, "The New Push for Middle East Studies," *Saudi Aramco World*, January/February 2003; Stanley Kurtz, "Saudi in the Classroom," *National Review*, July 25, 2007; Ben Shapiro, "When Harvard Met Saudi," *Human Events*, December 28, 2005.

49. Thomas, "America as Alma Mater."

50. Department of Education, www.nationalreview.com/kurtz/allforeigngiftsreport.html.

51. There is some controversy about Khalidi's connection to the PLO, and he has denied being a spokesman, but Martin Kramer has produced a number of items to document Khalidi's role with the PLO. Martin Kramer, "Khalidi of the PLO," October 30, 2008, http://sandbox.blog-city.com/khalidi_of_the_plo.htm.

52. Martin Kramer, www.geocities.com/martinkramerorg/2003_09_08.htm; Jacob Gershman, "Columbia Failed to Report Saudi Gift," *New York Sun*, January 30, 2004. Donors to the Said chair at Columbia: Yusef Abu Khadra, Abdel Muhsen Al-Qattan, Ramzi A. Dalloul, Richard and Barbara Debs, Richard B. Fisher, Gordon Gray Jr., Daoud Hanania, Rita E. Hauser, Walid H. Kattan, Said T. Khory, Munib R. Masri, Morgan Capital & Energy, Olayan Charitable Trust, Hasib Sabbagh, Kamal A. Shair, Abdul Shakashir, Abdul Majeed Shoman, Jean Stein, and United Arab Emirates.

53. Ann Mosely Lesch, "Promoting Academic Freedom: Risks and Responsibilities," 1995 MESA presidential address, *MESA Bulletin*, July 1996.

54. Bari Weiss, "New Columbia Hire Backed Academic Boycott of Israel," *New York Sun*, September 12, 2008.

55. Arthur Clark, "The New Push for Middle East Studies," *Saudi Aramco World*, January/February 2003.

56. "Educators to Saudi Arabia Program," Institute of International Education, www.iie.org/programs/aramco/; Rachel Ehrenfeld and Alyssa A. Lappen, "The Progress of Hassan al-Banna's Vision," *American Thinker*, November 24, 2006.

57. Zvika Krieger, "The Emir of NYU," *New York*, April 13, 2008.

58.   Chronicle of Higher Education, quoted in "New Coverage of Western Universities in the Middle East and South Korea and a List of Some Foreign Universities with Branches in Gulf Countries," *GSED—Global Studies in Education Digest*, April 2, 2008, http://gsed.wordpress.com/2008/04/02/articles-new-coverage-of-western-universities-in-the-middle-east-and-south-korea-and-a-list-of-some-foreign-universities-with-branches-in-gulf-countries/.

59.   Zvika Krieger, "Desert Bloom," *Chronicle of Higher Education*, March 28, 2008.

60.   Murawiec, *Princes of Darkness*, 51.

61.   Emerson, *American House of Saud*, 166.

62.   Ira Katznelson, chair, Lisa Anderson, Farah Griffin, Jean E. Howard, and Mark Mazower, "Ad Hoc Grievance Committee Report," Columbia University, March 28, 2005, www.columbia.edu/cu/news/05/03/ad_hoc_grievance_committee_report.html. See, for example, Joseph Massad, "The Gaza Ghetto Uprising," *Electronic Intifada*, January 4, 2009; Massad, "The Legacy of Jean-Paul Sartre," *Al-Ahram Weekly Online*, January 30–February 5, 2003, http://weekly.ahram.org.eg/2003/623/op33.htm.

63.   "Columbia Unbecoming," www.columbiaunbecoming.com (site no longer available); Douglas Feiden, "Hate 101, Climate of Hate Rocks Columbia University," *Daily News*, November 21, 2004; Jamie Glazov, "The Campus War Against Israel and the Jews: Joseph Massad," FrontPage.com, October 2, 2009; Deborah Passner, "The Columbia Battleground," Committee for Accuracy in Middle East Reporting in America, March 31, 2005.

64.   Katznelson et al., "Ad Hoc Grievance Committee Report." Among the many stories on the controversy at Columbia, see U.S. Commission on Civil Rights, "Campus Anti-Semitism," U.S. Commission on Civil Rights, Washington, D.C., November 18, 2005. Columbia president Bollinger declined to participate and Professors DeGenova and Dabashi submitted statements denying they were anti-Semitic or had made any anti-Semitic remarks. Sam Dillon, "Columbia to Check Reports of Anti-Jewish Harassment," *New York Times*, October 29, 2004; "Bollinger's Blindness," *New York Sun*, October 22, 2004; Jeffrey Amlin, "Columbia to Probe Faculty Remarks," *Harvard Crimson*, October 29, 2004; Nat Hentoff, "Columbia Still Unbecoming," *Village Voice*, March 4, 2005; Jacob Gershman, "Anti-Israel Professor Is Defended," *New York Sun*, October 26, 2004; Jacob Gershman, "Committee Investigating Bias May Have Known about Intolerance," *New York Sun*, November 2, 2004; Robin Finn, "At the Center of an Academic Storm, a Lesson in Calm," *New York Times*, April 8, 2005; N. R. Kleinfield, "Mideast Tensions Are Getting Personal on Campus at Columbia," *New York Times*, January 18, 2005; Alec Magnet, "Columbia Dean Admits Taking Saudi Junket," *New York Sun*, January 11, 2006.

65.   "Ad Hoc Grievance Committee Report," *Columbia News*, March 28, 2005; Karen W. Arenson, "Columbia Panel Clears Professors of Anti-Semitism," *New York Times*, March 31, 2005; Karen W. Arenson, "Panel's Report on Faculty at Columbia Spurs Debate," *New York Times*, April 1, 2005.

66.   Liel Leibovitz, "Battle of the Chairs," *Moment Magazine*, February 2006.

67.   Nathaniel Popper, "Israel Studies Gain on Campus as Disputes Grow," *Forward*, March 25, 2005.

68.   Michael C. Duke, "Rice U Program on Gaza 'Crisis' Perverted by Anti-Israel Advocacy," *Jewish Herald-Voice*, January 29, 2009.

69. Ilan Benjamin and Tammi Rossman-Benjamin, "The Faculty Is Far More Problematic," Scholars for Peace in the Middle East, http://spme.net/cgi-bin/articles. cgi?ID=3925.

70. "Convention News and Program Update," Modern Language Association of America, December 27, 2008; Resolution from the 2008 Delegate Assembly approved December 10, 2009, www.mla.org/governance/mla_resolutions/2008_resolutions.

71. Gary Schiff, *Middle East Centers at Selected American Universities* (New York: American Jewish Committee, 1981), 39.

CHAPTER 15: BRAINWASHING THE CHILDREN

1. Stanley Kurtz, "Saudi in the Classroom: A Fundamental Front in the War," National Review Online, July 25, 2007, http://article.nationalreview.com/print/?q=YjRhZjY wMjU4MGY5ODJmM2MzNGNhNzljMzk4ZDFiYmQ=.

2. National Resource Centers (NRC) Program and Foreign Language and Area Studies (FLAS) Fellowship Program, U.S. Department of Education, FY 2006–2009, www.ed.gov/about/offices/list/ope/iegps/nrcflasgrantees2006-09.pdf. The seventeen centers are Columbia, Georgetown, Harvard, NYU, Ohio State, Princeton, University of Arizona, Berkeley, UCLA, University of Chicago, University of Illinois, University of Michigan, University of Pennsylvania, University of Texas, University of Utah, University of Washington, and Yale.

3. Arthur Clark, "The New Push for Middle East Studies," *Saudi Aramco World*, January/February 2003.

4. Carol Karsch, "Propaganda in the Classroom," *Midstream*, March 1986; Arthur Clark, "The New Push for Middle East Studies."

5. Schiff, *Middle East Centers*, 10.

6. JTA, "Tainted Teachings," October 27, 2005, www.campus-watch.org/article/ id/2247.

7. Palestinian American Research Center, http://parc-us-pal.org. An earlier mission statement had mentioned cooperation with Israeli scholars. That has been deleted.

8. Jonathan Schanzer, "Follow the Money behind Anti-Israel Invective on Campus," *Camera on Campus*, Spring 2009.

9. Jonathan Schanzer, "PARC's Anti-Israel Polemics," National Review Online, July 11, 2008, http://article.nationalreview.com/363061/parcs-anti-israel-polemics/jonathan-schanzer.

10. Schiff, *Middle East Centers*, 38–39.

11. Mitchell Bard, *Rewriting History in Textbooks* (Washington, D.C.: AICE, 1993).

12. Gary A. Tobin and Dennis R. Ybarra, *The Trouble with Textbooks* (Lanham, Md.: Lexington Books, 2008).

13. William J. Bennetta, "How a Public School in Scottsdale, Arizona Subjected Students to Islamic Indoctrination," www.textbookleague.org/tci-az.htm.

14. Tobin and Ybarra, *Trouble with Textbooks*.

15. JTA, "Tainted Teachings," pt. 2.

16. Sandra Stotsky, *The Stealth Curriculum: Manipulating America's History Teachers* (Washington, D.C.: Thomas B. Fordham Foundation, 2004).

17. Ibid.

18. "From the Saudis to Your Children," *California Catholic Daily*, August 10, 2007.

19. "Propaganda, Proselytizing, and Public Education: A Critique of the Arab World

Studies Notebook," American Jewish Committee, February 2005, www.ajc.org/site/apps/nlnet/content2.aspx?c=ijITI2PHKoG&b=838459&ct=1054741.

20. William J. Bennetta, "Arab World Studies Notebook Lobs Muslim Propaganda at Teachers," October 8, 2003, www.textbookleague.org/spwich.htm.

21. "From the Saudis to Your Children"; Sarah Stern, "The Wahhabi Jihad for Young American Minds," *inFocus*, Winter 2008.

22. Joe Kaufman, "The Return of the CAIR Quran," FrontPageMagazine.com, February 27, 2008.

23. Valerie Strauss and Emily Wax, "Where Two Worlds Collide: Muslim Schools Face Tension of Islamic, U.S. Views," *Washington Post*, February 25, 2002; "Islamic Groups Hit Curriculum at Saudi School," *Washington Times*, August 2, 2004; Jerry Markson and Ben Hubbard, "Review Finds Slurs in '06 Saudi Texts," *Washington Post*, July 15, 2008; Gold, *Hatred's Kingdom*, 4.

24. Matthew Barakat, "Saudi Academy in Va. Revises Islamic History Books," *Washington Post*, March 12, 2009.

25. Cinnamon Stillwell, "U.S. Soldiers Learning Arabic at Wahhabist Islamic Saudi Academy," Pajamasmedia, May 10, 2008, http://cinnamonstillwell.blogspot.com/2008/05/us-soldiers-learning-arabic-at.html.

26. Valerie Strauss, "Muslim School Withdraws from Association—Saudi-Funded Academy Loses Accreditation—Va. Agency Had Raised Questions," *Washington Post*, July 11, 2002; Kirsten Downey, "Board Extends Saudi School's Lease," *Washington Post*, May 22, 2008; Michael Birnbaum, "Fairfax, Va., Board Approves Saudi Academy Plan," *Washington Post*, August 4, 2009.

27. U.S. Commission on International Religious Freedom, press release, June 11, 2008.

28. Center for Religious Freedom of Hudson Institute, *2008 Update*.

29. Khaled Abu Toameh, "On Campus: The Pro-Palestinians' Real Agenda," *Hudson New York*, March 24, 2009.

30. Catherine Philip, "West Turns Blind Eye to Friend It Dare Not Offend."

31. Abu Toameh, "Pro-Palestinians' Real Agenda."

CONCLUSION: THE ARAB LOBBY'S NEFARIOUS INFLUENCE

1. Urofsky, *We Are One*, 302.

2. Doreen Carvajal, "Britain, a Destination for 'Libel Tourism,'" *New York Times*, January 20, 2008.

3. Bill Gertz, "Inside the Ring—Coughlin Sacked," *Washington Times*, January 4, 2008.

4. Alan Dershowitz, *The Case for Israel* (Hoboken, N.J.: John Wiley & Sons, 2003), 183.

5. Schwartz, *Two Faces of Islam*, 291–92.

6. Pollack, "Saudi Arabia and the United States."

7. Baer, *Sleeping with the Devil*, 11.

8. "Reforms and Relations: Perspectives on the Kingdom—A Conversation with Amb Chas Freeman," SUSRIS, October 8, 2008, www.saudi-us-relations.org/articles/2008/interviews/081008-freeman-interview.html.

9. Mitchell G. Bard, *Will Israel Survive?* (New York: Palgrave, 2007), 221.

10. Interview with Hume Horan, November 3, 2000, transcript, ADST.

11. Ibid. When President Bush organized a peace conference in Annapolis, Maryland, in 2007, the Saudis insisted on going in and out the back door to avoid the Israelis.

12. Joseph Kraft, "Those Arabists in the State Department," *New York Times*, November 7, 1971.

13. Jackson Diehl, "Abbas's Waiting Game," *Washington Post*, May 29, 2009.

14. Randa Habib, "US Has New Mideast Peace Plan, Says Jordan King," *Sydney Morning Herald*, May 17, 2009; Tzvi Ben Gedalyahu, "Report: Obama's Master Plan for the Middle East," *Arutz Sheva*, May 6, 2009.

15. Allison Hoffman, "New York: A Peace of His Mind," *Jerusalem Post*, May 7, 2009; Christopher Dickey, "'Not the Same America,'" *Newsweek*, June 15, 2009.

16. Daniel Pipes, "Both Sides of Their Mouths," *Jerusalem Post*, August 4, 1993.

17. Bronson, *Thicker Than Oil*, 240.

18. David T. Dumke, "Saudi Arabia and Congress: Understanding the Tension," Saudi–US Relations Information Service, March 15, 2006.

19. Robert G. Kaiser and David B. Ottaway, "Saudi Leader's Anger Revealed Shaky Ties; Bush's Response Eased a Deep Rift on Middle East Policy," *Washington Post*, February 10, 2002.

20. *Near East Report*, August 15, 1973, 131.

21. Khaled Abu Toameh, "What Does 'Pro-Palestinian' Really Mean," *Hudson New York*, November 17, 2009, www.hudsonny.org/2009/11/what-does-pro-palestinian-really-mean.php.

22. An interesting case study of European behavior was the decision of the British government to release from prison the terrorist convicted of blowing up a Pan Am airliner over Lockerbie, Scotland. Reports indicated that Libya made the release of the terrorist a condition for concluding a multibillion-dollar oil and gas deal with British Petroleum. The British government denied there was any quid pro quo and insisted its decision was a humanitarian one based on the prisoner's ill health. In fact, he died shortly after being returned to Libya. Jason Allardyce, "Lockerbie Bomber 'Set Free for Oil,'" *Sunday Times*, August 30, 2009.

23. Kofi A. Annan, "10 Years After—A Farewell Statement to the General Assembly," United Nations, September 19, 2006, www.un.org/News/ossg/sg/stories/statements_full.asp?statID=4.

24. *New York Times*, December 17, 1991.

25. Benny Avni, "Bolton Scores U.N. on Stance toward Israel," *New York Sun*, January 13, 2006; Reuters, December 2, 2007.

26. "Israel's Bombardment of Gaza Is Not Self-Defence—It's a War Crime," *Sunday Times*, January 11, 2009; Bernard Josephs, "Dispute Over 'Biased' Gaza Inquiry Professor," *The Jewish Chronicle*, August 27, 2009.

27. "Excerpts from Interview with U.N. Ambassador Susan E. Rice," *Washington Post*, September 22, 2009.

28. House Resolution 867, approved 344–36, November 3, 2009. See also "Israel's Initial Reaction to the Report of the Goldstone Fact-Finding Mission," Israel Ministry of Foreign Affairs, September 15, 2009; Gerald M. Steinberg, "UN Smears Israeli Self-Defense as War Crimes," *Wall Street Journal*, September 16, 2009; "Israel's Analysis and Comments on the Gaza Fact-Finding Mission Report," Israel Ministry of Foreign Affairs, September 15, 2009; Jonathan D. Halevi, "Analysis: Blocking the Truth behind the Gaza War," *Jerusalem Post*, September 21, 2009.

INDEX